UNRAVELING CANDIDIASIS

THE PATIENT GUIDE

MARC J. BIELSKI, MD

LITTLE SPIRIT BOOKS

The information and advice contained in this book are based upon the research and the personal and professional experiences of the author. They are not intended as a substitute for consulting with a healthcare professional. The publisher and author are not responsible for any adverse effects or consequences resulting from the use of any of the suggestions, preparations, or procedures discussed in this book. All matters pertaining to your physical health should be supervised by a healthcare professional. It is a sign of wisdom, not cowardice, to seek a second or third opinion.

Little Spirit Books LLC
Prescott, AZ
littlespiritbooks.com

ISBN: 979-8-9888309-1-7

EDITOR: Carol Killman Rosenberg
COVER DESIGN & TYPESETTING: Gary A. Rosenberg

Printed in the United States of America

Contents

PART THREE CANDIDIASIS & THE IMMUNE SYSTEM

PART FOUR DIAGNOSING & TREATING CANDIDIASIS

Preface

Unraveling Candidiasis: The Patient Guide is the offspring of *Unraveling Candidiasis: The Perplexing Puzzle of Medical Maladies,* which contains detailed scientific and medical evidence to explain and understand how disease-causing yeast can precipitate and promote frequent, recurrent, and chronic illness (with or without the assistance of other infectious invaders, including harmful parasites, bacteria, molds, and/or viruses). More than 2,400 references are included, and many tens of thousands more were considered but were either redundant, weakly supportive, or irrelevant (the references for this book are listed there). The information in that book provides a foundation to create new and better ways to treat candidiasis, and many case studies are presented throughout the candidiasis connections chapters.

After completing the first book, it became clear to me that a patient guide was needed for two reasons:

- First, most candidiasis sufferers are not interested in the scientific and/or medical details or have the background to understand all the information. They just want to get better and as soon as possible. Yet, without some understanding of how candidiasis occurs, including its expressions and manifestations, few sufferers would be willing to start and continue anti-candidiasis therapy. More important, sufferers need a basic understanding of, and appreciation for, the components of therapy, or they will readily sabotage their recovery or quit. Therefore, this book is a reference guide to support sufferers through their journey from illness to wellness.

- Second, even the most knowledgeable candidiasis-minded physicians do not have time to explain the intricacies of candidiasis and its treatment approach to their patients, especially with respect to its ups and downs. So, *The Patient Guide* was created to assist physicians and healthcare practitioners who manage candidiasis sufferers in working better together.

Note: *Efforts were made to simplify the information in this book, but it might be too complicated for some readers. If this applies to you, rather than focusing on the specifics, just try to understand the basic information so you can know why you are being treated and what you need to do.*

Introduction

Candidiasis is the medical designation for yeast-related illness. Other names are *Candida-related complex, candidiasis hypersensitivity syndrome, chronic candidiasis syndrome, monilial hypersensitivity, Candida albicans*–related illness, *chronic mucocutaneous candidiasis*, as well as some less-formal designations. Regardless of its name, it involves the colonization of disease-causing yeast within the human body, promoting various symptoms, syndromes, illness, and disease. To make matters worse, candidiasis sufferers frequently have a variety of harmful parasites, bacteria, molds, and/or viruses within their bodies.

Candidiasis is real. This cause and contributor to a vast number of medical maladies has been documented, researched, and treated by holistic medical practitioners for years, decades, and much longer when you include and investigate the past. Although some books and many articles have been published on this topic, the information in this book strongly supports its existence. Yet, the mainstream medical community and industry ignores, dismisses, and hides information about it, including canceling and denying access to tests that reveal its existence and harm. Mainstream medical experts refuse to acknowledge the health problems instigated by disease-causing yeast. Opponents of candidiasis claim its legitimacy is circumstantial and speculative, which is why it is constantly maligned as a fictitious malady. Opinions aside, for everyone that suffers with it, candidiasis does exist, and it is all too real.

Only the most obvious cases of candidiasis are diagnosed and treated, leaving most sufferers to be overlooked. Since candidiasis is not taught or barely mentioned in medical school, most physicians are clueless. Any physician interested in learning more will discover that candidiasis is clouded in confusion and misinformation. How can physicians appreciate, understand, and even attempt to treat a condition they know almost nothing about?

Most people are well acquainted with some types of yeast, as a vital ingredient in making bread, baked goods, wine, beer, and more. When used in preparing foods and beverages, baker's yeast and brewer's yeast add flavor, body, and texture, as well as ferment carbohydrates into alcohol. From a culinary perspective, yeast is a helpful, innocent microorganism. In contrast, disease-causing yeast are far from innocent with respect to precipitating and causing illness within human beings.

Many types of yeast cause disease within the human body. Women suffering with vaginal yeast infections are aware of the problems and discomfort associated with the presence of their disease-causing yeast, both its infectious and allergic consequences. In most cases, vaginal yeast infections are a nuisance. Yet, this is just the tip of an enormous and extremely dangerous candidiasis iceberg. Since 90 percent of an iceberg's mass is hidden underwater, most of the illness resulting from candidiasis goes unnoticed, until it is too late.

Yeast exists almost everywhere on this planet. As a form of life, they were here before us. They live and survive in a diversity of environments and on numerous surfaces. Since yeast prefer warm, moist, and dark conditions, one of their favorite habitats is within the human body. Due to their prevalence, mainstream medicine believes any yeast within our gastrointestinal tract are normal, innocent inhabitants. When present in small amounts, they cause little harm. Yet, when the opportunity arises, these infectious invaders multiply and cause problems.

Yeast is a general term for microscopic organisms (fungi) that grow on dead, decaying plant matter and insects as well as on other surfaces and forms of life. Although they can be found almost everywhere, the yeast causing disease within human beings has a more restricted habitat, as they primarily exist within warm-blooded animals.

Candida-species organisms are the subgroup of yeast that promote candidiasis within human beings. Although there are nearly 200 related species of *Candida*, the medically significant ones, the disease-causing *Candida*-species organisms, comprise a small percentage. It is important to mention, some *Candida*-like infections are caused by yeast that are not *Candida*-species organisms; although these cases are infrequent, their prevalence is increasing.

More than 90 species of yeast have been found growing within human beings. At least 8 major and 17 less prominent disease-causing yeast occur with such regularity that it is difficult to dismiss their association with illness. *Candida albicans* is undeniably the most prevalent and prominent *Candida*-species organism connected with illness. In fact, when someone says "candidiasis," they are usually referring to an infection with *Candida albicans*—the most studied and researched member of the *Candida* family; more is known about it than any other species of *Candida*. However, other disease-causing *Candida*-species organisms also contribute to illness and should not be ignored, especially as their presence and prevalence increases. Therefore, when describing candidiasis, the more correct term is "disease-causing *Candida*-species organisms," because it includes *all* disease-causing members of the *Candida* family.

Every human being passing through their mother's birth canal is immediately introduced to disease-causing yeast, although it might be inconsequential. More significantly, contact can occur at almost any time and place because disease-causing yeast are all around us. They are within our air, water, and food, which is why most people have one or more disease-causing yeast residing within their gastrointestinal tract. Fortunately, people with a healthy population of beneficial (good) gastrointestinal bacteria (that compete with and suppress their reproduction) should not develop candidiasis. Unfortunately, one strong assault or many small invasions can deplete the beneficial bacteria, allowing the disease-causing yeast to reproduce and promote problems.

Disease-causing yeast can colonize and inflame the gastrointestinal tract, causing inflammatory bowel, irritable bowel, constipation, and other unpleasant and debilitating conditions. If they invade the gut wall and enter the blood, they can infect and colonize other tissues and organs, including the sinuses, lungs, vagina, bladder, and any other location that supports their survival. Infections of almost every organ and tissue have been reported; the medical literature abounds with case reports, discussions, and studies.

Given the chance, disease-causing *Candida*-species organisms are opportunists that readily reproduce and colonize their surroundings. Although many risk factors encourage the development of candidiasis, it typically arises as the beneficial bacteria decrease and lose their ability to suppress the reproduction of any disease-causing yeast.

How do disease-causing yeast cause harm? Yeast ferment carbohydrates, a chemical process that changes sugar (and grains) into alcohol; although it can cause problems, this is the least of our concerns. They also manufacture a variety of other substances (metabolites) much more harmful to the human body. In tiny amounts, their damage is insignificant. Yet, as the population of disease-causing yeast increases, their metabolites and antigens (substances that induce an immune response) will escalate, instigating and promoting various bodily disturbances that can cause serious injury and damage.

More concerning, certain disease-causing yeast, especially *Candida albicans*, can invade into and through the gut wall. When they cannot obtain nourishment within the gastrointestinal tract, they can transform, growing little "root-like" projections that produce enzymes (chemicals that break down certain substances). Their enzymes allow them to create tiny holes in the gut wall and enter the tissues to acquire nourishment. As their population grows, the gut wall's ability to function normally becomes impaired. After it loses its normal effectiveness as a barrier, leaky gut syndrome occurs, which permits inappropriate substances to enter the tissues, while other vital substances can leak out or are not absorbed. The larger the "holes" and more extensive the damage, the worse the situation.

To add insult, disease-causing yeast can invade deeper into the tissues, enter the blood, and colonize it. Their presence within the circulatory system provides access to every part of the body that can provide a habitat for their colonization and survival. This is the *infectious* side of candidiasis. It includes the localized, *direct* effects of disease-causing yeast residing within the gastrointestinal tract, tissues, and blood, including any accompanying inflammation. More significant and confusing for mainstream practitioners, infections with disease-causing yeast also *indirectly* instigate and promote numerous adverse consequences, including a multitude of disturbances that impair the immune, endocrine (hormone), and nervous systems, making matters even more complicated.

Candidiasis has another side that is equally disturbing. Disease-causing *Candida*-species organisms are renowned to be exceptional *allergy-inducing* troublemakers. Their presence within the human body encourages a diversity of sensitivities and hypersensitivities; typically, their colonization instigates or promotes allergies to the disease-causing yeast themselves and molds that are allergically cross-reactive, as well as many other harmful molds. In addition, candidiasis can instigate and/or promote a variety of other allergies, including to foods, environmental substances (pollens and dust), chemicals, or any other allergy-inducing substance that might be encountered. So, both the *infectious* and *allergic* aspects of candidiasis must be appreciated and addressed.

If candidiasis was this simple and easy to understand, it would have been widely accepted long ago. Instead, like a Rubik's Cube, candidiasis has numerous sides and a variety of contributors to its expressions and harm. Ernő Rubik, a Hungarian sculptor and professor of architecture, invented the standard Rubik's Cube as a 3x3x3 puzzle in 1974. Since then, cubes in increasing sizes and number of sides have been created. Solving them requires knowing the algorithms and moves that lead to the solution. Likewise, treating candidiasis involves understanding and unraveling all the pieces that need to be addressed and aligned to achieve wellness.

Why does candidiasis continue to be a confusing condition? Since every human being is unique, the symptoms and illness caused by candidiasis create an incredible amount of variability from one person to another, even when they have similar risk factors, infectious invaders, allergies, and so on. This point is difficult for most people and physicians to comprehend.

The variety and variability of candidiasis does involve genetics, including each person's unique bodily strengths and weaknesses. When you add the contributions of harmful parasites, bacteria, molds, viruses, the toxic effects of heavy metals, our modified food supply, including its chemicals, environmental antigens, and more, as well as an abundance of stress, it is easier to appreciate the great diversity of candidiasis symptoms, disorders, syndromes, illnesses, and diseases that can arise. Although there are similarities, no two sufferers can ever be the same. Most physicians have trouble accepting this, but it is what occurs, nevertheless.

Although candidiasis has been recognized since the dawn of medicine, the medical mayhem it causes is rarely appreciated. Most of the research has focused on the individual problems related to candidiasis. More recently, instead of looking at the forest or even the trees, the research has shifted toward the leaves and their parts. Dissecting the activities of disease-causing yeast into ever smaller pieces might uncover something interesting, but it is unlikely to reveal the intricacies and multisystem complexities of candidiasis. The mainstream medical community needs to appreciate that the human body is an ecosystem and candidiasis is a condition that upsets its balance and well-being. It takes time, effort, and patience to integrate all the obvious and obscure parts into a comprehensive understanding of the whole.

Disease-causing *Candida*-species organisms are easy to study, and laboratory analysis has revealed a great amount of information. In contrast, as a cause of illness, candidiasis involves intricate, highly complex interactions between disease-causing yeast and the bodies of human beings, which is impossible to study in a laboratory.

Most candidiasis research has been mediocre, involving poorly designed studies, improperly controlled parameters, and high levels of bias by the involved researchers. To complicate matters, candidiasis includes the covert presence of one or more additional infectious invaders, including harmful parasites, bacteria, molds, and/or viruses. This makes research much more difficult. Since medical investigators tend to focus on one variable at a time, their tunnel-vision approach prevents a clear view of the big picture. Optimally, the whole must first be appreciated and understood before a dissection can be performed. Later, when a dissection does occur, its findings are supposed to be integrated into the whole. Little of this approach has occurred with candidiasis research.

I gained an advanced understanding of the infectious and allergic behaviors of disease-causing yeast and the various presentations of candidiasis through observation, thirty-plus years of clinical experience, and an intense study of the medical and scientific literature. Here are some illuminating points I have learned through my training, research, and experience with patients:

- More people develop symptoms and illness from candidiasis every day. The sufferers are increasing, not decreasing. If the number of mild sufferers was truly appreciated, candidiasis would be immediately classified as an epidemic. Instead, it continues to be ignored, ridiculed, and even maligned.

- Most chronic and recurring medical maladies are directly or indirectly due to candidiasis and/or its adverse effects on blood-sugar metabolism.

- According to mainstream medicine, *candidiasis* is an infection with *Candida albicans*. In fact, there are 8 major and 17 less prominent disease-causing yeast. All of them can cause candidiasis and conditions that cannot be treated with a mainstream approach. Therefore, I suggest a new term, *atypical* candidiasis, to describe yeast-related illness that is caused by the less prominent disease-causing yeast. People with atypical candidiasis have infections with, as examples, *Rhodotorula*-species organisms and *Saccharomyces cerevisiae* (baker's and brewer's yeast). Compared to someone infected with the major disease-causing yeast, people with atypical candidiasis are not usually as sick, making them difficult to detect and diagnose. Even worse, the less prominent disease-causing yeast are often unaffected by antifungal medications, which is why some candidiasis sufferers do not respond to medical treatment.

- There is no widespread agreement or accepted explanation regarding the colonization of disease-causing *Candida*-species organisms within the gastrointestinal tract and the presence of their accompanying sensitivities and hypersensitivities (allergies). Some healthcare practitioners accept their allergic contributions can trigger an immune system response, but most only look for antibody-mechanisms related to immunoglobulin E (IgE). Although IgE is accepted as the antibody participating in allergies, about half of all allergies do *not* involve IgE (or other antibodies). In other words, for all the IgE-related sensitivities and hypersensitivities that manifest, an equal amount remains undetected and will not be treated.

- When allergies *are* considered, most practitioners typically look for sensitivities and hypersensitivities to foods, environmental substances, or chemicals. Few physicians consider allergies related to the presence of disease-causing yeast and harmful molds. This oversight ignores most candidiasis sufferers with strong allergies to disease-causing yeast and numerous harmful molds. Since most sufferers consistently manifest these allergies, it is important to test for them and, when identified, administer desensitization (allergy) immunotherapy, using injections or drops. There are many scientifically sound and clinically beneficial reasons to embrace this approach.

- Mainstream research believes that candidiasis exists within people with impaired immunity, thinking the disease-causing yeast only colonize them after their immunity fails. New theories and insight reveal that a persistent infection with disease-causing yeast promotes metabolic disturbances (especially, carbohydrate and lipid metabolism) that damage the immune system. Simply put, candidiasis impairs immunity. Candidiasis-minded physicians appreciate that chronic infections with disease-causing yeast frequently cause defects in cellular (cell-mediated) immunity, including *suppressed immunity* (inferior functioning cells), *depressed immunity* (fewer cells), and *suppressed-depressed immunity* (fewer, inferior functioning cells). Defective cell-mediated immunity is capable of instigating and promoting various abnormal immune system activities. This way of thinking has profound consequences for people suffering with immune system illnesses (like cancer, chronic viral illnesses, AIDS, and autoimmune disease), and is certain to alter the way they are approached, treated, and managed. Mainstream medicine cannot ignore the *candidiasis-cancer connection, candidiasis–chronic viral illness connection*, or *candidiasis–autoimmune disease connection*. Harmful parasites, bacteria, molds, and numerous viruses also contribute their ill effects and must be considered, found, and treated.

- Diagnostic tools are frequently inadequate, and no single test exists to definitively confirm candidiasis, a condition that is typically diagnosed by its symptoms. Unfortunately, most physicians refuse to make a diagnosis that primarily rests on clinical observations; in fact, current medical practice *demands* laboratory justification and verification of every health problem or symptom before a diagnosis can be delivered. There is an inherent contradiction in this approach to illness; it undermines the foundation of good medical practice, which is *diagnostic tests were created to support, not replace, good clinical observations*. In many cases of candidiasis, it is common to hear a doubtful mainstream physician protest, "Oh, you can't be sick, your blood tests look fine." If you are sick, your doctor's confidence about your results will provide little comfort or insight about your condition. If you still insist you are ill, you are likely to be told, "There's a nice psychiatrist I'd like you to see." Although some people could benefit from visiting a psychiatrist, most people *are* suffering with a condition that does not usually reveal itself by common laboratory testing. This nearsighted, scientific approach is unfair to the person suffering. Instead of treating a test result or number, candidiasis-minded physicians know it makes more sense to treat a patient with symptoms and illness. A symptom-oriented approach does not have to exclude good science because numerous tests do support the diagnosis of candidiasis, depending on the strength and weakness of each test.

- To date, no one has provided a suitable explanation for why some patients with *Candida*-negative stool cultures have symptoms, and why others, even with blatantly positive cultures remain asymptomatic. This "stool culture paradox" is now easily explained. Like any laboratory test, stool cultures have limited usefulness.

- No universal candidiasis cure has been discovered. When treatment fails, people assume they did not have it in the first place. Many candidiasis-minded physicians are often unaware of this condition's intricacies; the infection is often widespread and/or improperly treated. As a result, conservative or unsound approaches are virtually guaranteed to provide inadequate health benefits. In a large percentage of cases, especially those with severe illness, there are one or more participating infectious allies, including harmful parasites, bacteria, molds, and/or viruses. To effectively combat candidiasis, it is essential to see and align all the sides of the candidiasis puzzle. The treatment recommendations suggested in this book produce an overwhelming percentage of successes.

- Many sufferers do not respond, or poorly respond, to the commonly used antifungal medication nystatin. This occurs because it is not absorbed into the tissues and can only kill certain disease-causing yeast residing within the gastrointestinal tract; the disease-causing yeast within the tissues and blood are unaffected. In addition, there is a risk to its use because nystatin is a mold-made substance that may induce allergies and allergic reactions in sensitive people. Moreover, it may not work at all because disease-causing *Candida*-species organisms may mutate into nystatin-resistant forms. There are much better antifungal medications (chapter 19).

- Treating candidiasis using allergy shots or drops with *Candida albicans* antigen alone is usually ineffective, even though this type of therapy aims to stimulate the immune system to mount an attack against disease-causing *Candida*-species organisms. This method, which may take months to years to accomplish if it works at all, primarily addresses the *allergic* mischief of *Candida albicans* and rarely eliminates the *infection* with disease-causing yeast; it also does not address the presence of any harmful parasites, bacteria, molds, and/or viruses. The disease-causing yeast must be identified and eliminated with the appropriate therapeutic weapons, whether medications or natural preparations are used. In addition, antigen-antibody cross-reactions between disease-causing yeast and numerous molds encourage the existence of perpetual allergy symptoms. With respect to treating allergy symptoms, significantly better results are obtained when therapy is targeted against all the disease-causing yeast and harmful molds that cause reactions within a candidiasis sufferer.

- More than one-third of all candidiasis sufferers have difficulty maintaining a normal body temperature; typically, their internal thermostat has a lower-than-normal set point. Since immune system activities are temperature-dependent, optimal immunity is impossible with a subnormal body temperature. This handicap must be considered and addressed because immunity is vital for an effective assault against candidiasis. The nervous, endocrine (hormone), and immune systems are interconnected, forming the *neuroendocrine-immune connection*. Candidiasis can affect one or all these systems, and since they are interconnected, disturbances within one system are likely to be reflected within the others. The variety of illness that can arise is staggering. These disturbances will be described and explained throughout this book.

- A tremendous *candidiasis-parasite connection* exists and is commonly overlooked, which is why many sufferers are frequently resistant to standard anti-candidiasis treatment. Once the parasites are revealed and effectively treated, remarkable improvements often occur. Rather than collecting stool samples, the *anoscopy* (rectal swabs, chapter 17) is a better way to reveal the presence of parasites as well as the prevalence of disease-causing yeast.
- In most candidiasis sufferers, the colonization of disease-causing yeast encourages gut disturbances that promote some magnitude of malabsorption and nutritional deficiencies. All sufferers will benefit from an oral supplementation program that corresponds to their symptoms and illness. When sufferers are unable to tolerate oral supplements, especially those with impaired immunity, they require the intravenous administration of vitamins, minerals, and amino acids to assist in their treatment and recovery.
- During treatment, why is it necessary to kill the disease-causing yeast? How strict does your diet need to be? Must you remain yeast-free forever? Will they grow back? These are a few of the hundreds of questions to be considered, addressed, and answered in this book.

The above are only a few points; many more could have been added. The important message is that the infectious and allergic consequences of disease-causing yeast affect the human body directly and indirectly, blatantly and subtly, and overtly and covertly.

On October 25, 2022, the World Health Organization released its first-ever list of health-threatening fungi. They stated, "Emerging from the shadows of the bacterial antimicrobial resistance pandemic, fungal infections are growing, and are ever more resistant to treatments, becoming a public health concern worldwide." Their most dangerous ("critical") group includes *Cryptococcus neoformans* (an encapsulated yeast), *Aspergillus fumigatus* (a harmful mold), *Candida albicans*, and *Candida auris*. Like most mainstream physicians, they only recognize the obvious and advanced cases, and the subclinical presentations are consistently overlooked.

In contrast to mainstream medical thinking, candidiasis affects a much greater percentage of the human population than is currently appreciated, and the number of its sufferers is only increasing. If you have any frequent, recurring, or chronic illness, you are likely to be a candidiasis sufferer. In addition, with the increasing prevalence of long COVID (syndrome) sufferers, including its complex and diverse symptoms, it is highly likely that most of them are candidiasis sufferers.

Based on the information in this book, candidiasis might seem to be an overwhelming and insurmountable condition, but most sufferers should improve within weeks to months. More complex cases will take longer (appendix). In all cases, there is hope because this book describes and explains a comprehensive way to improve your health and well-being.

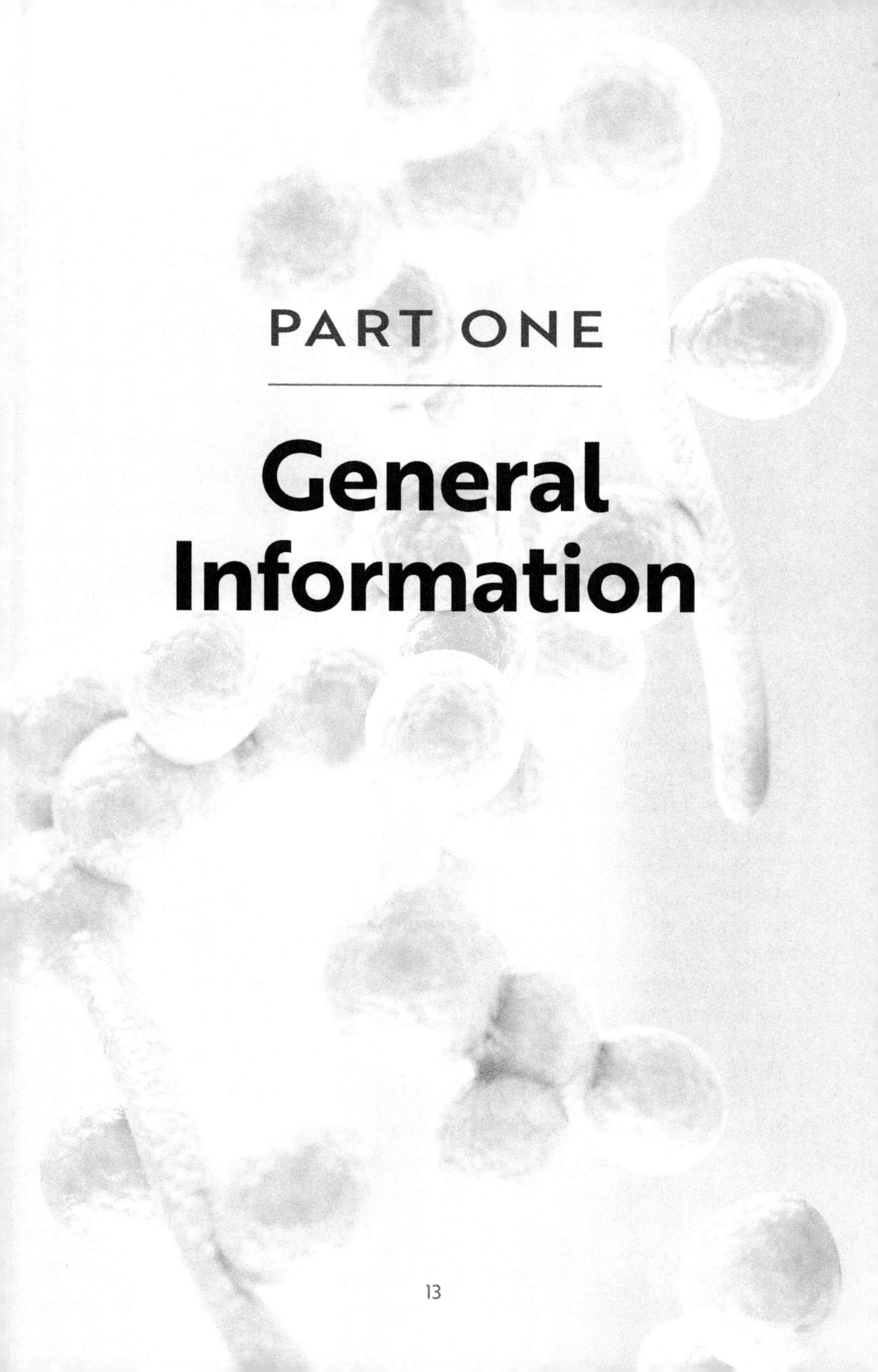

PART ONE

General Information

CHAPTER 1

Do You Feel Sick & Don't Know Why?

You feel sick. The length of time does not matter because all you want to do is to feel better. If you went to a doctor, you may have been diagnosed with an accepted illness, given a prescription for medication with a fancy-sounding name, and then told to return in a few weeks. If you had an acute illness, were treated with antibiotics or something else, and got better, you might have nothing more to do. However, if you develop frequent, recurrent, and chronic health problems, keep reading.

Although most medications used to treat chronic and recurring medical problems might alleviate someone's symptoms, they are unlikely to eradicate the actual cause of their suffering. Even worse, a symptom-oriented, drug-treatment approach forces someone to take medication for an extended duration, if not the rest of their life, or they risk getting worse. Over time, most people taking long-term medication do become worse, requiring more medication.

Speak to anyone suffering with a chronic or recurring medical problem. Ask them how many prescription and nonprescription drugs they have in their medicine cabinet. Ask them how many prescriptions they get filled each week, month, and year. How much money do they or their insurance company spend for it? If you are suffering with a chronic or recurring medical problem and willing to take one or more medications for the rest of your life, that medical approach is perfect for you. If you are in search of a better answer, read on.

In contrast, suppose you are sick, and your doctor is confused by your ill health. You have mysterious symptoms that come and go, no clear laboratory test abnormalities, or problems that do not fit into accepted medical parameters. How can you receive effective care when your physician cannot understand your illness? You are likely to feel frustrated and abandoned when your doctor proclaims, "I can't find anything wrong, so there's someone I want you to see." This is when you are referred to one or more specialists, and maybe a psychiatrist.

Since specialists only look for the signs and symptoms that pertain to their area of specialization, they cannot see the big picture. Instead of being considered a whole person, your health gets dissected into ever smaller parts with each specialist consulted. In return, you may end up seeing an allergist for your runny nose; a gastroenterologist for your heartburn, constipation, and bloating; an ophthalmologist for your dry eyes; and other physicians anxious to treat each of your symptoms one or two at a time. As a result, you end up taking numerous medications without substantial improvements. In many instances, depending on the combination of medications, including their side effects and interactions, you might feel even worse.

Although mainstream medical specialists believe they are administering good healthcare, a symptom-oriented approach eliminates their responsibility as healers. The goal of a healer is to "heal" you. Specialists can only heal symptoms they were trained to understand; they cannot treat health problems they do not. Therefore, if you suffer from a condition that adversely affects many parts of your body all at once, treating symptoms one at a time will do little to get you well. Considering you as a whole person, rather than assessing and treating your individual parts one at a time, is the secret to transcending your ill health.

In the big picture, it does not matter whether you have a name for your condition, disorder, syndrome, illness, or disease. In every case, something is wrong, and you only want to have it corrected and feel better. More to the point, if you are like most people who are suffering, you want a permanent solution, not a temporary fix; you would like to eliminate the cause of your ill health, not just suppress your symptoms.

In your search for wellness, you might have visited numerous doctors and a variety of specialists. Frustration may have motivated you to try "alternative" therapies. More likely than not, the results of your efforts have been mediocre or short-lived. Clearly, something is occurring within your body that is not being addressed by most therapies; obviously, if it was, you would feel better. You are running out of options. Time passes and you still suffer. Where do you turn next? What should you do? Where should you go? Who should you see? If this sounds all too familiar, you should consider candidiasis.

More people are experiencing chronic and recurring medical maladies than ever before. If you are lucky, you may never develop this type of illness, or it may only occur for a short time in your life and disappear forever.

More often, your illness will wax and wane over many years, worsening as time passes. Unfortunately, some people's daily existence, and even their lives, may be perpetually plagued and, ultimately, ruined by their chronic ill health. In a search for the cause of your illness, you may have found a doctor who cares enough to consider the big picture. Even when this is the case, most mainstream physicians are still likely to intricately dissect and examine you under a microscope. Regardless, if your doctor does not look in the right place, or does not know what to look for, this endeavor will be a complete waste of time. If this rings a bell . . . if you have been under this type of scrutiny . . . if you still have no clear answers, you need to consider candidiasis.

Mainstream medicine does not have all the answers with respect to combating chronic and recurring medical maladies. This explains why most people who visit their health practitioners often feel dissatisfied with their care. These same patients are frequently told they should "learn how to live" with their condition. Any sane person would find this frustrating, to say the least. Even more annoying, most physicians believe this approach is appropriate and good medicine. They hope your problem will someday be better understood and a medication or vaccine will become available to cure it. In the meantime, they believe they are doing their best for you. That is fine for them, but why must you "learn how to live" with your condition when treatment is available? Just because mainstream medicine does not recognize the problem, it does not mean one does not exist. If you are keeping an open mind, continuing to search for better answers, do not want to "learn how to live" with your health problem, and are not willing to wait forever for a magical cure that may never arrive, you must consider candidiasis.

Hopefully, you are now starting to think about candidiasis, a condition greatly misunderstood, underappreciated, and often maligned. How can you get the answers you need or the care you require? Since candidiasis is not taught or even mentioned in most medical schools, it continues to be a mysterious condition hidden behind a closed curtain. For numerous reasons, mainstream medical research has been unable to open this curtain, so it remains tightly closed. Meanwhile, your joints hurt. Your headaches are unbearable. You are bloated, confused, fatigued, and miserable. Your allergies are terrible. Anxiety and depression are a constant burden. *Oh, if I could only feel better,* you think, as you continue to hope for some salvation from your ill health. Your "candle of hope" may have even burned out altogether.

Fortunately, there is hope because all your symptoms, and more, can be understood and treated. This, of course, can only occur when you know where to look and what to look for. So, what is the answer? Whether you know it or not, the odds are great the colonization of disease-causing yeast is causing your suffering. Candidiasis is an infection with allergic consequences that can cause an incredible diversity of symptoms and illness. In addition, candidiasis frequently includes the adverse contributions of one or more harmful parasites, bacteria, molds, and/or viruses. So, instead of being sick and not knowing why, you must understand there is a cause of your suffering, and it is called candidiasis.

THE MANY MANIFESTATIONS OF CANDIDIASIS

Candidiasis involves a diversity and spectrum of symptoms, conditions, syndromes, disorders, illnesses, and diseases. Even if you are well informed, the confusion surrounding candidiasis must be clarified, especially with respect to its treatment. By the way, do not expect help from your doctor or other health practitioners; to them, candidiasis is a totally fictitious, phantom illness created by a group of hypochondriacs. As a result, most candidiasis sufferers have been abandoned by the mainstream medical community. What about the few candidiasis-minded healthcare providers out there? Unfortunately, for all their good intentions, many of them do not have great, or even consistent, success in treating candidiasis; usually, they lack the science or understanding to treat their patients effectively and completely. So, what should you do?

The wisest choice is to assume some responsibility and try to learn as much as possible about this overlooked and underappreciated health blight. After all, an educated patient truly cares about their health and, regarding candidiasis, is likely to know more than their doctor. When you are an active participant in decisions that involve your health and well-being, you become an asset to yourself as well as to your doctor.

If you think candidiasis is a new condition, you probably thought yeast was only notable for its culinary use. Although television commercials and magazine ads about vaginal yeast infections indicate its potential for medical mischief, this relatively mild manifestation of yeast-related illness sits at the top of a much larger and dangerous iceberg that resides underwater. When you look below the surface, you will realize candidiasis is a major cause of chronic and recurring medical problems, and its long-term mischief promotes debility and even death.

Most physicians cannot understand how one condition can cause such a diversity of medical maladies. Ignoring all the proof, mainstream medicine proclaims disease-causing yeast as innocent microorganisms beyond reproach, except in the most extreme cases. Opponents of candidiasis say everyone harbors some disease-causing yeast within them, and insist candidiasis is a fictitious condition that is difficult, if not impossible, to diagnose. Yes, candidiasis is a complicated condition, but it is far from fictitious.

To add fuel to the fire, mainstream physicians are quick to point out there is no one test to diagnose candidiasis. "How can this condition exist if it can't be proved with a laboratory test?" they ask. In contrast, the diagnosis of candidiasis should primarily be based on its symptoms and illness; although numerous tests exist to support its diagnosis (chapter 17), it cannot be determined by laboratory findings alone. Instead, the identification of yeast-related mischief rests and relies on sound clinical judgment and experience. The first step to understanding candidiasis is to be aware of its most common manifestations, including food allergies, fatigue, allergic rhinitis, metabolic immune disorders, headaches, abdominal bloating/gas, depression, constipation, abdominal pain, vaginitis, poor memory, itching, joint pains, sore throats, frequent colds, skin rashes, asthma, flu-like symptoms, PMS, diarrhea, muscle pains, and recurring urinary tract infections, as well as many other less-frequent symptoms.

How can disease-causing yeast cause so many different medical maladies? It involves a multitude of complex interactions between disease-causing yeast and the human body. Over time, as their population increases within the body, their presence, chemical activities, and allergy-inducing abilities instigate and/or promote numerous disturbances resulting in both *infectious* and *allergic* consequences. In addition, candidiasis is frequently exacerbated by the presence and undesirable contributions of one or more harmful parasites, bacteria, molds, and/or viruses. The symptoms and illness that arise are also determined by your body's inherited (genetic) strengths and weaknesses, your diet, the amount of stress in your life, exposures to toxins (like heavy metals, chemicals, and plastics), and anything else that harms you.

Typically, during candidiasis, the gastrointestinal tract and mucous membranes are the first areas colonized by disease-causing yeast and adversely affected. Since they can be in the air around us, the sinuses and respiratory tract are equally vulnerable, or these areas can become colonized if they spread from the mucous membranes.

As candidiasis progresses, the disease-causing yeast can become more aggressive, invade into the tissues, and then enter the blood. The longer the infection persists, the more it disturbs and damages the functioning of the immune, endocrine (hormone), and nervous systems. Candidiasis is virtually impossible to miss in some patients because of their symptoms and illness, whereas other patients require a high index of suspicion to avoid overlooking their yeast-related disturbances. Why does this variety exist? Since every person is different, every sufferer will not exhibit the exact same symptoms and illness. Candidiasis is far from a black-or-white, all-or-none illness. If it was clear-cut, it would be simple to diagnose.

Why is candidiasis not more fully appreciated and accepted? Unlike infections that readily induce fever or other obvious signs, indicating their presence, candidiasis is frequently a low-grade, stealth infection (subclinical) that produces less-obvious complications, including a spectrum of allergies. Unlike infections that assault the body over hours to days, candidiasis is a chronic condition that can take months to years to develop. Unlike other illnesses that have a definitive laboratory test to make their diagnosis, candidiasis does not have one solitary "you have it or you don't" lab test. Typically, candidiasis is first considered and later diagnosed because of someone's symptoms and illness; approximately 90 percent is based on the history obtained from the patient by carefully questioning and listening. Obviously, when mainstream medical reasoning is founded on laboratory testing, rather than by obtaining a thorough medical history, candidiasis is certain to be overlooked. Sadly, thorough medical histories are rarely taken.

According to Ross E. McRonald, M.D., a family physician, commenting in the July 15, 1999, issue of *Internal Medicine News* (32[4]:9), "Unfortunately, the medical history is disintegrating. It has become seriously incomplete, and the causes are manifold . . . An individual arriving at a new doctor's office rarely takes the time to complete a comprehensive medical history. The physician, under the pressure of an increased patient load, often omits a comprehensive history." When the covert tendencies of disease-causing yeast, its spectrum of manifestations, the presence of other infectious invaders, and the lack of a definitive laboratory test are all combined, the confusion surrounding candidiasis becomes easier to understand and appreciate.

It is no secret doctors like "black-or-white" diagnoses—if it is not *this*, then it is going to be *that*. This instills them with confidence, making their job easier. Currently accepted medical practice places its emphasis on treating symptoms and diseases, rather than identifying the cause of illness, particularly when its origins are nebulous or a mystery. Indeed, the less a doctor thinks about their patient's problem the better, especially when the average length of a typical office visit is a scant six minutes. In contrast, candidiasis is a condition that requires a doctor to obtain a thorough medical history, which certainly takes much more time than six minutes, before a diagnosis can be given. It is sad to say, but longer patient visits mean a physician will see fewer patients and, consequently, lose income. Therefore, due to time and economic constraints, it is not a diagnosis that is likely to be considered or entertained.

The fact that the mainstream medical community consistently overlooks candidiasis would seem bad enough, but something more disturbing frequently occurs that adds insult to injury. It is common for a candidiasis sufferer to visit numerous physicians, insist something is amiss, not be effectively treated, and become more desperate with each physician consulted. When nothing is found to be wrong, according to mainstream medicine's standards, a physician is likely to label a candidiasis sufferer a hypochondriac.

After this occurs numerous times, the attitude toward this patient changes; physicians run out of places to look for answers and the candidiasis sufferer gets less attention, eventually becoming a victim of neglect. By that time, they may be classified as having some type of mental illness. In fact, this is unsurprising because most sufferers do become depressed and anxious when they reach this point. In return, because they lack appropriate answers and do not know where to look, physicians will likely focus on the patient's mental state, saying their symptoms are due to depression, with possible anxiety, and they are likely to prescribe one or more medications. If the patient improves, which is often the case or there would not be so many people currently taking medication, psychiatric illness is confirmed. However, what most physicians do not know, and would not admit if they did, is many antidepressants have antifungal activity; the medication kills disease-causing *Candida*-species organisms and other fungi. So, the patient who appears to be suffering with a neurosis is really a candidiasis sufferer. However, once again, the diagnosis of candidiasis is missed. Even worse, this same patient may be sent for psychotherapy, which is likely to further complicate and delay their recovery.

Fortunately, a handful of doctors *do* recognize candidiasis as a legitimate medical condition and treat it accordingly. They appreciate that the human body has an inherent tendency toward wellness, believing everyone has the right to good health—the right to eat well, exercise, get a full night's sleep, decrease stress, and so on. If we waive any or all of these rights, illness is likely; although it is usually mild at first, it will be easily exacerbated as more insults are added. Using logic, candidiasis-minded physicians accept symptoms, conditions, disorders, syndromes, illnesses, and diseases without an obvious cause must result from something. These medical maladies cannot appear for no reason or from nowhere; ill health always has a cause. Yet, identifying the cause of mysterious medical maladies is not always easy. Fortunately, in 1961, a clinician named C. Orian Truss made the association between *Candida albicans* and chronic illness, but the history of candidiasis dates much further back in time.

A BRIEF HISTORY OF CANDIDIASIS

Billions of years ago, life began on this planet. At first, it was exceedingly simple; only single-celled organisms existed. In the beginning, there was plenty of room for all, and anything able to survive and reproduce could expand its population. As time passed, evolution rolled its dice, and changes occurred; some slowly, others quickly. As competition occurred, survival of the fittest became the standard for existence. "Fitter" forms survived and evolved, while the less-fit were likely to fade away and become extinct. As a result, life that adapted was able to colonize our mostly water-covered planet. This has taken about 3.5 *billion* years. Recent evidence reveals our ancestors evolved into human beings over the past 3.4 to 3.6 *million* years.

As more human beings populated our world, so did their problems and issues. Initially, our ancestors' most important concern was survival. As humankind progressed, we learned to avoid chaos by instituting order. Some people wrote laws to keep the masses orderly. Other people were designated to enforce these laws. Although different groups instituted their own laws, which varied from one group to another, these "rules" enabled humankind to live together as a whole and, in general, as peacefully as possible.

As humankind's knowledge and insight increased, it became clear there was a difference between health and disease. *Health* is considered the normal state of existence, while *disease* is abnormal. Initially, the roots of this thinking probably arose out of the need to survive, not individually, but as a group. Since the strength of a tribe depended on its hunters and gatherers, if one of them became injured or ill, the overall strength of the tribe decreased, which made everyone less likely to survive. Maintaining the strength-fitness of the people ensured the survival of the entire tribe. That is why some people became skilled at treating medical maladies. These "health restorers" or "healers" were often taught by the elders of the community, or they learned by trial and error. If a treatment helped an ill person regain their health, this method would be applied to others. Since there was a need for their services, most communities had at least one medicine man or woman. It is important to note these ancient healers were, unknowingly, doing research using a highly primitive form of case studies.

One day, a man named Hippocrates began to practice the art of healing. During his lifetime (circa 460–370 BC), modern science was in its infancy, so he could not conduct double-blind, placebo-controlled, random, crossover studies. If you could have discussed our current methods with Hippocrates, he probably would say it sounds interesting and of great value, but the results would take too long to achieve. Like every committed healer, he wanted to help the sick regain and maintain their health. Fortunately for his patients, he did not have to fight between mainstream and alternative medicine; during his time, there was no difference between them. Politics played no part in Hippocrates's practice; he simply used whatever worked to benefit the sick. Clearly, his only concern was healing. Since he was the first to practice medicine in a formalized way, Hippocrates later became known as the Father of Medicine. Feeling there should be some science to healing, he kept records, diaries, and other notes. He was a pioneer and brought new developments in medical management. Others recognized his efforts and respected him, and many followed in his footsteps. In his honor, every physician is supposed to take the Hippocratic Oath when they graduate from medical school, pledging their allegiance to Hippocrates's medical ethics and behavior.

Hippocrates was one of the first doctors to describe oral thrush and its manifestations; his description of this condition can be found in his work *Epidemics III*. This illustrates that disease-causing *Candida*-species organisms, as well as other fungi, were recognized and appreciated for their harm long ago. Hippocrates's observations prove candidiasis existed more than 2,500 years ago. After his work and observations, for the most part, candidiasis fell into obscurity.

We should appreciate that Hippocrates (and many of the physicians who followed him) did *not* have medical technology to assist their diagnosis. Hippocrates's practice of medicine was limited to obtaining a thorough *history* from the patient and performing a complete *physical examination*. Although he occasionally analyzed some bodily fluids, he appreciated the use of *auscultation* (listening to the internal organs, such as the heart and lungs), *percussion* (tapping areas of the body, like the chest, back, and abdomen), and *palpation* (touching an organ or area of the body). He knew these three tools, in addition to obtaining a history and observing the patient, would determine a patient's wellness or illness. These clinical tools have always been, and will continue to be, the crux of a correct diagnosis.

Moreover, good clinical observations do not always come without difficulty. Sometimes an old problem leads to an innovative discovery. For example, William Withering, M.D., a graduate of the University of Edinburgh in Scotland, was introduced to the "secret" treatment for "dropsy" (edema or water retention), a condition considered unmanageable at the time. Dr. Withering learned that one woman was using a combination of some two dozen herbs and had great success in treating patients with dropsy, even though numerous physicians had tried to treat them and failed. After analyzing the woman's herbal formula, Dr. Withering discovered the herb foxglove (*Digitalis purpurea*) was the active and effective ingredient. To confirm his theory, Dr. Withering selected 163 patients and treated them with foxglove. His success proved foxglove caused a loss of water (diuresis). In 1785, after 10 years of observations, he published a book on digitalis—a drug prepared from the seeds and dried leaves of foxglove, which has been one of the most respected and recognized preparations for treating congestive heart failure. It took an open mind, 10 years, and hard work to produce one notable discovery.

C. Orian Truss, M.D., from Birmingham, Alabama, graduated New York Cornell Medical College, and completed his postgraduate medical training at Bellevue Hospital in New York City, including being a chief resident. He then became an internist, specializing in allergies.

By coincidence and keen observations, Dr. Truss made a profound discovery. In 1961, he gave a desensitization (allergy) injection containing *Candida* antigen (the allergy-inducing part of *Candida albicans*) to a woman suffering with multiple chronic symptoms, including yeast vaginitis, severe headaches, and terrible depression. Although Dr. Truss administered the allergy injection to decrease the woman's vaginal symptoms, he was surprised when her headache and depression completely disappeared after 10 minutes. Unfortunately, the benefits were temporary because the woman returned the next morning with all her symptoms. Once again, Dr. Truss repeated the injection with the same results. After some thought, he concluded the *Candida* antigen injection effectively blocked the woman's symptoms.

In 1977, after 16 years of work and research, Dr. Truss presented his findings to the Academy of Orthomolecular Psychiatry in Toronto, Canada. He hypothesized multisystemic problems, previously unrelated to any causative agent, might result from an infection with *Candida albicans*. In 1983, he released *The Missing Diagnosis*, in which he proclaimed *Candida albicans* was the medical missing link—that is, it was responsible for numerous illnesses with no known cause. Although he primarily wrote his book for the public, he hoped to enlighten his colleagues and encourage followers. To strengthen his case, he published numerous scientific articles in the medical literature. Sadly, for all his hard work, only a handful of physicians attempted Dr. Truss's anti-candidiasis protocol. Most of the medical world remained silent. Like Columbus being ostracized for claiming that the world was round, the mainstream medical community refused to consider or accept a discovery based on simple observations, no matter how obvious. Like a judge delivering a death sentence, they deemed his work "anecdotal evidence" and announced it would never be accepted until double-blind, crossover studies were performed. Unfortunately, but understandably, Dr. Truss became frustrated, withdrew from the candidiasis controversy, and faded out of the spotlight.

Regardless, a revolution was underway. The news of Dr. Truss's discovery slowly spread. Successes with patients added to the growing need for more information. Demand triggered the creation of two additional books: *The Yeast Connection* by William G. Crook, M.D., and *The Yeast Syndrome* by John Parks Trowbridge, M.D., and Morton Walker, D.P.M. They became best sellers and enlightened the public about poly-systemic candidiasis syndrome. In addition, they also delivered a strong message to the mainstream medical community, which still insisted candidiasis was completely fictitious.

Even though mainstream medicine continued to ignore the treatment successes, the number of candidiasis believers increased, and more books were written. Many physicians have searched for the "yeast connection." The proponents of candidiasis are typically holistic and complementary physicians, but it also includes several other open-minded healthcare practitioners, like naturopaths, dietitians, acupuncturists, and more. Most surprisingly, a few mainstream physicians do embrace candidiasis. All of them accept that candidiasis is a legitimate condition.

The opponents have also been hard at work, hoping to eradicate any belief in candidiasis. They liken the proponents' efforts to the search for the Holy Grail. "Candidiasis looks great in theory," they say, "but it probably does not exist." They are quick to add there is no working definition for a "multisystemic candidiasis syndrome." Yet, how can a condition that adversely affects numerous bodily systems, producing multiple symptoms, be classified? In other words, the diverse presentations of candidiasis have prevented the establishment of a clear, working definition. Unfortunately, this all-or-none viewpoint has discouraged and prevented valid, scientifically designed research. After all, if something cannot be defined, how can it be understood and studied systematically?

Why does candidiasis get shortchanged when a working definition exists for a condition called chronic active Epstein-Barr virus (CAEBV)? Epstein-Barr virus was, at one time, thought to be the cause of chronic fatigue syndrome, yet studies to support its cause and effect are lacking. It should be noted, by the time we are adults, almost all of us have been exposed to Epstein-Barr virus, but only a small percentage develops and displays a persistent Epstein-Barr virus infection; usually, it involves people with impaired immunity. In contrast, not every person with deficient immunity and chronic fatigue has evidence of an infection with Epstein-Barr virus. So, at best, CAEBV would seem to be a subpopulation of patients with chronic fatigue syndrome. If mainstream medicine does not understand the intricacies of something simple like CAEBV, why does a working definition exist? Candidiasis has been much more studied and understood, but its working definition does not officially exist. This oversight is due to the complex nature of candidiasis; in essence, its inherent variability makes a precise working definition difficult by mainstream medicine's standards. Simply put, if candidiasis did not involve multiple manifestations, it would be easy to classify. This black-or-white thinking has hindered mainstream medicine's understanding of candidiasis.

Regardless, with respect to candidiasis, multiple symptoms and illness can and do belong to the same condition, whether it is accepted or not. To add confusion, the lack of one generally agreed-upon name has created dozens of designations, including *Candida*-related complex, candidiasis hypersensitivity syndrome, chronic candidiasis syndrome, monilial hypersensitivity, *Candida albicans*-related illness, chronic mucocutaneous candidiasis, and more. None of them are considered standard nomenclature. Even without a universally accepted designation, disease-causing yeast (and other harmful fungi) play an undeniable part in the development, maintenance, and enhancement of human illness and disease.

Nevertheless, the universe, including our planet, is in infinite color. Life does not appear to follow a "yes or no" plan. An organism does not have to *either* cause illness *or* be completely innocent. There are also shades of gray and tints of color. Human beings vary, and so do their interactions with disease-causing yeast. That is why candidiasis encompasses a broad spectrum of symptoms, conditions, disorders, syndromes, illnesses, and diseases. From annoying allergies to deadly cancers, candidiasis displays its many ugly faces and different personalities. Although there are similarities among its sufferers, it is important to appreciate disease-causing yeast are tiny tricksters capable of instigating and/or promoting a diversity of medical maladies; as a result, no two people are ever impaired the same way. Candidiasis is an *infection* with *allergic* consequences, so both tendencies must be considered and appropriately addressed. Since numerous other infectious invaders (harmful parasites, bacteria, molds, and/or viruses) often exacerbate candidiasis, uncovering, identifying, and eliminating their presence is essential. Moreover, the colonization of disease-causing yeast within the gastrointestinal tract causes malabsorption and nutritional deficiencies that must be addressed and treated. In addition, some sufferers have been exposed to toxic heavy metals and disruptive chemicals that should be assessed and treated. Although there are similarities among candidiasis sufferers, all of this will ultimately prove that there are more differences than most realize.

Yes, candidiasis is a legitimate condition. Yes, it can be diagnosed. Yes, it can be treated. However, according to one of the most important founders of medical microbiology, Louis Pasteur, "Where observation is concerned, chance favors only the prepared mind." So, if you have candidiasis and want to eliminate it, you must first learn as much as possible. You need to understand why certain things work and why others do not. You need to avoid sabotaging your recovery by making mistakes. At the same time, you should know what to expect. It is in your best interest to become an educated patient to make certain you are treated correctly. You are not expected or supposed to make your own decisions because a knowledgeable candidiasis-minded physician should be consulted.

QUESTIONING YOUR SUSPICIONS

Candidiasis is confusing. Although there are still missing pieces, the information in this book provides strong support for the existence of candidiasis and a request for more serious study and research to be done. The pieces can fit together and create a clearer picture when a basic tenet is followed: Candidiasis has two sides, *infectious* and *allergic*. Although one may be more prominent than the other, most sufferers have both. When this is combined with their genetic strengths/weaknesses, risk factors, environmental exposures, stress, and more (including the adverse effects of harmful parasites, bacteria, molds, and/or viruses), a diversity and spectrum of symptoms and illness results. Since every person is different, every sufferer is unique and must be diagnosed and treated as such. Remember, candidiasis is the underlying cause of most chronic and recurring medical maladies, not simply a set of symptoms.

Okay, so maybe it is candidiasis, you start thinking. Obviously, when you develop suspicions, it is a good idea to question them. The Candidiasis Questionnaire in this section will provide a better indication of whether candidiasis is participating in your medical problems and ill health. Your answers are not absolute proof because there are always exceptions. This questionnaire is only a tool to help point you in the appropriate direction.

Keep in mind, your score is only a number. In fact, it may change from season to season, week to week, and day to day. Its real value is its ability to indicate the *presence* of candidiasis. What it does not reveal is that you are a unique individual with a body that may compensate differently from someone else's. If you experience many of the symptoms on the questionnaire infrequently or only a couple constantly, the odds favor candidiasis.

Moreover, it does not matter whether your candidiasis is mild, moderate, or severe. Over time, your symptoms and illness are likely to worsen. The key is to recognize your problem early and treat it accordingly. Prevention is sound thinking and the secret to lifelong wellness. Yet, if you have moderate or severe candidiasis, please seek professional assistance.

CANDIDIASIS QUESTIONNAIRE

The following questionnaire is designed to determine if you may have candidiasis. It is divided into four sections: questions for adults and adolescents, questions for female adults and adolescents, questions for male adults and adolescents, and questions for children.

Answer all the questions that pertain to you (or your child). Adult women and adolescent girls should answer Sections A and B. Adult men and adolescent boys should answer Sections A and C. Young children only require Section D; obviously, a parent or guardian should answer.

Answer questions with a number between 0 and 5 (**0 = never; 1 = rarely; 2 = infrequently; 3 = occasionally; 4 = often; 5 = always**). After finishing, total each section and read the scoring directions at the end to determine your likelihood, or your child's, of having candidiasis.

A. Questions for All Adults and Adolescents

1. Have you taken frequent or prolonged courses of antibiotics? ______
2. Have you repeatedly used prednisone or another steroid? ______
3. Have you ever had or been treated for parasites? ______
4. Are you worse on warm or damp days, and/or in musty or moldy locations? ______
5. After enough sleep, do you experience low energy, tiredness, or persistent fatigue? ______
6. Do you have depression-anxiety, and/or frequently feel "blue" for no reason at all? ______
7. Are headaches, memory loss, irritability, moodiness, feeling "spaced out" or "in a fog" common complaints? ______
8. Do you have bloating, gas, belching, heartburn, abdominal pain or cramping, ulcers, diarrhea, and/or constipation? ______
9. Do you have or experience acne, rashes, hives, itching, or other skin eruptions? ______
10. Are you hypersensitive to odors, such as tobacco smoke, perfumes, fabric dyes, and household chemicals? ______
11. Do you suffer from frequent or recurring fluid retention? ______
12. Do you have a chronic runny nose or postnasal drip? ______
13. Do you have sinus problems or suffer with sinus headaches? ______
14. Do you suffer with allergies, asthma, or a chronic cough? ______
15. Do you have sore throats, colds, bronchitis, or other chronic or recurring infections? ______

16. Have you ever had cancer, a chronic viral illness, autoimmune disease, or any other illness that involves impaired immunity? ______

17. Do you have, or have you had, high blood pressure, heart disease, a stroke, or any chronic or recurrent cardiovascular problem? ______

18. Do you have elevated cholesterol and/or triglyceride levels? ______

19. Do you have body temperature disturbances or problems with your thyroid gland (for example, over or under activity, Grave's disease, or anything else)? ______

20. Do you frequently have cold hands and feet? ______

21. Do you have joint pains or arthritis? ______

22. Do you crave sugar or carbohydrates? ______

23. Do you suffer with hypoglycemia symptoms, including shakiness, sweating, dizziness, lightheadedness, and severe feelings of hunger if a meal is skipped? ______

Section A Total* ______

**Maximum Score = 115*

B. Questions for Adult and Adolescent Females

1. Have you ever used birth control pills, estrogen, or other female hormones? ______

2. Do you have chronic or recurring genitourinary symptoms, such as vaginitis, rectal burning or itching, urinary tract infections, or excessive urination during the day or night? ______

3. Do you have PMS, irregular menses, a low sex drive, or infertility? ______

4. Have you been pregnant two or more times? (Either 0 or 5) ______

5. Do you have difficulty becoming pregnant or carrying a pregnancy to full term? ________
6. Do you have vaginal burning, itching, or pain during intercourse? ________
7. Do you have menstrual problems or endometriosis? ________
8. Do you suffer with breast lumps or cysts? ________
9. Do you get hot flushes or flashes? ________

Section B Total* ________

**Maximum Score = 45*

C. Questions for Adult and Adolescent Males

1. Do you suffer with impotence? ________
2. Did you have any penile discharge? ________
3. Do you frequently need to urinate or feel burning and/or itching with urination? ________
4. Have you ever had a lump in one or both testicles? ________
5. Do you suffer with orchitis (inflammation involving one or both testicles)? ________
6. Do you suffer with prostatitis (inflammation of the prostate gland)? ________

Section C Total* ________

**Maximum Score = 30*

D. Questions for the Parents of a Young Child

1. Was your child a colicky baby? ________
2. Has your child ever received antibiotics? ________
3. Does your child have dark circles under his or her eyes? ________

4. Does your child have allergies? ________
5. Does/did your child suffer with eczema or contact dermatitis? ________
6. Does/did your child have continuous nasal congestion, drainage, or the sniffles? ________
7. Does/did your child suffer with chronic or frequent ear infections or tonsillitis? ________
8. Does/did your child suffer with a chronic cough, bronchitis, or asthma? ________
9. Is/was your child hyperactive, with or without a poor attention span? ________
10. Does your child have a history of bed-wetting? ________

Section D Total* ________

**Maximum Score = 50*

Scoring

For adult and adolescent females: Add the totals of Sections A and B. If your grand total score is between 50 and 104, you are likely to have moderate candidiasis. If your grand total score is above 105, it supports the likelihood of severe candidiasis.

For adult and adolescent males: Add the totals of Sections A and C. If your grand total score is between 35 and 84, you may have moderate candidiasis. If your grand total score is above 85, it supports the likelihood of severe candidiasis.

For young children: If your child's score on Section D is between 20 and 34, your child may have moderate candidiasis. If your child's score is above 35, it supports the likelihood of severe candidiasis.

CHAPTER 2

What Risk Factors Promote Candidiasis?

Unlike other illnesses, candidiasis is not a black-or-white, all-or-nothing, "you have it or don't" condition. There is an enormous gray area between good health and the most blatant case of candidiasis. Between these extremes, sufferers experience and demonstrate a diversity of symptoms and illness, ranging from mild to severe. In advanced cases, candidiasis can be debilitating, life-threatening, and even fatal. Since every person is a unique individual, each sufferer's condition will be exclusive to them, including their specific symptoms, illness, and history of why and how they developed their candidiasis.

Candidiasis involves the colonization of disease-causing *Candida*-species organisms within the human body. Initially, they populate the gastrointestinal tract, anywhere from the mouth to anus. Over time, they can invade further, into the tissues and blood. Do the disease-causing yeast just appear magically? No, they are normally present in small amounts within the gastrointestinal tracts of all human beings. Yet, healthy people have beneficial (good) bacteria that inhibit and suppress their growth; they keep the disease-causing yeast under control, preventing them from causing harm. Unfortunately, various circumstances and risky behaviors impair, injure, or even kill the beneficial bacteria, enabling the disease-causing yeast to reproduce and colonize their surroundings. Certain exposures are strongly associated with candidiasis, while others are a weak cause for concern.

As a medical condition, candidiasis involves the complex interaction between disease-causing yeast and their human host. In contrast to other illnesses, it has a multitude and diversity of risk factors. Simply put, a risk factor is anything that places you at risk for developing candidiasis. Major risk factors are more likely to instigate illness, while the minor ones are typically less troublesome. Yet, this does not mean minor risk factors are harmless because repeated or prolonged exposure to one or more can accumulate and cause significant disturbances. In fact, given enough time, every risk factor is a cause for concern. No matter how minor, the more risk factors someone is exposed to, the greater their chance to develop candidiasis. Confusingly, even though it has numerous prominent risk factors, there will never be a 100 percent correlation between exposure to any single risk factor and the development of candidiasis. In other words, a particular risk factor may be insignificant for one person and overwhelm someone else.

Since everyone is unique, each sufferer adapts or succumbs to candidiasis in their own way. People with similar histories of risk factors are *not* guaranteed to experience identical symptoms or illness. There is no one hard and fast rule, and numerous exceptions exist. With respect to candidiasis, a seemingly infinite variety of predisposing and compromising circumstances are known to promote its development. If you have candidiasis, want to avoid making mistakes, and get well, you need to understand and appreciate the risk factors that caused and continue to support your ill health.

THE MAJOR RISK FACTORS

Although some risk factors are more influential than others, and all affect sufferers to varying degrees, most cause some disturbance or reaction in everyone exposed. A specific factor may be the primary cause of one person's condition, but insignificantly affect someone else. Regardless of the risk factor, disease-causing yeast are opportunists that readily reproduce and colonize their environment when given the chance. Therefore, anything that increases their potential to do this, or alters the body's capacity to combat them, will accelerate the development of candidiasis as well as its associated problems and disturbances.

Note: The following risk factors are arranged alphabetically, not by importance or prevalence.

Allergies

If you experience a runny nose and watery eyes in the springtime, you know what it is like to have an allergy. If you wheeze in the fall, when ragweed is prevalent, you know what it is like to have an allergy. If you get bloating and gas every time you eat green pepper, you know what it is like to have an allergy. These are common allergies. If you break out in hives when you are exposed to cats, get blisters on your hands after you touch chlorinated bleach, or become depressed every time you eat bread or pasta, you also have allergies, even though these allergic manifestations are less common.

Candidiasis-minded physicians are aware that allergies can instigate and/or promote a diversity of symptoms and illness, including asthma, alcoholism, stomachaches, acne, hives, eczema, skin rashes, panic attacks, anxiety, depression, fatigue, migraine headaches, muscle and joint pains, and numerous other problems.

An *allergy* is an acquired and abnormal immune system response to a substance (*antigen*) that does not normally cause a reaction in someone else. Since healthy people do not develop allergies, it implies that people with allergies must be suffering from ill health. In general, allergies arise when someone's immune system becomes sensitive or hypersensitive; it produces inflammation and other undesirable immune system reactions that can stress the body and disturb its normal defense mechanisms. For example, food allergies within the gastrointestinal tract can inflame and impair the gut wall. In turn, a weakened gut wall allows disease-causing yeast to invade it, gaining access to the gut tissues. It also creates excessive mucus, protecting the disease-causing yeast from substances that kill them.

Most candidiasis sufferers experience allergies in one form or another; some are obvious, while others are not. Although allergies can precipitate candidiasis, it also works in reverse, because most sufferers, if not all, develop allergies after their candidiasis arises. Disease-causing *Candida*-species organisms are prominent antigenic organisms that instigate allergies, not only to themselves, but to numerous other things as well. So, sufferers develop allergies to disease-causing yeast, harmful molds, dust, pollens, foods, chemicals, and any other substances they may encounter.

Typically, allergies are divided into three major categories: 1) environmental, 2) food, and 3) chemicals. In candidiasis sufferers, there is also a fourth category that includes allergies to disease-causing yeast and harmful molds.

Classically, allergies are diagnosed by their ability to produce symptoms or a certain reaction when someone is exposed to a specific antigen. To uncover these allergies, testing can be performed in different ways; depending on the specific antigen, it can involve intradermal skin testing, drops placed under the tongue, or laboratory studies with a patient's blood, not to mention other less-reliable methods. Once it is diagnosed, mainstream physicians generally treat allergies with one or more medications that make someone less likely to react to their offending substances. The medication only suppresses the allergic reaction and does not eliminate the allergy.

If you have allergies, eliminating or avoiding your allergy-inducing substances is a better way to stop your symptoms; this works when foods are a problem, but is nearly impossible when you are allergic to environmental antigens. In addition, desensitization (allergy) injections or drops are often used to help make allergy sufferers less sensitive to their offending antigens.

Environmental Allergies

We do not live in a sterile bubble; if we did, no one would ever develop allergies. No matter where you live, your environment is teeming with substances that can induce allergic reactions in sensitive or hypersensitive people. Anything we touch, smell, or consume has the potential to trigger symptoms that can range from insignificant to debilitating. Environmental allergies typically include exposures to various plants, insects, and animals. In addition, disease-causing yeast as well as harmful and innocuous molds are also in our environment and can easily cause problems.

Disease-causing yeast often cause sensitivities and hypersensitivities to environmental substances. Through complicated immune system interactions, they instigate and/or promote a multitude of allergies (chapter 16). This also occurs in reverse because the persistent presence of specific antigens stresses a candidiasis sufferer's immune system, worsening their candidiasis. Atmospheric pollutants can be irritating and are basically unavoidable. Many environments are so allergically debilitating that some people must relocate to completely different surroundings to avoid perpetual discomfort.

Moreover, molds are organisms also classified as fungi, flourishing in the same warm and moist environments as disease-causing yeast. Since disease-causing yeast and molds are closely related, many of them cause similar allergic reactions that can precipitate or exacerbate a candidiasis sufferer's allergies. Therefore, allergies to disease-causing yeast and molds are important to test for and treat. Even worse, numerous molds can cause disease. These harmful molds can simultaneously infect the gastrointestinal tract and tissues, causing inflammation and illness. Some European researchers believe numerous different mold toxins (*mycotoxins*) can cause all sorts of chronic illness. For all their infectious and allergic contributions, molds must be considered as a prominent participant in candidiasis.

Food Allergies and Intolerance

If you suffer with lactose intolerance, you are likely to experience bloating, gas, and other unpleasant symptoms every time you consume dairy or dairy-containing foods. People with lactose intolerance have a deficiency of the enzyme *lactase* that breaks down *lactose* (a two-sugar carbohydrate) into its two individual sugars. Lactose needs to be broken down within the upper gut or it instigates symptoms within the lower gut. This is *not* an allergy. Instead, it is a food *intolerance*; an inability to tolerate a food that does not involve an allergic reaction, even though there may be abundant inflammation. As a result, the gastrointestinal environment (*microbiome*) may become irritated and inflamed, which, for numerous reasons, promotes the adverse effects of disease-causing yeast.

In contrast, when the immune system becomes sensitive or hypersensitive to the presence of one or more foods, someone can develop food *allergies*. Some foods strongly induce allergies and their symptoms, while others seem to be insignificant. In fact, virtually any food can produce an allergy if a susceptible person is exposed to it long enough. The most common food allergies involve corn, wheat, eggs, cow's milk, soy, chocolate, strawberries, and citrus fruits, but this is far from a complete list.

Allergies to foods commonly develop and arise during candidiasis, after leaky gut syndrome is established; disease-causing yeast invade into the gut wall and weaken it, allowing undigested food particles to enter the tissues and blood. Once someone becomes sensitive or hypersensitive to a specific food, subsequent exposures aggravate their immune system, setting the stage for other foods to cause similar reactions. Since every person is unique, their food-allergy profile will be just as individualized. Specifics aside, any food that irritates or inflames the gastrointestinal microbiome creates conditions that encourage the colonization of disease-causing yeast. Frequent food-allergy reactions can also, over time, impair the immune system. In other words, food allergies can compromise the body's ability to effectively combat any disease-causing yeast that are present and allow candidiasis to worsen.

Chemical Allergies

Repeated contact with certain chemicals can induce reactions and allergies that stress the immune system, which can precipitate or exacerbate candidiasis. If you are sensitive or hypersensitive, the chemicals used to clean or repair your house may be highly irritating. Some people are allergic to the materials used to construct their home; as examples, new carpeting, linoleum, paint, wallpaper, and furniture emit fumes and gases that affect susceptible people. Even items like newspapers, books, dish detergent, and certain types of cloth are known to instigate and promote health disturbances. Undeniably, people react to a wide variety of chemicals, and their allergic reactions can manifest as a diversity of symptoms and illness. Moreover, many people are allergic to the additives and other substances used in certain foods, which is why some people can eat the natural form of a specific food, but not the variations of that food prepared with additives.

Cancer

Few words scare people more than the word "cancer" because of its association with suffering and death. Fears aside, it is important to state being diagnosed with cancer does not guarantee a death sentence, as many people survive its ravages.

Cancer involves the presence of abnormal cells and tissue. Cancerous cells are generated in everyone virtually all the time. Normally, the immune system of healthy people protects them by eliminating the cancerous cells before they reproduce. Therefore, cancer seems to arise when the body's normal control mechanisms fail, allowing the abnormal cells to grow unregulated. Cancer can develop in any type of cell, tissue, or organ. Usually, it begins in one area and then spreads (metastasizes) or independently arises in other locations.

Cancer develops by a two-step process called *transformation*. In the first step, *initiation*, the genetic material of a normal cell undergoes a change that prepares it to become cancerous (abnormal). This change is often precipitated by some *carcinogen* (cancer-causing agent), such as being exposed to a toxic chemical or harmful radiation. All the body's cells are not equally susceptible to initiation by carcinogens; some cells are more susceptible because of a genetic flaw, assistance from an additional agent, or chronic physical irritation. Cells that do not make this transformation, *non-initiated cells*, do not become cancerous. In the second step, *promotion*, an initiated cell physically alters itself, becoming cancerous.

Suppressed immunity (inferior functioning cells) may make certain cells more susceptible to being initiated or may permit the transformation of initiated cells. Either way, this encourages the development of cancerous growths and populations of abnormal cells (as well as the proliferation of harmful viruses). Usually, the type and extent of cancer that arises is directly proportional to the magnitude of immune system impairment. A major cause of suppressed immunity is candidiasis (chapter 14); an infection with disease-causing yeast can hinder or impair the immune system's functioning. In addition to suppressed immunity, sufferers can manifest depressed immunity (fewer cells), and both suppressed-depressed immunity (fewer, inferior functioning cells). In fact, candidiasis sufferers consistently demonstrate abnormal immunity. Although cancer is a risk factor for promoting candidiasis, disease-causing yeast are a strong risk factor for developing cancer.

If candidiasis is not responsible for someone's cancer, it almost surely appears during their battle with it. Rather than strengthening the immune system, mainstream medicine focuses on destroying the cancer. Unfortunately, this approach further impairs a cancer sufferer's immunity and overall health. The two common anticancer treatments presently employed are chemotherapy and radiation therapy.

Chemotherapy uses one or more potent anticancer drugs—powerful subtoxic and mildly toxic agents that interfere with the cancer cell's chemical processes and metabolic functioning. Although they are administered to kill cancerous cells, many types of chemotherapy are highly effective at injuring or killing normal cells, especially immune cells. The hope is, after the cancer cells die, the cancer patient's normal cells will survive and reproduce, even though their impaired immunity often persists.

In contrast, *radiation therapy* is used to combat a cancer confined to a specific area; a patient is typically exposed to a series of treatments with X-rays, or they receive radioactive isotopes that are surgically implanted near their cancer. Excessive amounts of radiation, whether artificial or natural, can impair or poison the immune system, compromising its ability to function properly. In addition, severe tissue, cellular, and genetic damage can result from exposures to the radiation and often cause mild to severe radiation burns. The metabolic and immune system disturbances and damage caused by chemotherapy and radiation therapy are frequently profound, resulting in conditions that promote the support and growth of many opportunistic infectious invaders. So, infections with disease-causing yeast are likely to surface or, if already present, become severe.

Diet

Western society prefers convenience in food preparation. More prepackaged, processed, and fast foods are bought and consumed every day. Processing and refining foods compromises their nutritional value, as they often contain large quantities of salt, sugar, and chemicals. If you only eat foods to satisfy your taste buds, you may eat a limited selection that promotes nutritional deficiencies. Abnormal eating habits cause similar problems; for example, people who have anorexia or bulimia often have nutritional disturbances. Even vegetarian diets, if not practiced properly, can lead to deficiencies of vitamins, minerals, and essential fatty acids.

Vitamin and *mineral deficiencies* readily contribute to the development of candidiasis. Studies demonstrate that insufficient levels of vitamin A closely correlate with an increased incidence of mucocutaneous candidiasis, whereas elevated concentrations of vitamin A seem to protect against it. Other studies reveal a decreased intake of vitamins B1, B2, and B6 exacerbate infections with disease-causing yeast. A vitamin C deficiency may reduce someone's resistance to invasive candidiasis. Studies in mice have substantiated iron-deficiency anemia, serum-iron overload, copper excesses, and selenium deficiency are all capable of enhancing the presence, symptoms, and debilitation of candidiasis. Moreover, the current dietary recommended amounts of vitamins and minerals often fall below what most people require to be healthy, and those with illness or who engage in strenuous activity/exercise need to consume even more.

Protein deficiency also encourages the development of candidiasis. An inadequate consumption of dietary protein causes a deficiency of both essential and nonessential amino acids. This decreases the bodily production of numerous proteins and other protein-related substances. The body can temporarily compensate for a shortage and will use whatever protein is stored. Eventually, a lack of protein causes muscle tissue to be broken down for energy, a state called catabolism. Since protein is essential for a healthy immune system, a deficiency impairs immunity. In return, the immune system cannot effectively defend the body against the further invasion of disease-causing yeast.

Yet, what is included in the diet is often as detrimental as what is missing. Disease-causing yeast primarily use sugars and other carbohydrates for energy. Therefore, consuming excess carbohydrates, especially sugars, readily nourishes them, and candidiasis often becomes unavoidable. Unless you study every label, you cannot know how much sugar you consume. Processed foods and beverages frequently contain large quantities of sugar, not to mention salt and chemicals. Many people turn to fruits and juices to "eat healthy," but these items are basically simple carbohydrates. Fruits are natural foods and do contain nutrition, but they are not much better than sugar in the way they affect your health. With respect to candidiasis, juice is just sugar water and fruit is sugar with a peel. Being simple carbohydrates, fruit and juice are sources of energy and nutrition for disease-causing yeast.

Besides feeding them, consuming sugars or other carbohydrates adversely affects a sufferer's glucose tolerance (their ability to process sugar and regulate their blood sugar concentration), which exacerbates their symptoms and ill health (chapter 11). Sugars and other carbohydrates will only worsen candidiasis.

In addition, dietary disease-causing yeast can contribute to promoting candidiasis and worsen its symptoms. People with a healthy population of beneficial bacteria are not likely to develop candidiasis simply from ingesting disease-causing yeast, since a healthy population of beneficial bacteria competes with and suppresses the disease-causing yeast, inhibiting their colonization. In contrast, people with insufficient amounts of beneficial bacteria are at risk when they consume foods that contain living disease-causing yeast; these infectious invaders have a greater chance to colonize the gut. In addition, sufferers almost always experience allergies to disease-causing yeast, regardless of whether it is alive, dead, intact, or in pieces. The repeated consumption of foods or drinks containing disease-causing yeast, in any amounts, commonly provokes allergic reactions and their accompanying symptoms and illness.

Equally bad, if not worse, research reveals raw vegetables can be infected with parasites and harmful bacteria. For example, a study found eight different vegetables from Costa Rica were contaminated with fecal bacteria as well as the cysts (eggs) of numerous parasites, including *Endolimax nana*, *Entamoeba coli*, *Entamoeba histolytica*, *Giardia intestinalis*, and *Cryptosporidium-species* organisms. These infectious invaders can upset the gastrointestinal microbiome, promoting candidiasis. Similarly, foods containing molds, whether harmful or innocent, can provoke infectious and allergic reactions in sensitive or hypersensitive sufferers. For all these reasons, diet is a strong risk factor for developing candidiasis.

Dysbiosis

When the gut contains enough beneficial bacteria, a state of *eubiosis* is present and all is well. The beneficial bacteria competitively inhibit and suppress disease-causing yeast. Essentially, this decreases the available binding sites and nutrition available for the disease-causing yeast. In addition, some beneficial bacteria produce substances that inhibit or even harm them.

Anything that disturbs or disrupts the gastrointestinal microbiome and its beneficial bacteria creates conditions that encourage the reproduction and colonization of disease-causing yeast (as well as harmful parasites, bacteria, molds, and/or viruses). *Dysbiosis* is a general term to describe an imbalance of organisms within the gut, regardless of the dominant organism(s).

More precisely, candidiasis occurs when the primary infectious invader is disease-causing yeast; *dysbacteriosis* involves an infection with one or more harmful bacteria; *mycosis* is the presence of one or more harmful molds; and parasitic illness is usually named according to the organism present; as examples, *amoebiasis* involves an abundance of amoebas, whereas *giardiasis* describes an infection with *Giardia duodenalis*.

Many things can disturb or destroy the beneficial bacteria and create a dysbiosis. All the risk factors in this chapter can instigate and/or promote dysbiosis, but the most prevalent cause involves the use of antibiotics; although they are used to kill harmful bacteria, they also kill beneficial bacteria. Regardless of its cause, once dysbiosis exists, it is a strong risk factor for candidiasis.

Electromagnetism

Some researchers strongly believe repeated exposure to the powerful magnetic fields generated by electrical lines can decrease immunity and encourage the development of malignancies (cancers). Electricity running through a wire creates a magnetic field around it. Research indicates this perturbs cellular functioning, including cellular reproduction, and is especially concerning when it adversely affects immune cells, as impaired immunity hinders the fight against candidiasis or any other infectious invader.

All cells have a tiny difference in electrical charge between their inner and outer cellular membranes as well as between the inner-outer membranes of their internal organelles, including their energy-producing mitochondria and chromosome-containing nucleus. The concentrations of different chemical ions inside and outside of a cell creates a difference in electrical charge between its internal and external environments (chapter 4), which, it is hypothesized, magnetic fields can disrupt. Not only does this affect the cell itself, but it also impairs its ability to send messages to other cells. Experiments using exposures to high levels of electromagnetism have even generated abnormal (cancerous) cells.

The strength of any artificially generated electromagnetic field is directly proportional to the proximity of its electrical source. Since the strength of the field decreases exponentially as you move away, doubling your distance decreases your exposure to one-fourth the amount of radiation. In addition to power lines and electrical wires, other common items that generate electromagnetic fields include microwave ovens, hair dryers, electric toothbrushes, electric blankets, fans, air conditioners, televisions, stereos, personal computers, and cell phones. In fact, because any electrical current passing through a wire creates an electromagnetic field, the electrical wiring in the walls of your home might also be a reason for concern.

Research with *Candida albicans* reveals electrostatic forces may make, at best, a minor contribution to their adherence process. Although most studies have been inconclusive so far, avoiding or decreasing excessive electromagnetic exposure would seem prudent.

Emotions and Stress

There is a strong connection between your mind and body, each readily influencing the other; the state of your mind affects your bodily functions, and the health of your body influences how you think and feel. An abundance of research supports a mind-body connection. Since the nervous, endocrine (hormone), and immune systems are connected and interrelated, anything that influences one system directly or indirectly affects all. The mind-body connection can work to your advantage, have no noticeable effect, or cause you harm.

Happy relationships generally provide a greater sense of well-being. Through the mind-body connection, happy relationships give someone a greater capacity to withstand adverse circumstances and undesirable conditions or stimuli. Love has a strong positive effect, which is why couples in a happy marriage have the lowest incidence of illness. People with friends are consistently healthier than people without good social support systems. Work is another key area that affects health; people who enjoy their vocation feel more personal satisfaction than people who do not. Anything that has a positive effect on your mind and emotions will positively affect your body's functioning and overall health.

Yet, there is a downside. Regardless of whether it is perceived or unconscious, anything that increases emotional tension or causes unhappiness will have a negative influence on the body's functioning and health. Depression, anxiety, and other strong negative feelings almost always adversely affect the body. A lack of sleep can impair your thoughts and mood as well as compromise your health. Real or imagined job stress can cause profound bodily disturbances. Negative thoughts, emotions, and experiences will take their toll on your health and body. In contrast, negative stress is not always a bad thing because it can have a positive effect in the long run by teaching you how to react and adapt to different situations and experiences.

The effects of stress are highly subjective, making the contributions of your emotions and mental state to your body's health and functioning difficult to precisely measure. People respond to stress differently, and what adversely affects one person may have little or no effect on another. Generally, anything that helps you achieve a positive emotional state will be beneficial for your health, while negative experiences usually create bodily distress, undesirable alterations in its functioning, and even overt disturbances.

With respect to candidiasis, the mind-body connection works in two directions at once. Negative emotions and stress make you susceptible to developing candidiasis and worsen any of its symptoms and illness. Moreover, the presence of candidiasis, an infection with allergic consequences, is certain to have an undesirable effect on your emotions, mood, and thinking. Therefore, stress can precipitate and/or exacerbate candidiasis.

Endocrine System Functioning

The endocrine system encompasses numerous glands and the hormones they produce. Its purpose is to help regulate and fine-tune the body's internal activities and chemical functioning. Endocrine problems can cause metabolic disturbances that encourage candidiasis. Furthermore, since the nervous, endocrine, and immune systems are all interconnected (*neuro-endocrine-immune connection*), endocrine disturbances will adversely affect the nervous and immune systems, which can instigate and/or promote candidiasis. Once established, candidiasis can disturb or disrupt the *neuro-endocrine-immune connection*, inducing a variety of endocrine disturbances and/or dysfunctions. At the extreme, candidiasis can cause autoimmune disease involving one or more endocrine glands and their hormones. More commonly, *glucose intolerance* and *hyperinsulinism* are disturbances that typically occur in most candidiasis sufferers, exacerbating their ill health.

After you eat sugar, it is absorbed and then enters your blood, increasing your blood glucose concentration (more complex carbohydrates must be broken down first). Rather than remaining within the blood where most of it is not used, your body tries to move sugar into your cells and tissues where it is needed. *Insulin* is a hormone, manufactured by your pancreas, that allows sugar to exit the blood and enter the tissues and cells. When this functions normally, it is called *glucose tolerance*, and your sugar is processed appropriately. In contrast, *glucose intolerance* occurs when the metabolism of sugar and other carbohydrates is abnormal. In addition to some unpleasant symptoms that accompany blood sugar "highs" and "lows," glucose intolerance frequently instigates and/or promotes candidiasis. If this involves the incomplete absorption of sugar and carbohydrates, disease-causing yeast within the gut will be well-fed, as sugar is their primary source of energy. Alternatively, if absorption occurs properly, but the body is unable to effectively mobilize sugar into the tissues and cells, the blood sugar will remain elevated, nourishing any disease-causing yeast that reside within the blood. Unfortunately, this leads to more glucose intolerance, promoting a vicious cycle with numerous harmful metabolic consequences. Glucose intolerance does not usually occur spontaneously. Instead, the persistent presence of candidiasis impairs or disturbs a sufferer's ability to process sugar and other carbohydrates, which, in turn, fosters abnormal insulin levels—typically, hyperinsulinism.

Insulin is our primary blood sugar lowering hormone; its actions help move excess glucose out of the blood and into the tissues and cells. *Hyperinsulinism* occurs when a person's pancreas produces and releases too much insulin, resulting in insulin levels significantly greater than normal, but it can also include the prolonged release of insulin or its impaired degradation. Rapidly increasing levels of insulin encourages the precipitous transfer of glucose from the blood into the tissues and cells, often leading to a lowered blood sugar concentration. In addition, if the pancreas releases insulin for too long, the blood glucose concentration can stay lowered for an excessive length of time. When all is well, the hormone *glucagon* is released to help raise a lowered blood sugar concentration. Yet, when the release of glucagon is impaired, or when the blood sugar concentration falls too low, the hormone *epinephrine* is released to help raise a lowered blood sugar concentration; it triggers numerous undesirable symptoms with physiological and metabolic consequences. Disturbances involving any or all these hormones induce symptoms that further stress a candidiasis sufferer's ill health (chapter 11).

Moreover, elevated insulin levels are believed to promote *harmful oxygen-based free radicals*. When two oxygen molecules are paired together, they form O2, a beneficial, life-sustaining substance. If these atoms separate or lose an electron (a charged particle), they become reactive entities known as oxygen-based free radicals. These unstable molecules can cause chemical damage that promotes structural destruction in the cells and tissues. To combat excessive free radical activity, the immune system shifts into high gear, becoming hyperactive, which can greatly stress its effectiveness. To add insult, hyperinsulinism frequently promotes abnormalities in lipid (fat) metabolism, leading to *hypercholesterolemia* (excess cholesterol within the blood). Although elevated lipid levels and oxygen-based free radicals are associated with cardiovascular disease (chapter 7), including heart attacks and strokes, there is an equally dangerous risk: hyperinsulinism and hypercholesterolemia are two metabolic conditions that can impair and even harm immune system functioning (chapter 14).

Problems within the endocrine system strongly contribute to the disturbances and symptoms that arise during candidiasis, but disease-causing yeast are *not* innocent in this process because they directly instigate and/or promote glucose intolerance. In fact, *insulin-like substances* have been found in cultures of *Candida*-species organisms and *glucagon receptors* have been discovered on their cell membranes (chapter 11). The available evidence reveals there is a *candidiasis-endocrine connection*.

Genetics

You inherited your basic neuroendocrine-immune functioning and metabolic parameters, as well as your tendency to manifest inflammation, symptoms, and illness, from the genetic material of your ancestors. As a result, your genetics are the foundation for your interactions with the world. It dictates your predisposition to developing certain illnesses and your ability to tolerate or resist exposures to various substances, conditions, or even experiences. This can have a profound effect with respect to developing candidiasis. For example, cystic fibrosis is an inherited lung (congenital pulmonary) disorder. People born with this illness suffer with its associated problems and frequently develop and demonstrate candidiasis as well. People with breast cancer have a greater-than-average number of candidiasis sufferers among their blood relatives. Since some groups are more likely to develop candidiasis, there appears to be an inherited tendency to develop it, including a proclivity to have certain of its manifestations; one family may suffer with cancer, while another may have cardiovascular problems.

Immune System

Impaired immunity strongly contributes to developing and manifesting illness, regardless of its type. The immune system guards your health; it is the protective foundation for all your bodily processes. If it is competent, your experience with ill health is likely to be infrequent and minor. In contrast, when your immunity is compromised, you are likely to suffer with numerous, repeated infections or, even worse, afflictions like cancer or autoimmune disease.

Frequent assaults on the immune system decrease its ability to function properly with each battle taking a toll. Once someone's immunity is inadequate or impaired, they are predisposed to develop candidiasis and quickly succumb to its undesirable effects.

Certain illnesses involve conditions that encourage the proliferation and invasion of disease-causing yeast; for example, "food poisoning" promotes inflammation within the gastrointestinal tract that can injure or kill the beneficial bacteria, allowing disease-causing yeast to reproduce or invade into the gut wall. In general, anything that adversely affects your immune system can create problems that promote candidiasis.

Unfortunately, repeated infections can exacerbate candidiasis and hasten its effects in another way. Chronic sinus, ear, respiratory, and urinary tract infections necessitate the repeated use of antibiotics, which kill the beneficial bacteria, enabling the disease-causing yeast to proliferate and colonize these and other areas. Besides treating the harmful bacteria causing the acute infection, most mainstream physicians are unaware disease-causing yeast also grow within these areas, causing inflammation that predisposes their patient to subsequent bacterial infections. As a result, candidiasis participates in creating the vicious cycle of a bacterial infection, antibiotic use, killing beneficial bacteria along with the bad, proliferation of disease-causing yeast, more inflammation, another bacterial infection, and so on.

More problematic, chronic candidiasis can impair the immune system. Sufferers frequently experience suppressed immunity (inferior functioning cells), depressed immunity (fewer cells), or suppressed-depressed immunity (fewer, inferior functioning cells). As a result, impaired immunity hinders the body's ability to combat the yeast-related infection, enabling it to progress and further compromise immunity, and so on. This opens the door for the adverse contributions of other infectious invaders. Even worse, impaired immunity increases a sufferer's likelihood of developing chronic viral illnesses, cancer, or autoimmune disease, which, as it weakens their immunity further, allows their candidiasis to worsen.

Medications

Since the turn of the twentieth century, healthcare in the United States has been primarily based on the use of medications. In some cases, the use of a drug has been miraculous; for example, administering an anticoagulant in the emergency room may avoid the fatal effects of a heart attack or stroke, saving someone's life. More commonly, medications are used to make life more comfortable—for example, taking an antacid to ease an upset stomach or using an anti-pain drug to alleviate arthritis or a headache. Medications spell relief from suffering for millions of people every day, have cured countless numbers of infections that would have previously been deadly, and are essential tools during surgical procedures.

By themselves, medications are not bad or evil. Yet, problems can arise when they are indiscriminately used, or even abused. Most people do not think twice about popping a pill at the first twinge of a headache or asking their doctor for an antibiotic "just to play it safe." Although they might cure what ails you, medications do have a downside; they irritate your body in numerous ways. The frequent use of some drugs may make you tolerant to its effects, forcing you to take increasingly higher doses. Some microorganisms may be or become resistant to an antibiotic being used to treat an infection, requiring the use of other medications that may be less effective or more irritating. Certain conditions necessitate the daily use of medication, for example, diabetes and high blood pressure. Many medications are often overused and should be taken less often, at lower doses, or not at all. The most common medications that wreak havoc within the body are antibiotics, corticosteroids, hormonal contraceptives, and neutropenic drugs (immunity impairing). All of these can instigate and/or promote candidiasis.

Antibiotics

These drugs are one of the most (if not *the* most) accepted and prominent risk factors for developing candidiasis. Just ask the multitude of sufferers who first noticed their candidiasis symptoms after they finished or while they were taking an antibiotic.

Although they are infection-fighting medications used to destroy or inhibit the growth of harmful bacteria, most antibiotics also alter the gastrointestinal microbiome for the worse by killing the beneficial bacteria. Since they compete with the disease-causing yeast for space and produce substances that inhibit their growth, decreasing the population of beneficial bacteria allows the disease-causing yeast to proliferate and colonize their surroundings. This effect is not just confined to the gut because the epithelial tissue that covers most of the body's internal and external surfaces can also be colonized with disease-causing yeast when their populations of beneficial bacteria are disrupted with antibiotics; the prime locations are the sinuses, upper respiratory tract and lungs, bladder, and vagina.

Antibiotics are likely to promote candidiasis when they are taken for a prolonged period. Yet, even repeated, short courses can equally disturb the beneficial bacteria. Research reveals the more broad-spectrum the antibiotic, the greater the diversity of microorganisms it kills, and the more effective it is at eliminating the beneficial bacteria, even in the stomach's harsh, acidic environment. Medications that kill gram-negative, anaerobic bacteria (a type of bacteria) strongly disrupt beneficial bacteria, since a large percentage of them are also this type and similarly susceptible. Numerous antiparasitic medications have the same ability; in addition to killing their intended parasite, they eradicate a variety of beneficial bacteria. Moreover, as the beneficial bacteria are eliminated, numerous infectious invaders also gain the freedom to reproduce, including harmful parasites, bacteria, molds, and/or viruses.

Furthermore, antibiotics have another undesirable effect; some suppress the immune system and interfere with cell-mediated immunity (the ability of certain immune cells to directly attack some infectious invaders or to participate in the process without using antibodies). Anything that impairs immunity also compromises the body's ability to defend itself from the further invasion of disease-causing yeast.

In 2015, United States healthcare providers wrote nearly 270 million antibiotic prescriptions, a number slightly less than one course of antibiotics per person each year. This may not seem like much, but after a few years, it adds up. Antibiotics do not affect viruses, but many physicians prescribe them anyway to "cover the bases." As a result, antibiotics are among the most overprescribed, indiscriminately chosen, and inappropriately used medical tools. A reputable healthcare practitioner would not dare to supply other medications in the same manner.

Corticosteroids

Corticosteroids are steroid hormones used to suppress a hyperactive immune system, especially when there is significant inflammation; they have strong immune-suppressing and anti-inflammatory actions. Some medical experts believe corticosteroids work by depressing cell-mediated immunity, while others think they suppress the functioning of certain immune cells. Regardless, disease-causing yeast benefit when corticosteroids are used. In fact, disease-causing *Candida*-species organisms have been found to possess an *intracellular* (internal) *steroid-binding protein*. Evidence indicates corticosteroids may directly alter or encourage the proliferation and/or functioning of disease-causing yeast; for example, steroids increase the colonization of

Candida albicans within the stomach. An increase in the presence of candidiasis is a consistent finding with any form of corticosteroid therapy.

Hormonal Contraceptives

Birth control pills and other oral contraceptives are medications that raise a woman's levels of progesterone and/or estrogen, the sex hormones secreted by her ovaries. This tricks her body into believing it is already pregnant to prevent the release of a fertile egg. It is not without risk because oral contraceptives often cause an increased incidence of candidiasis; they alter the mucosal surface of the vagina, encouraging colonization with disease-causing yeast, even in women without yeast-related symptoms. This happens because numerous disease-causing *Candida*-species organisms possess an *intracellular* (internal) *binding protein* specific for *progesterone* and, theoretically, an excess of this hormone stimulates their further growth and proliferation. Some studies claim this effect is due to excess estrogen because disease-causing *Candida*-species organisms also possess an *intracellular binding protein* with a specificity for *estrogen*. Some studies demonstrate that *estradiol*, the most active form of estrogen, stimulates disease-causing yeast to transform from their less-aggressive, ovoid form into their more-aggressive, invasive form. Therefore, oral contraceptives are a risk factor for promoting invasive candidiasis.

Regardless of which hormone is guilty, oral contraceptives also adversely affect a woman's glucose tolerance, impairing her ability to regulate her blood sugar concentration, causing metabolic disturbances that can predispose her to or contribute to candidiasis.

Yet, even without taking oral contraceptives, normal month-to-month (cyclic) variations in the levels of female hormones can create immune system abnormalities and promote the proliferation and colonization of disease-causing yeast, which is why women seem to suffer with candidiasis more than men. Research repeatedly illustrates that the adherence of *Candida albicans* to vaginal epithelial cells is related to a woman's menstrual cycle. This effect is not only in the vagina; other research reveals that the menstrual cycle similarly affects the adherence of *Candida albicans* to buccal (cheek) epithelial cells as well.

Neutropenic Drugs

Neutrophils (immune cells) are responsible for a large percentage of the body's protection against infection and inflammation. In return, an inadequate number of neutrophils (neutropenia) greatly increases someone's risk for infection and inflammation. These drugs place the body at risk for candidiasis by interfering with the anti-*Candida* activity of neutrophils (in addition to impairing other immune cells; monocytes and macrophages). As a result, decreased neutrophil functioning promotes a loss of communication between all immune cells, impairing cell-mediated immunity (and possibly even delayed-type hypersensitivity reactions). Since a healthy immune system is required to control and combat candidiasis, any medication that impairs immunity will precipitate or exacerbate it.

Numerous drugs poison the immune system, causing neutropenia. Although some are described in this chapter, like chemotherapy agents, others do not fit into those categories and are mentioned here. For example, cimetidine (used for gastric and duodenal ulcers) decreases immunity, allowing disease-causing yeast to invade into ulcerated areas, delaying or preventing their healing. Some tranquilizers are highly associated with the presence of candidiasis. Any drug that alters metabolism in some way has the potential to impair immunity, creating disturbances that encourage the colonization of disease-causing yeast.

Metabolism

Your metabolism involves the physical and chemical processes within your cells, tissues, and organs. Some processes (catabolism) involve degrading substances to liberate energy for power or to provide materials to be used in various processes. Other processes (anabolism) create complex substances from simple ones, needed to perform a variety of functions.

The basic activities of your metabolism are inherited. Its functioning reflects the internal and external influences that affect it, whether discernible, microscopic, or invisible. As a result, it is sensitive to what is in your body, especially within your gastrointestinal tract and other tissues, as well as things in your immediate, external environment. A candidiasis sufferer's metabolism is often disturbed or damaged by the presence of disease-causing yeast, other harmful organisms, and the existence of any allergies as well as the adverse effects of allergy-inducing and toxic substances in their internal and the external environments.

Anything that disrupts metabolism in one place often initiates a cascade of compensatory consequences, which are often undesirable. For example, the long-term presence of an infection with disease-causing yeast adversely affects the liver's functioning, and, in return, this disturbs sugar and fat (glucose and lipid) metabolism (chapter 14). Under these conditions, it promotes *hypercholesterolemia*, an increase in the blood's cholesterol concentration. It occurs because the liver, an organ that normally participates in metabolism, shifts its duties to aid the immune system. To help the body eliminate a chronic infection, the liver undertakes its *acute phase response* (aka *acute phase reaction*); it decreases its production of metabolism-related proteins, while producing *acute phase proteins* that participate in nonspecific host defenses (a generalized type of immunity against infectious organisms that does not need to be directed against a specific organism).

In most candidiasis sufferers, an elevated concentration of blood cholesterol is an indicator of a long-term *infection* with disease-causing yeast. Since the endocrine system is also frequently disturbed during this process, *glucose intolerance* and *hyperinsulinism* often coexist and contribute to hypercholesterolemia. These disturbances frequently promote impaired immunity. During infections or inflammation, *lymphocytes* (immune cells) are often injured, sustaining cell membrane damage. Normally, cholesterol is used to repair their cell membranes. However, excess cholesterol in the blood encourages extra cholesterol to enter the cell membranes, increasing their viscosity; in return, a more rigid membrane inhibits the flow of nutrients and other substances into and out of the lymphocytes, negatively affecting their functioning. Over time, it can create suppressed immunity (inferior functioning cells), depressed immunity (fewer cells), or suppressed-depressed immunity (fewer, inferior functioning cells). Unfortunately, impaired immunity readily permits candidiasis to progress, which compromises the immune system further, creating a vicious cycle.

Since your metabolism is an important contributor to your health, any condition that disturbs or disrupts it impairs your body's ability to function normally. Moreover, because your metabolism is directly related to the functioning of your nervous, endocrine, and immune systems, any abnormal variations in your metabolism will promote a diversity of undesirable effects. Whether mild, moderate, or severe, this will create an environment that encourages the further colonization and invasion of disease-causing yeast.

Obesity

Being overweight places you at an increased risk of ill health. Obesity is an excess of body fat; usually, at least 25 percent above average. In the United States, obesity is the most common metabolic disease. In 2014, roughly 160 million Americans were obese or overweight—nearly 75 percent of men and more than 60 percent of women as well as almost 30 percent of children under age 20. In 2021, it was estimated 13 percent of adults, about 1.04 billion people, are obese worldwide.

Statistics reveal that obesity causes an increased incidence of diabetes, high blood pressure, and some cancers. For many reasons, including consuming excess carbohydrates, overweight people often have glucose intolerance and hyperinsulinism. In return, blood glucose and insulin disturbances may worsen their metabolism, including their metabolism of fats (lipids). These disturbances may hinder or impair the functioning of their immune systems.

Obese people have more body mass (cells and tissues), making it harder for them to move compared to a thin person. This places stress and strain on their cardiovascular system (heart and blood vessels), which worsens as their body weight increases. The extra mass must be perfused with blood to receive oxygen and nutrients as well as remove wastes. Areas that are poorly perfused will have compromised immunity; for example, many obese people have fungus-infected toenails. Areas where the skin overlaps (stomach folds, groin folds, the folds of the buttocks, or other skin folds) are warm, dark, and moist locations, providing a perfect habitat for the colonization of disease-causing yeast. Although obesity does not guarantee candidiasis, being overweight is an undeniable risk factor.

Parasites

Any parasite that enters the gut can promote an infection, whether it involves a protozoa parasite or a more highly developed organism like a tapeworm. *Parasite* is a general term for any organism that lives within us, on us, or at our expense, without contributing to our survival. With respect to candidiasis, a "parasite" refers to an internal infection with a protozoa or helminth worm (chapter 5). Parasites often cause great harm. If a parasite is aggressive, symptoms can occur quickly. In contrast, if it is less aggressive, symptoms may take months to years to surface or they will be mild and nonspecific, causing the parasite's presence to not be suspected or taken seriously. Although a parasitic infection may be localized to the gut, systemic symptoms and disturbances may also arise. In some cases, parasites can spread to the blood early in their infection, and then colonize other tissues and organs. In other cases, they can advance up the common bile duct and invade the liver, gallbladder, or pancreas, and then later gain access to the blood.

Normally, the beneficial bacteria protect us against a number of these infectious invaders; they inhibit or suppress them, hindering their mischief. As a result, many parasites can live within someone for years without them knowing they are infected. Some parasites are more persistent and aggressive than others, creating conditions that disturb and overwhelm the beneficial bacteria. Some of them produce and release numerous toxins and undesirable metabolites that directly injure the beneficial bacteria. Whether overt or covert, parasites cause harm.

An infection with one or more parasites predisposes someone to develop candidiasis. After candidiasis is established, the disease-causing yeast and harmful parasites frequently form a cooperative (symbiotic) relationship, creating an environment that permits their successful coexistence. In fact, these organisms often become codependent, relying on each other for their continued growth and support. Their combined undesirable effects are usually much worse than their individual effects combined.

Since parasites are infectious organisms, many instigate an immune system response that is often disadvantageous to the body of their human host; it promotes inflammation and other disturbances, while it does little to eliminate the parasite. Some parasites have surface antigens easily identified by the immune system, while others are unrecognizable and escape unnoticed; either way, the parasite causes trouble. More concerning, some parasites confuse a person's immune system into attacking their own body; numerous researchers and parasite experts believe some parasites can precipitate abnormal immune system reactions that promote autoimmune disease, with or without candidiasis.

Parasites are all around us. They can infect our food and water. As a result, even the most health-conscious person can be plagued with parasites. If you strictly adhere to an anti-candidiasis program (part 4), but do not achieve success, unidentified or improperly treated parasites should be considered. Unfortunately, most of the methods currently used to detect parasites are not sensitive enough to detect all parasites, or they are performed improperly. Since a high percentage of sufferers are simultaneously infected with one or more parasites, it is vital to suspect that parasites are present until proven otherwise.

Pregnancy

The more times a woman is pregnant, the higher her risk of developing candidiasis. This may result from the physiological alterations that accompany the hormonal fluctuations related to pregnancy and childbirth. Changes in the gastrointestinal tract and vaginal mucosa of expectant and new mothers can create conditions that promote the proliferation and colonization of disease-causing yeast in these and other areas; excessive levels of estrogen and progesterone may stimulate the estrogen and progesterone intracellular binding proteins of disease-causing yeast (whether estrogen, progesterone, or both, they can stimulate the binding proteins and encourage the further growth and proliferation of disease-causing yeast).

During pregnancy, women tend to alter their normal eating habits. Cravings are commonplace, especially for foods high in sugars and carbohydrates, which nourish disease-causing yeast. Moreover, weight gain is typical, which can be significant, making it difficult to lose weight afterward. Women who are pregnant more than once are likely to have experienced repeated weight gain and/or loss that adversely affects their metabolism; typically, it causes glucose intolerance and hyperinsulinism.

After birthing their baby, whether they are aware of it or not, many mothers are given antibiotics to prevent subsequent infections. Usually, they unknowingly receive the antibiotics intravenously, especially after an episiotomy (an incision to avoid lacerating their perineum during delivery) or any other invasive or surgical procedure that assisted their delivery, ranging from a forceps-assisted delivery to a cesarean section. Obstetricians prescribe antibiotics to avoid the infections that commonly follow these invasive procedures. Moreover, sometimes a newborn baby is given antibiotics for various reasons, which sterilizes their gastrointestinal tract, placing them at high risk for developing candidiasis early in life. However, a miscarriage or abortion may have similar effects and are also likely to promote candidiasis.

Sexual Intimacy

Sexual activity can transfer disease-causing organisms from one person to another. Some infectious disease specialists believe intimate kissing can transmit some infectious invaders from partner to partner. Intercourse may pass numerous infectious invaders from one partner's genitals to the other, but these invaders do not gain access to the gut, so there is a minimal chance of causing candidiasis. Yet, if someone acquires a sexually transmitted infection that requires antibiotics, their risk of candidiasis increases.

Oral gratification places the performer's mouth in proximity to the receiver's genitals and anus, making the transfer of infectious invaders likely. Any type of anal manipulation carries a high risk of transmission because it provides direct access to the infectious invaders residing within their partner's gastrointestinal tract and anus, including disease-causing yeast, harmful parasites, bacteria, molds, and/or viruses.

Sex must be considered a risk factor for candidiasis because it is an intimate avenue of communication for transmitting infectious invaders from one person to another. For example, research reveals male and female partners are likely to be infected with the same strains of *Candida albicans*. Therefore, to avoid reinfections and relapses, it is important for a candidiasis sufferer's sexual partner to also be treated, even in the absence of symptoms.

Substance Abuse

Some people cope with life by using substances such as alcohol, drugs, or tobacco. Regardless of the form, substance abuse is prevalent and, depending on the substance and amount used, it predisposes a user or abuser to develop candidiasis.

Alcoholism

Alcohol is the oldest mind-altering *drug* known to man. Yes, alcohol is a drug. A significant number of Americans consume alcohol in one form or another. Some of them are problem drinkers, drinking enough to cause problems in their life, and about 60 percent of the problem drinkers consume enough alcohol to become dependent on it.

The active drug in alcohol is *ethanol* (ethyl alcohol), and ingesting excessive amounts slowly ravages the body. The undesirable effects of "drinking" cause metabolic disturbances and alcohol-induced tissue damage. Alcohol primarily affects the gastrointestinal tract, especially the liver, but it also impairs and compromises the brain and nervous system. Since the brain governs nearly all the body's activities, alcohol's effect on the brain instigates numerous secondary problems. Although this is certain to adversely affect the nervous system, it can also cause impaired immunity and endocrine (hormone) disturbances.

Few alcoholics eat correctly and rarely obtain their required nutrition, which impairs their metabolism. Many alcoholics increase their exposure to yeast by consuming beverages that contain large amounts of it; notably, wines and unfiltered beers. Moreover, certain "hard" alcohols (spirits) are aged in oak or other wood casks and can become contaminated with mold.

Any of these may induce allergy symptoms and inflammation in sensitive and hypersensitive people. In addition, many alcoholic beverages contain sugar and carbohydrates, which adversely affect a drinker's glucose tolerance and nourishes their disease-causing yeast.

Researchers have determined chronic or frequent alcohol ingestion can cause leaky gut syndrome (chapter 3) by extracting-dissolving lipids (fats) within the gastrointestinal mucus, making the gut wall more easily assaulted and inflamed. This scientific evidence suggests that frequent drinkers and alcoholics are at high risk for developing candidiasis.

Drug Abuse

Drug abuse can involve doctor prescribed medications, over-the-counter drugs, and illegal substances obtained behind closed doors. Your doctor may prescribe tranquilizers, sleeping pills, or painkillers. Your pharmacy and grocery store sells many items that can cause addiction, including diet pills, cold medications, and numerous herbs. Although these substances are obtained legally, it does not mean they are less dangerous than what you get from your local drug dealer. In addition to the current pharmaceutical opioid epidemic, the most often used drugs are marijuana, depressants (hypnotics and tranquilizers), cocaine, heroin, amphetamines, and hallucinogens.

Drug abuse is a risk factor for candidiasis for numerous reasons. Some drugs suppress or depress immunity; for example, research revealed that morphine caused decreased immunity in mice, whereas amphetamines worsened *Candida albicans* infections on the tongues of rats. Impaired immunity impedes the body's ability to defend against disease-causing yeast. Certain drugs have allergic consequences. For example, numerous antibiotics precipitate allergic reactions in sensitive people—most commonly, penicillin and sulfa-containing drugs. Within the gut, these undesirable reactions cause inflammation and stress the immune system; either creates conditions that allow disease-causing yeast to proliferate or invade into the gut wall. By the way, some people have an allergy to marijuana, and smoking it can cause inflammation and stress their immune system, whether they know it or not.

In addition to the drugs, their route of administration can be a risk factor. Injecting a drug into the skin or blood can increase the potential for recurring infections, and this can weaken the immune system. Unsanitary practices, such as sharing needles, also places the user at risk for transferring infections and illness from one person to another.

Smoking

It is not definitively known whether smoking tobacco increases a person's risk for candidiasis. In contrast, in 2019, a study found that nicotine enhanced the biofilm thickness and adherence of oral-associated *Candida albicans* and *Candida parapsilosis*. This implies that smoking and vaping substances that contain nicotine can be problematic.

Although studies disagree, it is prudent to be cautious. Any substance known to promote the development of cancer cannot be deemed beneficial or innocently ignored. In fact, research reveals that smoking may suppress immunity; a study published in the *American Journal of Respiratory and Critical Care Medicine* stated, "Smoking may decrease the immunity of HIV-positive patients." Although it mostly involves the lung's immunity, it is a cause for concern because it may increase a person's likelihood of developing respiratory candidiasis.

Smoking can cause genetic abnormalities. One study found that smoking can damage sperm cells (agricultural pesticides used in tobacco farming might contribute to this effect). Another study showed it may impair fertility, claiming smoking can cause genetic damage in both sexes. Since all the cells in your body contain genetic material, all of them are susceptible to smoking's ill effects, especially the cells of your immune system.

The risk of tobacco use is usually associated with the amount inhaled. So, pipe and cigar smokers have a lower risk than cigarette smokers because they tend to inhale less. Yet, tobacco products have been found to contain up to 7,000 constituents, with hundreds being toxic chemicals and cancer-causing substances that provoke harmful oxygen-based free radical activity and bodily damage. Smoking can initiate injury and constriction of blood vessels, impeding the body's ability to transport and deliver oxygen and nutrients as well as eliminate wastes. Equally alarming, studies reveal that secondhand smoke is just as, if not more, harmful than smoking. Moreover, vaping and chewing tobacco have their associated risks.

Research demonstrates that exposing *1,3-beta-D-glucan* (a major component of fungal cell walls, especially *Candida albicans*) to cigarette smoke can increase inflammation in lung tissue. Simply put, if you have disease-causing yeast within your lungs, you are more likely to be sensitive and susceptible to the damaging effects of cigarette smoke. Therefore, even though smoking has not been definitively proven to promote candidiasis, there are enough warnings to make it highly suspect.

Sunlight and Ultraviolet Light Exposure

Sunlight contains frequencies of radiation beneficial to our optimal health; for example, sunlight converts the inactive forms of vitamin D to its active form. Sunlight also contains a specific frequency of radiation called ultraviolet (UV) light; a lack of exposure has been shown to promote the development of certain forms of candidiasis. Experiments with disease-causing *Candida*-species organisms demonstrate that their growth is sensitive to UV light, which inhibits them. UV radiation also impedes "delayed-type hypersensitivity" to *Candida albicans*, an allergic reaction involved in numerous skin conditions.

These findings help explain why sufferers of various skin conditions are often treated with UV light, with mixed to favorable results. Although UV light is unlikely to affect disease-causing yeast within the gut or blood, it may photo-inactivate numerous yeast-related toxins and metabolites within the epithelial (skin) cells. In addition, UV light may physically incapacitate or destroy disease-causing yeast (or other fungal organisms) living on or within the skin tissue. There is no denying that sunlight exposure can help combat candidiasis in some sufferers.

Since prolonged outdoor activities are associated with premature damage and aging of the skin, excess sunlight exposure can adversely affect someone's skin and establish an environment hospitable for the growth of numerous infectious invaders. Excessive sunlight exposure has also been associated with an increased risk of skin cancer.

Surgery

Surgery is an invasive procedure that places the body under strain, physically and mentally. Whether minor or extensive, it is often followed by disturbances in the body's normal functioning. Organs, tissues, and cells are often damaged when something is being repaired, adjusted, or removed. In the process, many bodily functions and systems suffer negative consequences. The more intrusive the surgery, the greater its adverse effect.

With any type of surgery, anesthesia is a potential health risk. Since postoperative infections are common, antibiotics are routinely administered before, during, and after procedures. In addition, a person's nutritional requirements increase after surgery. Any of these circumstances can contribute to promoting candidiasis.

An especially concerning form of surgery is organ transplantation, the replacement of a damaged organ with an identical one from a compatible donor. Transplant recipients often have impaired cell-mediated immunity. In addition, they routinely receive medications that suppress their immunity to prevent their immune system from recognizing their new organ as foreign and rejecting it. Since impaired immunity is a risk factor, it is not surprising that candidiasis frequently arises after bone-marrow, kidney, liver, and other organ transplantations.

Tissue Damage

The skin is an essential organ that performs many critical functions and metabolic processes, including preventing the assaults of infectious invaders, inhibiting the entry or loss of water, regulating body temperature, eliminating bodily toxins and wastes (especially urea and salt), and assisting in the production of vitamin D. Since it is connected to the nervous system, it gives us the ability to experience numerous sensations, ranging from pleasant to painful.

Extensive skin damage places great stress on the body, causing metabolic disturbances. The effect is not only localized to the area damaged; as injury increases, the bodily strain becomes more systemic and disproportionately greater, which is why a mild (first-degree) burn involving two-thirds of the body can be fatal. Depending on the type and amount of tissue damage, burns can be dangerous because of their risk of infection, dehydration, shock, and death. The localized and systemic complications of severe burns increase someone's risk for developing candidiasis and opportunistic infections more than any other type of tissue damage; burn victims are typically given large amounts of antibiotics and other medications as well as intravenous feedings, all of which readily promote the reproduction and colonization of disease-causing yeast.

Yet, damage to the skin does not have to be life threatening to increase someone's risk of candidiasis. Areas with decreased blood flow lose their normal protective functions and immunity, making them vulnerable to infection. The worst situation involves tissue that has lost its blood supply and died (infarcted) and tissue that is damaged (traumatized) after an injury or surgery. These areas create conditions that support the invasion and colonization of infectious invaders, which can progress further if the immune system is unable to effectively confine them to these locations.

Once an infection is entrenched, it can easily spread to adjacent areas. This may weaken immunity further and require the use of antibiotics; both are potent risk factors for the development of candidiasis.

Toxic Exposures

Almost anything we are exposed to in our environment has the potential to be harmful to our good health. Some substances are strongly toxic to the human body, producing disturbances and illness from even a small, one-time exposure. In contrast, other substances are much less disruptive, inducing problems only after a significantly large exposure or years of small exposures accumulate. Regardless, exposures to certain toxic chemicals and heavy metals can induce reactions and allergies, which stress the immune system and directly injure the body's cells, tissues, and organs. As a result, toxic exposures can increase someone's likelihood of developing candidiasis.

Toxic Chemicals

Frequent interactions with subtoxic substances or a one-time, blatant exposure can induce severe anatomical, physiological, and metabolic disturbances. Some chemicals are overtly poisonous, while others are grossly or microscopically caustic. Chemicals are all around us and are virtually impossible to completely avoid. Pesticides sprayed on crops eventually make their way into us. Numerous chemicals increase your likelihood of candidiasis; studies indicate that exposure to formaldehyde, pesticides, and dioxin (and its related compounds) instigate or exacerbate a sensitivity to disease-causing yeast and/or promote its colonization.

Our food supply is often contaminated with these toxic chemicals. In addition to receiving antibiotics and hormones, many animals are fed food and grain tainted with chemicals and toxins. Seafood from contaminated oceans and rivers commonly contains moderate to large amounts of chemicals, heavy metals, plastic residues, and other harmful substances. For example, polychlorinated biphenyls (PCBs) are plastic residues polluting our rivers and oceans, which contaminate the fish and other seafood we eat, and then our bodies.

Chemicals disturb endocrine (hormone) functioning; at least 51 common chemicals are known or suspected. Estrogen-like chemicals can accumulate within the body, especially the fatty tissues, so their effects can be long-lasting. Since disease-causing yeast have an intracellular (internal) estrogen-binding protein, estrogen-like chemicals can stimulate the growth of disease-causing yeast, promoting candidiasis. Moreover, disease-causing yeast have been found to bind with bisphenol A, a plastic present in many consumer products, including plastic bottles, that mimics the hormone estrogen. So, in addition to what you eat, harm can also result from the packaging materials that contain your foods and beverages.

It should be noted, using a rodent model of Gulf War syndrome, chemical exposure caused intestinal injury via leaky gut syndrome (chapter 3) and inflammation of the nervous system.

More disturbingly, genetically modified foods and some non-genetically modified foods have been treated with chemical weed killers to increase their harvest. The herbicide Roundup, a widely used and reportedly "safe" weed killer, has been associated with cancer of the lymph nodes and lymphatics, and there have been and are multiple lawsuits settled and ongoing. Roundup is the brand name of a systemic, broad-spectrum glyphosate-based herbicide. Researchers have determined that Roundup exposure is associated with neurobehavioral alterations, especially anxiety and depression-like behaviors, as well as adversely affects the beneficial gastrointestinal bacteria.

In short, chemical exposures and their toxicity can range from innocuous to deadly.

Heavy Metals and Mercury Amalgams

Lead can inhibit the body's ability to kill disease-causing yeast. Other common heavy metals are aluminum, arsenic, beryllium, cadmium, and mercury. In addition, gold, silver, nickel, and copper are metals that cause problems for susceptible people; for example, research reveals that nickel can cause skin allergies.

Although dentists use it less often than they used to, Hal A. Huggins, D.D.S., uncovered an association between candidiasis and silver dental amalgams filled with mercury; his candidiasis sufferers' symptoms significantly improved after removing their fillings. Furthermore, research reveals that candidiasis sufferers with mercury fillings have a 200 to 300 percent increase in glucose intolerance, hyperinsulinism, and hyperlipidemia—three components of *metabolic immunosuppression* (chapter 14). In fact, numerous studies support evidence of a *disease-causing yeast–bacteria connection* that can result in inflammation, decay, and illness.

Many candidiasis sufferers with mercury-containing dental fillings often have one or more swollen lymph nodes in their neck. When the node within their lymphatic system is traced back to the teeth it drains, it is common to discover the presence of decay in one or more silver fillings. Although most American dentists believe decay in these areas occurs because of harmful bacteria, German dentists discovered *Candida albicans* living beneath mercury-containing dental amalgams.

Dr. Huggins theorized, over time, silver dental fillings break down, liberating one or more byproducts of mercury decomposition (by methylation). Even worse, *Candida albicans* can convert inorganic mercury to *organic methylmercury* (a more easily absorbed form), with its concentration accumulating in direct proportion to the amount of disease-causing yeast within someone's mouth. Mercury byproducts are harmful to the beneficial bacteria that compete with disease-causing yeast, so the presence of these toxins encourages the proliferation and colonization of additional disease-causing yeast, with their increased production of harmful metabolites and/or toxins, creating a vicious cycle. More alarming, Dr. Huggins believed the absorption of one or more mercury metabolites encourages the disease-causing yeast to be resistant to antifungal medication. This implies that candidiasis sufferers with numerous amalgam fillings may have difficultly eliminating their disease-causing yeast.

Just as significant, mercury is a heavy metal that can suppress and depress the immune system. Impaired immunity promotes the further colonization of disease-causing yeast. Regardless of which happens first, candidiasis or silver fillings, mercury is harmful. This theory has been criticized and debated because the evidence is not precise and inconclusive. Yet, it is difficult to dismiss because many candidiasis sufferers demonstrate remarkable improvements after their amalgams are removed.

If you do have these fillings and are planning to have them removed, it must not be done indiscriminately; it is important to consult a trained professional familiar with their proper removal (by quadrants), coupled with a nutritional-intravenous program that eliminates (chelates) heavy metals from the body's cells and tissues.

Water

Water is essential for life. It comprises most of the weight and mass of the human body. It is required for the body's metabolic processes and other functions. As humans, we can exist without food for a prolonged period, but we cannot survive for long without water.

Water is equally important for everything else that is alive, which is why most of the food we eat contains some water, unless it was dehydrated. From a plain piece of fruit to a complicated gourmet recipe, all foods have some water within them. Regardless of whether it is a food or beverage, if the water it contains is tainted, problems are certain to follow.

Water can be contaminated with a variety of things, organic and inorganic, placing our health at risk. Organically, water can harbor disease-causing yeast as well as harmful parasites, bacteria, molds, and/or viruses. Inorganically, water can contain lead and other heavy metals, chemicals and toxins, plastic residues, radioactive elements, and other harmful substances. Depending on its origin, the water you ingest can be anything from a pure product to a lethal liquid. Unfortunately, most contaminants cannot be smelled, tasted, or seen. Therefore, it can be a long time before a certain contaminant is suspected, isolated, and finally verified.

Tainted water commonly affects the gut first. It may then be absorbed, causing a variety of systemic illnesses. Unclean or infected water used in cooking or to wash fruits and vegetables can also contribute to illness. Ice made from tainted water can be just as injurious to your health. Although essential, water can directly and indirectly instigate and/or promote candidiasis.

BEATING THE RISK FACTORS

A large variety of risk factors are associated with candidiasis. Some are more powerful or disruptive to your body than others. Some are well documented to participate and/or promote candidiasis. The contributions of others are speculative, while a few are controversial. Yet, they must all be considered to cause or contribute to the development of candidiasis in one way or another. The risk factors discussed in this chapter are not a complete and binding list. Indeed, there might be others to be discovered.

The ability to withstand the physical disturbances caused by a risk factor is important in the prevention of any illness, but this is especially true of candidiasis. A particular risk factor may represent a major part of one person's illness, while it has no effect on someone else. The more resistant you are to the risk factors, the less likely you are to develop an infection, allergy, or other manifestation of candidiasis. Some people seem to withstand the pressure exerted by these risk factors for prolonged periods before their health is compromised, whereas other people succumb after a little push. Most people fall somewhere between these extremes. In general, your resistance to candidiasis depends on your inherited (genetic) constitution and surrounding (environmental) circumstances as well as your emotional state, diet, and overall health. This is not written in stone because there are exceptions.

The good news is even if your constitution is poor and your risk factors are overwhelming, you can still transcend your candidiasis and be the winner. All you need to do is pinpoint the risk factors that weaken your body, especially your immune system, and eliminate or compensate for them accordingly. For example, do not refuse to ever take antibiotics again; instead, just use them when they are absolutely indicated. Here is another example: if you eat too much sugar, decrease your intake or, better yet, eliminate simple sugars from your diet.

The remaining chapters in this book will help you understand candidiasis and form a comprehensive plan of attack against it. However, since you did not become ill overnight, you are not likely to regain your health immediately or without making significant changes and sacrifices. So, if you are willing to make the commitment and put in the effort, good health is easily within your grasp.

CHAPTER 3

How Does Candidiasis Develop?

Candidiasis is a confusing medical condition. Some people are highly prone to develop it, while others do not, even after being exposed to its numerous risk factors. Some sufferers have severe symptoms and illness, while others have the most minor complaints, or none. Some patients readily respond to anti-candidiasis therapy, while others suffer endlessly. Clearly, there is no one, clear-cut way to describe the mischief of disease-causing yeast. Every person is unique, and each candidiasis sufferer is an individual with a history and body that is unique. This helps explain why candidiasis is so misunderstood. Mainstream physicians have trouble understanding this point, but it is a fact, nonetheless.

A large part of the confusion about candidiasis is because disease-causing yeast usually do not cause problems alone. Unlike test-tube research, we are exposed to an endless number of harmful substances and circumstances all the time, whether or not we know it. Therefore, candidiasis frequently involves the undesirable contributions of other infectious invaders, including harmful parasites, bacteria, molds, and/or viruses. These participants precipitate and exacerbate a candidiasis sufferer's ill health. Depending on the combination of infectious invaders present, as well as their capacity to cause harm, an assortment of manifestations and debilitation can arise. Mainstream physicians also have trouble understanding this point.

Moreover, the foundation for a human being's susceptibility to candidiasis often depends on their genetic inheritance—the complement of genes they receive from their biological parents. These genes are the tiny "blueprints" that endow their body with its inherent strengths—its ability to function effectively and its capacity to adapt to unfavorable circumstances. Yet, heredity has a downside because people also inherit genetic weaknesses, predisposing them to develop certain symptoms, diseases, and illnesses. In addition, a multitude of risk factors, some worse than others, plays a significant role in promoting candidiasis, and the greater the exposure, the higher the chance for illness. Hopefully, you are beginning to realize candidiasis is far from being a black-or-white, all-or-nothing condition. Since mainstream physicians are taught to classify and define illness, they have a major problem understanding this point.

Regardless of mainstream medicine's doubts and disbelief, candidiasis is real. Yes, its diversity and variability can be understood. In fact, it is essential to understand the intricacies of candidiasis to effectively treat it. This is done to avoid mistakes as well as achieve the quickest and best results. Even though it may seem confusing at first, when the pieces of the candidiasis puzzle are aligned and assembled, this medical malady is easier to appreciate.

A TYPICAL CASE OF CANDIDIASIS?

How does someone acquire candidiasis? What permits its development in the first place? What promotes its symptoms and illness? Why is there such a variety of manifestations? Why do some people suffer with severe symptoms, while others have hardly any? Why do some patients rapidly respond to treatment, while others show limited improvement followed by a brisk relapse? These questions illustrate how "typical" is not a word that should be used in the same sentence with "candidiasis."

Experience with candidiasis sufferers reveals there is no such thing as a "typical" case. Yes, there are similarities, but there are also a spectrum and variety of differences. Since each person's genetic individuality, history of illness, infections, allergies, environmental exposures, diet, experiences, and stress make them unique, no two candidiasis sufferers' symptoms and illness can ever be exactly alike. If that were not the case, candidiasis would be accepted as a legitimate malady and would be easy to diagnose and treat. In contrast, the manifestations and variations in its symptoms and illness has enveloped candidiasis within a web of confusion and frustration, not to mention doubt and disbelief. The presence of coexistent infections, toxin exposures, allergies, food intolerances, and other problems distort the picture further. Therefore, it is critical to appreciate that the multitude of symptoms and illness accompanying candidiasis make its misdiagnosis and mistreatment common occurrences for its sufferers.

Candidiasis is a highly variable condition. To examine the development and symptoms of any one case is like looking at tread wear on an automobile tire to assess the car's running condition. Although it indicates how a car interacts with the road surface, it cannot reveal the inner workings of the engine, much less the car's general condition and total activities. We cannot tell where it was driven, how fast or slow it goes, its age, and so on. Even though a single case of candidiasis answers some questions, it overlooks a multitude of others.

Rather than focus on specifics, consider the big picture of how someone progresses from wellness to candidiasis. Some people have a smooth and slow journey, while others find their trip to be bumpy and unpleasant. Since each person is unique, their development of candidiasis is similarly unique, although there are some common landmarks and milestones. Regardless of whether there are bumps, potholes, straight roads, or curves, when you travel along the Candidiasis Highway, your destination is guaranteed to be a town called "Illness."

On the Candidiasis Highway, a person starts by being healthy, moves along, is exposed to numerous candidiasis risk factors, and is transformed into a sick person with disease-causing, yeast-related symptoms and illness. Like any voyage, there is more than one way to get to your destination. The shortest route is a straight line, a fast trip from wellness to illness. This involves exposing someone to numerous candidiasis risk factors one after another, especially giving them an abundance of antibiotics that kill the gastrointestinal beneficial bacteria, which inhibit and suppress the growth of disease-causing yeast. Once the beneficial bacteria decrease, a high sugar or carbohydrate diet readily nourishes the disease-causing yeast, allowing them to reproduce and colonize their surroundings. Yet, few people take the fast route, and even fewer people drive into a ditch or off a cliff. As trips go, candidiasis is more likely to be slowly debilitating.

Fortunately, if enough beneficial bacteria are present, most healthy people can compensate and tolerate exposure to mild candidiasis risk factors. Typically, when a healthy person encounters a few mild risk factors, they can stay well, like how a new car is not damaged by a few small bumps and potholes. In fact, most people are frequently exposed to one or more mild candidiasis risk factors, but few of them develop candidiasis.

Exceptions exist because illness can follow mild exposures to the candidiasis risk factors. If you are driving too fast by not getting enough sleep, drinking alcohol, taking drugs, eating poorly, or any other harmful behavior, even small bumps may cause noticeable damage. So, living in the "fast lane" and partying all the time is like driving without tuning up your automobile; undeniably, it takes less effort to damage a car that is not running optimally. If you are driving a poorly manufactured car (a "lemon")—that is, if you have inherited a tendency to easily develop illness—you may be disturbed by bumps and potholes that would not harm someone driving in a better car.

As time passes and more risk factors are encountered, even the healthiest person is unable to withstand disturbances and damage. Sooner or later, being exposed to numerous, mild candidiasis risk factors or a few moderate ones can cause changes, leading to symptoms. If someone is generally healthy, their body may make the adjustments needed to return them to a state of well-being. In this situation, mild or insignificant symptoms typically arise. Usually, this person does not progress to overt candidiasis, unless they encounter other undesirable risk factors; the more bumps and potholes, the more damage they will sustain.

When the candidiasis risk factors are powerful, someone can quickly succumb. If you drive over a large bump or into a deep pothole, you can suffer great damage. In this case, there is no turning back; significant damage requires professional help to repair it. Any severe or repeated stressful events that readily disrupt or destroy the beneficial bacteria, especially the use of antibiotics, are certain to guarantee the development of candidiasis. If the beneficial bacteria are unable to inhibit and suppress the disease-causing yeast, they will reproduce and colonize their surroundings, with their increased presence and chemical activities promoting disturbances within their human host. Typically, candidiasis sufferers can develop metabolic (chemical) disturbances as well as problems within their nervous, endocrine (hormone), and immune systems. Unfortunately, impaired immunity allows the disease-causing yeast to advance further, creating a vicious cycle.

Regardless of whether it develops quickly or slowly, *candidiasis is present when disease-causing yeast dominate the gastrointestinal tract.* At first, their presence is insignificant, with little to no symptoms being evident. Later, their mischief becomes more pronounced, forcing many candidiasis sufferers to ask, "I never had this before, why now?" What they do not understand is that candidiasis often develops gradually. It is not an "absent one day, present the next" condition. Unlike the rapid onset of a bacterial infection or virus that forces you to quickly seek help, candidiasis tends to slowly compromise your health over many months to years.

After developing candidiasis, other problems are likely to follow. As candidiasis continues or progresses, it frequently precipitates and/or promotes disturbances that involve the immune, endocrine, and nervous systems. The symptoms and illness that arise often reflect someone's genetic strengths and weaknesses; their inherited tendency to manifest specific medical maladies. For example, some families are prone to develop bowel problems, others have elevated cholesterol levels, and others experience a high incidence of breast cancer. As the disturbances and damage continues, a candidiasis sufferer becomes increasingly compromised and unwell.

Even worse, in many sufferers, the disease-causing yeast do not remain within the gastrointestinal tract. Some of them can invade into and through the gut wall, enter the tissues, and advance into the blood, where they are free to travel throughout the body. Using dark-field microscopy (chapter 17), living disease-causing yeast are regularly seen within samples of blood taken from candidiasis patients, and not just the sickest ones. Once they are within the blood, they can colonize other locations. This often involves areas with poor blood flow, for example, the nail beds. Yet, poor blood flow is not an absolute requirement if there is impaired immunity; disease-causing yeast can infect the spleen, colonize the lungs, and even cause problems within the brain. In contrast, disease-causing yeast can spread from the gut and mucous membranes to other areas; they can advance to colonize the sinuses and Eustachian tubes, and even progress up the common bile duct to infect the gallbladder, liver, and pancreas. Infections of virtually every organ and tissue have been described in the medical literature.

In addition to its *infectious* side, candidiasis has an *allergic* side. Disease-causing yeast are prominent allergy-inducing microorganisms. Their presence frequently instigates and/or promotes undesirable, immune system sensitivities and hypersensitivities to various substances (chapter 16), including allergies to foods, chemicals, smoke, dust, pollens, animals, or anything else someone might be exposed to. Most candidiasis sufferers develop and demonstrate allergies to disease-causing yeast as well as many harmful molds. This often includes allergies to *Candida albicans*, baker's and brewer's yeast, and the molds *Trichophyton*, *Oidiomycetes*, and *Epidermophyton*. Rather than being the cause of candidiasis, these allergies are a consequence of its presence that acts to further aggravate and exacerbate illness.

This brief description of candidiasis's infectious and allergic sides is basic information. Since every person is unique, there are infinite ways to develop candidiasis. Although each sufferer has their own story to tell, they all have one thing in common: the loss or absence of their beneficial bacteria and the colonization of disease-causing yeast. The one constant is that candidiasis occurs because *disease-causing yeast are opportunists*; given the chance, they readily proliferate, colonize their surroundings, and cause illness. The variables involve someone's inherent health (strengths, weaknesses, and resilience) and environmental exposures (toxins, caustic chemicals, plastics, and more). This determines their susceptibility or resistance to develop candidiasis, the symptoms and illness they manifest, the debility they experience (acute, recurrent, or chronic symptoms), their tendency to succumb further, and their capacity to regain health.

Fortunately, most candidiasis sufferers should be able to improve—provided, of course, they are properly diagnosed, are appropriately treated, are motivated, have a positive outlook, and do what it takes to get well. With the basics covered, it is essential to understand the specifics to avoid making the mistakes that will sabotage your recovery.

YOUR HEALTH & WHAT AFFECTS IT

Although health is your most valuable commodity, most people take it for granted until they get sick. If you want to function optimally, be as healthy as possible, and feel the best you can, you must maintain (or restore) your good health.

Sadly, most people neglect their health, going through life ignorant or apathetic about what they need to do to stay well. Most people sabotage their wellness with unhealthy foods and beverages, drugs, lack of sleep, negative emotions, and numerous other harmful things and behaviors. Undeniably, a poorly maintained car will suffer in performance and is likely to break down prematurely. In the same way, your body is your lifelong vehicle. It transports you from one place to another. You live in it, eat in it, sleep in it, and so on. If you want it to last, you must treat it with care and respect, which requires knowing what is good and bad for it. You do not have the luxury of a lease, trading your body in for a new model every three years, so it is essential to be a concerned and responsible owner, gaining knowledge and understanding about your body's functioning. Yet, it is not helpful to be overly obsessed. Constantly focusing on your health can be stressful and counterproductive. In some people, this obsessive attitude can be harmful. For example, someone who follows a low-fat diet to an extreme, eliminating dietary fat, is likely to develop a fatty acid deficiency and its associated health problems.

Even if you are careful, you might be making mistakes. The current nutritional guidelines espoused by mainstream medicine may turn your good intentions into empty, or even harmful, efforts. It will be many years before mainstream physicians and nutritionists appreciate that the worst dietary culprit is *sugar*, not fat. Abundant evidence reveals diets favoring carbohydrates and denouncing fats cause more disease than it prevents. In fact, many populations had an insignificant incidence of diabetes, heart attacks, strokes, and similar medical maladies until they added sugar to their diet. Yes, some people do benefit from a low-fat diet because they also eliminate a lot of sugar and harmful ingredients with the fat. In any case, the best answer is to learn more and find out what works best for you.

Some things are out of your control. Adverse environmental conditions can hurt your body and promote illness, depending on their severity; for example, sun exposure may take years to progress to skin cancer, whereas radiation exposure can quickly be fatal if its dose is strong. Of course, it also depends on your susceptibility; what harms you may not hurt someone else. The most notable environmental risks to your health include exposure to dust, smoke, pollens, chemicals, or anything else that might make you sick. Some exposures can be minimized or eliminated, while others can never be avoided.

Your environment also encompasses the internal activities of your body, especially what occurs within your gastrointestinal tract (gut). Whatever enters your mouth (or anus) ends up within your gut, beneficial or harmful. Your gut is the prime location for the colonization of disease-causing yeast as well as harmful parasites, bacteria, molds, and viruses. Any of these infectious invaders can cause internal disturbances that impair your good health, often slowly and silently at first. So, your health is affected by two environmental components; your *external* and *internal* exposures, combining to produce the total effect the environment has on you. When you want to alleviate or correct any adverse bodily condition, illness, or disease, it is crucial to understand that both aspects must be addressed.

Other factors also affect your health. Anything that produces strain or tension can cause stress, which can influence your body and mind depending on whether it is perceived as positive, neutral, or negative. *Positive stress* beneficially affects your body in some way; as an example, being in love elevates your mood and charges you with energy. *Neutral stress* often has no noticeable effect, one way or the other. *Negative stress* adversely affects your well-being; for example, excess worrying may make you feel tired, induce stomach pain, cause your shoulders to be tight, and have other undesirable effects. Stress may also occur blatantly, innocently, or inconspicuously.

Stress affects your body in three major ways. It may *physically* affect your muscles, tendons, ligaments, and bones; *physiologically* alter your body's chemical, hormonal, and glandular functioning; or *psychologically* modify your emotions and intellect. Your physical, physiological, and psychological characteristics are not independent; normally, all three are interconnected and stay in a healthy balance (called homeostasis). However, like shortening one leg of a three-legged table, undesirable changes in one adversely affects the others. In addition, the interaction between stress and your body is a two-way process; external stimuli can alter your bodily activities and functions, while your internal activities, thoughts, and emotional perceptions influence your responses.

Most of your body's reactions to stress are tiny and temporary. Yet, tolerance to stress varies from one person to another, sometimes remarkably. One person may readily adapt to an unpleasant situation, while another may physically and emotionally break down or explode. The ability to adapt to stressful situations is called coping, and some people are better at it than others. Often, the type of strain does not matter. Rather, what is important is how the stress is perceived consciously, subconsciously, and unconsciously, which then affects your body physically, physiologically, and psychologically.

The stress you perceive is *subjective* and often reflects your previous experience with similar events. Human beings are products of their past experiences. Whether happy, sad, good, or bad, everything you experienced in your life determines who you are and what makes you unique. In addition, as a species, human beings are particularly notable for their ability to adapt to adverse circumstances. When we adapt, we learn what works and what does not. This enables our species to grow and evolve. Yet, if a stressor is strong or overwhelming, someone may regress or collapse entirely, regardless of their ability to cope. In most situations, what does not kill us makes us stronger, and past experiences provide the foundation for us to determine how we adapt and cope today. For example, you learn not to touch a lit match by getting burned. However, the ability to cope with a burn varies greatly; it may cause mild discomfort in one person, while the same burn may be excruciatingly painful for someone else. Clearly, there is a subjective component to stress. This is evident with respect to psychological stress because responses vary from one person to another. Personality differences, bodily characteristics, and individual idiosyncrasies often make psychological stress difficult to completely assess or predict. For example, one person's reaction to criticism may completely differ from someone else's response to the same comments.

Physical stress is more easily measured and, depending on the type of strain on the body, may be positive, neutral, or negative. *Positive* physical effects promote good health, whether they feel good or are imperceptible. *Neutral* stress has little or no noticeable effect. *Negative* physical stress will promote ill health. It is this simple. Sensations produce similar effects; positive, neutral, or negative. Tolerance to physical stress is commonly influenced by a person's mental capacity; for example, some people have a higher threshold for pain than others. This reflects our mind-body connection, with each part readily influencing the other.

Physiological stress is much more complicated than psychological or physical stress. Every illness is accompanied by metabolic (chemical) and physical disturbances, ranging from imperceptible to overtly irritating, which shift the body's balance from its normal set point. For example, a viral illness is often accompanied by a fever; the increase in temperature stimulates the immune system to combat the virus. External stimuli can have physiological effects on the body, but these often go unnoticed until they cause disturbances. Physiological reactions to external stimuli vary from one person to another because people inherit different strengths and weaknesses, enabling them to tolerate adverse circumstances differently. In addition, a person's specific physiological response reflects the state and health of their mind and body. Our mind-body connection influences our physical, physiological, and psychological functioning, with all of it staying in a healthy balance, that is, until we get sick.

So far, it should be clear that the foundation for your health reflects your strengths and weaknesses, including your inherited and acquired physical, physiological, and psychological constitution. All of these determine and affect your metabolism, your body's chemical activities and functioning. Since you are the product of your ancestors (parents, grandparents, and so on), your metabolism was inherited and reflects your genetic lineage. Basically, the stronger your genetics, the more resilient and adaptable your metabolism can be, especially when stressed. In contrast, genetics can put you at a disadvantage because some illnesses have an extremely high prevalence among blood relatives.

Your metabolism does not function independently and is greatly influenced by your internal and external environment—everything you are exposed to from foods you consume to the temperature and humidity in your surroundings. In addition, your psychological state affects your metabolism, your biological functioning influences your mental activities, and your state of mind affects your physical and physiological processes. With respect to the mind-body connection, genetics strongly contribute to your ability to withstand or succumb to pressure.

Why is your metabolism important? Your chemical functioning is the way your body manufactures and processes what you require and recycles or discards what you do not need. You have your own nutritional requirements that must be obtained on a regular basis. Some of the nutrients are considered *essential*; they cannot be made within your body and must be obtained from foods or supplements. The others are *nonessential*; they can be manufactured, using various nutrients as their building blocks. You must fulfill your need for essential nutrients to function optimally; a shortage leads to deficiencies that will produce chemical disturbances and, when prolonged, metabolic abnormalities.

Basically, your metabolism works like an assembly line that produces products called *metabolites*. If something is needed, production is stimulated, assuming there are raw materials available or retrievable from storage. Yet, production is not usually a simple, one-step process; metabolite A does not turn directly into metabolite B, as multiple steps are often needed. There are also numerous interconnections and interactions between different production lines, with most affected by the functioning within adjacent and connected production lines. If a fundamental component is defective or absent, the chemical machinery will stop; typically, one or more metabolites prior to the defect accumulates, with an absence of metabolites after the defect. Fortunately, your metabolism has some redundancy and overlap because the interconnecting production lines form a widespread network that often compensates for a single or insignificant disturbance. Yet, even under the best of circumstances, if a prominent production line suffers a major disruption, the results can be fatal.

Most of your metabolic production lines (*pathways*) are bidirectional, moving products forward and backward. When a certain metabolite is needed, more of it is manufactured with the building blocks that are available. If there is an excess of a certain metabolite, the surplus is degraded into its basic components, which are stored, used elsewhere, or eliminated. This is how your body avoids accumulating excess metabolites and effectively uses any superfluous amounts. Your metabolism is usually exceptionally efficient, and little gets wasted.

Metabolic processes generate waste. Some products are recycled, others are removed to create space, and certain (toxic) substances must be eliminated to prevent them from harming your cells and tissues. When waste removal is impaired, you become burdened with harmful metabolites, which adversely affects your metabolism and functioning. Since the liver and kidneys are the two major organs responsible for eliminating harmful metabolites, people with impaired functioning of their liver or kidneys are most likely to have metabolic disturbances.

Altered physiological processes adversely affect your body's functioning. Any imbalance weakens your capacity for optimum wellness. Metabolic disturbances can easily be instigated and/or promoted by one or more infectious invaders. For example, disease-causing yeast produce metabolites harmful to your cells and tissues; many of these chemicals have been, and can be, measured within the urine of a candidiasis sufferer. In short, the activities of disease-causing yeast will adversely affect your metabolism. Depending on the size of their population, this can cause disturbances ranging from insignificant to debilitating.

Your immune system usually protects your body from infectious invaders. However, it does not function alone because your immunity relies on your metabolism; the capacity to react and respond to infections and allergies is the result of a multitude of chemical and physiological activities. Immunity is further modified by your diet, nutritional status, exercise, sleep, mental activity, and numerous other contributors as well as the presence of any infections or allergies. The complex interrelationship between all these elements represents a person's *total* metabolism. Your immune system is one piece of the whole, not a separate entity, and its functioning is intricately involved with all your other physiological processes and pathways. When your immune system is impaired, a variety of abnormalities are certain, whether overt or inconspicuous. Moreover, your immune system interacts with your nervous and endocrine (hormone) systems, forming your *neuroendocrine-immune connection*. Anything that adversely affects one system indirectly alters the others, precipitating numerous secondary disturbances. So, your body has three major systems, numerous secondary systems, different organs, specialized tissues and cells, and a multitude of chemical activities that collectively enable you to be healthy. Anything that disrupts any part is likely to precipitate ill health.

If your body's metabolism compensates for an offending stressor, regardless of the type, you will most likely suffer few or no problems. In contrast, if your body cannot adapt or surmount some undesirable stress, you are likely to suffer. Repeated or prolonged exposure to one or more harmful stressors significantly increases your chance to develop illness. Typically, illness arises when the stress cannot be tolerated; sooner or later, an inability to compensate instigates or promotes one or more disturbances. Frequent or prolonged exposure to one or more of the candidiasis risk factors increases your chances to develop candidiasis. Even if your body and its beneficial bacteria can compensate, eventually, with repeated insults, a point of no return occurs when the disease-causing yeast colonize the gastrointestinal tract.

THE COLONIZATION OF DISEASE-CAUSING YEAST

Although candidiasis often arises from antibiotic use and a poor diet, any of its risk factors (chapter 2) can instigate and/or promote its development. The gastrointestinal tract of healthy people contains a significant population of beneficial bacteria, which perform numerous activities that help everything run smoothly. One of their most important functions is to inhibit and suppress infectious invaders that enter the gut. Since disease-causing yeast are virtually everywhere, they often gain access. When there are enough beneficial bacteria, the disease-causing yeast are suppressed and managed. The gut can also be assaulted by harmful parasites, bacteria, molds, and viruses. When a healthy population of beneficial bacteria is present, they outnumber and overwhelm these infectious invaders, unless one or more of them is aggressive or additional troublemakers arrive and contribute their mischief.

We are not completely dependent on the beneficial bacteria and have some nonimmune-related, gut antifungal defenses. For example, *lactoferrin* and *lysozyme* (aka *muramidase*) are substances present in various surface (exocrine) secretions, including saliva, which have varying bactericidal and antifungal activity; they can kill bacteria and fungi. *Salivary histatins* can bind to and kill *Candida albicans*. Yet, when these substances are in short supply or disease-causing yeast are resistant, they will be ineffective. Compared to the beneficial bacteria, these substances play a minor role, and their activities are likely to be important in other areas of the body.

During the development of candidiasis, certain risk factors can kill the beneficial bacteria, especially antibiotic use. As their population decreases, disease-causing yeast are no longer competitively inhibited, and being opportunists, they seize their chance, quickly multiply, and can colonize their surroundings. Although this usually occurs slowly, over months to years, if someone's immunity is compromised, illness can arise over days to weeks.

It is important to mention that there is a difference between disease-causing yeast and their non-harmful relatives. In fact, some species of yeast are beneficial because they compete with disease-causing yeast. For example, *Saccharomyces boulardii* is believed to be a non-harmful yeast that can lower the acidity of the digestive tract to create a more hospitable environment (microbiome) for the acid-loving, beneficial bacteria. Yet, seemingly non-harmful yeast may not be so innocent after all. Many candidiasis sufferers have sensitivities or hypersensitivities to *Saccharomyces cerevisiae* and may react allergically when they are exposed to *Saccharomyces boulardii*. Regardless of whether beneficial bacteria or non-harmful yeast are present, disease-causing yeast are aggressive, and, when given the chance, they will overwhelm any beneficial organisms within the gut.

As the population of beneficial bacteria decreases, other infectious invaders can also reproduce, including harmful parasites, bacteria, molds, and viruses. This unfavorably altered gastrointestinal microbiome is called *dysbiosis*. Once you reach this point, you have crossed the line and passed from wellness toward illness. Without appropriate intervention, there is usually no turning back, and things will only get worse.

Once dysbiosis is established, it creates conditions that encourage the further colonization of disease-causing yeast and allow other infectious invaders to increase their presence. Dysbiosis usually involves the participation of numerous infectious invaders acting together, with some being more aggressive than the disease-causing yeast. When they join forces, conditions within the gut are worse than just their additive effects. For example, many researchers appreciate that mixed bacterial and fungal co-infections are the most advanced and severe form of this condition. To add insult, numerous harmful bacteria (especially *Staphylococcus aureus*, *E. coli*, *Proteus*, and *Pseudomonas* species) are significantly more harmful in the presence of disease-causing yeast. This type of alliance is usually not discovered or suspected until a candidiasis sufferer fails to recover with appropriate therapy, including a strict sugar-free, yeast-free, mold-free diet with one or more courses of systemic antifungal medication.

More specifically, *dysbacteriosis* occurs when one or more harmful bacteria are present in notable numbers. So, candidiasis is often not simply about the disease-causing yeast. In fact, it may include the adverse contributions of a variety of harmful parasites, molds, and/or a multitude of viruses. The more infectious invaders present, the worse a candidiasis sufferer's health is likely to be.

Dysbiosis and dysbacteriosis can often be diagnosed with stool testing. If the samples are collected properly, they can reveal the presence of disease-causing yeast and harmful bacteria. If the laboratory is thorough, it will culture the infectious invaders, determining what drugs kill them effectively, helping healthcare providers choose the best therapy. However, stool testing is of limited value because it often misses or does *not* identify the presence of parasites. In most candidiasis sufferers, unless there is a significant infection, parasites are *not* typically found within their stool samples.

Parasites (chapter 5) are best diagnosed by anoscopy, a procedure that involves taking deep rectal swabs, staining them, and microscopically examining them for parasites (chapter 17). In addition, if disease-causing yeast are growing within the rectum, it will reveal their presence (as well as harmful bacteria when present in large amounts). Since parasites normally adhere to the gut wall, rectal swabbing can scrape them off and, after processing, expose them microscopically, even when they do not show up in stool samples. When parasites are present, therapy must include the use of antiparasitic medications and/or herbs. Most often, the disease-causing yeast should be eliminated before antiparasitic therapy is given. Many antiparasitic medications kill the beneficial bacteria, which encourages the further colonization of disease-causing yeast, worsening candidiasis. In addition, the disease-causing yeast can grow in masses that physically protect (biofilms) the parasites, making antiparasitic therapy ineffective. In contrast, some parasites are particularly aggressive and must be eradicated as fast as possible, even if it means making a candidiasis sufferer worse. Diagnosing parasites can be difficult because stool samples are often negative and the anoscopy is only as good as the technician who performs it and the parasitologist who assesses the sample.

The gut is not the only location that can be colonized with disease-causing yeast. They can also colonize the upper and lower respiratory tract (chapter 6), including the nasal passages, sinuses, and lungs. They enter these areas by being inhaled from the air, directly spreading from adjacently infected areas, or by traveling within the blood and access these tissues through inflamed or damaged blood vessels. Once they colonize these areas, they can promote localized and systemic symptoms, including inflammation and allergic reactions.

In addition, disease-causing yeast have a proclivity to colonize the vagina (chapter 13), which is why so many women have frequent vaginal yeast infections. Their colonization of the vaginal mucosa is not an innocent occurrence because they can inflame the cervix, promoting the growth of abnormal cells, as well as advance upward into the uterus, fallopian tubes, or further. Disease-causing yeast can also colonize the skin in other moist, warm, and dark regions, like the folds between overlapping skin—for example, between the leg and the genitals or the two folds of the buttocks near the anus. They can directly or indirectly affect the skin internally, causing a variety of chronic or recurring skin conditions (chapter 8).

Another prominent area that can readily be colonized is the bladder and urinary tract (chapter 13). As a result, many candidiasis sufferers have chronic or recurring urinary tract infections; typically, it involves a mixed bacterial-fungal coinfection. Research proves that some species of disease-causing yeast can survive and flourish within the bladder, especially *Candida glabrata* but also *Candida albicans*. In fact, *Candida glabrata* can survive even with a urine pH of 1, which is a particularly harmful, acidic environment. So, contrary to mainstream medical thinking, if a urinary tract infection sufferer has yeast in his/her "clean catch" urine specimen, it should *not* be dismissed as a contaminant. Both the disease-causing yeast and harmful bacteria must be treated or relapses are certain. To add insult, disease-causing yeast can invade into and through the bladder wall, causing interstitial cystitis. Unsurprisingly, most interstitial cystitis sufferers are discovered to be candidiasis sufferers (chapter 13).

It should now be evident that disease-causing yeast readily grow within the human body and on its surfaces. Numerous areas can be colonized. In small numbers, these infectious invaders are kept under control and are rarely a problem. Yet, as their population increases, their adverse effects escalate, especially when the beneficial bacteria are in short supply and the immune system is compromised. What makes these infectious invaders so problematic? In short, disease-causing yeast produce substantial amounts of harmful substances. In addition, many of their cellular components and some of their metabolites are strongly antigenic, inducing allergies, inflammation, and numerous undesirable consequences.

CANDIDIASIS-RELATED DISTURBANCES

As candidiasis progresses and the disease-causing yeast colonize the gastrointestinal tract, there is an accompanying increase in their waste products, metabolites, toxins, and allergy-inducing substances (antigens). The more disease-causing yeast, the greater their infection and worse its effect. Over time, the gut may become irritated, inflamed, injured, and even damaged. In return, this may instigate and/or promote functional disturbances, impairment, and even debilitation. Of course, it all depends on the amounts and concentrations of any offending substances as well as the participation of other infectious invaders.

Regardless of where they reside (the gut wall, tissues, or blood), disease-causing yeast perform a multitude of chemical processes and activities to survive. For example, sugar molecules and other simple carbohydrates are their fuel, but their metabolism of these seemingly innocent substances produces *ethanol* and *acetaldehyde* as waste products that are released into their surroundings. As their amounts increase, they become toxic to the cells and tissues. In addition, *Candida albicans* (and other fungi) produces *gliotoxin*, a chemical that poisons the liver enzyme *alcohol dehydrogenase*, which breaks down ethanol. Impairing alcohol dehydrogenase allows the concentration of alcohol within the blood to rise, worsening its harmful effects. Gliotoxin has other deleterious effects, including an ability to suppress immunity.

The multitude of harmful waste products, metabolites, and toxins disease-causing yeast release into their surroundings must be eliminated, or they become toxic, even to the disease-causing yeast themselves. In fact, this is how wine making occurs; when a certain concentration of alcohol is achieved, it physically poisons the yeast, effectively halting the fermentation process. Unfortunately for us, these harmful substances do not usually have a chance to injure the disease-causing yeast that manufacture them. Instead, they are frequently absorbed from the gastrointestinal tract, adversely affecting and injuring the cells lining the gut wall. If these substances enter the tissues and blood, they have the potential to harm all the cells, tissues, and organs of the body.

When a candidiasis sufferer is relatively healthy, these harmful substances are eliminated with minimal adverse consequences, especially when the amounts are relatively small. In contrast, since the liver and kidneys assist in the elimination of these undesirable metabolites and toxins, chronic sufferers often develop impaired liver and kidney functioning, so even small amounts can be deleterious. In short, the metabolic problems that occur within any sufferer reflect the amounts and concentrations of these harmful substances as well as their ability to tolerate and eliminate them from their body.

The presence of any harmful substance within the human body always alters the body's metabolism and chemical functioning in some way. Although the body tries to modify its internal activities to compensate, it loses its ability to do so with time and repeated insults, which weakens its metabolic functioning further. During candidiasis, decreased metabolic functioning exacerbates the body's fragility and susceptibility to additional insults. In return, this permits the further invasion and support of disease-causing yeast as well as other infectious invaders, creating a vicious cycle that worsens over time. Like a line of dominos being tipped over one after another, each having a minimal effect by itself, small insults promote additional insults that eventually cause a large disturbance.

An altered metabolism promotes secondary disturbances as well, especially immune system problems. Since a normal metabolism is essential for a healthy immune system, adverse changes in metabolism impair the immune system in some way; as a candidiasis sufferer's metabolism is increasingly disturbed, their immunity becomes impaired. Since chronic sufferers almost always have metabolic disturbances, they are susceptible to impaired immunity. Typically, the continuous presence of disease-causing yeast promotes *suppressed immunity* (inferior functioning cells). As a result, chronic sufferers often lose their ability to mount and support an effective immune assault against their disease-causing yeast and other infectious invaders, which only escalates their ill health. Although some immune cells can directly attack and destroy disease-causing yeast, they lose this ability, enabling the disease-causing yeast to escape unharmed. Once immunity is impaired, the disease-causing yeast can freely assault the gut wall and invade into the tissues.

Other immune cells produce substances that inhibit the transformation of disease-causing yeast from their less-aggressive form into their invasive form, so improper functioning of these immune cells permits invasive candidiasis. Even worse, when candidiasis is severe, it can lead to *depressed immunity* (fewer cells) and even *suppressed-depressed immunity* (fewer, inferior functioning cells). Impaired immunity can promote the development of some harmful medical maladies, including cancer, chronic viral illness, and autoimmune disease (chapter 14).

Furthermore, metabolism and immunity affect the nervous and endocrine (hormone) systems. These three systems form the *neuroendocrine-immune connection*. Candidiasis can disturb any or all these systems, instigating a spectrum of disturbances, symptoms, and illness. Candidiasis sufferers commonly manifest one or more hormone disturbances (chapter 11) as well as numerous undesirable nervous system symptoms (chapter 10).

During candidiasis, stress on the endocrine system can disturb one or more glands. Hormones are chemical messengers released from a gland that travel within the blood to their target cells and tissues to regulate their metabolism and functioning. Disruptions occur when a gland does not release its hormone or its target cannot respond. A common candidiasis endocrine disturbance involves the adrenal gland cortex, which produces a variety of hormones that assist metabolism, in addition to their anti-stress activity. Most notably, *cortisol* participates in long-term maintenance of our blood glucose concentration. Early in candidiasis, many sufferers develop adrenal cortical overactivity to combat their abundant inflammation, but this also promotes glucose intolerance (abnormal blood sugar regulation) that worsens their metabolism. When candidiasis is severe or prolonged, adrenal gland overactivity can lead to glandular exhaustion and then burnout; candidiasis, adrenal exhaustion, and chronic fatigue are related (chapter 15).

Another common disturbance involves the parathyroid glands, which regulate calcium and magnesium ion concentrations. Functional hypoparathyroidism occurs when the serum (blood) calcium and magnesium levels appear normal, but the amounts within the cells are lowered, causing numerous undesirable symptoms. Any gland and its hormones can be disturbed, with their associated symptoms (chapter 11).

Unfortunately, candidiasis is not just an infection. Disease-causing *Candida*-species organisms are extremely *antigenic*; they are strong inducers and promoters of allergies, including sensitivities and hypersensitivities to disease-causing yeast, molds, foods, dust, pollens, chemicals, and anything else someone is exposed to. So, the inflammation usually reflects two simultaneous, undesirable processes: *infection* and *allergies*.

To combat disease-causing yeast within the body, a healthy immune system produces antibodies targeted against them. These specific molecules bind to the disease-causing yeast so they can be identified and destroyed by certain immune cells. Depending on the location of the disease-causing yeast, as well as their populations and amounts, specific antibodies, called *immunoglobulins* (Ig), are produced; generally, IgA targets disease-causing yeast on mucous membranes, IgG is aimed against disease-causing yeast within the tissues and blood, and IgM is a larger molecule, produced early in the infection, confined to the blood. These antibodies can readily reveal the extent and severity of a candidiasis sufferer's infection, although there are exceptions (chapters 16 and 17). In short, the variable responses that occur and are expressed explain why the results of antibody titer testing (the antibody levels) tends to vary from one sufferer to another.

Undeniably, chronic candidiasis disturbs the body in numerous undesirable ways. So far, none of this requires the disease-causing yeast to be anywhere other than within the gut and on the mucous membranes. Healthier candidiasis sufferers can keep their infection confined, perpetually remaining in this state. Unfortunately, with additional insults, the infection is likely to progress, allowing the invasion of disease-causing yeast into their gut wall and tissues as well as into their blood.

INVADING INTO & THROUGH THE GUT WALL

For most of us, the gastrointestinal tract has several anti-yeast defenses that resist the assault of disease-causing yeast. Gastric (stomach) acid is a potent inhibitor of disease-causing *Candida*-species organisms. *Candida albicans* exhibits optimal growth within an environment of pH 7.4, an almost neutral, slightly alkaline condition. (pH refers to a fluid's acid-alkaline balance; seven = neutral, lower = acidic, higher = alkaline.) Fortunately for us, the activity of *Candida albicans* is completely inhibited at pH 4.5 or lower, the typical acid content of the stomach and uppermost small intestines.

If any disease-causing yeast do pass this first major obstacle, other challenges await. Certain cells lining the gut wall normally produce a beneficial layer of mucus, making it difficult for disease-causing yeast to approach and enter the wall. Normal peristalsis encourages the clearance of excess microorganisms; the wave-like contractions of the intestines, forcing its contents through, helps clear an overabundance of disease-causing yeast and other infectious invaders. Some gut cells and beneficial bacteria produce a variety of antibacterial substances that inhibit or compete with the infectious invaders. Localized antibodies, especially IgA, target disease-causing yeast on the gut wall and mucous membranes for attack and destruction by certain immune cells.

As the number of infectious invaders increases, inflammation within the gut wall and tissues occurs; they become irritated, swollen, impaired, and even injured. As a result, the gut wall becomes weakened and increasingly fragile, making it easier to disturb with each additional insult. Eventually, as the insults accumulate, the gut wall can be breached, which allows inappropriate substances to enter the tissues, while fluid and other substances can leak out.

Damage to the gut wall does not happen spontaneously. Instead, disease-causing yeast readily participate. Under optimal conditions, when they are well-fed, disease-causing yeast typically remain in their less-aggressive *ovoid* form. However, when their environment is compromised, some disease-causing yeast can transform into a more aggressive, invasive form called a *mycelium*, with a main body and numerous, extending branches called *hyphae* or *pseudo-hyphae*, like a tree-trunk and its branches. Even though the ovoid form can enter the gut wall and tissues when its survival is at stake, research reveals the mycelial form is much more effective at invading the gut wall; it produces enzymes that digest protein and other components within the gut wall, allowing it to more easily invade into the gut wall to obtain nutrition.

The mycelial form of disease-causing yeast can digest its surrounding tissue, creating tiny "holes" in the gut wall that allow undigested food particles and other inappropriate substances to leak through, a condition called *leaky gut syndrome.* In return, the wall and mucous membranes can become irritated, impaired, injured, and even damaged, from microscopic to grossly visible, localized, patchy, or widespread. Depending on the location and severity, colonization and invasion can cause or exacerbate one or more gastrointestinal problems, including oral thrush, esophagitis, gastritis, duodenitis, ulcers, irritable bowel syndrome, inflammatory bowel disease, colitis, spastic colon, and proctitis (chapter 4).

Furthermore, the presence of harmful parasites, bacteria, molds, and viruses participates in compromising the gut wall and its functioning. For example, disease-causing yeast and certain parasites, notably *Giardia duodenalis*, are often responsible for non-inherited *lactose intolerance. Lactose* is a two-sugar carbohydrate present in milk that must be broken down within the upper gut or it promotes annoying symptoms within the lower gut. Certain cells of the upper gut produce *lactase*, the enzyme that digests lactose, which is extremely sensitive to the health of the cells and tissues lining the gut wall. If the cells that manufacture lactase are inflamed or injured, a lactase deficiency occurs, followed by lactose intolerance and its symptoms. Conversely, after effective treatment, a candidiasis sufferer will often have their lactase production resume after their gut wall heals; since the production of lactase is sensitive to any disturbance within the gut wall, it is usually the first enzyme to be disrupted and last to return. Other enzymes can be similarly affected and further disrupt the gut's functioning.

Symptoms of gastrointestinal candidiasis can range from one extreme to the other, from severe constipation to frequent explosive and bloody diarrhea, which can further vary from hour to hour and day to day. In contrast, some sufferers have few bowel problems at all. Once again, every sufferer is unique.

Symptoms aside, the colonization of disease-causing yeast within the gastrointestinal tract and the presence of leaky gut syndrome frequently instigate and/or promote malabsorption. Depending on the circumstances, one or more nutrients will not be adequately absorbed, while fluids, minerals, and other substances can inappropriately leak out from the tissues, leading to imbalances and nutritional deficiencies. Although there are exceptions, almost all sufferers have some malabsorption, whether insignificant, mild, moderate, severe, or fatal (chapter 4).

As the gut wall is weakened, it becomes susceptible to attack by infectious invaders. Disease-causing yeast are frequently the first to assault. As the gut wall's integrity decreases, like a crumbling fortress, they easily invade, move through, and progress deeper into the surrounding tissues. This is often the beginning of the next detrimental development.

To maximize the absorption of nutrients, the gut is supplied with an abundance of blood vessels. Disease-causing yeast within the tissues that encounter these blood vessels can assault them, pass through, and enter the blood. This is when *gastrointestinal* candidiasis progresses to *invasive* candidiasis, and then eventually to *systemic* candidiasis. Simply put, the disease-causing yeast spread from the gut wall into the surrounding tissues and then enter the blood, where they gain access to virtually the entire body.

Once they invade into the gut wall, *systemic antifungal agents* are essential weapons for effective treatment. This explains why nonabsorbable medications, such as nystatin, are often ineffective; although it may kill disease-causing yeast within the gut, it cannot combat their presence within the tissues and blood. Someone with invasive or systemic candidiasis may feel better after taking it because the amount of disease-causing yeast and their harmful metabolites has decreased within their gut, but their overall condition has not been corrected and will return.

After entering the blood, disease-causing yeast usually transform back into their ovoid forms (or a cell wall–deficient form), which are better for traveling within the circulation and cardiovascular system; although the other forms do exist and can be seen within the blood. In fact, when blood is taken from a candidiasis sufferer and examined by dark-field microscopy (chapter 17), numerous cell forms are often visualized, including the invasive (mycelia), ovoid, and the immature form (syncitia). The form present, as well as its amount, corresponds with the severity of illness; typically, the more disease-causing yeast within the blood, especially the invasive form, the more ill a sufferer is likely to be. Again, there are exceptions, and some sufferers have minimal symptoms even with a significant amount of disease-causing yeast within their blood. Symptoms aside, their presence within the blood is proof of systemic candidiasis.

To add insult to injury, systemic candidiasis can progress further. Disease-causing yeast can colonize and infect other tissues and organs. They can travel within the circulation to any location with a blood supply.

Typically, disease-causing yeast infect and colonize areas of insufficient or poor blood flow, including damaged cells and tissues; injured or small capillaries may trap disease-causing yeast, forcing them to reproduce or die. If they are nourished, the disease-causing yeast are likely to remain within the blood. However, when the blood supply is insufficient, they can invade through the blood vessels, and then enter and infect the surrounding tissues. As a result, they can promote secondary infections in locations distant from their place of origin. Secondary sites are not guaranteed because the immune system will, if it is healthy and competent, do what it can to prevent this from happening.

CANDIDIASIS: IMMUNITY & IMPAIRED IMMUNITY

Disease-causing yeast are infectious microorganisms. In small numbers, they cause few or no problems. Yet, as their population increases, their presence creates a mass effect that instigates and/or promotes disturbances, symptoms, and illness. The colonization of disease-causing yeast is an infection that, typically, starts within the gastrointestinal tract and then progresses into the tissues, blood, and other areas of the body. If the disease-causing yeast are not suppressed in some way, every person who develops candidiasis would be destined to succumb to its ravages. Fortunately, this is not what happens. The immune system helps protect us from most foreign invaders, including disease-causing yeast. Although it is not perfect and makes mistakes, the overall goal of immunity is to protect the *"self"* (your bodily components) while destroying the *"nonself"* (the invader). During an infection, the immune system is supposed to recognize an infectious invader as being *foreign* or *nonself*, and then organize an appropriate response to combat its presence. In some cases, an infectious invader may not be appreciated or assaulted for one or many reasons, which allows it to reproduce and perpetually infect the body.

Typically, the condition of each candidiasis sufferer escalates until they reach their level of compromise, reflecting their specific combination of risk factors, infectious invaders, genetics, and so on. Thereafter, this person generally remains in a steady state of ill health; not getting better but not becoming worse. A sufferer can continue like this for years or even decades, unless pressure forces a change one way or the other; additional risk factors exacerbate illness, whereas appropriate therapy alleviates it. A large percentage of this burden falls on the immune system because it maintains candidiasis in this steady state. The stronger a sufferer's immunity, the better they can withstand the ill effects of candidiasis, and anything that impairs immunity will permit candidiasis to progress.

As mentioned earlier, one of the ways the immune system combats the colonization of disease-causing yeast is with antibodies—immunoglobulins (Ig). When the immune system functions normally, disease-causing yeast are usually recognized as foreign. After their presence is detected, certain immune cells may respond by manufacturing antibodies of one or more type, depending on where the disease-causing yeast reside and the length of their infection; typically, IgA targets disease-causing yeast on the mucous membranes and gut wall surface, IgG is aimed against disease-causing yeast within the tissues and blood, whereas IgM is produced early in the infection to assault disease-causing yeast within the blood. In fact, these anti-*Candida* antibodies can be measured in any candidiasis sufferer and their levels often correlates with the severity of their candidiasis. Confusingly, some sufferers demonstrate minimal or nonexistent antibody levels. Does this mean they are not actually suffering with candidiasis? No, because there are always exceptions to the rule.

An important exception concerns anti-*Candida* antibodies, which only detect antibodies against *Candida albicans* or an antigenically similar disease-causing yeast. If someone has symptoms and illness consistent with candidiasis, but does not have elevated anti-*Candida* antibodies, does this negate an infection with disease-causing yeast? This is when intradermal skin-testing with antigens of disease-causing yeast and harmful molds sheds light. Unless their immunity is severely impaired, most candidiasis patients have positive skin-test responses to one or more disease-causing yeast and harmful molds. So, an absence of anti-*Candida* antibodies with positive skin reactions to less prominent disease-causing yeast or harmful molds implies there is *atypical candidiasis*. For example, some sufferers have allergies to the less prominent species of disease-causing yeast called *Rhodotorula* and *Saccharomyces*, implicating them as being responsible and/or contributing to their symptoms and illness. Yes, it is still candidiasis, but instead of the major disease-causing yeast, it is caused by the less prominent disease-causing yeast. So, anti-*Candida* antibodies are useful but not 100 percent reliable.

Since antibodies are specific protein molecules that are basically nonfunctional by themselves, they require the assistance of other (antibody-dependent) immune cells to complete their intended effect; the antibodies bind with the disease-causing yeast and identify them as foreign, enabling other immune cells to recognize and destroy them. However, even without antibodies, certain immune cells can *directly* recognize disease-causing yeast as foreign and attack them. If everything is functioning properly, these two immune system processes (*antibody-dependent* immunity and *cell-mediated* immunity) would eliminate disease-causing yeast from the body. Unfortunately, this rarely occurs because a candidiasis sufferer's immune system, by itself, appears incapable of entirely eradicating them. At best, the disease-causing yeast are brought under control, allowing a chronic, low-grade infection to persist.

Many sufferers are not this lucky. As their candidiasis worsens, their immune system becomes increasingly impaired. This can cause *suppressed, depressed,* or *suppressed-depressed* immunity. Chronic candidiasis is a prolonged infection with disease-causing yeast that precedes and promotes deficient immunity. In fact, a significant percentage of chronic sufferers display some form of impaired immunity by laboratory testing, ranging from mild to severe. If impaired immunity preceded the candidiasis, there would be little or no immune system benefits after receiving anti-candidiasis therapy. Yet, immunity does improve in most sufferers after therapy, providing evidence that a prolonged infection with disease-causing yeast impairs immunity. How does this occur? It involves the liver's role in candidiasis.

The liver is the largest organ within the body, and its importance parallels its enormous mass of cells and tissue. Although it assists digestion by producing and releasing bile into the small intestine to promote the absorption of fats, this is a small part of its functioning. The liver's best-known duties involve *metabolism* and *detoxification.* Its metabolic activities involve manufacturing and/or regulating numerous metabolites, including carbohydrates, amino acids, and fats. It also produces several essential proteins, called *plasma proteins,* that circulate within the blood—most notably, our clotting factors. Moreover, the liver helps the body resist the harmful effects of drugs, chemicals, and toxins by degrading these substances (using enzymes) into their less-toxic counterparts through a process called detoxification. Once they are neutralized, the liver eliminates them in the bile or releases them into the blood. In addition, the liver acts as a warehouse for some minerals, fat-soluble vitamins (A, D, E, K), and vitamin B12.

This would seem to be enough to keep the liver perpetually busy, but it has another function that is vital for our good health. The liver is also an organ of *immunity.* It contains special immune cells, called *Kupffer cells.* If bacteria pass through the liver's blood vessels, these cells can engulf and destroy some of them, effectively filtering them out of the blood. The

Kupffer cells also help filter undesirable debris from within the blood, like old red blood cells.

Yet, the liver makes an even bigger contribution to immunity. It helps fight infections or inflammation with its *acute phase response*. In the presence of an infection or significant inflammation, the liver decreases its production of some metabolism-related proteins (especially albumin), while it increases its production of other proteins involved with *nonspecific host defenses*. It manufactures a group of proteins, *acute phase proteins*, that participate in a generalized form of immunity against infectious invaders. In many instances, this assists the immune system in combating an infection or inflammation. This is a tradeoff because, during its acute phase response, the liver sacrifices its metabolism and detoxification duties. So, chronic infections usually involve impaired metabolism, liver congestion, and an increased amount of toxins within the body. Over time, if the infectious invaders are not eradicated, they can establish a chronic infection that perpetually disturbs the liver's functioning. The worst situation involves someone with an unhealthy liver that has a persistent acute phase response; as their liver is increasingly burdened, their metabolism and detoxification are further impaired, so their immunity becomes even more compromised. What does all of this have to do with candidiasis? The acute phase response can be "turned on" by a variety of infectious invaders, and this certainly includes disease-causing yeast.

In most candidiasis sufferers, the presence of disease-causing yeast (the infection) triggers their liver's acute phase response, although the inflammation that occurs contributes as well. Basically, at the expense of its routine functions, a sufferer's liver shifts its activities to assist the immune system. In some sufferers, this does not eliminate their candidiasis or make it significantly better, but it does keep it from worsening, especially when their condition is mild and their immunity is competent.

Many candidiasis sufferers are not so lucky. Their immune systems are unable to combat or even control their disease-causing yeast. As a result, a persistent infection maintains their acute phase response; typically, the greater their infection and inflammation, the more pronounced their acute phase response. Contrary to its intended purpose, a persistent acute phase response can have numerous undesirable consequences. For example, it can impair their liver's ability to produce and regulate many essential metabolites, disturbing their metabolism overall. As a result, candidiasis sufferers commonly have blood sugar and cholesterol problems as well as disturbances involving their nervous, endocrine (hormone), and immune systems.

In addition, the liver's inability to detoxify and eliminate harmful substances can enable them to accumulate. In return, the body's cells, tissues, and organs will become increasingly poisoned, impaired, and injured; for example, an accumulation of ammonia can be toxic and even lethal. This also allows yeast-related toxins and metabolites to accumulate, with their adverse effects. The longer this continues, the greater the toll it takes. Therefore, in most sufferers, persistent candidiasis causes a continuous acute phase response that can instigate and/or promote a spectrum of metabolic abnormalities, the buildup of harmful toxins, disturbances in one or more systems, and compromised liver functioning. (It is essential to detoxify and strengthen the liver of every sufferer prior to therapy, especially when systemic antifungal medication will be used; chapters 18 and 19.)

Most candidiasis sufferers have some magnitude of liver impairment and congestion, often corresponding with the length and severity of their condition. Candidiasis burdens the liver, adversely affecting the body in a variety of undesirable ways. In return, the more the body is disturbed, impaired, or injured, the more the liver becomes compromised. This creates a vicious cycle that aggravates and exacerbates their health, which only worsens over time.

When disease-causing yeast are present in small numbers, the immune system, the body's police force, does not consider them to be a threat and pays little or no attention. In contrast, when they are causing an infection, it will defend the body and attempt to combat them. Obviously, there is a point between these two extremes when the immune system realizes the disease-causing yeast are a health threat and must be attacked. Every sufferer's immune system will respond to their yeast-related infection uniquely; some people's immunity is stronger and more resilient, while others have weaker immunity that is easily impaired. In all cases, once the disease-causing yeast are identified as an enemy, the immune system begins its assault.

If life was fair and the immune system was perfect, disease-causing yeast would be quickly eliminated, end of problem, no questions asked. Yet, this almost never happens. The immune system typically has a difficult time combating disease-causing yeast and is rarely able to eliminate them completely. It can only properly perform its duties when the disease-causing yeast are recognized as foreign. In some sufferers, this does not occur because disease-causing *Candida*-species organisms share identical cell surface antigens with some common gut bacteria as well as certain human blood components (group H antigens). This fools the immune system into thinking the disease-causing yeast belong in the body, like a wolf wearing a sheepskin to hide its identity from the flock. In this situation, the best a candidiasis sufferer can hope for is to have their disease-causing yeast kept under control.

To expect a happy ending is fairy-tale thinking because the disease-causing yeast are opportunists that seize any chance to advance their infection. In many sufferers, this is exactly what happens. Over time, additional or prolonged exposures to the candidiasis risk factors stress and weaken their body even more, permitting and promoting the further colonization of disease-causing yeast. As the amount and magnitude of their infection increases, the immune system must work harder to combat their mischief. If it can increase its activities, peace will be maintained but at a greater cost; it usually involves increased cell destruction and inflammation, which only stresses and impairs the sufferer's bodily functioning further. This usually creates and promotes a vicious cycle that only worsens.

The real trouble begins when the immune system is overwhelmed and can no longer keep the disease-causing yeast under control, which creates a *functional* deficiency in immunity; the immune system's strength and numbers are normal, but its functioning is insufficient. This allows the disease-causing yeast to expand their population and mischief. As the infection rages onward, increased cellular injury and inflammation disrupt the body's metabolism and the liver's functioning. This causes additional metabolic disturbances and the accumulation of toxic substances that disturb and injure the body's cells, tissues, and organs, including the liver itself. As the liver becomes increasingly compromised, the immune system becomes more deficient, a harbinger of dreadful things to come. When the immune system can no longer maintain its strength or numbers, *true* deficiencies in immunity occur. In short, the impaired immunity that arises during candidiasis is a result of the infection and its various adverse effects within the human body, especially the liver.

As the disease-causing yeast advance, any or all of the body's metabolic parameters may worsen. The endocrine (hormone) system is frequently disrupted in one or more places, further exacerbating metabolic disturbances (chapter 11). For example, a thyroid deficiency hinders the body's metabolism, while adrenal gland insufficiency impairs the body's ability to cope with stress, inflammation, and injury. In short, endocrine disturbances impair immunity. To add insult to injury, the presence of other infectious invaders (harmful parasites, bacteria, molds, and/or viruses) exacerbates and aggravates these disturbances. All these infectious invaders can coexist in one person. Remember, this is not a black-or-white condition. In fact, rather than infections with a single organism, mixed infections with many different infectious invaders are commonplace, and the more invaders present, the worse their combined effect.

After a candidiasis sufferer reaches this point, their condition is likely to worsen, with detrimental consequences. Regardless of its magnitude, *any* immune deficiency predisposes someone to a spectrum of undesirable, immune-related medical maladies. The most common involve dormant viruses, infectious invaders suppressed by a healthy immune system. Suppressed immunity allows one or more dormant virus to reactivate, creating infections that exacerbate a sufferer's ill health. Two notable examples are *Epstein-Barr virus* and *human herpesvirus;* although these viruses are present in an overwhelming percentage of adults, they only seem to cause chronic infections and problems in people with impaired immunity, which often includes candidiasis sufferers.

Some viruses may create conditions that promote the proliferation of disease-causing yeast through nutritional and metabolic disruptions; for example, hepatitis-related viruses impair liver functioning, which compromises metabolism and immunity further. In addition, the presence of a harmful parasite, bacteria, or mold is likely to impair immunity as well. At this point, asymptomatic people infected with human immunodeficiency virus (HIV) cannot suppress the virus and are likely to progress to acquired immunodeficiency syndrome (AIDS). Candidiasis, with or without other infectious invaders, appears responsible for the establishment of numerous chronic viral infections.

There are two more undesirable consequences of impaired immunity. Generally, healthy people do not develop cancer because a competent immune system protects the body against abnormal cells and growths. Normally, cancerous cells (cellular mutations and abnormalities) are generated within the body virtually all the time, but the immune system suppresses or eliminates them before they become self-sustaining. As a result, people with impaired immunity are known to be at significant risk for developing cancer. So, impaired immunity predisposes someone to cancer. Since chronic candidiasis, with or without other infectious invaders, causes impaired immunity, it is a strong risk factor for the development of cancerous cells and growths. In fact, most cancer patients, especially those with blood malignancies, are found to have candidiasis. Mainstream medicine claims the cancer came first and the candidiasis follows; if you believe cancer arises spontaneously, this is plausible. Yet, candidiasis-minded physicians disagree. They know that candidiasis can impair immunity, permitting cancers to develop; weakened immunity, combined with an abundance of harmful oxygen-based free radical activity, hinders the body's ability to repair cellular damage and causes metabolic and endocrine disruptions. Under these conditions, the immune system cannot suppress abnormal cellular interactions and formations, allowing cancerous cells and growths to generate in one or more areas. The type and severity of cancer is usually determined by numerous factors, including someone's genetics, internal infections and allergies, and their environmental exposures. The development of cancer is a serious manifestation of candidiasis.

Lastly, impaired immunity can encourage autoimmune disease, which involves the generation of cells and/or antibodies that attack one or more parts of someone's own body. Normally, the immune system can distinguish *self* from *nonself*, allowing it to determine what belongs within the body and what does not. It enables the immune system to attack infectious invaders without damaging the body. During prolonged candidiasis, things can go awry. The immune system often produces abnormal cells programmed to attack specific *self*-elements. Under normal circumstances, these cells are suppressed by a healthy immune system and cannot reproduce, so they cause little harm and do not survive for long. However, when candidiasis promotes suppressed and especially depressed immunity, these self-attacking cells can multiply. As a result, populations of cells programmed to attack specific cells, tissues, or organs can be generated, which disturb and damage their intended targets in a process called *cell-mediated autoimmunity*. Moreover, certain conditions may encourage the production of one or more self-directed antibodies that specifically bind to certain cells, tissues, or organs, targeting them for destruction by other cells in a process called *antibody-mediated autoimmunity*. Whether or not other infectious invaders are involved, prolonged candidiasis can cause both cell-mediated and antibody-mediated autoimmunity.

Since candidiasis can impair immunity, it can promote chronic viral illnesses, cancers, and autoimmune diseases (chapter 14). Although seemingly disparate, all these medical maladies share the same basic process: candidiasis weakens immunity before these problems arise. Yes, genetics play a role in determining someone's susceptibility to one or another, as does the presence of other infectious invaders. A sufferer is not destined to manifest any of these medical maladies or may develop them all. It depends on the circumstances surrounding each person's condition; after all, everyone is unique. Most of this involves the infectious nature of candidiasis, but its allergic consequences are equally troublesome.

CANDIDIASIS-RELATED ALLERGIES

Disease-causing yeast are strongly *antigenic*; they can instigate and/or promote a diversity of allergies (chapter 16). As a result, sufferers typically develop allergies to the disease-causing yeast themselves and molds that are antigenically similar. This effect can also become more generalized, since sufferers commonly demonstrate allergies to dust, pollens, foods, chemicals, animals, numerous harmful molds, and more. Most sufferers have symptoms that relate to both their infection and numerous allergies; rarely does a sufferer have one or the other. Moreover, the longer someone has candidiasis, the more allergies they are likely to develop. With respect to treatment and management, ignoring their allergies omits a large part of their condition. Why do these allergies occur? Why are they often associated with nutritional deficiencies? It involves the colonization of disease-causing yeast within the gastrointestinal tract and its associated leaky gut syndrome (chapter 4).

Anything that enters the gut has the potential to be absorbed, pass into the tissues, and find its way into the blood. Usually, there is a size constraint because particles larger than a certain size are prevented from passing into and through the gut wall, which is why food must be chemically digested by acids and enzymes before it is absorbed. Anything that hinders digestion, preventing food from being processed, causes malabsorption. The colonization of disease-causing yeast and the presence of other infectious invaders will adversely affect the gut wall's functioning and promote malabsorption. Candidiasis sufferers often develop nutritional deficiencies that further disturb and disrupt their metabolism and body's functioning. Significant inflammation can occur, making their immune system sensitive or hypersensitive to one or more offending substances.

Disease-causing yeast rarely remain confined within the gastrointestinal tract. Given the opportunity, they readily invade and enter the gut wall, creating leaky gut syndrome, as mentioned earlier. They can release enzymes that digest tiny "holes" that allow inappropriate substances and fluids to traverse the gut wall. Undigested food particles can enter the tissues and blood. The immune cells within the blood can recognize these incompletely digested food particles as *foreign* or *nonself* (unless there is severely suppressed immunity). To eliminate them from the blood, as well as the tissues, the immune system may manufacture and release protective antibodies, especially when there is significant inflammation and the immune system is being sensitive or hypersensitive. When this occurs, food particle–directed antibodies react with their intended targets, creating *antigen-antibody immune complexes*, which are recognized by other immune cells that sequester and eliminate them. When a food elicits an immune response, it causes inflammatory reactions that worsen with each subsequent exposure. A sufferer first becomes sensitive to an offending food and then hypersensitive; if untreated, their allergies only worsen. In addition, allergies to one food can generalize, triggering allergies to others. Anything that enters or resides within the gut can exacerbate this situation; it can induce allergies to molds, dust, pollens, chemicals, and more. This escalates the gut's inflammation, increasing the malabsorption and illness.

In addition, food allergies can cause undesirable consequences beyond the gut. For example, a person with joint pains that are not from a physical injury is likely to be suffering with inflammation from food allergies. In these people, antigen-antibody immune complexes are deposited in the linings of one or more joints, causing localized inflammation. The body tries to squelch and resolve these inflammatory "fires" by releasing cells and substances that produce discomfort, stiffness, and pain within these areas. A large portion of non-autoimmune arthritis is created this way (chapter 9).

At the extreme, food allergies trigger the immune system to become hypersensitive, especially when harmful parasites, bacteria, molds, and/or viruses exacerbate the inflammation. When it becomes hypersensitive, it more readily reacts to whatever it perceives as being a threat. Normally, the immune system recognizes and attacks disease-causing yeast because they have cell surface antigens that are recognized as being foreign or nonself. Yet, when the immune system is hypersensitive, it loses its ability to recognize and discriminate antigens properly, which causes confusion when there is suppressed, depressed, or suppressed-depressed immunity—that is, when the normal checks and balances are not working. Since disease-causing yeast have cell surface antigens like human blood group H antigen (a primary antigen expressed on the red blood cells of type O blood) and numerous other human tissue antigens, a hypersensitive immune system can be fooled into believing these self-antigens are nonself, and inappropriately attack any cells, tissues, or organs that contain them. When this happens, it can further react and produce cells programmed to directly recognize and destroy anything with these antigens, and/or it can create antibodies that target these antigens for other immune cells to recognize and destroy. As a result, the body initiates and maintains an inflammatory reaction directed toward itself (autoimmune disease), with numerous accompanying problems that reflect the areas adversely affected. This process is highly variable and frequently unpredictable. However, one thing is certain, if it is severe or prolonged, it will result in irreversible destruction of the cells, tissues, and organs that are targeted.

Although it is not definitively confirmed, some experts (both doctors and dentists) believe mercury-containing dental amalgams contribute to this process of self-reactivity and autoimmunity. How might they play a role? As mentioned in chapter 2, research reveals *Candida albicans* can convert the *inorganic mercury* in silver dental amalgams into its easily absorbed *organic methylmercury*. After organic methylmercury is absorbed, this heavy metal can impair and poison the immune system, which may instigate and/or promote the generation of these self-destructive cells and autoantibodies. It is important to mention clinical evidence reveals that some candidiasis sufferers do not fully recover until their mercury-containing fillings are removed.

YOUR CONDITION MAY VARY

Whether it develops quickly or slowly, in childhood or as an adult, if you want to be well, candidiasis is not for you. Twists, turns, and unexpected obstacles make candidiasis hazardous to your health if not downright detrimental. Avoiding candidiasis at all costs is your best bet. Yet, if you are a candidiasis sufferer, what can you expect from your condition? Unless you seek appropriate treatment, you can expect to get worse, not better.

Since disease-causing yeast are all around us, they are normally present within your gastrointestinal tract. Usually, the presence of beneficial bacteria inhibit and suppress the disease-causing yeast, keeping them under control. Exposure to the candidiasis risk factors (chapter 2) can disturb, injure, or kill the beneficial bacteria, allowing your disease-causing yeast to reproduce and colonize their surroundings. This is when the trouble begins.

At first, candidiasis is typically confined to the gut and mucous membranes. If circumstances permit, the disease-causing yeast can directly spread to the upper and lower respiratory tracts, including the sinuses and lungs, as well as progress up the common bile duct to infect the gallbladder, liver, and pancreas. The disease-causing yeast can invade into and through the gut wall, causing leaky gut syndrome with its associated problems—especially, malabsorption and nutritional deficiencies. At this point, *gastrointestinal* candidiasis has progressed to *invasive* candidiasis. Even worse, the disease-causing yeast can enter and colonize the blood, causing *systemic* candidiasis. This allows them to travel within the blood and take up residence where conditions favor their growth. In fact, infections of virtually every organ and tissue have been reported in the medical literature. To add insult, because of their strong allergy-inducing tendencies, disease-causing yeast can instigate and/or promote an abundance of sensitivities and hypersensitivities to a variety of substances, including foods, pollens, dust, chemical, and more, as well as to the disease-causing yeast themselves and numerous molds (harmful and harmless). So, candidiasis is an *infection* with *allergic* consequences. Moreover, the presence of other infectious invaders, including harmful parasites (chapter 5), bacteria, molds, and/or viruses, will accelerate a candidiasis sufferer's passage from wellness to illness.

Regardless of its magnitude, candidiasis can cause numerous disturbances. Its sufferers often manifest congestion of their livers and kidneys, two organs essential for removing wastes and toxins from the body. Since the liver is vital for metabolism (chemical functioning), liver problems cause numerous chemical disturbances. In addition, the liver assists the immune system, so liver problems impair immunity. Candidiasis can directly or indirectly cause chemical disturbances involving the brain and nervous system. Over time, one or more major glands may become disturbed, or even damaged, precipitating even more trouble. Therefore, the adverse consequences of candidiasis occur directly and indirectly.

With respect to its symptoms and illness, candidiasis affects the gastrointestinal tract (chapter 4), respiratory tract (chapter 6), cardiovascular system (chapter 7), skin (chapter 8), joints and muscles (chapter 9), brain and nervous system (chapter 10), endocrine system (chapter 11), genitourinary tract (chapter 13), and immune system (chapter 14). It can cause perpetual fatigue (chapter 15), and the development of allergies is common (chapter 16). Yet, this does not only apply to adults; children can easily be affected (chapter 12). So, candidiasis should be suspected as being the underlying cause or participating in the existence of any chronic, recurring, or frequent medical malady.

Since every person is a unique individual, no two candidiasis sufferers experience candidiasis the same way. Overall, the presentation of yeast-related symptoms and illness is highly variable, ranging from mildly innocuous to severely debilitating. Yes, there are many similarities as well. By definition, candidiasis begins with the colonization of disease-causing yeast. Once this occurs, a sufferer is well on their way to illness. The more it advances, the greater the disturbances they will acquire, making it increasingly complicated and difficult for them to return to a state of wellness. Unfortunately, most sufferers almost never improve without some form of anti-candidiasis therapy. So, the sooner a sufferer recognizes their condition and seeks help, the better their chance for recovery. Some sufferers will only need tweaking, while others require a comprehensive overhaul. In all cases, professional guidance from a candidiasis-minded physician or other healthcare practitioner is highly recommended to achieve the best results.

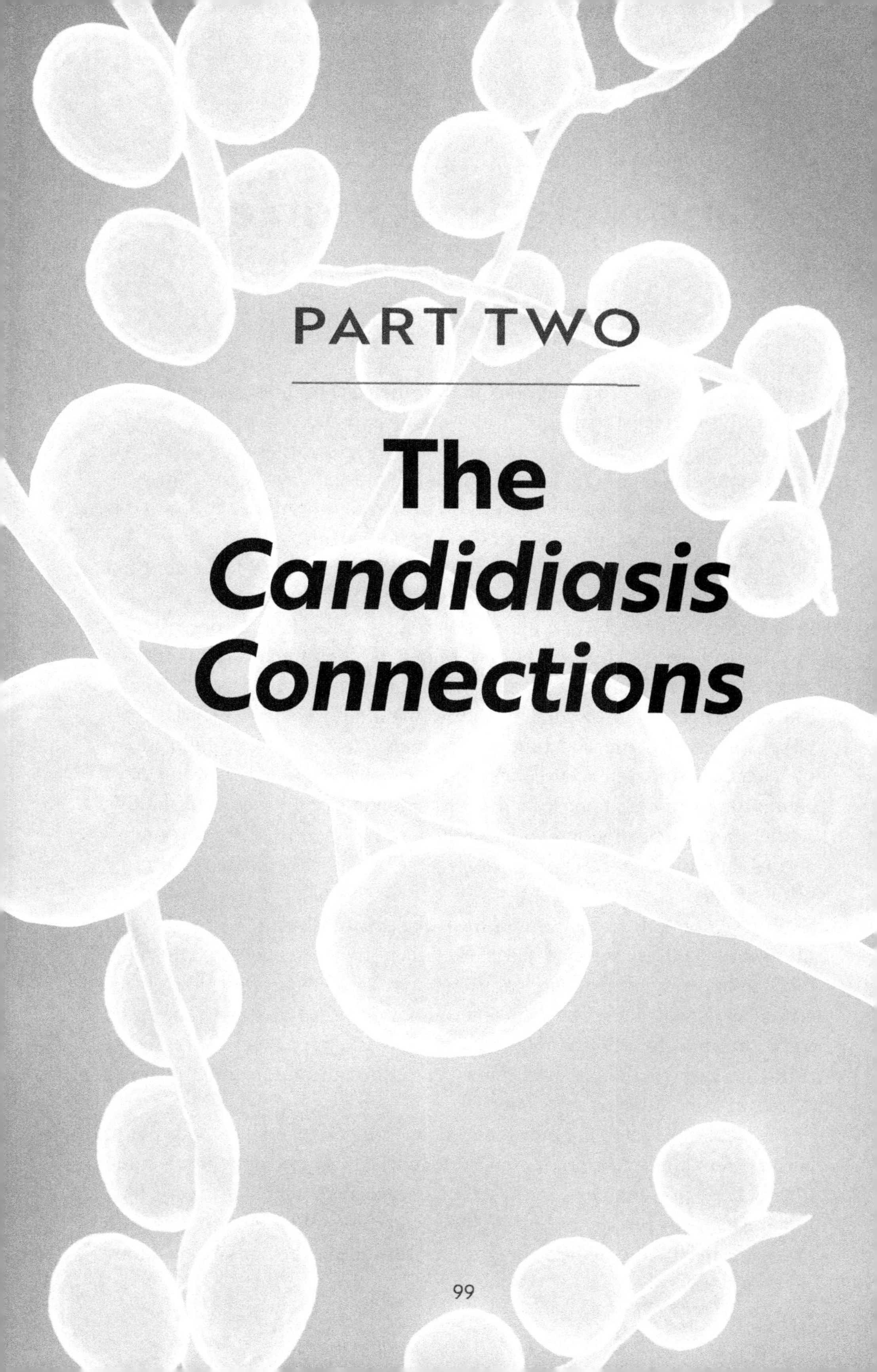

PART TWO

The *Candidiasis* Connections

CHAPTER 4

Gastrointestinal Problems

For most people, what happens within their gastrointestinal tract (gut) is a mystery; food and liquid enter at one end and unpleasant-smelling stuff exits the other. However, knowing how the gut works and functions is crucial to understanding where candidiasis almost always begins. Since the gut does not exist alone, the immune, endocrine (hormone), and nervous systems are essential for its activities and good health.

The average adult's gastrointestinal tract is roughly 23-feet long from mouth to anus. More amazingly, because of its folds, nooks, and crannies, its surface area is enormous (although various studies claim it approximates the size of a tennis court, in 2014, researchers determined it is about 440 square feet, or roughly half the size of a badminton court). It is functionally called the digestive tract, which includes the mouth, salivary glands, pharynx, esophagus, stomach, duodenum, small intestines, liver, gallbladder, pancreas, cecum, appendix, colon (ascending, transverse, descending, and sigmoid), rectum, and anus. Its main function is to alter foods and liquids so that they can be digested and absorbed, providing the body with energy and essential nutrients. During the process, waste is generated and must be eliminated.

The *upper* gut, from the mouth to the small intestines, digests food into ever smaller pieces and particles, which involves chewing, churning, mixing, and numerous chemical secretions. Most absorption takes place within the small intestines. Whatever is not absorbed passes to the colon to be prepared for elimination. Intestinal gas is a byproduct composed of nitrogen, carbon dioxide, and hydrogen, although one in three people's bodies also manufacture methane.

Depending on the complicating factors, gut problems can be acute or chronic, ranging from mild discomfort to marked distress to life-threatening illness. Food poisoning is a frequent occurrence, with almost everyone having at least one episode in their lifetime, regardless of whether it was mild or severe. In 2012 the Centers for Disease Control and Prevention concluded that during the past year, "48 million Americans suffered from domestically acquired foodborne illness associated with 31 identified pathogens and a broad category of unspecified agents." Since most people do not report mild events, the number of sufferers is much greater.

Most people have some type of malabsorption and nutritional deficiencies, suffer with food allergies, and have bloating and gas. Constipation and/or diarrhea are frequent complaints. Clearly, a diversity of symptoms, problems, illnesses, and disease arises within the gut, from mild symptoms like indigestion and heartburn to fatal medical maladies like cancer.

The gastrointestinal tract is a warm, moist, and nutritionally rich environment, which supports the growth of microorganisms. Many beneficial bacteria perform numerous activities to help the body digest and absorb food. We need them and their byproducts; for example, some produce vitamin K, required by the body to clot blood. Although your gut is within you, it is not a closed system and is part of your external environment because its two openings (mouth and anus) allow substances to enter and exit from your surroundings. Contamination occurs when an infectious invader gains entry, which can involve disease-causing yeast, parasites, bacteria, molds, and/or viruses.

Given all the solids and liquids that enter your mouth, the primary environment for the presence and colonization of disease-causing yeast is within the gut; they readily colonize the mucous membranes, anywhere from your nose and mouth to your anus. For them, it is a wonderful environment to exist within, survive, and reproduce. Fortunately for us, there are beneficial bacteria that live and survive within our gut. Normally, they prevent the infectious invaders from taking over. Unfortunately, disease-causing yeast are opportunists that wait for their chance to colonize their surroundings.

The beneficial bacteria's health is inversely proportional to the prevalence of candidiasis. In other words, the greater the population of beneficial bacteria, the less likely disease-causing yeast will cause problems. So, anything that injures or destroys the beneficial bacteria will permit the proliferation and colonization of disease-causing yeast. Numerous factors adversely affect our population of beneficial bacteria (chapter 2), encouraging the colonization and mischief of disease-causing yeast, creating *gastrointestinal candidiasis*. In addition, with respect to *invasive candidiasis*, evidence indicates disease-causing yeast do not tend to invade the gut wall unless the beneficial bacteria have been disturbed. So, the beneficial bacteria are essential for the health of our gut.

Research reveals some of the ways disease-causing yeast can infect the gut. Simply put, they can infect the gastrointestinal tract by directly adhering to the gut wall, sticking to its mucus, being trapped within it, or attaching to a microorganism (fungus or bacteria) colonizing the gut wall.

A multitude of studies establish candidiasis as a legitimate medical malady. Since the presence and assistance of the beneficial bacteria is essential to prevent this condition, candidiasis has been highly correlated and associated with the use and abuse of antibiotics (chapter 2). In fact, anything that disrupts the beneficial bacteria strongly predisposes someone to candidiasis, especially assaults by other infectious invaders. When the number of beneficial bacteria overwhelms the infectious invaders, little or no problems occur. When this balance is disrupted, problems will arise.

EUBIOSIS VERSUS DYSBIOSIS

Since microorganisms occur virtually everywhere, it is almost impossible to completely avoid them. Some are beneficial for us. Others cause little to no harm or instigate trouble only when they are present in large numbers (potentially harmful). In contrast, disease-causing microorganisms create problems; they can infect your foods and beverages, reside in the dust on your desk, live on the dead skin in your bedding, and float within the air you breathe. With respect to illness, most people appreciate infectious microorganisms spread by coughing or sneezing, but even shaking hands can transfer one or more infectious invaders. In addition, there are other ways to pass and spread these disease-causing troublemakers among us, and, unless you live in a bubble, there is no escaping them.

Normally, the body's surfaces form a protective barrier that prevents most infectious invaders from harming us. When all is well, these locations are colonized with beneficial bacteria that protect us against most infectious invaders. Within the gut, the beneficial bacteria maintain the gastrointestinal environment (microbiome) and assist the body to function better or more efficiently. In the best of times, the gut is colonized with a diversity of beneficial bacteria, and everything functions for our health and well-being.

Beneficial bacteria can prevent infectious invaders from colonizing the gut by competing with them for space and nutrients. Some of them produce and release substances that are injurious or deadly to one or more infectious invaders; for example, the species *Lactobacilli* release *peroxide,* a chemical that interferes with the growth of many infectious invaders. Simply put, the beneficial bacteria create "zoning laws" that prevent too many infectious invaders from inhabiting the gut. A healthy gastrointestinal microbiome is referred to as *eubiosis* (*eu* = true, *biosis* = state of life). When there are enough beneficial bacteria, the gut is usually healthy.

Believing this state of perfection will exist forever is wishful thinking. Since the gastrointestinal microbiome is not closed, it is often contaminated with a multitude of infectious invaders, including disease-causing yeast, parasites, bacteria, molds, and viruses. Most of these infections occur subtly, producing minor or no symptoms. They are managed and resolved by the beneficial bacteria and immune system; typically, the infection is mild and insignificant, with most people not even suspecting its presence. Unless an infectious invader is aggressive, it will be suppressed and competitively inhibited by the beneficial bacteria; they ensure infectious invaders that enter the gut do not produce illness, are unable to colonize these locations, and cannot invade deeper into the tissues.

In addition to the beneficial bacteria, the immune system assists in eliminating most infectious invaders or at least keeping them under control—that is, if the immune system recognizes them as being a problem or threat. Many infectious invaders instigate trouble, making their presence known to the immune system. Yet, eradicating every infectious invader is almost impossible because some escape the immune system's recognition, are not assaulted, or are too aggressive or resilient to be eliminated; any of these circumstances will permit a perpetual infection. Moreover, some infectious invaders frequently hang around too long, just waiting for their chance to cause illness.

In contrast, if an infectious invader causes a blatant infection, it can significantly disturb the gastrointestinal microbiome and its functioning. When an infectious invader is aggressive, problems and disturbances arise quickly. Depending on the infectious invader, its effect on the gut (and entire body) can range from insignificant to deadly, with the majority causing problems in between these extremes. In many cases, the troublemaker is not eliminated, and a constant low-grade (subclinical) infection persists. Over time, as more infectious invaders enter the gut, their combined presence becomes increasingly notable. Since every infectious invader has its strengths and weaknesses, their combined mischief is often worse when they enter an alliance, especially when they compensate for each other's deficiencies. Their prolonged presence eventually disturbs the beneficial bacteria, upsetting the gastrointestinal microbiome. Regardless of whether this occurs slowly or is quickly precipitated by consuming antibiotics or some other candidiasis risk factors, the beneficial bacteria can lose their stronghold. When the beneficial bacteria are injured or die, there is a point when they cannot suppress or inhibit the reproduction and colonization of the infectious invaders. When the gut's population of bacteria becomes unhealthy, it is termed *dysbiosis* (*dys* = abnormal, *biosis* = state of life). This is a general term that describes a lack of beneficial bacteria. Dysbiosis may or may not involve the presence of one or more infectious invaders, even though it almost always does.

Dysbiosis is not a true disease state. Rather, it is a prelude to illness, since a lack or loss of beneficial bacteria allows virtually all infectious invaders within the gut to reproduce. Infections with specific infectious invaders create inflammation and disturbances. When it is infected with one or more harmful bacteria, it is called *dysbacteriosis* (*dys* = abnormal, *bacteriosis* = growth of bacteria). An infection with a harmful mold creates a *gastrointestinal mycosis* (*mykes* = fungus, *osis* = condition). An infection with a harmful parasite is usually referred to by the name of the specific infectious invader; for example, *amoebiasis* denotes an infection with an amoeba. Viruses can cause similar problems and the condition is named according to the areas affected or the symptoms produced; for example, *gastroenteritis* is inflammation of the stomach and intestinal tract, accompanying an infection with a virus. When the infection involves disease-causing *Candida*-species organisms, it is called *candidiasis*.

GASTROINTESTINAL DYSBIOSIS

Anything that disrupts the body's internal balance instigates a reply by a chorus of compensatory mechanisms. When one or more infectious invaders are within the gut in large numbers, they create an infection with numerous primary and secondary undesirable reactions and responses. In most cases, their presence signals the immune system, the body's "police force," to be rapidly summoned into action. With most infections, the skirmishes are minor, and the immune system effectively controls the situation, continuing its assault until the invaders are eliminated. In many cases, the immune system retains a memory of the invasion so future contact with the same, or similar, infectious invader is quickly undertaken. The gastrointestinal immune system is extensive. Many researchers believe that, because of its mucosal lymphoid tissue and overall surface area, the gut mucosa is the largest immune system organ within the body.

Yet, the gut's immunity is not perfect. If an infectious invader, or alliance between two or more of them, is aggressive and mounts a strong offensive against their human host, the immune system can be partially or completely overwhelmed. If reinforcements are available, other immune cells are quickly enlisted and enter battle. Like any war, there are casualties. The longer the battle continues, the more inflammation, injury, and damage on both sides, involving the infectious invaders and the body of their human host. When an infectious invader is resistant to the immune system's best efforts, a perpetual infection ensues, causing problems that range from insignificant to debilitating.

As mentioned, the immune system can only function properly if it can correctly identify a harmful invader as foreign. Since it is not perfect, this recognition does not always occur. If some infectious invaders appear like one or more beneficial bacteria, the cells of the immune system may not be able to discern the difference. In this scenario, the immune system can become confused, with its behavior being unpredictable, erratic, and misdirected. Lacking distinguishing characteristics, some infectious invaders cannot be identified. In other cases, like ninjas, an infectious invader can hide or evade the immune system's detection; for example, several invaders can enter some of the body's cells and avoid being recognized by the immune system. Although there are other ways they can escape or confuse the immune system, identification does occur in most cases, and an assault will ensue.

DYSBIOSIS, DYSBACTERIOSIS & CANDIDIASIS

Many studies associate candidiasis with bowel disease. As an example, various researchers have obtained small intestine biopsies from people suffering with gastrointestinal disease and diarrhea, finding a significant number of the patients had fungal infections with varying rates. Forms of disease-causing yeast (blastospores, pseudomycelia, and mycelia) were seen on the patients' gut walls, with the most severe cases having their surface (epithelium) entirely covered with mycelia. In addition, some invasion of the gut wall by fungal *hyphae,* the more invasive form, is often noted. Because of their shape and characteristics, the fungi were classified as disease-causing *Candida*-species organisms. Although numerous disease-causing yeasts were found, the most prevalent infectious invader was *Candida albicans*. Simply put, the studied patients were suffering with *gastrointestinal candidiasis*. These studies provide indisputable proof that disease-causing yeast can invade the gut wall and cause gastrointestinal disturbances.

Almost everyone has some amount of disease-causing yeast within their gastrointestinal tracts. Normally, they are present in small or insignificant amounts, causing little or no trouble. This assumes there are enough beneficial bacteria to keep them under control, maintaining a state of eubiosis. However, in the presence of dysbiosis and/or dysbacteriosis, there is little to impede these infectious invaders from causing trouble and their inherently harmful nature becomes readily obvious. Disease-causing *Candida*-species organisms can colonize the entire gut, virtually anywhere from the mouth to the anus. A particularly undesirable consequence happens when disease-causing yeast, as well as some parasites, enter and migrate up the common bile duct and biliary tree, subsequently colonizing the gallbladder, liver, and pancreas, which can impair and damage these organs; in fact, numerous studies have reported infections of these organs. More often, when the beneficial bacteria decrease and one or more infectious invaders promotes inflammation, disease-causing *Candida*-species organisms can readily assault and enter the gut wall and tissues.

Disease-causing yeast are not the most harmful microorganisms that can infect the gut. Compared to other infectious invaders, they are usually much slower growing, and in small numbers create few problems, which is why candidiasis often takes months to years to arise. Unlike some infectious invaders that cause significant problems within minutes after entering the gut of their victim, disease-causing yeast are not overly aggressive and patiently wait for conditions that favor their growth. Inflammation and a lack of beneficial bacteria allow them to steadily colonize and impair the gut and its functioning. When other infectious invaders are also causing problems, the behavior and adverse effects of the disease-causing yeast can escalate. An abundance of research reveals the undesirable, additive effects (synergism) that occur when disease-causing yeast forms an alliance with harmful parasites, bacteria, molds, and/or viruses. The more infectious invaders and inflammation present, the more easily the disease-causing yeast invade into the gut wall and tissues. Simply put, the more troublemakers that attend a party, the greater the chance there will be trouble.

Although *Candida albicans* is the most notable troublemaker in its family and a major player in the candidiasis game, it does not play alone; there are 7 other major disease-causing yeast and 17 less prominent disease-causing yeast. The major culprits are the most strongly associated with illness. In contrast, the less prominent disease-causing yeast are often ignored, as they are thought to be noninvasive and have a weaker potential to instigate illness. With respect to invasion of the gut wall, only a handful of the most harmful, major disease-causing yeast are thought to be capable of undertaking this assault. Yet, recent findings contradict this with profound consequences for most candidiasis sufferers. A newly recognized version of candidiasis, called *atypical candidiasis*, involves infections with one or more less prominent disease-causing yeast, especially *Saccharomyces*-species and *Rhodotorula*-species organisms; these sufferers are usually not as ill and are frequently overlooked (chapters 3 and 17). More confusing, many candidiasis sufferers are infected with numerous disease-causing yeasts, creating another manifestation called *mixed candidiasis*.

The most knowledgeable candidiasis-minded experts accept the "rules of invasion" for disease-causing yeast; some major disease-causing yeast can invade into and through the gut wall, while others do not. Since a rule is a rule, with little room for exception, most of these experts would be shocked to learn one disease-causing yeast breaks the invasion rules. This troublemaker is commonly referred to as baker's and brewer's yeast. *Saccharomyces cerevisiae* is the formal name for the strains of microorganisms that comprise baker's and brewer's yeast; the microorganisms involved in making bread, wine, beer, and other fermented products. Previously, researchers noted it was noninvasive and rarely caused illness, so it was classified as a less prominent disease-causing yeast. Yet, this was an oversight because laboratory evidence reveals *Saccharomyces cerevisiae* readily grows hyphae when its survival depends on it. In short, it is capable of invading into the gut wall when it is starved.

Skin allergy testing consistently demonstrates that numerous candidiasis sufferers have allergic reactions to baker's and/or brewer's yeast, revealing that they are reacting to these microorganisms within their body. Where is the research to support these results?

Several British researchers implicate the contributions of *Saccharomyces cerevisiae* to Crohn's disease, a form of inflammatory bowel disease, because large amounts of antibodies against this microorganism were found in Crohn's patients (especially anti-IgA antibodies). Although eliminating dietary yeast improved the symptoms of the sufferers, implicating allergic reactions, most researchers think the yeast-produced toxins are more harmful than the disease-causing yeast's invasion into the tissues. In fact, research reveals that the *candidiasis-IBD connection* is more complicated than most medical practitioners understand, differing from each continent, country, region, group, and family that suffer with it.

The important point is that any disease-causing yeast that causes illness, directly or indirectly, should be considered a problem, especially if it can invade into the gut wall and tissues. Therefore, *Saccharomyces cerevisiae* can no longer be ignored or considered innocent of precipitating or participating in candidiasis. With respect to candidiasis, *all* disease-causing yeast must be considered guilty until proven innocent.

LEAKY GUT SYNDROME

Although it occurs in other areas, dysbiosis primarily arises within the gastrointestinal tract. Usually, it begins with an infection, following the invasion of a harmful microorganism, most often, a parasite or bacteria. Regardless of whether the infectious invader is eliminated quickly, slowly, or not at all, the presence of an infection disturbs the beneficial bacteria. If the infection is mild and short-lived, the beneficial bacteria often escape unscathed. In contrast, when the infectious invader is aggressive, a severe infection can injure or kill the beneficial bacteria, sometimes rapidly and significantly. In any case, the longer the infection, despite its severity, the greater the disruption and damage within the gastrointestinal microbiome. If the infection is controlled, but the infectious invader is not eliminated, it can colonize the gut, creating a perpetual infection that promotes problems according to its harmful nature. In most people, rather than developing after a single infection, dysbiosis usually follows numerous infections with increasing numbers of infectious invaders that collectively compromise the health of the beneficial bacteria and the gastrointestinal microbiome.

Dysbiosis arises when the population of beneficial bacteria decrease, or they are eliminated from the gut, and an unhealthy or unbalanced grouping of microorganisms remains. This is a prelude to disease because it allows disease-causing yeast and other infectious invaders to reproduce, colonize their surroundings, and cause trouble. So, dysbiosis promotes candidiasis as well as the reproduction and colonization of harmful parasites, bacteria, molds, and viruses.

Exceptions aside, the mischief caused by most of these infectious invaders first occurs within the gastrointestinal tract. However, since the gut is proficient at absorbing toxins, metabolites, antigens, or anything else harmful within it, systemic effects are common. In general, debilitation often reflects the harmful activity of the infectious invaders present. Yet, this is usually a temporary condition because, as someone's condition escalates, only one obstacle prevents these harmful microorganisms from gaining further access to the body: the thickness and integrity of their gut wall. With the repeated insults and assaults that accompany each and every infection, this natural barrier gets irritated, inflamed, impaired, and even injured. Initially, the gut wall becomes only mildly irritated, with few problems. As insult leads to injury, it can become severely inflamed and leaky, creating leaky gut syndrome. Although numerous disease-causing troublemakers can contribute to this process, the most effective and efficient gut wall invaders are the disease-causing yeast.

A variety of circumstances encourage or promote the invasion of disease-causing yeast into and through the gut wall. First, there is a mass effect, and the more disease-causing yeast present, the greater their combined mischief. As the size of their population increases, their living space and resources become scarcer, so disease-causing yeast must spread to new areas to survive; in return, these locations are colonized and harvested for nutrition. Thereafter, lacking additional space or to obtain enough nutrients, they can invade into the gut wall. Once the gut is sufficiently colonized, the only place for them to go is into the gut wall, granting them further access to the tissues and blood. This effect can also be self-inflicted; when a candidiasis sufferer stops eating sugars or other carbohydrates, their disease-causing yeast will become hungry and may aggressively search for food, invading the gut wall and its tissues for nourishment. This explains why many sufferers initially feel better when they stop eating sugars and simple carbohydrates, because they are starving their disease-causing yeast. After some time, when their disease-causing yeast become more aggressive, they frequently feel worse than ever. Although it may temporarily lessen their symptoms, an anti-candidiasis diet without other therapeutic interventions (chapter 18) will almost never cure a candidiasis sufferer.

During invasion, some disease-causing yeast, notably *Candida albicans*, can transform into a more aggressive, invasive form called a *mycelium*, which consists of a main body with many projections (like a tree with roots). The tiny projections release enzymes that chemically digest holes through or between the cells lining the gut wall, aiding their invasion and advancement into the tissues, where they can consume the nutrients in these areas. *Candida albicans* is particularly invasive because it can produce four enzymes, including *hyaluronidase*, *chondroitin sulphatase*, *proteinase*, and *phospholipase*. Strains of *Candida*-species organisms lacking one or more of these enzymes are less invasive or even noninvasive. *Candida albicans* in the blood of human volunteers produces significantly more *phospholipase* than noninvasive strains. So, disease-causing yeast, especially *Candida albicans*, can invade into the tissues, progress further, and then enter and colonize the blood. Additional research reveals that transformation into a mycelium is *not* an absolute requirement for tissue invasion because the less aggressive, ovoid form has been found to invade into the gut wall; since this form is not suited for invasion, its presence within the gut wall is probably incidental, following the invasion of an aggressive form, or it could have reverted to its ovoid form after its nutritional needs were met.

The invasion of disease-causing yeast into the gut wall is frequently assisted by other infectious invaders, with aggressive troublemakers causing significant inflammation and injury to the gut wall. Whether it occurs quickly or slowly, this weakens the gut wall; since inflamed and injured cells cannot heal or reproduce normally, the number of cells within the gut wall decreases, impairing its effectiveness as a barrier to invasion. Simply put, the greater the number of infectious invaders, the more likely the disease-causing yeast can invade into the gut wall, creating leaky gut syndrome.

So, what exactly is leaky gut syndrome? Normally, the gut wall absorbs essential nutrients, while it prevents the entry of infectious invaders, dietary and bacterial proteins, numerous toxins, and an assortment of antigens (allergy-inducing substances). Leaky gut syndrome arises when the wall of the gastrointestinal tract becomes injured or damaged; like a leaky container, this allows inappropriate substances to enter the gut wall, while fluids, proteins, and other essential bodily substances can ooze out. Depending on the extent of invasion, it may occur in a localized area, in patches, or involve a substantial portion of the gut.

Typically, the gastrointestinal problems that accompany leaky gut syndrome reflect disturbances of the gut wall in the areas adversely affected. Since the gut functions in an assembly-line fashion, from breaking up food within the mouth, to its absorption in the small intestines, and then its elimination by the anus, a disturbance in one area often precipitates problems further along within the gut, regardless of whether leaky gut syndrome exists there or not. The larger the area impaired, the more it disturbs gastrointestinal functioning, which promotes more widespread problems. The other major factors contributing to leaky gut syndrome include impaired digestion, intestinal toxemia, a deficiency of one or more basic mucosal (gut wall) nutrients, and oxidative tissue injuries.

In addition to the colonization and activities of disease-causing yeast, damage from leaky gut syndrome involves the inflammation that accompanies the presence of inappropriate substances within the gut wall and tissues. Once the gut wall is compromised, the "holes" allow undigested food particles and other inappropriate substances within the gastrointestinal tract to pass through the gut wall and enter the tissues, irritating and inflaming these areas. Although some substances are inherently troublesome, causing overt damage, most inappropriate substances are less injurious, promoting inflammation and injury proportional to the amount that "leaks" into the tissues as well as the immune system's response to their presence. In addition, if the blood vessels within a "leaky" area are inflamed and weakened, the inappropriate substances may pass through and enter the blood, instigating more widespread problems.

As the gut wall becomes increasingly impaired, inappropriate substances enter the tissues and blood in greater amounts and do not disappear or leave by magic. Instead, it is the immune system's responsibility to eradicate inappropriate substances from these areas. A part of being the human body's police force involves eliminating unwanted trespassers, regardless of whether they are infectious invaders, undigested food particles, or anything else that is not supposed to be within the body. For this to occur, the immune system must recognize an inappropriate substance as foreign and then signal some of its cells to attack and eliminate it. Usually, when an inappropriate substance is present, the immune system may make it more identifiable by having some of its cells manufacture little tags (*antibodies*) that target the inappropriate substance and bind with it, speeding up its process of elimination (chapter 16). The production of antibodies requires an inappropriate substance to have one or more *antigens*, components recognized as foreign. This triggers the immune system to produce antibodies specifically targeted against them. When this occurs, the specific antibodies bind with their intended antigens, forming *antigen-antibody immune complexes* within the tissues and blood; their intended purpose is to signal other immune cells to quickly grab and eliminate these targeted, inappropriate substances. Unfortunately, the cleanup is rarely easy, and the result is often inflammation, injury, and even damage.

When everything works well, the inappropriate substances are eliminated, but usually at a cost to the body. Although the immune system has the best of intentions, the actual process of removing inappropriate substances from the tissues causes additional irritation and injury that aggravates the situation and fosters a vicious cycle. Misdirected or confused immunity may arise under these circumstances and instigate undesirable reactions against someone's own cells, tissues, or organs, creating autoimmune disease (chapter 14).

Although its problems range from insignificant to debilitating, most leaky gut syndrome sufferers do not experience doom and gloom. Typically, they develop allergies to one or more foods (as well as other substances within their gut). Normally, food is broken down until it is small enough to be absorbed; the resulting pieces must be a certain size, or they cannot cross the cell membranes of a healthy gut wall. As a food is digested, the antigens it contains are usually broken down and cause little to no allergic consequences. In contrast, when the gastrointestinal tract is "leaky," incompletely digested food particles can inappropriately pass through the gut wall, enter the tissues, and then the blood. The greater the damage to the gut wall, the larger the undigested particles that enter the tissues, increasing the opportunity for allergic consequences. The more extensive and pronounced the leaky gut syndrome, the greater the number and larger the size of allergy-inducing (antigenic) particles that are absorbed.

Under the best of circumstances, if a small undigested food particle enters the tissues, it will be attacked and quickly eliminated, especially when it lacks notable antigens or a food is rarely consumed. In contrast, if an undigested food particle has notable antigens, is frequently eaten, and eludes rapid elimination, it can promote allergic consequences, regardless of whether it enters the blood or not, even though it often does. This is how leaky gut syndrome promotes sensitivities and hypersensitivities (allergies) to a diversity of foods.

Although food allergies have only been recently understood, even the ancient Greeks knew that various foods could elicit a broad range of reactions; diarrhea is probably the most annoying among them. Since the early 1900s, food allergies have been recognized as an etiological component of inflammatory bowel disease, not to mention other gastrointestinal illnesses. Food allergies range from mild, self-limited episodes to severe reactions with an abundance of irritation and inflammation. The length of a reaction caused by an allergy-inducing food varies; some people have a brief encounter, while others suffer with symptoms for a week or two. Why does this variation exist? For food allergies to develop, the immune system must first recognize an undigested food particle as foreign. Once this occurs, two types of processes are thought to contribute to the development of food allergies: IgE-mediated immune reactions and non-IgE-mediated reactions.

Briefly, *IgE-mediated* reactions involve repeated exposures to food antigens that stimulate certain immune cells to produce IgE (immunoglobulin E) antibodies. If antibodies are produced to target a specific food, an antigen-antibody response will occur every time that offending food is eaten, promoting antigen-antibody complexes that trigger immediate inflammation and secondary reactions (directly and indirectly). This is a rapid way of identifying and eliminating the presence of a specific food particle. Although methods to establish IgE-mediated food allergies are common, these reactions represent less than 25 to 30 percent of all food allergies. Since IgE-mediated foods reactions are a smaller part of the food allergy picture, they appear to be the exception rather than the rule.

In contrast, most food allergies evolve by *non-IgE-mediated*, reactions. This process reflects the activity of certain immune cells that become sensitive or hypersensitive to the presence of specific food antigens. Certain immune cells directly recognize the invading food particles and then assault and eliminate them. This is a contact phenomenon that contributes to longer-lasting inflammation, and, although there are immediate effects, their indirect, secondary, and prolonged responses are often the most debilitating.

Regardless of whether one or both processes contribute, it results in food sensitivities and hypersensitivities. Moreover, allergic reactions do not only happen within the tissues and blood; they can also arise within the gut. In addition to the physical presence and mischief of the infectious invaders, food allergies also play a part in the production of a sufferer's symptoms. Because of its diversity, leaky gut syndrome involves numerous adverse consequences, variations, and manifestations.

When leaky gut syndrome is present, undigested food particles are the most common inappropriate substance to pass through the gut wall and enter the tissues, where they often induce allergies. If the inflammation and injury escalate, entire infectious invaders or their pieces and byproducts may traverse the gut wall. Even though the immune system tries to impede these assaults, with increasing damage and ingress into the tissues, one or more infectious invaders can gain access to the blood vessels and blood. At this point, symptoms that were previously localized within the gut (abdominal bloating, distention, flatulence, diarrhea or constipation, colicky pains, and so on) become more systemic; fatigue, joint and/or muscle aches and pains, skin rashes (hives, eczema, and psoriasis), allergies and multiple chemical sensitivities, neurological complications (depression, memory loss, poor concentration, and anxiety), and various other problems. So, leaky gut syndrome is far from a black-or-white condition. Instead, a spectrum of symptoms and illness manifests, with the disturbances reflecting the presence and contributions of the infectious invaders, whether simply disease-causing yeast or a consortium of harmful parasites, bacteria, molds, and/or viruses.

- **Gastrointestinal candidiasis:** Disease-causing yeast are within the lumen (center) or on the surface of the gut wall. It may or may not create leaky gut syndrome.
- **Invasive candidiasis:** Disease-causing yeast assault and enter the gut wall, creating leaky gut syndrome.
- **Systemic candidiasis:** Disease-causing yeast invade into the blood vessels within the gut wall, enter the blood, colonize the circulatory system, and may attack and infect other areas of the body.

The scientific evidence to support leaky gut syndrome is difficult to dismiss and its acceptance is increasing. Rather than having an obscure cause, it seems that candidiasis is involved. In fact, candidiasis, dysbiosis, and leaky gut syndrome are found to participate in most recurring and chronic gut problems, especially inflammatory bowel disease and irritable bowel syndrome.

INFLAMMATORY BOWEL DISEASE

Inflammatory bowel disease (IBD) is a chronic condition within the lower intestines, involving inflammation from *unknown* or *mysterious* origins. Mainstream medicine refers to any illness with an obscure cause as "idiopathic." Since every illness must have a cause, what is the origin of IBD?

IBD has two presentations: *Ulcerative colitis* involves inflammation and ulceration of the *superficial* gut wall, mucosa, and submucosa, anywhere from the proximal colon to the anus. In contrast, *Crohn's disease* traverses the *entire* gut wall, and its inflammation commonly occurs in the distal small intestine and colon, although it can develop in other areas as well.

A 2014 report by the Crohn's & Colitis Foundation of America stated that about 1.6 million Americans suffered with IBD (an increase of about 200,000 since 2011), with as many as 70,000 new cases diagnosed each year in the United States. Moreover, *microscopic colitis* is being found with increasing frequency, which implies that there may be many more mild sufferers who would add to the incidence of this illness.

IBD has numerous characteristics. It invariably involves disturbances (pathology) within the colon, but it can also cause disease within the small intestines. In addition to gut disturbances, systemic complications (extra-intestinal symptoms) may also occur. Some studies indicate that IBD may predispose someone to carcinoma (cancer) of the colon. Who develops it?

IBD appears to be genetically inherited because it tends to arise in members of the same family.

Numerous symptoms are common among IBD sufferers, including low-grade fevers, abdominal pain and tenderness, bouts of diarrhea (occasionally bloody, with cramping), loss of appetite and weight, and anal fissures (crack-like sores) that may lead to fistulas (abnormal anatomical passages from the anus to another area).

Because IBD involves inflammation and disturbances within the gut, sufferers regularly and repeatedly develop and demonstrate multiple nutritional deficiencies. There are many reasons, but four groups of contributing factors are the most significant, including decreased oral intake, malabsorption, increased requirements, and nutrient loss—excessive secretion.

Scientific evidence suggests abnormalities within the gastrointestinal microbiome and its population of beneficial bacteria are associated with the development of IBD. Sufferers frequently have increased amounts of harmful bacteria within their gut. They often experience fever and toxemia (blood poisoning by bacteria-produced toxins), implying their gut is absorbing harmful bacteria and/or their toxins and harmful metabolites; in fact, harmful bacteria are regularly identified within blood cultures taken from IBD patients. Certain antibiotics improve this condition, especially in sufferers with significant dysbacteriosis; after antibiotics destroy and eliminate their harmful bacteria, improvements often follow. IBD patients fed by intravenous routes experience some improvement; besides correcting nutritional deficiencies in these sufferers, it is thought a lack of food within their gut starves any infectious invaders residing there, making them less active and mischievous.

Researchers appreciate that undesirable changes in gut permeability usually precede a flare-up of Crohn's disease symptoms; so, an exacerbation of leaky gut syndrome is a prelude to IBD. Some investigators have noted a direct relationship between the presence and extent of leaky gut syndrome and the severity of Crohn's disease by measuring *lactulose* and *mannitol* intake in patients. Following an oral challenge with these two sugars, measuring the urinary excretion of lactulose and mannitol can determine intestinal permeability. Lactulose is poorly absorbed by a healthy gut, so it does not enter the blood and will not be eliminated within the urine. Yet, as someone's gut becomes more "leaky," their urine ratio of lactulose-to-mannitol will increase. Since the magnitude of Crohn's disease is proportional to the lactulose-to-mannitol ratio, the symptoms of Crohn's disease directly reflect the severity of gut wall impairment and its increased permeability. Simply put, there is an *IBD–leaky gut syndrome connection*. Since leaky gut syndrome involves the invasion of disease-causing yeast into and through the gut wall, candidiasis appears to be the real cause of IBD, with or without other infectious invaders, including harmful parasites, bacteria, molds, and/or viruses. Yet, evidence for a mixed infection does exist and is increasing.

However, being candidiasis-minded does not always guarantee success. One study involved a group of patients who did not respond to a food-allergy elimination diet and small doses of nystatin; a nonabsorbable antifungal agent that only kills disease-causing yeast within the gut. Since it did not work, does it mean disease-causing yeast were not causing illness? On the contrary, when systemic antifungal medication was administered, dramatic clinical improvement occurred; in return, this group of IBD sufferers eliminated their candidiasis and food allergies. So, in addition to recognizing the *candidiasis-IBD connection*, it is also vital to understand how the disease process works. Specifics aside, the study illustrated the ability of disease-causing yeast to invade into and through the gut wall, and then enter the tissues and blood. Therefore, the use of systemic antifungal agents is essential, and more than one course of therapy may be required.

Fortunately, some mainstream physicians are waking up about IBD and the best way to treat its sufferers. It involves the appropriate, individualized treatment of their candidiasis and dysbiosis, including the multitude of infectious invaders that participate in their disease process. Therefore, anyone who suffers with or treats IBD should become aware of the *candidiasis-IBD connection*.

IRRITABLE BOWEL SYNDROME

Irritable bowel syndrome (IBS) might seem to be a less-aggressive variant of IBD, but it is *not* a disease. In fact, it is a more complicated and confusing bowel problem than IBD. Although it does not have definitive characteristics like IBD, it is a significant medical problem. Its prevalence ranges from 9 to 23 percent worldwide, with an incidence rate of about 18 percent. When this paragraph was written in January 2023 there were about 8 billion human beings on Earth, with roughly 1.44 billion people suffering with some magnitude of IBS. Dissecting the IBS piece of the candidiasis puzzle is not easy because many pieces must be mentioned.

For the record, *irritable bowel syndrome* is an improper name for this medical malady; after all, "irritable" refers to an emotionally fragile person who is cranky or to a child who is hyperactive. "Irritable" is an inappropriate term for a functional disorder because it implies there is an underlying psychological basis to this condition, rather than the existence of an anatomical and physiological problem causing psychological distress. Admittedly, a mind-body connection exists and, yes, stress and emotions do instigate and promote illness. Numerous publications accept there is a *mind-body/stress-IBS connection.*

Other publications profess a dietary connection. Mainstream medicine has advanced various dietary approaches to IBS. The FODMAP diet has been recommended, involving dietary restrictions of short-chain fermentable carbohydrates, especially the low fermentable oligosaccharides, disaccharides, monosaccharides, and polyols. Research demonstrates the low FODMAP diet leads to clinical response in 50-80% of IBS patients with improvements in bloating, flatulence, diarrhea, and global symptoms. If they knew the sugars that were eliminated nourished disease-causing yeast, they would know why the diet is effective.

More simply, the gastrointestinal microbiome, its flora, determines its state of health, from wellness to illness. Multiple studies consistently show that subjects diagnosed with IBS have a disrupted gut microbiome. (Note: If you think that taking probiotics and synbiotics [a mixture of probiotics and prebiotics] is the simple cure, think again; the differences in their composition and concentrations varies widely across studies and has prevented strong recommendations on their use in IBS.)

Most important, as a designation, IBS ignores its association with candidiasis, the presence and contributions of other infectious invaders, allergic sensitivities/hypersensitivities, and the visceral reactions within the gut wall and its musculature. In medical school, students are told a basic tenet: *If it looks like a horse and runs like a horse, unless it has black-and-white stripes, do not classify it as a zebra.* So, the cause of IBS might be more understandable than mainstream medicine realizes.

IBS is the diagnosis gastroenterologists give to roughly 50 percent of their patients. It is defined as a functional disorder of the lower gastrointestinal tract with an *absence* of structural defects or demonstrable organic participants. Simply put, the lower gut functions abnormally, and without anatomical problems or other causes, mainstream medicine is unsure why. Although its primary features are abdominal discomfort and altered bowel habits, there are a diversity of presentations, with symptoms ranging from mild to severe, and acute to chronic. In general, the common symptoms include diarrhea, constipation, or both, including abdominal pain, excessive mucus production in the colon, flatulence and/or belching, nausea, loss of appetite, and occasional anxiety and/or depression.

Mainstream medicine separates IBS features and symptoms into three clinical types: the *diarrhea-predominant* form, the *constipation-predominant* form, and the *pain-gas-bloating* form. Although all three forms of IBS have different names and symptoms, they are closely related. If all the presentations are really variations of the same syndrome, how can the spectrum of IBS range from diarrhea to constipation? Candidiasis that is *noninvasive* and self-limited, without other infectious invaders, tends toward constipation. In contrast, *invasive* candidiasis creates leaky gut syndrome, promoting food allergies and inflammation, which upsets the gut's functioning, causing diarrhea. Moreover, the presence of harmful bacteria, parasites, molds, and/or viruses often induces diarrhea, although pain, gas, and bloating are common. So, the type of IBS regularly reflects the gut's collection of infectious invaders and their accompanying mischief. In some cases, one infectious invader's mischief cancels the effects of another. As an example, there are candidiasis sufferers who have relatively normal gut functioning. Why? Their disease-causing yeast encourage constipation, while other infectious invaders tend to loosen their stool; their effects cancel each other and there is a relatively normal bowel movement, usually with an abundance of bloating and gas, and possibly mucus. Therefore, the *candidiasis-IBS connection* is often confused and missed. In fact, with bowels that are seemingly normal, candidiasis is consistently overlooked.

IBS is less debilitating than IBD, and the big difference between the two conditions is IBS involves less insult and invasion of the gut wall; the problem is often confined within the gut interior. Why is it limited? In most cases, a strong immune system is probably a person's best defense against the invasion of their disease-causing yeast, keeping them from advancing to IBD.

Disease-causing yeast are regularly involved with gut disturbances. Many reports describe the association between disease-causing *Candida*-species organisms and gut illnesses. Furthermore, mainstream medical research reveals that numerous infectious invaders contribute to IBS. Some researchers admit that IBS is related to an allergy within the gut. Food allergies and intolerances are considered, but allergies to disease-causing yeasts and molds are often ignored. To add confusion, since everyone is unique, every candidiasis sufferer has their own sensitivities and hypersensitivities to allergy-inducing substances and toxic substances, including heavy metals.

In addition to the infectious and allergic contributions to IBS, there is an essential piece of the IBS puzzle, which is often overlooked and ignored by mainstream physicians. It affects IBD sufferers and other people with chronic and intermittent gastrointestinal problems and also contributes to all medical maladies. In short, every evolved, physical form has its *anatomy*, including its cells, tissues, and organs. Its functioning is called its *physiology*. Cells that function normally and optimally keep us healthy. Cells that function abnormally cause problems, ranging from overactive (*hyperactive*) to underactive (*hypoactive*). This can occur for a myriad of reasons, but this discussion pertains to the electrical charges of cells. Basically, the inside and outside of cells have different electrical charges. Although this involves tiny charges, when many cells have an internal charge that is increased or decreased, abnormal cellular functioning occurs. This can result in hyperactivity, hypoactivity, variable, or irregular symptoms. Why does it happen? Infections and allergies can create immune system reactions, including endocrine (hormone) and nervous system problems, that disturb the cells of the body and their ability to effectively maintain their normal internal charge. Trauma, surgical or nonsurgical (acute, chronic, or repetitive insults), can create areas of tissue strain, injury, damage, and scarring that disturbs the cells in those and adjacent locations. In addition to abnormal cellular functioning, traumatized areas have restricted/abnormal movement and decreased/abnormal circulation, worsening the situation. Food insensitivities and nutrient deficiencies often participate, as well as the strong contributions of stress. Medical research supports the connection between visceral (intestinal) hypersensitivity and IBS.

To add further insult, *Candida*-species organisms can form *biofilms*—a thin, resistant layer of microorganisms that forms on and coats surfaces. As their numbers increase, the density of cells within their biofilm(s) escalates, creating more adverse effects as well as antifungal resistance. This is part of the reason some candidiasis sufferers are difficult to treat; they often require prolonged or repeated courses of antifungal therapy, rotating different types of antifungal medications and other substances as the layers of their *Candida*-species biofilm(s) are cleared. In addition, *Candida*-species biofilms can provide a protective habitat for other infectious invaders, including harmful molds, parasites, bacteria, and viruses.

In summary, IBS has components of IBD, but it is not a disease. Its variability has numerous contributors, including acute and chronic infections, allergies, food intolerances and sensitivities, nutritional deficiencies, and more. Often, there are anatomical and physiological disturbances that agitate, aggravate, and exacerbate the situation. An understanding of all the puzzle pieces is essential to improving and even curing the symptoms of IBS sufferers.

OTHER GASTROINTESTINAL PROBLEMS

If you search PubMed.gov, there are more than 1,000 articles about *Candida* esophagitis, so a *candidiasis-GERD connection* is highly likely. In addition to the infection on the surface of the esophagus, some physicians think persistent GERD is a food allergy, which is consistent with the allergic mischief of disease-causing yeast.

The evidence to support a *candidiasis–gastric ulcer connection* is undeniable. It usually includes the participation of other infectious invaders, including *Helicobacter pylori* (a bacteria) and *Giardia duodenalis* (a protozoa parasite, chapter 5). Other contributors can include *Campylobacter*-like bacteria and one or more viruses. Clearly, gut maladies are a mix of infectious invaders, working together to ensure their survival at the expense of ours.

Malabsorption occurs when one or more substances is not appropriately absorbed. The symptoms are often related to the areas of the gut affected. Regardless of its location, impaired digestion prevents the complete breakdown of food and effective absorption of all its nutrients, which impedes the assimilation of fats, proteins, carbohydrates, vitamins, minerals, water, and electrolytes. Although candidiasis is not responsible for every case, given its diversity of gut disturbances, a *candidiasis-malabsorption connection* must be considered in anyone who manifests some amount of malabsorption and their accompanying nutritional deficiencies.

Lactose intolerance is an inability to appropriately digest lactose-containing foods. Although some people are born with this problem, if you were well and developed a lactase deficiency, you should be suspicious of a disturbance within your gut. However, disease-causing yeast do not usually create this havoc alone because one or more parasites can initiate or participate in this process; since the jejunum is the prime location for *Giardia duodenalis*, it is suspected of participating in the development of non-inherited lactose intolerance. In addition, one or more harmful bacteria, as well as harmful molds, may also contribute their ill effects.

Celiac disease primarily affects the small intestine. It is considered a chronic autoimmune disorder that is related to gluten intolerance. There seems to be a genetic tendency to develop it, which can occur at any age.

It affects 1.4 percent of people worldwide, with a greater prevalence in certain regions. After ingesting foods that contain wheat, rye, or barley (and certain varieties of oats), there is an inflammatory reaction within the small bowel that can shorten the gut wall villi, leading to villous atrophy, promoting malabsorption and often anemia. The disease process involves several different autoantibodies that can harm various organs. Classic symptoms include diarrhea, abdominal bloating, malabsorption, and appetite loss. Its presence in children can promote developmental problems. Confusingly, there may be none, mild, or a diversity of symptoms that affect various parts of the body. Mainstream medicine believes its only effective treatment is the strict avoidance of gluten and foods it contains. However, in 2023, A.A.H.S. Al-Janabi et al. stated, "A variety of Candida spp. can be found as a natural commensal fungus in various parts of the human body. This fungus may be associated with various diseases such as celiac disease (CD). Gliadin, component of the gluten protein complex that is mostly found in wheat, is the main inducer of CD. A number of studies have demonstrated that patients infected with Candida can develop CD, and vice versa. C. albicans is presumed to induce CD because it has a protein homologous to gliadin in its cell wall called Hwp1." Although more research needs to be done, in addition to leaky gut and food allergies, it seems Candida albicans can directly trigger the production of antibodies and autoantibodies (chapter 14) against its gliadin-like, cell wall protein in people who are genetically susceptible. Other disease-causing yeast may also have this cell wall protein and contribute to the process. So, if you suffer with celiac disease, anti-candidiasis therapy might not be a cure, but it could greatly improve your symptoms and decrease your reactivity to ingested gluten.

Halitosis often results from dysbiosis and candidiasis within the esophagus and stomach; these areas are colonized with disease-causing yeast as well as other harmful microorganisms. Disease-causing yeast can convert (metabolize) dietary carbohydrates into *ethanol* (a form of alcohol). In addition, these tiny living factories also metabolize numerous foods. As a result, all sorts of inappropriate chemical reactions occur, producing undesirable solid, liquid, and gaseous byproducts. In the process, many volatile gases are exhaled, and a noxious odor (bad breath) occurs. Fortunately, this problem quickly resolves with appropriate anti-candidiasis treatment.

Chronic candidiasis is likely to be associated with the increasing prevalence of *nonalcoholic fatty liver disease* (NAFLD), aka *metabolic (dysfunction) associated fatty liver disease* (MAFLD), which is the excessive accumulation of fat within the liver without a definitive cause like alcohol consumption, viral hepatitis, or the use of some liver-damaging medication. Two types of NAFLD are known: 1) *nonalcoholic fatty liver* (NAFL), and 2) *nonalcoholic steatohepatitis* (NASH), which involves inflammation and can progress to liver cirrhosis. With more people experiencing gastrointestinal candidiasis and the incidence of systemic candidiasis increasing, disease-causing *Candida*-species organisms have been found to colonize and infect the liver. It has been thought that it only occurs in immunocompromised people and those with significant liver disease or viral infections. Yet, it is likely many candidiasis sufferers experience some magnitude of liver colonization because the liver has an extensive blood supply and participates in filtering out (destroying) bacteria and dead blood cells within the blood. Regardless of their location, *Candida*-species organisms can produce numerous toxic substances that can inflame and injure liver cells. In return, as disease-causing yeast travel within the blood and pass through the liver, they may become trapped, and, if they adapt and survive, they can colonize and cause harm in one or more areas of the liver.

Some physicians think bacterial infections of the gallbladder may trigger *gallstones* because the DNA of bacteria has been found in extracted gallstones and biliary sludge. Yet, it seems unlikely that harmful bacteria take up residence within the gallbladder unless its environment is compromised, and this certainly includes the presence and mischief of disease-causing yeast. Coinfections with disease-causing yeast and other infectious invaders are the rule rather than the exception. In addition, elevated blood cholesterol levels are thought to contribute (chapter 7).

More concerning problems occur when disease-causing yeast colonize and compromise the pancreas, the organ located behind the stomach. Since it has a rich blood supply, its blood vessels are susceptible to insults and injury by disease-causing yeast toxins. In addition, disease-causing yeast traveling within the blood can get trapped and take up residence in areas with poor perfusion (decreased blood flow). Any insults or injury within the pancreas will have significant consequences. Inflammation of the pancreas is called *pancreatitis* and common causes include gallstones and the chronic ingestion of alcohol. Chronic *pancreatitis* has been associated with pancreatic cancer. The medical literature reveals acute pancreatitis can progress to pancreatic *necrosis* (cell death), and even though bacterial infections are thought to cause most cases, it should be clear this is unlikely to occur without the participation of disease-causing yeast.

CLEANING UP YOUR GUT

The gastrointestinal tract is the primary location for the mischief and harm of disease-causing yeast and other infectious invaders. If the information to support their adverse contributions was simple to interpret and understand, the *candidiasis-gastrointestinal connection* would be commonly accepted and more frequently treated.

Normally, disease-causing *Candida*-species organisms are present in small numbers within the gastrointestinal tract. When all is well, a healthy population of beneficial bacteria suppresses and inhibits these opportunistic infectious invaders, preventing them from causing harm. Yet, certain undesirable circumstances can injure or kill the beneficial bacteria (chapter 2), allowing the disease-causing yeast to colonize their surroundings, alone or by cooperating with other infectious invaders, including harmful parasites, bacteria, molds, and/or viruses. Undeniably, the situation becomes worse when disease-causing yeast invade into the gut wall, creating leaky gut syndrome with its increased gut wall permeability. To add insult, disease-causing yeast can progress further, entering the tissues and blood vessels, and travel throughout the body. Regardless of their location, as their population increases, disease-causing yeast directly and indirectly initiate and promote a variety of undesirable reactions, symptoms, and illness. Since their primary residence is within the gut, gastrointestinal disturbances are common.

Generally, most cases (if not all) of inflammatory bowel disease and irritable bowel syndrome are associated with candidiasis. Other problems, like malabsorption and gut ulcers, are also closely connected. Even worse, since disease-causing yeast instigate and promote most of their mischief within the gut, gastrointestinal cancers often result from the presence of candidiasis; disturbed gut functioning damages the gut cells, and the impaired immunity associated with chronic candidiasis (chapter 14) allows abnormal cells to transform into cancerous cells.

So, if you have a chronic or recurring gut malady, you are likely to be a candidiasis sufferer. To reclaim your health, you must eradicate the disease-causing yeast within your gastrointestinal tract, gut wall and tissues, and your blood. It is also essential to identify and eliminate other infectious invaders, including harmful parasites, bacteria, and molds. Since all of them can easily contribute to your gut symptoms and illness, any untreated troublemakers that remain will upset your gastrointestinal microbiome, promoting relapses. To decrease inflammation within your gut, you should avoid allergy-inducing foods as well as foods and beverages containing disease-causing yeasts and harmful molds. Since the beneficial bacteria are critical to the health of your gut, they must also be restored.

With a thorough anti-candidiasis program (chapter 18), most candidiasis sufferers can eliminate their disease-causing yeast and other infectious invaders, reestablishing the health and functioning of their gut. Inflammatory bowel disease, irritable bowel syndrome, ulcers, lactose intolerance, malabsorption, and halitosis can be corrected. More amazing, precancerous gut polyps have disappeared in some candidiasis sufferers. With the incidence of nonalcoholic fatty liver disease increasing, people who suffer with this condition are likely to be candidiasis sufferers. Therefore, an appreciation and understanding of the *candidiasis-gastrointestinal connection* will eventually enable most gastrointestinal disturbances to be treated and eliminated.

CHAPTER 5

The Candidiasis-Parasite Connection

When you hear the word *parasite,* do you think of the alien invaders that appear in so many movies? If so, think again because, unlike those sci-fi villains, the parasites that infect us do not have grand plans to conquer the Earth and enslave all its people.

Another misconception is that parasites are trying to possess your body and mind, instigating illness in the process. This gives them far too much credit. Most parasites have no brain or heart. Even the most complex parasites have rudimentary nervous systems. Since they cannot experience emotions like love or hate, parasites cannot have malicious motives. On the contrary, they have the simplest agenda, which is to survive, so they behave in ways that ensures their survival and well-being.

Although they feed off living beings, most parasites are not hunters and do not seek their prey. Instead, most of them eke out their daily existence, biding their time until they find a more suitable home, usually within a warm-blooded animal or human being. Parasites are unknowingly encountered by chance, although some behaviors greatly increase the odds of being infected—for example, drinking contaminated water, consuming unwashed produce, or eating undercooked meat. Parasites have no preference for who they infect, human being or animal. Like disease-causing yeast, they are unbiased, equal-opportunity infectious invaders.

People living in poor countries, where sewage exposure and poor hygiene are common, are frequently infected with parasites, ranging from relatively innocuous, microscopic inhabitants to incredibly large tapeworms and other harmful infectious invaders. If you travel to those locations, you can easily become infected with one or more parasite and, in addition to returning with pictures of your trip, you will arrive home with those infectious invaders as souvenirs. More alarming, after getting past customs, these ingested illegal immigrants can spread their infection to others.

Parasites were only thought to be prevalent in poor countries, but not anymore. Estimates indicate that roughly one in six Americans harbors one or more of these infectious invaders. Although numerous studies corroborate these numbers, anoscopy (chapter 17) detection demonstrates that mainstream estimates are low, because rectal swab samples reveal that parasites exist within 50 to 90 percent of the patients tested.

Most parasites that infect us remain undetected. They make us feel sick and cause illness. Yet, most people, including physicians, are unaware of their presence. Although they exist in a variety of shapes and sizes, most of the parasites infecting people in the United States are too small to be seen without a microscope, making their detection an active effort.

More disturbing, the number of people infected with parasites increases every day. As a result, parasites covertly cause or contribute to significant infectious disease. This situation is worsening because numerous activities carry a high risk of transmitting them from one person to another. Sadly, for all the illness and debilitation they instigate and cause, most parasites remain undetected or are overlooked by mainstream health providers.

Since the immune system is often able to control the parasite's initial infection, most people who harbor them become chronic carriers with minimal to no symptoms and are totally unaware of their plight. Therefore, someone can have parasites without the symptoms to prove it.

Numerous parasites evade the immune responses of their human host, and by escaping its assault, they are not eliminated and perpetually infect their host. For example, some parasites can mutate their cell surface antigens so they are not easily recognized by the human immune system, whereas other parasites can alter their susceptibility to certain drugs. These reasons, and others, illustrate why parasites are often overlooked. In the big picture, because of their covert behaviors and activities, parasites are rarely considered when illness is diagnosed. Even when they are suspected, they are not usually found because mainstream medicine's methods to identify them are less than reliable. As a result, most people with infections are missed, which explains why attempts to avoid the spread of parasites have been unsuccessful. How can you prevent the spread of an infectious organism when you cannot accurately determine who is infected? If most parasitic infections are missed, how can eradication be possible?

By definition, a *parasite* is an organism that lives on or within another living being. Parasites obtain their nourishment, and often benefit, at the expense of their host. Compared to disease-causing yeast, which are normal citizens of the gastrointestinal tract (in small numbers), parasites are true trespassers, and their presence is not to be taken lightly.

Parasitogenesis is the relationship established between a parasite and its host. Once this occurs, *parasitocenose* is the environmental (ecological) system formed between them. Depending on the parasite (and other circumstances), some people develop and manifest drastic disturbances, while others have mild symptoms or none.

Because of their harmful nature, parasites have attracted an abundance of medical attention. Physicians and scientists investigate and identify parasites, although the percentage they detect is small compared to the population of people infected. Some parasites are considered blatantly harmful, and, when found, efforts are made to rapidly eradicate them. In contrast, many induce illness more casually, and mainstream medicine makes no recommendations about them. This laidback approach does not help people suffering with symptoms related to an infection with these less-aggressive, infectious invaders.

The question used to be *"Guess who's coming to dinner?"* Now it is "Who prepared the dinner," and "Where and how was it prepared?" Depending on the circumstances, almost anything that touches or enters your mouth can be contaminated with parasites, conferring these infectious invaders. Yes, the most obvious means of transmission is by ingesting contaminated food and water because that directly transfers the parasites into your body. Yet, there are also a variety of other prominent routes for transmitting parasites.

The purpose of this chapter is to make an essential point: Parasites are major illness-causing allies in a large percentage of candidiasis sufferers. Using anoscopy, candidiasis experts find parasites infecting 50 to 90 percent of their patients. Abundant evidence indicates that parasites and disease-causing yeast form a close alliance, and their combined effects can drastically harm their human host; their combined, undesirable efforts are greater than their individual harmful behaviors added together. So, if a candidiasis sufferer desires to fully regain their health and prevent a relapse, in addition to their disease-causing yeast, their parasites must be found and treated.

The presence of parasites helps explain why a variety of symptoms and illness arises among candidiasis sufferers; typically, the manifestations of candidiasis reflect the combined mischief of the disease-causing yeast and one or more parasites (as well as any harmful bacteria, molds, and viruses). A sufferer's inherited bodily strengths and weaknesses (their genetic tendencies) also play an important role in the disease process because their genetics determine their proclivity to develop specific symptoms and illness, which includes their ability to resist or succumb to these disturbances.

Parasites belong to the animal kingdom (unlike fungi, bacteria, or viruses) and are classified into two groups: protozoa and helminths (worms).

PROTOZOA

In general, protozoa are unicellular organisms, measuring 1 to 10 millimeters in size, making them much larger than bacteria and viruses. Typically, since they readily multiply after entering their host, only a small amount is required to instigate illness or disease.

Because most protozoa are often overlooked or are undetected, their infections manifest as a chronic condition or illness. The effects of their infestations range from mild symptoms, like fever, chills, and so on to life-threatening conditions that can involve inflammation of the brain (encephalitis). Optimally, a healthy immune system should destroy any trespassing parasites, eliminating their infection. Yet, this does not happen nearly as often as we would like. On the contrary, gastrointestinal tract infections with protozoa evoke a diversity of immune system responses, and immunity to protozoa varies from one extreme to the other.

Major protozoan diseases

Malaria, African trypanosomiasis (Gambian sleeping sickness and Rhodesian sleeping sickness), Chagas disease (South American trypanosomiasis), leishmaniasis (visceral, cutaneous, and mucocutaneous), toxoplasmosis, babesiosis (piroplasmosis), amoebiasis, *giardiasis, trichomoniasis,* balantidiasis, coccidiosis, and sarcosporidiosis. (*Pneumocystis carinii* was previously classified as a protozoon, but it is now considered a fungus.)

HELMINTHS

Helminth worms are multicellular organisms with well-developed organ systems. The worm's range in size from 1 centimeter to 10 meters in length. Although they do not reproduce within their host, their population increases with repeated exposures. The severity of their infection is proportional to their quantity; the presence of a few may only create minor problems, while an abundance of certain helminths can induce severe to deadly illness. (There are three categories of worms: tapeworms, flatworms/flukes, and roundworms.)

Major helminthic diseases

- **Cestodes (tapeworms):** *Diphyllobothrium latum* (broad or fish tapeworm), *Dipylidium caninum* (dog tapeworm), *Echinococcus granulosus* (hydatid tapeworm), *Hymenolepis nana* (dwarf, mouse, or rat tapeworm), *Taenia saginata* (unarmed or beef tapeworm), and *Taenia solium* (armed or pork tapeworm).
- **Trematodes (flatworms, or flukes):** blood flukes (*Schistosoma haematobium, Schistosoma mansoni, Schistosoma japonicum*), intestinal flukes (*Gastrodiscoides hominis, Fasciolopsis buski, Heterophyes heterophyes, Metagonimus yokogawai*), liver flukes (*Clonorchis sinensis, Fasciola hepatica, Dicrocoelium dendriticum, Opisthorchis felineus*), and lung flukes (*Paragonimus westermani*).
- **Nematodes (roundworms):** *strongyloidiasis, capillariasis, hookworm disease, cutaneous larva migrans, trichostrongylus, gnathostomiasis, primate nematodiases, ascariasis, toxocariasis, anisakiasis, trichuriasis, enterobiasis* (pinworms), *trichinellosis* (trichinosis), *angiostrongyliasis, filariasis* (dracunculiasis, lymphatic filariasis, tropical eosinophilia, loiasis, *Mansonella ozzardi* infection, perstans filariasis, dirofilariasis, onchocerciasis).

The immune response to helminths is variable, ranging from mild to severe to fatal. Disturbingly, the most prominent human tapeworms (*Diphyllobothrium latum, Taenia solium,* and *Taenia saginata*) do not evoke a response, which means the immune system does not respond to or react against them; it is a reason why they can infect our bodies for years without being detected. (Since helminth infestations are uncommon in the United States and other Westernized countries, this chapter focuses on protozoa. However, this does not mean you or your doctor should ignore infections with helminth worms.)

Yes, parasites reside among us and in great numbers. Even the most meticulously clean and healthy people can become unknowingly infected. If you are well, you may or may not have a parasite. In contrast, if you have any chronic or recurring medical malady, there is an excellent chance you are infected with one or more parasites. Unless you have notable gut symptoms, like persistent diarrhea, your parasites may not even be suspected or detected. So, what can you do? Keep reading and learn more.

COMMON ROUTES OF TRANSMISSION

Most parasites escape the recognition and responses of their host's immune system, so their infections are often chronic. There are many methods of eluding and evading the immune system; these include *intracellular life cycles* (parasites hiding within cells are difficult to assault), *antigenic phenotype switching* (parasites alter their surface receptors to confuse the immune system), and *acquired drug resistance* (medications that kill them become ineffective). Moreover, these attributes make the creation of effective antiparasitic vaccines virtually impossible. Combine the inability to produce vaccines with the ability of most parasites to avoid the immune system's assault, adding in the fact that most parasites are overlooked or are undetected, and you will realize parasites can instigate or cause illness for a long time. The amount of people infected with parasites will only increase unless something is done to halt their invasion.

Sadly, to expect mainstream medicine to take this seriously is wishful thinking. Since they do not have reliable methods to detect parasites and identify far too few of them, mainstream physicians do not realize the magnitude and scope of the parasite problem. With so many people harboring one or more parasites, ignoring their presence is a major oversight. The blame results from ignorance; if you do not know what to look for, or suspect the presence of parasites, you will not find them, especially if your methods for detection are unreliable. As the amount of time spent with a doctor decreases, it is unsurprising most physicians miss or overlook the presence of parasites. In contrast, considering their presence requires an inquisitive healthcare professional who obtains a thorough medical history. How long did you spend with your physician during your last visit? Like most patients, it was probably about five to six minutes, including your physical exam, your doctor's advice, and maybe getting a prescription or two. Since parasites are an uncommon conversation topic, the odds of discussing them in this brief interlude are virtually nil.

What can be done about the widespread prevalence of parasites? A great deal, but care, persistence, and patience are needed if their collective presence is to be reduced among our population. What will it take to stop their spread? Awareness, but not on the part of the doctors because they do not acknowledge that this problem exists. Every person who reads this book must become aware of parasites. Does it mean you are required to precisely diagnose which parasites are infecting you? No, in the bigger picture, it is more valuable to understand how they contribute to your ill health. Rather than becoming an expert, you should determine if parasites are likely to be present within you, or even a possibility. If you are a good detective, you will be able to inform your physician about your discovery. How can you uncover if you have a parasite? Like any detective, start by looking for clues. Consider the most common ways parasites are transmitted and how they can get to you. Since these harmful infectious invaders travel by various routes to invade their host, several questions can help reveal their presence.

Questions for Parasite Sufferers and Their Sexual Partners:

- Do you travel frequently?
- Do you drink, swim, or bathe in any type of untested water, indoors or outdoors?
- Do you frequently eat out?
- Do you enjoy eating raw fruits and vegetables, and do you clean them thoroughly?
- Do you like eating raw or undercooked fish, meat, or poultry?
- Do you have pets in your household, or are you exposed to animals or rodents?
- Do you work in a hospital, day-care center, sanitation center, or a garden?

If you answered "yes" to any question, there is a good chance you are infected with one or more parasite, and a thorough investigation should be undertaken. If you think you are off the hook because all your answers were definitive "no's," do not dismiss the possibility you may harbor one or more of these infectious invaders because they may have infected you by other means. Remember: *The vast majority of people infected with parasites are totally unaware of their presence.* Furthermore, determining their presence or absence by symptoms alone is often unreliable because there is no one absolute rule.

Gastrointestinal parasites existed long before human beings walked on this planet. Yet, medical science has only accepted these infectious invaders in the last 200 years. For all the illness it has caused, amoebic dysentery (a gut infection with an amoeba) was only first recognized at the beginning of the twentieth century. Over the last 60 years, parasitic infections have increased, especially infestations with protozoa—most notably, amoebiasis and giardiasis. Some reasons for this increase include the conditions during the World Wars, locations with poor sanitation, and increased immigration, emigration, and tourism. In addition, dining out has become a popular pastime, and there is an upward trend toward unconventional sexual practices that involve a high risk of transmitting parasites from one person to another.

Louis Parrish, M.D., was a parasitologist (parasite expert) in New York City. In 1990, he published *The Protozoal Syndrome*. Virtually every homosexual or bisexual AIDS patient in his practice was infected with at least one parasite. At that time, because of his findings, he estimated roughly 25 percent of the New York City metropolitan population was infected with parasites; the number of infected people was in the millions. Why did New York City become an epidemic location for parasite infestations? This is only supposed to occur in unsanitary conditions, tropical areas, and poor countries, is it not? Well, if that is what you think, wake up and count the parasites. Contrary to popular thought, developed countries are just as likely to have a high incidence of parasites; especially, *Giardia duodenalis* and *Entamoeba histolytica*. Officially, this problem is not completely recognized, believed, or admitted, but it exists, nonetheless. How could this have happened?

Unwashed hands that remain soiled with fecal material may readily spread parasites from an infected person to other people. Ingesting raw seafood contaminated with parasites may present a source of transfer, in addition to eating unpeeled or unwashed fruits and vegetables. For example, one study found that eight different vegetables from Costa Rica were contaminated with cysts (eggs) of numerous parasites, including *Endolimax nana, Entamoeba coli, Entamoeba histolytica, Giardia intestinalis,* and *Cryptosporidium-species* organisms.

Dr. Parrish conducted an informal study at a health convention in a large New York City hotel. The men's room attendant was asked to count the number of men who washed their hands over a two-hour period. Only 60 of 112 lavatory users washed their hands, a mediocre 54 percent. Equally poor hygiene has been observed in women's restrooms. This may be one reason why parasitic infections are reaching *epidemic* proportions. Regardless of the type of restroom visit, contact with fecal material knowingly or unknowingly is one of the most prominent ways to obtain parasites from another person, and a lack or deficiency of handwashing is a primary way to spread parasites from one person to another.

Animals can harbor parasites and transmit them to human beings. Cats, dogs, birds, and rodents can carry a variety of parasites, which can be passed to humans by direct contact with or exposure to their fecal matter. Pets that roam outdoors are not immune to these infectious invaders and often become infected. In addition, certain protozoa are directly transferred to human beings by insect exposure and their bites.

Taking a vacation to an exotic location can be a fun, relaxing, and rewarding experience, unless it includes a parasitic infection. Many countries are well-known habitats for these infectious invaders. Yes, traveling does put you at a high risk for acquiring parasites, especially visits to poor countries or unindustrialized areas, but you can still easily get infected at home.

All too frequently, parasites are sexually transmitted. Anal manipulation, oral-anal contact, anal sex, and other unconventional sexual practices are avenues for spreading fecal matter, including any parasites within it. If a woman is infected with parasites and they spread to her vagina, oral sex can pass her infection to her sexual partner. Intercourse does not readily spread parasites, but it is not completely risk-free. Sharing rectal cleaning devices, inappropriate colon irrigation, coprophagia, and inserting items into the rectum for stimulation are all risk factors for the transmission of parasites.

While there is a high prevalence of parasite infestations among homosexual people, it encompasses fewer than 30 percent of the people infected with protozoa, so it is naive to think that parasites are exclusive to them. To obtain a proper diagnosis, someone's sexual activities must be questioned, regardless of their stated preferences. Sex is not necessarily the most frequent means of transmitting parasites, but it is a prominent route of spread in many people.

WITH OR WITHOUT PARASITES: CANDIDIASIS SYMPTOMS

Candidiasis can develop without the assistance of other infectious invaders (chapters 3 and 4). If the risk factors for candidiasis (chapter 2) disturb the beneficial bacteria, the proliferation and colonization of disease-causing yeast within the gastrointestinal tract will easily occur. However, the more infectious invaders that participate in disrupting and impairing someone's gut, the more quickly they will succumb to candidiasis.

Candidiasis sufferers do not develop the condition simply by having disease-causing yeast within their gut, because it takes more than their physical presence to produce problems. When someone does not have enough risk factors or has taken the necessary steps to compensate for their exposures, it is unlikely their disease-causing yeast will colonize their gut and instigate problems. This does not mean these people are immune to candidiasis. On the contrary, they only need to be exposed to more or stronger candidiasis risk factors; in fact, a few risk factors are so potent they can promote candidiasis in almost everyone given enough time.

Since most parasite infestations remain undetected or are overlooked, most parasites can constantly infect and disturb their host's gut. Depending on their aggressiveness, a parasite will sooner or later undesirably alter the gastrointestinal environment (microbiome), creating conditions that are virtually guaranteed to promote the colonization of disease-causing yeast and their accompanying mischief. A parasite infestation is a major risk factor for the development of candidiasis. It explains why most sufferers have infections with one or more parasites.

When someone's gut is healthy and a parasite suddenly appears, their beneficial bacteria are usually able to inhibit or suppress its proliferation, at least at first—that is, unless the parasite is aggressive. In fact, parasite suppression is why most infected people remain totally unaware, unsuspecting, and mostly asymptomatic. If a parasite is nonaggressive, it must be patient and wait for something else to upset the gut before it can reproduce in significant numbers. Antibiotics, drugs that suppress immunity, and many of the other risk factors will adversely alter the gastrointestinal microbiome (chapter 2), disturbing or killing its population of beneficial bacteria. Once this occurs, idle parasites and disease-causing yeast (as well as harmful bacteria, molds, and viruses) can proliferate and instigate illness. The result is a coinfection with both disease-causing yeast and one or more parasites (as well as the other infectious invaders present). This does not only occur within the gut because other areas can be similarly affected; for example, a vaginal yeast infection is often associated with *Trichomonas vaginalis*, a parasite that causes a foul-smelling discharge and burning sensation within the vagina of an infected woman.

In the big picture, it does not matter which came first, the disease-causing yeast or the parasite, because either will cause problems. With respect to a candidiasis sufferer's symptoms and illness, the specifics do matter. Since each person is a unique individual, no two sufferers can ever manifest identical problems. There are similarities, but they cannot have the same symptoms and illness because a diversity of factors adversely affects someone's health, specific symptoms, and illness. Regardless, the infectious invaders present significantly contribute to the development and magnitude of someone's symptoms and illness.

When disease-causing yeast are the sole infectious invaders, a candidiasis sufferer's condition mostly reflects their presence and mischief, the toll the environment takes on their body (including dietary disturbances or deficiencies), and their inherited tendencies to develop or resist the development of certain symptoms and illness. The fewer infectious invaders present, the less complicated a sufferer's condition is likely to be. These people are usually the easiest candidiasis sufferers to treat.

In comparison, an infection with one or more parasites can cause a diversity of consequences. A parasite infestation is likely to promote candidiasis slowly when a nonaggressive parasite is involved, or quickly if the parasite is notably harmful. The greater the number of parasites present, the worse the infection. A candidiasis sufferer's ill health will reflect the participation of all their adverse contributors.

If someone is infected with a nonaggressive parasite, an organism suppressed or not virulent enough to disturb their gut, they may harbor the infectious invader for long periods of time with little to no ill effects. However, as exposures to additional candidiasis risk factors occur and their beneficial bacteria are disrupted or killed, their disease-causing yeast can proliferate. Once this occurs, a nonaggressive parasite can increase its numbers. This person eventually develops candidiasis, with symptoms and illness reflecting the combined presence of their disease-causing yeast and an infection with a nonaggressive parasite. In many instances, the nonaggressive parasite is so passive the person appears like a candidiasis sufferer without parasites. (The presence of parasites within these people is often overlooked, ensuring a future relapse after treatment.)

Obviously, the worst scenario involves an infection with an aggressive parasite because it can produce overt symptoms and illness. A gut infection with an aggressive parasite creates conditions that readily disrupt the beneficial bacteria, promoting the rapid onset of candidiasis. Thereafter, a sufferer develops symptoms and illness that represent the combined mischief of the disease-causing yeast and an infection with an aggressive parasite. In many cases, these infectious invaders create an alliance much worse than their undesirable effects simply added together. In addition to the disease-causing yeast, the aggressive parasite must be identified and appropriately treated to ensure a complete recovery and prevent a relapse. Furthermore, the greater the variety of parasites, the worse a sufferer's health is likely to be.

The important conclusion: The variability of a candidiasis sufferer's symptoms and illness relates to the mischief of their disease-causing yeast as well as to the type and variety of parasites infecting them. Confusingly, sufferers with similar parasites can manifest a diversity of symptoms, whereas seemingly identical problems can occur with unrelated parasites. So, there is no one absolute rule. Since harmful bacteria, molds, and viruses can also contribute their ill effects, numerous infectious invaders participate to collectively promote a sufferer's symptoms and illness. When genetic, environment, and dietary contributions are included, it is easy to understand why a spectrum of symptoms and illness exists among candidiasis sufferers.

Determinants of Candidiasis Symptomatology:

- **Genetics:** inherited bodily strengths, weaknesses, and proclivity to develop specific symptoms, illness, and disease.
- **Metabolic functioning:** the body's chemical activities and internal functioning as well as any resulting metabolic disturbances.
- **Environmental influences:** exposure to allergy-inducing substances and various toxins.
- **Dietary contributions:** a person's diet, including any excesses or deficiencies.
- **Parasites:** alone, many, or in certain combinations can promote significant debilitation.
- **Dysbacteriosis:** any of a multitude of disease-causing bacteria.
- **Mycosis:** any of a multitude of disease-causing molds.
- **Viral infection:** any of a multitude of disease-causing viruses.
- **Secondary immune system responses:** includes the production of antibodies, autoantibodies, or the lack of an appropriate immune system response.

A more important conclusion: Treating a candidiasis sufferer without attending to their parasites (or other infectious invaders) is unlikely to produce substantial improvement in their health, and, because of the likelihood of a relapse, improvements that occur are often temporary. Harboring an untreated parasite, even a nonaggressive one, virtually guarantees a candidiasis sufferer will relapse sooner or later.

SYMPTOMS OF PARASITIC INFECTIONS

The clinical picture of protozoa infestations ranges from healthy, unsuspecting carriers to severe (and even fatal) gastrointestinal and systemic complications. Gut manifestations are separated into *primary* and *secondary* symptoms. Diarrhea is the most common primary symptom, which is usually watery stool, with or without the presence of mucus and/or blood. Abdominal cramps and pain are the second most frequent primary symptom. There are numerous secondary symptoms, including flatulence, abdominal bloating, foul-smelling stools, heartburn/esophageal reflux, constipation, vomiting, and nausea.

Parasites can cause problems almost anywhere along the length of the gut, from one end to the other. Typically, a specific parasite will colonize a location that has a gastrointestinal microbiome favoring its survival. In contrast, some parasites can reside within numerous areas. Their symptoms and problems usually relate to the area(s) they inhabit as well as any secondary effects these disturbances cause.

Furthermore, a parasitic infection can produce symptoms beyond the gut. These *extraintestinal* symptoms are often more debilitating than their typical gut symptoms. For example, intense fatigue is a common extraintestinal symptom. Yet, when a person lacks significant gut symptoms, fatigue is rarely associated with a parasitic infection. (Many extraintestinal symptoms are like the symptoms experienced by candidiasis sufferers and, since these two conditions often occur together, it is difficult to distinguish between them.)

Among all the extraintestinal symptoms that accompany infections with protozoa, the psychological manifestations are probably the most debilitating. These can include moderate to severe depression with suicidal tendencies, nightmares with peculiar and vivid dreams, irritability and mood swings, spacey feelings or feeling like you are in a "fog," personality changes, attention deficit hyperactivity disorder (especially in children), dyslexia, and insomnia.

Other extraintestinal symptoms include weight loss and anorexia (loss of appetite), disturbed taste and/or smell, abnormal acute hearing, and complaints of partial or total hair loss. Urinary-genital symptoms are common and differ between the sexes. Men may experience acute inflammation of the skin covering the glans of their penis (balanitis), perianal or penile irritation, inflammation of the prostate gland (prostatitis), and acute inflammation of the seminal vesicle (vesiculitis). Women tend to have vulvar ulcers, inflammation of the cervix (cervicitis), inflammation of the vagina (vaginitis), and pelvic inflammatory disease. Both can have decreased libido.

An increasing body of information confirms a cause-and-effect relationship between parasites and allergies that has been considered controversial. It is unclear if parasites trigger allergic reactions or whether allergies are an undesirable consequence that occurs when the human host's protective mechanisms respond to the parasite's invasion. Many parasites have antigens that can be appreciated as foreign, so it is likely these infectious invaders can trigger sensitivities and hypersensitivities, either directly or indirectly.

The medical community needs to become aware of the widespread presence of parasites and their contributions to ill health. When this occurs, physicians will acknowledge that there is more to be learned about the harm caused by these seemingly common infectious invaders: they *must* be taken seriously and eradicated accordingly.

THE COMMON PROTOZOA

Giardia duodenalis is the most common protozoa in the United States, with an estimated 2 million cases occurring in 2011. Also, in 2011, it was estimated that 200 million people in Asia, Africa, and Latin America had symptomatic infections, which are often a self-limited clinical illness characterized by diarrhea, abdominal cramps, bloating, weight loss, and malabsorption. In addition, asymptomatic infections occur frequently, especially in developing countries.

Giardia duodenalis preferentially colonizes the mucosal linings of the *duodenum* and *jejunum* (the uppermost parts of the small intestines), where it can attach to the mucosal cells of the gut wall and cause gastroenteritis. Unlike other gut infections, diarrhea is a relatively infrequent and unreliable symptom, so many infected people do not suspect its presence; as a result, they become a carrier of the parasite, readily spreading it to others whenever and wherever the opportunities arise. There are two forms of *Giardia duodenalis*: the active *trophozoites* are often observed when there is severe diarrhea, whereas their dormant *cysts* (eggs) enable it to spread from one person to another. Simply put, the trophozoites are the "parent" parasite and the cysts are their inactive "eggs." Most mainstream physicians believe the trophozoites of *Giardia duodenalis* can only reside within the duodenum and jejunum of the small intestines. Although they would consent that passage of the cysts to the large intestines is possible, they believe the trophozoites cannot reside within this lower location, being a too-harsh environment for their survival. This narrow viewpoint is repeatedly refuted when anoscopy, again and again, demonstrates otherwise. Contrary to popular medical thought, *Giardia duodenalis* can also exist in locations other than the small and large intestines. Yet, given the diversity of illness it creates, it is often overlooked or ignored.

Entamoeba histolytica is a common parasite. It usually resides within the gut, feeding on bacteria and the tissues of its host. The trophozoite is its infectious form, causing symptoms and illness. During an active infection, when diarrhea is present, trophozoites are eliminated within the host's watery stool. Fortunately, its trophozoites are sensitive organisms that quickly expire outside of a host, impeding the spread of its infection. In the absence of diarrhea, the trophozoite can transform into a cyst, a form resistant to adverse environmental conditions, including inhospitable temperatures. Spread from one person to another usually occurs by direct contact or consuming contaminated food and water. After a cyst enters the small intestine, it opens like a seed, releasing the trophozoite, which is passively transported to the colon, the location where the parasite matures, multiplies, and repeats this process.

Although *Entamoeba histolytica* is not a blatantly harmful protozoa, an infrequent, undesirable complication occurs when its trophozoites enter the mucous membranes of the lower gut wall, producing one or many encapsulated lesions, called *abscesses*, which are areas of dead cells, tissue, and organisms. In advanced cases, the abscess expands, causing bleeding (hemorrhaging) and swelling (edema) of the gut wall (mucosa). Even worse, if the parasite enters the blood and then the portal vein, it can infect the liver and lungs, causing abscesses, illness, and debilitation in these locations. Over time, this can have profoundly undesirable, and even deadly, consequences for its host.

Most people infected with *Entamoeba histolytica* do not develop tissue invasion. Instead, their symptoms are usually mild or absent. One study found 2 to 40 percent of people infected with *Entamoeba histolytica* had cysts within their stool samples, meaning 60 to 98 percent do not. So, if an infected person has mild or no symptoms and an absence of cysts within their stool samples, a certain amount of suspicion is required or their *Entamoeba histolytica* infestation will be overlooked or missed. Moreover, infected people without symptoms are unsuspecting carriers of this parasite.

An increasing number of reports reveal certain systemic illnesses are associated with parasitic infections. For example, an infection with

Blastocystis hominis has been related to infectious arthritis. Yet, most mainstream physicians disagree and consider *Blastocystis hominis* to be totally harmless, preferring not to treat it when it is found. They need to reconsider because numerous reports suggest that *Blastocystis hominis* is not innocent. A few studies note about two-thirds of patients with gut symptoms had *Blastocystis hominis* within their stool samples. In other studies, the most prevalent symptom of an infection is abdominal pain associated with diarrhea and/or constipation. Although its presence may be common, *Blastocystis hominis* is far from harmless. On the contrary, it is a legitimate infectious invader. Even more alarming, it has been found to have the undesirable characteristics of both a fungus and protozoa; so, it has the harmful traits of both disease-causing yeast and an amoeba, a discovery that narrows the connection between them.

Other noteworthy, though poorly known, parasites associated with human disease:

- *Endolimax nana* is a small amoeba. It resides within the colon and cecum of the lower gut. It can cause acute problems, but its chronic presence is related to arthritis and hives (urticaria).
- *Dientamoeba fragilis* produces gut symptoms, including diarrhea, abdominal discomfort, and excessive flatulence. It is an amoeba that does not have a cyst stage, so it is only transmissible by directly ingesting the living organism.
- *Entamoeba hartmanni* is a weak parasite. Basically, it is a smaller version of *Entamoeba histolytica*, and similar symptoms and debilitation are possible.
- *Entamoeba coli* is an amoeba, usually noninvasive, transmitted by ingesting cysts.
- At least four species of *Cryptosporidium* are known: *Cr. parvum*, *Cr. muris*, *Cr. Bailey*, and *Cr. meleagridis*. *Cr. parvum* is primarily responsible for human disease. Following ingestion, the parasite invades the gut wall. Common symptoms are watery diarrhea associated with weight loss, nausea, and dehydration. Alarmingly, *Cr. parvum* is a threat to our water supply because its *oocysts* can survive chlorination and filtration. Moreover, this infectious invader can sometimes be inhaled and may produce a respiratory infection.
- *Cyclospora cayetanensis* (a protozoa) is increasing its presence within the water supply, and it is also able to cause diarrhea.

In clinical practice, using anoscopy, most patients are found to harbor one or more parasites. They cause gastrointestinal and extra-gastrointestinal symptoms, and the prevalence of their infections is lower or higher in different diseases and illnesses. Therefore, these parasites should not be considered harmless because all of them are detrimental to your good health. Yes, you might be able to live with a parasite, but why should you have to?

DIAGNOSING PARASITIC INFECTIONS

The presence of a parasitic infection is preferentially determined by anoscopy (chapter 17) because stool specimens have proven to be less accurate. Unless there is an active infection, often with diarrhea, the number of parasites may be too small to show up within a stool sample. Many protozoa have enzymes that enable them to attach to the gut wall or live within its layer of mucus. If these infectious invaders are not actively removed by rectal swabbing, their presence will not be revealed. In addition, some parasites are extremely sensitive to conditions outside the body; as a result, they expire within a stool sample, liberating their cellular contents, leaving little evidence of their presence. (Stool specimens are better for identifying and culturing harmful bacteria, as well as disease-causing yeast, including their sensitivities to antifungals.) It is also possible to obtain and assess fluid samples from the stomach and duodenum (gastric and duodenal aspirates), especially when *Giardia duodenalis* is suspected and other methods have failed. Since any procedure is only as good as the "expert" performing it, false negatives are common; that is, although the procedure did not obtain or observe the parasite, it was present anyway. Obviously, this delays a patient's treatment or dismisses it altogether.

Many protozoa elude detection, and several other tests may help diagnose the presence of these hidden infectious invaders or can, at least, be used to increase the index of suspicion. However, these supplementary tests are not 100 percent reliable or guaranteed to definitively prove the presence of parasites in every person. Therefore, they should be considered secondarily, using their findings to point you or your doctor in the right direction.

ELIMINATING YOUR PARASITES

Clinical experience with candidiasis sufferers demonstrates that 50 to 90 percent are infected with one or more parasites. Although parasites can be harmful by themselves, there is a *candidiasis-parasite connection*. Anything that disturbs the gut and its beneficial bacteria will permit the colonization of both disease-causing yeast and parasites as well as harmful bacteria, molds, and viruses. Unless there are significant symptoms within the gut, such as unrelenting diarrhea, parasites are likely to be ignored or missed by most healthcare practitioners. Since diarrhea has proven to be an unreliable symptom, parasites have been consistently overlooked in most candidiasis sufferers, providing another reason why they do not get better when treated or readily relapse after therapy is finished. In other words, parasitic infections are not always obvious. In fact, most infected people are completely unaware they harbor these infectious invaders, making them unsuspecting carriers.

If you suffer with candidiasis, consider the possibility that you are also infected with one or more parasites, especially if your anti-candidiasis therapy has been less than successful. You may have to convince your doctor you need to be tested. The best procedure for revealing parasites is the anoscopy because of its ability to uncover most parasites, even in asymptomatic, unsuspecting carriers. Although it is less accurate, collecting multiple stool samples may prove the point as well, but they are much less sensitive to the presence of parasites. Yet, neither method is 100 percent perfect, and, when both are negative, others laboratory tests can help raise your suspicions. In some cases, a parasite is present in such small numbers that it will not be noted until some of the disease-causing yeast are eliminated, which gives it room to reproduce and reveal itself. Regardless of which arrived first, your disease-causing yeast and parasites must *both* be addressed, or a complete recovery is impossible.

The most frequent parasitic infections involve protozoa, especially *Giardia duodenalis* and *Entamoeba histolytica*. In addition, *Blastocystis hominis*, previously thought to be an innocent interloper, is now recognized for its illness-causing ability. Other parasites appear with such regularity that their association with human illness is difficult to dismiss.

Many parasites do not stay localized within the gut; some can colonize other areas, including the liver and lungs, making systemic treatment necessary. (Note: Helminth worms are not discussed because their presence is rare in the United States; even so, these infectious invaders can cause significant illness and must be eliminated when found.)

Suppose you have a parasite, what should you do? First, do not panic, and do not rush to kill it, because many people treated for parasites cannot eliminate them. Although some parasites are resistant to the drugs routinely used to eradicate them, there is a more significant reason why parasites are difficult to eliminate. The presence of disease-causing yeast may impede their destruction. For many reasons, the colonization of disease-causing yeast can create a gastrointestinal microbiome that protects or shields parasites. So, if you want to greatly increase your odds of eliminating your parasites, your physician should initially focus on eliminating your candidiasis and healing your leaky gut syndrome. Once your disease-causing yeast are gone, your parasites will be more vulnerable to any therapy aimed against them. In addition, do not ignore the possibility that your parasites are infecting areas outside of your gut.

Now you have a choice: do you treat with medication or herbs? Some parasites are better treated with medication, while others do not respond to manufactured drugs and mandate the use of certain herbs. Some people believe herbs are superior because they are natural substances, but this is not always the case. Other people say medications are better, but these are only as good as the parasites they are targeted against and will not work if the parasite is resistant to the drug. Your doctor may make this choice for you. In any case, you want to use what works best.

Medications Commonly Used to Eradicate Parasites

- Infections with *Giardia duodenalis* are treated with metronidazole (Flagyl), quinacrine (Atabrine), furazolidone (Furoxone), and tinidazole (Fasigyn).
- *Entamoeba histolytica* requires the use of iodoquinol (Yodoxin), metronidazole (Flagyl), paromomycin (Humatin), and tinidazole (Fasigyn).
- Tinidazole (Fasigyn), a less-toxic relative of Flagyl, is effective against *Giardia duodenalis* and *Entamoeba histolytica*. Since it only takes from one to five days to eliminate the trophozoites (parent parasite), it must be followed by paromomycin (Humatin) for 7 days or iodoquinol (Yodoxin) for 20 days to kill any cysts (eggs) that remain.
- Many herbal preparations are also available, some better than others, and if they have a broad spectrum of coverage, they can eradicate numerous parasites. Often, herbal preparations take longer to work and may need to be used for two months or more. Rather than recommending any product here, it is best to consult with a healthcare provider to achieve optimal results.

CHAPTER 6

Respiratory Problems

The primary purpose of your respiratory system involves inhaling air into your lungs so that oxygen can enter your blood as well as allowing carbon dioxide to exit your blood and be exhaled. The cells and tissues of your body require oxygen to functional optimally. Conversely, carbon dioxide is produced as a cellular waste product and excesses must be removed or it functions as a poison. Yet, so much more is happening.

Respiration involves transporting oxygen into the lungs with inspiration and expelling carbon dioxide during expiration. Numerous anatomic and physiologic activities enable the lungs to exchange these two gases between the air and blood. In addition, the respiratory system includes the nose, sinuses, mouth-pharynx (oropharynx), and extrapulmonary airways (for example, the trachea) as well as the thoracic cage and respiratory muscles. The respiratory system does not function alone, because other systems are involved, including the cardiovascular system (blood vessels), reticuloendothelial system (lymph nodes and vessels), and nervous system (brain, spinal cord, nerves). The respiratory system also has direct connections with the immune system as well as its own distinct immunity. Moreover, the respiratory system indirectly participates in numerous metabolic (chemical) activities.

Even though the air surrounding you is usually clear and cannot be seen, do not assume it is harmless because all sorts of nasty stuff can float in what appears to be clean air. At the extreme, during a fire, it is obvious the air is blatantly dirty. Breathing unclean air causes all sorts of health problems, especially if you are sensitive or hypersensitive to the particles it contains. In some cases, the repeated inhalation of tobacco smoke or harmful chemicals plays a role in causing cancer. In other instances, exposure to carbon monoxide or other noxious gases causes death. Air is also a good medium for the spread of infection. A variety and diversity of infectious invaders can be transmitted from one person to another, using water droplets suspended in the air as vehicles of transportation. As a result, coughing and sneezing can easily spread one or more infectious invaders (usually viruses such as SARS-CoV-2, the cause of COVID-19, for example).

Since we constantly breathe in airborne "junk" from our external environment, our respiratory system is at risk to be disturbed, impaired, and injured. Acute respiratory illnesses are the most common medical maladies to plague human beings; they are responsible for the greatest percentage of absences from school and work. Even worse, as the population density increases, forcing us even closer, there is a greater prevalence of respiratory illness. Fortunately, most people's immune systems can combat and recover from acute respiratory disturbances. In contrast, chronic respiratory illnesses range from mildly annoying to debilitating, reflecting anything from a simple cough to a major illness that involves airway obstruction (for example, obstructive pulmonary disease).

The three common respiratory complaints are coughing, chest pain, and difficulty breathing (dyspnea). Less frequent respiratory disturbances include chronic sinus infections, sneezing, runny nose, postnasal drip, congestion, and other mild annoyances. Problems with the respiratory system often necessitate the use of one or more medications, which provide long-term support for most people with chronic respiratory illness.

Coughing is a protective mechanism that clears the airways of excessive secretions and harmful substances. Since healthy people seldom cough, an acute or chronic cough implies an underlying medical problem. A chronic cough may reflect a sensitivity or hypersensitivity to certain substances (allergies) and, as a result, be nothing more than a nuisance. In contrast, a chronic cough may accompany a serious condition like cancer. Depending on the cause, coughing is either *productive* (notable secretions) or *nonproductive* (dry or irritating).

Since respiratory illness and cardiovascular illness can masquerade as each other, it is essential to distinguish between them. It is vital to uncover if there is a history of chest pain and/or shortness of breath as well as other less prominent, identifying symptoms.

Warning: If blood is within your respiratory secretions (hemoptysis), whether frequent or occasional spotting, it must be considered an indicator of trouble until proven otherwise. In most cases, do not panic, because posterior nosebleeds may trickle blood down the back of your throat, where it can be coughed up. In any case, if there is blood, a physician *must* be consulted.

Worst cases aside, with respect to most recurring and chronic respiratory maladies, candidiasis is directly and indirectly involved. The same risk factors that promote the proliferation and colonization of disease-causing yeast within the gastrointestinal tract encourage their presence *on* and *within* the respiratory tissues. The respiratory tissues are a warm, moist, and dark environment (microbiome), a perfect habitat for the growth and nourishment of disease-causing yeast (and other fungi). Fortunately, the respiratory system is under the immune system's protection and does its best to prevent this from happening. The respiratory system also has some non-immune defenses. Since its defensive capabilities are not perfect, aggressive and resistant disease-causing yeast can assault and infect the respiratory tract and tissues.

How does disease-causing yeast infect the respiratory tract? They can be inhaled and colonize the surface of the airways or lungs when conditions permit. They may spread from the nasal passages or nasopharynx (nasal part of the throat), migrate downward, and colonize the trachea, bronchial tree, and lungs. Alternatively, in the presence of gastrointestinal candidiasis and leaky gut syndrome, disease-causing yeast can enter the blood, travel through the blood vessels of the lungs, get trapped, and take up residence. In any case, the colonization of disease-causing yeast within the lungs and airways may prevent or inhibit the respiratory system's immunity, allowing harmful bacteria, molds, viruses, and parasites to colonize and infect these locations. For example, *Candida albicans* and other fungi can produce a harmful toxin, *gliotoxin*, that can suppress immunity (chapters 10 and 14), encouraging infections within the respiratory tract.

To add insult, the respiratory system can indirectly be affected by the colonization of disease-causing yeast within the gut, especially when leaky gut syndrome is present. Their mischief induces inflammation and allergic reactions, including producing toxins and other harmful substances that can be absorbed. This can indirectly irritate, agitate, and aggravate the nasal passages and airways. Even worse, persistent respiratory candidiasis predisposes someone to numerous opportunistic infections that would not occur in a healthy person. Since recurring respiratory infections require treatment, especially the frequent use of antibiotics, chronic candidiasis creates a vicious cycle that further compromises someone's health.

If you suffer with chronic or recurring respiratory symptoms or illness, or frequent acute infections, consider the *candidiasis-respiratory connection*. Numerous respiratory conditions are directly or indirectly caused by candidiasis with or without the assistance of other infectious invaders. The most common manifestations include recurring common colds (upper respiratory infections), allergic rhinitis, chronic postnasal drip, chronic laryngitis (hoarseness), acute and chronic sinusitis, chronic coughing, chronic bronchitis, and asthma.

IT'S YEAST & MOLD, NOT THE "COMMON" COLD

Contrary to popular opinion, there is no such thing as a common cold. Despite its universal acceptance and widespread use, the term is inaccurate. It does not refer to a specific illness caused by a single, common infectious invader. Instead, upper respiratory tract infections are "common" because of their prevalence and frequency; typically, most children and adults develop three to five upper respiratory infections each year. Since numerous infectious invaders can cause problems within the upper respiratory tract, "common cold" is a nonspecific term, referring to a variety of infections. The symptoms of each infection differ because each infectious invader has its characteristics and prefers to assault certain locations. Many viruses predominantly infect the upper-middle respiratory passages; their manifestations typically include pharyngitis, laryngitis, croup, and bronchitis.

- **Pharyngitis:** inflammation or an infection within the pharynx, the passageway that allows air to flow from your nasal cavity to your larynx and food to travel from your mouth to esophagus. Its symptoms usually include a scratchy, sore throat and occasional pain with swallowing. Various other symptoms often accompany this illness, reflecting the number and variety of infectious invaders instigating the inflammation or infection.

- **Laryngitis:** inflammation or an infection within the larynx, an organ composed of muscle and cartilage, residing below the root of the tongue and at the top of the trachea. In general, it manifests as hoarseness of the voice. There may also be difficulty when talking, pain when coughing or clearing the throat, and fever.

- **Croup (laryngotracheobronchitis):** a childhood illness that produces high-pitched, noisy, inspiratory respirations (stridor), hoarseness, and a brassy cough. It is related to laryngitis because of its acute, significant swelling within the larynx and mucus secretions that obstruct the upper airway. There is usually fever, coughing, wheezing, and shortness of breath. Children with this illness are prone to develop hyperreactive airways (asthma).

- **Bronchitis:** inflammation or an infection within the bronchial passages, the two main airways leading from the trachea to the lungs (the bronchi) or the smaller subdivisions of the bronchial tubes (bronchioles). This illness usually presents as a cough (productive or nonproductive) and fever. Other symptoms are common.

When any of these medical maladies occur once or infrequently, it is most likely a chance encounter with an infectious virus. In contrast, when respiratory illness is chronic or recurring, candidiasis is virtually guaranteed. The colonization of disease-causing yeast within the respiratory tract promotes inflammation and disturbances in the infected areas, encouraging colonization and mischief by other infectious invaders as well. Chronic candidiasis can impair the immune system's ability to combat or eliminate these infectious invaders, allowing viruses to cause problems occasionally, frequently, or continuously. In addition, allergies to disease-causing yeast and harmful molds can trigger the airways to become sensitive or hypersensitive to these infectious invaders. When someone is exposed to the antigens of these infectious invaders, regardless of whether they are eaten or inhaled, their airways can become hyperreactive. These circumstances can promote persistent inflammation within the respiratory tract and induce many accompanying symptoms.

So, is candidiasis the cause of most common colds? Not by itself. You still need an infectious invader, usually a virus, to instigate illness. Yet, candidiasis does make someone more susceptible to succumbing to an infection as well as less able to eliminate it.

The typical symptoms of a common cold often include a high fever, headaches, body aches, coughing, and a runny nose. However, these symptoms are not exclusive to common colds. Why is this important? If you experience any or all these symptoms, a common cold may not be your problem. Instead, you may have candidiasis-related allergies.

ALLERGIC RHINITIS & NASAL ALLERGIES

People who suffer with nasal allergies regularly have clear nasal secretions and repetitive sneezing as well as itchy eyes, nose, and throat. *Allergic rhinitis* is a general term describing inflammation of the nasal mucous membranes in response to an allergy-inducing substance (antigen), regardless of the substance. There are more specific terms, like *hay fever* or *rose fever*; *hay* and *rose* refer to the time of year when the antigen is present (hay = late summer or autumn; rose = spring), and *fever* implies inflammation of the nasal passages. These are not the only two types of nasal allergies because a multitude of "fevers" exist. Although the designation of each reflects the name of the allergy-inducing substance, as well as the time of year it presents, all the "fevers" have similar symptoms.

According to 2017 statistics, 10 to 30 percent of adults and as many as 40 percent of children in the United States suffer with allergic rhinitis, representing more than 60 million people. An allergy to pollen is the most frequent cause of nasal allergies, followed by sensitivities and hypersensitivities to dust, dust mites, animal dander, feathers, tobacco, foods, and medications. Reactions to mold spores and disease-causing yeast are extremely prevalent, which is unsurprising because candidiasis promotes and causes most allergies (chapter 16).

Basically, *postnasal drip* is allergic rhinitis, except that the allergy-induced secretions flow down the back of the nasal passages into the throat, where they are swallowed or spit up. Postnasal drip tends to occur without other allergy symptoms and its seasonal association is less obvious, often making its presence a mystery or nebulous. If you think of postnasal drip as a different form of allergic rhinitis, it is easier to decipher its cause. Many people suffer with postnasal drip continuously, implying they have numerous, subtle allergies almost all the time. Once again, since postnasal drip is allergy-related, candidiasis is a prominent instigator and participant in its causation and recurring or chronic symptoms.

Physicians who specialize in ear, nose, and throat problems understand that there is a strong relationship between allergic rhinitis and sinusitis. Mainstream researchers are searching to find the medical "missing link" between allergies, allergic rhinitis, and sinusitis. Some mainstream physicians believe allergies cause sinusitis and their treatment approach mirrors their thinking; that is, if you treat someone's allergies, they should not have sinusitis. Yet, this point of view is not consistently effective because classical allergy treatments rarely benefit *both* allergic rhinitis and sinusitis. If both are related, what benefits one should benefit the other. Since this does not consistently occur, mainstream medicine's way of looking at these medical maladies is out of focus.

With respect to understanding and treating allergies, allergic rhinitis, and postnasal drip, mainstream allergists are also off track. Since they are unaware or do not appreciate the cause of these medical maladies, they treat them as illnesses. As a result, their approach is illness-oriented, with therapy aimed at the inflammation and immune system reactions that accompany allergies. Antihistamines, steroids, and other medications are commonly prescribed to suppress allergy mechanisms and responses. Allergy shots may be used to make someone less reactive to one or more offending substance, but they do not eliminate what is triggering their allergic reactions in the first place. Although their therapeutic arsenal may help control symptoms, allergy sufferers will probably need to take medication for the rest of their life. Yes, they might be able to live this way, but why should they when there is a better way to address allergies?

Allergies, allergic rhinitis, and postnasal drip are really symptoms of an underlying problem. Disease-causing yeast are the infectious invaders that promote allergies, allergic rhinitis, and postnasal drip (chapter 16). The longer candidiasis is present within someone's body, the greater their likelihood of developing allergies. The colonization of disease-causing yeast directly and indirectly promotes inflammation and immune system disturbances that induce sensitivities and hypersensitivities to a variety of substances—in fact, to almost anything encountered in someone's external or internal environment, which commonly includes allergies to inhaled substances, foods, and chemicals. In addition, most candidiasis sufferers develop subtle to severe allergies to numerous disease-causing yeast and harmful molds. Unless someone has some magnitude of candidiasis, allergies rarely occur. Since candidiasis precipitates and instigates most people's sensitivities and hypersensitivities, when it is appropriately treated, most (if not all) allergies markedly improve and often disappear. Moreover, disease-causing yeast can be assisted by harmful parasites, bacteria, molds, and/or viruses; all the harmful participants need to be identified and eliminated in allergy sufferers.

Therefore, it is critical to test and treat candidiasis sufferers, especially those with allergies, for sensitivities and hypersensitivities to disease-causing yeast and harmful molds. In fact, sufferers of allergic rhinitis and postnasal drip are frequently allergic to numerous disease-causing yeast and harmful molds; their body's reactions to these infectious invaders precipitates their inflammation and nasal allergies. Since disease-causing yeast and harmful molds are highly antigenic microorganisms, their presence within the body can promote allergies to them. Even after the infection with disease-causing yeast is eliminated, exposure to any of these allergy-inducing troublemakers causes inflammation and allergic reactions in anyone who is sensitive or hypersensitive to their presence. Because disease-causing yeast and harmful molds are present within many common foods and beverages, symptoms can arise when they are consumed. Some people experience *immediate-type* hypersensitivities, effects that occur quickly and resolve over a day or two. Other people have *delayed-type* hypersensitivities, an allergic reaction that takes time to develop and lasts for days, a week, or longer. All of this depends on how sensitive or hypersensitive someone is to a specific antigen, how often it is encountered, and the amounts of exposure. Besides eliminating foods and beverages that contain disease-causing yeast and harmful molds, reducing a person's sensitivity or hypersensitivity to them is warranted—typically, using a process called *desensitization* (chapter 18).

Confusingly, some sufferers of allergies, allergic rhinitis, and postnasal drip do not demonstrate sensitivities or hypersensitivities to disease-causing yeast or harmful molds when they are allergy tested. Does this mean that candidiasis is not present within these people? No, because many sufferers develop suppressed immunity that hinders their immune response. At the extreme, severely suppressed immunity creates a state of *anergy*, involving a partial or total lack of responsiveness to one or more allergy-inducing substances. If you understand this point, you can appreciate how candidiasis can be missed. When a person with suppressed immunity demonstrates a lack of positive reactions to allergy testing with disease-causing yeast and harmful molds, impaired immunity is to blame, not an absence of allergies. Clinically, the lack of a positive response causes these people to be mistaken for normal, and their candidiasis is overlooked. So, relying completely on positive test results to confirm the presence of allergies and candidiasis can sometimes lead to a big mistake; it misses the candidiasis sufferers who have suppressed immunity. Keep in mind, tests were designed to support, *not* make, the diagnosis.

The *candidiasis-allergy connection* is consistently ignored by mainstream medicine, and its practitioners remain stolid and steadfastly closed-minded. The allergy-inducing tendencies of disease-causing yeast and harmful molds are readily dismissed. Although disease-causing yeast have antigens that are similar (cross-react) to some molds accepted by mainstream allergists, an anti-candidiasis bias continues to pervade mainstream medicine. This does not make sense and exists to the detriment of all allergy sufferers.

MOLD ALLERGIES & NASAL SYMPTOMS

Experience with candidiasis sufferers reveals disease-causing yeast and harmful molds can instigate and promote nasal allergies. Even though there is a growing acceptance for mold-induced allergies, particularly involving the respiratory system, mainstream physicians continue to disregard the detrimental contributions of disease-causing yeast.

With respect to their role in illness, especially nasal allergies, molds are often overlooked or ignored in children and adults. There are greater than 10,000 molds (chapter 16). Because of their prevalence, diversity, and ability to survive in almost any climate, molds occur nearly everywhere and are almost impossible to avoid. Like disease-causing yeast, many molds are highly antigenic; they are strong inducers of allergies. A large percentage of year-round nasal allergy sufferers (*perennial* allergic rhinitis) demonstrate symptoms when exposed to one or more molds. Yet, mainstream physicians and allergists often ignore this connection. If mold allergies significantly contribute to the production of nasal symptoms and are not considered or evaluated, how can people with nasal allergies be effectively treated? Moreover, how can optimal desensitization therapy be designed and administered? The answer is it cannot. In fact, most perennial allergic rhinitis sufferers do not significantly improve with mainstream therapy, and even fewer are cured.

Furthermore, disease-causing yeast are as problematic (if not more), and they are regularly ignored or dismissed. This is surprising because disease-causing yeast and harmful molds are related; both are classified as *fungi*. They are so closely related that disease-causing yeast have similar antigens (allergically cross-react) to three common mold species: *Trichophyton*, *Oidiomycetes*, and *Epidermophyton* (TOE). Basically, disease-causing yeast and TOE share allergy-inducing components; allergic reactions to one can trigger allergic reactions to the others. Therefore, someone who is allergic to the molds TOE is likely to develop allergy-related symptoms when exposed to disease-causing yeast. In addition, someone allergic to disease-causing yeast will react similarly when exposed to TOE. Clearly, the gap between mold allergies and allergies to disease-causing yeast is not wide.

In contrast to TOE, allergies to disease-causing yeast are unappreciated or disregarded. If both types of infectious invaders are related, especially their ability to induce allergies, why does this bias exist? Disease-causing yeast are not accepted by mainstream physicians because their minds are closed. Some of them admit, "Everyone is allergic to *Candida albicans*," which is why an extract containing *Candida albicans* antigen is often used to test if a person's immune system functions properly; since *Candida albicans* is one of the most antigenic microorganisms known, the absence of a reaction indicates that someone's immune system is suppressed. Yet, the same physicians will add, "Although everyone is allergic, there is no evidence allergies to *Candida albicans* contribute to someone's symptoms." They diffused the bomb before it exploded; they believe everyone may be allergic to *Candida albicans*, but it has nothing to do with anyone's symptoms or illness. Although their approach ignores the undesirable contributions of disease-causing yeast, does it make sense? After all, if you are allergic to disease-causing yeast, being exposed to it would seem likely to induce inflammation and allergies. Do you believe exposures to disease-causing yeast have nothing to do with your symptoms? On the contrary, if everyone is allergic to disease-causing yeast, maybe it is playing a role in illness that is greatly unappreciated.

Mainstream physicians tend to focus on treating symptoms rather than addressing the causes of illness, especially when its origins are obscure or mysterious. Disease-causing yeast, TOE, and other harmful molds are not always directly linked to someone's symptoms and illness. Unlike some bacteria that rapidly promote infections, disease-causing yeast and harmful molds are not as aggressive and grow slowly, making their adverse contributions less notable or nebulous. Because of their stealthy behavior, the mischief of disease-causing yeast and harmful molds is often overlooked. In contrast, a cause-and-effect approach notices the more obvious, illness-associated culprits. For example, since hay fever symptoms arise in the late summer and fall, sufferers are tested for sensitivities to certain pollens, grasses, and other antigens pervading the environment at that time of year. Even though it includes environmental contributions, it misses the circumstances that caused someone to develop allergies in the first place. Whether appreciated or not, candidiasis can disturb the immune system, instigating allergic sensitivities and hypersensitivities. Thereafter, allergies to disease-causing yeast, TOE, and other harmful molds can contribute to the illness. This indirect relationship is rarely considered or examined, and these allergy-inducing infectious invaders are often undetected and go untreated. As a result, most allergy sufferers rarely improve substantially.

This approach is not meant to ignore environmental antigens or the benefits of allergy injections for nasal allergy sufferers, as effective management includes desensitization (allergy) injections with the appropriate environmental antigens. For example, if someone is sensitive to ragweed, it is preferable to desensitize them with injections containing its antigen(s). Antigen-specific desensitization helps a person's immune system combat their allergies; it makes them less likely to react when exposed to specific antigens, reducing their symptoms and discomfort. Yet, the use of allergy shots alone misses what causes someone to have allergies in the first place. Since candidiasis promotes most allergy sufferers' symptoms, the presence and adverse effects of disease-causing yeast needs to be addressed as well as the contributions of any other infectious invaders. Eliminating all their infectious invaders and treating their allergies greatly decreases the burden on their immune system. Not only is this the best approach to patient care and management, but it is also the best form of prevention; if the cause of a person's allergies is eliminated, additional sensitivities and hypersensitivities are unlikely to arise.

Do not underestimate the importance of allergies to disease-causing yeast and harmful molds in the production of nasal allergies and respiratory illness. Although these allergies may be less than obvious, they are far from nonexistent. In addition to environmental contributions, foods and beverages that contain these antigens can cause as much discomfort and illness in anyone who is sensitive or hypersensitive to them.

THE MYSTERY OF SINUSITIS

Although estimates vary depending on the source, sinus infections afflicted 31 million Americans in 2019, and chronic sinusitis affects about 12.5 percent of all people worldwide.

Whether it is acute or chronic, mild or severe, sinusitis is always uncomfortable. Many cases are debilitating because of their involved intense pain, pressure, and headache. Even worse, in rare circumstances, a sinus infection can progress and become life-threatening. If you ever had a sinus infection, you know how much discomfort sinusitis can cause. How can such a seemingly small infection confined to the sinuses create such undesirable consequences?

Sinusitis is a general term for the inflammation or infection that exists within one or more of the four pairs of air-filled bony cavities that surround the nasal passages (eight in total). Basically, you can think of these locations as little, warm, moist, and dark caves protruding from your nasal passages. These areas are covered and protected by a layer of epithelial tissue (mucous membranes). The sinuses normally communicate with the nasal passages through small openings. If there is an infection of the mucous membranes and tissues within one (or more) of the sinuses, the inflammation and swelling can obstruct the flow of air into and out of the involved sinus(es). When it is blocked, negative air pressure increases inside it, which can produce pain and other symptoms, like fever. If the obstruction is significant, fluid secretions accumulate, exacerbating the situation. In addition to the actual infectious invaders that cause a sinus infection, this allows other less-harmful bacteria to proliferate and contribute their mischief.

When everything is added together, you have one or more infected, clogged, and painful sinuses, commonly accompanied by a headache, difficulty concentrating, and fever. To add insult, your misery is not likely to be confined to your sinuses because it can adversely affect your entire body, causing lethargy or fatigue.

The common symptoms of an *acute* sinus infection include a thick and greenish nasal discharge, fever, headache, and facial pain and/or pressure. Only a small percentage of upper respiratory infections produce the sudden onset of sinusitis. Yet, some people seem to suffer with repeated sinus infections, which implies most cases of acute sinusitis really represent the flare-up of an underlying chronic sinus problem. In other words, if you suffer with one or more sinus infections a year, rather than these being distinct and unrelated events, you are probably experiencing some amount of low-grade inflammation within your sinuses that predisposes you to develop a sinus infection when certain conditions occur. The more sinus infections you have each year, the more likely this situation becomes.

Chronic sinusitis typically accompanies repeated or persistent insults to the nasal passages. Recurrent upper respiratory and sinus infections, with their inflammation, promote degenerative changes within the mucous membranes lining the sinuses, inhibiting the sinuses from draining their secretions. This usually creates conditions that permit the development of a simultaneous bacterial infection, resulting in a flare-up or case of acute sinusitis. Candidiasis-minded physicians appreciate that chronic sinusitis is rarely the result of a bacterial infection alone, although sufferers are at risk for acute episodes. Regardless of the number of acute episodes someone experiences, the inflammation within their sinuses is constant. When it is severe, chronic sinus-related illness occurs, with symptoms that often include dull pain over the infected sinus or sinuses, a thick discharge (clear, yellowish, or greenish), nasal congestion, postnasal drip, and a decreased sense of smell. By the way, acute sinusitis and chronic sinusitis are not two separate and distinct conditions, but the same illness with differing magnitudes.

Since their function is unknown, it is a mystery why the sinuses even exist. Yet, a lack of purpose does not prevent the sinuses from causing a great amount of misery. The most frequent sinus problem is the development of infections. Since the sinuses cannot be removed, acute and chronic sinus infections must be treated. Mainstream medical therapy involves antibiotics and decongestants; antibiotics eliminate the infection, and decongestants decrease inflammation and swelling, allowing the sinuses to open and drain their secretions. Sinusitis does not always include an infection; inflammation from any cause can swell the mucous membranes lining the sinuses, producing symptoms. If sinusitis is not always due to an infection, why are antibiotics used in virtually every case? More to the point, why are antibiotics administered when inflammation, rather than an infection, is really the problem?

Although antibiotics are effective at eliminating the active infection in acute sinusitis, they do little to prevent recurring or chronic sinusitis. In other words, recurring or chronic sinusitis does not reflect a persistent bacterial infection, or antibiotics would permanently eliminate it. Yes, chronic sinusitis sufferers do develop bacterial sinus infections, but these episodes are the exacerbation of an underlying condition. Episodes of acute sinusitis occur after a chronic sinus condition is established. Since healthy sinuses do not become infected, something must be happening within the sinuses of chronic sinusitis sufferers that predisposes them to repeated infections. Because inflammation can create conditions that permit the development of an acute sinus infection, something must be causing the inflammation. Numerous physicians accept allergies cause inflammation within the sinuses of allergy suffers, promoting a sinus infection. In fact, many sinusitis sufferers are also allergy sufferers. Therefore, when you think "sinus infections," you should also be thinking "allergies." This insight alters how sinus infections should be approached, treated, and managed.

Although allergies can promote mucous membrane inflammation within many sinusitis sufferers, the "sinusitis story" is far from over. Allergies do not develop for no reason, and inflammation does not arise without a cause. Something must be occurring within the sinuses of sinusitis sufferers that predisposes them to develop both allergies and sinus infections. What could it be? In addition to their ability to colonize the gut, disease-causing yeast can invade into and live within the nasal passages and mucous membranes of the sinuses. As a result, their continuous presence can contribute to the persistent inflammation that encourages sinusitis as well as allergies within these areas. If the inflammation is mild, an upper respiratory infection or significant allergic reaction can promote acute sinusitis. As the amount of inflammation increases and the density of *Candida*-species organisms escalates, forming a biofilm (chapter 4), chronic sinusitis and its symptoms becomes more likely.

Regardless of whether the sinuses are partially or completely obstructed, the presence of disease-causing yeast within the nasal passages and sinuses promotes a respiratory microbiome that allows harmful bacteria to reproduce and cause acute infections. Over time, degenerative changes permit the development of recurring or chronic sinusitis. Since antibiotics kill harmful bacteria but do not disturb the disease-causing yeast, sinusitis sufferers are virtually guaranteed to relapse after antibiotic therapy; in fact, this is a common occurrence. Moreover, antibiotics often make sinusitis worse in the long run because they kill off any beneficial bacteria that may reside within the nasal passages and sinuses (as well as the gut), allowing the disease-causing yeast to increase their numbers and harmful effects.

Just when you thought allergies were totally to blame, it seems disease-causing yeast are the real culprits behind sinusitis. Therefore, most sinusitis sufferers should be treated with systemic antifungal medication to eliminate the disease-causing yeast within their nasal passages and sinuses. Most sufferers can eradicate their sinusitis using this approach, even when their allergies are not immediately addressed. Nevertheless, because disease-causing yeast have both infectious and allergic tendencies, treating someone's allergies is equally important, especially their sensitivities and hypersensitivities to disease-causing yeast and harmful molds. With this approach, most sufferers quickly become ex-sinusitis sufferers.

In contrast to candidiasis, research reveals that harmful molds may contribute to chronic sinusitis, especially allergy-related cases. Does this mean harmful molds are responsible for chronic sinusitis and not disease-causing yeast? Not necessarily, because disease-causing yeast tend to *invade* tissue surfaces and unless they form a biofilm, they are difficult to detect, while harmful molds grow on the surface and are easier to collect. Although harmful molds may contribute, candidiasis-minded physicians will continue to consider disease-causing yeast the primary cause of chronic and recurring sinusitis.

COUGHING & BRONCHITIS

The air we inhale contains all sorts of substances, ranging from harmless to harmful. Exposures can irritate the tissues within the lower respiratory tract, making them sensitive or hypersensitive to one or more of these substances. Typically, this is related to the presence of allergies or an inflammatory cause. The more harmless the substance, the greater the amounts needed or the longer the exposure required to induce problems. In contrast, certain substances are caustic or toxic in small doses and rapidly damage the lower respiratory tissues. Although the respiratory system is within the body, it is in constant contact with our external environment and at risk for injury when circumstances permit. Exposing the lower respiratory tract to inhaled irritants can lead to a chronic cough, simple chronic bronchitis, asthmatic bronchitis, chronic obstructive bronchitis, and asthma. When these medical maladies are considered objectively, they all appear to be related, being variations of the same theme. Yet, someone's specific condition often reflects the adversely affected areas of their respiratory tract.

The external environment does strongly contribute to the development of respiratory sensitivities and hypersensitivities, but its contributions alone do not explain why people develop these reactions in the first place; after all, if the external environment was totally to blame, everyone would experience these medical maladies. Something else must be occurring within the respiratory systems of certain people that predisposes them to develop these problems. Like the nasal passages and sinuses, the tissues of the lower respiratory tract can become colonized with disease-causing yeast. The more persistently and chronically irritable and inflamed someone's respiratory tissues, the greater the likelihood they have respiratory candidiasis, warranting the use of systemic antifungal medication. In addition, the airways of some people may also be infected with harmful parasites, bacteria, and molds, which must also be appropriately addressed.

The most uncomplicated lower respiratory tract condition is coughing, the mechanism that protects our lower airways from the inappropriate inhalation of harmful substances. The action of coughing helps to forcefully remove foreign material and clear excess secretions from within the lower respiratory tract. (Sneezing performs a similar function within the upper respiratory tract and nasal passages.) A cough can be consciously produced, but most coughing results from the reflex stimulation of the cough receptors within the nose, oropharynx, larynx, trachea, and large central bronchi; receptors agitated by an irritating substance send messages to the brain to produce a cough. During a cough, the rapid flow of expired air often loosens and expels particles and secretions from the surface of the respiratory tissue (mucosa).

Coughs can be *acute* (lasting fewer than three weeks) or *chronic* (lasting at least three to eight weeks). A *productive* cough clears secretions that accumulate when there is excess production, deficient clearance, or the presence of some physiological abnormalities. Although this is a crucial defense mechanism, as a symptom it indicates the presence of both acute and/or chronic inflammation. In contrast, a *nonproductive* cough reflects irritation after a mechanical, chemical, thermal, or inflammatory insult. Typically, the cough reflex becomes sensitive or hypersensitive to relatively harmless stimulants, making this type of cough rather annoying. Since healthy people rarely cough, a *chronic cough* is a symptom that indicates the presence of an underlying problem, usually the presence of persistent inflammation. In most cases, it results from the presence of allergies to disease-causing yeast and harmful molds, which is consistent with postnasal drip being the single-most common cause of a chronic cough. Moreover, a chronic cough may involve the colonization of disease-causing yeast in areas that have cough receptors; persistently irritating one or more of these receptors triggers a recurring cough. As a result, inhaled substances within the external environment can readily exacerbate someone's condition. Other chronic cough causes include asthma and gastroesophageal reflux disease (acid reflux/heartburn), especially in nonsmokers who have normal chest X-rays. In fact, chest X-rays are normal or stable in greater than 90 percent of people with a chronic cough. In comparison, respiratory-related cancers occur in less than 2 percent of the cases of chronic cough and are unlikely in nonsmokers.

Moving downward, *chronic bronchitis* is a condition of the bronchial passages involving increased mucous secretions, decreased (ciliary) clearance, and a tendency to develop infections. Although allergies can contribute, the presence and colonization of disease-causing yeast within the lower respiratory tract is often to blame, creating inflammation that encourages infections with harmful bacteria, molds, parasites, and viruses. Medical research reveals that *Candida*-species organisms can participate in bronchitis, which is why chronic bronchitis often disappears when systemic antifungal medication is prescribed, providing proof of its association with respiratory candidiasis.

Since many chronic bronchitis sufferers experience some magnitude of smooth muscle constriction of their airways, this illness becomes difficult to distinguish from asthma. In fact, simple chronic bronchitis should really be considered a relatively mild form of asthma.

ASTHMA

In 2012, researchers at BMC Public Health wrote, "The global prevalence of doctor diagnosed asthma in adults was estimated to be 4.3%, while the prevalence of wheezing was estimated to be 8.6%. The five countries with the highest prevalence were Australia (21.5%), Sweden (20.2%), United Kingdom (18.2%), Netherlands (15.3%), and Brazil (15.3%)."

According to the Asthma and Allergy Foundation of America website (2022), "Approximately 25 million Americans have asthma (1 in 13), including 8% of adults and 7% of children." Half of the sufferers are diagnosed between ages 2 and 17. In contrast, one-third are diagnosed after age 30. Children, age 10 or younger, have symptoms and are debilitated the most often, usually because of their smaller airways. In addition, children develop upper respiratory infections more frequently, which precipitates episodes of asthma. More concerning, the incidence of asthma is increasing, including asthma-related deaths.

In general, asthma arises in people with hyperreactive or hypersensitive airways; acute or chronic exposures to bronchial irritants provoke an asthma "attack," or *bronchospasm*. Although the main feature of bronchospasm is constriction of the bronchial smooth muscles, it is often associated with bronchial wall swelling (edema) and an abnormal production of mucus. To diagnose asthma, the bronchospasm must be severe enough to produce noticeable symptoms, usually wheezing or shortness of breath. Sinusitis and allergic rhinitis are frequently related to bronchial asthma, promoting prolonged episodes. It is no coincidence these connections exist because all are related to the presence of allergies and respiratory candidiasis.

Technically, asthma involves "reversible hyper-responsiveness of the tracheobronchial smooth muscle." Simply put, the trachea and bronchi of asthma sufferers are hyperreactive to numerous irritating stimuli that cause their air passages to constrict and narrow, which is spontaneously or therapeutically reversible. Most asthmatics are well acquainted with their wheezing, coughing, and shortness of breath (dyspnea). The onset, severity, and duration of asthma usually differs from one person to another. Its symptoms often present as recurring "attacks." Since many asthmatics frequently feel like they are suffocating, anxiety often ensues. In rare cases, an insufficient flow of air can become life-threatening or fatal.

Asthma sufferers are classified into two groups: *Extrinsic* asthma presents in children, has seasonal fluctuations, and involves a well-defined history of allergies to inhaled antigens. In contrast, *intrinsic* asthma arises after age 30, occurs throughout the year (perennial) and is more severe, usually has no allergic contributors, and is responsible for less than 10 percent of all sufferers. Confusingly, greater than 80 percent of asthma sufferers have characteristics common to both groups. Regardless of whether allergies to inhaled antigens trigger an allergy attack, bronchospasm is present in all cases, implying the existence of unknown hypersensitivities.

Mainstream medicine claims to understand the physiological abnormalities and processes of asthma; the presence of hypersensitive airways leads to beta-adrenergic blockage of the smooth muscles lining the airways, producing cyclic nucleotide imbalances that encourage the release of inflammatory mediators from the mast cells. Simply put, you get inflammation and constriction of the airways. Although asthma is a real illness, mainstream medicine does not appreciate its origin. All illnesses have causes, whether known or not. Abundant evidence, as well as treatment successes, demonstrates a prominent *candidiasis-asthma connection.*

The simplest research reveals that exposure to *Candida albicans* antigen can provoke bronchospasms in susceptible people. Various studies demonstrate that the airways of asthmatics are sensitive or hypersensitive to exposures of disease-causing yeast, specifically *Candida albicans.* Although this readily supports a *candidiasis-asthma connection,* it is only the tip of the iceberg.

Instead of disease-causing yeast, many mainstream physicians focus on harmful molds. Rather than discussing the scope of their research, consider one mold. Numerous studies note that patients with moderate to severe asthma also suffer with athlete's foot, caused by the fungus *Trichophyton tonsurans* (the "T" in TOE); they had positive intradermal skin testing and positive reactions to bronchial challenge testing with this fungal antigen extract, evidencing allergies, with their pulmonary function tests decreasing significantly. Yes, asthma symptoms can be instigated by an allergic reaction to it, and there is an *allergy-asthma connection* with this mold. However, this is only a subgroup of all asthmatics. In contrast, asthmatics without athlete's foot and athlete's foot sufferers without asthma will react to different molds, as there are over 10,000 molds. Obviously, regardless of which mold causes asthma, it makes sense to eliminate it. Yet, disease-causing yeast are closely related and are equally, if not more, guilty. Why are molds accepted and disease-causing yeast ignored when both are likely to play a role in asthma?

As for the cause of asthma, there are two opposing viewpoints, even though both are related. On one side, *Candida albicans* antigen can provoke an asthma attack, evidencing a *candidiasis-asthma connection.* On the other side, many physicians believe that an allergy to one or more molds is the cause. So, it is not one or the other, but both disease-causing yeast and molds contributing to most cases of asthma.

Since *Candida albicans* is antigenically (allergically similar) to *Trichophyton tonsurans,* exposure to the antigen of either organism can produce the same reaction (bronchospasm). In fact, when tested, most candidiasis sufferers are also allergic to *Trichophyton tonsurans.* Since most asthmatics, if not all, have candidiasis and are allergic to disease-causing yeast, it makes sense that they would also be allergic to this mold. So, what appears to be an allergy to *Trichophyton tonsurans* is really candidiasis in disguise—something you would not realize, unless you were looking for it.

How can this be validated? By approaching the treatment of asthma from the direction of candidiasis. When asthmatics are treated with Diflucan (a systemic antifungal medication that kills disease-causing *Candida*-species organisms and a few other molds, but not *Trichophyton tonsurans*), their condition greatly improves and is cured in many cases. By eliminating the disease-causing yeast colonizing an asthmatic's airways, the inflammation and hyperreactivity responsible for their asthma attacks decreases. Even though it is also important to treat their accompanying allergies to decrease their respiratory sensitivities and hypersensitivities, the cause of their asthma is primarily due to the colonization of disease-causing yeast within their lower respiratory tract. Yes, other infectious invaders can contribute their ill effects and must also be appropriately eliminated to achieve wellness.

What about the contributions of viruses? Numerous investigators know that viral upper respiratory infections can extend episodes of asthma for as long as five to six years. This means, after the bronchial smooth muscles of an asthma sufferer become hypersensitive, they are susceptible to continuous hyperreactivity with repeated upper respiratory infections. Since antibiotics are routinely used to treat these acute infections, they further promote the colonization of disease-causing yeast within an asthma sufferer's lower respiratory tract, aggravating their *respiratory candidiasis* and its symptoms (asthma). The colonization of disease-causing yeast, including their infectious and allergic consequences, is a risk factor for additional infections. Even worse, chronic candidiasis can suppress immunity, including respiratory immunity, making asthma sufferers more likely to succumb to frequent viral (and bacterial) respiratory infections. Regardless of the specifics, with respect to respiratory illness, unless you know what to look for and where to look, the *candidiasis-asthma connection* will likely be missed.

MAGNESIUM DEFICIENCY: THE ASTHMA TRIGGER

In 1912, Dr. Friedrich Trendelenburg, a German surgeon, speculated that magnesium can relax bronchial smooth muscles, implicating that a magnesium deficiency exists within asthma sufferers. Many studies have supported and confirmed the beneficial effects of this essential mineral in asthma. Basically, a magnesium deficiency can promote bronchospasm within asthma sufferers, while magnesium administration can relax the smooth muscles lining their airways.

How does a magnesium deficiency occur? Unless a dietary deficiency is to blame, it usually involves an abnormality of the *parathyroid glands*, the two pairs of glands behind the thyroid gland (chapter 11). Their decreased functioning is called *hypoparathyroidism*, involving a deficiency of *parathyroid hormone* secretion. In short, if someone's intake of calcium is normal, but they have a magnesium deficiency, hypoparathyroidism will promote low serum concentrations of both minerals.

Specifics aside, *functional hypoparathyroidism* is the most common hormone disturbance among candidiasis sufferers (chapter 11). European physicians appreciate that many patients with functional hypoparathyroidism have *normal* calcium levels; low serum magnesium levels can occur with a normal concentration of serum calcium. Since serum calcium concentrations are routinely measured while magnesium concentrations are not, functional hypoparathyroidism is often overlooked.

This is crucial with respect to asthma. Since functional hypoparathyroidism is the most common candidiasis hormone disturbance, serum magnesium deficiencies (hypomagnesemia) often plague candidiasis sufferers. Those with asthma will be more likely to have contraction or hypersensitivity of their bronchial smooth muscles. So, a candidiasis-related hormone deficiency seems associated with asthma. When the physical presence and colonization of disease-causing yeast within the airways is added in, the magnitude of this malady becomes more compelling.

MÉNIÈRE'S DISEASE: CHRONIC EAR INFECTION?

Ménière's disease plagues middle-aged and elderly people. Sometimes, its presence can be debilitating. Usually, it involves hearing loss and *tinnitus*, recurring episodes of abrupt and frequently severe dizziness (*vertigo*) accompanied by a sensation of fullness, pressure, or ringing within the ear. It is usually one-sided but may progress to include both. Mainstream physicians claim that "recurring endolymphatic hypertension" is the problem, reflecting the inflammation and dilatation of the *endolymphatic sac* of the internal ear. Supposedly, after enough time, this causes the hair cells within the endolymphatic sac to become damaged and waste away (atrophic), precipitating the symptoms that accompany this medical malady. Why is it included here? The middle and internal ear are part of the upper respiratory tract; the Eustachian tube connects the oropharynx to the middle ear, which is adjacent to the internal ear.

Although this explains the mechanics of a person's hearing loss, it ignores their episodes of dizziness. In addition, it overlooks what causes their endolymphatic sac to be inflamed and dilated as well as what instigates their tinnitus. Yes, mainstream medicine appreciates the process and recognizes that allergies might participate, but they do not know its origin. Yet, illnesses do not arise without a cause. Something is responsible for Ménière's disease, regardless of its mysterious or obscure origins. Fortunately, the answer involves knowing where to look and what to look for.

Objectively, Ménière's disease behaves like a chronic middle ear infection, except that the inflammation involves the internal ear instead. Most, if not all, chronic middle ear and/or internal ear infections demonstrate a relationship with the colonization of disease-causing yeast and allergies, whether or not it is obvious (chapter 12). So, it is no coincidence most Ménière's disease sufferers also have numerous allergies and poor nutritional health. Frequently, rather than environmental allergies, the inflammation and dilatation of their endolymphatic sac results from allergies to disease-causing yeast and harmful molds; this effect, over the long term, can explain the degenerative changes that promote hearing loss.

The *tinnitus* is believed to arise from inflammation constantly exciting (enervating) the *vestibulocochlear* nerve, the eighth cranial nerve, which carries impulses from the internal ear to the brain. In return, this produces a constant ringing or hissing in one or both ears. How might this happen? In addition to direct inflammation, the nerve can be irritated or compressed by an inflamed *vagus nerve,* the tenth cranial nerve, the major nerve supplying the gut. If there is inflammation or a chronic condition within the gut (for example, gastrointestinal candidiasis), the vagus nerve can become chronically irritated and inflamed. Since its path to the brain crosses the vestibulocochlear nerve, inflammation of the vagus nerve can compress the vestibulocochlear nerve, causing it to be irritated and inflamed.

Furthermore, the episodes of dizziness may reflect a combination of middle ear and/or internal ear inflammation combined with fluctuations in a person's blood glucose concentration. Since glucose is the brain's primary source of energy, severe or prolonged decreases in someone's blood sugar concentration can deprive their brain of fuel, encouraging episodes of lightheadedness or dizziness. In addition, a lowered blood sugar concentration can trigger the release of hormones to raise it; one or more hormones (for example, *epinephrine*) may participate in inducing dizziness. Alternatively, because candidiasis sufferers often have insufficient adrenal gland functioning, a deficiency of certain adrenal hormones may precipitate periods of low blood pressure that can contribute to these episodes as well as any hormones released to compensate for a lowered blood pressure. In contrast, increases in blood pressure can engorge the blood vessels nourishing the endolymphatic sac, increasing its inflammation and dilatation. In any case, the presence and allergies to disease-causing yeast and harmful molds appear to contribute the greatest ill effects.

Since chronic ear infections, allergies, and blood sugar disturbances are all related to candidiasis, not to mention blood pressure problems, there is a *candidiasis–Ménière's disease connection*. Moreover, when the candidiasis is appropriately addressed, the episodes of dizziness often significantly improve, if not disappear entirely. In many cases, the tinnitus equally improves and often abates. (In fact, during and after treatment, younger candidiasis sufferers with tinnitus frequently state that the ringing within their ears is gone or greatly improved.) Unfortunately, with respect to the hearing loss, its permanence relates to the damage sustained over time; in general, as the inflammation and resulting damage increase, the benefits of therapy decrease. Regardless, appropriate anti-candidiasis intervention is certain to bring some relief to Ménière's disease sufferers as well as to people who suffer with these symptoms separately—for example, tinnitus sufferers.

BREATHING EASIER

Candidiasis primarily involves the colonization of disease-causing *Candida*-species organisms within the gut. By itself, *gastrointestinal candidiasis* (chapter 4) can disrupt the gut's functioning as well as promote other bodily disturbances, directly and indirectly. As it progresses and the gut wall is weakened, the establishment of leaky gut syndrome permits numerous allergy-inducing substances to be absorbed, which can sensitize or hypersensitize the immune system to them. This creates more disturbances within the gastrointestinal microbiome; for example, it exacerbates the inflammation within the gut wall and tissues. If the allergy-inducing substances enter the blood, they can adversely affect other areas that are sensitive or hypersensitive to their presence. In this way, a sufferer's diet and gastrointestinal microbiome can undesirably influence the tissues within their upper and lower respiratory tract. In addition to environmental allergies, many candidiasis sufferers with respiratory problems discover they are sensitive or hypersensitive to disease-causing yeast and harmful molds, allergies that strongly contribute to inflammation within their respiratory tissues. Eliminating foods and beverages that contain or are made with these infectious invaders, dead or alive, often enables sufferers to decrease their respiratory inflammation and symptoms. Although this is not a cure, it frequently makes them feel better.

For numerous reasons, disease-causing yeast can gain entry to and colonize the airways and respiratory tissues, causing localized inflammation and other adverse reactions that promote a variety of respiratory symptoms. Their presence and colonization also make these areas sensitive or hypersensitive to various external environmental substances, exacerbating a sufferer's symptoms and illness with each exposure. The respiratory manifestations of candidiasis depend on the areas adversely affected and can include frequent "common colds" (upper respiratory infections), allergic rhinitis, chronic postnasal drip, chronic laryngitis (hoarseness), acute and chronic sinusitis, chronic coughing, chronic bronchitis, and asthma. Even uncommon conditions like Ménière's disease have an association with candidiasis and allergies. You can suffer with one problem or a combination of many. There is no hard and fast rule. Each manifestation reflects many factors that encourages its development. Yes, genetics play a role because you must have a susceptibility to develop certain illnesses in the first place.

Asthma is a special manifestation of candidiasis. Although allergies strongly contribute, the bronchial (airway) hyperreactivity and hypersensitivity usually results from the colonization of disease-causing yeast within the airways, including their direct *infectious* and *allergic* effects. Chronic candidiasis often promotes *functional hypoparathyroidism*, an endocrine (hormone) disturbance that contributes to the bronchospasms that characterize asthma; a sufferer can develop low levels of parathyroid hormone that decrease their body's serum magnesium ion concentration. Since magnesium effectively relaxes bronchial smooth muscle tissue, functional hypoparathyroidism creates a magnesium deficiency that can allow contractions of the smooth muscles lining the small airways within susceptible people.

With respect to treating respiratory candidiasis, the best place to start is within the gut; eliminating disease-causing yeast helps heal the gut wall, decreasing leaky gut syndrome. Eliminating foods and beverages containing disease-causing yeast and harmful molds reduces inflammation within the gut and respiratory tract. *Respiratory candidiasis* necessitates systemic antifungal medication, drugs that enter the blood and diffuse to the sinuses and airways, killing disease-causing yeast within these areas. This explains why nonabsorbable antifungal agents (like nystatin) are rarely effective in treating *respiratory candidiasis.* In addition, it is wise to test people with chronic respiratory symptoms for various allergies, especially to disease-causing yeast, harmful molds, foods, pollens, and dust. Even after their candidiasis is eliminated, their allergies often continue unless treated; desensitization (allergy) injections are used to teach their immune system not to react against their offending substances, which further decreases their respiratory inflammation. In addition, correcting an asthmatic's magnesium deficiency encourages their airways to be less hyperreactive. Equally important, harmful parasites, bacteria, and molds may contribute, and they must be considered, revealed, and treated appropriately.

Once the *candidiasis-respiratory connection* is appreciated, chronic and recurring respiratory illnesses are easier to understand and treat. Yet, the treatment results are not always quick or easy. There are likely to be complications, for example, the presence of other infectious invaders or severe allergies. Fortunately, from clinical experience, the benefits of an anti-candidiasis approach enable most sufferers of chronic respiratory problems to breathe easier.

CHAPTER 7

Cardiovascular Complications

As you know, blood is the viscous, dark-red liquid that fills our blood vessels. It contains a mixture of fluid and cells. Its primary citizens are the microscopic red blood cells; in addition to giving blood its color, they transport inhaled oxygen from the lungs to the cells and tissues, where it is exchanged for the potentially toxic carbon dioxide that is returned to the lungs and exhaled. The blood also transports a variety of substances essential for our health, including water, vitamins, minerals, amino acids, glucose, hormones, cellular chemical messengers, and more, as well as helps eliminate waste—most notably, lactic acid, urea, and carbon dioxide. Circulation is the name for this process.

When the body functions normally, our circulation keeps everything in balance and *what enters* equals *what exits*. The blood performs several other beneficial functions as well. It is a proficient heat absorber and distributor, enabling us to be warm-blooded. It participates in immune system activities; immune cells, white blood cells, inhabit the blood and use it to move throughout the body. Clearly, there is more to blood than just its red color.

The plumbing system that contains and carries blood within the body is comprised of arteries, capillaries, and veins. In addition, all self-contained plumbing systems require a pump. The heart is the "living pump" that incessantly circulates blood throughout the entire body. The blood flows within the blood vessels at a rate proportional to our activities and metabolic requirements; as our needs increase, the rate of flow is greater. In total, the cardiovascular (circulatory) system includes the blood, heart, and a network of interconnecting vessels. Even though blood is a vital component, cardiovascular disease typically excludes abnormalities of the blood. Instead, it focuses on the medical maladies that disturb or disrupt the functioning of the system's pump and pipes, the heart and blood vessels. (Because of its connection with the immune system and role in metabolism, blood abnormalities are classified as immune system or metabolic disturbances.)

Classically, cardiovascular illness encompasses blockage or damage of the blood vessels supplying the heart, brain, various organs, and peripheral areas. Since its symptoms are often absent, most cases remain undetected until the disturbance or damage is advanced. Most cardiovascular maladies appear abruptly—as a heart attack, coronary artery–related chest pain (angina), stroke, or infarction of an extremity (claudication). Some of these events often precipitate sudden death. Atherosclerosis and hypertension ("hardening of the arteries" and "high blood pressure") are the two primary processes responsible for subtly injuring our blood vessels, which is why these illnesses are referred to as "silent killers."

The common *major* risk factors for developing cardiovascular illness include age, sex (males have a higher risk), hypertension, cigarette smoking and environmental tobacco smoke exposure, plasma levels of "bad" and "good" cholesterol (LDL and HDL), and diabetes. The less prominent contributors are obesity, lack of exercise, personality type, and stress. Since mainstream medicine has expanded to consider it to be an infectious process, it is thought that various pathogens are involved in promoting atherosclerosis (inflammation); the more pathogens someone is infected with the greater their chance for illness. The most prominent known culprit is *Chlamydia pneumoniae. Helicobacter pylori* and *cytomegalovirus*, as well as *herpesvirus simplex type 1*, have been implicated. Many more pathogens are also considered problematic.

Numerous risk factors contribute to the development of cardiovascular illness. Yet, none of the risk factors, major or minor, are guaranteed to instigate illness in everyone, which is when genetics plays a role—your inherited, familial tendency to develop certain medical maladies. Even if cardiovascular illness is prevalent within your family, there is no guarantee you will develop it because everyone is unique. So, there must be more to cardiovascular disease than its risk factors and a genetic predisposition.

Although the physical mechanics (pathophysiology) are well understood, for all the answers that exist, some vital questions remain: What are the actual causes of cardiovascular illnesses? What *precipitates* the blockage or damage within blood vessels that leads to disease? What causes someone's cholesterol levels to be elevated? What instigates blood pressure problems? Does mitral value prolapse cause serious problems? What do hypercholesterolemia, atherosclerosis, hypertension or hypotension, and mitral valve prolapse have in common? Are these difficult questions to answer? Not when you know where to look and what to look for, especially when you consider that cardiovascular disease has an infectious component. For the most part, mainstream medicine ignores the most prevalent infectious invaders—disease-causing yeast. So, the answers to all these questions can be easily summed up: Disease-causing yeast can adversely affect the cardiovascular system in various ways, and the evidence is too compelling to be dismissed. Typically, the longer someone's candidiasis has existed, the greater their resulting disturbances and damage. The *candidiasis–cardiovascular disease connection* has been consistently overlooked until now.

HYPERCHOLESTEROLEMIA: ELEVATED CHOLESTEROL LEVELS

If you stand on a busy street corner in a large city and question the passing pedestrians, they are more likely to know their cholesterol level than who represents them in government. Does this mean people are not interested in politics? No, it illustrates the emphasis mainstream medicine places on knowing your cholesterol level. Why are cholesterol levels so important? Cardiovascular disease, especially atherosclerosis, has been associated with elevated levels of cholesterol; usually, the more elevated, the greater the risk of disease. Elevated cholesterol levels (*hypercholesterolemia*) are not commonly associated with concrete symptoms and are most often discovered by a blood test. Therefore, mainstream medicine believes it is in every person's best interest to have their cholesterol level checked periodically. Is this wise and does it make sense? The answer requires understanding the basics of cholesterol.

Cholesterol is a waxlike substance manufactured within the liver. In contrast to the doom and gloom touted by mainstream physicians, cholesterol is vital for our good health; it is an essential component of our cell membranes, it is used to manufacture numerous hormones, and it is a free radical scavenger. You need cholesterol within your body and would die without it. Nevertheless, there are two extremes. With too little cholesterol, you cannot maintain your health, and excesses are associated with cardiovascular illness. Therefore, the goal is to have a cholesterol level somewhere in between—a level providing enough cholesterol but not too much.

Cholesterol enables the membranes of healthy cells to have integrity and *fluidity*; lipids, proteins, minerals, and more enter and exit appropriately. In addition, cholesterol is a free radical scavenger; it can neutralize free radicals. Although this is a vast subject with intricate details, there are some basic points to understand.

Free radicals (unstable atoms or molecules) that contact the cell membrane can bind and crosslink cholesterol molecules as well as damage them, decreasing membrane integrity and fluidity. As less oxygen enters a cell, energy production by its mitochondria decreases, and being deprived of oxygen, more free radicals are released, creating a vicious cycle. Insults and damage to the cell wall decrease its ability to transport substances in and out of the cell. So, *excesses of free radicals promote cellular damage and death.*

Cholesterol also functions as a free radical scavenger within the blood. After being produced, cholesterol enters the blood and binds with *lipoproteins*. Cholesterol molecules that encounter a free radical and are oxidized selectively bind to *low-density lipoproteins*, forming *LDL cholesterol*, called "bad" cholesterol because it is toxic to blood vessel walls in various ways. In contrast, unoxidized cholesterol preferentially binds to *high-density lipoproteins*, forming *HDL cholesterol*, referred to as "good" cholesterol. Simply put, LDL cholesterol can deposit on the artery walls, while HDL cholesterol scours the walls, freeing the adherent cholesterol so it can return to the liver. When all is in balance, cholesterol is deposited and removed with no buildup. Yet, if there is too much LDL cholesterol or too little HDL cholesterol, deposits on the artery wall can accumulate, leading to atherosclerosis.

Mainstream medicine believes that LDL cholesterol excesses are associated with a high-fat diet, lack of aerobic exercise, and a genetic predisposition to have elevated cholesterol levels. If you have an elevated total cholesterol level, most mainstream physicians initially recommend diet and lifestyle changes—usually, decreasing dietary fat and getting regular aerobic exercise. If your level does not notably improve, your physician might prescribe a cholesterol-lowering medication. The downside is, in addition to its cost, you must take it forever because its effect is not permanent. In some people with hypercholesterolemia, these drugs barely work at all. In any case, something important is being missed. Since cholesterol-lowering drugs do not permanently correct elevated levels, it implies that there is a chronic, underlying problem not being addressed. In other words, elevated cholesterol levels are a *symptom* of a deeper problem. To make this clear, there are a few more important points about cholesterol to consider.

Cholesterol is manufactured within the liver and is the product (*metabolite*) of the *metabolic pathway* producing it. Decreased amounts within the blood means the liver is underproducing or it is being consumed-eliminated at an increased rate. In contrast, excesses imply overproduction, or it is not used-cleared appropriately. Production usually depends on the difference between the concentrations of its precursors and final form; the greater the amounts of *fatty acids* and *triglycerides* present, the stronger the push toward production, whereas their scarcity impedes production. Typically, there is a balance between the *supply* of precursors and the body's *demand* for cholesterol, called a *steady state*. If demand increases, the metabolic pathway is stimulated to produce more, and when demand decreases, its pathway is slowed down. When all is well, someone's steady state involves a healthy balance between the amount of cholesterol needed and the amount produced, with demand equaling supply.

Since cholesterol is manufactured from fatty acids and triglycerides, dietary excesses are thought to increase production, causing hypercholesterolemia. This is how mainstream medicine approaches elevated cholesterol levels, especially levels of LDL cholesterol. Except for people with the genetic tendency to overproduce cholesterol (*familial hypercholesterolemia*), excesses of dietary precursors are thought to be the problem, which is why dietary changes are recommended. Yet, this perspective does not always work in reverse or apply to everyone because decreasing the intake of dietary fatty acids and triglycerides does not correct all cases of hypercholesterolemia, and consuming excess dietary fat does not always cause elevated unhealthy cholesterol levels. Mainstream physicians also believe increasing HDL cholesterol levels helps prevent atherosclerosis and cardiovascular disease. Since aerobic exercise can raise HDL cholesterol levels, it is included as part of cholesterol management. Once again, there is a problem with this thinking because its benefits do not apply to everyone.

If diet and a lack of aerobic exercise caused hypercholesterolemia, dietary changes and aerobic exercise should decrease and correct elevated cholesterol levels in virtually everyone, but this is not the case; most people who reduce their dietary fat have modest LDL cholesterol level benefits, and aerobic exercise often produces only modest increases in HDL cholesterol levels. Although many people improve, like taking cholesterol-lowering drugs, they need to continue a low-fat diet and aerobic exercise for the rest of their life, or their LDL cholesterol level is almost certain to elevate. Since diet and exercise do not permanently correct the problem, there must be a chronic, underlying issue that is not being addressed in people with hypercholesteremia.

It is important to appreciate that the body functions in the most efficient way possible. It does not deviate from normal or shift its metabolic processes for no reason or without a cause. So, elevated LDL cholesterol levels must occur for a reason. Since cholesterol is a vital component of every cell membrane, elevated levels imply there is an increased demand to repair damaged membranes or manufacture new cells. What promotes cellular damage or the need for more cells? There are several possibilities, but the most likely cause is a chronic infection and/or persistent inflammation. These conditions trigger certain immune cells to send a chemical signal to the liver; however, the extra cholesterol needed is often less than the strength of the signal sent (the immune cells overreact) and the liver produces excesses that enter the blood. If elevated cholesterol results from a chronic infection and/or persistent inflammation, it is a *symptom* rather than a disease or illness. How might this occur?

Although its primary purpose involves metabolism, the liver has another role. Under certain conditions, it participates in immunity with its *acute phase response*. During an infection or inflammation, the liver decreases its synthesis of *albumin* (a protein) and produces-releases large amounts of *acute phase proteins* that are involved in *nonspecific host defense* (a generalized form of immunity, not specifically directed). This is supposed to be a short-term, beneficial assist for the immune system to combat illness. However, any chronic infection (especially chronic candidiasis) prolongs its acute phase response, creating numerous undesirable consequences. The presence of chronic candidiasis promotes the production of (at least) two chemical cellular messengers (*tumor necrosis factor* and *interleukin 1*) that inhibit the production of *lipoprotein lipase*. This enzyme enables fat and muscle cells to use triglycerides, so decreased amounts raise serum triglyceride levels, causing *hypertriglyceridemia*. This usually triggers increased LDL cholesterol levels, causing hypercholesterolemia. Furthermore, lowered HDL cholesterol levels can also result. *Apoprotein CII* is a lipoprotein lipase cofactor that is recycled from circulating HDL. As lipoprotein lipase levels decrease, less apoprotein CII is needed, so HDL production decreases. Simply put, the presence of *chronic candidiasis can cause increased LDL cholesterol levels and lowered HDL cholesterol levels*.

In addition, *insulin* (the major blood sugar–lowering hormone) is required to maintain normal lipoprotein lipase levels. To raise lowered levels, more insulin may be released and *hyperinsulinism* can occur, precipitating or worsening *glucose intolerance* (chapter 11). Insulin excesses or its prolonged presence promotes free radical damage and cellular chemical injuries that increase the body's demand for cholesterol.

Let us return to cholesterol acting as a free radical scavenger within the blood. Free radicals are atoms or molecules with one or more unpaired electrons in its outer shell. Within the body, biological free radicals can undesirably react with various substrates, including lipids, proteins, and

DNA. In contrast, antioxidants are substances that neutralize free radicals; they can be made within the body or supplied by foods, beverages, and nutritional supplements. *When all is well, free radicals are neutralized and cause no harm.*

During an infection or inflammation, free radical production can increase and become excessive, overwhelming the antioxidant defenses. As their amounts escalate, free radicals and oxidants cause *oxidative stress.* Oxygen molecules (O_2) that split apart participate in the oxidative stress and cellular damage. Since blood carries oxygen from the lungs to the cells, numerous studies reveal that oxidative stress participates in cardiovascular disease. Cholesterol molecules that scavenge free radicals become oxidized, creating *oxysterols;* they cannot be incorporated into cell membranes and cause numerous adverse effects, including reducing cell proliferation, inducing cell differentiation, modulating gene expression, binding with proteins, and much more. This would explain why the liver produces excesses of cholesterol when the demand is not as great as the amount produced. In other words, the injured or damaged cells never receive the amount of cholesterol they need to make repairs, so they continue sending their signal to make more. Yet, in the presence of an infection or inflammation, especially chronic candidiasis, the cholesterol is oxidized before it can reach the cell, and since the cell is still sending its signals for more, LDL cholesterol levels in the blood can elevate.

Although many mainstream physicians rarely appreciate how free radicals contribute to unhealthy cholesterol levels, they often recommend taking *antioxidants,* substances that inhibit oxidation, like vitamin E, vitamin C, and more. For example, studies show that low blood levels of vitamin E are statistically 100 times more significant as a predictor of coronary heart disease than elevated LDL cholesterol levels within the blood. Moreover, the long-term benefits of vitamin E seem to be cumulative because some studies reveal the greatest benefit occurs when it is consumed daily for at least 30 years.

Although diet and lack of aerobic exercise can contribute to unhealthy cholesterol levels, free radical damage seems to be the bigger problem. An acute infection and its short-term free radical damage might have adverse effects, but after the infection resolves, the body returns to its steady state. In contrast, chronic infections and their inflammation create persistent disturbances. So, chronic candidiasis with or without the help of other harmful infectious invaders is a more significant problem to consider in people with unhealthy cholesterol levels. Chronic candidiasis is both an *infectious* and *allergic* illness. *Gastrointestinal candidiasis* with leaky gut syndrome enables undesirable substances to enter the blood, promoting free radical oxygenation. Moreover, dark-field microscopy reveals that many chronic candidiasis sufferers have disease-causing yeast *living within their blood*, directly escalating the number of free radicals produced within their arteries and veins. Equally concerning, chronic candidiasis can cause sensitivities and hypersensitivities (allergies) that further increase the amount of free radical damage. Once chronic candidiasis is established, it can become a vicious cycle because research reveals that *Candida*-species organisms grow better in lipid-rich environments. Since elevated total cholesterol levels can sustain chronic candidiasis, it helps explain why both conditions are related.

Over time, as these disturbances continue, the immune system becomes impaired. *Metabolic immunosuppression* (chapter 14) details how chronic candidiasis sufferers often develop *glucose intolerance*, *hyperinsulinism*, *hyperlipidemia* (hypercholesterolemia and/or hypertriglyceridemia), and *impaired immunity*. It reveals why unhealthy cholesterol levels should be considered a *symptom* of chronic candidiasis. In fact, many candidiasis sufferers experience great improvements in their unhealthy cholesterol levels after receiving anti-candidiasis therapy. However, to be complete, the contributions of other factors also need to be considered and addressed, including infectious invaders, the adverse effects of toxic heavy metals, endocrine-disrupting plastics, and much more. This viewpoint differs significantly from mainstream medical thinking. Regardless, profoundly elevated cholesterol levels often fall precipitously when candidiasis is appropriately addressed and eliminated.

Wait, how do low-fat diets decrease total cholesterol levels and prevent cardiovascular problems? The most notable diet is probably the Pritikin Diet, a diet low in fats, cholesterol, and protein. The fact that it works would seem to refute the connection between disease-causing yeast and cardiovascular illness, would it not? No, because there is a catch. Even though complex carbohydrates and fruit are permitted, all refined sugars and grains are completely *forbidden*. This appears to be the crux of this diet's success. Moreover, foods are supposed to be eaten raw or minimally cooked, the closer to their natural state the better. An additional aspect of the program involves regular exercise, which is always recommended. So, the benefits appear to follow the elimination of refined sugar/grains rather than fat, which keeps a person's insulin levels from becoming excessively high or low, while effectively starving their disease-causing yeast. By the way, not only is the diet somewhat difficult to follow, but it does not work for everyone, especially those with more chronic or severe forms of candidiasis.

The conclusion is simple: there is a *candidiasis-hypercholesterolemia connection*. A persistent infection with disease-causing yeast, as well as its accompanying inflammation, can stimulate the liver to overproduce cholesterol. This increases LDL cholesterol and can also decrease HDL cholesterol. Although dietary changes and exercise are recommended, eliminating chronic candidiasis is the key to permanent results and achieving true wellness. In addition, the presence of many other long-term infectious invaders can contribute to stimulating the liver's acute phase response and be involved in this process, either directly or indirectly, including harmful molds, bacteria, parasites, and/or viruses. Improvements may not occur until all the culprits are appropriately addressed and eliminated, resolving the continuous acute phase response that occurs for as long as any chronic infection or inflammation is present within the body.

ATHEROSCLEROSIS

Atherosclerosis, sometimes called "hardening of the arteries," affects people of all ages. It occurs when *plaque*, deposits of *lipid* (cholesterol and lipoproteins), accumulates on the inner surface of a blood vessel wall. As its interior (lumen) is slowly narrowed, its rate of blood flow decreases, which can continue until the blood vessel is functionally compromised or blocked. Impaired blood flow decreases the delivery of oxygen and vital nutrients to the cells and tissues, as well as compromises their ability to eliminate wastes. When the flow rate is severely limited or suddenly stopped, the cells and tissues supplied effectively "starve" and can die (infarct). Atherosclerosis within a prominent or vital blood vessel will cause more undesirable consequences than when it occurs within an insignificant blood vessel.

In most people, the accumulation of plaque is a slow and insidious process, taking years to decades to promote problems. Since small insults can progress to significant injury, atherosclerosis is responsible for a large percentage of disability and deaths. Symptoms like chest pain, headaches, intermittent pain in a leg, and more may accompany the narrowing of blood vessels within certain areas of the body. It might seem absurd to state, but if you have symptoms related to cardiovascular disease and go to a doctor to address the problem, you are lucky because atherosclerosis is frequently a silent killer; in fact, many cases arise suddenly and without warning, often occurring as a fatal heart attack or stroke.

Is candidiasis associated with atherosclerosis? Can disease-causing *Candida*-species organisms contribute to or cause heart attacks, strokes, peripheral vascular disease, and more? Does candidiasis have anything to do with the presence of plaque? The answer to all these questions is yes. There is a *candidiasis-atherosclerosis connection.*

The prior section supported a *candidiasis-hypercholesterolemia connection.* A chronic infection with disease-causing yeast, including its inflammation, stimulates the liver's acute phase response, promoting the overproduction of cholesterol. In addition to increasing LDL cholesterol, a prolonged acute phase response promotes a decrease in HDL cholesterol. How does this cause atherosclerosis? LDL cholesterol is deposited on the inner walls of arteries, while HDL scours the walls, enabling adherent cholesterol to return to the liver. When all is well, cholesterol is deposited and removed equally with no accumulation. Yet, if there are excesses of LDL cholesterol or too little HDL cholesterol, plaque can build up, causing atherosclerosis. Since chronic candidiasis promotes increases in LDL cholesterol and decreases in HDL cholesterol, this alone supports a *candidiasis-atherosclerosis connection.* Yet, there is much more to be understood before this case can be considered closed.

It is important to note that an elevated LDL cholesterol level, by itself, does not guarantee atherosclerosis. If your HDL cholesterol level increases in proportion to your LDL cholesterol level, and you have a healthy *ratio* between them, you may be no worse off than someone with normal cholesterol levels. Even with a markedly elevated LDL cholesterol level and a decreased HDL cholesterol level, there is also no guarantee atherosclerosis will develop. Wait, if an elevated total cholesterol level always precipitates atherosclerosis, why do some people develop atherosclerosis without having unhealthy levels? Yes, elevated total cholesterol levels are associated with atherosclerosis, but they do *not* guarantee that it develops within everyone. Does this negate the connection between hypercholesterolemia and atherosclerosis? No, it means in addition to unhealthy cholesterol levels, something else must contribute to atherosclerosis. What is the missing "piece" of the "atherosclerosis puzzle"?

If you ever made scrambled eggs in a good-quality, nonstick pan, you are aware the eggs only begin to stick to the pan after it is scraped or loses its coating. Similarly, LDL cholesterol has a notorious proclivity for adhering to the linings of injured or damaged arteries. In short, *injury* or *damage* to the blood vessel walls allows LDL cholesterol to deposit, accumulate, and form the plaque that creates atherosclerosis. With mild injury or damage, increased levels of LDL cholesterol are needed to promote plaque buildup. In contrast, with significant injury or damage, even normal LDL cholesterol levels can lead to atherosclerosis. In most people with atherosclerosis, both processes occur simultaneously. Therefore, *unhealthy cholesterol levels* and *damage to the blood vessel wall* are both required for the accumulation of plaque. What process is responsible for injuring or damaging the linings of blood vessels?

The most obvious way blood vessels are injured or damaged is by trauma. Overt injuries range from seemingly inconsequential to permanent disruption or debilitation. Acute traumatic episodes can precipitate undesirable cardiovascular complications (like a stroke or heart attack); if someone has fragile/weak blood vessels, a sudden insult can cause them to rupture. Yet, overt injury is not considered part of the atherosclerosis disease process. Instead, it characteristically encompasses *covert* injury or damage to the blood vessel linings that slowly accumulates over years to decades. The process responsible for this injury and damage has not been universally realized and much less accepted. Rather than being easily visualized, the injury and damage accompanying atherosclerosis reflects a process occurring on a *chemical* level, involving harmful oxygen-based free radicals. Although they were discussed in the previous section, it is important to understand how they damage the inner wall of arteries.

After two *oxygen* atoms join, they form O_2, which is a life-sustaining, chemically unreactive substance; the joined oxygen atoms have no free electrical charge, making them stable and unable to cause problems. However, when oxygen molecules lose an electron or split into individual atoms, they become charged particles that are reactive chemical entities called *oxygen-based free radicals*; their harmful chemical activities injure and damage cells and tissues. When this process occurs within blood vessels, the insults to the vessel walls allow LDL cholesterol to be deposited and plaque to accumulate, leading to narrowing and/or weakness in one or more areas. Since oxygen is vital for our existence, the generation of oxygen-based free radicals within our bodies is unavoidable. Fortunately, when you are in good health, in addition to the amounts of antioxidants within the food and beverages you ingest, your body generates antioxidants that neutralize your oxygen-based free radicals.

Unfortunately, adverse conditions can increase the production of oxygen-based free radicals beyond your body's ability to neutralize them. Although their harm is on a chemical level (magnitudes below the microscopic level), their insults are additive, leading to significant problems and disturbances over time. Like smoldering embers that spread and instigate a huge fire, excesses of oxygen-based free radicals initiate chemical reactions that inflict injury and damage within a diversity of cells and tissues. Under these circumstances, the body's free radical defenses become ineffective. Yet, this is far from hopeless because, if it is functioning properly, the immune system is signaled to assist in fighting and eliminating excess free radicals. How does this occur?

Once the immune system perceives that excess free radical activity is a threat, it becomes hyperactive and puts out these chemical "fires" as fast as its cells are able, a type of defense that can be effective for short-term insults. Yet, in the presence of chronic or persistent excesses of free radical activity the immune system can become stressed and impaired. In return, adverse conditions that hinder immunity decrease the body's ability to neutralize excesses of oxygen-based free radicals. Therefore, *impaired immunity* encourages atherosclerosis and cardiovascular disease. So, we now have a third contributor to atherosclerosis. In addition to elevated cholesterol levels and damage to the linings of blood vessels, impaired immunity can promote atherosclerosis by its inability to completely combat the free radical activity that injures and damages the linings of blood vessels.

Furthermore, plaque can harden, decreasing the elasticity of blood vessels, which is why atherosclerosis is sometimes called "hardening of the arteries." What causes plaque to harden? Although lipid deposits contribute to the accumulation of plaque, these cholesterol-laden masses are not completely rigid. For plaque to harden, the mineral *calcium* must be incorporated, which solidifies it like cement; other substances can contribute, but calcium is primarily responsible. How does this happen?

In addition to being an ingredient of bones and teeth, calcium ions circulate within the blood (in a dissolved state). When everything is in balance, all remains well. However, if there is illness, infection, or inflammation, certain forms of calcium can precipitate out of solution (the dissolved forms transform) and can be incorporated into plaque. As a result, a part of the blood vessel wall, the *basement membrane*, may thicken, decreasing the vessel's elasticity and its ability to filter beneficial substances through it and eliminate wastes. As the blood vessels lose their elasticity, the heart must work harder to push the same volume of blood through them, and the blood pressure will increase proportionately. Clearly, atherosclerosis is a risk factor for a variety of cardiovascular problems, general ill health, and much more than just a consequence of consuming too much fat.

If you enter "free radicals" in the search bar of the National Library of Medicine, the results will include more than 368,000 publications (as of January 2023). The research reveals that excesses of oxygen-based free radicals can be generated during times of *infection*, *inflammation*, and *stress*—conditions that adversely alter or place increased demands on the body's chemistry and its chemical functioning. There are also other equally significant reasons that are often overlooked. Sometimes, in the pursuit of knowledge, dissecting the parts into ever smaller pieces and looking at them too closely puts the "big picture" out of focus. This is what has happened with cardiovascular disease as well as a multitude of other medical maladies. To sort this out, consider the risk factors that promote cardiovascular disease: The *major* risk factors include age, being male, hypertension, cigarette smoking and exposure to tobacco smoke, plasma levels of LDL ("bad") and HDL ("good") cholesterol, and diabetes. The less prominent risk factors are obesity, lack of exercise, personality type, and stress. To set the record straight, instead of considering each risk factor separately, they will be combined to find the common thread linking them all.

When objectively analyzed, all the cardiovascular disease *risk factors* involve *metabolic abnormalities* (chemical disturbances) that directly or indirectly promote excesses of harmful oxygen-based free radicals. This includes a diversity of problems, from hormone imbalances to exposures to toxic substances. Anything that upsets the body's chemistry and functioning creates conditions that increase free radical activity. Each risk factor can adversely alter the body's chemistry or functioning in some way; the magnitude determines whether a risk factor is major or minor. Although these are the obvious contributors to cardiovascular illness, there is a more significant, much less appreciated metabolic disturbance contributing to most of the risk factors, if not all. In short, most of the risk factors are directly or indirectly associated with *blood sugar disturbances*.

Since any chemical imbalance within the blood can adversely affect its vessel linings, blood sugar disturbances are associated with atherosclerosis. In fact, the inability to properly metabolize glucose is a strong risk factor for cardiovascular illness. The most well-known blood sugar disturbance is diabetes (chapter 11); due to an absence or insensitivity to *insulin*, the hormone that allows glucose to exit the blood and enter cells/tissues, normal concentrations of blood sugar cannot be maintained. Unless they are meticulously managed, people with diabetes experience abnormally elevated blood glucose concentrations. Since diabetes is strongly associated with cardiovascular illness, most sufferers eventually develop and succumb to cardiovascular complications, regardless of whether it involves their small (microvascular) or large (macrovascular) blood vessels. If the main diabetes defect is an inability to maintain a normal blood sugar concentration and its primary sequalae is cardiovascular disease, it seems that atherosclerosis is closely related to blood sugar disturbances and *glucose intolerance.*

Although diabetes is the most obvious manifestation of glucose intolerance, it is not the only expression, nor the most common. Another type may exist in as much as two-thirds of the population. *Reactive hypoglycemia* involves abnormal glucose metabolism (chapter 11), a condition in which a person's fasting blood sugar concentration is normal, but their ability to chemically process glucose is abnormal. Usually, after ingesting glucose, their blood sugar concentration increases much greater than normal and then decreases significantly below its fasting level. As a result, people with reactive hypoglycemia experience frequent blood sugar "highs" and "lows" with symptoms that reflect their blood sugar levels. Since its symptoms are diverse and none are 100 percent reliable, reactive hypoglycemia is often missed or not suspected. Yet, it is a legitimate condition that can be verified by a *five-hour glucose tolerance test*; the patient swallows an amount of glucose, and their blood sugar concentration is measured at regular intervals, revealing their metabolic response to glucose. What happens on a chemical level? After ingesting glucose, insulin release is delayed, allowing the blood sugar concentration to increase above normal. Insulin is eventually released, but it is either excessive and/or it persists too long. Increased amounts of insulin within the blood, *hyperinsulinism*, precipitates excessive and/or prolonged decreases in the blood glucose concentration. In response, other hormones are released to assist in raising blood glucose to its normal fasting concentration. Since reactive hypoglycemia is a form of glucose intolerance that is rarely revealed, as much as two-thirds of the population is, unknowingly, at risk for atherosclerosis.

It is important to appreciate that insulin is not an innocent participant in this process. Its inappropriate release promotes glucose intolerance. Regardless of whether too little or excesses are released, when and for how long, glucose metabolism is adversely affected. In fact, research reveals that hyperinsulinism is associated with an increased risk of cardiovascular (coronary heart) disease, especially when someone has an elevated fasting insulin level. Since insulin can stimulate fat (lipid) production within arterial cells/tissue and induce arterial smooth muscle cells to grow and proliferate, it can contribute to the accumulation of plaque as well as thickening and narrowing of the arterial wall. Other research reveals that hyperinsulinemia is associated with hypertriglyceridemia (excess triglycerides), with or without lowered HDL cholesterol levels; both lipid disturbances are risk factors for cardiovascular problems. Moreover, many researchers believe that excess amounts or the prolonged presence of insulin is associated with an increased generation of oxygen-based free radicals.

So, hyperinsulinism adversely contributes its harm in two ways; it causes glucose intolerance and promotes free radical activity that injures or damages the linings of blood vessels. Usually, this is a slow process that occurs over years to decades. In contrast, what happens when there is too little insulin—for example, in insulin-dependent diabetes? When too little insulin is released or the body's cells are insensitive to its presence, the blood sugar concentration can increase markedly above normal. In return, excess blood glucose allows more water to remain within the blood vessels, raising blood pressure and stressing the vessel linings. Furthermore, like excesses, an absence of insulin can also injure or damage the blood vessel linings (over time). Therefore, an excess or absence of insulin are both risk factors for cardiovascular complications.

Most blood sugar disturbances involve the overproduction or prolonged release of insulin. Since it is released in response to excess glucose within the blood, high-carbohydrate meals can promote hyperinsulinism, regardless of whether the carbohydrates are simple (like sugar) or complex (like rice). So, ingesting excess carbohydrates can promote cardiovascular disease. In contrast to fat, a high-carbohydrate diet is more likely to contribute to atherosclerosis. This point may be controversial, but it is accurate, nonetheless.

The pieces of the atherosclerosis puzzle can now be combined. Ingesting an abundance of carbohydrates increases the blood sugar concentration, encouraging the overproduction or prolonged release of insulin. During glucose metabolism, there is a limit to how much glucose can be stored, as *glycogen*. If more glucose must be stored, it is chemically changed into fatty acids and triglycerides, elevating total cholesterol and triglyceride levels (hyperlipidemia). Moreover, hyperinsulinism can increase the generation of harmful oxygen-based free radicals, leading to injury and damage of the blood vessel linings. These circumstances encourage the formation of plaque, which can incorporate calcium and harden. Although atherosclerosis is a complicated process, hopefully, it can now be more easily understood.

Instead of just dietary fat, there are many contributors to the atherosclerosis process, including glucose intolerance, hyperinsulinism, hyperlipidemia (hypercholesterolemia, hypertriglyceridemia), and impaired immunity. We have a process, but we do not yet have an identifiable cause.

This assortment of metabolic and immune system disturbances does not arise for no reason. Something must cause or contribute to these disturbances. If you understand that excesses of harmful oxygen-based free radicals are generated during times of infection, inflammation, and stress, the answer is clear. Candidiasis is an *infection* with *allergic* consequences that usually involves abundant *inflammation*. Yes, chronic candidiasis can instigate and aggravate all these metabolic disturbances and impair the immune system's ability to combat excesses of free radicals. *Metabolic immunosuppression* (chapter 14) explains why candidiasis sufferers often develop *glucose intolerance, hyperinsulinism, hyperlipidemia* (hypercholesterolemia, hypertriglyceridemia), and *suppressed immunity* (inferior functioning cells), *depressed immunity* (fewer cells), or *suppressed-depressed immunity* (fewer, inferior functioning cells). Since chronic candidiasis can promote the metabolic and immune system disturbances that appear to contribute to atherosclerosis, it now seems clear that there is an irrefutable *candidiasis-atherosclerosis connection*.

It is important to summarize these points: The prevalence and severity of cardiovascular disease is related to consuming excess simple carbohydrates, especially sugar; in fact, many people with blood sugar disturbances develop some type of cardiovascular problem, notably diabetes sufferers. Yet, most blood sugar disturbances are primarily or secondarily related to the adverse effects of chronic candidiasis. In addition to their direct effects, carbohydrates are fuel for disease-causing yeast, promoting their growth and colonization. Since most hyperlipidemia (hypercholesterolemia, hypertriglyceridemia) significantly improves when candidiasis is treated and eliminated, or even when carbohydrate consumption is markedly reduced, it implicates disease-causing yeast in causing cholesterol disturbances. Moreover, chronic candidiasis can impair immunity, allowing free radical damage to escalate. Therefore, candidiasis appears to be a strong promoter of atherosclerosis, and the more severe the infection and length of time it is present, the more likely this becomes.

Admittedly, the *candidiasis-atherosclerosis connection* does not hold true 100 percent of the time, but it does apply to most people who develop atherosclerosis. (The exceptions involve people with *familial hypercholesterolemia*, an inherited tendency to develop significantly elevated cholesterol levels, increasing their risk of cardiovascular complications.) Yes, chronic candidiasis readily contributes to cardiovascular illness in numerous ways. Once you appreciate this process in general, the specifics become more compelling.

As a condition, candidiasis involves the colonization of disease-causing *Candida*-species organisms within the gastrointestinal tract as well as other tissues. Disease-causing yeast are infectious invaders that produce numerous metabolites, wastes, and toxins that can be absorbed within the gut and then enter the tissues and blood. Some of these substances can directly injure/damage the blood vessel linings and wall. These substances remain within the blood until they are deactivated by the liver, eliminated by the kidneys, or move into one or more tissues or organs. If the liver and/or kidneys are congested or injured, the elimination of yeast-produced substances is impaired, allowing them to accumulate within the blood, as well as within the organs, tissues, and cells, and increase their harm. Since the liver and kidneys are not immune to the adverse effects of these harmful substances, they are likely to suffer, which creates a vicious cycle that promotes additional disturbances and compromise.

What are these mysterious, yeast-related "substances" and how can they contribute to cardiovascular disease? *Candida albicans* and other disease-causing yeast are known to manufacture numerous harmful byproducts that can adversely affect the cardiovascular system in various ways. Most notably, these include an *adrenaline-like substance* that can increase heart rate, an *angiotensin-like substance* thought to lower blood pressure, *insulin-like substances* that promote decreases in the blood sugar concentration, and a harmful substance, *gliotoxin*, that produces damaging free radicals, suppresses immunity, injures the liver enzyme that degrades alcohol (alcohol dehydrogenase), and adversely alters the brain's cells and their chemistry (chapter 10).

Moreover, Japanese research from June 1967 through April 1978 proved that a strain of *Candida albicans* produced a harmful toxin, called *canditoxin*. This work was never followed up and only scant information is known about its harmful effects. In addition, disease-causing yeast readily ferment sugars and carbohydrates into *ethanol* and *acetaldehyde*, which can be absorbed into the blood and then enter the organs, tissues, and cells, where they exert their toxic effects. Any or all these substances can upset a candidiasis sufferer's metabolism and cardiovascular functioning.

Optimally, these harmful substances are deactivated by the liver and/or filtered out of the blood by the kidneys and eliminated. Yet, when an infection with disease-causing yeast is present for a long time, this is not usually the case. With lengthy infections, especially chronic candidiasis, the liver decreases its metabolic functions to assist the immune system in fighting the disease-causing yeast. During its acute phase response, the liver manufactures numerous proteins that support the immune system's ongoing fight. As a result, the liver participates in both metabolic and immune system activities. Over time, this compromises the liver's functioning; with chronic candidiasis, *both* metabolism and immunity eventually suffer (chapter 14). As the liver's detoxification duties become impaired, harmful yeast-related substances can accumulate within the blood, organs, tissues, and cells, instigating a cascade of harmful oxygen-based free radical activity and other toxic effects. If it progresses, the liver will be unable to manufacture a significant amount of acute phase proteins, and immunity falters. Once again, this creates a vicious cycle that encourages further disturbances.

Remember, chronic candidiasis is not a black-or-white condition; it contributes to cardiovascular illness in various ways, including through disturbances in the endocrine system (chapter 11), immune system (chapter 14), and nervous system (chapter 10). It also encourages malabsorption and nutritional deficiencies that compromise cardiovascular functioning.

So far, the harm does not require disease-causing yeast to be anywhere other than within the gastrointestinal tract. Yet, if they invade into the gut wall, enter the tissues, and access the blood, their adverse effects increase. They can survive within the blood by consuming glucose and other nutrients. In return, they produce metabolites, wastes, and toxins that directly exert their harmful effects. Various researchers support the *candidiasis-atherosclerosis connection*. It is important to summarize their findings. Disease-causing yeast, especially *Candida albicans*, can adhere to blood vessel linings. Contracted or damaged linings with exposed extracellular matrix proteins greatly increase adherence. In the presence of platelets, *Candida albicans* markedly increases its adherence. It can also adhere to aggregated platelets. Its ability to adhere is dependent on the presence of calcium. The release of prostacyclin by endothelial cells can prevent this. Unfortunately, the presence of *Candida albicans* can inhibit prostacyclin release. Moreover, their cell wall components within the blood can trigger free radical reactions that induce microvascular disease. The conclusion is, undeniably, *Candida albicans* within the blood can promote cardiovascular disease.

Can disease-causing yeast really get into the blood and do this? Yes, in fact, when blood samples are taken from candidiasis sufferers and examined by dark-field microscopy, disease-causing yeast are frequently identified; typically, the amount correlates with the severity of their condition. This is much more common than you might realize. Since most candidiasis sufferers have immune systems that keep their infection from escalating, as beneficial as this is, it also prevents their condition from being detected.

What about researchers who claim that, instead of disease-causing yeast, harmful molds are responsible for atherosclerosis? Admittedly, harmful molds are fungi. As such, they also have 1,3-beta-D-glucan within their cell walls, so their presence can trigger microangiopathy. Moreover, numerous harmful molds produce toxins (*mycotoxins*) capable of injuring-damaging the cardiovascular system. Yet, without chronic candidiasis and its leaky gut syndrome (chapter 4), harmful molds are unlikely to enter the tissues or blood; researchers have discovered that patients with *noninvasive* fungal infections had low levels of 1,3-beta-D-glucan within their blood. The same can be said for mycotoxins. So, in most people, chronic candidiasis seems to be the cause and promoter of atherosclerosis. If harmful molds play a role, their presence is frequently secondary.

What about other infectious invaders? Research implicates the mischief of *Chlamydia pneumonia* because it has been found within atherosclerotic plaques. Although classified as bacteria, this infectious invader primarily lives within cells. Most people are exposed to it, but not everyone succumbs, implying that immunity is essential, and impaired immunity allows it to cause mischief. Since chronic candidiasis can impair immunity (chapter 14), *Chlamydia pneumonia* is not likely to be the primary atherosclerosis troublemaker. Moreover, without leaky gut syndrome or the increased respiratory permeability (chapter 6) that accompanies chronic candidiasis, this infectious invader is unlikely to enter the blood in the first place. The same can be said for most other infectious invaders.

To be complete, there is another way disease-causing yeast contribute to cardiovascular illness. Since they are highly antigenic infectious invaders, their presence induces allergies to themselves and other substances. During chronic candidiasis, many sufferers manufacture various anti-yeast antibodies; these proteins target disease-causing yeast, identifying them for attack by certain immune cells, although there are exceptions (chapters 3 and 17).

In any case, the presence of yeast-antigen alone or yeast-antigen that forms an immune complex with its anti-yeast antibody can trigger the generation of harmful oxygen-based free radical activity within the cardiovascular system as well as within any organs, tissues, or cells they enter; this is certain to encourage impairment, injury, and even destruction. Far from obvious, this effect slowly accumulates over months to years, or even decades. Even though it is a slow process, it must not be ignored. So, allergies may promote cardiovascular disease in some people.

Wait, what about excesses of the amino acid homocysteine and cardiovascular disease? In 2007, Kilmer McCully, M.D., claimed that the accumulation of homocysteine damages cells, contributing to cardiovascular disease as well as to premature aging. Homocysteine is metabolized within the liver through the *methyltetrahydrofolate cycle*, so it accumulates if there is a decrease in any of the enzymes that convert it to other forms. Since folate (folic acid), vitamin B6, and vitamin B12 are cofactors in this process, as well as other nutrients, deficiencies promote increases in homocysteine. Like elevated cholesterol levels, homocysteine cannot accumulate for no reason. Once again, the answer is chronic candidiasis and a prolonged acute phase response that decreases the liver's metabolic activities; over time, it decreases its ability to convert homocysteine into its other forms. In addition, *gastrointestinal candidiasis* encourages malabsorption, producing nutritional deficiencies that are associated with increased levels of homocysteine. So, homocysteine itself is unlikely to cause cardiovascular damage by promoting the generation of excess free radicals. Instead, it is more likely to reflect an abnormal metabolism. What is causing this? Once again, chronic candidiasis appears directly or indirectly responsible for atherosclerosis and cardiovascular illness.

Other evidence associates elevated blood uric acid levels and atherosclerosis in minority and elderly patients. Yet, excesses of uric acid do not occur without a cause. Indeed, excess uric acid can also be associated with candidiasis (chapter 9). So, this is further support for a *candidiasis-atherosclerosis connection*.

Researchers found *anti-endothelial antibodies* in some men, implying atherosclerosis may involve autoimmune disease. Other research shows that *antibodies to oxidized low-density lipoproteins* (LDL) relate to the magnitude of atherosclerosis. Different research sheds light on *anti-phospholipid antibodies* and their connection to cardiovascular illness. So, in addition to all the other causes previously presented, it is important to mention that autoimmunity can contribute to cardiovascular illness. Are these coincidental findings? No, because there is a *candidiasis–autoimmune disease connection* (chapter 14). Once again, disease-causing yeast steps into the spotlight.

Unquestionably, if someone has symptoms related to atherosclerosis, it is essential to treat them in order to make them feel more comfortable and prevent deadly consequences. Yet, any intervention aimed only at treating someone's symptoms is unlikely to completely stabilize their condition, much less reverse it. In general, atherosclerosis continues to advance unless its underlying cause is corrected. So, all the infectious invaders that are contributing their ill effects must be treated. Since there is a prominent *candidiasis-atherosclerosis connection*, it is critical to eliminate disease-causing yeast to prevent the advancement of cardiovascular disease, disability, or even death.

BLOOD PRESSURE: HIGHS & LOWS

Simply put, *blood pressure* is the tension created when blood presses against the arterial walls, which can be measured by certain devices. Several factors contribute to blood pressure, including the *contraction* of the heart's ventricles, the *resistance* of the arteriolar and capillary vessels, the *elasticity* of the arterial walls, and the *volume* and *viscosity* of the blood. Blood pressure reflects how efficiently the heart and blood vessels are performing their jobs.

When blood pressure is measured, two numbers are reported. The *systolic* pressure (higher number) is the pressure generated when the heart's ventricles contract, forcing blood into the vessels; this is the maximum pressure exerted within the blood vessels. The *diastolic* pressure (lower number) occurs when the ventricles are relaxed and refilling with blood; this is the lowest pressure exerted within the blood vessels. The *pulse pressure* is the difference between the systolic and diastolic numbers and is important because it characterizes the tone of the arterial walls, their ability to stretch and contract in response to the blood pushed through them. A normal pulse pressure is about 40 points, so over 50 or under 30 is abnormal.

Blood pressure is more complicated than it first seems, ranging from low to normal to high, with pulse pressures that can be small, normal, or large. Yet, most physicians are only concerned when a patient's blood pressure is chronically high or low. As a result, the most notorious blood pressure disturbances are hypertension and hypotension. Is candidiasis a condition that can adversely affect a person's blood pressure? Yes, but an appreciation of how this occurs requires a deeper understanding of what is happening.

Hypertension is an elevated blood pressure. Typically, it is diagnosed when the blood pressure is above 160/95. To detect this condition early and prevent undesirable consequences, some physicians classify 140/90 as mild or borderline hypertension. Why is it important to recognize hypertension early? Since most people cannot feel an elevated blood pressure, this malady is called "the silent killer," remaining undetected until misfortune strikes. Therefore, regular blood pressure checks are essential for early detection and prevention.

In general, blood pressure tends to increase with age and is usually associated with the development and advancement of *atherosclerosis*; hypertension accompanies hardening of the arteries. Moreover, it also involves some gender, race, and environmental differences. Increased body weight is a strong risk factor. Classically, an excessive intake of salt has been highly associated with it, but only a small percentage of people demonstrate significant blood pressure benefits after salt is removed from their diet.

Why do health practitioners consider hypertension a serious and dangerous problem? Since it is rarely felt, they consider it a "silent, ticking time-bomb" waiting to explode and kill its victim. Although it sounds overly dramatic, high blood pressure can cause one or more blood vessels to be suddenly damaged or rupture, and the consequences can be exceedingly unfortunate when it involves vessels supplying the essential organs. Depending on the location, this can cause disturbances ranging from mild to debilitating to fatal; severe episodes can precipitate a heart attack, stroke, or kidney failure, leading to sudden death.

Hardened arteries impair the heart's ability to pump blood. Since there is a *hypertension-atherosclerosis connection*, and a *candidiasis-atherosclerosis connection*, there must also be a *candidiasis-hypertension connection*. In short, chronic candidiasis promotes atherosclerosis, and as the arteries harden, it leads to hypertension. Since it is a potent risk factor for hypertension, eliminating chronic candidiasis is the best way to prevent this malady. This is not about reversing atherosclerosis or controlling hypertension. Rather, it is about its causation.

There is more to this story. Hypertension appears to reflect someone's nutritional status and sugar intake. Usually, it is more prevalent in developed societies. Since a Westernized diet often includes an abundance of sugar and other carbohydrates, hypertension seems related to excessive consumption. So, to avoid atherosclerosis and hypertension, sugar consumption should be reduced and even eliminated. By itself, sugar is not inherently bad. Yet, after being consumed, sugar can adversely affect glucose metabolism (glucose intolerance), which is why blood sugar disturbances are associated with hypertension. As an example, mainstream cardiologists know that people with diabetes, the most exaggerated blood sugar disturbance, are at risk for developing atherosclerosis and high blood pressure. Since an elevated blood sugar concentration (hyperglycemia) is associated with an increased risk of cardiovascular disease, diabetes sufferers readily develop atherosclerosis. Taken further, since atherosclerosis is a strong risk factor for hypertension, it is unsurprising that diabetes sufferers often develop it. So, there seems to be a *glucose intolerance–hypertension connection* and a *candidiasis–glucose intolerance connection* (chapter 11), providing further support for a *candidiasis-hypertension connection*.

What about hypertension sufferers without diabetes? They are likely to have *reactive hypoglycemia*, a type of glucose intolerance that promotes blood sugar "highs" and "lows," following the consumption of sugar and other carbohydrates. When their blood sugar concentration is elevated, more water is retained within their blood (due to osmotic pressure), which increases their blood volume, raising their blood pressure. Later, when their blood sugar concentration is decreasing rapidly or below normal, several hormones are released to raise their blood sugar toward normal. Among these, *adrenaline* can precipitate a rapid heart rate (often palpitations) and increase blood pressure. These people are easily identified because their blood pressure is often normal in the morning before breakfast and increases after meals. A five-hour glucose tolerance test with regular blood pressure measurements can readily confirm this process. Many people with reactive hypoglycemia have a form of high blood pressure, *labile hypertension*, that fluctuates; their blood pressure varies from normal to elevated and may or not involve atherosclerosis. In any case, reactive hypoglycemia is frequently associated with candidiasis, providing further evidence of a *candidiasis-hypertension connection*.

In addition, research reveals that a large percentage of hypertension sufferers have an elevated or prolonged release of *insulin* (hyperinsulinemia). Since as much as 50 percent of hypertension sufferers are found to have glucose intolerance and hyperinsulinism, there seems to be a *hyperinsulinemia-hypertension connection*. In fact, research shows that decreasing the insulin dose given to non-insulin-dependent diabetes patients lowers their blood pressure. Other research demonstrates that non-insulin-dependent diabetes patients have an increase in blood pressure after initially receiving insulin. Different researchers propose various mechanisms, but none fully explains what is occurring. Similarly, research with blood pressure–lowering drugs reveals an inability to significantly decrease hypertension-related debilitation or death, or hyperinsulinemia, implying that the underlying disturbance responsible for hypertension continues even when the blood pressure is controlled with medication. Since hyperinsulinemia is readily associated with candidiasis, all of this adds more support for a *candidiasis-hypertension connection*.

Moreover, another contributor to hypertension is rarely appreciated. Regardless of the type, allergies can cause excess fluid retention within someone's cells and tissues, including their cardiovascular system; it increases blood volume and raises blood pressure. In fact, experience with chronic candidiasis sufferers demonstrates that, in sensitive or hypersensitive people, hypertensive episodes occur after consuming allergy-inducing foods and beverages as well as after exposure to the antigens of disease-causing yeast and harmful molds. In short, this supports an *allergy-hypertension connection*. Since there is a *candidiasis-allergy connection* (chapter 16), this adds evidence to a *candidiasis-hypertension connection*.

The pieces can now be combined. Chronic candidiasis is responsible for *metabolic immunosuppression* (chapter 14), a condition involving glucose intolerance, hyperinsulinemia, hyperlipidemia (hypercholesterolemia and/or hypertriglyceridemia), and impaired immunity. Over time, this can promote atherosclerosis and hypertension. In addition, it can cause numerous chemical and hormone disturbances, making someone's glucose metabolism especially sensitive to their dietary intake of excessive sugars and carbohydrates. It can also instigate a variety of allergies, causing excessive fluid retention, thereby increasing blood pressure. Moreover, an infection with disease-causing yeast may directly alter blood pressure. Research reveals that *Candida albicans* produces an *adrenaline-like substance* that, in large amounts, may increase heart rate and blood pressure. Also, *Candida albicans* can trigger atherosclerosis, leading to narrowed blood vessels, as well as inhibit prostacyclin release, favoring the contraction of blood vessels as mentioned in the last section. In summary, the *candidiasis-atherosclerosis-hypertension connection* is difficult to ignore.

With respect to treating hypertension, most sufferers experience some improvement in their blood pressure after all dietary sugars and many complex carbohydrates are eliminated. However, the greatest benefits occur when chronic candidiasis is eradicated, which corrects the true cause of the problem. Unfortunately, if moderate-severe atherosclerosis is present, the improvements will be more limited. (*Warning:* If you are going to be treated for candidiasis and take antihypertensive drugs or heart medication, you must be carefully monitored by a physician to avoid episodes of low blood pressure.)

What about the other blood pressure extreme, hypotension? Surprisingly, most physicians are not concerned about it. Since low blood pressure does not suddenly damage or rupture blood vessels, it would not seem to be a dangerous condition. Yet, having low blood pressure can cause people to faint, fall, and hit their head. Even worse, it can cause someone to pass out while driving a car. Chronic hypotension is not normal. Indeed, it should be considered a signal that there is something wrong. In other words, rather than being considered an illness, hypotension is really a *symptom* of an underlying problem.

Hypotension occurs when systolic and diastolic blood pressures decrease below normal. Typically, it arises during episodes of shock or other adverse circumstances, like a severe loss of blood. Although it is supposed to be a life-saving mechanism, certain conditions can cause its perpetual presence, including infections, fever, cancer, anemia, and some obscure illnesses. Usually, these problems are readily identified and frequently corrected.

There is a form of low blood pressure, *idiopathic hypotension*, that is more troubling and prevalent throughout the population. A significant number of people, especially women, persistently suffer with it; recurring lightheadedness and dizziness is common, and some of them have frequent fainting spells. Since it has no known or appreciated cause, this mysterious malady has many physicians and researchers confused. The best they can do is give medication to raise blood pressure. Even when this works, it only treats the symptom and completely ignores its cause. As far as mainstream medicine is concerned, there is no cause. Although it may not be readily apparent, there is a cause. What is being missed? It is not a coincidence that most idiopathic hypotension sufferers also have cold hands and feet. Few physicians realize that both problems are related to the poor perfusion that accompanies chronic candidiasis. In fact, other candidiasis symptoms are also common among people with idiopathic hypotension. Yet, until it is diagnosed, the *candidiasis–idiopathic hypotension connection* is not appreciated.

How does chronic candidiasis decrease blood pressure? The *adrenal glands* assist the body with stress. Some of its hormones help maintain a normal blood pressure. Chronic candidiasis can overstress the glands (chapter 11) and lead to adrenal exhaustion (hypoadrenocorticism). When a sufferer's adrenal glands are functionally impaired, their blood pressure usually decreases, and pressures of 90/60 or lower often occur. In addition, the liver and kidneys assist in maintaining a normal blood pressure. What does this have to do with chronic candidiasis? Since sufferers frequently have impaired functioning of their liver and kidneys (as well as their lungs), chronic candidiasis can contribute to low blood pressure. In addition, disease-causing yeast may directly promote this process. As an example, *Candida albicans* can manufacture an *angiotensin-like substance* that is thought to lower blood pressure (probably by inhibiting angiotensin release or blocking its receptors).

Hypotension is not as life-threatening as hypertension, but it is not a state of wellness and should be treated accordingly. If no permanent atherosclerosis or adrenal gland destruction occurred, eliminating chronic candidiasis usually reverses this condition. In addition to raising a sufferer's low blood pressure, it returns warmth to their fingers and toes. Sometimes this is a slow process, taking weeks to months, because their organs and glands need to recover from years of compromise. So, a detoxification program aimed at regenerating the cells of their liver and kidneys, as well as nutritional support for the adrenal glands, will facilitate their recovery.

Although rare, a confusing presentation arises when a chronic candidiasis sufferer with apparently normal blood pressure is treated and subsequently develops hypertension. Why would this occur? The most likely scenario is that they have the effects of both atherosclerosis and idiopathic hypotension. In other words, hardening of their arteries raises their blood pressure, while decreased adrenal gland, liver, and kidney functioning precipitate a lower blood pressure. These two conditions compensate for each other, resulting in a normal blood pressure. If a candidiasis sufferer's blood pressure increases significantly during or after therapy, medication may be indicated. Therefore, it is essential to monitor blood pressure carefully during treatment, especially the older the person or the longer they have suffered with chronic candidiasis.

There is little doubt that candidiasis can precipitate blood pressure disturbances in a variety of ways. Depending on the circumstances, either extreme may occur, hypertension or hypotension. Fortunately, these can be improved or even corrected—that is, if you are willing to consider the *candidiasis–blood pressure connection.*

MITRAL VALVE PROLAPSE & ARRYTHMIAS

Like a door that opens and closes between two rooms, the *mitral value* regulates the flow of blood between the heart's left *atrium* and left *ventricle.* The left atrium receives oxygenated blood from the lungs. The mitral valve prevents the backflow of blood, maximizing its oxygen content, and when the left ventricle contracts, blood is pushed into the aorta, the major blood vessel providing access to virtually all the cells and tissues of the body.

In contrast, if the valve functions improperly or is impaired, it cannot perform its job optimally, which allows blood to flow backward from the left ventricle into the left atrium. The reverse leakage is called *mitral regurgitation* and is classified as mild, moderate, or severe. *Mitral valve prolapse* (MVP) is its primary cause; the mitral valve closes ineffectively, allowing the backward flow or turbulence of blood.

Specifics aside, MVP is known to be much more prevalent among candidiasis sufferers. Various researchers claim there is a *mitral valve prolapse–thyroiditis connection.* Since a *candidiasis–thyroid connection* exists (chapter

11), it should be unsurprising there is a *candidiasis–mitral valve prolapse connection*.

Many people with MVP experience panic attacks and arrhythmias (abnormal heart rates or rhythms). Mainstream cardiologists attribute these symptoms to the MVP, believing that the improper valve closing and its regurgitation are responsible. Can one valve cause these symptoms? It is unlikely. Many people with MVP also have candidiasis and thyroiditis disrupting their metabolism, including their heart's ability to function normally. Moreover, most candidiasis sufferers have glucose intolerance, which can trigger the release of hormones that induce a rapid heart rate and cause heart muscle irritability. They also have malabsorption, leading to nutritional deficiencies, especially the minerals that regulate heart rate and its contractions. An important mineral deficiency involves magnesium. Like asthma sufferers (chapter 6), reduced tissue magnesium levels can increase the likelihood of arrhythmias. The regular use of *magnesium orotate* has shown to provide clinically valuable improvements in MVP patients, as well as in preventing and treating cardiac arrhythmias, regulating blood pressure, and improving the function of the autonomic nervous system. Other researchers reveal that dietary magnesium intake is associated with a reduced risk of coronary heart disease.

So, it seems that the symptoms attributed to MVP reflect candidiasis-related disturbances, including its leaky gut syndrome and malabsorption. Can this be proven? In the absence of cardiac damage, MVP symptoms often disappear when candidiasis is eliminated, dietary sugars are avoided, and nutritional deficiencies are corrected. Can it be this simple? No, because some patients' arrhythmias are only eliminated after receiving allergy injections that desensitize their immune system against disease-causing yeast and harmful molds (chapters 17 and 18) as well as other allergy-inducing substances. This implies that an allergic reaction to disease-causing yeast and harmful molds may contribute to their arrhythmia. Since there is a *candidiasis-allergy connection* (chapter 16) and an *allergy-arrythmia connection*, this supports a *candidiasis-arrhythmia connection*.

With rare exception, MVP by itself does not cause symptoms. Yet, people with MVP have often been told before dental procedures: "Since you have mitral valve prolapse, antibiotic prophylaxis is needed to prevent endocarditis." Basically, *endocarditis* is inflammation within one or more of the membranes covering the heart; it can promote improper heart functioning and/or damage. It can occur during an infection or from an abnormal immune system reaction, either as a primary disorder or associated with an illness. Regardless, does giving antibiotics to MVP sufferers prevent endocarditis? Obviously not, because there are many reports of prophylaxis failure; even with antibiotics, some MVP sufferers develop endocarditis. Although a dentist may prefer to be on the safe side, a good defense can be a bad choice because antibiotics are a potent risk factor for developing candidiasis (chapter 2).

Fortunately, research led to major guideline changes for antibiotic prophylaxis and dental procedures in 2007 (updated 2021) by the American Heart Association: "1. Only an extremely small number of cases . . . might be prevented . . . 2. . . . prophylaxis . . . is reasonable only for patients with underlying cardiac conditions associated with the highest risk of adverse outcome. 3. For patients with these underlying . . . conditions, prophylaxis is reasonable for all . . . procedures that involve manipulation of gingival tissue or the periapical region of teeth or perforation of the oral mucosa. 4. Prophylaxis is not recommended . . . solely on an increased lifetime risk of acquisition of infective endocarditis. 5. Administration . . . is not recommended for patients who undergo a genitourinary or gastrointestinal tract procedure."

If you have candidiasis, be thankful for these changes because antibiotics are a strong risk factor for instigating and promoting candidiasis. Since their routine administration can cause more harm than good, these agents should not be used indiscriminately. Yet, if you do require antibiotics, it is wise to also undertake some type of anti-candidiasis therapy.

HONORABLE MENTIONS

There are a few medical eye-related maladies that have a strong association with candidiasis either directly or indirectly, including macular degeneration, glaucoma, and cataracts. And, although it could have been included in a previous section, *thrombocytopenia* (low platelet count within the blood) deserves a brief discussion.

Macular degeneration, often referred to as age-related macular degeneration, usually occurs in older people. In 2020, it was estimated that greater than 190 million people are affected worldwide, which is expected to increase to 288 million by 2040 as the elderly population escalates. It involves damage to the macula of the *retina,* the thin layer of tissue lining the back interior of the eye. The *macula* is the yellowish oval area surrounding the *fovea,* the area of sharpest vision. It does not lead to complete blindness but results in a gradual loss of central vision. There are two forms. The "dry" form includes *drusen* (cellular debris) that damages light-sensitive cells, whereas the "wet" form has blood vessels that grow under the macula, enabling blood and fluid to leak into the retina. Unfortunately, no cure or treatment exists that reverses the damage. Increasing age, genetic factors, and smoking tobacco are considered risk factors. Yet, the pathologic process is not well known, and some theories include oxidate stress, mitochondrial dysfunction, and inflammation. Does this sound familiar? Given the information provided in this chapter, it seems wise to determine if macular degeneration sufferers have candidiasis, with or without the presence of other infectious invaders. Although their vision might not improve, eliminating their candidiasis should prevent it from worsening.

Glaucoma affects roughly 70 million people worldwide. It involves damage to the optic nerve, or retina, leading to vision loss, and is the second-leading cause of blindness after cataracts. There are two types with various subtypes. In *open-angle* glaucoma (*wide angle, chronic simple*), the angle for fluid (*aqueous humor*) drainage within the eye is open, but its exit through the *trabecular meshwork* is impaired; it develops slowly, and there is no pain. In *closed-angle* glaucoma (*narrow angle, acute congestive*, and *normal-tension*) the *iris* obstructs the trabecular meshwork, impeding the drainage of fluid; it can arise suddenly with (or without) severe eye pain, blurred vision, a mid-dilated pupil, eye redness, and nausea, or it can develop slowly and progress over time. It is diagnosed when the pressure within the eye is 21 mmHg or higher. Although there are numerous risk factors, its cause remains elusive. One study involved 41 glaucoma patients and 30 age-matched controls. Upper gastrointestinal endoscopies and mucosal biopsies detected *Helicobacter pylori* in 88 percent of patients and 47 percent of controls. Using therapy, *H. pylori* was eradicated in 83 percent of patients, and after two years, the subgroup with chronic open-angle glaucoma was improved.

The case for an association between candidiasis and *H. pylori* (chapter 4) provides indirect evidence for a *candidiasis-glaucoma connection*. Moreover, the *canal of Schlemm* is an endothelial-lined tube that is covered and held open by the trabecular meshwork, creating resistance against the outflow of aqueous humor within the eye's anterior chamber. Since its tissue is like the tissue within blood vessels, it can become inflamed for the infectious and allergic reasons stated in this chapter, which can hinder the outflow of fluid, raising pressure within the eye. More to the point, some candidiasis sufferers with certain types of glaucoma have had their intraocular pressure decrease to normal after treatment. Yes, glaucoma is a complicated disease with obscure origins, but the adverse contributions of candidiasis are worth considering.

Cataracts occur when the lens of the eye becomes cloudy or opaque.

They typically arise slowly and can develop in one or both eyes. Approximately 20 million people are blind worldwide because of cataracts. Over time, clumps of protein or yellow-brown pigment accumulate within the lens, reducing the amount of light transmitted to the retina. Common risk factors include diabetes, chronic use of steroids, smoking tobacco, excess sunlight exposure, and alcohol consumption. Numerous diseases (metabolic and nutritional) are associated with their development as well as with the presence of various infections. The lens is composed of up to 60 percent proteins, as well as collagen, and does not directly connect with the blood or nerves. Instead, the aqueous humor provides it with energy and flushes away waste products. Given the expansive list of causative factors, it seems any process within the body that involves free radical damage and inflammation could precipitate the deposition of protein clumps or pigment within the lens. Simply put, candidiasis may contribute to the development of cataracts, and although treatment is unlikely to reverse the damage, it should slow or stop its progression.

Last, but not least, is *thrombocytopenia*, which involves abnormally low levels of platelets. Since its presence impairs the blood's ability to coagulate, it can lead to prolonged or excessive bleeding. Its medically accepted causes are diverse and varied, including decreased platelet production, increased destruction, medication-induced suppression, and more. Given all the mischief disease-causing yeast can create within the blood, candidiasis is rarely considered. Although research reveals an acute infection within the blood can lower the platelet count, systemic candidiasis seems to be a strong contributor to thrombocytopenia. Therefore, chronic candidiasis, especially when it is systemic, can create conditions that lower the platelet count. Fortunately, many candidiasis sufferers with thrombocytopenia improve when their candidiasis is treated.

IMPROVING YOUR CARDIOVASCULAR HEALTH

The *candidiasis-cardiovascular connection* is hardly ever appreciated. Unless you understand both conditions, the connection between them is rarely made.

Chronic candidiasis is a lengthy infection that stimulates the liver's *acute phase response*, decreasing its metabolism to assist the immune system in fighting the disease-causing yeast. In return, a prolonged acute phase response can promote glucose intolerance, hyperinsulinism, hyperlipidemia (hypercholesterolemia and/or hypertriglyceridemia), and impaired immunity (chapter 14). So, chronic candidiasis can contribute to cardiovascular disease in many ways, including unhealthy cholesterol levels, hardening of the arteries, high or low blood pressure, abnormal heart rhythms, palpitations, and more. Mitral valve prolapse is more prevalent among candidiasis sufferers, although the reason has not yet been determined.

Everyone has some amount of disease-causing yeast within their body, but small amounts are not a problem. In contrast, billions can instigate disturbances, injury, and damage. If you have candidiasis, are you doomed to develop cardiovascular disease? No, but your risk for problems is increased. Typically, an inherited genetic weakness predisposes someone to develop cardiovascular complications, yet its absence does not guarantee you will never develop cardiovascular disease. Although every candidiasis sufferer does not have cardiovascular illness, the longer and more systemic their candidiasis, the greater the toll it takes on their body and the greater the chances of developing cardiovascular complications.

If you have cardiovascular disease, do you have candidiasis? There is not a 100 percent guarantee, but the odds are great you have some magnitude of it. Therefore, if you want to improve your cardiovascular health, your disease-causing yeast must be eliminated. These and other infectious invaders should be identified and appropriately eradicated, including harmful molds, parasites, and bacteria. Since most cardiovascular illness involves some type of glucose intolerance and hyperinsulinemia, dietary changes should be made, especially the elimination of simple sugars as well as excesses of complex carbohydrates. In addition, chronic candidiasis commonly creates nutritional deficiencies, which should be corrected. It is wise to also address and treat any associated allergies. Not to be outdone, in some people, heavy metal toxicity contributes its ill effects, and this must be considered and addressed.

Although the association between cardiovascular disease and candidiasis is controversial, it is real. If you have cardiovascular problems, a candidiasis-minded approach will not hurt you. At best, you may discover that candidiasis is responsible for your cardiovascular problems and greatly benefit from anti-candidiasis treatment. In any case, the *candidiasis-cardiovascular connection* is compelling, and the information that supports its existence is difficult to ignore.

CHAPTER 8

Skin Manifestations

Your *skin* is probably your best-known feature because it is the part of you everyone sees. Although its color is its most obvious characteristic, your skin does not exist for its cosmetic purposes. Like the exterior of a house, your skin functions to protect the interior of your body from your external environment. Simply put, the skin is the body's natural, protective covering. It is the part of us that directly and unceasingly interfaces with the world. Rather than being a passive shell, it is an organ, performing numerous critical functions and metabolic processes essential to our sustenance and survival. As an example, in the presence of sunlight, certain substances within the skin help convert the inert form of vitamin D into its metabolically active version. In short, your skin functions like a selective covering, preventing certain substances from entering and exiting your body, while allowing others to pass through.

The technical name for the skin is *epidermis* or *integument*. It has two layers. The *epidermis* is the external layer, and its growth progresses from interior to exterior; as its cells mature, they flatten, die, and form a dead layer of tough *keratin* that is pushed outward until it is eventually sloughed off. *Melanin* within the epidermis is the substance that provides its color. *Langerhans cells* within the epidermis and dermis are immune cells (macrophages) thought to participate in allergic reactions, especially, contact dermatitis and delayed-type hypersensitivity. The *dermis* is the more massive layer, comprised of a mixture of proteins, collagen, and mucopolysaccharides as well as water, elastic fibers, blood vessels, nerves, lymphatic channels, glands, hair, and some cells. Furthermore, both layers rest on a deeper layer of fat-containing, subcutaneous tissue, the *panniculus adiposus*.

The skin is the body's largest organ. Like other organs, it contains living cells that must constantly receive nutrients and oxygen, as well as remove wastes. Fortunately, the skin has a profuse blood supply, much more than it needs, making it relatively low maintenance. Its abundance of blood vessels assists the skin in performing another vital function, which involves body temperature regulation. In addition, the skin has two types of sweat glands. The *eccrine sweat glands* produce perspiration, a liquid that prevents the body from overheating. The other gland has two parts: The *apocrine glands* make an oily, colorless secretion, while the *sebaceous glands* synthesize lipids (fats) and sometimes hair. Moreover, nails are specialized areas of the skin. Undoubtedly, there is more to skin than what you can see.

The skin is not an isolated organ. The entire skin is supplied with nerves that connect it with the central nervous system and brain, creating a *skin–nervous system connection*. This two-way association enables us to sense our external environment and interact with it; signals are sent from the skin to the brain and interpreted, and then a signal is returned to the skin to influence its activities. For example, anxiety produces perspiration, whereas touching something hot triggers you to withdraw your hand. Since the immune system protects the skin from infections and/or injuries, there is a *skin–immune system connection*. The skin is also influenced by numerous hormones, evidencing a *skin–endocrine system connection*. Taken together, there is one all-encompassing *skin-neuroendocrine-immune connection*.

Since our skin is in direct contact with our external environment, it can be impaired, injured, or damaged. Commonly, the skin is traumatized, burned, or chemically poisoned. Damage to the skin will adversely affect the way it functions; generally, the more extensive the damage, the worse the outcome. Although cancer of the skin is undesirable, it is often localized and can be surgically removed. In contrast, burns can be much more dangerous and may become life-threatening when severe or extensive. The skin can be invaded and colonized by one or more infectious invaders, either from the outside surface inward or from within the body outward. Fortunately, under most circumstances and adverse situations, the skin repairs itself and heals. When it is injured or infected during an isolated incident and heals, there is little cause for concern. In contrast, a chronic or recurring skin malady is not normal but a signal that there is an underlying problem adversely affecting the skin's health.

When all its functions and connections are considered, it is easy to appreciate that, if something is wrong within the body, it should adversely affect the health of the skin. Since most chronic illnesses and diseases disturb the *neuroendocrine-immune connection* in some way, the skin can be harmed in the presence of chronic illness and disease. In fact, numerous illnesses and diseases frequently involve the skin, producing a variety of epidermal manifestations. Since it connects with the immune system, it participates in immune system regulation; *dendritic* cells and *Langerhans* cells recognize, react to, and present antigens (allergy-inducing substances) to the immune system, regulating its functioning. If a medical malady or condition persistently impairs immunity, it can harm immune cells within the skin, compromising the skin's health. In addition, most illnesses and diseases disturb the nervous and endocrine (hormone) systems, which can escalate the disarray. Therefore, any chronic or recurring skin condition should be considered evidence that something undesirable is happening within the body, which is promoting a skin disturbance. Simply put, most chronic or recurring skin conditions really represent symptoms of a more significant, deeper problem. So, the cause of most chronic or recurring skin conditions will be found within the body, not on its surface.

An acute or one-time skin problem is unlikely to involve candidiasis. In contrast, recurring and chronic ailments often reflect its adverse contributions, whether externally, internally, directly, or indirectly. Chronic candidiasis is an *infection* with disease-causing yeast that has *allergic* consequences, which can undesirably alter the *neuroendocrine-immune connection*. Since there is a *skin-neuroendocrine-immune connection* and a *candidiasis-neuroendocrine-immune connection*, there must be a *candidiasis-skin connection*. In fact, abundant scientific evidence supports this connection. Yet, on a simpler level, it is readily confirmed each time a candidiasis sufferer is appropriately treated and their chronic or recurring skin problem disappears. (It is important to note other infectious invaders—harmful parasites, bacteria, molds, and viruses—should be considered, identified, and treated accordingly.)

THE CANDIDIASIS-SKIN CONNECTION

The *candidiasis-skin connection* has been appreciated for thousands of years. Disease-causing yeast have a long history of promoting skin infections. Commonly, their colonization produces oral thrush and diaper rash in infants with immature immunity as well as oral thrush in older people with impaired immunity. Decreased immunity or areas of poor circulation allow disease-causing yeast in the external environment to directly colonize the skin's surface; they are all around us and invade the skin when conditions permit (they prefer warm, moist, and dark locations, explaining why the mouth and genital area are often assaulted). Although these superficial manifestations involve disease-causing yeast externally infecting the skin and mucous membranes, they are a small percentage of all candidiasis-induced skin maladies. In the big picture, disease-causing yeast are more proficient at internally causing a diversity of skin ailments, ranging from unpleasant-appearing conditions like psoriasis to deadly illnesses like cancer. Therefore, it is important to understand that candidiasis can instigate and promote skin disturbances, both externally and internally.

Although most candidiasis sufferers do not have diaper rash or oral thrush, they often have the white-coated tongue of oral candidiasis. Instead of disease-causing yeast externally assaulting their skin, sufferers are more likely to experience skin conditions resulting from their internal effects. Dark-field microscopy (chapter 17) reveals that many sufferers have disease-causing yeast living within their blood; the skin has an abundance of blood vessels, and they can readily travel throughout the skin layers. Since they adhere better to contracted or injured blood vessels (chapter 7), poorly perfused or damaged areas provide locations for their colonization. If their food supply is limited, to survive, they may invade through the vessel wall, access the skin or nail beds, take up residence, and cause epidermal disturbances.

Since chronic candidiasis is primarily a gastrointestinal infection, how does it cause skin problems? Disease-causing yeast are infectious invaders that produce a variety of toxins, metabolites, wastes, and antigenic (allergy-inducing) substances. In small amounts, these substances do little to no harm. When chronic candidiasis is present, these substances can be produced in large amounts, causing significant disturbances. How does this adversely affect the skin? Typically, many sufferers have leaky gut syndrome (chapters 3 and 4), which enables many of these harmful substances to be absorbed from the gut into the surrounding tissues. Disease-causing yeast can also weaken and invade the gut wall, and colonize the surrounding tissues, where their harmful substances can easily enter the blood vessels. Regardless of where they physically reside, if the harmful substances they produce enter the blood, they can travel to the vessels supplying the skin, diffuse through the vessel walls and enter the skin itself; areas with weakened or damaged blood vessels make this likely. Once these substances are present within the skin, they are directly harmful to the cells and tissues or recognized as foreign, triggering an immune response. In either case, this is likely to instigate inflammation and other undesirable immune system reactions that can precipitate chronic skin ailments.

Research reveals that *Candida antigen-antibody immune complexes* circulating within the blood can be deposited within the skin. If the immune system is competent and recognizes the complexes as foreign (harmful), efforts are made to eliminate them, which produces inflammation and tissue damage in the process. Fortunately, these immune complexes are large and infrequently pass through the blood vessel wall, unless there is notable injury or damage, and do not cause most candidiasis-related skin conditions. If antigen-antibody immune complexes are not the problem, what is? Research reveals that *Candida albicans* can activate the classical and alternative complement pathways. Their *free* antigens are small enough to enter the skin, where they trigger the *complement system*, a group of proteins that helps the immune system's defenses. Although the activation of the complement system signals immune cells to attack and remove the *Candida* antigen, it also causes inflammation and localized damage. In addition, *gliotoxin* is a harmful substance produced by fungi, including *Candida albicans* (chapter 10), that can damage and reduce the number of epidermal Langerhans cells, decreasing the skin's immunity for up to 13 weeks. This explains why some recurring skin conditions have flare-ups and can go into remission; they worsen during periods of increased exposure to fungal antigens and toxins, and then improve when the exposure is minimal. In contrast, people with skin ailments that never disappear implies they are constantly being exposed to fungal antigens and toxins. Recurring and chronic skin ailments do not occur for no reason. Indeed, something must cause them. Although the finger of guilt points to candidiasis, there is more compelling evidence.

The skin is a peripheral organ under the same influence and control as the other end-organs of the body; for example, its two-part sweat glands are highly sensitive to a deficiency or excess of *androgens* (a hormone). Since the skin is influenced by the endocrine (hormone) system and chronic candidiasis often disturbs endocrine functioning (chapter 11), candidiasis-related endocrine abnormalities frequently disturb or impair the skin's functioning. Simply put, candidiasis can decrease the body's production or release of one or more hormones and, depending on the hormones involved, adversely affect the skin's functioning. So, candidiasis can internally compromise the skin's functioning in more than one way.

Because there is a *skin-immune connection*, autoimmune reactions contribute to some chronic or recurring skin conditions. For a variety of reasons, *autoantibodies* to peripheral cells and/or tissues may arise that are targeted to assault specific skin components; the immune system manufactures antibodies that inappropriately attack and destroy someone's own cells and/or tissues. Commonly, *anti-melanocyte* antibodies, *antinuclear* antibodies, *rheumatoid factor* antibodies, and other "anti-self" antibodies can cross-react with certain skin cells and components. Depending on the severity of the assaults, the undesirable consequences range from inflammation to injury and from damage to destruction. Since there is also a *candidiasis-immune connection*, chronic candidiasis can instigate and promote autoimmune disturbances, including the production of autoantibodies (chapter 14).

Confusingly, a large percentage of autoimmune disease does not involve autoantibodies because none are detected. So, what is occurring, and can candidiasis be involved? Yes, candidiasis can also instigate and promote direct *cell-mediated* autoimmunity, which can precipitate and cause damage. Yet, this type of autoimmunity is unlikely to be detected, much less associated with candidiasis. Moreover, autoimmune disease is not the only way candidiasis adversely affects immunity, causing skin problems. The persistent presence of disease-causing yeast can induce *suppressed immunity* (inferior functioning cells), *depressed immunity* (fewer cells), or *suppressed-depressed immunity* (fewer, inferior functioning cells). In turn, impaired immunity prevents the skin from effectively combating the presence of any infectious invader, whether it is a disease-causing yeast, mold, parasite, bacteria, or virus. The more the immune system is impaired, the greater the likelihood a chronic skin ailment will arise.

In addition, the skin is connected to the nervous system through its *skin-neuroendocrine-immune connection*. It is supplied with an extensive network of nerve endings and the nervous system influences its functioning; the brain regulates and integrates the skin with other areas of the body. Since there is a *neuroendocrine-immune connection*, disrupting the endocrine and/or the immune system will adversely alter the nervous system. Moreover, there is a *candidiasis-neuroendocrine-immune connection*, so chronic candidiasis can undesirably affect the nervous system directly (chapter 10). Because candidiasis can disturb or disrupt the nervous system and the skin is under the control of the nervous system, this adds to the ways candidiasis can instigate and promote chronic or recurring skin ailments.

Furthermore, candidiasis is an infection (with allergic consequences) that increases the body's metabolic and nutritional requirements. This escalates when other infectious invaders are present, including harmful parasites, bacteria, molds, and/or viruses. As a result, the colonization of disease-causing yeast (and other infectious invaders) within the gut promotes malabsorption and nutritional deficiencies. Inadequate absorption of vitamin A, vitamin E, and essential fatty acids is common among candidiasis sufferers and harmful to their skin's health. Deficiencies of other vitamins and minerals impair the skin's ability to repair itself and heal. Dietary deficiencies, especially a lack of protein, have adverse consequences. Yet, when a sufferer is appropriately treated and their nutritional deficiencies are corrected, it is common to notice great improvements in the health of their skin.

Mainstream physicians think disease-causing yeast only cause occasional, superficial skin problems, unless someone has impaired immunity. Conversely, candidiasis-minded physicians appreciate yeast-related skin disturbances range from mild, localized redness with intermittent itching to bizarre, unrestricted rashes that involve several forms of primary and secondary skin elements. Many epidermal problems are externally or internally associated with candidiasis, directly and indirectly, although chronic and recurring skin maladies are the most notable. A partial listing of candidiasis-mediated skin disorders includes persistent acne, psoriasis, vasospastic disorders with localized, bluish-discolored cyanotic fingers followed by erythema/redness (for example, Raynaud's phenomenon), aphthous ulcerated lesions, gingivitis, foot and heel ulcers, hand eczema (aka housewife's eczema), contact dermatitis, folliculitis, hyperkeratosis (dry skin), and hives. The hair manifestations of candidiasis encompass dull, dry, thin, oily, or sparse hair, as well as nonhereditary baldness or hair loss. A candidiasis sufferer can also have brittle, fragile, flaking nails with frequent discoloration and abnormal pigmentation. Since a long-term infection with disease-causing yeast can impair immunity, viral warts and cancers of the skin are more common among chronic candidiasis sufferers.

To summarize, candidiasis can externally and internally promote chronic and recurring skin ailments in a variety of ways. Typically, the surface of the skin and the nails are easily accessible locations for the external colonization of disease-causing yeast. Because they prefer dark and moist environments, especially the intertriginous folds, they readily colonize locations where skin contacts adjacent skin (for example, under the breast or the groin folds of heavy people). Moreover, chronic candidiasis can disturb the functioning of the nervous, endocrine, and/or immune systems, which can undesirably affect the skin's functioning. Lastly, it can promote a variety of nutritional deficiencies and metabolic disturbances that impairs the skin's ability to optimally function as well as to repair itself and heal. When the puzzle pieces are joined and viewed objectively, it is difficult to dismiss the *candidiasis-skin connection*.

CHRONIC MUCOCUTANEOUS CANDIDIASIS

Many mainstream medical practitioners are aware that *chronic mucocutaneous candidiasis* (CMCC) is the most accepted, yeast-related skin manifestation.

This ailment involves a persistent infection of the skin, nails, and mucous membranes with disease-causing *Candida*-species organisms; it is almost always *Candida albicans*. Its onset is distributed within three age groups: infancy/childhood, adolescence, and the adult years. Although each group has its characteristic manifestations and predisposing factors, the symptoms that arise usually relate to the bodily locations adversely affected as well as to the accompanying failure of a sufferer's endocrine organs. Unfortunately, endocrine organ failure frequently occurs and is responsible for hormone disturbances that can be significant.

Skin or mucous membrane biopsies from CMCC sufferers have disease-causing *Candida*-species organisms living within these areas. Although the disease-causing yeast are usually in their *hyphal* (invasive) growth phase, their colonization is mostly confined to the epidermis. If deeper invasion of their skin is infrequent and limited, why do CMCC sufferers consistently demonstrate a strong, localized inflammatory response? After all, deep invasion is usually necessary to instigate antigen-antibody reactions that produce inflammation. Moreover, CMCC sufferers classically have defective immunity, impairing their ability to produce anti-*Candida* antibodies. If the inflammation that arises within their skin is unlikely to represent antigen-antibody reactions, what process is involved?

Numerous findings indicate *complement system activation* is responsible for instigating the inflammation associated with their cutaneous lesions. The presence of *Candida albicans* within their skin activates their complement system; in fact, deposits of *complement factor C3* are found within the dermal-epidermal junctions of their lesions. So, instead of antigen-antibody interactions, the epidermal manifestations of CMCC sufferers represent the undesirable activities of the complement system. This illustrates the role of complement activation in instigating candidiasis-related skin disturbances.

CMCC sufferers often develop areas of their skin that do not have pigmentation (*vitiligo*). They also frequently have a complete loss of scalp hair (*alopecia totalis*). Both manifestations are common in people with endocrine (hormone) disturbances, as normal functioning is required to maintain skin coloring and the growth of hair. In addition, some CMCC sufferers have *anti-melanocyte antibodies*, which is evidence that a loss of skin coloring involves an autoimmune process; these people produce autoantibodies programmed to attack their melanocytes (the skin cells containing *melanin*, the pigment providing skin color). This reveals how autoimmunity can participate in candidiasis-related skin ailments.

The skin disturbances of CMCC involve numerous undesirable processes. The superficial, epidermal skin manifestations reflect the direct mischief of disease-causing *Candida*-species organisms colonizing these locations. The immune system tries to combat the infection, but because defective immunity is common among CMCC sufferers, antibodies against *Candida albicans* are usually not produced, allowing the infection to become prolonged. In the process, the skin ailments advance to include the secondary effects of a chronic infection with *Candida albicans*, including complement activation, endocrine disturbances, and autoimmune reactions; all of these can easily promote epidermal inflammation.

CMCC is the most accepted example of how candidiasis precipitates or promotes skin disturbances. Yet, CMCC is uncommon. Does this mean candidiasis-related skin ailments are also uncommon? On the contrary, most chronic and recurring skin ailments are often associated with candidiasis. Why is this scarcely known? Since most chronic and recurring skin ailments are not as obvious as CMCC, their connection with candidiasis is missed or ignored. If you suffer with any chronic or recurring skin ailment and are wondering what is causing it, you would be wise to consider the *candidiasis-skin connection*.

COMMON CANDIDIASIS CUTANEOUS CONDITIONS

If you are a candidiasis sufferer, you are likely to have a skin ailment associated with the chronic presence of your disease-causing yeast. Your face and eyelids may be red and swollen. You may have dryness and flaking over your nose and lips (nasolabial seborrhea). Your constantly chapped lips may cause you to develop small, painful cracks at the corners of your mouth that are frequently covered with a yellowish crust. You are likely to have dry and hard skin that feels like sandpaper. You may not want to take off your socks or swim in public places because you do not want people to see your infected, discolored, ingrown, or strange-appearing toenails. Even worse, you are likely to complain of skin irritations and rashes, which are often accompanied by itching that can range from uncomfortable to unbearable.

Admittedly, not all candidiasis sufferers develop skin ailments. Usually, there must be an inherited (genetic) weakness, predisposing someone to develop specific conditions, which is why certain medical maladies occur more frequently among members of the same family. Yet, even without a genetic predisposition, prolonged or severe circumstances can cause the most stout and healthy person to develop ailments they normally would not. How can such diversity exist? Since every human being is a unique individual, no two candidiasis sufferers ever develop identical skin ailments, even though there are often similarities. Among sufferers, the entire spectrum of skin ailments varies from insignificant, isolated lesions to diffusely widespread disturbances that precipitate severe complications.

If you have candidiasis and do not have significant yeast-related skin manifestations, you are fortunate. Does this mean you never will? No, given enough time, you are likely to develop some skin disturbance, even without a genetic predisposition. Why? Candidiasis involves the colonization of disease-causing yeast within your gut, creating conditions that promote malabsorption and a spectrum of nutritional deficiencies. Since your skin is composed of cells and tissue that require a variety of nutrients, candidiasis will disturb your skin's health and functioning in some way. The more significant or prolonged your malabsorption, the greater the toll it takes on your skin. This weakens your skin's defenses, making it susceptible to the direct assault and colonization of disease-causing yeast as well as other infectious invaders. Unless your candidiasis is eliminated, the situation will only worsen.

If you presently suffer with a candidiasis-related skin ailment, can you develop more? Yes, like any infection, its undesirable effects can spread. Fortunately, it is extremely rare for a sufferer to develop the entire spectrum of yeast-related skin disturbances. Since numerous factors, especially genetics, contribute to the expression of candidiasis symptoms, it is exceedingly unlikely anyone can succumb to them all, developing the entire spectrum of yeast-related skin ailments. Among all sufferers, severe skin manifestations are the exception, rather than the rule. So, most sufferers are somewhere in the middle of the range, between wellness and severe illness. Severe skin ailments are not prevalent, but neither is complete wellness. So, if you have candidiasis, you are almost guaranteed to have some candidiasis-related skin problem, sooner or later.

The good news is most chronic and recurring skin disturbances can be corrected when candidiasis is properly treated. Yet, few people ever go to a candidiasis-minded physician to treat their skin ailments. Instead, mainstream dermatologists are consulted. You might think a skin specialist is the best person to diagnosis and treat skin ailments, but they are not. They rarely consider that skin ailments reflect someone's disturbed inner health. Most dermatologists miss or overlook the *candidiasis-skin connection*, even when other yeast-related symptoms are present. Yet, if the association between candidiasis and skin ailments is clear, why is it missed? Although dermatologists are experts in understanding the skin's anatomy and functioning, their focus and methods usually embrace the skin as a discrete entity. Disease-causing yeast are rarely identified as the cause of skin ailments, and the presence of a few skin disturbances is unlikely to make this obvious. Using a narrow-sighted approach, the best they can do is suppress or alleviate the symptoms accompanying your skin manifestations, until you have a flare-up or your condition spreads. Since treating a person's symptoms does not correct the real cause of their problem, you should appreciate why most people with chronic and recurring skin ailments continue to suffer rather than being permanently cured.

This anti-candidiasis bias should not exist. After all, most physicians, including dermatologists, are taught that skin lesions are often associated with various diseases and illnesses. If you look in an internal medicine textbook, you will learn that skin lesions can accompany infectious diseases, gastrointestinal diseases, renal diseases (kidney problems), hematological diseases (blood disorders), rheumatic illnesses (joint maladies), and many other medical maladies. The point is: Anything that undesirably disturbs your internal health will often manifest itself within your skin. In other words, most skin ailments result from an internal disturbance working its way outward. Since your gastrointestinal tract is part of your internal environment, chronic or recurring skin ailments can easily accompany a gut disturbance related to the presence and colonization of disease-causing yeast as well as other infectious invaders, including harmful parasites, molds, bacteria, and/or viruses. Therefore, a candidiasis-minded approach is a better way to treat chronic and recurring skin ailments.

The most common skin ailments include psoriasis (2 to 3 percent of the worldwide population, about 200 million), seborrheic dermatitis (3 to 5 percent worldwide, roughly 320 million), eczema (2.4 percent worldwide, 192 million), and acne (9.4 percent worldwide, 752 million).

Psoriasis

Psoriasis usually disfigures the elbows and knees with chronic or recurring, silver-red, scaling patches. Some people develop lesions on their scalp and face as well as other areas. The lesions are a cosmetic problem, rarely causing discomfort. Most psoriasis sufferers live with their condition or take medication to suppress their lesions. In contrast, anti-candidiasis therapy often produces dramatic improvement, curing many cases of psoriasis.

For some people with mild candidiasis, improvements of their skin lesions follow the use of probiotic supplements and eliminating dietary sugars by reestablishing a healthy population of beneficial bacteria and starving their disease-causing yeast.

Mainstream medicine accepts psoriasis as being "without cure" but knows it can improve or enter remission with or without certain therapies. If mainstream physicians conceded that disease-causing yeast precipitate or promote these epidermal lesions, psoriasis would be more curable. Understanding how candidiasis contributes to the production of epidermal disturbances helps clarify a mystery surrounding psoriasis. Long-wavelength ultraviolet (UV) light exposure has benefitted some psoriasis sufferers; it decreases their lesions, but it is not known how or why. An appreciation of candidiasis reveals two possibilities: Disease-causing *Candida*-species organisms may be present within the cutaneous lesions of certain psoriasis sufferers and their adverse sensitivity to UV light makes phototherapy effective; exposure kills the disease-causing yeast within the lesions, improving their appearance. In addition, UV light might inactivate the complement components that promote skin disturbances. Depending on the extent of the candidiasis, both processes may occur. Although UV-light exposure may benefit some psoriasis sufferers, the real therapeutic solution involves eliminating their disease-causing yeast.

Many studies reveal an association between *Candida*-species infections and psoriasis, but their conclusions put the cart before the horse. In other words, most studies conducted by the mainstream medical community are biased against the *candidiasis-skin connection*.

Seborrheic Dermatitis

Seborrheic dermatitis often occurs in the scalp area. Its physical appearance resembles greasy scaling on a yellow-red base, without wasting or disruption of the hair follicles. When severe, it is considered a form of psoriasis and may represent an alternate expression. If there is a *candidiasis-psoriasis connection* and a *psoriasis-seborrheic connection*, it makes sense there would be a *candidiasis–seborrheic dermatitis connection*. Logic aside, according to mainstream medical experts, the etiology of seborrheic dermatitis is a mystery. If its cause is not evident, how can dermatologists effectively treat it? They cannot because they do not know what they are treating. Although its origin is obscure, something must cause seborrheic dermatitis, as it cannot exist for no reason. Once again, you would be wise to consider candidiasis.

Specifics aside, many studies do support a *candidiasis-psoriasis–seborrheic dermatitis connection*. Moreover, harmful bacteria may contribute. Since the problems caused by disease-causing yeast are frequently assisted by other infectious invaders, this is unsurprising.

In addition to the infection, allergies to disease-causing yeast may contribute to skin ailments. This is consistent with the dual nature of candidiasis; it is an infection with allergic consequences. So, when candidiasis sufferers are treated, their *infection* and *allergies* must be addressed.

Allergies to harmful molds can also promote symptoms, including skin ailments. In fact, a group of molds, called *dermatophytes*, can colonize the skin and cause disturbances. In the big picture, sensitivities and hypersensitivities to numerous harmful molds induce inflammation and allergy symptoms in susceptible people. Furthermore, disease-causing yeast and some harmful molds are closely related; their similar antigens (allergy-inducing parts) cause identical inflammation and allergic consequences (chapter 16). If you suffer with a chronic or recurring skin ailment, consider the allergic contributions of harmful molds (as well as their infectious presence). Simply stated, candidiasis-related skin ailments can involve numerous infectious invaders, and their combined contributions escalates the medical malady, whether it is a skin ailment or another illness.

Eczema

Eczema (atopic dermatitis) is highly associated with allergies, occurring in all age groups. Seasonal variations contribute to the flare-up of an eczema sufferer's symptoms, including skin itching, superficial inflammation, redness, small and weeping blisters, crusting scales, and different types of papules (pimples). The areas of the body most afflicted are the cheeks, front of the neck, and folds of skin at the joints of the upper and lower extremities. Since there is an *eczema-allergy connection* and a *candidiasis-allergy connection* (chapter 16), there must also be a *candidiasis-eczema connection*.

Psoriasis is associated with seborrheic dermatitis, and it is likely that eczema is a related variation. The separation between these skin ailments may reflect eczema's close relationship with allergies and immunoglobulin E (IgE) reactions, causing lesions with certain characteristic allergy symptoms.

Fortunately, like the people who suffer with psoriasis and seborrheic dermatitis, eczema sufferers often improve when their candidiasis is treated. Yet, because of its strong association with allergies, efforts must be made to address and treat the sensitivities and hypersensitivities of eczema sufferers to facilitate a complete recovery. As for the research, many studies implicate candidiasis, but few make a definitive connection, again evidencing the anti-candidiasis bias prevalent among mainstream physicians.

Acne

Acne typically plagues teenagers, but many candidiasis sufferers know it can become a problem at any age. Its blemishes are usually confined to the face, upper chest, back, and shoulders—areas adjacent to the sebaceous glands, which synthesize lipids and sometimes hair, implying an endocrine (hormone) disturbance may play a role. Acne is not just a cosmetic annoyance because it can cause skin damage with permanent scaring. An important factor and early sign in its development is the presence of greasy skin or seborrhea that, in turn, promotes blackheads, whiteheads, and/or pustules. Although mainstream medicine considers acne to have an obscure origin, antibiotics are frequently used with moderate success; most likely, its benefits result from eliminating harmful bacteria within the gut (dysbacteriosis). The missed clue is greasy skin or seborrhea is an early sign during the development of acne. Since there is a *candidiasis–seborrheic dermatitis connection* and a *seborrhea-acne connection*, there must be a *candidiasis-acne connection*, which is why acne sufferers treated with anti-candidiasis therapy often eliminate their blemishes. Yes, an infection with disease-causing yeast is the primary problem, but many acne sufferers also have a strong allergy component to their ailment as well as the adverse contributions from other infectious invaders (parasites, bacteria, and/or molds). Obviously, all these troublemakers need to be identified and treated effectively.

Psoriasis, seborrheic dermatitis, eczema, and acne are the skin ailments most associated with candidiasis. Classically, all of them are medically listed as separate conditions. Yet, when the real cause and contributors are considered, they have much in common. The colonization of disease-causing yeast with its *infectious* and *allergic* consequences, and the contributions of other infectious invaders are the main ingredients that instigate and promote these epidermal ailments. Since the skin takes time to heal, some of these cutaneous disturbances can take a long time to resolve. Although topical therapy may benefit some people, if you suffer with any of these skin ailments, an anti-candidiasis approach is the best way to achieve a speedy recovery.

THE CANDIDIASIS-HIVES CONNECTION

The skin ailments just discussed are usually cosmetic disturbances. Yes, they are unpleasant. Yes, they may cause psychological problems and emotional pain. Yes, in some cases, they can permanently damage the skin. However, they are unlikely to completely disrupt someone's life. In stark contrast, hives (chronic urticaria) can greatly disturb someone's everyday existence. For example, the severe itching that frequently accompanies this condition prevents some people from sleeping, effectively ruining their quality of life. Although it is not the most prevalent candidiasis-related skin malady, it affects about 1 percent of the worldwide population of all ages, about 80 million people.

Chronic urticaria usually involves the sudden eruption of temporary epidermal lesions, wheals, or papules associated with severe itching, ranging from annoying to greatly disturbing. Allergies are thought to instigate or promote the episodes, which can arise from contact with irritating environmental substances or result from an internal disturbance. Therefore, if a chronic urticaria sufferer's allergies can be identified and avoided, their eruptions can be reduced or eliminated. Yet, the cause of the eruptions is often unknown, prolonging their episodes endlessly. At best, mainstream medicine can only treat the symptoms. Because of its prominent allergy component, antihistamines are routinely used to decrease the inflammation and allergic responses; they are only effective at reducing the discomfort of each episode and almost never eliminate the condition, which requires an appreciation of its true cause. Mainstream medicine knows that allergies are involved and is unaware of what is responsible for chronic urticaria. Since there is a *chronic urticaria–allergy connection* and a *candidiasis-allergy connection* (chapter 16), there must be a *candidiasis–chronic urticaria connection.*

Candidiasis has been known to be associated with chronic urticaria, especially allergies related to disease-causing yeast. When female patients were tested with *Candida albicans* antigen, 35 percent had type-1 or type-3 allergic reactions, while 60 percent demonstrated type-4 delayed reactions. Since type-4 reactions last for days to weeks, it explains why urticaria episodes are frequently prolonged. In contrast, testing with *Saccharomyces cerevisiae* antigen produced type-1 and type-3 reactions in 29 percent of the women, without any type-4 reactions. Yes, baker's and brewer's yeast can trigger urticaria episodes, but their effect is usually immediate and short-lived, while exposure to *Candida albicans* antigen produces more persistent disturbances. Do these results mean allergies to disease-causing yeast are only responsible for 29 to 60 percent of chronic urticaria episodes? No, because the impaired immunity (anergy) that accompanies chronic candidiasis (chapter 14) may cause some patients to appear falsely negative.

In addition to disease-causing yeast allergies, harmful molds and their allergies frequently contribute to chronic urticaria. Numerous researchers have revealed that disease-causing yeast *and* harmful molds can both play an important role in the development of chronic urticaria. Candidiasis-minded physicians who skin test patients for reactions to numerous yeasts and molds commonly uncover a spectrum of allergies to both. Yet, these allergies would probably not exist if candidiasis, an *infection* with disease-causing yeast, was not present (chapter 3).

Confusingly, most of the research involving the *candidiasis–chronic urticaria connection* misses an essential point. Mainstream physicians do not appreciate how common candidiasis is within the general population. When a study reveals the healthy controls have about the same amount of disease-causing yeast as the evaluated patients, the contributions of candidiasis are dismissed. Even though the supporting research has not been perfect, a *candidiasis–chronic urticaria connection* exists.

ALLERGIC CONTACT DERMATITIS

Contact dermatitis is a red, itchy rash. It is usually confined to the skin areas that are exposed to some substance, but there are exceptions and other areas may be involved. An estimated 15 to 20 percent of the worldwide population have it, about 1.4 billion people.

Irritant contact dermatitis, which accounts for 80 percent of cases, involves skin cell damage from exposure to various substances, including solvents, detergent, soap, bleach, hair dye, and more. It can also occur from touching nickel-containing objects and from overwashing the hands with soap and hot water or wearing scratchy wool. Caustic and toxic substances will undoubtedly damage skin cells, depending on the strength of the offending substance or amount of exposure. This type of contact dermatitis is avoidable and is not involved with candidiasis.

In contrast, *allergic contact dermatitis,* which accounts for 20 percent of cases, arises one to two days after skin contact with an environmental substance that triggers an allergic reaction, producing irritation and inflammation that promotes itching, redness, and a variety of skin lesions. For example, touching poison ivy can produce a significant reaction in sensitive people. Yet, contrary to its superficial appearance, allergic contact dermatitis does not occur *on* the skin; after all, most of the epidermis is composed of dead, keratinized cells. Instead, its effects are mostly within the dermis, or deeper, depending on someone's allergic sensitivity and the spread of their response. Since it occurs *within* the skin, it reflects the body's internal response to externally contacted substances (antigens). In short, the inflammation and skin lesions are the way the body "pushes" these offending antigens out, so they can be eliminated.

According to the National Eczema Association, "It [allergic contact dermatitis] bears some of the same symptoms as the six other types of eczema. But unlike atopic dermatitis, the most common and difficult-to-treat form of eczema, it doesn't run in families and isn't linked to other allergic conditions such as hay fever or asthma." In other words, it does not seem to involve a genetic predisposition.

Since allergic contact dermatitis is related to eczema, and there is a *candidiasis-eczema connection*, as well as a *candidiasis-allergy connection*, there must be a *candidiasis–allergic contact dermatitis connection*. Moreover, contact dermatitis and chronic urticaria have much in common, except that the reaction of contact dermatitis is usually localized to the affected area. The existence of a *candidiasis–chronic urticaria connection* is further support for a *candidiasis–allergic contact dermatitis connection*. In fact, most contact dermatitis sufferers have skin sensitivities or hypersensitivities that are instigated or promoted by candidiasis; the presence of disease-causing yeast causes their skin to become sensitive or hypersensitive to certain substances. Even though the research is lacking, when allergic contact dermatitis sufferers have their candidiasis appropriately treated (its infection, allergies, and the contributions of other infectious invaders), their skin hyperreactivity often resolves and disappears.

THE WAY TO A HEALTHY COMPLEXION

Almost anything within your external or internal environment can interact with your body, eliciting a reaction. The risk is greater for an organ with a significant blood supply, like the skin. Circulating blood traveling through the skin's profuse capillary network can transport harmful substances that can be deposited within the skin layers (epidermis and dermis), including undesirable toxins, metabolites, wastes, antigens, antigen-antibody immune complexes, and activated complement components. In turn, these substances can initiate a variety of cutaneous disorders, although the activated complement components and their reactions appear responsible for most, with localized (or systemic) inflammation arising secondarily.

Since healthy people have healthy skin, any chronic or recurring epidermal abnormality indicates the presence of some unseen or unrecognized disturbance. The goal is to determine what is instigating or promoting these skin ailments. An abundance of evidence reveals that most skin ailments are not attributable to external environmental causes, so the attention should be focused inward. In fact, most environmental exposures do not promote epidermal reactions unless something within the body causes the skin to be sensitive or hypersensitive; otherwise, everyone would always react to the same things all the time. Although some topical medications may provide relief for some skin ailment sufferers, most of them simply suppress symptoms, producing temporary relief. Since skin disturbances reflect a deeper problem, relapses are destined to follow because their cause was not addressed. Skin lesions can be acute, recurring, or chronic. Acute problems usually resolve by themselves with only minor support. Yet, frequent acute episodes suggest a recurring problem, implying there is a continuous ailment with periods of remission. So, a chronic epidermal disturbance is almost guaranteed to represent the presence of an internal imbalance.

The *candidiasis-skin connection* has been appreciated for thousands of years, but this association has only recently entered the scientific limelight. In short, the colonization of disease-causing yeast, especially *Candida albicans*, within the body can cause chronic or recurring skin disturbances, and it may make someone susceptible to acute episodes as well. The presence of these living, growing, reproducing, and dying infectious invaders can interfere with our internal processes, creating disturbances that can be visibly evident on the skin's surface. Typically, this involves an *infection* with disease-causing yeast as well as the *allergies* they promote (sensitivities and hypersensitivities). In addition, the skin is closely interconnected with the functioning of the nervous, endocrine (hormone), and immune systems. Since chronic candidiasis can adversely affect the *neuroendocrine-immune connection*, this increases the odds a sufferer's skin will be disturbed, impaired, or injured. Disease-causing yeast can grow on the skin's surface, but the epidermal manifestations they instigate or promote usually occur within the deeper layers. The most notable and well-known candidiasis-related skin disturbance is chronic mucocutaneous candidiasis, but it only affects a small percentage of all sufferers. More commonly, candidiasis causes psoriasis, seborrheic dermatitis, eczema, acne, chronic urticaria (hives), and allergic contact dermatitis. In addition, numerous other skin manifestations have been directly or indirectly associated with candidiasis.

Regardless of the anti-candidiasis bias among mainstream physicians, the *candidiasis-skin connection* exists. Although eliminating the disease-causing yeast *infection* is essential, many skin ailments involve *allergies* to disease-causing yeast and harmful molds, which must also be addressed and treated. Candidiasis-minded physicians know that other infectious invaders (harmful parasites, bacteria, molds, and/or viruses) often add their adverse effects, contributing to the skin disturbances. Therefore, attending to the *candidiasis-skin connection* is the best way to treat most people suffering with chronic or recurring skin ailments. Because the skin can be slow to heal and allergies may take a long time to resolve, some people may not have notable changes for months. So, if you want to improve your complexion or eliminate your unsightly epidermal lesions, you would be wise to consider the *candidiasis-skin connection* and seek out a candidiasis-minded physician for treatment.

CHAPTER 9

Arthritis

Most people wake up in the morning, get out of bed, wash, dress, eat breakfast, and go to work, never thinking how effortlessly all of this is done. In contrast, millions of arthritis sufferers awaken with one or more stiff, swollen, and/or painful joints, making it difficult to do something simple like get out of bed. Some arthritis sufferers' hands are so affected they cannot open a jar. Other sufferers have problems with their ankles, knees, and hips, making them unable to walk. Arthritis might not be life-threatening, but its debilitation, ranging from minimal to profound, ruins the quality of life for almost 88 percent of the 350 million people who suffer with arthritis worldwide.

Arthritis is the general term for inflammation of one or more joints, usually with pain, swelling, and (often) structural changes. You might know your elbow and knee are joints, forming movable connections between their adjacent bones, but there are also slightly movable joints and completely immovable joints; in short, there are many types of joints with their different characteristics (the specifics are unimportant). Simply put, a *joint* is the anatomical location where two bones connect; in fact, "joint" derives from the Latin *junctio*, meaning "a joining." Joints are usually composed of *fibrous connective tissue* and *cartilage*, which are susceptible to inflammation and injury. Since most joints are in constant use and under incessant stress, they are highly prone to injury and inflammation.

Chronic arthritis worsens as you age, with complications that often promote debilitation. In contrast, some cases of acute arthritis can induce significantly rapid devastation within one or more joints. If you think only gray-haired grandmothers have arthritis, think again, because young people can develop arthritis, even children. According to 2020 statistics by the U.S. Centers for Disease Control and Prevention, 60 percent of arthritis sufferers are between the ages of 18 and 64. Almost 60 million Americans have arthritis, and more sufferers are diagnosed every day. It is a leading cause of work disability, involving annual medical costs and lost earnings greater than $303.5 billion. Although some people's symptoms wax and wane, most suffer endlessly and require the constant use of medication, which is not without risk because large quantities of high-dose nonsteroidal anti-inflammatory drugs (NSAIDs) cause gut complications, usually "silent" ulcers that are medication-induced.

Most arthritis sufferers want to eliminate their illness, but mainstream medicine's approach to treatment does not provide cures. Since they believe joint pain and inflammation result from the presence and activity of numerous chemical mediators, its practitioners routinely use anti-inflammatory medications to impede or inhibit these substances and chemical processes. When it is ineffective, other medications may be added to suppress the immune system, impeding its cells from participating in the production of pain, inflammation, and joint destruction. An inhibitory and suppressive approach does not cure arthritis. Although anti-inflammatory medications and immunosuppressive agents might reduce or eliminate symptoms, they do not address their underlying cause. If you want to eliminate an illness, you must address its cause. With respect to *infectious arthritis*, this can be done without much difficulty; once the infectious invader is identified, an appropriate medication is used to kill it, eliminating the infection. In contrast, most other forms of arthritis have obscure or mysterious origins. When you realize that the cause of a chronic or recurring ailment is obscure or unknown, you should immediately suspect the contributions of candidiasis.

Research supports a *candidiasis-rheumatoid arthritis connection*. Can the other types of arthritis be associated with candidiasis? The answer is not simple because it depends on the circumstances involved with each type. Yet, without candidiasis, it is unlikely someone will suffer with arthritis. (The exceptions involve chronic joint pain from trauma that produces permanent joint damage or a joint-attacking infection.)

The presence of disease-causing yeast may or may not instigate or promote joint pain (*arthralgia*); after all, there are plenty of candidiasis sufferers who do not have arthritis or arthralgia. Moreover, candidiasis is not responsible for every case of arthritis. It does not cause infectious arthritis, which involves a small percentage of arthritis cases and is promoted by many different, harmful invaders that assault one or more joints. So, what is the cause of joint pain and inflammation in most arthritis sufferers? Since the origin of most types of arthritis is obscure or mysterious, candidiasis is highly likely.

What can determine if an infection with disease-causing yeast is causing or contributing to arthritis? In general, the fewer joints adversely affected, the less likely candidiasis becomes. In other words, the more widespread the arthritis, the greater the chance of having candidiasis, although this is not a hard-and-fast rule because cases of *Candida* septic arthritis confined to a single joint have been reported. Similarly, the more chronic or recurring the joint pain, the more likely there is long-term candidiasis. Yes, these statements are generalizations, and there are always exceptions. For example, osteoporosis involves bone loss and does not usually involve pain, but there is a *candidiasis-osteoporosis connection* as well. Since every person is a unique individual, there are a diversity of exceptions. This means that candidiasis can be readily evident or its presence may be covert. In any case, unlike the law, it is in your best interest to consider candidiasis *guilty* of instigating or promoting arthritis until proven innocent.

Is candidiasis solely to blame for all cases of arthritis? No, numerous infectious invaders may promote joint disturbances, including harmful parasites, bacteria, molds, and/or viruses. In addition, the symptoms of arthritis (or arthralgia) can be precipitated or exacerbated by food and environmental allergies, chemical sensitivities, and adverse reactions to mercury-containing dental fillings, toxic heavy metals, chemical toxins, and other harmful substances. So, almost anything within your environment, internally and externally, that is harmful can trigger a series of chemical reactions and immune system responses that induce joint inflammation and pain. Arthritis is a complicated illness with numerous unappreciated and unrecognized contributors, explaining why its origins remain obscure and mysterious.

Although not every case of arthritis involves candidiasis, a large percentage do, especially the chronic and recurring types. Since candidiasis is an infection with allergic consequences, it can promote localized and systemic illness, which often includes the cells and tissues of the joints. When significant, the resulting pain and inflammation may encourage anatomical disturbances, leading to significant joint destruction; over time, this can facilitate biomechanical disabilities as well as fractures. Can this undesirable course of events occur from the presence of candidiasis? Yes, but the typically slow disease-process that accompanies most cases of arthritis has made its association with candidiasis less than obvious, if not totally obscure. Regardless, the *candidiasis-arthritis connection* is obvious when you know where to look and what to look for.

HOW MANY JOINTS ARE AFFECTED?

If you randomly choose 1,000 arthritis sufferers and question them, you will discover that each has a unique history of when they first noticed their joint pain or inflammation, how slowly or quickly it progressed, which joints were involved, and so on. If you examined them, you would be forced to conclude that arthritis is really a variable illness. The number and location of joints adversely affected, the amount of pain and inflammation, the debilitation and destruction that arise, and so on are all part of the disease process. Since every sufferer is a unique individual with their own expression of illness, it makes more sense to consider arthritis as not being a single, discreet malady, but a spectrum of diverse manifestations.

Specifics aside, arthritis can be separated into two classes; monoarticular arthritis adversely affects a single joint, whereas polyarticular arthritis insults more than one joint. Understanding the difference between these general classes will help reveal whether disease-causing yeast are contributing their harmful effects to each type of arthritis.

Most people with *monoarticular arthritis* either have a joint infection (septic arthritis) or an irritation of their joint (synovial) linings from the deposition of harmful crystals (gout or pseudogout). Because of their dramatic and sudden inflammation, these illnesses require rapid medical intervention to protect the involved joint(s) from permanent damage and to ensure the sufferer's comfort and well-being. Fortunately, monoarticular arthritis is often reversible, and relapses are frequently preventable. Although it usually involves only one joint, it can be instigated by diseases involving more than one joint. So, you can have pain and inflammation within many joints before you experience an episode of monoarticular arthritis. How can you tell the difference between a case of mild chronic arthritis that flares up and monoarticular arthritis? Typically, monoarticular arthritis is characterized by the rapid onset of pain, swelling, and excess fluid involving a single joint; a consistently notable sign is redness around the joint (peri-articular erythema), a physical finding unique to these illnesses.

In contrast, although it may initially affect a single joint, *polyarticular arthritis* impairs more than one joint. Its chronic nature (slow development and progression) usually involves a relaxed approach to diagnosis and management. Numerous diseases cause diffuse inflammation and destruction of the joint linings, including rheumatoid arthritis, osteoarthritis (degenerative joint disease), multisystemic diffuse inflammatory disorders, and polyarthritis of the vertebrae.

Can any conclusions be made at this point? On the surface, monoarticular arthritis does not seem to be associated with candidiasis because of its sudden onset and often identifiable origins, while the chronic and more mysterious nature of polyarticular arthritis makes the mischievous contributions of disease-causing yeast more likely. Although this would seem the obvious conclusion, do not assume nature agrees with our thinking or follows our rules. In fact, both classes of arthritis can involve candidiasis, and a discussion of each type will illuminate the *candidiasis-arthritis connection*.

INFECTIOUS ARTHRITIS, GOUT & PSEUDOGOUT

The most common manifestations of monoarticular arthritis are infectious arthritis, gout, and pseudogout. All three are lumped together because of their ability to adversely affect a single joint. Yet, each illness is distinct, with its own characteristics and disease process. Even though these medical maladies have well-known origins, are they candidiasis-related? Yes, once their true underlying disease process is revealed.

Infectious Arthritis

Infectious arthritis classically occurs abruptly in about 20,000 Americans each year, with similar numbers in Europe. It is a bacterial infection within a single joint (*bacterial arthritis*) that frequently results from a bacterial infection within someone's blood. Less commonly, bacterial arthritis follows a traumatic injury that directly introduces (inoculates) infectious invaders into a joint. Rarely, it happens when an infection within a bone (*osteomyelitis*) spreads to an adjacent joint. Infectious arthritis is usually classified by its gonococcal or non-gonococcal origins, although tuberculosis is an infectious invader that may be involved. Harmful bacteria are not the only troublemakers. *Viral arthritis* involves multiple joints and is caused by many viruses. Lyme disease almost always adversely affects the joints of its sufferers. Other noteworthy, but infrequent, forms of infectious arthritis are syphilitic arthritis and fungal arthritis (disease-causing yeast and harmful molds).

Since numerous infectious invaders are known to be responsible, infectious arthritis does not seem to be candidiasis-related, unless disease-causing yeast are identified in a culture of fluid taken from an infected joint. Is something being missed? Yes, the presence of a joint infection does not explain why infectious arthritis occurs in the first place. Obviously, a traumatic injury that directly introduces bacteria into a joint, causing infectious arthritis, is highly unlikely to result from candidiasis. What about the other infectious arthritis sufferers? Most of them do not have trauma-induced illness. Instead, their condition arises from a bacterial infection within their blood or from a bone infection. Since healthy people do not have this ailment, why would these people have bacterial infections within their blood or develop osteomyelitis that spreads to an adjacent joint? Usually, both conditions involve impaired immunity; someone's immune system cannot effectively defend their blood and bones from an assault by these infectious invaders. What could cause impaired immunity? A long-term infection with disease-causing yeast can impair a candidiasis sufferer's immunity (chapter 14), predisposing them to develop infections with harmful bacteria, viruses, molds, and parasites. At the least, candidiasis is a risk factor for developing infectious arthritis (except for traumatic joint injuries).

Yet, the answer is more compelling when you realize where these infectious invaders reside. The mucous membranes, gastrointestinal tract, and respiratory tract are ideal locations for the growth and colonization of harmful bacteria. When someone is healthy, their body can keep these infectious invaders from causing trouble. When the colonization of disease-causing yeast within the gastrointestinal tract causes leaky gut syndrome (chapters 3 and 4) or inflammation within the respiratory tract (chapter 6), harmful bacteria can assault these weakened barriers, gaining access to and infecting the tissues and blood. With respect to viral arthritis, chronic candidiasis can impair immunity, encouraging the proliferation of one or more joint-infecting viruses (chapter 14). Except for traumatic injuries that directly induce a joint infection, there appears to be a *candidiasis–infectious arthritis connection*.

Gout

Gout is an illness that most frequently afflicts middle-aged and elderly men. In 2017, it was estimated there were 7.44 million cases worldwide. Although its precise causation is poorly understood, its incidence is associated with an elevated serum concentration of uric acid; this condition, *hyperuricemia*, reflects the *abnormal metabolism of purine* (the parent compound of numerous substances that comprise nucleoproteins, which aggregate to form things like DNA and RNA). The resulting hyperuricemia is *primary* when it occurs because of an error in metabolism and *secondary* if it manifests as the result of another disease. Greater than 99 percent of *primary* gout is *idiopathic*, meaning its cause remains unknown, whereas less than 1 percent is associated with an enzyme defect or metabolic error. Secondary hyperuricemia is acquired; numerous diseases promote excess purine production, an increased production and degradation of nucleoproteins, or a decreased clearance of uric acid. The reason this information is important will soon become evident.

Even though four stages are recognized, the characteristic gout "attack" is usually an intensely painful monoarticular arthritis involving the large toe, although it may also affect the bones and ligaments of the foot and knee (rarely, the heel or ankle). During an attack, abnormal purine metabolism promotes the excessive formation and release of *monosodium urate crystals* that are deposited within the fluid and linings of a specific joint, causing pain and inflammation. After the initial episode, numerous relapses frequently follow, which may endanger more than one joint. In addition, gout can have widespread adverse consequences; for example, circulating monosodium urate crystals can be deposited within the tissues of the kidney, promoting renal disease and systemic illness. Some gout sufferers are prone to develop kidney stones. How does this occur? Free uric acid and urate salts are insoluble in water. After these substances filter through the kidneys, they enter the urine, where they can precipitate out of solution, crystallize, and form kidney stones; in turn, this can instigate renal disease, not to mention a multitude of closely related disturbances. For all that is known about gout, the exact mechanism and cause of these disturbances is incompletely understood.

Can candidiasis be related to gout? Certainly, an inherited defect in purine metabolism is a byproduct of your genetics and not likely to be yeast-related; fine, but this describes fewer than 1 percent of primary hyperuricemia sufferers. In contrast, since greater than 99 percent of primary hyperuricemia has mysterious (idiopathic) origins, candidiasis is a possible cause; after all, many illnesses with no definable cause often involve an infection with disease-causing yeast, which frequently promote metabolic disturbances. If secondary hyperuricemia results from illnesses that indirectly alter purine metabolism, increasing uric acid production, can candidiasis be part of the cause? Looking deeper, numerous diseases, illnesses, and conditions are readily associated with the colonization of disease-causing yeast, so candidiasis may indirectly be responsible for secondary hyperuricemia as well. Therefore, candidiasis is likely to be related to gout. Is there evidence to support this thinking?

Some holistic physicians are aware that most gout sufferers have abnormal blood sugar regulation (*glucose intolerance*) with an increased or prolonged release of insulin (*hyperinsulinism*). Is this coincidental, or does it contribute to gout? *Insulin* is the blood sugar–lowering hormone that, in normal amounts, causes little harm. However, an excessive or prolonged release of insulin can trigger the generation of harmful free radical reactions (chapter 7) that may injure various metabolic pathways, including purine metabolism. In short, hyperinsulinism can promote increases of uric acid. Yet, why would someone have glucose intolerance and hyperinsulinism in the first place?

Metabolic immunosuppression (chapter 14) explains how a long-term infection with disease-causing yeast can promote glucose intolerance and hyperinsulinism, as well as hyperlipidemia and impaired immunity, in candidiasis sufferers. So, by promoting hyperinsulinism, candidiasis could cause an increased serum uric acid concentration. Is this speculation? No, when gout sufferers are treated with an anti-candidiasis approach, dramatic improvements often occur. Moreover, simply eliminating carbohydrates from the diet of a gout sufferer, especially simple carbohydrates, frequently drops their uric acid levels into the normal range, accompanied by a rapid decrease in their symptoms (by starving their disease-causing yeast).

Candidiasis can adversely affect purine production for other reasons. Normally, the liver is an organ of metabolism, including its ability to process, produce, and regulate amino acids, the building blocks of nucleoproteins. In the presence of a significant or prolonged infection, especially chronic candidiasis, the liver decreases its metabolic activities to assist the immune system in fighting the infection; during its *acute phase response*, the liver produces and releases numerous proteins to assist immunity (chapter 14). As its metabolic duties decrease, the liver may not properly metabolize purine, resulting in increased uric acid levels. In addition, a chronic infection takes its toll on the body, instigating an increased recycling of cells, and if purine metabolism is compromised, the uric acid level can elevate. To add insult, chronic candidiasis sufferers often have decreased kidney functioning, which can impair their uric acid excretion, promoting increased levels. Although some will disagree and claim this is speculation, it explains why treating candidiasis often eliminates someone's gout permanently.

With respect to mainstream medical therapy, allopurinol is often the drug of choice for managing gout. Typically, it reduces the serum uric acid level in one to two weeks by inhibiting the enzyme *xanthine oxidase*. Is this how it really works? Not according to A. V. Constantini, M.D., the retired head of the World Health Organization. In 1992, he published research stating that harmful molds and their toxins (*mycotoxins*) are responsible for most chronic illnesses. He claims allopurinol works because it has *anti-fungal* activity; it kills disease-causing yeast and harmful molds; eliminating candidiasis improves glucose intolerance and hyperinsulinism, decreases the generation of harmful free radicals, and turns off the liver's acute phase response, improving metabolism. Moreover, killing disease-causing yeast and harmful molds eliminates a group of infectious invaders that produce numerous harmful toxins and metabolites as well as trigger inflammation and allergic reactions within the body. Regardless of whether disease-causing yeast, harmful molds, or both are to blame for hyperuricemia, all the evidence points toward the existence of a *candidiasis-gout connection.*

Pseudogout

Pseudogout is an illness mostly confined to the elderly of both sexes. Estimates vary, but 4 to 7 percent of American adults are thought to be affected. Clinically, its joint changes appear nearly identical to gout. Although almost any joint can be disturbed, the knees, wrist, and hands are the most victimized. Instead of uric acid, the arthritis involves the deposition of *calcium salts*—specifically, *calcium pyrophosphate dihydrate crystals.* The precise origin of pseudogout remains ambiguous. Yet, if calcium salts are deposited within and around a joint, it makes sense they would first have to be elevated within the blood. Why would there be an increase in calcium salts? Using gout as an example, excesses of calcium salts are likely to reflect increased production, decreased breakdown, and/or decreased elimination.

Can candidiasis be involved? Yes, because abnormal calcium metabolism frequently occurs among its sufferers. Why? Calcium metabolism depends on the *parathyroid glands*, which produce *parathyroid hormone*; it regulates the blood *calcium* ion and *magnesium* ion concentrations (chapter 11). Candidiasis sufferers often have *functional hypoparathyroidism*—abnormal hormone functioning, leading to low levels of calcium and magnesium within their cells and tissues, as well as increased blood levels of phosphorus, even though their blood levels appear normal.

You might think that because functional hypoparathyroidism promotes lowered levels of calcium, it seems unlikely to cause calcium salt deposition. On the contrary, a diet high in calcium in someone with functional hypoparathyroidism increases calcium salt production because the dietary calcium that enters their blood is impaired from entering their cells and tissues, leading to calcium excesses, and with elevated amounts of phosphorus, the materials for creating calcium pyrophosphate dihydrate crystals are readily available. These crystals can be deposited within and around susceptible joints. (This may be missed because most levels are measured after fasting many hours.) Moreover, decreased liver and kidney functioning, typical among candidiasis sufferers, exacerbates the situation. Less commonly, sufferers can develop *hyperparathyroidism*, an excessive secretion of parathyroid hormone. Generally, this produces elevated serum calcium ion levels (hypercalcemia) that could stimulate the production of calcium salts, encouraging their deposition within one or more joints. Regardless of an increase or decrease in parathyroid hormone, there appears to be support for a *candidiasis-pseudogout connection*.

OSTEOARTHRITIS

Although relapses are common, monoarticular arthritis is usually an *acute* illness. In contrast, polyarticular arthritis is more prevalent, frequently long-lasting, and progressive. Depending on someone's circumstances, polyarticular arthritis may arise *primarily* within their joints or occur *secondarily* because of another systemic disturbance.

Osteoarthritis is the prominent cause of joint pain and its disabilities in middle-aged and elderly people. Since it is a progressive degenerative disease, its presentations range from extremely mild to severely debilitating. In general, osteoarthritis involves degeneration of the joint cartilage, bony remodeling, and the overgrowth of abnormal areas of bone, producing the undesirable, age-related joint changes that are frequently observed. Sooner or later, an alteration within the joint's metabolism and functioning cause anatomical alterations that lead to biomechanical disturbances. It is estimated that 500 million adults are affected, and 90 percent of the population will have this type of arthritis by their eighth decade of life.

What is it like to have osteoarthritis? Many sufferers with mild illness would not know they have it, except for the bony changes that make their malady evident. Yet, as their disease progresses, a typical sufferer is likely to awaken with joint stiffness that may slowly resolve or linger throughout the day. When stiffness is present, it often includes a deep aching pain. There is also likely to be variable thickening of the joint tissues as well as excessive synovial fluid within the affected joints (effusions). Although the initial anatomical disturbances are minor, they tend to worsen, leading to marked instability and disability as time passes.

The most common type of osteoarthritis is *idiopathic*, which has no known cause and appears unrelated to local or systemic disorders. The secondary presentations are clinically indistinguishable and are attributable to various prior insults and/or disturbances.

Because of its degenerative nature, candidiasis might appear to have little influence in instigating or promoting osteoarthritis. Yet, like a magician with a trick up his sleeve, there is more going on than meets the eye. The deposition of *calcium crystals* is known to complicate osteoarthritis and may promote much of its pain and inflammation. One study found that 42 percent of osteoarthritic knees had effusions containing *calcium pyrophosphate dihydrate crystals*, and these crystals or *calcium apatite crystals* were present in 60 percent or more of the tested subjects. Since 42 percent of these crystals are involved with pseudogout, similar metabolic changes seem to be involved with osteoarthritis. If the abnormal calcium metabolism of pseudogout can be traced to a parathyroid gland disturbance resulting from chronic candidiasis, as discussed previously, the same process can participate in osteoarthritis sufferers, at least in 42 percent of them; including the other calcium salt crystal raises the total to over 60 percent. Yes, it is not 100 percent, but it is evidence for a *candidiasis-osteoarthritis connection*, nonetheless.

More compelling evidence was noted when researchers intravenously injected 40 rats with a nonlethal dose of *Candida albicans* cells. Joint swelling (experimental osteoarthritis) was induced in 24 rats, with two or more joints affected in 10 of them. (Was it a coincidence 24/40 = 60 percent?) Since dark-field microscopy often reveals disease-causing yeast living within blood samples of candidiasis sufferers, their physical presence within the blood is likely to contribute to the development and progression of osteoarthritis.

Does the pain only involve the deposition and presence of calcium crystals or is something else occurring? If the crystals were the only cause, they would be present within the joint fluid of every sufferer with pain. Since crystals are not a universal finding, they cannot be completely responsible. So, what else can contribute to the joint pain?

Obviously, anatomical changes that disturb a joint's functioning and movement can create pain and disability within and around a joint. Although this occurs in many osteoarthritis sufferers, other sufferers exhibit anatomical disturbances (bony changes) without significant symptoms or pain. So, joint changes do not guarantee pain. Conversely, the complete absence of joint changes, or only minor bony alterations, does not ensure that there will be no pain because many sufferers complain of significant pain without evidence of any notable joint disturbances. Since bony changes are not consistently associated with pain, is there something else that can cause joint pain?

Numerous foods allergies are known to adversely affect the joints, causing inflammation and pain. Classically, the nightshade vegetables (tomatoes, potatoes, peppers, eggplant, paprika, and tobacco) are appreciated as being guilty of this mischief. Once these items are eliminated from someone's diet and immediate external environment, their allergy-inducing effects diminish, and their joint pain frequently decreases and may disappear. In addition, because most osteoarthritis sufferers have allergies to many other foods, it is important to identify all their allergy-inducing foods and eliminate them from their diet.

How does someone become allergic to foods? Most allergies develop when disease-causing yeast colonize the gastrointestinal tract and cause leaky gut syndrome (chapter 4); undigested food particles can inappropriately enter the tissues and blood, inciting the immune system to react against these substances, instigating food allergies in the process. After candidiasis is eliminated, these irritating food particles cannot assault the gut wall, which alleviates someone's food allergies and their inflammation. Simply put, joint pain (arthralgia) is a *symptom*, and candidiasis is often its cause. This provides evidence for a *candidiasis-arthralgia connection*. In the bigger picture, it helps explain much of the pain and inflammation that accompanies osteoarthritis. Moreover, allergies to disease-causing yeast and harmful molds may also contribute (chapter 16).

Except for those with previous trauma, most osteoarthritis sufferers can be helped by accepting that there is a *candidiasis-osteoarthritis connection* and seeking appropriate treatment. When found early, an anti-candidiasis approach can eliminate pain and inflammation as well as prevent progression of anatomical disturbances. Even if it advanced, treating candidiasis can alleviate symptoms and slow or halt its progress. In fact, appreciating the *candidiasis-food allergy-arthralgia connection* is a simple way to decrease, and even eliminate joint pain, inflammation, and stiffness. There is nothing to lose for trying, other than your joint pain.

RHEUMATOID ARTHRITIS

Rheumatoid arthritis is a chronic, systemic type of arthritis that often arises in midlife, between ages 30 and 50. Roughly three of four sufferers are women. Almost 14 million people worldwide have it, and, as of 2017, more than 1.36 million people in the United States were afflicted. Research reveals that approximately 7 percent will develop crippling arthritis within five years. By 10 years, more than 50 percent will stop working because of their disability.

Typically, a sufferer's joints demonstrate an inflammatory pattern of involvement, *symmetrically* affecting the cells and tissues within and around their joints. Over time, the inflammation may progress to include the adjacent bone. Because it is a systemic illness, it may instigate and promote generalized inflammation within a variety of tissues and organs.

Most rheumatoid arthritis sufferers (about two-thirds) experience the slow onset of their illness, which frequently evolves over weeks to months. During this time, there may be several nonspecific complaints, including malaise, fatigue, and weight loss, as well as intermittent, diffuse musculoskeletal pain. Since these symptoms often mimic a chronic viral illness or flu-like condition, the diagnosis is not readily evident. In contrast, about 20 percent of rheumatoid arthritis sufferers experience an abrupt onset of illness, over a few days or less, making their malady more obvious. Initially, the arthritis tends to involve their smaller joints and then often progresses to adversely affect almost all.

A *positive rheumatoid factor* can be found in 50 to 95 percent of sufferers, signifying the presence of self-reactive antibodies targeted to attack the cells and tissues of their joints. After these autoantibodies bind to cells or tissues, certain immune cells mistakenly recognize them as foreign and attack them. The number of autoantibodies frequently, but not universally, determines the disease severity. Yet, if the rheumatoid factor is *negative*, implying no autoantibodies, it does not mean there is no rheumatoid arthritis (or other types of autoimmune disease). In short, autoantibodies are *not* required for autoimmune disease. So, what happens in these people? Instead of autoantibodies, *cell-mediated autoimmunity* (chapter 14) is responsible for their joint destruction; for numerous reasons, certain immune cells directly attack cells and tissues that are mistakenly recognized as foreign. In either case, rheumatoid arthritis involves destruction of a person's joints by their own immune system, and it includes cell-mediated destruction, with or without autoantibodies.

So, rheumatoid arthritis is an autoimmune disease. This type of disease disturbs the entire body, explaining why rheumatoid arthritis has numerous, adverse systemic consequences. In fact, a variety of non-joint symptoms are common among its sufferers, ranging from barely noticeable disturbances to major systemic complications that are localized or generalized. The tissues tending to be adversely affected are the skin, heart, lungs, nervous system, and eyes. Classically, this can produce subcutaneous nodules, muscle wasting (atrophy), inflammation of the lung's linings (pleurisy) that may promote scar tissue (pulmonary fibrosis), inflammation of the membranes surrounding the heart (pericarditis), swollen lymph nodes (lymphadenopathy), impaired immunity (leukopenia), and a reduction in the number of circulating red blood cells (anemia). Given the scope and magnitude of its effects, it can advance to become a diverse, systemic, inflammatory disorder. Rheumatoid arthritis is a much more serious illness than the other major types of arthritis because once autoimmunity arises, it is often difficult, if not impossible, to reverse. At least, this is what most mainstream physicians will tell you.

The American College of Rheumatology has criteria to diagnosis rheumatoid arthritis. Depending on the number, it is labeled as *classic, definite,* and *probable*. The criteria were created to distinguish it from disorders that mimic it. They were also created to name a disease. Yet, creating criteria that help define and name a disease is not the same as identifying its cause. In fact, even after years of intensive investigation, its etiology and origins remain a mystery. Mainstream medicine has studied the contributions of nutrition, metabolism, and the endocrine system. They have considered familial (genetic) inheritance, geographical prevalence, occupational risks, and psychosocial factors. Their conclusion is that rheumatoid arthritis most likely results from *immune system abnormalities,* which may involve one or more infectious invaders. In short, rheumatoid arthritis is an autoimmune disease that may have an infectious cause. Yes, it arises in the presence of impaired immunity (chapter 14), but immune system abnormalities do not occur for no reason. Although there may be exceptions, one or more infectious invaders *must* be present within most rheumatoid arthritis sufferers, or their immunity would not be impaired. Which infectious invader is most likely to impair immunity and is not being recognized?

In 1995, Gus J. Prosch, Jr., M.D., et al. stated, "All arthritics, by virtue of their weakened immune system, suffer also from candidiasis, or 'organisms of opportunity' similar to candidiasis. Arthritics who are presumed to already have a weakened immune system, and who are obviously suffering from candidiasis, certainly don't need another factor to further stress their immune system!" Simply put, they believe the weakened immunity of arthritis sufferers enables disease-causing *Candida*-species organisms to reproduce and colonize their surroundings. In return, an infection with disease-causing yeast further weakens their immunity. Although they recognized an association between arthritis, weakened immunity, and candidiasis, they put the cart before the horse by claiming that candidiasis results from the arthritis and weakened immunity. Moreover, they do not discuss why arthritis sufferers develop impaired immunity in the first place. So, what is really going on?

In the November 5, 1998, issue of *Medical Tribune,* an article titled "Drug for Crohn's disease said to help treat arthritis patients' pain." It stated, "Rheumatoid-arthritis sufferers may someday find relief from their aching joints and crippling lethargy with a new drug that affects the immune system by inhibiting tumor necrosis factor alpha (TNF-alpha)." *TNF-alpha* is a chemical mediator involved with inflammatory cell activity; it increases in the presence of inflammation and infection. Unsurprisingly, chronic candidiasis is an *infection,* with *allergic* consequences, that promotes the production of TNF-alpha, which can cause significant *inflammation,* leading to chronic joint pain. So, it appears a *candidiasis–rheumatoid arthritis connection* is possible. Furthermore, this evidence indicates that candidiasis would precede the development of rheumatoid arthritis.

A chronic infection with disease-causing yeast can disturb and impair the immune system, leading to *suppressed immunity* (inferior functioning cells), *depressed immunity* (fewer cells), or *suppressed-depressed immunity* (fewer, inferior functioning cells). *Metabolic immunosuppression* (chapter 14) explains how candidiasis can compromise the immunity of candidiasis sufferers. In certain people, it permits abnormal cells targeted to inappropriately attack the cells and tissues of their joints to reproduce. In short, a decrease in the amount of "good" immune cells allows one or more "bad" cells to achieve prominence and instigate trouble. Although autoantibodies are common among rheumatoid arthritis sufferers, they are not required for the disease process. Basically, chronic candidiasis encourages direct cell-mediated insults to one or more joints, with or without the presence of self-reactive antibodies.

Since evidence exists to implicate *Candida albicans* in contributing to rheumatoid arthritis, this understanding can be used to treat other autoimmune joint diseases as well. Numerous other joint maladies are related to rheumatoid arthritis, including *ankylosing spondylitis, Reiter's syndrome, juvenile chronic arthropathy, peripheral arthropathy, spondylarthritis,* and *psoriatic arthropathy.* Since many have no identifiable autoantibodies, most are likely to involve direct cell-mediated autoimmunity. Although there is some genetic predisposition to develop these illnesses, the origin of each is incompletely understood or remains obscure. Like rheumatoid arthritis, illness cannot arise without a cause. Since there is a *candidiasis–autoimmune disease connection* (chapter 14) and there seems to be a *candidiasis–rheumatoid arthritis connection,* the other autoimmune joint illnesses are probably also related to candidiasis. Their differences are likely to reflect the way they manifest within different people as well as reflect the presence of various infectious invaders.

Furthermore, many systemic illnesses have arthritis as a prominent component. Even though rheumatoid factor is absent, other autoantibodies may be involved. These medical maladies include *systemic lupus erythematosus* (SLE), *systemic sclerosis* (scleroderma), *Sjögren's syndrome, polyarteritis nodosa*, and *polymyalgia rheumatica*. In addition, a wide variety of diseases are associated with arthritis, and there are some miscellaneous forms as well. Clearly, there is a great diversity of joint maladies, and the cause of most, if not all, is still not precisely determined. An investigation to uncover the culprits involved with these forms of arthritis is likely to reveal the presence and adverse contributions of disease-causing yeast, with or without the assistance of other infectious invaders, including harmful parasites, bacteria, molds, and/or viruses. Some associations for candidiasis have been described, and further investigations are certain to strengthen this position.

In summary, rheumatoid arthritis and the other autoimmune-related presentations of arthritis are closely associated with chronic candidiasis. Since these illnesses typically involve impaired immunity, the presence of other infectious invaders is not uncommon, explaining why many rheumatoid arthritis sufferers are frequently found to harbor one or more harmful parasites, bacteria, molds, and/or viruses. With this understanding, rheumatoid arthritis sufferers now have a chance to improve, and even eliminate, their pain and suffering forever. Although there are no guarantees, an appreciation for the *candidiasis–rheumatoid arthritis connection* should provide great hope for all rheumatoid arthritis sufferers.

RHEUMATOID ARTHRITIS & FOOD ALLERGY

Food allergies contribute to many types of arthritis. If you have rheumatoid arthritis, you may have discovered that eating certain foods exacerbates your symptoms. Typically, the nightshade vegetables (tomatoes, potatoes, peppers, eggplant, paprika, and tobacco) are common culprits. Although all sufferers are not sensitive to these vegetables, most demonstrate allergies to one or more foods. Is this a coincidental finding? No, because there is a *candidiasis-rheumatoid arthritis-food allergy connection*. Rheumatoid arthritis is not a gastrointestinal condition, even though gut symptoms are not uncommon among its sufferers. Since candidiasis primarily arises within the gut before advancing and affecting other areas of the body, rather than resulting from rheumatoid arthritis, candidiasis is the primary promoter of food allergies. How does this happen? The colonization of disease-causing yeast within the gut can cause inflammation and injury to the gut wall, creating leaky gut syndrome (chapters 3 and 4). This creates areas where inappropriately digested food particles can pass through the gut wall, enter the surrounding tissues, and then the blood. When this occurs, these substances are often recognized by the immune system as foreign. As a result, food allergies and inflammation result. In fact, candidiasis can induce a variety of food allergies, which can greatly increase someone's inflammation and aggravate their rheumatoid arthritis (or other symptoms).

Moreover, decreased amounts of hydrochloric acid within someone's stomach and digestive system (*hypochlorhydria*) can contribute to food sensitivities by slowing down the activity of *pepsin*, the enzyme that initiates protein digestion. Many proteins are allergy-inducing (antigenic) in their predigested state, but when properly metabolized, they are degraded into their amino acids and peptides, which do not usually retain an ability to precipitate or cause allergies. In short, if an ingested protein is not cleaved into small pieces, an increased quantity of allergy-inducing food particles will interact with the cells and tissues. An abundance of protein-derived antigens can inflame the gut wall, impairing its ability to function properly. In turn, this allows undesirable substances to be absorbed, contributing to or exacerbating leaky gut syndrome. Impaired gut functioning enables arthritis sufferers to absorb enormous amounts of intact and partially digested allergy-inducing food particles. So, a *food allergy–rheumatoid arthritis connection* should be taken seriously.

Is this a new realization? No, because food sensitivities have been noted for thousands of years. Many physicians agree and have explored this issue. When rheumatoid arthritis sufferers are tested, most of them demonstrate allergies to specific foods (and environmental chemicals). Fortunately, the adverse effects of food allergies can be avoided by eliminating the allergy-inducing foods, and scientific evidence supports this thinking. Studies revealed eliminating allergy-inducing foods produced significant benefits in both subjective and objective parameters, which persisted for as long as the foods were avoided.

The surprising efficacy of an elimination and rotation diet has been appreciated by many physicians that treat similar patients. For example, one study reported a successful 10-year follow-up of 100 arthritis patients treated with dietary modifications. After a decade, 33 percent of them continued to remain symptom-free.

How do food allergies promote joint pain? The contributions of TNF-alpha were mentioned, and there may be other ways as well. Usually, exposing an arthritis sufferer to a heavy load of allergy-inducing food particles (antigens) promotes abundant inflammation. It is thought that this directly stimulates the cell membrane receptors that control the activity of pain neurons.

Although candidiasis and food allergies participate in the mischief of rheumatoid arthritis and are frequently underappreciated, a *candidiasis-food allergy-rheumatoid arthritis connection* does exist and must not be ignored. Addressing and treating rheumatoid arthritis patients with this approach is certain to improve their ill health.

RHEUMATOID ARTHRITIS & OTHER INFECTIOUS INVADERS

Although there are exceptions, the more persistent and systemic the arthritis, the greater the chance chronic candidiasis is its underlying cause. Yet, disease-causing yeast do not usually cause mischief alone. Candidiasis sufferers commonly have one or more other infectious invaders, including harmful parasites, bacteria, molds, and/or viruses.

Is there evidence to associate parasites with rheumatoid arthritis? In 1979, Dr. Roger Wyburn-Myson reported that almost all his rheumatoid arthritis patients harbored a protozoa parasite within their tissues (an amoebae of the genus *Naegleria*). Once this parasite was determined to be the culprit, it was grown in the laboratory and administered to animals. In return, the test subjects developed and displayed various stages of rheumatoid arthritis as well as arthritic tissue changes. So, at least one parasite is scientifically associated with rheumatoid arthritis, but there are more.

Another physician reported treating more than 1,500 arthritic patients with antiparasitic medications, achieving a 60 to 70 percent success rate, which is strong evidence for the participation of parasites in arthritis. Not bad, considering that candidiasis was not addressed.

What about harmful bacteria and other related microorganisms? *Lyme disease* is caused by a tick bite that transmits a spirochete called *Borrelia burgdorferi*. This infection promotes numerous symptoms and is well known for its ability to cause a specific type of arthritis called *Lyme arthritis*. Since rheumatoid arthritis sufferers can have Lyme disease, it is important to determine if this situation exists; eliminating their *Borrelia burgdorferi* is likely to improve their condition. Many others infectious invaders are related to arthritis, especially the species of harmful bacteria called *Proteus*, *Klebsiella*, *Salmonella*, *Shigella*, and *Yersenia*. There is such an abundance of harmful bacteria that it is difficult to associate most of these infectious invaders directly with rheumatoid arthritis. Nevertheless, stool cultures reveal that rheumatoid arthritis sufferers are usually infected with one or more harmful bacteria within their gastrointestinal tract, producing *dysbiosis* and *dysbacteriosis* (chapter 4), which readily disrupts their gut's functioning. Identifying and eliminating the presence of any harmful bacteria is important to improve a rheumatoid arthritis sufferer's health.

Undeniably, harmful parasites, bacteria, and molds can contribute to causing or exacerbating rheumatoid arthritis. Yet, do viruses also play a role? *Epstein-Barr virus* (EBV) is a member of the herpesvirus family and well known for its ability to cause *infectious mononucleosis*. A multitude of research connects EBV with rheumatoid arthritis. In short, EBV can cause the production of autoantibodies, many rheumatoid arthritis sufferers have evidence of an EBV infection, and rheumatoid arthritis patients have weakened immunity, making them unable to properly combat EBV. Despite the close relationship between rheumatoid arthritis and EBV, the researchers concluded that EBV is probably not the cause of rheumatoid arthritis.

Indeed, EBV is probably an innocent bystander in rheumatoid arthritis or an opportunistic infectious invader at best. By adulthood, virtually everyone has been exposed to EBV. In people with healthy immunity, EBV remains a peaceful, sleeping virus. In contrast, candidiasis can impair immunity, allowing these (and other) dormant viruses to become active (chapter 14). Therefore, the same conditions that encourage EBV replication also instigate or promote rheumatoid arthritis; that is, chronic candidiasis encourages both conditions. How does EBV contribute to rheumatoid arthritis? After EBV is activated, an EBV infection is likely to further weaken a candidiasis sufferer's immunity. This effect exacerbates immune disturbances, promoting the production of *self*-reactive cells and autoantibodies. (This may represent the presence of an EBV infection within certain tissues and the body's attempt to eradicate the virus from these areas.) Although EBV does not directly cause rheumatoid arthritis, its presence exacerbates and aggravates a person's condition and ill health.

Undeniably, numerous infectious invaders can contribute to promoting or causing rheumatoid arthritis, including harmful parasites, bacteria, molds, and/or viruses. Yes, these infectious invaders can create trouble on their own and often do when they are aggressive. Yet, few notable problems often arise unless candidiasis is also present. In fact, without candidiasis and its ability to cause leaky gut syndrome and weaken immunity, most of these infectious invaders seem to cause little harm within most people. In contrast, when candidiasis is present, the undesirable effects of these troublemakers are greatly amplified. So, if someone has arthritis, it is essential to identify and eliminate all their participating infectious invaders.

COULD THE PAIN BE FIBROMYALGIA?

About 4 million adults suffer with fibromyalgia in the United States, and almost 1 in 20 people, or 5 percent, are affected worldwide. It is a chronic condition in people of all ages, but most sufferers are diagnosed during middle age. Women are twice as likely as men to have it. Rather than classified as a disease, this ailment is considered a syndrome with many associated symptoms; in fact, its proper designation is *fibromyalgia syndrome.*

Fibromyalgia syndrome is a condition that typically involves pain. Since it shares many similarities with arthritis, these two conditions are often confused with one another. Having one does not exclude the other, and people can have both. Yet, it is possible to tell these two conditions apart. Typically, fibromyalgia involves neck and shoulder pain, morning stiffness, fatigue, and sleep disturbances. Although these symptoms can be present in an arthritis sufferer, fibromyalgia pain is usually associated with someone's *muscles* and *connective tissue*, not their joints. Therefore, unlike arthritis, diagnosing fibromyalgia depends on a minimum number of body points that are tender when touched.

Most medical experts believe fibromyalgia syndrome is closely related to chronic fatigue syndrome, and both are thought to represent manifestations of the same disorder. Since there is a *chronic fatigue–fibromyalgia syndrome connection* and a *candidiasis–chronic fatigue connection* (chapter 15), there must be a *candidiasis-chronic fatigue-fibromyalgia syndrome connection.*

Research reveals the involvement of disease-causing yeast in fibromyalgia syndrome. Using the *citric acid cycle* of metabolism, disease-causing yeast and other fungi can produce numerous harmful metabolites, including *citramalic acid, tartaric acid, 3-oxoglutaric acid,* and *carboxycitric acid.* Among these, tartaric acid is specifically known to be destructive to muscle tissue (as well as citramalic acid). It is thought, therefore, that the overproduction of tartaric acid by disease-causing yeast (and other fungi) in susceptible people causes the muscle damage of fibromyalgia syndrome. Furthermore, for many reasons, chronic candidiasis can promote excesses of *lactic acid*, a substance that can make muscles more prone to fatigue.

Some physicians believe that fibromyalgia syndrome is related to a decreased flow of lymph thorough the *lymphatic system. Lymph* is a fluid created within all the tissue spaces of the body. After its formation, it flows into small vessels that lead to larger vessels, and eventually enters the blood. Lymph contains *proteins* (serum albumin, serum globulin, serum fibrinogen), *salts, organic substances* (urea, creatinine, neutral fats, glucose), *water,* and immune cells called *lymphocytes.* Decreasing the flow of lymph increases the amounts of these substances within the affected muscles, leading to increased pressure and pain within these areas. It is not known whether candidiasis can decrease lymphatic drainage, but the presence of citric acid cycle metabolites is certain to exacerbate this condition as well as the inflammation that accompanies the *infectious* and *allergic* contributions of disease-causing yeast.

The evidence supports a *candidiasis–fibromyalgia syndrome connection,* especially when the chronic presence of disease-causing yeast adversely affects the nervous (chapter 10), endocrine (chapter 11), and immune systems (chapter 14). One or more other infectious invaders may actively participate and need to be addressed accordingly. Moreover, holistic physicians also consider the adverse contributions of toxic heavy metals because many sufferers improve with detoxification. Instead of having no hope, fibromyalgia syndrome sufferers now have a good chance to regain their wellness.

OSTEOPOROSIS: DISEASE, SYNDROME, OR SYMPTOM?

Although it is not initially associated with pain, *osteoporosis* is a malady that can eventually involve an incredible amount of debilitation and may even lead to death. It occurs when bone is broken down faster than it is manufactured, resulting in decreased bone density, which compromises the bone's integrity and ability to provide mechanical support. Fractures are more likely and, when advanced, may happen spontaneously. In the United States, about 10 million people over age 50 have osteoporosis, and more than 200 million people suffer with it worldwide. According to the International Osteoporosis Foundation, one in three women and one in five men over age 50 will have osteoporotic fractures in their lifetime.

Although osteoporosis is known to be associated with a diversity of disorders, 60 percent of men and 80 percent of women have osteoporosis *without* a definitive origin. On the contrary, something must be responsible for causing a decrease in bone density whether or not it is recognized.

To understand osteoporosis, it is important to know how bone is regulated. As a tissue, bone performs four functions. It provides rigid *support and protection* for the soft tissues, *assists movement*, and *harbors immature red and white blood cells* within its marrow. Bone is also an enormous *reservoir* (about two-thirds of its weight) for numerous *essential minerals*, especially calcium, phosphorus, magnesium, and sodium. Bone is constantly remodeled, and *parathyroid hormone* maintains its complex structure (chapter 11); it is released in response to low serum levels of calcium ions, which stimulates bone to liberate calcium and phosphate ions. In addition, this hormone affects the kidneys by increasing calcium and magnesium reabsorption and the excretion of phosphate and bicarbonate, and it also enhances the absorption of calcium within the intestines (indirectly with vitamin D). In a healthy person, parathyroid hormone raises the calcium ion concentration to normal, and then its levels decrease until it is needed again. Normally, bone is broken down (resorption) equal to the rate it is formed, ensuring a steady state and continuous stability in adults. Since a loss of bone density occurs in osteoporosis sufferers, something must be causing bone to be degraded faster than it is made.

Is it a coincidence that a significant number of elderly candidiasis sufferers have osteoporosis? Conversely, why do most osteoporosis sufferers have one or more candidiasis-related symptoms, especially gut problems? Is there a *candidiasis-osteoporosis connection*? Indeed, the prominent risk factors for osteoporosis include *endocrine* (hormone) *disturbances* and *gastrointestinal diseases*. Both are exceedingly common among candidiasis sufferers (chapters 4 and 11). Osteoporosis sufferers and candidiasis sufferers have much in common. Is there really a *candidiasis-osteoporosis connection*?

Since chronic candidiasis frequently promotes malabsorption, leading to deficiencies of dietary calcium and magnesium, bone is signaled to supply these minerals to maintain normal levels within the blood. Over time, this can cause a loss of bone. At the least, osteoporosis sufferers should be assessed for malabsorption. Yet, the cause of malabsorption is another story altogether. In most gut illnesses, candidiasis and leaky gut syndrome are responsible for malabsorption, with or without the help of other infectious invaders. With few exceptions, most cases of osteoporosis appear to arise secondary to candidiasis.

What about hormone disturbances? Since estrogen replacements have stabilized the course of some sufferers, *estrogen deficiencies* are associated with osteoporosis. Unsurprisingly, estrogen deficiencies are extremely common among candidiasis sufferers (chapter 11), providing more evidence for a *candidiasis-osteoporosis connection.*

More likely, the endocrine disturbance involves *abnormal* parathyroid hormone activity. Malabsorption precipitates a low concentration of serum calcium ions (and magnesium ions). Normally, this promotes hyperparathyroidism, increasing calcium absorption and its conservation. Yet, in the presence of malabsorption, diet is not a significant source of calcium. So, conservation and bone resorption must escalate, and excessive bone loss occurs. Some candidiasis sufferers do manifest hyperparathyroidism.

In contrast, candidiasis sufferers often have a deficiency of parathyroid hormone; in fact, *functional hypoparathyroidism* is the most common candidiasis-related endocrine (hormone) disturbance (chapter 11). It involves a decrease of calcium and magnesium ions within the cells and tissues, while the blood's calcium ion concentration is normal. The body cannot resupply the cells and tissues because there is a functional hormone deficiency. Why does this occur? Parathyroid hormone is sensitive to the presence of magnesium ions, and a severe or prolonged decrease of magnesium inhibits its release. Normally, a lack of parathyroid hormone should result in low blood levels of calcium, but this is not what happens, and the bone continues to supply these minerals, resulting in bone loss. (Calcium and magnesium ion levels do eventually fall below normal.) So, a deficiency of parathyroid hormone will cause a loss of bone. Various studies demonstrate that, while estrogen is important, a deficiency of parathyroid hormone is integral to osteoporosis. As a result, parathyroid hormone replacement seems to be more important than estrogen replacement.

When osteoporosis occurs in someone without a definitive cause, attempting to correct a hormone disturbance only treats the symptom. Alternatively, most osteoporosis sufferers should be investigated for chronic candidiasis because this will correct the malabsorption and endocrine disturbances that are likely to instigate and promote their malady. Using an anti-candidiasis approach to treatment, osteoporosis can be prevented and even reversed.

ELIMINATING YOUR ACHES & PAINS

In every person's lifetime, it is not uncommon to wake up with one or more stiff, achy, or painful joints. When this occurs after too much strenuous work or exercise, there is little cause for concern. Applying ice to decrease pain and inflammation, a few days of rest, and a massage are certain to return that person to a state of good health.

In contrast, when someone's joint pain results from arthritis, there is a reason for concern. Although pain and inflammation involving one or more joints are common symptoms, the real problem is that many types of arthritis frequently promote progressive debilitation and disability.

Arthritis is not a single illness but a variety of manifestations that may involve one joint or many. As a result, the effects of arthritis can be localized or widespread. Even worse, the most severe types are not just joint disturbances but systemic illnesses.

Arthritis can arise from age-related changes (osteoarthritis), infections (infectious arthritis), metabolic disturbances (gout and pseudogout), and autoimmune diseases (rheumatoid arthritis and many other types of arthritis). Each type has numerous implications, reflecting its origin, development, and course. It is important to distinguish arthritis from fibromyalgia syndrome because the approach to treatment and management, although similar, is not the same. Moreover, a loss of bone (osteoporosis) can occur in the absence of arthritis and, although it may not initially cause pain, in the long run it can lead to an abundance of debilitation, nonetheless.

Acute infectious arthritis must be immediately addressed to save a person's joint from imminent destruction. In addition, gout and pseudogout should be quickly treated to decrease its accompanying pain and suffering. In contrast, the chronic types of arthritis typically involve therapy aimed to comfort its sufferer and provide mobility for their affected joints. As a result, medications that decrease inflammation and pain are routinely used, which typically produce numerous undesirable side effects and adverse complications like gut ulcers. Due to the nature of autoimmune diseases, many people with rheumatoid arthritis (and its related types of arthritis) are destined to progressively deteriorate over time, which eventually precipitates biomechanical abnormalities and debilitation.

Why does arthritis develop? Although there is some inherited genetic tendency to develop it, mainstream medicine does not know exactly why most cases develop. Its experts can explain much of the way it works (its pathology) and reveal numerous factors associated with it, but its cause is often poorly understood. For most sufferers, the best mainstream medicine can do is treat symptoms. This means that, except for infectious arthritis, mainstream physicians cannot eliminate (cure) the arthritis. Are these sufferers destined to slowly deteriorate with every passing moment?

There is hope because a better solution is available. Abundant evidence indicates that chronic candidiasis can instigate and promote the undesirable disturbances and joint symptoms that produce most types of arthritis, directly and/or indirectly. The colonization of disease-causing yeast is an *infection* with *allergic* consequences. In return, it can promote pain and inflammation within one or more joints. Moreover, the colonization of disease-causing yeast within the gut can cause leaky gut syndrome, leading to the absorption of various undigested foods that induce food allergies, which increase an arthritis sufferer's pain and inflammation. With respect to rheumatoid arthritis, chronic candidiasis can impair and confuse the immune system, resulting in the generation of immune cells that are inappropriately programmed to attack someone's own joints and tissues; this may or may not involve the presence of self-directed autoantibodies, although it frequently does. Specifics aside, all of this indicates that there is a *candidiasis-arthritis connection*.

Is candidiasis the sole cause of arthritis? No, it can occur with other infectious invaders, including harmful parasites, bacteria, molds, and/or viruses. In addition, it may be instigated or exacerbated by chemical sensitivities, chemical toxicities, toxic heavy metals, and environmental irritants and allergies. Anything within an arthritis sufferer's body or external environment can contribute to causing or aggravating their joint disturbances.

If you suffer with arthritis, what can you do? Eliminating your candidiasis is the best way to reestablish a state of good health. It is also essential to uncover, identify, and eradicate all the infectious invaders contributing to your ill health. Attending to your food allergies is critical. Some sufferers need to address their environmental allergies. Since most sufferers are allergic to numerous disease-causing yeast and harmful molds, they must be tested (chapter 17), and desensitization (allergy) injections are frequently important (chapter 18). In fact, some arthritis sufferers will not eliminate their pain and inflammation unless they receive these injections to treat their allergies.

Although the bony changes of osteoarthritis may be an inevitable consequence of aging, it and the other types of arthritis do not have to ruin your life. Understanding the *candidiasis-arthritis connection* and getting proper treatment can make freedom from joint pain a reality for the millions of people who suffer with arthritis.

CHAPTER 10

Psychological & Neurological Manifestations

If you suffer with candidiasis, you have probably experienced its mental confusion, fogginess, concentration difficulties, memory problems, and other brain-related symptoms. You probably thought your lightheadedness and dizziness meant something was amiss, so you sought medical help. After visiting one or more doctors, numerous tests, and being told "We can find nothing wrong," you were probably confused. With respect to these candidiasis symptoms, seeking help from mainstream physicians is a waste of time because they have no answers. You can visit one doctor or 100 and, for the most part, you will still be told "We can find nothing wrong."

Depending on the doctor's specialty, you may learn that you have numerous different problems, like irritable bowel syndrome, psoriasis, an elevated cholesterol level, and so on. This will confuse your situation further because mainstream physicians are unlikely to connect the dots and reveal your underlying problem. Or you may have a more serious problem, like schizophrenia, bipolar disorder, severe depression, multiple sclerosis, parkinsonism, headaches, seizures, or some other life-disrupting mental disturbance. Once again, if you do not know that these medical maladies are, directly or indirectly, associated with candidiasis or how to treat it, little can be done to help you. A physician can have the best of intentions, but if they are not looking for something or searching in the right place, they will not find the answer.

Why does an anti-candidiasis bias exist? When a physical exam and laboratory tests do not reveal abnormalities, mainstream physicians do not know where to turn. Lacking answers, it is easy to blame stress and emotional disturbances. Yes, some people experience stress and suffer with emotional disturbances, which contribute to their unhappiness and ill health, but it does not eliminate the possibility that something *real* is causing or exacerbating their compromised mental health. Because of the *mind-body connection*, an unhappy mind can disturb health, and a sick body can promote mental disturbances. For example, the flu is a systemic illness that causes people to feel tired, lethargic, and depressed; it also impairs their memory, ability to concentrate, and so on. Psychological and neurological symptoms must include some physical disarray, whether or not it is obvious.

Which candidiasis sufferers develop mental manifestations? First, you must have some inherited genetic tendency to develop an illness, and psychological and neurological illnesses are no exception. This is influenced by your body's inherent strengths and weaknesses, and exacerbated by stress, diet, lack of sleep, adverse environmental exposures, and many other factors. Add it up, and there is no way to know for sure who will develop candidiasis-related mental manifestations. Yet, one thing is certain, the longer you have candidiasis and the more severe it is, the greater the chance it will adversely affect your body. So, sufferers with chronic and/or severe illness are the most likely to have mental manifestations.

With respect to instigating or promoting psychological and neurological illnesses, candidiasis is rarely considered, even though C. Orian Truss, M.D., from Birmingham, Alabama, discovered and established an association between candidiasis and depression over 40 years ago. In addition, Dr. Truss noted that other clinically respected psychiatric symptoms were primarily or secondarily attributable to an infection with *Candida albicans* (candidiasis), including poor concentration, memory loss or deterioration, feeling "spacey" or "in a fog," anxiety disorders, behavioral problems, and a diversity of phobias (fears).

Confusingly, the mental manifestations of candidiasis are highly variable, ranging from minor concentration difficulties to severe psychiatric illness, which may include harmful and irrational behaviors like suicide and homicide. The colonization of disease-causing yeast within the gut and other tissues is an infection that produces abundant inflammation as well as allergic consequences. A persistent infection can upset the body's metabolism and chemistry, indirectly affecting the brain and its functioning. Moreover, disease-causing yeast produce a variety of harmful substances that can be absorbed, travel within the blood, and diffuse across the *blood-brain barrier*, directly altering the brain's chemistry and functioning. In many sufferers, numerous allergies and their allergic reactions can further cause or exacerbate these disturbances. In addition, chronic candidiasis can upset the gut, causing malabsorption and nutritional deficiencies that will adversely alter the brain's chemistry and functioning.

None of this should be surprising because the nervous, endocrine, and immune systems are all interconnected, forming one vast *neuroendocrine-immune connection*. Since there is a *candidiasis-endocrine connection* (chapter 11) and a *candidiasis-immune connection* (chapter 14), it implies that there is a *candidiasis–nervous system connection*. Yes, chronic candidiasis can promote psychological and/or neurological manifestations. Typically, its *psychological* manifestations involve *abnormal brain functioning* without structural (anatomical) disturbances. Psychotic and neurotic behaviors, undesirable thoughts, and abnormal thinking occur when the brain's chemical messengers (neurotransmitters) are disturbed or altered.

A *neurosis* is a psychological or behavioral disturbance with *anxiety* (nervousness) as its primary component. To cope with it, people learn *defense* mechanisms like denying a problem exists or develop *fears* (phobias) that exclude them from situations that produce anxiety. In contrast, a *psychosis* includes a significant *distortion* or *disorganization* of someone's mental processes and emotional responses. Because this impairs their ability to recognize reality, communicate, and relate to other people, they have difficulty coping with life's ordinary daily demands. Usually, neuroses are anxiety-causing emotional or behavioral disorders that do *not* interfere with reality; they may cause distress and discomfort, but the affected person is mostly in tune with the world. In contrast, people with psychoses are out of touch, having thoughts that range from mildly unrealistic to bizarre, accompanied by completely innocent to overtly dangerous behaviors. (These two categories are further classified according to their origins.)

The brain is not separate from the rest of the body and interacts with the endocrine and immune systems through the *neuroendocrine-immune connection*. So, conditions that disturb one system can disturb all. Chronic candidiasis is a systemic illness, and its ability to impair the brain's chemistry and functioning is profound. Although not every psychological disturbance and neurological illness is associated with its presence, it frequently contributes to or causes a large percentage of persistent and recurring brain-related maladies, from mild disturbances like difficulty concentrating to mental illnesses like schizophrenia, from transient cerebral symptoms like headaches to life-destructive neurological illnesses like multiple sclerosis. Moreover, disease-causing yeast are often assisted by other infectious invaders, so it is essential to uncover the presence and contributions of all these troublemakers and treat them accordingly.

There is a *candidiasis-neurological connection*, and disease-causing yeast can instigate and promote a variety of psychological and neurological illnesses. Before discussing specific illnesses, it is important to understand brain chemistry and how candidiasis disrupts it.

BRAIN CHEMISTRY & YOUR MOOD

The human *brain* is a highly complex anatomical organ located within the skull. It has about 14 to 16 billion cells within its cerebral cortex and 55 to 70 billion within its cerebellum. Although details about the operations of its individual cells are known, modern science does not really understand how they cooperate in groups or how millions of cells interact together.

Brain activity has three processes: anatomical, electrical, and biochemical. Its *anatomy* determines its function as well as the part of the body it regulates through the nervous system. Specifics aside, there are two broad classes of cells (*neurons* and *glial cells*). *Electrical* processes involve an electrical signal sent lengthwise along a nerve cell until it reaches its end. Since the signal cannot traverse the gap (*synapse*) between two adjacent cells, information is passed onward by releasing chemical messengers (*neurotransmitters*) into the gap between the cells. After being released, these substances diffuse across the synapse until they contact the membrane of the next cell, which generates an electrical signal within it, continuing the message onward. So, an electrical process triggers a *biochemical* process, generating another electrical process, and so on. Although its anatomy is its framework, the electrical and biochemical processes send and receive all the brain's information at the physical level.

The human brain performs and governs many complicated and intricate bodily functions. Since its activity involves three processes, problems can arise from anatomical, electrical, and/or biochemical disturbances. Most mental manifestations involve a known or suspected disturbance within the brain's *chemistry*. Since its functioning reflects its chemistry, its neurotransmitters are essential; more than 60 have been identified, and the behavior of most remain unclear. Regardless, the important ones are the catecholamines (*epinephrine* and *norepinephrine*), acetylcholine, and many amino acids (especially *glutamate* and *gamma-aminobutyric acid*).

Where do neurotransmitters arise? They are manufactured within nerve cells, near their synapse. After being released and stimulating the next nerve cell, they are either degraded within the synapse or absorbed and reused. (Confusingly, neurotransmitters may have dissimilar effects in different areas of the brain and nervous system.) This reveals the potential for some serious problems if one or more neurotransmitter is not produced or released in sufficient quantities, if an inappropriate one is released, if it is not degraded or reabsorbed, and so on. Clearly, any of this can adversely alter the brain's chemistry and, in turn, its functioning.

In addition, there are *neuromodulators*, with short-range activity, that enhance or diminish neurotransmitter activity. The best known are *endorphins*, *somatostatin*, and *substance P*, as well as other *neuropeptides*. To complicate matters, there are also *neurohormones*. Taken together, neurotransmitters, neuromodulators, and neurohormones reveal the brain and nervous system's incredible complexity. Therefore, disrupting the brain's chemistry must affect its functioning. In many cases, this does not even require a major disruption.

Consider a few of the most common and important neurotransmitters. *Epinephrine* and *norepinephrine* are mainly responsible for elevating mood and for providing feelings of assertiveness, confidence, and alertness. *Serotonin* has a calming effect, inducing relaxation as well as sleep (it balances epinephrine and norepinephrine). *Dopamine* stimulates sexual arousal and assists with your movements and coordination. *Acetylcholine* participates in controlling your movements and is vital for your memory. *GABA* (gamma-aminobutyric acid) inhibits anxiety and stimulates mental acuity. An increase or decrease in any one or all can profoundly alter your mental state, thoughts, movements, coordination, and more.

In short, your mental state and mood are determined by your inventory (profile) of neurotransmitters. With respect to mood, "happiness" is a subjective feeling that occurs when the brain's chemicals are in healthy (balanced) proportions; as a result, someone experiences enthusiasm, desires to achieve, mental acuity and sharpness, assertiveness, and willpower. In contrast, "sadness" reflects an abnormal balance of chemicals, promoting a loss of desire, depression, apathy, lethargy, concentration difficulties, and suicidal thoughts (when severe). The more abnormal the neurotransmitter levels, the greater the disturbances.

Research reveals the brain's neurotransmitters can be affected and controlled by a single meal. Ingesting an abundance of protein can increase epinephrine and norepinephrine levels, causing hyperactivity. In contrast, a high-sugar, low-protein meal produced fatigue, sleepiness, loss of stamina, decreased willpower, and concentration difficulties. The blood sugar concentration can also contribute to someone's mood. For the most part, the brain uses blood *glucose* (sugar) as its primary source of energy, and when its concentration decreases too fast or falls below a certain level, the brain is essentially starved of fuel. This can produce a diversity of symptoms, including mental confusion, disorientation, deteriorations in short-term memory, difficulty concentrating, depression and crying spells, headaches, irritability and impatience, incoherent speech, emotional instability and mood swings, blurred vision, focal or generalized seizures, coma, and possibly death (if severe), not to mention bizarre behaviors.

Eating one "bad" meal will, at most, temporarily alter your mood. Yet, eating one bad meal after another may be responsible for someone's mood swings: The sugar from one meal hypes them up. Then, when their blood sugar concentration falls, they come down and eat more sugar, which hypes them up, until they crash again, and so on. Many people ride this nutritional roller coaster day after day, never realizing that their improper diet participates in their mood swings.

To compound the problem, a high-sugar, protein-deficient meal will not contain enough of the building blocks required to make neurotransmitters. This becomes more evident when someone consumes a bad diet for a long time. When you consistently have an improper diet, the recurring deficiency of certain nutrients is destined to disturb, and even impair, your brain's chemistry and functioning. How does this happen? Most neurotransmitters are constructed from amino acids obtained from your gut when it digests and absorbs dietary proteins. If your supply or delivery of dietary protein is deficient or impaired, it can cause a proportionate, or even exaggerated, disturbance in the production of your neurotransmitters. Although your body and brain can compensate with certain adjustments, it can only go so far or last so long. The consistent consumption of a bad diet, especially high in sugar and low in protein, is certain to eventually cause notable biochemical disturbances, disturbing the brain's chemistry and functioning, promoting an adversely altered mental state.

Can an unbalanced diet cause psychological and neurological illnesses? Although a bad diet can cause problems, it is unlikely to be responsible for the biochemical disarray that accompany these illnesses; indeed, a bad diet is more likely to cause short-term symptoms that are often mild and reversible. When someone's mental manifestations are more prolonged or pronounced, something notable must be going on. What could it be? The answer lies within the gastrointestinal tract. If the gut cannot completely digest dietary proteins, their amino acids will not be available for absorption. Moreover, even if dietary protein is completely broken down, their amino acids cannot be effectively absorbed when the gut wall is not functioning normally. Minor gut disturbances cause few problems that can produce significant consequences over time. In contrast, a major gut disturbance, like starvation or malabsorption, may readily create nutritional deficiencies, promoting marked biochemical disturbances. In any case, these disturbances frequently lead to altered mental states.

Biochemical disturbances and mental manifestations are directly associated with the health of the gastrointestinal tract. Yes, one unbalanced meal may make someone feel "high" then "low," but it is not likely to cause persistent mental manifestations. In contrast, a chronic gut disturbance is certain to instigate or promote nutritional deficiencies that adversely alter neurotransmitter levels. It seems obvious that chronic psychological and neurological illnesses must involve some perpetual gut problem. So, what is happening?

Research reveals that roughly 100 million neurotransmitters exist along the length of the gastrointestinal tract, and every type within the brain is also found within the gut. In 1998, Michael D. Gershon, M.D., author of *The Second Brain,* stated, "The brain in the bowel has got to work right or no one will have the luxury to think at all." In other words, if the gut is not working properly, the brain cannot function normally.

Whether recognized or not, most gut disturbances are related to the presence of an infection. More than 400 species of bacteria have been identified in the feces of a single person. Yet, when there is a healthy population of beneficial bacteria, the infectious troublemakers are suppressed and unable to cause harm. Many researchers and clinicians appreciate that gastrointestinal dysbiosis is related to mental and psychological problems. Numerous studies reveal that irritable bowel syndrome (IBS) is associated with anxiety, depression, and a decreased ability to cope with stress. Some physicians appreciate the link between severe IBS and psychosocial disorders. Other researchers have found an association between IBS and mental disorders, including abnormal intestinal permeability in patients with chronic psychiatric disorders like schizophrenia. Since there is a *candidiasis–inflammatory bowel connection* and a *candidiasis–irritable bowel syndrome connection* (chapter 4), candidiasis lies behind most gut maladies. The presence of other infectious invaders, including harmful parasites, bacteria, molds, and/or viruses, only exacerbates the situation. In addition to being an infection, candidiasis has allergic consequences with abundant inflammation (chapter 16). As a result, it can disturb the gut and its functioning, impairing its ability to properly digest proteins and absorb their amino acids. These circumstances lead to malabsorption, nutritional deficiencies, and biochemical disturbances. Therefore, most chronic mental manifestations are really *symptoms* of a bigger problem, which is candidiasis.

Many candidiasis-minded physicians are aware that candidiasis sufferers often have cerebral symptoms, such as dizziness, poor concentration, and mood swings. Sufferers usually have malabsorption, as well as poor diets, which instigates and promotes a persistent chemical imbalance, especially involving their neurotransmitters. This explains why depression and feeling "blue" are common among sufferers. In fact, when someone feels depressed and "blue" for no reason, you should immediately suspect candidiasis, both its *infectious* and *allergic* consequences. Undeniably, stress and emotions do influence your state of mind and can make you feel less than happy. Yet, when your mental state is exaggerated, or your condition is frequent or chronic, you should suspect that you have candidiasis until proven otherwise.

Candidiasis promotes psychological and neurological illnesses by upsetting the gut and its functioning. This causes nutritional deficiencies that instigate or promote disturbances within the brain's production of neurotransmitters, leading to an adversely altered mental state. Moreover, chronic candidiasis frequently worsens glucose tolerance, promoting *reactive hypoglycemia*; the blood sugar concentration becomes more labile, with exaggerated highs and lows (chapter 11). This can promote significant mood swings, alternating periods of feeling normal or "high" interspersed with times of feeling sad or "low." Since reactive hypoglycemia encourages sugar cravings, it creates a vicious cycle; when a candidiasis sufferer's blood sugar drops, they get hungry and consume more sugar. Eating excesses of sugar promotes blood sugar disturbances and readily nourishes their disease-causing yeast, encouraging their proliferation and further colonization.

By promoting malabsorption, nutritional deficiencies, and reactive hypoglycemia, candidiasis *indirectly* promotes disturbances that undesirably alter neurotransmitter levels, adversely affecting a sufferer's mental state. In addition, since certain minerals are used to create an electrical charge and signal along a nerve cell, malabsorption-related mineral deficiencies can cause electrical disturbances within the brain. To add insult to injury, disease-causing yeast can *directly* disturb the brain's chemistry, which can greatly impair the brain's functioning. How does this occur? Disease-causing yeast produce toxins, metabolites, and waste products and also have an abundance of allergy-inducing substances (antigens). In small amounts, their influence is minimal or goes unnoticed. When candidiasis is significant, it can instigate and exacerbate psychological and neurological illnesses.

THE ACETALDEHYDE HYPOTHESIS

With rare exception, candidiasis involves some magnitude of gastrointestinal disturbance (chapter 4). Since the gut is where our food (dietary proteins, carbohydrates, and fats) is digested and absorbed, the more significant the candidiasis, the greater the malabsorption of essential nutrients. Since the brain's chemistry and functioning depend on its supply of neurotransmitters, which are constructed from biochemical precursors (protein-derived amino acids), the more significant the candidiasis, the greater the brain is disturbed. Although this is an indirect influence of candidiasis, its direct contributions can be equally, if not more, debilitating.

In most people, disease-causing yeast are normal inhabitants within their gut in small numbers. Healthy people have beneficial bacteria that competitively inhibit their disease-causing yeast, keeping them under control. Yet, the beneficial bacteria can die off or be killed for numerous reasons (chapter 2), allowing the disease-causing yeast to reproduce and colonize their surroundings. (When this happens, other infectious invaders gain similar freedom and increase their numbers as well.)

As living organisms, disease-causing yeast take in nutrition and release waste and other substances into their surroundings. Many of their substances harm the body. When present in small numbers, their effects are insignificant. In contrast, when they dominate the gastrointestinal environment (microbiome), they produce substantial amounts of chemical metabolites, waste products, toxins, and many other undesirable substances, which are allergy-inducing (antigenic) or non-allergy-inducing (nonantigenic). As their substances increase, they are absorbed in greater amounts. This situation can greatly disturb the brain's chemistry and its functioning.

As space becomes scarce and/or the disease-causing yeast are starved of nutrients, they can become aggressive and invade into the gut wall. By inflaming and weakening the gut wall, numerous inappropriate substances can "leak" in and out of the gut's tissues, a condition called leaky gut syndrome (chapters 3 and 4), which permits their infection to spread, increases the absorption of their undesirable substances, and promotes many allergic consequences, including food allergies. Furthermore, disease-causing yeast may invade deeper and enter the blood, take up residence, travel to more distant locations, and infect other areas of the body when possible. Obviously, this only increases the disturbances present.

Typically, a candidiasis sufferer's symptoms reflect the magnitude of their *infection* with disease-causing yeast as well as its *allergic* consequences.

Yes, genetics do contribute; your inherited strengths and weaknesses frequently determine what type of symptoms and illness you develop, explaining why certain medical maladies are prevalent among members of the same family. Yet, even in healthy people, the magnitude of their candidiasis and the length of time it has been present can eventually instigate or promote great disturbances.

Candidiasis disturbs the body's chemistry and its functioning, depending on its severity. Since the nervous, endocrine (hormone), and immune systems are interconnected, forming the *neuroendocrine-immune connection*, candidiasis can undesirably alter any or all these systems. So, the nervous system will be adversely affected in some way, directly or indirectly. This explains why sufferers often experience one or more symptoms related to altered or impaired brain functioning. Moreover, this effect will be exacerbated by other undesirable circumstances within the gut, including food allergies and the presence of other infectious invaders.

To summarize: The beneficial bacteria can be killed or die off, allowing disease-causing yeast to reproduce. As their population escalates, the production and presence of their undesirable substances increases accordingly, including their harmful metabolites, wastes, toxins, and allergy-inducing (antigenic) tendencies. These can be absorbed by the gut, enter the tissues and then the blood, and then travel through the blood vessels supplying the brain. Some substances are small enough to pass through the blood-brain barrier and enter the brain, directly disturbing its chemistry. This situation becomes worse if the disease-causing yeast invade into the gut wall, creating leaky gut syndrome, because many inappropriate substances can enter the tissues and blood, especially undigested food particles. Although these particles are likely to trigger an immune response, instigating food allergies, they also adversely affect the nervous system. As a result, food allergies can exacerbate mental disturbances. Even worse, the presence of "leaky" blood vessels within the brain (for example, Alzheimer's disease) allows more harmful substances to enter it. In addition, the predominant species (and strain) of disease-causing yeast can make a big difference in the disturbances; although there are similarities, not all disease-causing yeast are equally harmful. The presence of other infectious invaders adds to the problem.

Furthermore, chronic candidiasis can impair the body's ability to manage these deleterious substances. Normally, the liver helps clear these harmful substances and toxins from the body. However, the presence of a chronic infection or inflammation impels the liver to shift its activities away from its chemical duties (metabolism) to assist the immune system. The liver's *acute phase response* is supposed to be a short-term boost to immunity. Since the immune system is rarely able to eliminate candidiasis, a persistent acute phase response occurs, hindering or impairing the liver's metabolic activities, which allows these harmful substances to accumulate. Obviously, this only worsens a candidiasis sufferer's symptoms.

To appreciate the chemical disturbances that arise within a sufferer's brain, consider the acetaldehyde hypothesis by Dr. Truss. Disease-causing yeast within the gut and other locations are known to produce *ethanol* (alcohol) and *acetaldehyde* as byproducts of their metabolism. These two toxic substances can be absorbed and enter the blood (the situation is worse, when disease-causing yeast reside within the blood). Once these substances are within the blood, ethanol can exert its characteristic effects, whereas acetaldehyde becomes more harmful as its concentration increases.

Normally, the liver degrades (detoxifies) acetaldehyde to *acetate* using a zinc-requiring enzyme (*aldehyde dehydrogenase*). However, this chemical catalyst is deficient in up to 60 percent of Asian people and 5 percent of Americans and Europeans. Dr. Truss believed people with this deficiency cannot degrade acetaldehyde, allowing it to accumulate and saturate the body's organs, tissues, and cells. Being a toxic chemical, prolonged exposure or large amounts promote injury by free radical reactions and peroxidation (chapter 7). More to the point, acetaldehyde is suspected of being able to cross the blood-brain barrier. After entering the brain, it is thought to block the connections between brain cells (synapses) as well as inhibit the synthesis of *acetylcholine*, which decreases the functioning of the autonomic nervous system. Acetaldehyde may also bind with or be incorporated into neurotransmitters, creating *pseudo-neurotransmitters* (false messengers) that readily disrupt the brain's functioning.

You do not need an aldehyde dehydrogenase deficiency to accumulate acetaldehyde. A persistent acute phase response can compromise the liver's metabolic functioning, including its ability to degrade acetaldehyde (and ethanol). Over time, this can increase the concentration of acetaldehyde (and ethanol), which damages the liver, creating a vicious cycle. Therefore, sooner or later, a candidiasis sufferer is certain to develop mental manifestations, which only worsens as their condition continues.

Any substance that adversely influences the brain's chemistry will disturb or impair its functioning. Most mainstream physicians protest, claiming that disease-causing yeast cannot manufacture significant amounts of alcohol to cause a problem. On the contrary, the evidence to support the ill effect of ethanol is provided by *auto-brewery syndrome*. People diagnosed with it had candidiasis with a strain of disease-causing yeast that produced excessive amounts of ethanol, making them feel constantly drunk. Although most sufferers do not have disease-causing yeast that produce that much, ethanol must play a notable role because many sufferers claim they feel drunk without ever ingesting an alcoholic beverage, especially after consuming sugar or high-carbohydrate meals. Acetaldehyde also brings forth frowns of disbelief from mainstream physicians. Yet, if ethanol is absorbed from the gut, why would acetaldehyde not be? Since it is also produced by disease-causing yeast, its ability to cause problems would seem equally likely. Although this is a working hypothesis, the biology, physiology, and metabolism of disease-causing yeast make it credible.

Evidence supports another way disease-causing yeast promote mental manifestations. Research has revealed that *Candida albicans* produces a substance called *gliotoxin*. (Other fungal organisms also produce it, including *Aspergillus fumigatus*, *Penicillium bilaii*, and *Gliocladium* species.) Gliotoxin is known to inactivate *alcohol dehydrogenase*, the liver enzyme responsible for degrading (detoxifying) alcohol. In turn, this allows the amount of ethanol within the body to increase. The presence and ill effects of gliotoxin are certain to mirror someone's total population of disease-causing yeast (and harmful molds). An important question that needs to be answered is: Since it has been documented to disrupt a single liver enzyme (alcohol dehydrogenase), can gliotoxin harm other enzymes? If *acetaldehyde dehydrogenase* were similarly affected by gliotoxin, this would lend strong support for a *candidiasis–mental manifestation connection*. Research demonstrated that gliotoxin is toxic to different types of nervous system cells, including astrocytes and oligodendrocytes. A gliotoxin analogue of glutamate was toxic to glial cells. So, gliotoxin impairs metabolism and is directly toxic to numerous nervous system cells.

Therefore, it seems highly likely that most manifestations of psychological illness are associated with candidiasis. Moreover, except for medical maladies arising from an anatomical insult, most neurological illnesses probably have a similar affiliation with candidiasis. Undoubtedly, this is further exacerbated by the presence of other infectious invaders.

Although stress does contribute, without the chemical disturbances of candidiasis, emotional turmoil alone is not likely to produce most mental manifestations, especially those involving an altered reality (psychoses). What determines the psychological or neurological illness someone develops? In addition to the presence and contributions of other infectious invaders, the severity and length of time candidiasis is present is a strong factor. Yet, the greatest factor must be someone's inherited genetic tendency to develop a particular illness; in fact, numerous psychological and neurological illnesses involve some genetic weakness or defect, but without candidiasis disturbing the brain's chemistry, these manifestations would be unlikely to develop.

The good news is that unless there is permanent anatomical damage, eliminating candidiasis is likely to normalize a person's brain chemistry, freeing them from the chains of their psychological or neurological illness. If you think this sounds too good to be true, read on and the benefits of an anti-candidiasis approach will become apparent.

ANXIETY, PHOBIAS & PANIC ATTACKS

Anxiety, phobias, and panic attacks are a daily experience for hundreds of millions of people worldwide, preventing them from living a normal life. Can candidiasis be involved?

Anxiety is an unpleasant mood with feelings of apprehension. Unlike *fear*, it usually involves an anticipation of future events, including feelings of difficulty, distress, and danger. Anxiety is not completely bad; normal levels help us avoid unpleasant situations or events. In contrast, when someone's anxiety is excessive, inappropriate, or lacking a cause, it is abnormal. So, how can you tell the difference between normal and abnormal anxiety? Basically, anxiety has three presentations: as a normal response to threats or danger, as a component of another psychiatric illness, or as a self-limited condition.

The most common manifestation of anxiety is *phobias* (fears). Having one phobia (for example, a fear of being within tall buildings) is usually an inconvenience because it only limits you in certain situations. This type of phobia often arises during childhood, and avoiding the inciting situation is the typical solution. Additional phobias or generalized fears are more problematic because each has its own restrictions and further limits someone's activities. Anxiety can be expressed as inappropriate feelings, disturbed thinking, or physical maladies. Its symptoms are variable but frequently include headaches, tremors, nervousness, shortness of breath, heart palpitations, gastrointestinal problems or distress, frequent urination, and many others. Episodes of anxiety may involve choking, sweating, flushing, abnormal sensations, weakness, lightheadedness, chest tightness, and hyperventilation.

If enough phobias exist, or they are severe, *panic attacks* can occur with symptoms that may or may not relate to any specific fear. Since the experience is often spontaneous and confusing to its victim, it creates *anticipation* anxiety, the fear of another attack, which worsens someone's phobias, encouraging a generalized avoidance of anxiety-provoking situations. When panic attacks are extreme, people frequently refuse to leave their home. What is a panic attack like? Feelings of uneasiness typically progress to a severe panic state over 10 to 15 minutes, which usually resolves during the following hour.

Normal anxiety results from psychological stress or a rational fear; it typically persists while the inciting stress or fear is present. Severe anxiety is an exaggeration of normal anxiety, persisting much longer with significant and even life-disruptive symptoms; it may or may not have a clear inciting event or cause. Panic attacks are an extreme form of severe anxiety that limits or disrupts someone's life. Yes, normal anxiety is unavoidable. In contrast, because of their chronic and exaggerated nature, severe anxiety and panic attacks are not normal. Although psychological stress or some fear can precipitate all three conditions, severe anxiety and panic attacks must have some physical process that contributes to their presence.

At the physical level, panic attacks usually involve a rapid fall in someone's blood sugar concentration, or an inappropriately lowered concentration, triggering the release of their blood sugar–raising hormones, notably epinephrine and norepinephrine. Panic attack sufferers often have severe glucose intolerance, which usually manifests as *reactive hypoglycemia* (a profoundly labile blood sugar concentration). Candidiasis can promote blood sugar disturbances (chapters 11 and 14), which is why its sufferers frequently manifest glucose intolerance. As a result, eating an abundance of sugar or complex carbohydrates can cause someone's blood sugar concentration to increase and then rapidly fall, even below its fasting level. A rapid fall in the blood sugar concentration, as well as an abnormally lowered concentration, precipitates the release of epinephrine and norepinephrine, triggering the shakiness, nervousness, and so on that is associated with panic attacks. Moreover, the presence of disease-causing yeast can adversely alter the brain's chemistry, disturbing someone's thinking; this helps maintain or may further generalize their fears and anxiety. Therefore, there appears to be a *candidiasis–panic attack connection*.

Severe anxiety is similarly associated with candidiasis, but there tends to be less glucose intolerance. As a result, severe anxiety sufferers do not get the extreme physical symptoms that accompany panic attacks.

Yet, disturbed thinking can be just as notable in both conditions, lasting for a long time. This implies that severe anxiety and panic attacks involve candidiasis adversely affecting the brain's chemistry and functioning. Although psychological treatment may be necessary, the best way to treat these conditions is with anti-candidiasis therapy.

Many people with psychological or psychiatric illness have excellent responses from anti-candidiasis therapy. Although formal studies are still needed, it seems candidiasis, diet, nutritional deficiencies, and allergies are the instigators and promoters of most mental manifestations. Of course, other infectious invaders are likely to participate.

Mild or infrequent anxiety is a normal part of life. Yet, severe anxiety and panic attacks should not be considered normal. If you suffer with persistent anxiety or have panic attacks, these point to something being amiss at the physical level. Although stress and emotions (psychological factors) do contribute, you should appreciate that there is a *candidiasis-severe anxiety-panic attack connection*. So, comprehensive anti-candidiasis therapy should be included as an important part of treating and eliminating these conditions.

PMS: DEPRESSION, ANGER & ANXIETY

The mental manifestations of *premenstrual syndrome* (PMS) are often more debilitating than its physical expressions. This condition occurs before a woman's monthly menstruation, and its symptoms range from minimal to severe anxiety and/or depression as well as anger, mood swings, sugar cravings, and other common complaints.

Yes, there is a *candidiasis-PMS connection* (chapter 13). Over the years, many candidiasis-minded physicians have treated long-term PMS sufferers with frequent depression, anxiety, and anger using nystatin (nonabsorbable, oral antifungal medication) and a yeast-free diet with good results. Even better improvements occur when systemic antifungal medications are used with a holistic approach that also identifies and eliminates other infectious invaders.

With respect to promoting PMS symptoms, research reveals that *Candida albicans* has receptors for the female hormone's *estrogen* and *progesterone* (as well as corticosteroids). It seems the same hormones that stimulate the colonization of disease-causing yeast are also involved in the development and manifestation of PMS symptoms. Somehow, the combination of estrogen, progesterone, and candidiasis cause certain women to manifest depression, anxiety, and anger. Moreover, since candidiasis can cause significant glucose intolerance, its presence can precipitate exaggerated blood sugar "highs" and "lows," sugar cravings, irritability, nervousness, and so on—basically, the same manifestations that occur with severe anxiety.

To summarize: Candidiasis adversely affects a woman's endocrine (hormone) system, glucose tolerance, and metabolism. In turn, PMS sufferers can develop abnormal estrogen and progesterone levels and have cravings that cause them to consume a diet high in sugar. Both conditions nourish and stimulate the receptors of *Candida albicans*, encouraging their further growth and metabolic activities. This creates a vicious cycle that worsens over time. Depending on the severity of a woman's candidiasis and amount of glucose intolerance, the presence of disease-causing yeast can adversely alter her brain's chemistry, producing mental manifestations like depression, anxiety, and anger. In addition, allergies to disease-causing yeast and harmful molds, as well as environmental and food allergies, are likely to participate.

Some researchers have a different conclusion about the origin of PMS symptoms. They believe that the colonization of *Candida albicans* during the luteal phase or following the use of antibiotics and/or steroids causes the release of *canditoxin*, inducing PMS symptoms. Since canditoxin has not been clearly identified, their assumption is a speculative and simple answer to a complex problem. In contrast, *gliotoxin* may be the chemical culprit, causing the mental manifestations; in fact, hormone excesses may stimulate the appropriate receptors of *Candida albicans*, stimulating their metabolic activities, including gliotoxin production. Although this may contribute to mental manifestations, it is only part of the big picture.

The *infectious* and *allergic* consequences of candidiasis can disturb the nervous, endocrine, and immune systems. With respect to PMS, both the endocrine (hormone) and nervous (brain) systems are affected. In addition, because candidiasis is an infection that induces allergies, the immune system is also certain to be disturbed. This is understandable when you consider there is one encompassing *candidiasis-neuroendocrine-immune connection*. Specifics aside, the latest evidence points to a *candidiasis-PMS connection*.

DEPRESSION & BIPOLAR DISORDER (MANIC DEPRESSION)

Have you ever felt sad? Of course. Everyone, at one time or another, feels sad or "blue." You may have lost a job, or a loved one may have passed on. It is normal to feel sad after losing something or someone important to you. Although the length of time varies, this is a temporary situation for most people; after grieving and perhaps some soul-searching, this feeling usually abates. Yet, if someone is persistently sad, especially for no reason, they probably have depression. If their depressed mood is interrupted with episodes of inappropriate euphoria, they are likely to suffer with bipolar disorder.

In the summer of 2022, roughly 22 percent of American adults revealed that they had symptoms of depressive disorder. It is estimated that about 280 million people suffer with it worldwide. Although more than 7 percent of adults are diagnosed, the highest rates occur in people ages 12 to 25. Sadly, 80 to 90 percent of suicides are associated with a diagnosis of depression or manic depression.

According to the American Psychiatric Association's *Diagnostic and Statistical Manual of Mental Disorders,* Fifth Edition, major *depression* requires at least five of the following symptoms for a period of two weeks or longer: A depressed mood, a markedly diminished interest or pleasure in activities, a significant weight loss or loss of appetite, an inability to sleep (insomnia) or sleeping excessively (hypersomnia), slowed movement (psychomotor retardation) or hyperactivity (agitation), a loss of energy, feelings of worthlessness or guilt, a decreased ability to concentrate, and recurring thoughts of death or suicide. (At least one *must* be a depressed mood most of the day, nearly every day, or a markedly diminished interest or pleasure in all or almost all daily activities nearly every day.) Moreover, a psychotic or neurotic presentation is possible, depending on whether the depressed person is experiencing a loss of reality.

Since there is a *mind-body connection,* depression commonly involves multiple physical complaints and symptoms, making it a complex, emotional, physiological, and metabolic condition. Does depression have a physical cause? According to mainstream medicine, there are risk factors that precipitate it, but its exact origin is mysterious or poorly known. Although there may be a genetic tendency to develop it, an inherited weakness does not explain why some people get depressed and others do not. Lacking a cause, mainstream physicians can do little more than administer antidepressant medication, hoping to correct the adversely altered brain chemistry associated with depression. At best, this may make someone feel better, but it usually does not eliminate their depression; after all, when most depressed people stop taking medication, they frequently feel worse, forcing them to perpetually use medication.

Research reveals that depressed people have an adversely altered brain chemistry, and this is how antidepressant medication is thought to work. Yet, the cause of their chemical disturbance is unappreciated. Since illness cannot arise without a cause, something must be responsible for the chemical disarray of depression. Since chronic candidiasis can disturb the brain's chemistry and functioning, disease-causing yeast seem like the real culprits, with or without the participation of other infectious invaders. In fact, depression is one of the most prominent candidiasis-related mental manifestations.

Research shows a connection between disease-causing yeast, depression, and mental disturbances. As an example, sertraline (Zoloft) is a drug classified as a *selective serotonin reuptake inhibitor* (SSRI), reflecting its mechanism of action. It is used to treat depression, obsessive-compulsive disorder, posttraumatic stress disorder, premenstrual dysphoric disorder, social anxiety disorder, and panic attacks. Its effects may be different than assumed because research showed that it displayed *antifungal* activity against *Candida auris*, including inhibition of its growth and biofilm production. So, a drug used to treat mental disturbances may be effective because of its ability to kill disease-causing yeast.

Bipolar disorder (manic-depressive psychosis) is more complex, with an altered reality as a consistent finding. Typically, this illness involves two experiences: periods of marked, emotional "highs" (mania) and periods of extreme, despondent "lows" (depression). Regardless of whether occasional or persistent, a sufferer's emotional episodes are often interspersed with remissions of variable length. Only about one-third of its sufferers are ever treated, and untreated cases only worsen over time. In 2022, it was estimated that 2.8 percent of Americans and 46 million people worldwide suffer with bipolar disorder.

The emotional *high* (mania) involves feelings of euphoria and elation accompanied by abundant energy and restlessness. Its sufferers frequently enjoy confidence and a quick wit. Since their inhibitions are often ignored, they tend to behave inappropriately. During an attack, their symptoms tend to worsen and delusions may arise, which can cause their thinking to be disorganized and confused. In contrast, their despondent *low* (depression) manifests as sadness, hopelessness, a loss of confidence, and feeling miserable. There may be intense feelings of self-blame or guilt. Their activity may be increased or slowed to the point of unresponsiveness. Delusional thoughts may occur, especially bizarre or grandiose ideas. When their thinking is disturbed, they will usually deny all contrary evidence, clinging steadfastly to their opinions. During this time, suicide is a real threat. Moreover, depending on someone's delusions and circumstances, homicide becomes a possibility. Bipolar disorder is not just a mental illness because physical symptoms and complaints are extremely common among its sufferers.

Who gets bipolar disorder and why? Like other illnesses, there seems to be a genetic tendency to develop it; research indicates that a specific region on chromosome 18 appears to be the area affected. Although this reveals that certain people are predisposed, not everyone with this weakness will manifest it. Something must trigger the expression of these "bipolar disorder" genes, promoting episodes of illness in certain people. Like depression, bipolar disorder involves changes within the brain's neurotransmitters levels. Presently, lithium is often the leading medication for treating it, but because it has a wide spectrum of activity, it is not known how it works. It is important to emphasize that lithium does not permanently correct the illness because its sufferers typically relapse after discontinuing its use.

So, what could cause sufferers to have disturbed neurotransmitter levels? The presence of altered levels should quickly implicate candidiasis. If there is a *candidiasis-depression connection* and depression is major component of bipolar disorder, there must be a *candidiasis–bipolar disorder connection.* Since depression is a prominent symptom among candidiasis sufferers, the despondent "lows" (depression) of bipolar disorder can readily be explained by candidiasis undesirably altering the brain's chemistry and functioning. What causes the emotional "highs" (mania)? Bipolar disorder is an illness that combines a chemical disturbance within the brain with a labile or exaggerated blood sugar concentration. Once again, this can reflect the mischief of candidiasis because there is a *candidiasis–glucose intolerance connection* (chapters 11 and 14).

How does candidiasis and glucose intolerance cause episodes of bipolar disorder? Like many people with poor judgment or decreased inhibitions, its sufferers often consume inappropriate diets, especially foods high in sugars and carbohydrates, as well as yeast-containing foods, caffeine-containing beverages, and alcohol. The episodes of mania usually relate to an increased blood sugar concentration that is sustained while sugary foods and beverages are consumed. (Moreover, caffeine and alcohol exacerbate these circumstances; for example, evidence indicates that caffeine can increase glucose intolerance, causing exaggerated blood sugar "highs," and alcohol contributes its harmful effects.) The increased consumption of sugar and simple carbohydrates readily nourishes the disease-causing yeast, fueling their chemical activities (including their release of harmful toxins, metabolites, wastes, and more), which further disturbs the brain's chemistry and functioning. This readily explains why a sufferer's symptoms worsen during an attack, especially why their thinking often becomes delusional; the presence of increased concentrations of yeast-produced substances (notably ethanol, acetaldehyde, and gliotoxin) can greatly disturb their brain's chemistry.

Regardless of how "hyped up" they are, a bipolar disorder sufferer cannot sustain their behavior forever. Sooner or later, their blood sugar concentration falls, producing the depression that typically follows their manic episodes. Since glucose is the brain's primary source of energy, when their blood sugar falls below a certain concentration (usually, about 60 mg/dL), their brain will not obtain enough energy and symptoms of being "low" are common. Moreover, ingesting caffeine and alcohol without drinking appropriate amounts of water may produce dehydration, not to mention a hangover, which further contributes to making someone feel ill. Also, consuming allergic foods or beverages or those that contain disease-causing yeast or harmful molds can adversely affect their immunity, "depressing" their nervous system. Since allergic consequences can last for days and even weeks, this may be why the episodes of depression last much longer than the episodes of mania. Obviously, nutritional deficiencies will only compound the disturbances that are present. Lastly, environmental allergies contribute to depression in some bipolar disorder sufferers.

Fortunately, some physicians do appreciate this way of practicing medicine. People with depression and bipolar disorder have demonstrated incredible improvements when they are treated with an anti-candidiasis approach. This produces a subjective sense of well-being and health, and improves their neurotransmitter levels, which can be objectively measured for confirmation. Therefore, when depression or bipolar disorder is present, you would be wise to consider the contributions of candidiasis.

OBSESSIVE-COMPULSIVE DISORDER

Do you know someone who needs to repeatedly wash their hands, even when they are not dirty? What about someone who constantly checks to make sure their oven is off? Or how about someone who must count to 10 every time something goes wrong? These behaviors, under normal circumstances, are not out of the ordinary. Yet, they do become abnormal when they are repeatedly performed to temporarily cancel or alleviate some obsessive thoughts—distressing, negative emotions such as fear, disgust, doubt, and feeling incomplete or inadequate.

Obsessive-compulsive disorder (OCD) is a complex neurological-psychological condition that produces various bizarre behaviors, ranging from mild to severe to incapacitating. In 2022, its prevalence was estimated to be 2 percent worldwide, or roughly 160 million people. About 80 percent of OCD sufferers demonstrate *compulsive* behaviors. These repeated, purposeful activities are often performed for certain reasons or in specific ways to temporarily suppress or dismiss an obsessional thought and its disruptive consequences. The recurring *obsessions* are usually continuous or intrusive thoughts, ideas, images, themes, or songs that are painful, abnormal, or blatantly bizarre. Since only 15 percent have obsessions severe enough to be abnormal, this implies that most OCD sufferers have a mild form of illness, with only a small percentage significantly compromised. Moreover, this ailment is underdiagnosed because many OCD sufferers experience an urge for secrecy, even to the point of marked paranoia. Rather than simply being a psychiatric illness, physical and neurological symptoms are extremely common among OCD sufferers. This immediately implies that OCD is a part of a bigger problem.

OCD is frequently accompanied by numerous typical psychiatric symptoms, including anxiety, fear, phobias, and profound depression. Suicide, suicidal attempts, and self-inflicted injuries are regular consequences. Pulling out someone's own hair (*trichotillomania*) is a common behavior among children with OCD. In psychodynamic terms, OCD sufferers are thought to be caught between inwardly and outwardly aggressive feelings, leading to conflicts with their family, boss, job, and/or the authorities. Compulsive behaviors can involve excessive handwashing, double-checking, or desires to clean. Sexual maladjustments or disturbances usually occur and can be expressed as irrational fears of being contaminated, contracting AIDS, and/or being exposed to sexually transmitted diseases. Females may demonstrate frigidity, while males can have erectile difficulties or ejaculation problems.

An abundance of research indicates that OCD is effectively treated with medications that prevent the reuptake of *serotonin* within the gap between nerve cells. Evidence demonstrates that sertraline, a *selective serotonin reuptake inhibitor,* which was mentioned in the previous section, is effective in treating these people. The common conclusion is that sertraline's effectiveness reveals that OCD sufferers have a shortage of serotonin and adversely altered neurotransmitters levels. In contrast, researchers found this drug has antifungal activity against *Candida auris*, implying that OCD could be a mental manifestation of candidiasis. Once again, candidiasis can disrupt the brain's chemistry and functioning. In susceptible people, it instigates or promotes OCD. Is there support for this thinking?

Since candidiasis involves nutritional deficiencies, alternative medicine physicians often treat OCD with dietary modification, nutritional supplements, vitamins, and probiotics. Most sufferers have an abnormal glucose tolerance test (sometimes markedly), so patients are given a low- or zero-carbohydrate diet (it does not eliminate candidiasis but undernourishes disease-causing yeast, slowing their metabolism and activities). In addition, large doses of *tryptophan* have been given; tryptophan is an amino acid that crosses the blood-brain barrier and is converted to serotonin, improving OCD symptoms. Moreover, short-term psychotherapy and long-term counseling are regularly employed.

Yes, someone must be susceptible to developing OCD, and a large emotional component is part of this mental manifestation. As a result, psychotherapy is necessary but unlikely to produce notable improvements alone because something is occurring at the physical level. The key to achieving long-lasting improvements is to eradicate candidiasis as well as the presence of any other infectious invaders. In 1995, William Shaw, Ph.D., revealed that the colonization of disease-causing yeast and harmful molds is responsible for numerous mental illnesses; the presence of fungal metabolites can be measured using the *urine organic acid test*. The metabolites of disease-causing yeast and harmful molds have been found within OCD sufferers, and Dr. Shaw discovered that these people frequently have metabolites from harmful (*propionic*) bacteria as well. Other studies lend further support to the participation of many troublemakers, and candidiasis can be exacerbated by numerous infectious invaders. In return, all of them must be identified and addressed.

Since chronic candidiasis promotes nutritional deficiencies, causes glucose intolerance, adversely alters the brain's chemistry, and more, the evidence supports a *candidiasis-OCD connection*. So, an anti-candidiasis approach is certain to help OCD sufferers.

SCHIZOPHRENIA

Schizophrenia is a psychosis, involving bizarre thinking or thoughts. Sufferers typically experience hallucinations, delusions, and altered or inappropriate interpersonal interactions. In addition, their mental (cognitive) ability and mood are abnormal. It frequently disrupts and destroys the lives of its sufferers and negatively influences the lives of those around them. Although it is not as common as many other mental disorders, in 2022, it was estimated to affect about 24 million people worldwide (0.32%).

This illness is only diagnosed when there is an absence of any demonstrable anatomical or functional cause. It can present any time, but most frequently arises during adolescence and early adulthood. Its onset can be sudden or gradual, and its course may be limited or persistently debilitating. There seems to be a genetic predisposition to develop it, but not every susceptible person does. Since its exact cause remains unknown, and illness cannot occur without a cause, this suggests a *candidiasis-schizophrenia connection*. Is this possible? Yes, but you must first understand the basics of schizophrenia.

Hallucinations (especially auditory) and delusions are its most characteristic brain-related manifestations. Typically, *hallucinations* involve hearing a person's own thoughts aloud, voices commenting about their actions, or several voices in a conversation. *Delusions* are false beliefs that are often dramatic and strongly embraced, including anything from control over a person's own body and actions to the workings of the world. Occasionally, they might think their mind is controlled by an outside force. Language skills and interpersonal interactions are consistently abnormal. The best-known symptom relates to abnormal emotional expressions; usually, the person is distant, unresponsive, and "cold" to others. With respect to posture and movement, disturbed stance and mobility are common.

Can schizophrenia be related to candidiasis? The first clue to revealing this relationship is that this illness has no identifiable origin. When a cause is not appreciated, you should think of candidiasis. Is there support for this thinking? Yes, because abundant evidence associates the health of the gut with schizophrenia. Simply put, this illness can worsen with short exposures to certain inciting substances. Since schizophrenia is influenced by the gut's activities and candidiasis is primarily a gastrointestinal illness, this supports a *candidiasis-schizophrenia connection*. Another clue is that depression and suicidal impulses afflict about half its sufferers. Since there is a *candidiasis-depression connection*, this adds support.

Schizophrenia involves gross distortions in thinking and behavior, which implies that the brain chemistry and functioning of its sufferers is greatly disturbed. Treatment routinely includes antipsychotic medications, which increase or decrease certain neurotransmitters. Because of its scope, more than one drug is often needed. These drugs almost never cure schizophrenia, requiring its sufferers to take them indefinitely. In contrast, although antipsychotic medication might be needed, it makes sense to address what is causing their brains to be adversely affected. Candidiasis can directly and indirectly compromise the brain's chemistry and functioning, and often significantly, with its *infectious* and *allergic* consequences.

Admittedly, schizophrenia is not only caused by candidiasis because there seems to be a genetic predisposition to develop it, and there are psychological components. Regardless, candidiasis is a major trigger for its mental deterioration. Most schizophrenia sufferers develop the disorder in their late adolescence or early adulthood. This is usually when their diets are the least appropriate, their hormones are in full swing, the adverse effects of antibiotics or birth control pills start to accumulate, drugs and alcohol are used, and they are exposed to many other risk factors that promote candidiasis (chapter 2). In addition to disease-causing yeast, research supports that other infectious invaders contribute their adverse effects.

Schizophrenia sufferers have improved when their candidiasis was appropriately addressed, both its *infectious* and *allergic* contributions. In addition, the greater the number of infectious invaders present, the more a person's body and brain are likely to be disturbed. Research implicates the contributions of numerous parasites, a harmful mold called *Aspergillus*, members of the *Clostridia* species of bacteria, and other troublemakers. As a result, addressing all these infectious invaders is essential and certain to provide remarkable benefits for schizophrenia sufferers everywhere. With this appreciation, it becomes difficult to dismiss a *candidiasis-schizophrenia connection*.

MEMORY PROBLEMS

Most people are unaware that even the simplest tasks require us to retrieve, as well as store, information from our brain. For example, if you must do something, you may simply remember how you did it in the past and repeat the behavior. If you need to do something you never did before, you have to figure out how to do it; usually, you will consider similar experiences in your past, and then try to do the task until you get it right. Our ability to remember contributes to our intellect and, in the bigger picture, everything becomes meaningless without it; after all, if you cannot remember people, places, or something you just did, you would have no more awareness than a bacteria or plant. As a result, memory is one of the brain's most vital activities.

Although the concept of memory is easily defined, deciphering how it works and fails is another story. In short, memory can be disturbed if there is anatomical, electrical, and/or biochemical disarray. Anatomical disturbances can easily promote defective memory; for example, people who have had a head injury, stroke, or suffer with dementia often experience memory problems. Yet, most people with memory disturbances have not had an anatomical insult or injury, implying that electrical and biochemical disturbances are likely to be involved. So, what causes most memory problems? (This discussion refers to memory problems that occur without an identifiable cause, not substance-related memory problems that involve drinking alcohol or taking drugs.)

Candidiasis sufferers often experience *short-term memory* deficits. Basically, *acetylcholine* is a critical neurotransmitter for memory and the presence of candidiasis can compromise the brain's ability to produce and/or release it. As a result, sufferers regularly experience poor short-term memory. *Long-term memory* (for old events) is usually unaffected, so it is probably not as sensitive to altered acetylcholine levels. So, candidiasis seems the cause of the *biochemical disturbances* that adversely affect memory. Moreover, it consistently promotes malabsorption, leading to nutritional deficiencies; since certain minerals are used to generate and propagate electrical signals along nerve cells, candidiasis can cause electrical disturbances that also contribute.

Candidiasis sufferers also frequently experience a decreased ability to *concentrate*, the capacity to mentally focus on an immediate activity or problem. Many sufferers complain of feeling like they are "in a fog." This symptom means there is a breakdown in the brain's ability to pass information from one area to another. It can reflect a biochemical and/or electrical disturbance. Specifics aside, memory problems and an inability to concentrate are the result of the brain being inappropriately influenced, directly and/or indirectly, by the presence and adverse activities of disease-causing yeast.

If you suffer with poor memory or an inability to concentrate, there is good news. Once your candidiasis is eliminated, you are almost guaranteed to experience drastic improvements.

HEADACHES

Does any of this sound familiar? It is four o'clock in the afternoon, when suddenly, for no obvious reason, you develop a headache. Whenever it is humid or raining, you get a headache accompanied by pain around your sinuses. At certain times of the year, you develop weeks of headaches that seem almost unbearable. After you eat or drink something, you develop a visual disturbance lasting about a half hour, and then, as it fades, you get a severe migraine. For the people who suffer, headaches are more than a pain in their head. Depending on their severity, they can range from uncomfortable to incapacitating. The good news is that most headaches can be eliminated when you understand their causation.

Headache is a term used to describe head pain from a nontraumatic origin. They are classified by their timing and/or severity. Once a serious or life-threatening cause is ruled out (for example, a brain tumor), most headaches are thought to occur from stress and muscle tension. Mainstream physicians treat most headaches with a pain reliever. In certain cases, like migraine headaches, they use a special medication to impede the physical process that triggers the pain. Each year, about 45 million Americans complain of headaches, and it is estimated that roughly 15.8 percent of the world's population (1.264 billion people) experience a headache every day, with 7 percent experiencing a migraine (88.48 million). Why are so many people suffering?

Some physicians appreciate there is an *allergy-headache connection*. Since there is a *candidiasis-allergy connection* (chapter 16), there must be a *candidiasis-headache connection*. Moreover, many headaches occur when someone's blood sugar concentration rapidly falls, so glucose intolerance can promote headaches. Since there is a *candidiasis–glucose intolerance connection* (chapters 11 and 14), it further supports a *candidiasis-headache connection*. Does this mean all candidiasis sufferers have headaches? A significant percentage do, but not all. Instead, it means if you suffer with headaches, you are likely to have candidiasis.

What types of headaches plague candidiasis sufferers? The most common are *vascular headaches*, including migraines, tension headaches, and cluster headaches. These do not involve an anatomical defect. Vascular headaches result from a vasoconstriction and vasodilatation event; an artery constricts, dilates, triggers some nerve endings, and pain occurs.

Migraine headaches are far from rare events because more than 88 million people suffer with them every day. This means that candidiasis is a bigger problem than most people and physicians realize. If this is true, why is a *candidiasis-headache connection* not recognized? Since candidiasis is generally ignored and unrecognized when present, the connection is unappreciated, and its cause is overlooked. In addition, rather than being the direct result of candidiasis, most migraine headaches appear to be an indirect result; in susceptible people, candidiasis induces allergies and blood sugar disturbances that cause certain blood vessels to vasoconstrict and then vasodilate, producing migraines.

What kind of allergies trigger vascular headaches? Environmental and food allergies are both capable of triggering inflammation within the body. Normally, vasoconstriction is a protective mechanism that helps the body decrease blood flow to injured or damaged areas, preventing the loss of blood. Yet, the presence of irritating, allergy-inducing substances can trigger the release of numerous chemicals that can initiate vasoconstriction followed by vasodilation and the development of a vascular headache. Evidence also indicates that this can accompany the presence of *Candida albicans* within the blood (chapter 7).

If you have vascular headaches, but do not suffer with seasonal allergies, postnasal drip, or any identifiable food allergies, can an allergy contribute to your problem? Yes, because most candidiasis sufferers are allergic to one or more disease-causing yeast and harmful molds. Foods, beverages, or locations contaminated with these infectious invaders, alive or dead, can easily trigger vascular headaches. For example, many mainstream physicians believe that wine and cheese instigate headaches because of the *sulfites* they contain. Yet, wine and most cheese are fermented using either yeast and/or molds, or contaminated with them, so they contain their antigens, inducing allergic reactions in sensitive people. In addition, many wines and other alcoholic beverages are aged in oak casks, which are often contaminated with mold. So, the answer is not as simple as sulfites. Yes, this chemical sensitivity may exist within some people, but they are regularly found to be candidiasis sufferers. Since most migraine sufferers are not tested for allergies to disease-causing yeast and harmful molds, this association is hardly ever appreciated.

How does glucose intolerance contribute to vascular headaches? A rapid and/or profound decrease in someone's blood glucose concentration, especially below their fasting level, can cause certain blood vessels to vasoconstrict then vasodilate, precipitating vascular headaches. How? A rapid fall means glucose is quickly moving out of someone's blood into their cells and tissues; since water follows the sugar, it causes sensitive blood vessels to constrict. In addition, when the blood sugar concentration drops to a certain point, it triggers the release of hormones that assist in raising the concentration to its fasting level. *Epinephrine* is a prominent blood sugar–raising hormone that can also constrict blood vessels. This explains why many migraine sufferers often develop headaches after eating lots of sweets or fruit, drinking juice, or ingesting high-carbohydrate meals. Moreover, consuming simple carbohydrates and lots of complex ones readily nourishes disease-causing yeast, promoting their growth and associated mischief.

When a headache sufferer keeps a thorough record of all the foods they consume, glucose intolerance and allergies are revealed to be the cause of most of their headaches. Since there is a *candidiasis-glucose intolerance-allergy connection*, most headache sufferers also have numerous candidiasis-related symptoms. Even though most are not recognized as candidiasis sufferers, there is a *candidiasis-headache connection*, nonetheless. Moreover, other infectious invaders are likely to contribute. Experience demonstrates that parasites frequently infect migraine headache sufferers. So, if you are a headache sufferer, an anti-candidiasis program that identifies and eliminates all your infectious invaders should alleviate your headaches permanently.

SEIZURES

If you suffer with a seizure disorder, your condition may not exist for no reason. If you have blatantly abnormal brain activity or some anatomical defect that precipitates your seizures, the following may not apply. Nevertheless, there is hope for a large percentage of seizure sufferers, including a way to possibly discontinue taking medication (with medical supervision).

A *seizure* is a single occurrence of a sudden, uncontrolled electrical disturbance within the brain that involves changes in behavior, movements, or feelings as well as alterations in consciousness. There are four types, classified by their presentation, length, and frequency: focal, generalized, combination focal and generalized, and unknown. *Epilepsy* is a neurological condition that involves two or more unprovoked seizures. In 2015, 1.2 percent of Americans were diagnosed with epilepsy—roughly 3 million adults and 470,000 children. Recent estimates reveal more than 50 million people suffer with epilepsy worldwide.

Epilepsy involves repeated and/or spontaneous episodes of hyperactive brain functioning that induce seizures. It is *primary* when it has no apparent origin and *secondary* when there is a discernible anatomical abnormality. Although confusion, memory loss, and fatigue are common, seizure sufferers may also have impaired consciousness, involuntary movements, a disturbed autonomic nervous system, and/or psychic-sensory symptoms. Seizures range from annoying to debilitating and can even be fatal.

Is there a *candidiasis-seizure connection*? Admittedly, not all seizures are caused by candidiasis because anatomical disturbances, defects, or damage can promote abnormal brain activity, leading to seizures. In contrast, a large percentage of epilepsy sufferers have no discernible anatomical (structural) defect, implying that something more mysterious is occurring. So, what is responsible for their seizures?

A low blood glucose concentration (*hypoglycemia*) can trigger seizures in susceptible people. Since the brain cannot store fuel, blood glucose is the brain's almost exclusive source of energy. A rapid decrease or significantly low concentration of blood glucose hinders the amount of glucose that can cross the blood-brain barrier, nourishing the brain's cells and tissue. When the blood glucose concentration falls below a certain amount (about 60 mg/dL), the brain is effectively starved of energy, which induces symptoms like confusion, memory loss, and fatigue. If the brain is deprived long enough, chemical (metabolic) disturbances arise. In susceptible people, this triggers hyperactivity or inappropriate activity within certain areas of their brain, precipitating seizures. Since candidiasis can promote glucose intolerance (chapters 11 and 14), it can readily contribute to causing seizures in certain people, which depends on the severity of their glucose intolerance and threshold for abnormal brain activity. (Numerous studies demonstrate that a ketogenic diet—a high-fat, adequate-protein, low-carbohydrate diet—alone decreases seizures, but it requires strict compliance.)

Many food and environmental *allergies* are associated with seizures. Allergies to disease-causing yeast and harmful molds can also be irritating. In sensitive or hypersensitive people, exposure to allergic (antigenic) substances triggers an excessive release of certain chemicals that instigate inflammation and swelling, such as histamine, prostaglandins, interleukins, and more. In some people, these reactions promote biochemical and electrical disturbances that induce seizures. So, allergies can trigger seizures. Since there is a *candidiasis-allergy connection* (chapter 16) and allergic reactions can induce seizures, this supports a *candidiasis-seizure connection.*

Hormone and chemical (*metabolic*) disturbances can upset the body's internal balance, producing seizures in some people. Since candidiasis can adversely affect the body's endocrine (hormone) system and its chemical activities (chapter 11), it can indirectly promote seizures. More commonly, sufferers manifest a particular hormone disturbance that may precipitate seizures, although it is rarely appreciated. *Functional hypoparathyroidism* occurs when their blood calcium ion and magnesium ion levels are normal, but the amounts within their cells and tissues are decreased. This impairs their cellular activities and functioning as well as creates chemical (metabolic) disturbances. Convulsions are well accepted as being a symptom of functional hypoparathyroidism. However, since the serum magnesium and calcium ion concentrations appear normal by laboratory tests, it is often difficult to connect seizures with this candidiasis-related hormone disturbance. Regardless, hormone and chemical disturbances are common among candidiasis sufferers and can readily contribute to seizures.

Since the brain's activity and functioning depends on its neurotransmitters, a biochemical disturbance alone can precipitate seizure activity in certain people. Once again, candidiasis can adversely alter the brain's levels of neurotransmitters and directly precipitate seizures. In addition, certain substances produced by disease-causing yeast (specifically, gliotoxin) may cause one or more areas of the brain to become irritable or hyperexcitable, which may effectively lower someone's threshold for having seizure activity. The same may be said for ethanol and acetaldehyde. In other words, certain substances produced by disease-causing yeast can trigger seizure activity in susceptible people.

Furthermore, *malabsorption* can cause mineral deficiencies. Since certain minerals are required to generate electrical signals along nerve cells, deficiencies can induce electrical disturbances that promote abnormal brain activity, leading to seizures. Since candidiasis frequently involves malabsorption, especially when there is leaky gut syndrome, this adds more evidence for a *candidiasis-seizure connection*. To add insult to injury, malabsorption worsens all the previous parameters, making seizure activity more likely.

Seizures always have a cause, whether it is discernible or not. Although anatomical disturbances may precipitate or promote a seizure, in many cases, the cause of someone's seizures is mostly unknown. Therefore, an understanding of the *candidiasis-seizure connection* should give seizure sufferers a better approach to treatment as well as a chance to eliminate their condition.

NEURODEGENERATIVE DISEASES

All *neurodegenerative diseases* have one thing in common—various cells of the central nervous system stop working or die. Although Alzheimer's disease (AD), multiple sclerosis (MS), and Parkinson's disease (PD) are discussed in this section, other notable expressions are amyotrophic lateral sclerosis (ALS), Huntington's disease (HD), multiple system atrophy (MSA), and prion diseases. There seems to be a genetic predisposition to develop some of these diseases. Other causes include medical conditions such as alcoholism, a tumor, and a stroke, as well as exposures to toxins (heavy metals, chemicals, plastics, etc.) and viruses.

Alzheimer's Disease & Dementia

It is important to mention that *dementia* is a broad term, describing a range of symptoms that impair someone's ability to perform their daily activities. Common symptoms include a decline in memory, changes in thinking, poor judgment and/or reasoning, decreased focus and attention, language changes, and behavior changes. These can occur from aging or result from the candidiasis-related psychological and neurological manifestations discussed in this chapter. In 2020, there were more than 55 million people living with dementia worldwide, and this number is expected to double every 20 years (78 million by 2032 and 139 million by 2050). In 2019, the global economic costs related to dementia were reported to be 1.3 trillion U.S. dollars.

There are many different types and causes of dementia, but *Alzheimer's disease* (AD) is the most common; it is thought to contribute to 60 to 70 percent of cases. In 2022, according to the Alzheimer's Association, AD was estimated to affect 6.5 million Americans, which is expected to double by 2060. The worldwide prevalence is about 33 to 38.5 million people.

Alzheimer's disease is thought to be caused by a combination of age-related changes within the brain, involving genetic, environmental, and lifestyle factors. The risk factors for AD include age, alcohol consumption, aluminum ingestion, concussion, cerebral hypoperfusion, diabetes, homocysteine, hypercholesterolemia, hypertension, obesity, pesticides, pollution, physical inactivity, sleep disruption, and smoking. Except for trauma, self-induced abuse, and toxin exposures, all of these are risk factors for developing candidiasis and its manifestations. (Holistic physicians are aware that other toxic metals can contribute and are more problematic than aluminum.)

There are four stages of AD: 1) preclinical, involving brain changes without disease signs, 2) mild early, cognitive problems, 3) moderate, middle, and 4) severe, late.

In 1901, Alois Alzheimer, a German psychiatrist and neuropathologist, observed a 51-year-old female patient in a Frankfurt asylum who had strange behavioral symptoms, including a loss of her short-term memory. After the patient died on April 8, 1906, Dr. Alzheimer acquired her medical records and brain, which were taken to a laboratory in Munich. Using the newly developed *Bielschowsky stain*, he identified the amyloid plaques and neurofibrillary tangles that later became the brain anomalies indicative of AD. Since then, another noted feature is the loss of connections between neurons within the brain. The initial damage involves parts of the brain that participate in memory, including the *entorhinal cortex* and *hippocampus*. As AD progresses, it can adversely affect areas within the cerebral cortex that are involved with language, reasoning, and social behavior. With further insults, many other brain areas are damaged.

AD is a brain disorder involving a mental deterioration that occurs in middle or old age because of degenerative insults within the brain (and nervous system). *Amyloid plaques* are aggregates of misfolded proteins that arise in the spaces between nerve cells, whereas *neurofibrillary tangles* are abnormal accumulations of a "tau" protein that collects inside neurons. In a healthy brain, certain *glial cells* perform valuable functions; *microglia* are supposed to engulf and destroy waste and toxins, whereas *astrocytes* assist in clearing plaque and cellular debris. In AD, the microglia and astrocytes surround the neurons but fail to perform their debris-clearing functions. Even worse, they release inflammatory chemicals that further damage the neurons they are supposed to protect.

The acetaldehyde hypothesis was previously mentioned in this chapter. In short, disease-causing yeast can manufacture *acetaldehyde* (and *ethanol*), which can be absorbed, circulate throughout the blood, and enter the brain. Since it is a toxic chemical, prolonged exposure or large amounts can promote injury by free radical reactions and peroxidation (chapter 7). Within the brain, it is thought to block the connections between brain cells (synapses), which is consistent with the findings in AD. It also inhibits the synthesis of acetylcholine, decreasing the functioning of the autonomic nervous system. It may bind with or be incorporated into neurotransmitters, creating pseudo-neurotransmitters (false messengers) that readily disrupt the brain's functioning. So, the presence of chronic candidiasis can certainly contribute to the brain degeneration that occurs in AD. In addition, disease-causing yeast (as well as *Aspergillus fumigatus*, *Penicillium bilaii*, and *Gliocladium* species) produce *gliotoxin*, which suppresses immunity and is toxic to different types of nervous system cells, including astrocytes, oligodendrocytes, and glial cells. This provides further evidence for a *candidiasis-AD connection*.

Vascular problems are thought to contribute to AD, so there is an *AD-cardiovascular connection*. This can involve reduced blood flow within the brain, decreasing the amount of oxygen needed for proper functioning. More concerning, it may cause injury or damage to the *blood-brain barrier* (BBB), which is a vital immunological feature within the central nervous system. The BBB is the interface between the blood vessels and interstitial fluid within the brain, and it is composed of four types of cells (*endothelial cells, pericytes, astrocytes,* and *microglia*). It usually protects the brain from harmful substances, while allowing glucose and other needed factors to enter the brain tissue. It also forms a structural-functional barrier that prevents various microorganisms circulating within the blood from entering the brain, including disease-causing yeast, molds, bacteria, parasites, and/or viruses.

In AD, a damaged BBB allows harmful substances to access the brain, while glucose is prevented from entering. This adds to the inflammation and vascular problems within the brain's cells and tissue. In short, AD is a cause and consequence of vascular problems within the brain. Since there is a *candidiasis-cardiovascular connection* (chapter 7) and an *AD-cardiovascular connection*, this lends more support for a *candidiasis-AD connection*. Because chronic candidiasis is a persistent *infection* with *allergic* consequences, the constant inflammation and free radical damage can certainly contribute to the vascular disturbances that occur in AD. Moreover, the four types of cells comprising the BBB can directly and/or indirectly be adversely affected by the chronic presence of disease-causing yeast, including their infectious and allergic inflammation and toxins, so the pathology that occurs in AD is consistent with chronic candidiasis. Yet, there are other possibilities. Once the BBB is injured or damaged, one or more microorganisms may gain direct access to the brain tissue, causing various insults and harm.

Various researchers appreciate that there is a fungal contribution to AD, although other infectious invaders may participate, including harmful molds, bacteria, parasites, and/or viruses. So, there is a *candidiasis-AD connection*. Since the neurodegenerative damage that occurs in AD is typically irreversible, the benefits of anti-candidiasis therapy are likely to prevent or decrease the incidence of AD, as well as slow or stop its progression in AD sufferers.

Multiple Sclerosis

Multiple sclerosis is not usually life-threatening, but it can be scary. After all, it is a condition that involves degeneration of the nervous system. At present, there is no cure, which means it is progressive in most of its sufferers. About 2.8 million people suffer with it worldwide, and its prevalence is increasing.

Multiple sclerosis (MS) is a disease that involves the brain, optic nerve, and spinal cord. Normally, nerve cells have a conductive covering, their *myelin sheath*, that assists in the rapid propagation of electrical signals from one cell to another. By a process called *demyelination*, MS involves injury and damage to the myelin sheath. Depending on its extent, degenerated areas can easily disrupt nervous system activities. Typically, its associated symptoms include weakness of one or more extremities, one-sided vision loss (optic neuritis), incoordination, and abnormal sensations. Less prominently, there are bladder problems; dizziness (vertigo); hearing loss; pain of the face, extremities, body, or joints; and altered intellectual abilities.

MS has been recognized and described for decades, but its origin remains obscure. Mainstream physicians think that MS is caused by an overactive and misdirected immune system. Therefore, mainstream medical care relies on immunosuppressive medication—ocrelizumab (Ocrevus)—to prevent disease progression.

Something must be responsible for MS. Undeniably, a combination of factors is required to develop it. First, there must be an inherited genetic predisposition or weakness to develop MS when certain circumstances permit. Since everyone with this weakness does not develop MS, something else must promote this disease. So, what is the inciting factor?

The simple way to understand MS is to blame abnormal immunity, but it is not the complete answer. Yes, MS sufferers have it, but why it exists is another question altogether. Although some experts suggest that MS has an infectious origin, most physicians believe it represents an autoimmune process; certain immune cells get programmed to inappropriately assault someone's own myelin sheaths. Typically, this includes self-reactive cells, with or without the presence of autoantibodies. So, what causes it? There is a *candidiasis-autoimmune connection* (chapter 14); chronic candidiasis encourages impaired immunity, allowing self-reactive cells to arise that attack someone's own cells and tissues. If these self-reactive cells (and/or autoantibodies) are specifically directed to assault the myelin sheath of nerve cells, MS will occur. Although many infectious invaders often participate, especially parasites, candidiasis can by itself initiate and maintain MS. Research reveals that *Chlamydia pneumonia* plays a role in MS, but like its participation in cardiovascular illness, an infection with this harmful bacteria is likely to occur secondary to candidiasis (chapter 7).

Moreover, gliotoxin may play a strong role in promoting MS. Since gliotoxin is toxic to glial cells, astrocytes, and oligodendrocytes, its persistent presence in MS sufferers may prevent their nerve cell damage from being repaired. (In addition to disease-causing yeast and harmful molds, MS sufferers may have another source of gliotoxin. *Multiple sclerosis retrovirus* has been described by researchers and appears to cause its infected host cells to secrete a gliotoxin. Because of the *candidiasis–chronic viral illness connection* (chapter 14), candidiasis is likely to be responsible for the impaired immunity that permits this virus to cause trouble in MS sufferers. In other words, even if the virus does play a role in MS, its persistent presence is the result of chronic candidiasis.)

Furthermore, MS is not the only neuromuscular illness suspected of being associated with candidiasis. Other prominent examples include Parkinson's disease, essential tremor, myoclonus, motor tics, amyotrophic lateral sclerosis (ALS), spinocerebellar degenerations, neuromyelitis optica, diffuse sclerosis, traditional sclerosis, inflammatory neuropathies, Bell's palsy, acute brachial neuritis, trigeminal neuropathy, some types of muscular dystrophy, dermatomyositis/polymyositis, myasthenia gravis, and Lambert-Eaton myasthenic syndrome (LEMS). Basically, the abnormalities of each illness reflect variations on a common theme. In general, each illness represents cell-mediated autoimmunity, with or without autoantibodies, that is promoted by chronic candidiasis.

Research reveals that MS sufferers have increased amounts of *Candida*-species organisms. As far back as 1974, Dr. R. L. Swank noted, "If treated early in the disease, before significant disability had developed, a high percentage of cases remain unchanged for up to 20 years." There can never be a 100 percent cure rate if the nerve cells and tissue have been irreversibly damaged, but the likelihood of a promising prognosis increases with anti-candidiasis therapy. Yet, this does not mean advanced cases should be considered hopeless. On the contrary, eliminating the infectious invaders triggering this disease is likely to arrest its progress and maintain someone's health in the long run. Indeed, after the body is given its greatest chances to heal, improvements may even occur.

Parkinson's Disease

Although his symptoms began in 1991, actor Michael J. Fox revealed he was diagnosed and being treated for Parkinson's disease (PD) in 1998. Stories and reports appeared all over the news, and the message was clear: PD is a mysterious illness that was no longer confined to the elderly. Since most of its victims become progressively disabled, it is a life-disrupting illness. Concerningly, the prevalence of PD has doubled in the past 25 years, and it is estimated that more than 10 million people suffer worldwide. About 1 million Americans have it and roughly 60,000 new cases are diagnosed each year.

PD is a neurodegenerative condition, and its symptoms reflect the death of dopamine-producing nerve cells within the brain, causing a deficiency of the neurotransmitter *dopamine*. Idiopathic PD is the most common type and results from death of the pigmented dopaminergic neurons of the *substantia nigra pars compacta* and can include other cells as well.

PD has four components, including tremor at rest, rigidity, bradykinesia (decreased autonomic, spontaneous, and voluntary movements), and a loss of postural reflexes. PD sufferers do not need all four components, but bradykinesia is almost universal. There are different categories, including idiopathic, early-onset, familial, secondary, and atypical. Although idiopathic PD is the most prevalent, its origin remains unknown. More concerning, the worldwide population has not doubled over the past 25 years, so the increased incidence of PD is disproportionately greater than genetics alone—regardless of whether a genetic defect or proclivity to develop this condition exists. Something must be impelling more people to develop this neurological illness. Since candidiasis can disturb the brain's chemistry and functioning, is it involved in PD?

Depending on the species and strain of disease-causing yeast, its direct and indirect effects can create biochemical disturbances in susceptible people, promoting PD. Moreover, the most common candidiasis-related endocrine (hormone) disturbance may strongly contribute. *Functional hypoparathyroidism* (chapter 11) occurs when the calcium and magnesium ion levels within someone's blood are normal, while the amounts within their cells and tissues are decreased. This impairs their cells' activities and functioning as well as creates chemical (metabolic) disturbances. As a result, their symptoms reflect low levels of one or both minerals, and typically include muscle spasms, spasticity, and twitches, fatigue, emotional highs and lows, and impaired sensitivities (paresthesias). A common, but less prevalent manifestation of PD is *classic parkinsonism*. Therefore, PD can arise from a candidiasis-induced hormonal disturbance. Since the serum concentrations of magnesium and calcium may (falsely) appear normal, this relationship is often missed.

Yet, there is more to PD than a biochemical disturbance. It involves an abnormality within the *substantia nigra*, a part of the brain that helps control movements, as well as participates in chemical signaling within the brain that affects learning, mood, judgment, decision-making, and other processes. Why is this area adversely affected? Some people may have an anatomical or genetic weakness that makes them susceptible to insults within this location. If this is true, what causes the injury or damage? Research demonstrates that the substantia nigra may be susceptible to attack by the immune system. So, in some people, PD may be an autoimmune disease, involving the adverse contributions of (self-reactive) autoantibodies, and/or self-reactive cells (cell-mediated immunity). Since there is a *candidiasis-autoimmunity connection* (chapter 14), this is further support.

Yet, there is more evidence. *Candida albicans* and other fungi (including *Aspergillus fumigatus, Penicillium bilaii,* and *Gliocladium* species) produce gliotoxin. Different researchers have shown that gliotoxin can adversely affect brain cells and alter neurotransmitter levels, producing symptoms that mimic PD, which makes a *candidiasis-PD connection* highly likely. Moreover, gliotoxin is toxic and injurious to a variety of brain cells, including astrocytes, oligodendrocytes, and glial cells, so its harmful effects within the brain can be more widespread.

Therefore, PD may represent a combination of candidiasis-related mischief. Its direct and indirect effects can adversely alter the brain's neurotransmitter levels, with both their *infectious* and *allergic* consequences. Functional hypoparathyroidism is likely to contribute. Gliotoxin and other harmful substances may directly disturb and injure the brain's chemistry and functioning. Autoimmunity seems to participate in the disease process. A variety of allergies can promote or exacerbate PD symptoms. In addition, holistic physicians regularly test for heavy metal toxicity and, if positive, treat with a detoxification program. So, a *candidiasis-PD connection* seems obvious. Moreover, some of the nonprimary forms of PD may be related.

Treated early in the disease, anti-candidiasis therapy is certain to improve PD; that is, unless irreversible brain damage has occurred. Although disease-causing yeast appear to be the prominent troublemakers, they may be assisted by other infectious invaders. Therefore, PD should no longer be considered a mysterious illness. In fact, this thinking should provide a renewed hope for treating all its sufferers.

In summary, regardless of genetics, multiple microorganisms can participate in causing neurodegenerative diseases, and their alliances-interactions (including their metabolic activities and toxins) can certainly contribute to these illnesses. Moreover, other substances like toxic heavy metals, chemicals, plastics, and anything else that is deleterious to the brain's cells and tissues can participate in escalating the pathology of AD, especially if they cross the blood-brain barrier and enter the brain's cells and tissue. Since every person is unique and there are diverse contributors to the injuries and damage that occur in all the manifestations of neurodegenerative disease, no two sufferers are likely to ever have the exact same symptoms and illness, although there may be similarities. From a holistic perspective, candidiasis-minded physicians accept there may be numerous contributors to an illness, but in many, if not most, cases of neurodegenerative disease, disease-causing yeast contribute to creating an internal environment and gastrointestinal microbiome that favors their infectious, allergic, and inflammatory contributions with or without the assistance of other harmful infectious invaders.

ALCOHOLISM

Researchers are familiar with the ability of *Candida albicans* to *ferment* carbohydrates; basically, sugars and other carbohydrates are metabolized into *ethyl alcohol*. When this occurs within the gut, it is nearly impossible to avoid absorbing the ethyl alcohol. Candidiasis sufferers can produce and absorb moderate amounts of alcohol, depending on the species (and strain) of disease-causing yeast present, their severity of colonization, and their bowel transit time. Like drinking alcohol-containing beverages, the ethanol absorbed is likely to promote confusion, heavy-headedness, and mental fogginess. In rare cases, it has even produced drunkenness without ingesting any alcohol (*auto-brewery syndrome*).

In general, *alcoholism* is a disease that involves a period of alcohol abuse. Its diagnosis includes alcohol dependence and/or tolerance. Alcohol is a toxic substance, and excesses may instigate or promote an abundance of bodily disturbances, including numerous neurological disorders. Alcoholism does not usually refer to the moderate ingestion of alcohol but arises when someone is unable to control their consumption of alcohol or alcohol-containing beverages, which ends up creating social problems and/or causing bodily harm.

There are numerous psychological factors that can cause someone to use and abuse alcohol. Yet, many holistic physicians suggest that alcoholism is really a *symptom* of allergies to the ingredients within alcoholic beverages, including wheat, yeast, grapes, hops, malt, potatoes, and other substances. Since there is a *candidiasis-allergy connection* (chapter 16) and candidiasis can promote allergies to foods, disease-causing yeast, harmful molds, and more, this supports a *candidiasis-alcoholism connection*. Alcoholics often crave their most allergic foods, which establishes a vicious cycle; the worse they get, the more they desire to ingest their problematic foods. In the process, their tolerance to alcohol arises, so more can be consumed without feeling its ill effects, and dependence is not far behind.

Most alcoholics are frequently found to have marked glucose intolerance. Many alcoholic beverages contain an abundance of sugar and carbohydrates, especially wine and fruity drinks. In addition to the alcohol, someone will usually feel a "high" when their blood sugar concentration is elevated and "low" when it is rapidly falling or low. Often, as an alcoholic's blood sugar concentration falls, more alcohol is consumed to maintain their "high," creating a vicious cycle. This is a variation of a sweet tooth, and explains their cravings, but its object of affection is alcohol or alcohol-containing beverages. Since there is a *candidiasis–glucose intolerance connection* (chapters 11 and 14), most alcoholics readily demonstrate signs and symptoms of candidiasis. Some mainstream physicians think this reflects alcohol-induced stress, but candidiasis was probably present long before their alcohol addiction. After all, candidiasis sufferers regularly crave sugar and alcoholic beverages. In fact, leaky gut and inflammation have been found to be greatly increased in alcoholics, and it correlates with their depression and alcohol cravings. Since candidiasis is the primary contributor to leaky gut syndrome, it adds direct support for this connection.

Moreover, allergies to numerous ingredients contained within alcohol may alter the brain's chemistry, creating a "high" when these substances are consumed. The next day, the brain's chemistry may have a rebound or withdrawal effect, creating a "low" that subconsciously encourages someone to consume alcohol again. It is no surprise to find alcoholics are regularly allergic to numerous foods, disease-causing yeast, and harmful molds. Consuming beverages that contain these allergy-inducing substances (antigens) can contribute to their illness.

Alcoholism is thought to arise in certain personality types that experience various forms of psychosocial stress. Yet, it is also a physical illness, reflecting a manifestation or symptom of glucose intolerance and allergies. Since these conditions are candidiasis-related, a *candidiasis-alcoholism connection* is virtually guaranteed. When alcoholics are treated for their candidiasis, allergies, and glucose intolerance, their cravings for alcohol frequently disappear.

HONORABLE MENTION

Another neurological condition occurring with an increasing incidence among candidiasis sufferers is carpal tunnel syndrome, which involves inflammation of the *median nerve* in one or both wrists, producing mild to severe pain that may progress to marked debilitation. There must be a candidiasis connection because some sufferers' symptoms disappear after only two weeks of anti-candidiasis therapy. Admittedly, not all carpal tunnel syndrome sufferers are candidiasis sufferers. Yet, a percentage of them do have candidiasis, and their condition is likely to reflect candidiasis-related muscle spasms and/or joint pains associated with food allergies, nutritional deficiencies, hormone disturbances, and/or generalized inflammation. Most sufferers do not care why an anti-candidiasis approach works and are only grateful that it does.

Why do certain people develop carpal tunnel syndrome? Most of the muscles that control hand movements are in the forearm. Tendons from the bottoms of these muscles pass through the wrist and insert into the bones of the fingers and hand. Most cases of carpel tunnel syndrome are related to repetitive activities of these muscles; when someone strains or pulls any of these muscles, inflammation and injury arise, which promotes spasms and fibrous adhesions (scar tissue). This affects the ability of these muscles to properly contract and exert force on their tendons. If this occurs in a significant location, tendons can be pulled askew, causing them to become irritated and inflamed, generating pain. In these cases, deep tissue massage of the injured muscles is often exceptionally beneficial.

If you are suffering with carpal tunnel syndrome and want to avoid surgery, you would be wise to consider an anti-candidiasis approach combined with deep tissue massage (or acupuncture). Fortunately, most carpal tunnel syndrome sufferers discover that this combination is so effective that surgery becomes completely unnecessary.

CAN YOU REGAIN YOUR MENTAL HEALTH?

Of all the illnesses you can develop, psychological and neurological problems are often the most life disruptive. After all, these maladies frequently lead to a loss of mental and/or neurological functioning, which may involve a loss of reality. If you suffer with a psychological or neurological illness, you have the chance to regain your mental health.

The brain's anatomy forms its foundation; the precise location and structural integrity of its integrated parts is required for the brain's proper functioning. Yet, the brain's electrical activity and biochemical processes are what enlivens this collection of cells and tissues. Since it functions on three levels, the brain can be compromised by anatomical, electrical, and/or biochemical disturbances. Before you can eliminate your mental manifestation, you must first understand what kind of disturbance you have.

Anatomical disturbances are the easiest to diagnose; usually, there was a head injury, stroke, or other brain insult. A significant insult will damage the brain, impairing its structural integrity and functioning. These insults typically promote neurological consequences, but psychological illnesses can occur as well. Although there is contrary evidence, it is accepted that little can be done to heal an anatomically damaged brain. So, if you have experienced an anatomical insult, your recovery is likely to be limited. In contrast, most psychological illnesses and many neurological illnesses do not involve an anatomical insult and reflect electrical and/or biochemical disturbances. If you suffer with this type of a mental manifestation, the odds of regaining your mental health are increased. Moreover, even if you had an anatomical insult, your situation is far from hopeless because many people with them have accompanying electrical and biochemical disturbances, and benefit when these are addressed and treated.

According to mainstream medicine, most psychological and neurological illnesses have obscure or mysterious origins. Yet, illness cannot arise for no reason. This means your illness must have a cause, whether recognized or not. Without an anatomical insult, electrical and/or biochemical disturbances cannot occur by magic. Why do they exist? Since the building blocks (precursors) for your brain's neurotransmitters and electrical activities are obtained from your diet, an improper diet can adversely affect your brain's functioning. Typically, this only produces minor mental manifestations that are often reversible when your diet improves. If your diet is the culprit, consulting a nutritionist should provide rapid relief from your mental problems.

Suppose you changed your diet and have no significant improvements in your mental health, what does this mean? Most likely, you are not absorbing essential nutrients from your gastrointestinal tract. You are probably suffering from malabsorption, promoting more exaggerated biochemical and electrical disturbances. In some cases, this can be treated with megadoses of vitamins, minerals, amino acids, and other supplements. Although this may prove efficacious, it does not address the cause of your malabsorption. In most cases, *gastrointestinal candidiasis* is responsible (chapter 4). This means, if you truly want to correct your problem, you must eliminate your candidiasis as well as any other harmful infectious invaders.

Can candidiasis cause psychological and neurological illnesses? Absolutely. The colonization and adverse activities of disease-causing yeast, and other infectious invaders, can greatly disturb the brain's functioning. Chronic candidiasis is often associated with a variety of mental manifestations, including moodiness, anxiety, phobias, panic attacks, PMS-related mental problems, depression, bipolar disorder (manic-depression), obsessive-compulsive disorder, schizophrenia, memory problems, concentration difficulties, various headaches, seizures, neurodegenerative diseases, alcoholism, carpal tunnel syndrome, and probably much, much more. Unfortunately, adults are not the only ones affected; children can have mental manifestations as well (chapter 12).

It is important to understand that candidiasis can affect your brain directly and indirectly. In addition to malabsorption, disease-causing yeast produce numerous substances that are directly harmful to your brain, especially ethanol, acetaldehyde, and gliotoxin. Candidiasis promotes glucose intolerance and allergies that can indirectly impair your brain's functioning. It can cause a variety of endocrine (hormone) disturbances, especially functional hypoparathyroidism, which also instigates or promotes mental manifestations. Even more troubling, it can impair immunity, leading to the production of self-reactive cells and/or autoantibodies that precipitate autoimmune disease–related neurological illnesses. When all of this is considered, there seems to be an irrefutable association between candidiasis and mental manifestations.

Once you appreciate the *candidiasis–mental manifestation connection*, you are in a position of power. Instead of simply taking a medication to impede your symptoms or slow the progression of your mental malady, you can now address its true cause with a comprehensive anti-candidiasis program that will help you regain and restore your mental health.

CHAPTER 11

Endocrine-Hormone & Metabolic Disturbances

Your *endocrine system* includes your glands and their chemical messengers. Its purpose is to regulate your body's functioning, and a delicate balance must be achieved for optimal health. Maintaining this balance, *homeostasis*, is its primary duty. Yet, your endocrine system does not act alone; together with your nervous and immune systems, all three form your *neuroendocrine-immune connection*. The balance between them maintains homeostasis, and a disturbance in one system is guaranteed to influence the others. If an endocrine problem arises, it will disrupt the immune and nervous systems in some way. Alternatively, if there is a problem with the immune or nervous systems, the endocrine system will be adversely affected to some extent.

Each gland produces and releases one or more hormones that influence a specific organ or tissue. Hormones are unique chemical messengers that interact with a specific target. Basically, a hormone is released from its gland, enters the blood, and circulates until it reaches its target organ or tissue. The target identifies its hormone with receptors that bind with it, like a key fitting in a lock. The target's functioning, and sometimes its structure, is then altered. Although more than 50 hormones are produced by the human body, there are three basic types: *amino acid analogs* and their derivatives, *polypeptides*, and *steroids*.

Endocrine problems (*endocrinopathy*) often accompany and exacerbate the symptoms and manifestations of candidiasis. Since the *infectious* and *allergic* consequences of disease-causing yeast disturb the immune and nervous systems (chapters 10 and 14), candidiasis can indirectly cause endocrine disturbances. Moreover, research reveals that it can *directly* disturb endocrine functioning. Chronic mucocutaneous candidiasis (CMCC) (chapter 8) is associated with multiple endocrinopathies, including hypoparathyroidism, hypothyroidism, adrenal insufficiency, hypoadrenocorticism, Addison's disease, diabetes mellitus, pernicious anemia, and ovarian insufficiency. This condition—aka *candidiasis endocrinopathy syndrome* (CES)—reflects hormonal abnormalities secondary to candidiasis. The genetic contributions have not been established, but its cause is thought to involve abnormal and/or defective immunity. Regardless, it proves that candidiasis can significantly disturb endocrine system functioning.

Researchers found *Candida albicans* contains a special *corticosteroid-binding protein* that has a high affinity for binding with human *corticosterone* and *progesterone*. In short, disease-causing yeast, especially *Candida albicans*, can interact with and disturb the endocrine system by binding with steroids and other hormones. Other research proved that disease-causing yeast can produce *steroid-like substances*, which may disturb their human host. So, disease-causing yeast can disrupt the endocrine system directly and indirectly.

Moreover, *Candida albicans* has an *estrogen-binding protein* that adheres to mammalian *estrogens* with high affinity, and the gene encoding this protein appears to be inhibited by *estradiol*. This shows *Candida albicans* can directly interact with female sex hormones. Although this may explain why many female candidiasis sufferers have menstrual irregularities, it does not reveal why disease-causing yeast have this protein in the first place. What is its purpose? Research indicates that estradiol helps trigger disease-causing yeast to transform from its noninvasive to its invasive form. So, after entering a host and being exposed to their hormones, this binding protein allows disease-causing yeast to determine if it is within an environment (microbiome) suitable for tissue invasion.

Different research supports a *candidiasis-endocrine connection*. There is a strong association between the amount of anti-*Candida* antibodies and the activities of *estradiol* and *progesterone*. Simply put, candidiasis can induce autoimmune activities that disturb the functioning of these sex hormones. Since there is a *candidiasis–autoimmune disease connection* (chapter 14) and a disturbed immune system can affect the endocrine system, candidiasis immune disturbances can promote endocrine disturbances.

So, *Candida albicans* can interact with the endocrine system directly and indirectly through the *sex* hormones (estrogens and progestins) and *steroid* hormones. Moreover, baker's and brewer's yeast (*Saccharomyces cerevisiae*) have similar proteins, but they are less active. In addition, other disease-causing yeast can instigate or promote endocrine disturbances.

Research also reveals that *Candida albicans* can produce *insulin-like substances*, and they have *glucagon receptors* on their cell membrane surface.

With respect to blood sugar regulation, this implies that candidiasis has three consequences: Insulin-like substances may lower a sufferer's blood sugar concentration, promoting *hypoglycemia* and *glucose intolerance.* Since glucagon is the primary blood sugar–raising hormone, glucagon receptors on *Candida albicans* may compete for a sufferer's available glucagon, making it difficult for them to raise a lowered blood sugar concentration. Moreover, these effects encourage the excess release of two other blood sugar–raising hormones (*epinephrine* and *cortisol*) that contribute their undesirable effects. In addition, the insulin-like substances may bind with a sufferer's insulin receptors, promoting insulin resistance and diabetes. Since many people with diabetes have candidiasis, this is unsurprising.

Although most of the information is technical, it must be included to understand the *candidiasis-endocrine connection.* If you suffer with candidiasis, depending on its extent and severity, one or more of your glands are likely to be impaired, compromised, or damaged. For different reasons, the hormone's intended effect on its target can cause increased or decreased activity. This will aggravate or exacerbate your candidiasis-related manifestations and overall ill health. If it progresses, severe endocrine disturbances can arise. There is a *candidiasis-endocrine connection,* and, even though more needs to be learned, there is enough information to support its existence.

ENDOCRINE FUNCTIONING & ITS INTERACTIONS

The endocrine system is a multitiered, complex collection of parts, functioning on many levels. Regulation occurs by transferring information from one level to another, and hormones are usually used to send messages between its parts. Messages are sent downward from the top and upward from the bottom. This cascade of control assists in maintaining homeostasis, promoting the optimum operation of all our systems and metabolism. It enables the body to sustain a constant temperature, weight, height, mood, fluid balance, digestion, and so on; that is, unless there is a problem.

In general, the central nervous system governs the endocrine system. When it senses a physiological effect is required, a stimulus is sent to an area of the brain, the *hypothalamus,* which passes the message to the pituitary gland, using a *"releasing"* hormone. Once it is notified, the *pituitary gland* releases a specific *"trophic"* hormone that travels within the blood to its intended *gland,* where it stimulates the release of a *"glandular"* hormone. After its release, it travels within the blood to its intended *target* organ or tissue, where it triggers its *physiological effect.* Specifics aside, this interconnected sequence demonstrates the nervous and endocrine systems are closely related, creating a *neuroendocrine connection.*

From a functional perspective, the nervous system could be considered part of the endocrine system, as it actively participates in maintaining homeostasis, but the two systems work differently. Since the parts of the endocrine system are widely separated, the blood is used to send messages from one location to another. In contrast, the areas of the nervous system are closely connected and integrated, so messages only travel a short distance. Instead of hormones, nerve cells usually release *neurotransmitters* into the immediate vicinity of their target cells; functionally, these chemical messengers behave like short-range hormones (chapter 10). Nervous system communication is like handing someone a note, whereas the endocrine system transfers information like placing a message into thousands of bottles that are tossed into a river; sooner or later, one of these bottles encounters its intended recipient at the river's edge. The nervous and endocrine systems are closely interrelated and functionally overlap.

Both systems function together to ensure our internal balance, governing almost all the body's chemical (metabolic) activities. Yet, there is a third part. The immune system interacts with the nervous and endocrine systems. Certain immune cells, *lymphocytes*, respond to an infection by elaborating *cellular* hormones. Using these chemical messengers, lymphocytes can directly communicate with the *neuroendocrine connection*. Conversely, the nervous system influences the immune system through the *hypothalamic-pituitary-adrenal axis* (HPA); *glucocorticoids*, from the adrenal glands, seem to be the most important hormones for regulating the immune system. This implies that all three systems are integrated and interconnected, forming one encompassing *neuroendocrine-immune connection.*

This relationship is not a true democracy because there is an inherent hierarchy. In general, the nervous system oversees everything, including the endocrine and immune systems. It produces neurotransmitters that regulate the brain's *hypothalamus*, which then influences all the body's other physiological activities. This stepwise, waterfall-like functioning permits a great amount of flexibility. If there is a disturbance within one location, other areas can often compensate. Maintaining homeostasis is easier when there are many levels of involvement and integration.

With respect to the endocrine system, there are four levels. The *pituitary gland* is the highest, residing at the lower brain within a well-protected depression of bone. It is anatomically and functionally composed of two parts. The *anterior pituitary* produces six major hormones, while the *posterior pituitary* manufactures two. The *trophic* hormones of the anterior pituitary trigger their target glands to release *glandular* hormones. The pituitary gland is closely connected to the nervous system, communicating with the hypothalamus via the *hypothalamic-hypophyseal portal circulation*; each pituitary hormone is regulated by one or more hypothalamic hormones. This integrates the brain and central nervous system with the endocrine system to achieve maximum control over all the involved components. If a target gland fails or insufficiently functions, a reduction in its hormones is sensed by the hypothalamus, and it will increase the secretion of one or more of its hormones to compensate.

The next endocrine level involves the *thyroid gland*. It resides at the front of the neck and is one of the most vital (and controversial) endocrine glands. It secretes *thyroid hormone* in proportion to the metabolic needs of the peripheral tissues and cells; like a thermostat, it adjusts the body's chemical activities to match its needs. Abundant evidence reveals that the anterior pituitary and thyroid gland have a close relationship. Through a *pituitary-thyroid connection*, it allows the first and second endocrine levels to interact. Basically, a thyroid hormone deficiency stimulates the hypothalamus to produce *thyrotropin-releasing hormone* (TRH), which triggers the pituitary gland to release *thyroid-stimulating hormone* (TSH) into the blood. When TSH reaches the thyroid gland, it promotes thyroid hormone production. Eventually, thyroid hormone accumulates, inhibiting the production of TRH by the hypothalamus.

Iodine is incorporated into thyroid hormone, and the production of thyroid hormone depends on its availability; normally, iodine is obtained from dietary food and water. To make thyroid hormone, iodine is combined with *tyrosine* (an amino acid) to form T4 (thyroxine) within the thyroid tissue. To exercise its influence, T4 must be converted to T3 (triiodothyronine), its more physiologically active and potent form. Both T3 and T4 regulate a multitude of metabolic enzymes, including those needed for growth and the use of energy. As a result, in states of depleted (hypo-) or excessive (hyper-) thyroid functioning, significant (and often dramatic) metabolic disturbances are virtually guaranteed.

Hypothyroidism occurs when the thyroid produces inadequate amounts of T4, leading to underactivity or inferior functioning. Sufferers are often tired and feel cold, especially in their hands and feet (peripheral tissues). They are likely to have dry skin, decreased immunity, and other problems, including depression, constipation, headaches, a low or absent libido, muscle weakness, poor memory, PMS (in women), and more. Since these symptoms match many common candidiasis-related symptoms, a *candidiasis-hypothyroid connection* is evident. In contrast, *hyperthyroidism* or overactivity involves excess T3 and/or T4, increasing the body's *basal* (resting) *metabolic rate*. Its typical symptoms are protruding eyeballs (exophthalmos), enlarged thyroid (goiter), a tremor of the hands/fingers, altered bowel habits, exaggerated nervousness, irritability, weight loss, increased heart rate, palpitations, excessive sweating, heat intolerance, and others. Many of these symptoms are common among candidiasis sufferers, supporting a *candidiasis-hyperthyroid connection*. So, candidiasis sufferers can have thyroid glands that are underactive, normally active, or overactive. In any case, a *candidiasis-thyroid connection* exists and is difficult to dismiss.

The third level is comprised of the two *adrenal glands*. Each of these pyramidal-shaped glands rests on the topmost portion of a kidney (in the abdomen). The adrenal gland has two parts, its outer *cortex* and inner *medulla*. Even though they are considered separate, they share a common blood supply and have a capacity to integrate their functioning. The adrenal medulla produces and stores *dopamine*, *norepinephrine*, and *epinephrine*—the hormones involved in the fight-or-flight response that occurs when someone is in situations that are threatening, exciting, apprehensive, scary, and so on. More commonly, the medullary hormones stimulate metabolism, increase blood pressure, and depress appetite (they are shorter acting than the cortical hormones). In contrast, the adrenal cortex secretes a variety of hormones, including the *glucocorticoids* that act mostly on carbohydrate metabolism, the *mineralocorticoids* that affect sodium and potassium metabolism, and the *androgens*, *estrogens*, and *progestins* that are vital for reproduction.

A significant percentage of candidiasis sufferers have insufficient adrenal functioning, called *hypoadrenalism* or *hypoadrenocorticism*. Rather than an anatomical defect, it involves a *functional* deficiency of the adrenal cortical hormones, producing symptoms that often include fatigue, malaise, dizziness, low blood pressure, allergies, palpitations, anxiety attacks, shortness of breath, glucose intolerance (especially reactive hypoglycemia), and more. Since sufferers frequently manifest these symptoms, this reveals a *candidiasis-adrenal connection*. When you appreciate that disease-causing yeast have a corticosteroid-binding protein and can produce one or more steroids, this association becomes more notable.

The bottom, or fourth, level of hormonal interactions involves the sex glands (gonads). Even though they are within the pelvis, the sex glands are regulated by the glands residing at the higher levels. The female endocrine system is more complex. *Estrogens* are a group of hormones produced within the ovarian *follicles* (as well as the adrenal cortex) and are responsible for promoting the growth and development of the vagina, fallopian tubes, and uterus. They also help the maturation and maintenance of a woman's secondary sex features, including breast enlargement, deposition of fatty tissue within the lower body and hips, onset of menstruation, and more. Ovarian tissue disturbances present as disorders of the menstrual cycle, infertility, androgen excesses, and/or premature development (precocious sexuality). *Progesterone*, the other major female hormone, has several functions primarily related to fertility. (*Androgens*, mostly male hormones, are also present in females; the average woman has about 10 percent less androgen [DHEA] than the average man.) Since they have three sex hormones, women may manifest a deficiency of estrogen, progesterone, and/or androgen. Although the production of every hormone is often interrelated and there is likely to be some overlap, each abnormality has its idiosyncrasies. So, women can have an *estrogen deficiency*, a *progesterone deficiency*, and an *androgen deficiency*. Although men manufacture and use estrogens (in smaller amounts), their *sex gland disturbances* involve abnormal *androgen* functioning, which can cause altered sperm production (spermatogenesis), improper sex development (differentiation), disturbed sexual maturation, delayed puberty, and/or decreased libido. Because of the *candidiasis–sex gland connection*, any of these endocrine disturbances can arise in candidiasis sufferers.

The *parathyroid glands* are considered separately. They are four small glands at the back of the thyroid gland. They secrete *parathyroid hormone*, which regulates *calcium* and *phosphorus* metabolism and affects *magnesium* metabolism. Disturbances can involve decreased or increased hormone secretion. Although candidiasis can cause *hyperparathyroidism*, the most common candidiasis-related endocrine disturbance is *functional hypoparathyroidism*. In either case, there is a prominent *candidiasis-parathyroid connection*.

Last, but not least, is the *pancreas*. Although this gland releases *pancreatic juice* directly into the small intestine to aid the digestion of food, it plays a large role in regulating the blood sugar concentration. The pancreas has areas called the *islets of Langerhans* that contain three types of cells. The *alpha* cells release *glucagon*, a blood sugar–raising hormone. The *beta* cells secrete *insulin*, a blood sugar–lowering hormone. The *delta* cells produce *somatostatin*, which inhibits the release of insulin, glucagon, growth hormone (from the anterior pituitary), and gastrin (from the stomach). The most notable pancreatic disturbances produce diabetes or glucose intolerance. Since candidiasis sufferers frequently have glucose intolerance and many diabetics are known to have candidiasis, there appears to be an undeniable *candidiasis-pancreas connection*.

To summarize, the endocrine system is composed of four levels: the pituitary gland, thyroid gland, adrenal glands, and sex glands. In addition, the parathyroid glands and pancreas are involved. In the big picture, the endocrine system readily interacts with the nervous and immune systems to form the *neuroendocrine-immune connection*. Something that disturbs the functioning of the endocrine system is likely to directly promote endocrine abnormalities. The endocrine system is also susceptible to indirect assaults because anything that adversely affects the nervous or immune systems will instigate endocrine disturbances.

Candidiasis is an *infection* with *allergic* consequences that often involves significant inflammation. As a result, it can adversely affect the functioning of the nervous, endocrine, and immune systems. So, it can directly and indirectly disturb endocrine functioning. Therefore, sufferers frequently demonstrate disturbances that involve one or many of their endocrine glands, demonstrating a *candidiasis-pituitary connection*, a *candidiasis-thyroid connection*, a *candidiasis-adrenal connection*, a *candidiasis–sex gland connection*, a *candidiasis-parathyroid connection*, and a *candidiasis-pancreas connection*. Since each abnormality has its own characteristic symptoms and consequences, once a sufferer's symptoms are known, their disturbance can be revealed. Confusingly, the presence of more than one disturbance readily complicates the situation in some sufferers, making it difficult to assess their situation.

Why is it important to appreciate these candidiasis-related endocrine disturbances? If you are a candidiasis sufferer, you are likely to have one or more of them. Since these hormones are vital for optimal functioning, intervention is sometimes necessary before beginning anti-candidiasis therapy. Yet, in many cases, endocrine intervention is unnecessary. Unless there is glandular destruction, when their candidiasis is appropriately treated, most sufferers' endocrine disturbances disappear.

THYROID HORMONES, BODY TEMPERATURE & METABOLISM

In 1989, Ernest L. Mazzaferri, M.D., commented, "Thyroid function tests have certain limitations that must be recognized before they can be used effectively. Most important is the physician's awareness that the tests do not replace good clinical judgment and should not be used alone to confirm a diagnostic impression or to dictate therapy." In other words, rather than treating someone according to their laboratory test results, a physician needs to be aware of the patient's condition. Laboratory testing was created to support, not replace, a physician's diagnosis. With respect to endocrine functioning, laboratory testing does not always reveal what is truly occurring within someone's body. This is when good clinical judgment is essential.

What does this have to do with the thyroid hormone system? *Hypothyroidism* (underactivity) and *hyperthyroidism* (overactivity) are two states of abnormal thyroid functioning, and both are often confirmed by laboratory testing. Yet, there is another state that is usually ignored or overlooked. *Hypometabolism* occurs when someone's metabolism is decreased, even when their thyroid function testing is normal. How can this happen? Normally, the thyroid gland produces its hormone in proportion to the metabolic needs of the peripheral tissues and cells (*euthyroid*). Since the thyroid gland regulates metabolism, it is sensitive to dietary changes. For example, starvation reduces the amount of circulating T3, decreasing the body's chemical activities to conserve resources. In contrast, a low-carbohydrate diet may increase the conversion of T4 into T3, accelerating metabolism. Since diet influences its activities, someone can become *hypometabolic* without being hypothyroid. So, even if your thyroid gland functions normally, you may have a slowed metabolism. In this situation, your thyroid gland releases sufficient T4 into your blood, but its conversion to T3 is decreased. Because T3 is the more active form of thyroid hormone, a deficit of T3 slows the chemical activities of your peripheral tissues and cells, producing hypometabolism. Since your test results would indicate normal thyroid functioning, your problem is likely to be missed. This has created a major controversy between mainstream endocrinologists and holistic/integrative physicians.

Mainstream endocrinologists claim that slowed thyroid functioning can *only* be determined when an abnormality is revealed by thyroid function testing. In contrast, holistic/integrative physicians appreciate that the thyroid gland regulates the body's metabolism, including maintaining the body's temperature, and they are aware decreased thyroid hormone activity often causes temperature deviations, especially to the low side. Yet, this perspective based on glandular functioning and scientific logic, as opposed to laboratory values, is only appreciated by a small number of physicians in the United States. This approach is not meant to replace thyroid function testing. Instead, it is used to identify people who suffer with a slowed metabolism, even when their thyroid hormone testing appears normal.

If you think this is a new approach to thyroid gland functioning, you are mistaken. In the 1950s, Broda Barnes, M.D., Ph.D., discovered a strong association between decreased body temperature and slowed thyroid gland functioning. According to him, "No physician can afford to deny a patient any help he can give. Only the cost of a thermometer and a willing ear are needed." As a result, some physicians diagnose deficient thyroid functioning when a patient demonstrates a lowered body temperature.

How does this work? When everything is functioning optimally (homeostasis), your body's normal temperature is 98.6 degrees Fahrenheit (37 degrees Celsius). An increase of 1 to 1.5 degrees produces a *fever*, increasing your metabolism and the activities of certain enzymes, cells, and hormones; typically, this occurs to combat an infection or other bodily assault. Conversely, similar temperature deviations below normal should elicit their characteristic symptoms, reflecting a decreased metabolism and the suboptimal activities of certain enzymes, cells, and hormones. Although there is no common term for this condition, it make logical sense and is scientifically sound, nonetheless.

In 1991, E. Denis Wilson described *Wilson's thyroid syndrome*, a condition involving an average body temperature lower than normal with routine thyroid function blood tests that appear normal. Instead of assessing the activity of the thyroid gland with thyroid hormone testing, Dr. Wilson believes physicians should focus on the functioning of the entire *thyroid hormone system*. This approach reveals hypometabolism when hypothyroidism is not evident. How does this happen? The thyroid hormone system begins at the brain's *hypothalamus* with the release of TRH, which signals the pituitary to liberate TSH into the blood. TSH eventually reaches the thyroid gland, where it stimulates the production of T4 (thyroxine). Since T3 is the more active form, T4 must be converted into T3. Most T4 is converted into T3 within the peripheral tissues. So, even with normal T4 levels, if the conversion to T3 is deficient, someone will develop *functional hypothyroidism* and hypometabolism. Unfortunately, routine thyroid function blood tests would appear normal, causing this disturbance to be overlooked. Although Wilson's thyroid syndrome explains how hypometabolism can occur, it does not reveal *why* it develops in the first place. Indeed, Wilson's thyroid syndrome must have a cause.

Dr. Wilson realized that stress-induced metabolic and endocrine disturbances can induce low body temperature patterns. Simply put, stress can disrupt endocrine functioning, which impairs metabolism and promotes a lowered body temperature. Stress evolves and accompanies many events, such as divorce, financial difficulty, surgery, accidents, death of a loved one, work and family problems, and more. Its adverse effects may not cease after a problem has resolved, as most physical symptoms tend to persist. So, stressful situations can elicit long-term, undesirable effects in susceptible people, especially a lowered body temperature. In fact, a multitude of symptoms are consistent with the adverse effects of stress, including anxiety and panic attacks, depression and irritability, mood swings, poor concentration and memory deterioration, constipation and irritable bowel syndrome, migraine headaches, easy weight gain (or loss), hair loss, PMS (in women), decreased libido, cold or heat intolerance, and many others. Does stress cause a lowered body temperature and Wilson's thyroid syndrome, or is something else responsible?

The list of stress-related symptoms matches many common manifestations of chronic candidiasis. This implies that there is an association between stress and candidiasis. In fact, stress is a risk factor for developing it (chapter 2). Since stress adversely affects the nervous, endocrine, and immune systems, and a disturbance to the *neuroendocrine-immune connection* impairs the body's ability to combat the reproduction and colonization of disease-causing yeast, it can promote candidiasis. Yet, candidiasis can weaken the *neuroendocrine-immune connection*, making the body more susceptible to stress. This can work either way or both ways at once, and only worsens over time, which means ever smaller insults can cause disproportionately larger disturbances. If stress leads to a lowered body temperature and promotes candidiasis, there must be an association between candidiasis and a lowered body temperature.

Candidiasis is an *infection* with disease-causing yeast and their *allergic* consequences. It promotes significant inflammation and other adverse effects, which can directly and indirectly disturb the *neuroendocrine-immune connection*. Once established, candidiasis readily disrupts the body's homeostasis. In return, this makes it difficult for a sufferer to maintain their optimal internal balance, including their body temperature. Although this is a simplified explanation, the specifics are more compelling.

Candidiasis is a condition that frequently causes malabsorption. Moreover, its sufferers often eat an abundance of carbohydrates. Both can promote protein deficiencies. Since *tyrosine* is an amino acid incorporated into thyroid hormone, protein deficiencies can create a tyrosine deficiency that decreases the production of thyroid hormone. Although this would produce hypometabolism and a lowered body temperature, it is a state of *hypothyroidism* and should be evident by laboratory testing. In fact, many candidiasis sufferers have hypothyroidism revealed by laboratory testing, demonstrating a *candidiasis-hypothyroidism connection*.

In contrast, hypometabolism in the absence of hypothyroidism arises more subtly. The liver and kidneys are the most active tissues that convert T4 into T3. Since candidiasis sufferers frequently have decreased liver metabolism as well as impaired kidney functioning, their conversion of T4 into T3 would decrease. Why? To combat a chronic infection, especially with disease-causing yeast, the liver decreases its metabolic activities to assist the immune system. Its *acute phase response* is supposed to be a temporary solution, but chronic candidiasis can cause it to become prolonged (chapter 14). So, it impairs the liver's metabolism, including its ability to convert T4 into T3, leading to hypometabolism. It may also encourage the liver to make a mistake that exacerbates this problem. In addition to T3, the liver normally creates some *reverse T3*, a mirror image form of T3 that is *not* metabolically active; this probably occurs to prevent excess T3 and a state of hypermetabolism. When the liver's metabolism is impaired, instead of converting T4 into T3, it may mistakenly convert T4 into reverse T3. An increased amount of (nonactive) reverse T3 promotes hypometabolism. Like the liver, kidney functioning can become impaired in chronic sufferers, impeding its conversion of T4 to T3, contributing to hypometabolism. So, candidiasis can readily promote hypometabolism in the absence of hypothyroidism. Although measuring reverse T3 may sometimes reveal this situation, there is no guarantee because the conversion of T4 into (active) T3 is often the underlying problem. You should appreciate that Wilson's thyroid syndrome is not an independent medical malady but the result of an infection with disease-causing yeast and that other infectious invaders may contribute their harm as well.

Moreover, states of increased thyroid functioning, *hyperthyroidism*, can be associated with candidiasis. The most common is *Graves' disease*. Although it an illness of unknown origin, an autoimmune process is suspected. Since there is a *candidiasis–autoimmune disease connection* (chapter 14), a *candidiasis-hyperthyroidism connection* is likely. In contrast, autoimmune disease of the thyroid gland can lead to hypothyroidism. How can it produce both overactive and underactive thyroid conditions? Typically, hyperthyroidism is thought to involve an autoimmune process that stimulates the release of thyroid hormone, whereas hypothyroidism involves glandular destruction that impairs the release of thyroid hormone. Once autoimmune disease exists, it is not an easy process to stop. As a result, eliminating someone's candidiasis is likely to greatly improve their health, but it may not completely correct their autoimmune thyroid disease.

Hypothyroidism, hyperthyroidism, and hypometabolism are all manifestations associated with candidiasis. Although exceptions exist, hypothyroidism and hyperthyroidism are usually revealed by routine thyroid hormone testing. The diagnosis of hypometabolism requires an understanding of the way the thyroid hormone system functions, especially the relationship between metabolism and body temperature; typically, even when someone's routine thyroid hormone testing appears normal, hypometabolism is evident if they have a lowered body temperature. All three abnormal states cannot arise for no reason. Indeed, candidiasis can directly and indirectly disturb the functioning of the thyroid gland and its hormone system. Therefore, if you have a lowered body temperature and a state of hypometabolism, or if your thyroid is overactive or underactive, chronic candidiasis is likely to be causing your disarray, including your symptoms and illness.

THE ADRENAL GLANDS

In 1855, Thomas Addison described the histories, clinical presentations, and biopsy results of patients with a condition that bears his name, *Addison's disease*. It is medically known as *primary adrenocortical insufficiency* and involves abnormal functioning of the *adrenal cortex*, usually accompanied with destruction of the gland. Its symptoms include weakness, fatigue, malaise, weight loss, and gastrointestinal problems. Since candidiasis sufferers often have gut problems as well as fatigue, weakness, malaise, and weight loss, we can infer that candidiasis is related to disturbances of the adrenal cortex. Instead of Addison's disease, candidiasis sufferers frequently manifest a different type of adrenal gland abnormality.

Although the symptoms of candidiasis imply the presence of a deficiency and/or imbalance of adrenal cortex hormones, is there evidence to support this claim? In 1955, John Tintera, M.D., described a "syndrome . . . recognized in a group of over 200 patients" that was termed *hypoadrenocorticism*, which represented a subclinical version of Addison's disease. Unlike true Addison's disease, this form of *adrenal insufficiency* does not require the adrenal cortex to be destroyed. So, rather than an anatomical problem, hypoadrenocorticism involves a disturbance of the gland's *functioning*. As a result, there is *inferior* production and/or activity of various adrenal cortex hormones, which is accompanied by a variety of symptoms and/or illness that corresponds to the hormones adversely affected.

What hormones are involved? The *glucocorticoids* (cortisol, corticosterone) primarily affect carbohydrate metabolism. The *mineralocorticoids*, especially *aldosterone*, regulate sodium and potassium metabolism. And *dehydroepiandrosterone* (DHEA) is an androgenic substance that produces or stimulates the development of male characteristics. The cortex also produces reproduction-related hormones, including *androgens* (17-ketosteroids), *estrogens* (estradiol), and *progestins* (progesterone). Hypoadrenocorticism promotes many symptoms, including anemia, sluggishness, weakness, weight loss, low blood pressure (hypotension), hypoglycemia (occasionally), nausea, vomiting, diarrhea, abnormal skin changes, and mental changes. The adrenal cortex also secretes estradiol and progesterone, so menstrual irregularities are common. Since all these symptoms frequently manifest among candidiasis sufferers, this readily supports a *candidiasis-hypoadrenocorticism connection.*

Moreover, cortisol and cortisone are important anti-inflammatory hormones. Candidiasis is an *infection* with *allergic* consequences that produces abundant inflammation. To decrease inflammation, sufferers need to produce and release excess cortisol and cortisone. At first, their adrenal glands increase production, but over time, the adrenal cortex of many sufferers becomes "tired" or "exhausted" and production decreases, which worsens their symptoms and exacerbates their ill health. Typically, the worst cases of chronic candidiasis promote adrenal exhaustion as well as chronic fatigue; this is part of the *candidiasis–chronic fatigue connection* (chapter 15).

Hypoadrenocorticism and its relationship to alcoholism was first described in 1949. Since there is a *candidiasis-alcoholism connection* (chapter 10), this lends further support for a *candidiasis-hypoadrenocorticism connection.*

Researchers performed animal experiments with *adrenal cortical extract*, revealing hypoglycemia (glucose intolerance) can accompany a glucocorticoid deficiency. Other investigators found a lack of adrenal cortical hormones did not inhibit insulin activity or degrade it quickly; *insulin* is the body's primary blood sugar–lowering hormone, and excesses or its prolonged presence promotes a lowered blood sugar concentration and hypoglycemia. There is a *candidiasis-glucose intolerance connection* (chapter 14) and *hypoadrenocorticism–glucose intolerance connection*, so this readily supports a *candidiasis-hypoadrenocorticism connection.*

In the bigger picture, hypoadrenocorticism does not just accompany candidiasis; it is an endocrine disturbance that arises because of its presence. In fact, *Candida albicans* has an intracellular *corticosteroid-binding protein*. Early in candidiasis, when cortisol excesses are likely, this binding protein may function to stimulate the reproduction, colonization, and/or invasiveness of disease-causing yeast. In addition, this binding protein may compete with the body for cortisol. In turn, a lack of available cortisol causes a functional deficiency. It may exacerbate the effects of stress, stimulating the excessive production of cortisol, until the adrenal cortex becomes exhausted or fails. Although speculation, disease-causing yeast may also produce one or more substances (metabolites) that may directly or indirectly suppress or injure the adrenal cortex. Candidiasis-related malabsorption may also contribute by instigating or promoting deficiencies of the precursors that are used to construct these hormones.

More could be added, but the point is made. If you are a candidiasis sufferer and any of this describes your experience, you are likely suffering with candidiasis-related hypoadrenocorticism.

SEX GLAND DISTURBANCES

Your sex glands assist in developing your male or female body, including your secondary sex characteristics. They also enable you to have a libido. They are under your pituitary gland's control and produce hormones that correspond to your gender. Women have *ovaries* that primarily manufacture estrogen and progesterone, but they also produce some androgens. In contrast, men have *testicles* that create androgens (although men do make and use estrogens in small amounts). So, there are three basic sex hormones: estrogen, progesterone, and androgens. As mentioned earlier, women have all three and may have a deficiency of estrogen, progesterone, or androgens. Men primarily use androgens and tend to only manifest androgen deficiencies.

Estrogens induce the development of a woman's secondary sex characteristics and enable her to have a menstrual cycle. Therefore, an *estrogen deficiency* often involves prolonged menstrual cycles with poor blood loss, and occasional menstrual pain and cramping. Victims of this malady tend to have dry mucous membranes (including the vagina), pain during intercourse, and tiredness or fatigue. Depression is a frequent complaint. A significant percentage of female candidiasis sufferers have symptoms that reflect an estrogen deficiency.

Progesterone influences a woman's uterus, preparing it to implant a fertilized egg. If it implants, progesterone controls the development of the woman's placenta and mammary glands. Since it primarily affects the second half of a woman's menstrual cycle, a progesterone disturbance is likely to arise before or during her menses. Usually, a *progesterone deficiency* involves severe *dysmenorrhea* (painful periods) with abundant menstrual blood loss. Sufferers can have extensive swelling as well as breast enlargement and engorgement (particularly before their period). Anxiety and irritability are common. Since these symptoms often occur among female candidiasis sufferers and there is a *candidiasis-PMS connection* (chapters 10 and 13), a progesterone deficiency is a frequent manifestation of candidiasis.

Why are estrogen and progesterone disturbances common among candidiasis sufferers? Research demonstrates that disease-causing yeast, especially *Candida albicans*, can interact with, as well as disturb, the endocrine system by binding with steroid hormones and sex hormones. *Candida albicans* has been found to have a *corticosteroid-binding protein* capable of binding *progestins* and *corticosteroids*. In addition, *Candida albicans* has an *estrogen-binding protein* that binds with *estrogens* and is inhibited by *estradiol*. Since estradiol has been shown to stimulate disease-causing yeast to transform from their less-invasive form into their more invasive form, an estrogen-binding protein is a way disease-causing yeast can sense they are within a suitable host and a microbiome appropriate for their invasion. Their corticosteroid-binding protein may serve a similar purpose, particularly in men. (The more binding proteins, the greater their chance for survival, as they can become more sensitive to their surroundings.) Not to be outdone, baker's and brewer's yeast (*Saccharomyces cerevisiae*) have similar proteins, which reveals that many disease-causing yeasts can participate in this mischief.

Disease-causing yeast can also compromise the immune system, inducing autoimmune disease (chapter 14). Research reveals that candidiasis promotes an autoimmune disease that impairs the functioning of estradiol and progesterone. They can produce steroid-like substances and may also produce estrogen-like and progesterone-like substances. In large amounts, any of these impostors can assist in disturbing a sufferer's endocrine system and internal environment. For these reasons and more, candidiasis can readily instigate or promote estrogen and progesterone disturbances, both directly and indirectly. Because estrogen and progesterone are essential female hormones, it is not surprising that women suffer with candidiasis more than men.

Moreover, since there is a significant correlation between anti-*Candida*, anti-ovarian, and anti-thymocyte antibodies (an immune cell within the thymus), *ovarian autoantibodies* are thought to be involved. How does this arise? The surface antigens of disease-causing yeast, ovarian follicles, and T lymphocytes are somewhat similar, so antibodies targeted to attack disease-causing yeast may be inappropriately misdirected, assaulting ovarian tissue instead. Ovarian autoantibodies can initiate and sustain an assault against ovarian tissues, which may promote functional impairment and progress to destruction of the ovaries. Either way, ovarian hormone deficiencies are typical. Conversely, early on, ovarian receptors may be stimulated by certain autoantibodies to liberate excess ovarian hormones. Yet, as the gland becomes increasingly impaired, ever smaller amounts of hormone are produced and a deficiency ultimately follows. Therefore, a diversity of presentations is typical among female candidiasis sufferers.

Androgens stimulate the development of male characteristics and include the hormones *testosterone* and *androsterone*. Although primarily male hormones, as mentioned, women also have them. As a result, an *androgen deficiency* is one of the most overlooked deficiencies within women. An androgen deficit encourages decreased muscle tone (muscular hypotrophy), weakness, and obesity, notably within a woman's abdomen and hips. Usually, there is a lack of assertiveness and self-confidence and an absent or decreased libido. Emotional instability is common. Female candidiasis sufferers often have symptoms consistent with an androgen deficiency.

Although men make and use estrogens in small amounts, as mentioned, they are primarily dependent on androgens, so male sex disturbances typically involve abnormal *androgen* functioning. It causes altered sperm production (spermatogenesis), improper sex development (differentiation), disturbed sexual maturation, delayed puberty, and/or a decreased libido. Many of these are common among male candidiasis sufferers.

Like the other endocrine glands, candidiasis can disturb the sex glands, both directly and indirectly. Female candidiasis sufferers commonly have estrogen deficiencies, progesterone deficiencies, and/or androgen deficiencies. Since they can have one or more disturbance, women tend to display a variety of symptoms as well as experience infertility (chapter 13). In contrast, men only seem to develop androgen deficiencies. Regardless of your sex, if you are a candidiasis sufferer, you are likely to have some magnitude of sex hormone disturbance, and eliminating your candidiasis is the best way to correct it.

THE PARATHYROID GLANDS

The body has two small pairs (four) of *parathyroid glands* residing at the back of the thyroid gland. Their decreased functioning, *hypoparathyroidism*, is closely related to candidiasis. In 1985, Leo Galland, M.D., claimed that hypoparathyroidism is the most common candidiasis-related endocrine (hormone) disturbance.

Mainstream medicine believes most cases of hypoparathyroidism are *idiopathic*; they appear spontaneously and without a known cause. This condition has been described as *multiple endocrine deficiency-autoimmune-candidiasis syndrome* (or *juvenile familial endocrinopathy-hypoparathyroidism-Addison's disease-moniliasis syndrome*). Although its designations are a mouthful, an association between decreased parathyroid gland functioning and candidiasis (moniliasis) is within the names for this condition. Since candidiasis instigates and promotes many endocrine disturbances, including subclinical Addison's disease (hypoadrenocorticism), it makes sense it can cause hypoparathyroidism. It can also cause autoimmune disease (chapter 14). This evidence alone suggests a *candidiasis-hypoparathyroidism connection*. Why are the parathyroid glands so important, and how does candidiasis disturb them?

Calcium is an essential mineral with a multitude of functions. It assists in maintaining a regular heart rhythm, transmitting nerve impulses, causing muscle growth and contractions, forming blood clotting, decreasing blood pressure, and developing normal bones and teeth. In return, calcium deficiencies are associated with colon cancer, muscle cramps, nervousness, palpitations, brittle nails, eczema, hypertension, joint pains (arthralgia) and rheumatoid arthritis, elevated cholesterol levels (hypercholesterolemia), tooth decay, rickets, insomnia, and numbness in the arms and legs. Although its presence is thought to prevent osteoporosis, large amounts of calcium or its improper metabolism appears to encourage kidney stones and/or kidney disease as well as interferes with the absorption of zinc (another essential mineral).

The glands produce *parathyroid hormone*, which regulates the blood calcium ion concentration. In short, decreased parathyroid gland activity causes a parathyroid hormone deficiency, resulting in a lowered concentration of serum calcium ions, *hypocalcemia*. What does this have to do with candidiasis? Parathyroid hormone deficiencies are common among candidiasis sufferers, and their symptoms often reflect hypocalcemia.

Magnesium is another essential mineral. It is required for the activities and functioning of numerous metabolic enzymes, participates in maintaining calcium and potassium levels, assists in keeping the serum at its proper acid-base balance (pH) for optimal functioning, and is necessary for bone formation. The plasma magnesium ion concentration also affects parathyroid hormone release. Lowered levels of serum magnesium will stimulate the release of parathyroid hormone, raising *both* the calcium and magnesium concentrations.

Although parathyroid hormone is also influenced by the blood's acid-base balance (pH) and phosphate ion concentration, the serum calcium and magnesium ion concentrations are more important. The release of parathyroid hormone is primarily affected by a decreased calcium ion concentration and secondarily by a decreased magnesium ion concentration. Once again, what does this have to do with candidiasis? In addition to a lowered serum calcium ion concentration, a parathyroid hormone deficiency can cause a lowered serum magnesium ion concentration, *hypomagnesemia*. As a result, candidiasis can cause parathyroid hormone deficiencies and symptoms related to hypomagnesemia.

How does candidiasis participate? Normally, a low plasma concentration of calcium or magnesium ions triggers the release of parathyroid hormone, raising the concentrations of these minerals. However, a chronic *infection* or significant *stress* can cause a severe or prolonged decrease in the magnesium concentration that adversely affects parathyroid gland functioning. This impairs the release of parathyroid hormone or decreases its efficacy, producing a state of hypoparathyroidism. In turn, this causes a lowered concentration of calcium ions and magnesium ions, causing hypocalcemia and hypomagnesemia. Candidiasis is an *infection* with *allergic* consequences that often instigates and promotes hypoparathyroidism. Even worse, its involved malabsorption often exacerbates these mineral deficiencies, especially magnesium. When a sufferer's serum magnesium ion concentration falls low enough, their parathyroid glands become functionally impaired; that is, their activities decrease. Because they regulate the concentration of both minerals, candidiasis sufferers frequently manifest symptoms related to both hypocalcemia and hypomagnesemia.

Rather than an overt disturbance, most candidiasis sufferers often have a subtle version, called *functional* hypoparathyroidism. The parathyroid glands are composed of chemically active cells and tissue that require magnesium to function optimally. Since sufferers frequently have magnesium deficiencies, their parathyroid glands become impaired; the lower their serum magnesium ion concentration, the more likely this becomes. Depending on its severity and duration, their symptoms are a combination of *hypomagnesemia* and *hypocalcemia*, including muscle spasms, spasticity and twitches, fatigue, emotional highs and lows, and impaired sensitivities (paresthesias). The less common symptoms are mental retardation, improper tooth development, lenticular cataracts, skin problems, intestinal malabsorption, congestive heart failure, classic parkinsonism, and convulsions.

Since functional hypoparathyroidism causes a lowered serum calcium ion concentration, you might think this endocrine disturbance is easy to diagnose; that is, a routine blood test should reveal a calcium ion concentration below normal. On the contrary, European physicians found that most patients with functional hypoparathyroidism have serum calcium ion concentrations that are *normal*. So, most sufferers are undiagnosed. This condition is also called *latent tetany* (or spasmophilia) because its symptoms reflect a lowered calcium ion concentration. It is notable in France (about 15 percent of the population), Germany, and the United States (according to Dr. Galland). Because a lowered magnesium ion concentration contributes to this disturbance, a decrease in serum magnesium should be more prevalent than a calcium ion disturbance. Can this be detected? It is unlikely because the serum magnesium ion concentration is rarely measured. Magnesium deficiencies are common among sufferers, and functional hypoparathyroidism usually reflects a deficit of magnesium ions, as opposed to a deficiency of calcium ions. In the bigger picture, the combination of calcium and magnesium ion concentrations permits a great deal of symptom variability among all candidiasis sufferers.

There are various plausible explanations that may contribute to the disarray, but they are not the most likely reason for a *candidiasis–magnesium deficiency connection*. If you are aware of its risk factors (chapter 2), you know that candidiasis does not require a magnesium deficiency to develop. On the contrary, candidiasis is an *infection* with disease-causing yeast that promotes abundant inflammation and *allergic* consequences. The associated malabsorption and inappropriate magnesium-deficient diets of most sufferers further exacerbates the situation. Because magnesium is essential for the body's chemical activities (metabolism), its need is increased in sufferers. So, once a magnesium deficiency exists, candidiasis only makes it worse.

Alternatively, excesses of parathyroid hormone, *hyperparathyroidism*, may accompany candidiasis, although it is uncommon. Generally, this causes an increased serum calcium ion concentration, *hypercalcemia*. Most hyperparathyroidism is *idiopathic*; it has no known cause. Instead of a mysterious or nebulous origin, the presence of candidiasis can promote excesses of parathyroid hormone. A lowered serum magnesium ion concentration that does not lead to impaired glandular functioning may trigger excesses of parathyroid hormone to raise the magnesium concentration to normal, promoting increases in the serum calcium ion concentration that cause numerous disturbances. In fact, once their candidiasis was corrected, many patients with notably elevated calcium concentrations remarkably improved.

Also, hypoparathyroidism and hyperparathyroidism can reflect autoimmune disease, which may involve misdirected cells and/or autoantibodies targeted to attack the cells and tissue of someone's own parathyroid glands. If this assault destroys the gland or stimulates the release of parathyroid hormone, a deficiency or excess of parathyroid hormone may result. Since there is a *candidiasis–autoimmune disease connection* (chapter 14), disease-causing yeast can be responsible for either manifestation. Unfortunately, once this begins, it is difficult to stop.

Regardless of its origin, functional hypoparathyroidism is extremely prevalent among candidiasis sufferers. Because their serum calcium ion concentration is often normal and magnesium concentrations are almost never measured, this disturbance is almost always missed. True hypoparathyroidism and hyperparathyroidism also appear candidiasis-related but are much less common. If you are a candidiasis sufferer, you are likely to have some magnitude of magnesium deficiency and manifest some type of a parathyroid gland disturbance. Since magnesium is vital for your body's optimal functioning, including your immunity, you would be wise to have this condition identified, diagnosed, and appropriately treated.

THE PANCREAS: GLUCOSE TOLERANCE, HYPOGLYCEMIA & DIABETES

Note: *This section contains information that may be too complicated for many readers. It involves metabolic disturbances that occur in most candidiasis sufferers and the details had to be included to support their existence. (There is a summary paragraph at the end of this section.)*

The *pancreas* is a small organ below the sternum (breastbone) and toward the back. It is really two glands in one. Using a series of ducts that empty into the main pancreatic duct, the pancreas secretes *pancreatic juice*, a fluid that contains *sodium bicarbonate* and the enzymes *trypsinogen*, *chymotrypsinogen*, *elastase*, *carboxypeptidase*, *pancreatic lipase*, *nucleases*, and *amylase*. It acts to digest food within the small intestine, preparing it for absorption. Like the other endocrine glands, the pancreas secretes hormones that enter the blood. The pancreas has unevenly scattered, compact groups of cells (*islets of Langerhans*) that contain three distinct types. The *alpha* cells release *glucagon*, a blood sugar–raising hormone. The *beta* cells secrete *insulin*, our primary blood sugar–lowering hormone. The *delta* cells produce and release *somatostatin*, which inhibits the release of insulin and glucagon; somatostatin can affect growth hormone (from the anterior pituitary) and gastrin (from the stomach). In addition to its rich blood supply, the islets have an extensive network of nerves and ganglion cells, enabling the pancreas to be influenced by the nervous system (not to mention the immune system).

What does this have to do with candidiasis? First, its sufferers often have *malabsorption*; they are unable to, or poorly, absorb one or more substances, leading to a variety of nutritional deficiencies (chapter 4). Since pancreatic enzyme supplements often improve a sufferer's ability to absorb nutrients, it implies candidiasis can promote a *deficiency* of pancreatic juice and its enzymes. This shortage is likely to reflect a protein deficiency because enzymes are primarily manufactured from protein. Many sufferers have protein-deficient diets and/or poorly absorb dietary proteins, so they are unable to produce enough pancreatic enzymes. Regardless of its cause, a lack of pancreatic juice will exacerbate a sufferer's malabsorption and nutritional deficiencies, worsening their health. This is common, especially among candidiasis sufferers with significant gastrointestinal symptoms.

In contrast, a problem within the pancreas can instigate or promote blood sugar disturbances. Like the other endocrine glands, candidiasis can adversely affect the functioning of the islets of Langerhans. Since the islets produce insulin and glucagon, the hormones that primarily regulate blood sugar, compromised islet functioning commonly causes blood sugar disturbances. Blood sugar abnormalities, *glucose intolerance*, range from mild to severe. Yet, before you can appreciate the abnormal, you must first understand what is normal.

The beta cells react to sugar and glucose ingestion by producing and releasing *insulin*, which stimulates glucose to exit the blood and enter the cells, with excesses being stored as glycogen. Thereafter, any remaining glucose is stored as fat. (It also promotes the construction of bodily proteins.) Normally, as the blood sugar concentration falls, so does the insulin level. This slows the entry of glucose into the cells, limiting the lowest concentration the blood sugar can obtain. When all is well, insulin secretion decreases, until minimal amounts are present. If the beta cells respond by releasing appropriate amounts of insulin, the blood sugar concentration will fall over a few hours, until it returns to its fasting concentration.

Glucose tolerance is the way someone reacts to consumed dietary carbohydrates, especially glucose. It is best assessed with a *five-hour glucose tolerance test*. After fasting overnight, a sample of blood is drawn to determine someone's fasting blood glucose concentration. Then, they drink an amount of glucose proportional to their body weight. Blood samples are obtained at 30 minutes, hour 1, hour 2, hour 3, hour 4, and hour 5. (Six-hour tests were once common, but significant changes rarely occurred after five hours. Conversely, tests of three hours or less miss the late fluctuations.) When the values are obtained, they can be graphed, yielding a *blood sugar curve*. Every person has their unique response (metabolism) to glucose. Insulin levels can be measured at the same times to assess an *insulin response curve*, but only the fasting and hour-two values are routinely taken, as the others tend to be superfluous. An elevated insulin level supports *hyperinsulinism*. The more abnormal all of this is, the more medically significant its consequences.

The most common candidiasis-related blood sugar disturbance is *hypoglycemia*. How does it arise? Chronic candidiasis can promote excesses of insulin (*hyperinsulinism*) or its prolonged presence (*functional hyperinsulinism*). As a result, too much glucose exits the blood, causing the blood sugar concentration to decrease below normal. Depending on its severity, this can precipitate many undesirable symptoms, including an inability to concentrate, confusion, incoherent speech, headache, blurred vision, bizarre behavior, focal or generalized seizures, stupor, coma, and rarely death. Most often, the symptoms are mild and not experienced long. Moreover, they are likely to differ from one person to another as well as from one episode to another, even within the same person. Many of these symptoms are common among sufferers, evidencing a *candidiasis-hypoglycemia connection*.

There are numerous types of hypoglycemia. Many drugs, an excessive consumption of alcohol, and the presence of a significant infection can cause *induced* hypoglycemia. In contrast, candidiasis sufferers typically exhibit *reactive hypoglycemia*. Up to two-thirds of the United States population may have this condition, but it is not usually diagnosed because its symptoms are often variable and inconsistent. What is reactive hypoglycemia? Someone's fasting blood sugar concentration is normal, while their *reaction* to glucose is exaggerated. Their blood sugar concentration usually increases much higher than normal and then decreases significantly below its fasting amount. Their beta cells are initially slow to react and then release too much insulin, causing an exaggerated increase in their blood sugar concentration, followed by a pronounced decrease. Why is this a problem?

When the blood sugar concentration falls precipitously, or too low, it must be raised to normal. As a result, the blood sugar–raising hormones (*contra-insulin*) are released, promoting numerous undesirable symptoms. Mainstream medicine misses this form of hypoglycemia because they typically use a three-hour test, and the most significant changes are often evident after the third hour. Reactive hypoglycemia may arise from numerous endocrine disorders, including pituitary gland failure, severe hypothyroidism, adrenal gland exhaustion, and rare insulin-producing tumors of the pancreas. Moreover, any illness that impairs or damages the liver's functioning can adversely affect blood glucose regulation. Since there is a *candidiasis-endocrine connection* and chronic candidiasis can compromise the liver's metabolism, a *candidiasis–glucose intolerance connection* seems certain (chapter 14).

In contrast, *true* hypoglycemia is rare. It is defined as having a blood sugar level below 60 milligrams of glucose per 100 milliliters of blood, even after ingesting glucose. These people may be poor sugar absorbers with a deficiency or absence of their blood sugar–raising hormones. Why would sugar be unable to enter their blood? They may lack the required transport systems to adequately absorb it. More likely, an abundance of disease-causing yeast within their gut may preferentially use the sugar before it is absorbed. Furthermore, since disease-causing yeast can invade into and through the gut wall, candidiasis may injure or damage its host's sugar transport mechanisms. In addition, disease-causing yeast within the blood may directly consume their host's blood glucose. This would prevent someone's blood glucose concentration from increasing, hinder their release of insulin, and slow, delay, or impair the movement of glucose into their cells and tissues. To add insult, these people may have an adrenal gland disturbance, leading to a lack of epinephrine and cortisol, causing persistent hypoglycemia. All these circumstances point to the presence of candidiasis.

Since chronic candidiasis can promote excesses of insulin or its prolonged presence, there is a *candidiasis-hyperinsulinism connection* (chapter 14). Excesses of insulin or its sustained presence can be detrimental. Many physicians believe hyperinsulinism encourages chronic disease. Elevated insulin levels are believed to trigger the generation of harmful oxygen-based free radical reactions within the blood (chapter 7). In short, these highly volatile molecules or substances can damage cell components, accelerating aging and other destructive processes. Since research reveals that elevated insulin levels can injure arteries and veins, causing cardiovascular disease, free radical reactions may also compromise other systems. For example, they are thought to promote cancer, autoimmune diseases, and various other problems.

Researchers have discovered that *interleukin-1* (IL-1), an immune system chemical messenger, can cause hypoglycemia associated with increased insulin levels and, under certain conditions, IL-1 increases insulin secretion in the presence of glucose. Why is this important? Candidiasis is an infection with disease-causing yeast that can stimulate the release of IL-1, promoting insulin excesses. This helps to explain why sufferers frequently have hyperinsulinism as well as hypoglycemia. Other researchers found that, under different circumstances, IL-1 inhibits the production of insulin, which may promote insulin-dependent diabetes. Also, IL-1 is harmful to the pancreatic beta cells, which may encourage diabetes. This explains why diabetes sufferers are frequently candidiasis sufferers. In the big picture, chronic candidiasis can cause excesses of insulin encouraging hypoglycemia, while shortages favor diabetes.

There is also evidence that hyperinsulinism can result from autoimmune activities because patients with hypoglycemia can have *islet-stimulating autoantibodies* that trigger the release of insulin. Since there is a *candidiasis–autoimmune disease connection*, it adds further support for a *candidiasis-hyperinsulinism connection* (chapter 14). (People with consistently elevated levels often have noncancerous, insulin-producing islet tumors, whereas people without tumors have excessive or hyperactive beta cells. Although increased amounts of insulin may occur in people with cancerous pancreatic beta cell tumors, they are rare [about one in a million] and are usually discovered quickly because of the profound hypoglycemia and symptoms they cause.)

Confusingly, some people with reactive hypoglycemia do not have hyperinsulinism. In fact, their insulin levels are normal. Instead, their adrenal cortex is under-functioning, which creates *functional hypoadrenocorticism*. Since a cortisol deficiency impedes the degradation of insulin, it remains within the blood too long, promoting hypoglycemia—a condition called *functional* hyperinsulinism. A cortisol deficiency also makes someone's long-term blood sugar regulation more difficult. They often have a deficiency or decreased response to glucagon, with an increased secretion of epinephrine (even with a cortisol deficiency). Unfortunately, epinephrine excesses cause many unpleasant symptoms. Candidiasis is often involved in this disturbance.

Moreover, the adverse effects of hypoglycemia involve more than just insulin. A severe decrease in the blood sugar concentration triggers the alpha cells to release glucagon. In general, *glucagon* breaks down stored liver glucose (glycogen), liberating it into the blood within minutes, and stimulates the liver to produce glucose. Glucagon is the most predominant blood sugar–raising hormone, but it has short-term actions. Therefore, various other disturbances arise when the blood sugar concentration decreases too much, stays low for too long, or there is a problem with glucagon secretion.

The adrenal glands maintain the blood glucose concentration during a prolonged fast, preventing hypoglycemia. The adrenal *medulla* produces the *catecholamines*, epinephrine and norepinephrine. The *cortex* creates *glucocorticoids*, most notably cortisol. When glucagon cannot raise a low blood sugar concentration by itself, the adrenal glands release *epinephrine*; it acts within minutes, stimulating glucose production, promoting the use of liver glycogen, increasing the absorption of glucose by the intestines, and decreasing the use of glucose by nonessential tissues. It also inhibits insulin release by the pancreas, while stimulating the release of glucagon.

All these effects make as much glucose available as possible, causing the blood sugar concentration to rise. If there is an absence of glucagon, for whatever reason, epinephrine assumes the role of a short-term blood sugar–raising hormone. Epinephrine is normally released during the fight-or-flight response. In turn, excesses precipitate many characteristic symptoms, including (most notably) sweating, palpitations (strong heart-beats), tachycardia (fast heart rate), hunger, tremors, and anxiety. Someone can also manifest hypertension, chest pains, and shortness of breath. Since many candidiasis sufferers regularly experience these symptoms, they seem to have an advanced form of reactive hypoglycemia. (*Norepinephrine* acts similarly, except it is released from the end of nerve cells, stimulating adjacent cells and tissue. It also stimulates the liver to break down glycogen and release glucose.) To make matters worse, a deficiency of glucagon and epinephrine impairs someone's short-term recovery from hypoglycemia, even when their insulin levels are low.

Cortisol decreases hyperinsulinism by countering or degrading circulating insulin. It also promotes the production of glucose and stimulates glucose precursors to go to the liver. Rather than initially participating, cortisol has a delayed onset of action, with a more long-term effect. By counteracting insulin, cortisol prevents the blood sugar concentration from falling further, and it can raise it toward normal. If the glucocorticoids, especially cortisol, are not properly produced or secreted in the presence of a normal insulin response, there will be no antagonist to circulating insulin, promoting functional hyperinsulinism. The prolonged presence of insulin can excessively lower the blood sugar concentration, causing hypoglycemia. An absence of cortisol can promote severe hypoglycemia because research reveals a cortisol deficiency impedes the secretion of epinephrine. These circumstances can cause severe blood sugar lows that precipitate the development of many undesirable symptoms.

A cortisol deficiency can arise when severe stress weakens or exhausts the functioning of the adrenal glands, causing the underproduction of glucocorticoids. A deficiency impairs the degradation of insulin, promoting functional hyperinsulinism and hypoglycemia. In addition, it inhibits epinephrine secretion, exacerbating glucose intolerance. Since cortisol has anti-stress, anti-inflammatory, and anti-allergic actions, low levels encourage a vicious cycle. Normally, cortisol prevents tissues and cells from being broken down and assists in reducing fat deposits. So, a deficiency leads to poor protein metabolism (muscle wasting) as well as weight gain (increased fat deposition). Since there is a *candidiasis–adrenal gland connection*, candidiasis sufferers can easily develop a cortisol deficiency, and decreased cortisol levels only exacerbate their ill health.

Conversely, excess cortisol will degrade too much insulin, encouraging an elevated blood sugar concentration, as well as inhibit the release of growth hormone. Since *growth hormone* helps regulate the long-term blood sugar concentration, a deficiency can prolong hypoglycemia. It also influences numerous metabolic processes and promotes growth within almost the entire body. In adults, it helps the body adapt to stress and nutritional imbalances. Therefore, cortisol excesses cause the body to be more susceptible to insult, injury, and damage, as well as compromise its ability to properly repair itself. In short, cortisol excesses promote growth hormone deficiencies that readily worsen a candidiasis sufferer's health.

One or the other extreme of cortisol production may occur during illness. Initially, to eliminate an infection or adapt to stress, the body usually responds by producing excess cortisol. If the illness or stress continues, the adrenal cortex can become "tired," impairing the body's ability to recover, which can lead to adrenal cortex exhaustion or failure (hypoadrenocorticism) and a cortisol deficiency. Either way, candidiasis can disrupt the functioning of the adrenal cortex. In turn, the disturbances that arise encourage the additional reproduction and colonization of disease-causing yeast, creating a vicious cycle.

Alternatively, glucose intolerance can involve an elevated blood sugar concentration (*hyperglycemia*). *Diabetes* is an illness that involves hyperglycemia. It is usually classified as type 1 (juvenile) or type 2 (adult onset) as well as insulin-dependent or non-insulin-dependent. Can diabetes really be associated with candidiasis?

An article titled "Nearly All Diabetics Have Upper GI Disorders" appeared in the March 1, 1999, issue of *Internal Medicine News*, reporting statements made by Dr. Kenneth L. Koch at the annual postgraduate course of the American Diabetes Association. He said, "Nearly 90% of all diabetic patients have upper gastrointestinal symptoms . . . Because symptoms tend to be vague and nonspecific . . . patients will not necessarily link them to their diabetes." Since most diabetes sufferers have these symptoms and there is a *candidiasis-gastrointestinal connection* (chapter 4), it suggests a *candidiasis-diabetes connection*. Moreover, since diabetes is a form of glucose intolerance and there is a *candidiasis-glucose intolerance connection*, this further indicates that there is a *candidiasis-diabetes connection*. Even so, diabetes does not arise the same way in everyone, implying that candidiasis instigates and promotes diabetes in different ways.

Type 1 diabetes involves hyperglycemia arising prior to adulthood. Usually, it reflects a failure of insulin production. Since its cause is unknown, some physicians think it involves a viral insult, while others believe harmful molds may produce toxins (mycotoxins) that injure the pancreas. More likely, an infection with disease-causing yeast instigates or promotes this illness, with or without other infectious invaders. How? There is a *candidiasis–autoimmune disease connection* (chapter 14) and misdirected cells (cell-mediated autoimmunity) may cause damage to someone's own pancreas, with or without the assistance of autoantibodies. Because the cells and tissues of the pancreas cannot be injured or damaged for no reason and autoimmunity does not require the presence of autoantibodies, cell-mediated autoimmunity can be the mysterious process responsible for this type of diabetes. Moreover, the early ingestion of cow's milk may play a role (chapter 12). Equally concerning, heavy metal toxin exposures that block the insulin receptors can participate. Whatever its cause, this type of diabetes is insulin-dependent; patients must receive insulin to properly metabolize their dietary carbohydrates.

In contrast, *type 2 diabetes* is much more prevalent. It can be insulin-dependent or non-insulin dependent. Type 2 diabetes has many etiologies. Someone may have damaged or malfunctioning beta cells, impairing their ability to produce any, or enough, insulin. As a result, glucose is unable to exit their blood, causing hyperglycemia. In contrast, there may be *insulin resistance*; as someone's weight increases, more insulin must be produced to move their blood glucose into an increased number of cells. Eventually, the insulin receptors on their cell surfaces become less sensitive or unreactive to the insulin released, behaving as if they are "resistant" to it. In addition, as mentioned above, holistic physicians are aware that heavy metal toxicity can cause insulin resistance. Whatever the mechanism, the result is an elevated blood sugar concentration.

People with insulin-dependent diabetes often have a deficiency or absence of glucagon. This occurs because damage to their islets compromises their alpha cells and beta cells. Why is this important? Since glucagon is the primary blood sugar–raising hormone, its absence or shortage hinders their recovery from hypoglycemia. As a result, epinephrine becomes their active blood sugar–raising hormone, promoting its characteristic fight-or-flight symptoms. Even worse, deficiencies involving both glucagon and epinephrine can cause severe or prolonged hypoglycemia. To elevate a profoundly depressed blood sugar concentration or in response to candidiasis, excessive cortisol production may initially occur, inhibiting the release of growth hormone. This causes increased lability and worsening of their glucose tolerance. If the adrenal glands reach the point of exhaustion or candidiasis suppresses them, hypoadrenocorticism will arise, leading to decreased secretion of epinephrine, an increased incidence of illness and infections, and a decreased ability to cope with stress. This explains why diabetes sufferers experience so many medical problems.

Although there is an inherited genetic tendency to develop diabetes, candidiasis appears to precipitate and/or promote hyperglycemia and its associated complications. This might be a bold statement, but there is a *candidiasis–glucose intolerance connection* (chapter 14) as well as a *candidiasis-autoimmunity connection*. In addition, the most prominent sequela of diabetes is cardiovascular disease, and a *candidiasis-cardiovascular connection* (chapter 7) further supports a *candidiasis-diabetes connection*.

So far, candidiasis seems to indirectly promote diabetes. Yet, it can also *directly* cause diabetes. *Candida albicans* has glucagon receptors on its cell surface and can produce *insulin-like substances*. Both can contribute to hyperglycemia. In diabetics, these insulin-like substances may strongly bind with their insulin receptors, preventing them from responding to their own insulin; this promotes insulin resistance, and hyperglycemia results. Moreover, their glucagon receptors may compete for a diabetic's available glucagon, causing the excessive release of the other secondary blood sugar–raising hormones (epinephrine and cortisol) that may excessively raise their blood sugar concentration and contribute their undesirable effects. Eventually, this creates a vicious cycle that worsens over time.

As candidiasis promotes diabetes, its sufferers become more susceptible to candidiasis. Since disease-causing yeast primarily use sugar as fuel, they readily reproduce when there is an excess of glucose. So, the blood and tissues of diabetes sufferers are favorable habitats (microbiomes) for disease-causing yeast. Although there are exceptions, it is wise to assume that most diabetics have candidiasis until proven otherwise. Since candidiasis is an *infection* with *allergic* consequences that stresses the body, and disease-causing yeast secrete toxins and other harmful metabolites that can worsen diabetes, it makes sense to treat diabetes sufferers for candidiasis. In fact, treating them frequently improves their blood sugar control significantly, not to mention preventing the adverse effects of their diabetes. (Benefits also occur with an anti-candidiasis diet that has decreased amounts of complex carbohydrates).

Yes, there is a *candidiasis-pancreas connection*. A deficiency of pancreatic juice can cause malabsorption and a variety of nutritional deficiencies. Moreover, disturbances involving the pancreatic islets adversely affects glucose metabolism. The resulting glucose intolerance can range from mild episodes of hypoglycemia to significant hyperglycemia. The greater the intolerance, the more adversely it affects someone's health. In addition, candidiasis places great stress on the body, especially the functioning of the adrenal cortex. Over time, it can promote a cortisol deficiency and reduced epinephrine secretion, which exacerbates glucose intolerance, worsening someone's symptoms and illness. Yes, you might have inherited your tendency to develop glucose intolerance, but without the harmful contributions of candidiasis, it is unlikely it would develop into overt disease. Equally concerning, other infectious invaders and heavy metal toxicity may contribute, making diagnosis and treatment more confusing and complicated. Nevertheless, educated candidiasis-minded physicians know that the benefits of anti-candidiasis treatment are worth the effort.

GETTING YOUR GLANDS WORKING AGAIN

If you have a thyroid problem, you are usually told to take a medication. If other glands develop low hormone levels, you may be prescribed hormone replacements. Or you might have glandular overactivity, requiring some type of medical intervention. More often, you are likely to suffer with an imbalance involving one or more of your hormones without being aware of it. Even worse, your physician is probably unaware of it as well. How can this occur? Although you have symptoms, laboratory testing shows your hormone levels are normal, so the diagnosis is missed. If your results are normal, how can you have an endocrine disturbance? Instead of a deficiency or excess of a hormone, you have a *functional* disturbance; your hormones are abnormally functioning. Yet, why are you suffering with this problem in the first place? There is not any easy answer because the origin of most endocrine disturbances is unknown or mysterious. Since illness cannot occur without a cause, something must be responsible. This is when it is wise to consider the contributions of candidiasis.

Your endocrine (hormone) system is a multilevel, interconnected collection of glands that are sensitive to your body's internal and external environment. It begins within your nervous system, with signals forwarded from your brain's hypothalamus to your pituitary gland. Depending on your need, your pituitary releases hormones that signal specific target glands, including your thyroid, adrenal, or sex glands. After being stimulated, your target gland releases one or more hormones to influence certain tissues and cells. An extensive feedback mechanism exists, enabling your endocrine system to be tightly regulated. Moreover, your parathyroid glands and pancreas are also part of your endocrine system, even though they are not under the influence of your pituitary gland.

Your endocrine system closely interacts with your nervous and immune systems, forming your *neuroendocrine-immune connection*. All three perform in concert to achieve *homeostasis*, your balanced state of optimal functioning. An abundance of cellular chemical messengers, numerous hormones, and the propagation of electric signals by nerve cells allows all your systems to communicate. This normally keeps everything in balance, whereas a disturbance in one system is certain to adversely affect the others in some way.

Candidiasis is an *infection* with disease-causing yeast, producing an abundance of inflammation and *allergic* consequences. The presence of disease-causing yeast-related toxins, metabolites, byproducts, and/or allergy-inducing substances greatly stresses the body and its systems. As a result, candidiasis can adversely affect the body's functioning and well-being. The immune system of most sufferers tries to eradicate their disease-causing yeast, but this rarely occurs, and their disarray and disturbances only worsen over time, creating a vicious cycle.

Candidiasis can *directly* compromise the endocrine system, with or without help of other infectious invaders. Moreover, candidiasis-induced problems within the nervous and/or immune systems will *indirectly* disrupt the endocrine system. Yes, there is a *candidiasis-endocrine connection*. As a result, sufferers may present with disorders of their pituitary gland, thyroid gland, adrenal glands, sex glands, parathyroid glands, and/or pancreas. Any glandular abnormality causes problems with its hormones as well as the cells and tissues they influence. Since the entire endocrine system is interrelated, problems with one gland often indirectly disturb others. The *candidiasis-endocrine connection* helps explain why candidiasis presents with great variability. This can be confusing for a physician attempting to understand and diagnose candidiasis, not to mention the patient who suffers with it. When you add in the harmful contributions of other infectious invaders, the symptoms of candidiasis can become more confusing. It explains why candidiasis is an exceedingly variable condition with no two sufferers ever having the same illness and symptoms.

In candidiasis sufferers with an overt endocrine disturbance, laboratory testing is likely to reveal a problem; for example, the level of some hormone is high or low. Yet, laboratory testing is rarely helpful when they have a *functional* deficiency because the level of some hormone appears normal, while it functions abnormally. This is when a sufferer's symptoms can reveal the problem. Of course, a high index of suspicion must first exist, or a functional deficiency of some hormone will not be considered.

If you have an endocrine disturbance, you are likely to be a candidiasis sufferer. And if you are a candidiasis sufferer, you probably have one or more endocrine disturbances, whether or not you know it. A thyroid problem may produce overactivity or underactivity, or even a subtle state of slowed metabolism (hypometabolism). Mild candidiasis may stimulate your adrenal glands, but as it progresses, your adrenal glands can become exhausted, promoting hormone deficiencies (especially hypoadrenocorticism) or even glandular failure. A problem within your sex glands may lead to a deficiency of estrogen, progesterone, and/or androgens with their symptoms. A parathyroid gland disturbance typically promotes underactivity, leading to lowered calcium and magnesium ion concentrations, although overactivity can infrequently occur. Confusingly, any of these disturbances can be present with apparently normal hormone levels. If your pancreas is disturbed, you are likely to have a deficiency of pancreatic juice and malabsorption as well as blood sugar disturbances, ranging from hypoglycemia to hyperglycemia (diabetes). These are the most notable and well-known candidiasis-related hormone disturbances. Yet, there are more pieces that need to be discovered.

If you are a candidiasis sufferer or have an endocrine disturbance, how do you treat it? Yes, you can take a hormone replacement, but this is usually Band-Aid therapy, aimed at treating your symptoms rather than their cause. Because of the *candidiasis-endocrine connection*, it makes more sense to eliminate your candidiasis. This will address the cause of your endocrine malady. Although hormone replacement therapy is sometimes unavoidable, most sufferers discover that their endocrine disturbances resolve and disappear after their disease-causing yeast (and other infectious invaders) are eliminated. In addition, since allergies also promote abundant inflammation and a variety of disturbances, they must be addressed as well.

CHAPTER 12

Pediatric Manifestations

Any pediatrician will tell you children are not "little adults." Their immature bodies, especially their immune systems, make them more fragile and susceptible to a variety of disturbances. In contrast, children do not suffer with the age-related problems and degenerative diseases that plague adults, so they often recover from illnesses quickly. Although there are significant differences between children and adults, they do share one thing in common: with respect to candidiasis, both groups are equally susceptible. Disease-causing yeast do not care whether they colonize and infect the young or the old. Candidiasis and its characteristic symptoms can and does arise during infancy and childhood.

Since their immune systems are not as developed as adults, children commonly suffer with frequent upper respiratory infections ("common" colds). These tend to decrease as a child's immunity matures. Yet, considering the incredible number of infectious invaders and allergy-inducing substances that are around them, a child's immunity protects them quite well. Except for common colds, the presence of a chronic or recurring medical problem is not normal; so, if a child suffers with one, something must be wrong. Since illness cannot arise without a cause, *something* must be responsible. What could it be? Like adults, candidiasis is probably to blame. This is rarely recognized or appreciated by mainstream physicians, so parents are skeptical. As an example, one mother succinctly stated, "My daughter is so young, how can she have already gotten candidiasis?" On the contrary, age has nothing to do with developing and suffering with candidiasis.

Given inopportune circumstances, children readily develop candidiasis. Normally, at birth, as a baby passes through their mother's birth canal, they are exposed to and acquire some of their mother's beneficial bacteria, which are supposed to colonize and protect their gastrointestinal tract. Why is this important? Like adults, children must develop and maintain a population of beneficial bacteria, which competitively inhibit the colonization of disease-causing yeast and other infectious invaders (chapters 3 and 4). Anything that prevents the establishment of a healthy population of beneficial bacteria (or that kills them off) creates an environment that permits the proliferation and colonization of disease-causing yeast as well as harmful parasites, bacteria, molds, and/or viruses. So, if a newborn's mother has candidiasis, instead of being inoculated with some beneficial bacteria at birth, they will be introduced to the disease-causing yeast inhabiting their mother's vagina. Although a cesarean section, the surgical removal of a baby through the lower abdomen, avoids the direct exposure of a newborn to their mother's disease-causing yeast, it also prevents them from being inoculated with some of her beneficial bacteria. Since most infants are not fed yogurt or given probiotic-containing supplements, without a source of beneficial bacteria in their diets, they cannot develop a healthy population, so candidiasis is highly likely.

The repeated use of *antibiotics* and an abundance of dietary *sugar* are strong risk factors for candidiasis (chapter 2). Sugar and sugary foods readily nourish disease-causing yeast, promoting their reproduction and colonization. Even worse, foods that contain disease-causing yeast and mold (like cheese) can directly populate a child's gut, speeding this process along. Children readily develop candidiasis, and it is much more prevalent than currently appreciated.

When it is present, the most obvious indication is oral *thrush*, the presence of a whitish coating on a child's mouth and tongue. If thrush was always present, candidiasis would be easy to diagnose. Since thrush is not frequently evident, candidiasis is not suspected and missed. For it to be revealed, there must be a high index of suspicion. An adult's symptoms often assist in illuminating their problem, but children are not good at describing their symptoms, so the younger the child, the more difficult it becomes. For example, a child might tug or rub their ear when an ear infection is present, hold their stomach with gastroenteritis, or become lethargic when infected with a virus. More confusing, two children may react differently to the same problem. With respect to treating children, their inability to communicate usually leads to a symptom-directed approach—for example, repeatedly prescribing antibiotics to treat recurring ear infections rather than revealing why a child has this problem in the first place. For these reasons and more, candidiasis is regularly ignored and overlooked within most children.

Whether recognized or not, children can and do develop candidiasis. After all, children commonly suffer with a diversity of candidiasis-related maladies, including gastrointestinal disorders, asthma, allergies, rashes, and more. In contrast, several candidiasis-related disturbances are specifically associated with children, including chronic ear infections, attention deficit hyperactivity disorder, autism, and Tourette syndrome.

If a child is suffering with a chronic or recurring medical problem, you would be wise to consider candidiasis because there is a good chance the child's health can be drastically improved. In the bigger picture, an appreciation for the *candidiasis–pediatric connection* should provide a basis for eliminating most chronic and recurring childhood illnesses.

CHRONIC EAR INFECTIONS

A middle ear infection (*otitis media*) might seem like a relatively minor problem, but it can cause tremendous physical and financial burdens. Middle ear infections are more than a minor inconvenience. For example, the most frequent pediatric surgery in the United States involves placing tubes within the ears of children with chronic fluid behind their *tympanic membrane* (otitis media with effusion). Yet, most chronic ear infections can be eliminated or even avoided when you are aware of what is really occurring.

Otitis media is common among children. Since the passageways of their inner ear and airways of their lungs are smaller than adults, inflammation and swelling produce significant disturbances. As a result, children have a greater susceptibility and incidence of ear, nose, and throat infections. In fact, 50 to 85 percent of children under age three will experience a case of otitis media, and roughly 80 to 90 percent of them will have it with an effusion before age five. In 2019, there were 119 million prevalent cases, with 360 million incident cases worldwide.

An abundance of antibiotics is prescribed to treat middle ear infections, with three to six months of repeated therapy often being common. Unfortunately, the use of antibiotics disturbs and destroys the beneficial bacteria within these children, permitting the proliferation of disease-causing yeast as well as other infectious invaders. In turn, candidiasis can impair a child's immunity (chapter 14) and induce allergies (chapter 16). It also makes these children susceptible to more viral assaults, creating a vicious cycle. For example, once a child manifests respiratory allergies, their incidence of bronchitis and ear infections greatly increases.

In addition, food allergies are associated with chronic middle ear infections. As an example, several studies show that 30 to 40 percent of children with recurring ear infections have cow's milk allergies. Is this pertinent? Yes, because candidiasis can readily instigate and promote food allergies (chapters 4 and 16). Since there is a *candidiasis–food allergy connection* and a *food allergy–otitis media connection*, it supports a *candidiasis–otitis media connection*. More disturbing, if candidiasis is present early enough, a child can develop food allergies before a specific food is eaten. How does this happen? In addition to beneficial antibodies, mother's milk can contain a variety of allergy-inducing particles (antigens). During breastfeeding, a susceptible child may become sensitive or hypersensitive to certain food antigens, even before that food is eaten, especially cow's milk, eggs, and corn. So, there is a big difference between treating an ear infection with an antibiotic and understanding why it occurred in the first place.

Mainstream medicine believes that the sudden onset of a middle ear infection, *acute* otitis media, is caused by a bacterial infection. Yet, some observations made between 1977 and 1986 are concerning: 1) The number of children under age 10 increased by 9 percent; 2) The number of office visits for otitis media increased by 136 percent; and 3) The amount of antibiotics prescribed only increased by 51 percent. These statistics point out a large disparity between the size of the pediatric population, the number of office visits for ear infections, and the amount of antibiotics prescribed for it. In short, although there was a fivefold increase in their use, antibiotics were prescribed for otitis media less than 40 percent of the time. If the incidence of otitis media really increased at such an accelerated rate, the relatively conservative use of antibiotics indicates that bacterial infections are *not* the real cause of this prevalent childhood malady.

So, what is? Most mainstream physicians would say "viruses." In short, if a child with acute otitis media does not respond to antibiotic treatment within 48 hours, antibiotic resistance is unlikely to be the problem. Rather, they have a viral infection, and antibiotics do not kill viruses. Yet, despite the absence of harmful bacteria, two, three, and even four courses of antibiotics are often prescribed for persistent otitis media. If the first antibiotic is not effective, it is doubtful additional prescriptions will help. Unfortunately, this type of therapy is far from harmless because it eradicates the beneficial bacteria that keep the disease-causing yeast under control. As an example, one study revealed a virus was involved in 32 percent of the children with acute otitis media and bacteria in 18 percent, so what is responsible for acute otitis media in the remaining 50 to 70 percent of children?

Nasal allergies can cause acute ear infections. Since there is a *candidiasis–nasal allergy connection* (chapter 6), candidiasis can induce nasal allergies that promote acute otitis media. So, an increase in the number of office visits for otitis media means increasing numbers of children have *nasal allergies*. Under these circumstances, the use of antibiotics only creates a vicious cycle because it worsens a child's candidiasis, aggravating their allergies, and so on.

Antibiotics have their usefulness, even when allergies are present. When bacteria within a child's middle ear proliferate and spread, severe earache, fever, and discomfort may arise, and if it is significant, it can cause a loss of hearing or rupture a child's eardrum (tympanic membrane), so antibiotics are appropriate. Although they are a strong risk factor for promoting candidiasis, bacterial infections necessitate antibiotic intervention. In contrast, *serous* otitis media involves an accumulation of fluid behind the eardrum that is not infected with bacteria, making antibiotics worthless. In this situation, the best approach involves identifying the *allergy*-instigating culprits (antigens) that are causing a child's nasal allergies and congestion, and then eliminating them and/or administering desensitization (allergy) injections. Unfortunately, the hearing disability is often notable regardless of the therapy.

Some researchers have found that elimination diets are useful for patients with otitis media and multiple food allergies, and the cytotoxic test (chapter 17) is helpful in planning their elimination diets. Simply put, there is a significant cause-and-effect relationship between food allergies and recurring ear infections with fluid.

Undeniably, bacteria and viruses do cause acute ear infections. Yet, the presence of chronic or recurring ear infections implies that something is perpetually amiss; typically, allergies cause inflammation, creating an environment (microbiome) that encourages infections. In either case, something must be responsible for the conditions or circumstances that permit ear infections to develop in the first place. So, regardless of whether bacteria and viruses are involved, something must cause the allergies and congestion that promote ear infections. Because of the *candidiasis–otitis media connection*, most children with ear infections are likely to have candidiasis. How does it cause ear infections? By definition, candidiasis arises when disease-causing yeast colonize the gastrointestinal tract. In the process, they can also infect the mucous membranes, including the sinuses, nasopharynx, and eustachian tubes. The presence of disease-causing yeast within these areas can *directly* cause inflammation.

Since the opening between a child's inner ear and nasopharynx (their eustachian tubes) are smaller than adults, the colonization of disease-causing yeast within these areas enables them to become easily swollen, congested, and even blocked. This inhibits the drainage of secretions from their middle ear, causing increased pressure and pain. It also provides a medium for a secondary bacterial or viral infection. Moreover, by instigating allergies, candidiasis can *indirectly* precipitate inflammation and swelling in these areas. Since there a *candidiasis-allergy connection* (chapter 16), a *candidiasis–nasal allergy connection* (chapter 6) and a *candidiasis–food allergy connection* (chapter 4), disease-causing yeast can indirectly promote inflammation and congestion of the mucous membranes. In addition to food and environmental allergies, this includes allergies to disease-causing yeast and harmful molds. To prove this point, test any child with chronic or recurring ear infections for allergies to disease-causing yeast and harmful molds because it is highly likely they will have positive reactions.

Antibiotics are engineered to be effective against bacteria, not viruses. Many doctors say antibiotics cannot hurt. On the contrary, their frequent use in the treatment of a viral or allergy-caused ear infection is harmful because they indirectly promote the colonization of disease-causing yeast. Unfortunately, this encourages further allergic reactions and the accumulation of additional fluid, creating a vicious cycle. Yes, a percentage of children with ear infections do benefit from antibiotics—those caused by a bacterial infection. However, most do not, because frequent or recurring ear infections involve *allergies* and *candidiasis*.

Some children outgrow their ear infections without being treated for candidiasis. Yet, this does not occur without some risk because research shows there is a cause-and-effect relationship between otitis media and learning disabilities. Since there is an *otitis media–learning disabilities connection* and a *candidiasis–otitis media connection*, this implies the presence of a *candidiasis–learning disabilities connection*.

Although learning disabilities can accompany the hearing losses that are often associated with ear infections, candidiasis can just as easily be blamed. How can disease-causing yeast cause learning problems? Because of the *candidiasis-neurological connection* (chapter 10), candidiasis can directly and indirectly disturb the brain's chemical messengers (neurotransmitters), which can impair someone's thinking and thought processes as well as their mood. This is not to be taken lightly because learning disabilities affect up to 10 percent of all school-age children. Costly interventions are frequently required to avoid serious educational disabilities. If these children were treated for candidiasis, these interventions would be much less needed or even unnecessary.

In a letter to William G. Crook, M.D., Allan Lieberman, M.D., of the Center for Occupational and Environmental Medicine in Charleston, South

Carolina, stated, "I treat almost every patient I see, including children with hyperactivity, behavior, and learning problems, using a therapeutic trial of the anti-*Candida* program. The dramatic results I've obtained in so many encourage me to continue this approach. I've found young children with recurring respiratory and ear infections seem to really benefit. So do children, especially teenagers, with chronic depression."

Medical researchers are starting to realize that the microbiome of the nasal membranes, as well as the inner and outer ear, contributes to otitis media. There is evidence to support a fungal contribution to otitis media with effusion. Other research makes the case for certain bacteria being protective, like the beneficial bacteria within the gut. So, it seems that when the beneficial bacteria within the middle ear or eustachian tube are deficient or die, the microbiome is compromised, allowing opportunistic invaders to colonize these areas. Since disease-causing yeast, especially *Candida albicans*, can invade into tissues to survive (leaky gut syndrome, chapter 4; sinusitis, chapter 6) as well as form a biofilm that enables other fungi and bacteria to colonize these areas, it creates an environment suitable for a mixed infection, which is why the prevalent organisms tend to vary from one geographical region to another and from one study to the next.

Fortunately, once a child's candidiasis and allergies are treated, their ear infections almost always disappear forever. Unfortunately, the indirect effects of middle ear infections can involve long-term physical (and financial) burdens, including learning disabilities and developmental problems. So, it is important to diagnose and treat all children with candidiasis, even if they outgrow their ear infections. All of this means chronic and recurring ear infections can be eliminated and their accompanying learning disabilities can even be reversed when you are willing to consider candidiasis as a strong contributor to these medical maladies.

ATTENTION DEFICIT DISORDER & HYPERACTIVITY

A notable learning disability is *attention deficit disorder* (ADD). When hyperactivity is present, it is also a behavioral problem. To be accurate, attention-deficit/hyperactivity disorder (ADHD) is not a disease because there are no notable anatomical changes. Since mainstream medicine is unaware of its origin, it is termed a "disorder." Yet, even a disorder must have a cause, so something must be responsible for ADHD. Because an infection with disease-causing yeast can directly and indirectly disturb the brain's neurotransmitters (chapter 10), candidiasis can cause disordered or abnormal thinking, promoting learning difficulties. Is this speculation? No, because this phenomenon is real and extremely likely. After all, adult candidiasis sufferers often feel like they are "in a fog" and have difficulty concentrating, memory problems, dyslexia, and other mental manifestations that can impair their thinking and learning. Although young children cannot effectively explain their symptoms, candidiasis causes the same undesirable disturbances within them, including blood sugar disturbances (chapters 11 and 14) that encourage emotional "highs" (periods of elation) followed by "lows" (periods of depression). In adults, this typically reveals itself as episodes of mania and depression (bipolar disorder), ranging from mild to severe (chapter 10). Candidiasis-related blood sugar disturbances within children produce episodes of hyperactivity and lethargy. In turn, this can cause behavior problems and learning difficulties. So, instead of having no origin, ADHD appears to be a childhood manifestation of candidiasis, with or without glucose intolerance.

Different studies estimate that the prevalence of ADHD among children ranges from 2.2 percent to 17.8 percent. In the United States, 9.8 percent of children have been diagnosed. The incidence includes 2 percent of children ages 3–5, 10 percent ages 6–11, and 13 percent ages 12–17. At this point, there seems to be at least one "problematic" child in every classroom. These children are difficult to deal with, tend to cause trouble, and constantly test the patience of others. They are often the reason for their teachers' agitation, parents' frustration, and peers' curiosity. Why is ADHD so common? It has increased because the number of children with candidiasis has increased. Without treatment for candidiasis, many of these children eventually grow up to be adults with ADHD. In 2020, the worldwide prevalence of people with persistent adult ADHD was 2.58 percent (139.84 million), with symptomatic adult ADHD being 6.76 percent (366.33 million). These are staggering numbers.

In the bigger picture, a more complete list of childhood behavioral problems includes ADD, hyperactivity, hostility, unexplained fatigue and exhaustion, moodiness, tantrums, and depression (some physicians add headaches). The number of these "difficult to raise and teach" kids is significant. Specifics aside, physicians have been puzzled by these pediatric maladies for years. According to mainstream medicine, most, if not all, of these problems have unknown or mysterious origins, making them difficult to treat and harder to cure. Yet, these behavioral problems can be easily explained.

The presence of *candidiasis* directly and indirectly disturbs a child's brain chemistry, producing these problems (chapter 10). Because of *glucose intolerance*, the number and frequency of blood sugar "highs" and "lows" triggers significant changes in a child's mood, behavior, and more (chapters 10 and 11). For example, when their blood sugar concentration is elevated, feelings of euphoria, excitement, and overactivity are common. Conversely, when their blood sugar concentration is decreasing or below normal, they typically manifest lethargy, sleepiness, and concentration difficulties. In addition, a decreasing or low blood sugar concentration stimulates the release of numerous secondary hormones, causing aggressiveness and other undesirable behaviors (chapter 11). Even worse, candidiasis promotes additional disturbances by inducing a variety of allergies (chapter 16), including sensitivities and hypersensitivities to pollens, dust, chemicals, and foods as well as to disease-causing yeast and many harmful molds. These allergies can readily disturb the brain's chemistry and functioning, producing adverse cognitive consequences (chapter 10).

Do allergies contribute? ADHD children have been found to be sensitive to foods, food additives, inhalants, and chemical contaminants. Many of them are also sensitive to the metabolic products of *Candida albicans.*

Some physicians claim to have successfully treated these children using an elimination diet (the Feingold Diet). Although numerous studies were performed, the results were unclear, and no definitive conclusions were reached. Yet, other studies have supported the role of diet in ADHD children. As an example, children with "hyperkinetic syndrome" that were treated with a diet containing only simple foods (an oligoantigenic diet) had significant improvement, with 21 children (28%) achieving a normal range of behavior. Other symptoms were corrected as well—notably, headaches, fits, and abdominal pains. More revealing, the symptoms reappeared when suspicious foods were reintroduced. (Forty-eight different foods were found to cause reactions.) So, the presence of a *candidiasis-food allergy connection* (chapter 4) and a *food allergy–ADHD connection* supports a *candidiasis-ADHD connection.*

In addition to allergies, dietary *sugar* has been strongly associated with hyperactivity. Moreover, sugar causes more hyperactivity when it is combined with other carbohydrates (for example, sweetened breakfast cereals). This makes sense because blood sugar disturbances escalate as a child's intake of carbohydrates increases. Research and clinical experience shows significant improvements occur in hyperactive youngsters as their sugar intake is reduced. Why does sugar exacerbate ADHD? A diet high in sugar promotes glucose intolerance, involving the *candidiasis-glucose intolerance-ADHD connection*. When tested, most hyperactive children demonstrate *glucose intolerance* and increased *insulin* levels (*hyperinsulinism*). Although this chemical (metabolic) disturbance can be inherited, it usually arises or worsens in the presence of *candidiasis* (chapters 11 and 14). Eliminating sugar and carbohydrates helps stabilize a child's blood sugar concentration, preventing the blood sugar "highs" and "lows" that alter their mood and behavior.

Due to the trend toward "low fat" foods, children are consuming more sugar, juice, and fruit than ever. Although many parents mistakenly believe that sugar is harmless, diets high in simple carbohydrates readily contribute to most children's emotional and behavioral "highs" and "lows" (and other symptoms). Because of their smaller size, if an average 10-year-old drinks a 12 ounce can of soda, it is equivalent to an adult drinking two to three cans. Depending on the brand, with roughly 9 to 11 teaspoons of sugar in a can, it is a significant amount of glucose for a child. To add insult, the *caffeine* within many drinks, chocolate, and other foods also contributes to hyperactivity because it is a central nervous system stimulant and raises the blood glucose concentration. Caffeine is also a *diuretic*, causing dehydration, which can encourage a child to drink more, creating a vicious cycle.

What about juice? Its simple carbohydrates also adversely affect a child's blood sugar concentration. Yes, there is some nutrition, but the amount of simple carbohydrates is about the same as soda. Again, the serving size is often disproportionate to the child. Okay, what about fruit? Similarly, one apple for a child is equal to an adult eating two to three. Although fruit does contain nutrients, it can alter a child's blood sugar concentration. Moreover, all types of sugar readily nourish disease-causing yeast, regardless of whether the sugar is "natural" or processed.

Even though the evidence strongly supports a *candidiasis-ADHD connection*, most physicians are not listening. Instead, they have been turning to an easy solution, which is treating these children with a drug called Ritalin. According to 2019 statistics, in the United States, Ritalin is prescribed for 69 percent of children with ADHD ages 6 to 11 and 62 percent ages 12 to 17, with the total estimated prescriptions that year of more than 14.23 million.

Although Ritalin does help some children with ADHD, it is a Band-Aid remedy; it covers the problem but does not eliminate it. It does not treat the cause and, at best, only treats a child's symptoms. So, once a child starts taking this drug, they are likely to use it for a long time. Since Ritalin has undesirable side effects, there are risks to its use. So, before Ritalin is given to an ADHD child, parents and physicians should consider the contributions of candidiasis, glucose intolerance, allergies, nutritional deficiencies, chronic viral illnesses, and the effect of toxins on the child, as any or all of these can promote abnormal symptoms and behaviors. Parents will be amazed how quickly their ADHD youngster calms down soon after starting an elimination diet and being treated for candidiasis.

Most parents care about their children, want the best for them, and mean well. Embracing the easiest or most convenient treatment is not the best solution. So, Ritalin and other Band-Aid therapies are not the best answer. Instead, it is important to consider anything that can directly or indirectly cause a child's symptoms. This often includes the adverse contributions of candidiasis, glucose intolerance, and allergies. In addition, other infectious invaders may also participate. So, with respect to treating ADHD, the first step is to appropriately diagnose and correctly treat a child's candidiasis. Eliminating sugar from their diet will prevent them from having blood sugar "highs" and "lows," stabilizing their mood. Since sugar and carbohydrates nourish disease-causing yeast, eliminating these substances lessens the adverse effects of their candidiasis.

It is also important to test ADHD children for sensitivities and hypersensitivities to a variety of substances; the most frequent offenders are disease-causing yeast, harmful molds, food additives, various foods, classroom and/or household chemicals, dust, and pollens. If possible, all the substances that induce an allergic reaction should be removed from a child's diet and from their immediate environment. Equally important, a child with ADHD should receive a desensitization (allergy) injection program that includes their appropriate antigens, or long-lasting improvements may not occur.

Fortunately, the prevalence of ADHD can be halted and even reversed. For this to occur, an understanding and appreciation of the *candidiasis-ADHD connection* is required, and appropriate action must be taken.

AUTISM

Autism (infantile autism, autism spectrum disorder) was first described by Leo (Chaskel Leib) Kanner, M.D., in 1943, as an incapacitating mental, behavioral, and emotional disorder "characterized by severe distortions in multiple aspects of development." Since then, the features of autism have been updated to include impaired social relatedness, a severe deficiency of communication skills, and inappropriate and/or unusual responses to the environment. In other words, autistic children frequently appear totally unaware or out of touch as well as helpless and unable to exist independently (even as a teenager).

Although interpersonal interactions tend to vary, withdrawal and self-absorption are typical. Because hyperactivity or hyperkinesis is often present, and commands are frequently not understood, controlling these children is usually difficult. Autistic children typically demonstrate repetitive obsessive movements. Verbalization ranges from complete silence to mumbling. When an autistic child can talk, grammatical problems are common—for example, using "you" instead of "I" when referring to themselves.

Bernard Rimland, Ph.D., the director of the Autism Research Institute, founder of the National Society for Autistic Children, and author of *Infantile Autism,* shared some disturbing statistics: The institute's rate of autism went from 1 percent during 1965–1969, to 5 percent during 1970–1989, to 8 percent during 1990–1993, and to *17 percent* by 1994–1995. (Admittedly, part of this may reflect a greater awareness of autism.) During the early 1990s, more than 10 million hyperactive and autistic children were diagnosed in the United States (four to five out of every 10,000 children, or 0.045%). In 2022, estimates suggest that 1.8 percent of American children have autism, with a worldwide prevalence of 1 percent (about 80 million). Eighty percent of autistic children are intellectually disabled. As much as 25 percent experience seizure disorders by their adolescence.

Most studies suggest that autism arises from a direct organic insult within a child's brain and central nervous system. Although mainstream medical treatment includes major tranquilizers, lithium, antidepressants, vitamins, and psychotherapy, their effectiveness is poorly established. More often, these are usually considered hopeful interventions because it is estimated that only 1 to 2 percent of these children ever become fully functional.

In addition, the incidence of autism is thought to parallel the use of antibiotics, especially for ear infections. Autistic children have more ear infections than neurotypical children, and the severity of their disorder can be correlated with their number of infections. Since there is an *autism–otitis media connection* and a *candidiasis–otitis media connection,* this suggests the presence of a *candidiasis-autism connection.* Can autism be associated with candidiasis? Yes, children with autism have been found to have increased intestinal permeability (chapter 17), evidencing leaky gut syndrome, a prominent complication of candidiasis (chapters 3 and 4).

In support of a *candidiasis-autism connection,* William G. Crook, M.D., revealed, "In my own practice during the past four years, I've seen and treated over 500 patients with a wide variety of mental and nervous system symptoms that appear to be yeast connected. The response of most of these patients has been gratifying, even exciting." Dr. Rimland took this further and stated, "There is some evidence, still very controversial, that implicates a *Candida* infection as an important cause of autism in at least a small portion of the children."

Although Dr. Rimland admitted that a small percentage of children have candidiasis and autism, his admission is a *conservative* estimate. Since most autistic children cannot complain about their symptoms, this places the burden on their caregivers. With respect to candidiasis, most physicians are unaware, unconvinced, unable to recognize, or do not appreciate its complexity. Candidiasis is regularly overlooked or ignored, and most autistic children are never given a chance to benefit from anti-candidiasis intervention. Yet, with a careful and thorough approach, many autistic children do demonstrate improvement with anti-candidiasis therapy, especially when you consider that 98 to 99 percent do *not* improve with mainstream therapy. This does not even consider the undesirable contributions of other infectious invaders.

Since there is a prominent *candidiasis–mental manifestation connection* (chapter 10), autism may reflect an extreme form of candidiasis-related brain impairment. If this is true, adults should develop autism. In a sense, they do. For example, adults with candidiasis often have brain "fog," concentration difficulties, and memory problems. Depression, schizophrenia, and other psychiatric disturbances are common among adult candidiasis sufferers. Children express their symptoms differently because their bodies are immature, more fragile, and less able to compensate, especially with regard to insults involving their brains and nervous systems. In turn, a *candidiasis-autism connection* is missed. Similarly, autistic children are known to have a high incidence of seizure disorders without anatomical defects. Although this involves severe glucose intolerance and nutritional abnormalities, there is a *candidiasis-seizure connection* (chapter 10). All the available evidence points to candidiasis, with or without other infectious invaders.

Compelling evidence is provided by William Shaw, Ph.D., a biochemist and founder of Great Plains Laboratory in Lenexa, Kansas). Dr. Shaw has studied autistic children as well as children with severe developmental delays and other neurological abnormalities. By measuring *organic acid* levels within the *urine* of autistic children, he discovered the presence of chemicals (metabolites) that are not manufactured within the human body.

Instead, these compounds are produced by disease-causing yeast, harmful molds, and bacteria:

- *Arabinose,* a five-carbon sugar (probably produced from *arabitol,* a sugar alcohol made by *Candida albicans*) was found in 80 to 90 percent of more than 500 autistic children tested.
- *Tartaric acid, citramalic acid, 3-oxoglutaric acid,* and *carboxycitric acid* are metabolites of the Krebs cycle (a sequence of chemical reactions that use oxidation to release stored energy) that enable disease-causing yeast and harmful molds to generate energy.
- *Furans* are substances made by a species of mold, *Aspergillus.*
- *Dihydroxyphenylpropionic acid* is often present (as well as within schizophrenics) and thought to be a metabolite of a harmful bacteria called *Clostridia* (one or more members of its family may play a role). This acid is believed to inhibit the conversion of dopa to dopamine, adversely affecting the brain's chemistry (neurotransmitters).
- Moreover, other substances produced by disease-causing yeast can adversely affect the body and brain, including ethanol, acetaldehyde, and gliotoxin (chapter 10).

The bad news is that any or all these metabolites may instigate and promote autism. Therefore, disease-causing yeast, harmful molds, bacteria, and parasites must all be considered as participants in autism. Yet, according to Dr. Shaw, there is good news. In 2000, he reported that treatment with an oral antifungal medication (nystatin, not absorbed) and drugs against *Clostridia*-species organisms cause these chemicals to decline, and simultaneously improve an autistic child's clinical symptoms.

In 2020, S. Baker and W. Shaw published a case study of an autistic child who had urine biological markers consistent with *Aspergillus* species colonization within the gut. The child was initially treated with *Saccharomyces boulardii* (a probiotic) and had a strong die-off (Herxheimer) reaction. The major intervention involved increasing doses of Sporanox (itraconazole), a systemic, broad-spectrum antifungal that kills disease-causing yeast and other harmful molds, including *Aspergillus.* The child had a complete recovery from all autistic symptoms, and developed "excellent academic, athletic, and musical skills. The recovery coincided with a marked reduction of urine markers of *Aspergillus* colonization."

The first study involved numerous children who received a nonabsorbable antifungal medication (nystatin), and although the results were encouraging, the latter case study with a systemic antifungal medication reveals the benefits of treating disease-causing yeast and harmful molds that reside beyond the gut, within the tissues and the blood.

If candidiasis is appropriately addressed from a multifaceted direction, a large percentage of autistic children should improve. Although Dr. Shaw's work supports the contributions of numerous infectious invaders, there is another side to autism that must be considered. *Allergies* are closely associated with psychological symptoms, so they consistently contribute to autism. Is this surprising? No, because there is a *candidiasis-allergy connection* (chapter 16). Since candidiasis is an infection with allergic consequences, both sides must be addressed. Candidiasis can induce allergies to a variety of substances, including disease-causing yeast, harmful molds, foods, chemicals, pollens, dust, and more. Any of these can precipitate and exacerbate a child's mental symptoms, promoting autism.

Because autistic children suffer with gut problems that correlate with the severity of their disorder, medical research is beginning to appreciate that the gastrointestinal microbiome contributes to autism in children. Several studies have found abnormal gut bacteria in autistic children. Moreover, other researchers revealed that autistic children had twice the number of *Candida*-species organisms versus neurotypical subjects. One researcher did a systematic literature review and noted that there appears to be a high prevalence of *Candida albicans* in children with autism. In return, some research has attempted to alter the gut's microbiome toward normal.

Indeed, a *candidiasis-autism connection* is difficult to refute. In addition, harmful parasites, bacteria, molds, and/or viruses can contribute. All the infectious invaders need to be uncovered, identified, and treated. Equally important, autistic children must be evaluated for a variety of allergies and treated accordingly. Many parents may think this is too aggressive, time consuming, or expensive, but the results are certain to be worth the effort.

COW'S MILK . . . DOES IT REALLY DO A BODY GOOD?

Although Frank A. Oski, M.D., director of the Department of Pediatrics at Johns Hopkins University School of Medicine, was a strong advocate of mainstream medicine, he suspected that most infants who consume cow's milk develop "mini" gastrointestinal bleeding, and those with a significant loss of iron and red blood cells can develop anemia. When consumed during the first two years of life, inappropriate brain development can occur. He hypothesized that, since iron is an essential nutrient for the formation of a child's brain and nervous system, the microvascular gut damage that accompanies cow milk consumption can cause a loss of blood and iron, leading to brain and nervous system problems. Other physicians agree, but they are unaware of the bigger picture.

Instead, the insults are consistent with the microscopic bleeding and inflammation of the gut wall that accompanies leaky gut syndrome (chapter 4). So, it appears that cow milk consumption encourages candidiasis and leaky gut syndrome; a prominent ingredient is *lactose*, a mild sugar that nourishes disease-causing yeast. In addition, cow's milk is known to be one of the five most common food *antigens*; as an allergy-inducing food, it can induce substantial inflammation. When all these undesirable effects are combined, consuming cow's milk instigates inflammation, upsets the gut flora, and nourishes disease-causing yeast, promoting candidiasis.

Moreover, research reveals children exposed to cow's milk formulas early in life are more likely to have *insulin autoantibodies*, which are often the first sign of islet cell autoimmunity in prediabetic children. In short, early exposure to cow's milk is a risk factor for type 1 diabetes. Why might this occur? Cow's milk contains *bovine insulin*, which cross-reacts with human insulin. When consumed early in life, before a child's immunity is mature, the presence of bovine insulin can trigger the production of antibodies against it in susceptible children. If these antibodies also react against human insulin, they can assault the pancreas (its beta cells), leading to type 1 diabetes (chapter 11).

Human beings have consumed cow's milk (another mammal) for thousands of years. Yet, except for us, no other mammals drink milk after infancy. This implies that cow's milk is not as beneficial as most people think. In fact, 50 percent of human beings do not consume any dairy products and do not have a calcium deficiency. Unfortunately, about 51 percent of dairy products are contaminated with antibiotics, and manufacturers often use "recombinant bovine growth hormone" (rBGH) to increase milk production within their cows. Obviously, consuming milk is not without risk. As a result, The Physicians Committee for Responsible Medicine wants to "free Americans from dairy products by the year 2050."

Although antibiotics kill the infectious invaders that contaminate milk, they also kill your beneficial bacteria when you drink the same milk. Antibiotics are one of the prominent risk factors for developing candidiasis (chapter 2). Why is rBGH a problem? Although it increases milk production, scientific evidence from Europe indicates that rBGH milk contains *pus* from cow udder infections. When an ailing cow is discovered, antibiotics are routinely administered to combat their infection. Since these medications are systemically absorbed, saturating the cow's cells and tissues, they enter their secretions, producing *antibiotic-containing milk*. So, the milk from these cows is likely to be contaminated with antibiotics. Fortunately, most Westernized countries sell milk labeled "rBGH-free."

Cow's milk is not an innocent food. Its consumption can instigate or promote candidiasis, especially leaky gut syndrome. In some children, this can cause anemia as well as brain and nervous system problems. In susceptible children, it may increase their likelihood of type 1 diabetes. When you consider its adverse consequences, cow's milk "might *not* do a body good."

TOURETTE SYNDROME

Tourette syndrome is a neurological disorder that generally arises in children between ages 2 and 17 and affects them throughout their life. Its motor symptoms involve rapid, involuntary movements called *tics*. Classically, this includes *vocal tics*, which are expressed as sniffling, throat clearing, repeating words or phrases of others, shouting, or even obscenities. Recent estimates report 0.3 percent of American children ages 3 to 17 have the diagnosis, but studies imply that there are about an equal number of undiagnosed children. Overall, it is thought to affect at least 1 percent of the worldwide population.

For years, tics were embraced as nervous habits. Yet, research suggests that Tourette syndrome is a legitimate neurological disorder reflecting a *chemical imbalance* within the brain. This is supported by the fact that certain medications, *dopamine antagonists* and *alpha-adrenergic drugs*, are routinely used to treat tics. Since they do not work in all cases and are not curative, they must not be addressing the actual cause of the problem. So, what is responsible? Since candidiasis can directly and indirectly alter the brain's chemistry and its functioning (chapter 10), there is likely to be a *candidiasis–Tourette syndrome connection.*

Is there evidence? Tourette syndrome is related to attention-deficit/hyperactivity disorder (ADHD), which also involves stuttering and *dyslexia*, a learning disability that includes reading and spelling confusion. Since there is a *Tourette syndrome–ADHD connection* and a *candidiasis-ADHD connection*, there is a *candidiasis-ADHD-Tourette syndrome connection*. A significant percentage of children with learning difficulties have impaired immunity, and candidiasis can cause *metabolic immunosuppression* (chapter 14), which adds further support. In addition, Tourette syndrome is associated with *obsessive-compulsive disorder*, a condition that can be a mental manifestation of candidiasis (chapter 10). Keep in mind, candidiasis often includes the participation of other infectious invaders; for example, an infection with a harmful bacteria called *Streptococcus* may trigger Tourette syndrome in susceptible children.

Although an *infection* with disease-causing yeast is likely to be the primary cause, its *allergic* consequences strongly contribute. One of the prominent instigators of Tourette syndrome is allergies, including sensitivities and hypersensitivities to foods, pollens, dust, chemicals, and more. Since there is a *candidiasis-allergy connection* (chapter 16) and a *candidiasis–food allergy connection* (chapter 4), this strengthens the case for a *candidiasis–Tourette syndrome connection*. Confusingly, typical allergy symptoms may not be present, so a high index of suspicion in required.

Since illness cannot occur without a cause, the available evidence points to candidiasis. How can it promote Tourette syndrome? Disease-causing yeast, with or without other infectious invaders, produce numerous chemicals (metabolic) and allergy-inducing substances, as well as cause allergic reactions, that can adversely affect the functioning and development of a child's brain and nervous system. The symptoms vary from one youngster to another and depend on a variety of factors. Usually, the younger the child, the more impaired they are. Conversely, the sooner treatment begins, the greater their chance for improvement.

In 1994, S. G. Crawford et al. determined that children with reading difficulties and their families often suffer with immune and autoimmune disorders, especially involving the gut and thyroid gland. So, *subclinical hypothyroidism* has been associated with ADHD, and many cases improved with thyroid hormone replacement therapy. Yet, this more likely reflects the direct or indirect consequences of candidiasis causing endocrine (hormone) disturbances (chapter 11). Yes, a lack of thyroid hormone is important to treat, but candidiasis is the real problem to be addressed. After all, the existence of a *candidiasis-hypothyroidism connection* and a *hypothyroidism-ADHD connection* implies that candidiasis, hypothyroidism, and ADHD are all related.

Although Tourette syndrome has been a mystery, an infection with disease-causing yeast seems to be its cause, with or without the adverse contributions of other infectious invaders. In addition, its sufferers often have a variety of allergies, including sensitivities and hypersensitivities to disease-causing yeast, harmful molds, foods, pollens, dust, chemicals, and more, which should be identified and treated accordingly. Moreover, sufferers of Tourette syndrome and other psychological manifestations are frequently found to have hypothyroidism. Yes, treatment with thyroid hormone replacement may be beneficial, but addressing their candidiasis is likely to provide the real cure.

A HEALTHY CHILD IS A CANDIDIASIS-FREE CHILD

Children's bodies are resilient, having accumulated less long-term damage than adults. Yet, it is normal for a child to have an occasional cold or two, until their immunity matures. In contrast, a chronic or recurring medical problem is *not* normal and implies something is amiss. Since children are not usually able to fully explain their symptoms or what they are feeling, cases of childhood candidiasis are often difficult to identify. An adult might admit to having excess gas and bloating, while a child may just hold their stomach or complain of a "bellyache." Unless a physician is familiar with candidiasis, they are likely to address the symptoms and totally overlook their cause. In the meantime, the child's malady worsens. So, with respect to candidiasis within children, a high index of suspicion must always be present.

It is easy to be fooled into thinking that candidiasis only affects adults. Since children are susceptible to the same risk factors, they develop and express candidiasis just as often. Disease-causing yeast do not discriminate and readily seize any opportunity to cause harm, especially in the immature bodies of children. The manifestations of candidiasis specific to children include chronic ear infections, attention-deficit/hyperactivity disorder, autism, and Tourette syndrome. Once mainstream medicine appreciates the *candidiasis-pediatric connection*, most of these childhood maladies can be properly treated and eliminated.

If you are a parent, what can you do to help your child avoid candidiasis? Make sure your child establishes a population of beneficial bacteria as soon as possible. Your child should take antibiotics only if necessary. A lack of beneficial bacteria and the use of antibiotics encourage the colonization of disease-causing yeast. You might want to avoid giving your child cow's milk and products that include it or foods that contain yeast and molds, like cheese. Certainly, do not feed them excesses of sugar or sugar-containing foods, which readily nourish disease-causing yeast. With a little effort, you can make sure your child never develops candidiasis and enjoys their food.

What if your child has candidiasis? The first step is to take your child to a candidiasis-minded physician. In many childhood maladies, in addition to an infection with disease-causing yeast, allergies are playing a major role. It is important to address both the infection and allergies. Moreover, children are not immune to harmful parasites, bacteria, molds, and/or viruses, and these must be identified and addressed as well. When needed, you should not be afraid to let your child use a systemic antifungal medication that is prescribed by a knowledgeable and experienced candidiasis-minded physician; this is the best way to eliminate disease-causing yeast from their tissues and blood, avoiding a future relapse.

If your child never develops candidiasis, they are likely to have few health problems, other than an occasional cold or two. Conversely, if your child has candidiasis, good health can be reclaimed, but it may take some time, so patience is required.

CHAPTER 13

Female Genitourinary Problems

Candidiasis is not exclusive to women, but with respect to the genitourinary system, women do suffer with candidiasis-related problems more than men.

The genitals, the organs of reproduction and their accessories, are essential for the continued existence of our species. In contrast, the urinary system functions to eliminate waste products and excess water, and includes the kidneys, ureters, bladder, and urethra. Together, these comprise the *genitourinary system*. Like other areas of the body, this system can be directly colonized with disease-causing yeast as well as indirectly affected by the *infectious* and *allergic* contributions of candidiasis elsewhere within the body.

Because of their anatomy and physiology, women can develop and manifest numerous candidiasis-related genitourinary disturbances, including vaginitis, dysmenorrhea, vulvodynia, endometriosis, infertility, PMS, chronic or recurring urinary tract infections, and interstitial cystitis. These manifestations comprise the *candidiasis-genitourinary connection*.

To be complete, clinical reports also support a connection between candidiasis and prostatitis, balanitis, balanoposthitis, epididymitis, epididymo-orchitis, premature ejaculation, partial and complete male impotence (including decreased sperm production), decreased libido, female frigidity, and orgasmic abnormalities in both sexes. Although a lack of space prevents a discussion of these topics, candidiasis sufferers have improved or cured many of these maladies with treatment, so their connection to candidiasis should not be ignored.

VAGINITIS & VAGINOSIS

Almost 30 percent of American women between ages 14 and 49 suffer with vaginitis or vaginosis, accounting for about 10 million doctor visits a year. The worldwide prevalence is 23 to 29 percent.

Vaginitis is a disease process with inflammation of the vagina or vaginal tissues. Symptoms can include a vaginal discharge or secretion, odor, itching or irritation, burning sensations, uncomfortable to painful sexual intercourse (dyspareunia), and painful urination (dysuria). In contrast, *vaginosis* sufferers have no inflammation even with significant symptoms. The most common types are bacterial vaginosis, vulvovaginal candidiasis, and trichomoniasis. Less than 10 percent involve noninfectious causes, and result from atrophy, irritants, allergies, and inflammatory processes.

Before vaginitis is officially diagnosed, it is essential to distinguish it from a *urinary tract infection,* which usually elicits *internal* pain during urination. Although a urinary tract infection is rarely dangerous, it is concerning because its problematic infectious invader(s) can travel from the bladder up the urinary tract to infect one or both kidneys, precipitating dire consequences. By contrast, vaginitis/vaginosis is about five times more prevalent and involves *external* pain. Although infrequent, both maladies can cause illness in the same woman.

Even though bacteria may be present, most vaginal *infections* are promoted by disease-causing yeast because the mucous membranes of the vagina are an excellent environment (microbiome) for their colonization. In turn, the symptoms of vulvovaginal candidiasis often include uncomfortable itching, a burning sensation, and an odorless, white, "cheese-like" discharge. *Trichomonas vaginalis* is a parasite responsible for the remaining cases and is usually (not exclusively) transmitted sexually. *Nonspecific vaginitis* is often ascribed to *Gardnerella vaginalis*, but other infectious invaders can participate, including gonorrhea, chlamydia, and the herpesviruses. In contrast, *allergic vaginitis* encompasses vaginal irritation without any infectious invaders or obvious inflammation, and may involve sensitivities or hypersensitivities to disease-causing yeast, harmful molds, environmental substances, chemicals, and foods. These two extremes are not exclusive because many cases of infectious vaginitis also include the participation of allergies, so this should always be considered. Understandably, allergy-related vaginitis only resolves after the allergy-inducing (antigenic) substances are identified and treated.

The remaining type of vaginitis is different from the other two, although they can overlap. *Hormonal vaginitis* typically occurs in postmenopausal women and those without ovaries (from surgical removal). After a woman goes through the menopausal transition, diminished estrogen production cannot appropriately stimulate her vaginal epithelium, causing it to thin (atrophy). As a result, the symptoms of hormonal vaginitis include painful intercourse, vaginal itching, dryness, and burning. Rarely, there is a watery discharge.

The most prominent form of vaginitis is *candidiasis* related. Studies show almost 70 percent of females suffer with vulvovaginal candidiasis at least once in their lifetime, and it will occur multiple times in about 50 percent of women. Moreover, since its incidence has greatly increased, there has been a significant decline in trichomonas and gonorrhea vaginitis. The increase reflects the greater prevalence of candidiasis in general. Many of the risk factors (chapter 2) that promote candidiasis disturb the gut and vaginal microbiomes, encouraging the colonization of disease-causing yeast within these areas (and others), especially the use of antibiotics. Most women have their first (as well as subsequent) vaginal yeast infection while taking or after using an antibiotic. Like the gut, the vaginal tissues are normally supposed to be colonized with beneficial bacteria, microorganisms that compete with most infectious invaders (explaining the historical use of yogurt douches for women with vulvovaginal candidiasis). When the beneficial vaginal bacteria are disturbed or killed by antibiotics, disease-causing yeast are permitted to reproduce and colonize their surroundings.

The vagina's proximity to the anus readily allows disease-causing yeast and other infectious invaders to directly spread from the gut to infect the vagina. This explains the recurring nature of *Candida* vaginitis, and why most cases cannot be cured without eradicating *Candida albicans* from the gut. Although the vagina is where symptoms are experienced, it appears the gut is the reservoir for the disease-causing yeast and other infectious invaders that colonize the vaginal tissues (except for any transmitted by sex). As candidiasis has increased, so has candidiasis-related vaginitis. To eliminate vulvovaginal candidiasis and its symptoms, treatments and remedies aimed at eradicating disease-causing yeast within a woman's vagina only provide temporary relief. The perpetual presence of disease-causing yeast within the gut is a continuous source of reinfection, until they are eliminated.

Disease-causing yeast colonize the vagina because they have, especially *Candida albicans*, enzymes that assist their adherence and invasion into the vagina's mucosal surface, causing infectious disturbances and inflammation. (Historically, vinegar has been used as a douche. Supposedly, it works by destroying the adhesion enzymes, hindering disease-causing yeast from sticking to the vaginal wall. Also, by making the vagina more acidic, vinegar impedes the transformation of *Candida albicans* into its invasive form.)

The vagina is not completely defenseless. Certain immune cells (neutrophils), in the presence of lactoferrin-containing cervical mucus, have anti-*Candida* activity. In normal women, disease-causing yeast trigger the release of certain cellular chemicals that boost vaginal immunity. Research reveals women with recurring vulvovaginal candidiasis have altered levels of these chemicals. Therefore, impaired vaginal immunity contributes to recurring vulvovaginal candidiasis. Disease-causing yeast can promote impaired vaginal immunity. Research demonstrates *Candida albicans* has a specific cell wall glycoprotein (*mannan*) that strongly inhibits cellular immunity. Equally concerning, disease-causing yeast can produce and release numerous harmful substances; for example, *gliotoxin* is an immune system-suppressing substance produced by *Candida albicans* and other fungi (chapter 10). Women with severe vulvovaginal candidiasis were found to have significant levels of gliotoxin, which can impair their vagina's immunity and prolong their infection with disease-causing yeast. To summarize, disease-causing yeast usually spread from the gut to infect the vagina and impair its immunity. Once its defenses are compromised, vulvovaginal candidiasis results.

Candida albicans is the most prominent vaginal infectious invader; it is present 40 to 75 percent of the time, depending on the patient population studied. Other disease-causing yeast have been found to cause vaginitis, including *Candida tropicalis, Candida guilliermondii, Candida glabrata, Candida parapsilosis*, and even *Saccharomyces cerevisiae* (common baker's and brewer's yeast). Considering this variety, in 1995, P. Nyirjesy et al. commented, "Because non-*Candida albicans* species are responsible for a significant number of chronic fungal infections and are more resistant to therapy with fluconazole (Diflucan), fungal cultures are a valuable aid in confirming the diagnosis and selecting appropriate therapy." Fortunately, these researchers found that vaginitis involving non-*Candida albicans* species organisms could be eliminated with boric acid suppositories in 85 percent of their patients. Unfortunately, the suppositories do not address their gut reservoir of disease-causing yeast, so relapses are likely. Depending on the specific infectious invader, medication and/or natural anti-candidiasis agents can be used to achieve a much greater and longer-lasting cure rate (chapter 18).

What about allergic vaginitis? Its cause is often mysterious, forcing the women with it to suffer endlessly; after all, if the cause is not addressed, it cannot be cured. An unknown cause does not mean one does not exist. Since there is a *candidiasis-allergy connection* (chapter 16), as well as a *candidiasis–allergic rhinitis connection* (chapter 6), it seems likely allergic vaginitis is candidiasis-related. Indeed, for most candidiasis sufferers, it is an *infection* with *allergic* consequences.

How do vaginal allergies arise? The female genital tract has its own immune tissues and immunity. In addition to immune cells, the vagina has antibody-associated (humoral) immunity. *Immunoglobulin A* (IgA) is the antibody that most frequently protects the interior surface of the vagina. The vagina can produce IgA antibodies against disease-causing yeast. The prolonged presence of *Candida albicans* can promote the continuous production of IgA anti-*Candida* antibodies, causing inflammation and symptoms. In contrast, some researchers discovered a high correlation between vulvovaginal candidiasis and the presence of vaginal IgE antibodies. Regardless of the antibody, vaginal allergies can arise and accompany vaginal candidiasis. Yet, there are exceptions.

Research reveals estrogen suppresses the production of these antibodies. Therefore, the level of these antibodies is often lower during ovulation and much greater in the post-ovulatory state. Why is this significant? The sex hormones can affect cervical-vaginal antibody levels, which is why a woman's symptoms may vary during her menstrual cycle. In contrast, women with vulvovaginal candidiasis that results from another disease-causing yeast may have low levels of anti-*Candida* antibodies, since they are primarily targeted against *Candida albicans*. Does this mean these women do not have antibody-mediated immunity? No, it simply means they are not making anti-*Candida* antibodies. In fact, they may be producing antibodies targeted against other disease-causing yeast; unless these are measured, they will not be identified.

In addition to antibodies, women with chronic or recurring vulvovaginal candidiasis often have excess *prostaglandin E2* (PGE2); it inhibits immunity and stimulates disease-causing yeast to transform into their invasive form. Excesses encourage vulvovaginal candidiasis, favoring its continuous presence and creating a vicious cycle. Since allergies induce excesses of PGE2, women with vulvovaginal candidiasis must be suffering with vaginal allergies. In fact, its amount correlates with the levels of allergy related IgE antibodies. What does this mean? Simply put, women with chronic or recurring vulvovaginal candidiasis have vaginal allergies, especially to disease-causing yeast. This illustrates the importance of testing sufferers for sensitivities to disease-causing yeast and harmful molds as well as a variety of other substances. In addition to eliminating their disease-causing yeast, these women should receive desensitization (allergy) injections, or they will perpetually react to their allergy-inducing substances; even though their infection is gone, their allergies will cause symptoms. Immunotherapy (chapter 18) is valuable and frequently mandatory to successfully resolve this malady, whether a woman's allergies are overt or subtle. After all, vaginal tissues can produce antibodies against numerous fungal organisms, and if desensitization therapy is not used, a woman's allergy-related symptoms are likely to persist. Yes, there is a *candidiasis–allergic vulvovaginitis connection*.

Furthermore, hormonal vaginitis can also be a manifestation of candidiasis because there is a *candidiasis-endocrine connection* (chapter 11). Candidiasis is associated with a variety of endocrine disturbances, including an estrogen deficiency. *Candida albicans* (and other disease-causing yeast) has a *protein* that *binds corticosterone* and *progesterone* with high affinity. It also has an *estrogen-binding protein* that attaches to mammalian estrogens with high affinity. So, disease-causing yeast are hormone sensitive. This explains why candidiasis often worsens during steroid hormone treatment, birth control use, multiple pregnancies, and other situations of steroid and hormone excess. These intracellular binding proteins can stimulate disease-causing yeast to transform into their invasive form (chapter 11). Although speculative, the female hormones may also increase or accelerate the reproduction of disease-causing yeast, their survival time, or their ability to instigate illness. This demonstrates that candidiasis is influenced by the hormonal status of its host.

When you add all the ways disease-causing yeast can instigate and promote problems, it appears most vaginal disturbances must involve candidiasis. If someone suffers with this problem, the disease-causing yeast within their vagina must be eliminated and so must their relatives within their gut to avoid reinfections. Sufferers should be evaluated for allergies to disease-causing yeast and harmful molds and various other substances. Keep in mind, certain clothing may contribute to their problem. For example, women who wear panty hose experience about three times the incidence of vaginal yeast infections; wearing panty hose prevents drying, creating a wonderful microbiome for disease-causing yeast.

Fortunately, most women who have received a comprehensive anti-candidiasis program aimed at treating their infection and allergies have eliminated this annoying and uncomfortable medical malady. If you suffer with this problem, knowledge of the *candidiasis-vulvovaginitis connection* and seeking out appropriate treatment can lead you to a similar success.

DYSMENORRHEA

Many women experience menstrual pains of varying degrees. Although some consider this part of being a woman, good health and dysmenorrhea (difficult and painful menstruation) do not go hand and hand. The prevalence of dysmenorrhea varies greatly; estimates range from 16 to 91 percent in women of reproductive age, with severe pain in 2 to 29 percent of the women studied. Overall, 84.1 percent of women admit that they have had menstrual pain, and 43.1 percent state they have had it numerous times.

The *primary* form of dysmenorrhea involves a functional disturbance, inflammation, new growth(s), and/or other anatomical factors. *Secondary* dysmenorrhea may result from inflammation, infection, tumors, and anatomical or orthopedic problems. Both types are closely related. Because of their potential lethality, professional evaluation is mandatory to rule out cancerous or abnormal growths. (Susan M. Lark, M.D., further classifies it into three distinct groups, including primary spasmodic, primary congestive, and secondary; a discussion of each is beyond the scope of this book.)

Healthy women do not have dysmenorrhea, so when it is present, something must be amiss. Since a woman's menstrual cycle and menstruation are regulated by her hormones, the presence of pain implies that something is wrong on the endocrine (hormone) level. Because there is a *candidiasis-endocrine connection* (chapter 11), candidiasis can cause the hormone disturbances that accompany dysmenorrhea.

Yet, more is occurring than just a hormone disturbance. During menstruation, dysmenorrhea sufferers have significantly greater amounts of *prostaglandin F2 alpha* (PGF2 alpha), a substance that promotes uterine contractions. Because it can trigger irritable bowel syndrome symptoms, a major candidiasis manifestation (chapter 4), disease-causing yeast may be responsible for surpluses of this inflammatory substance. Since most dysmenorrhea sufferers also have candidiasis, PGF2 alpha excesses must be associated with both conditions. Moreover, increased amounts of PGE2 occurs in the presence of allergies, including vaginal allergies, discussed in the previous section. Elevated amounts of both substances support a *candidiasis-dysmenorrhea connection*.

PGF2 alpha levels are reduced by magnesium, so dysmenorrhea sufferers must have a magnesium deficiency. Because magnesium keeps the uterine muscle (*myometrium*) relaxed, correcting a magnesium deficiency inhibits the muscle spasms and spasticity that produce the symptoms of dysmenorrhea. Although a lack of dietary magnesium can cause deficiencies, malabsorption is usually responsible. It is common among candidiasis sufferers (chapter 4). In addition to a lowered concentration of magnesium, chronic candidiasis often promotes a lowered concentration of calcium. This frequently involves a hormone disturbance, called *functional hypoparathyroidism* (chapter 11); the mineral concentrations appear normal within the blood but are decreased within the cells and tissues. In short, calcium and magnesium deficiencies commonly arise during chronic candidiasis, and, because their concentrations within the blood are normal, this is usually overlooked.

So, dysmenorrhea is likely to result from hormone disturbances and a deficiency of magnesium. Since there is a *candidiasis-endocrine connection* and candidiasis can cause malabsorption, leading to a magnesium (and calcium) deficiency, this supports a *candidiasis-dysmenorrhea connection*. In the absence of a significant abnormality or exceptional disturbance, dysmenorrhea is often associated with candidiasis; most sufferers will be found to be candidiasis sufferers. When their disease-causing yeast are appropriately addressed and their magnesium deficiency is corrected, their dysmenorrhea commonly disappears. In addition, it is important to address the contributions of allergies to disease-causing yeast and harmful molds because they may exacerbate the symptoms. When they are treated from this perspective, most dysmenorrhea sufferers improve substantially.

VULVODYNIA

Vulvodynia is a malady that involves chronic discomfort of a woman's *vulva*, her external genitals, including her vagina. This condition usually includes a feeling of "rawness," burning, irritation, and stinging. Its severity can range from uncomfortable to debilitating.

A study in the United States noted that almost 16 percent of women experience this medical malady throughout their lives, while 8 percent of women have symptoms at some point in their life by age 40. Unfortunately, its victims are frequently told, "We're sorry, but not much can be done for you." On the contrary, William G. Crook, M.D., author of *The Yeast Connection*, believed that the prevalence of vulvodynia was so great that it warranted an entire chapter in his book *The Yeast Connection and the Woman*.

Vulvodynia is not a rare or limited condition. In 1999, Julius F. Metts, M.D., stated, "Vulvodynia is a problem most family physicians can expect to encounter. It is a syndrome of unexplained vulvar pain, frequently accompanied by physical disabilities, limitation of daily activities, sexual dysfunction, and psychologic distress." Since vulvodynia involves symptoms like vaginitis, it is likely to be associated with candidiasis.

What causes the pain? *Oxalates* are chemical irritants. Studies have found elevated urine levels of *oxalates* (hyperoxaluria) in vulvodynia patients. The consensus is that they are probably nonspecific irritants that aggravate the pain rather than being the cause of the condition. Other contributing factors are increased sexual sensitivity and abnormal skin conditions. In contrast, given its *infectious* and *allergic* consequences, candidiasis is the primary problem.

To appreciate this, you must know that there are four groups of vulvodynia sufferers, as follows:

- **Candidiasis sufferers** are one of the most important, and most physicians think pain in the vulvar region reflects vaginitis. When a vaginal culture appears "negative" for infectious invaders, these women are rarely treated with an anti-candidiasis program or antifungal medications. As a result, the origin of their misery is commonly overlooked.
- **Hypersensitivity vulvodynia** is typically triggered by one or more allergies; it usually involves sensitivities to foods and chemicals. Yet, the presence of allergies to disease-causing yeast and harmful molds makes candidiasis highly likely. Most cases of hypersensitivity vulvodynia are closely related to the candidiasis sufferers' group, and characteristics of both groups are often demonstrated simultaneously.
- **Metabolic vulvodynia** involves physiological disturbances associated with an abnormal metabolism of oxalates. Many of the changes may reflect the presence of candidiasis; the existence of a *candidiasis-gout connection* (chapter 9) demonstrates that candidiasis sufferers can have elevated oxalate levels. Therefore, this group may be related to the first two groups.
- **Neuromuscular vulvodynia** sufferers have neurological or muscular contributions to their pain. Frequently, these women have strained or "pulled" a groin muscle. Improper healing forms scar tissue that may encourage chronic pain. It can also result from a traumatic event, such as a fall. In return, a favorable response occurs with physical therapy, muscle massage, and/or muscle relaxants. Like dysmenorrhea, some of these women may have a magnesium deficiency and can be candidiasis sufferers as well.

The women in the candidiasis and hypersensitivity groups overlap those in the metabolic group. This is understandable because candidiasis is an *infection* with *allergic* consequences that also involves metabolic disturbances. Since elevated oxalate levels are a metabolic disturbance, it implies that hyperoxaluria is a consequence of candidiasis. Except for the neuromuscular category, vulvodynia patients should benefit from an anti-candidiasis approach. Yet, since magnesium deficiencies may be present in some neuromuscular vulvodynia sufferers, many of these women may similarly benefit from an anti-candidiasis approach.

Although vulvodynia has been a mystery, chronic candidiasis seems to play a big role in most vulvodynia sufferers. In addition to an infection with disease-causing yeast, allergies must be considered because a significant amount of the vulvar pain is allergy-induced. In other words, most vulvodynia sufferers demonstrate relief when their disease-causing yeast are eliminated, but persistent allergic reactions can cause perpetual symptoms, discussed previously. As a result, desensitization (allergy) injections are essential. Fortunately, as a woman's candidiasis and allergies disappear, so will her vulvar pain.

ENDOMETRIOSIS

If you are a woman with this problem, you are well acquainted with its main symptom, which is *pain, pain*, and *more pain*. It is estimated that 2 to 10 percent of American women between ages 25 and 40 have it, while roughly 10 percent of women and girls of reproductive age suffer with it worldwide. Almost 200 million women are estimated to experience severe pain during intercourse, chronic pain within their pelvic region, pain with bowel movements, and pain with exercise. This description barely describes the amount of misery it involves. To add insult, many endometriosis sufferers are infertile.

Endometriosis is the presence of an "ectopic endometrium located in various sites throughout the pelvis or within the abdominal wall." *Ectopic* means abnormal or out of place. So, this condition involves anomalous uterine tissue in areas where it should not be, including virtually every organ of the female genital tract, the peritoneum (the sac lining the abdominal cavity), and even the gastrointestinal tract. Mainstream medicine accepts that most cases of endometriosis are related to dysmenorrhea. Since there is a *candidiasis-dysmenorrhea connection*, this implies that there must also be a *candidiasis-endometriosis connection*.

How does endometriosis develop? In 1920, John Sampson proposed the *theory of reflux menstruation*, more commonly called the *theory of retrograde menstruation*; instead of draining normally out of the uterus opening (the *cervix*), menstrual fluid backs up or flows retrograde into the fallopian tubes, and then enters the peritoneal cavity. Endometrial cells are carried with the fluid, entering areas where they should not. If the conditions encourage their proliferation, sites of ectopic tissue form.

Looking deeper, why do some women have an abnormal menstrual flow? Often, this probably reflects the continuous inflammation of their endometrial tissues, especially their cervix, preventing their menstrual fluid from draining appropriately. The inflammation is probably secondary to an infection, which is likely to involve the participation of disease-causing yeast. Candidiasis also instigates localized allergies (within the vagina, cervix, and uterus), exacerbating the inflammation. Both its *infectious* and *allergic* consequences can promote an *inflammatory* environment that inhibits the normal drainage of menstrual fluid into the vagina. As a result, some fluid and cells may flow upward into the fallopian tubes, progressing further into inappropriate areas. Many women are suspected of experiencing these circumstances at one time or another, but only a small percentage develop endometriosis. Regardless of its frequency, the presence of any anomalous endometrial cells and tissue within areas other than the uterus should be considered abnormal.

Since women with healthy immunity do not have this problem, it implies that endometriosis sufferers have abnormal immunity. In fact, endometriosis has many similarities with cancer—most notably, the presence of abnormal cells. In both maladies, the immune system does not recognize or appropriately respond to the abnormal cells, and they are not eliminated. Since there is a *candidiasis–impaired immunity connection* (chapter 14), two prerequisites are needed for candidiasis to cause endometriosis. It must promote *infectious and/or allergic inflammation* within the uterus, causing congestion. In turn, this leads to improper drainage of menstrual fluid and cells, encouraging their retrograde passage up the fallopian tubes. For these cells to colonize, proliferate, and function within these areas, candidiasis must *impair the immune system*, keeping it from recognizing and eliminating these anomalous cells. This supports a *candidiasis-endometriosis connection*.

It is estimated that 5 to 15 percent of endometriosis sufferers have gut lesions, including growths within the rectum, sigmoid colon, ileum, appendix, cecum, and so on. Since gastrointestinal maladies are common among candidiasis sufferers, these two conditions are related. Dr. C. Orian

Truss was one of the first to note that a high percentage of endometriosis patients also suffer with candidiasis. In Mary L. Ballweg's 1988 book *Overcoming Endometriosis*, a chapter titled "The Endometriosis-Candidiasis Link" stated that endometriosis sufferers often respond to anti-candidiasis therapy. It also included the following quote from Dr. Truss: "It is unquestionable that there's a very high association of endometriosis with chronic candidiasis." Additional observations note that women with endometriosis often experience asthma and eczema, food and chemical hypersensitivities, autoimmune diseases, chronic fatigue syndrome, and viral illnesses. In short, endometriosis sufferers frequently have other candidiasis manifestations related to impaired immunity. In 1996, Ballweg took a stronger stand in an Endometriosis Association newsletter: "In looking back over the Association's sixteen-year history, it's fair to say that no other approach to endometriosis treatment has given as consistent and long-term positive results as has treatment for *Candida albicans* allergy/infection and its related problems."

The prominent Endometriosis Association admitted that endometriosis is closely related to candidiasis, so it indirectly endorsed a *candidiasis-endometriosis connection*. The prime locations for the colonization of disease-causing yeast are within the gastrointestinal tract and the female genital tract. These are also the most common areas adversely affected with the symptoms of candidiasis. Understanding this association makes the *candidiasis-endometriosis connection* difficult to ignore. In fact, endometriosis sufferers treated with a comprehensive anti-candidiasis approach often have dramatic improvements as well as cures.

INFERTILITY

Infertility describes a condition in which an ovulating woman cannot get pregnant despite having carefully timed unprotected sex for at least one year. It also pertains to a woman incapable of maintaining a pregnancy to full term. In the United States, it involves about 19 percent of heterosexual women ages 15 to 49 with no prior births. It is a worldwide condition, and its rates are rising. It is estimated that 48 million couples have this problem globally. The pain is often *psychological*, not physical, and involves the frustration of not becoming pregnant, not completing a pregnancy, not giving birth, not having a child, and not creating a family.

The main cause of infertility is *polycystic ovary syndrome* (PCOS). According to the Centers for Disease Control and Prevention, it affects about 6 to 12 percent of American women of childbearing age (as many as 5 million). PCOS involves an inability to ovulate and excesses of free testosterone (*anovulation* and *hyperandrogenism*). It is the most common endocrine disturbance among young women, but its cause remains unknown. When an illness has an obscure origin, think candidiasis. Women with PCOS often have many metabolic problems, including central obesity, *hypertension*, *abnormal lipid profiles*, *glucose intolerance*, and *atherosclerosis*. Since all these problems have connections with candidiasis (chapters 7, 11, and 14), including androgen problems, this supports a *candidiasis-infertility connection*.

Other causes for infertility are also well known, especially *pelvic inflammatory disease*, which is an infection within the uterus, fallopian tubes, and adjacent pelvic structures. Infections with *chlamydia* are prominent instigators of this condition and should be diagnosed and treated. Yet, what is the cause of infertility when a woman has no bacterial infection, or it has been treated and she still cannot become pregnant?

Instead of bacteria, an infection with disease-causing yeast is much more likely to cause infertility. Women who cannot become pregnant often have other common manifestations of candidiasis like irritable bowel syndrome, asthma, chronic sinusitis, acne, psoriasis, fatigue, and more. So, infertility sufferers are likely to be candidiasis sufferers. In fact, an abundance of reports confirm anti-candidiasis treatment benefits a large percentage of infertility sufferers.

Although many cases of infertility reflect endocrine (hormone) disturbances, candidiasis can disturb one or more of the female hormones and alter the levels of the male hormones (chapter 11). In turn, this can inhibit the release of an egg, causing anovulation. A hormone disturbance can also adversely affect the uterine lining, making the implantation of a fertilized egg impossible or unable to support a fetus. So, candidiasis can *indirectly* instigate or promote infertility by adversely affecting one or more hormones involved with reproduction.

In addition, candidiasis can *directly* cause infertility. By creating biofilms, it can impair the microbiome needed to appropriately fertilize and implant an egg as well as support the development of a fetus. Like the inflammation in endometriosis, the localized *infectious* and *allergic* consequences of disease-causing yeast within a woman's reproductive tract can cause significant inflammation, preventing an egg from being fertilized, implanting, and/or maturing. In addition, IgA-mediated and/or IgE-mediated (allergic) reactions may prevent a fertilized egg from effectively implanting, like the way an intrauterine device (IUD) works—that is, by creating an inflammatory environment and an inhospitable microbiome for the implantation and survival of a fertilized egg. One or more inappropriate prostaglandins may contribute to this process. Moreover, many women with candidiasis have fertility problems that continue even after eliminating their disease-causing yeast until their allergies are treated. Therefore, it is vital to test infertile women for allergies to disease-causing yeast and harmful molds and use desensitization (allergy) injections when appropriate to eliminate their inflammation.

Candidiasis can lead to infertility in another way. Research reveals that some women may be making *infertility-linked antibodies* that cause their uterus to be unreceptive to an embryo; their immune system mistakes the pregnancy for a disease and, as a result, attacks the growing embryo. Since there is a *candidiasis–autoimmune disease connection* (chapter 14), it provides further support for a *candidiasis-infertility connection*. Other research shows that some women have anti-sperm antibodies targeted to assault sperm, preventing it from fertilizing their egg. Although it involves a different autoantibody, the general disturbance is the same.

This brief discussion demonstrates that most infertile women are likely to be candidiasis sufferers. Yes, other infectious invaders may contribute and should be appropriately addressed. Unless there are intrauterine adhesions or scarring, after their candidiasis is diagnosed and completely treated, including both its infectious and allergic consequences, many infertile women discover they can quickly become pregnant.

PREMENSTRUAL SYNDROME (PMS)

The mental symptoms of premenstrual syndrome (PMS) range from mild irritation to severe anxiety and/or depression as well as anger, mood swings, sugar cravings, and more (chapter 10). Since *Candida albicans* (and other disease-causing yeast) have receptors that bind *estrogen* and *progesterone* (as well as corticosteroids), they are sensitive to the female hormones. Disease-causing yeast are most affected just before menstruation when a woman's hormone levels are changing. So, the same hormonal disturbances that encourage the colonization of disease-causing yeast also promote PMS symptoms. In short, there is a *candidiasis-PMS connection*. The undesirable combination of estrogen, progesterone, and candidiasis makes susceptible women likely to manifest depression, anxiety, and anger. Candidiasis can also cause and aggravate a woman's glucose intolerance and its symptoms, including the accompanying fight-or-flight sensations produced by an excessive release of her blood sugar–raising hormones (chapter 11). All of this can create significant symptoms.

The origin of this disturbance is possibly related to the acetaldehyde hypothesis (chapter 10). Basically, disease-causing yeast can produce *ethanol* and *acetaldehyde*. When they are within the blood, these chemicals can enter the brain, where they may alter the concentration, amount, or proportion of one or more of the brain's neurotransmitters. Typically, this produces or increases the neurotransmitters that are responsible for feelings of depression, anxiety, and hostility. In addition, *gliotoxin* may participate and cause similar disturbances.

Certain nutrients are beneficial for sufferers of PMS and other menstrual irregularities. As a result, PMS may represent a dietary deficiency, malabsorption, or the preferential use of these nutrients by disease-causing yeast. Specifics aside, the important point is that a woman's diet may primarily or secondarily contribute to their PMS and its symptoms.

Although the precise origin of PMS is controversial, any woman with more than infrequent or mild PMS is likely to be a candidiasis sufferer, and treating PMS sufferers reveals that most of them do benefit from an anti-candidiasis program.

CHRONIC URINARY TRACT INFECTIONS

Some women develop one *urinary tract infection* (UTI) after another. Other women get a UTI after they have intercourse, which can psychologically and/or physically ruin their love life. Others develop a UTI only once or twice a year, which is something they may tolerate and learn to live with. Although it occurs less commonly, men can have a UTI. Statistics show that between 1990 and 2019, UTI cases per year increased from about 252.2 million to more than 404.6 million. It is estimated that 10 in 25 women (40 percent) and 3 in 25 men (12 percent) will have UTI symptoms during their lifetime.

By definition, a UTI occurs when the urinary tract (usually, the bladder and urethra) becomes infected with harmful bacteria. UTIs are not dangerous unless the infectious invader(s) progresses up the ureters to infect one or both kidneys, instigating severe illness that may become life-threatening. The most associated symptoms are pain with urination (*dysuria*), frequent urination (*urinary frequency*), and a sudden urge to empty the bladder (*urgency*). In contrast, it may not involve any symptoms, especially during pregnancy.

UTIs can occur for a variety of reasons. If it is treated, a one-time infection is usually not of concern. In contrast, chronic or recurring UTIs are not normal. So, something must be happening within the urinary tracts of women who suffer repeatedly. What could it be? The most well-known answer is anatomical; women have a shorter urethra than men, making it easier for bacteria to spread from the opening of their urethra, upward into their bladder. Since the most prevalent harmful bacteria are known inhabitants of the gut (*E. coli*, *Staphylococcus*, *Klebsiella*, *Proteus*, and others), the proximity of a woman's anus to her urethra permits these infectious invaders to readily spread from her anus to the opening of her urethra.

It is important to mention that women with anatomical disturbances are at a much greater risk for UTIs. Typically, their bladders do not empty completely, or they have defects that promote reinfection (like a cystocele). An anatomical disturbance is likely to warrant surgical correction and must not be quickly dismissed or casually overlooked.

In contrast, the urinary tracts of most of women with frequent UTIs do not have anatomical abnormalities. Instead, something is occurring within the bladders of susceptible women that causes them to develop repeated UTIs. What could it be?

First, there is a more pressing question: Is it a coincidence that most UTI sufferers also have some type of gastrointestinal disturbance? No, because the infectious invaders that assault their urinary tracts must come from somewhere. The gut is a colossal breeding ground that can spread infectious invaders from a woman's anus to her urinary tract. After antibiotics are taken for a UTI, it should be gone for good, but this is not what happens, implying that there is still an underlying problem that was not addressed. What is being missed? Like candidiasis within the gut, the urinary tract can become colonized with disease-causing yeast (as well as harmful molds), creating a microbiome predisposed to repeated bacterial infections.

Classically, harmful bacteria are accepted as the sole cause of UTIs, while disease-causing yeast and harmful molds are consistently overlooked or ignored. Regardless of this bias, disease-causing yeast can and do infect the bladder and urinary tract; for example, *Candida albicans* and *Candida glabrata* are the number-one and number-two most common disease-causing yeast involved with UTIs, although others have been noted as well. (Yet, when these infectious invaders are found in a clean-catch urine sample, they are often dismissed as contaminants, even when the woman who performed the test confirms she did it properly.) In fact, research shows that *Candida albicans* and *Candida glabrata* are coconspirators, being synergistic in their behavior; *Candida albicans* releases enzymes that aid the adherence of *Candida glabrata* to the surface of the bladder wall.

After colonizing the urinary tract, disease-causing yeast can enter a synergistic relationship with many harmful bacteria; each benefit from the other's presence and prevent the others from taking over completely. When antibiotics are administered, they might kill the harmful bacteria, but they do not eradicate the disease-causing yeast, which maintains a microbiome highly susceptible to reinfection. Since disease-causing yeast can form colonies that grow in "sheets," creating biofilms, they may physically protect some harmful bacteria from administered antibiotics, explaining why a UTI can reappear as soon as the antibiotic is discontinued; although the active infection is reduced, some harmful bacteria survive to reinfect the urinary tract, and possibly become resistant to the antibiotic in the process.

This also explains why women with this problem often have a flare-up or develop a UTI soon after starting a systemic antifungal medication (like Diflucan); as the disease-causing yeast are killed, the harmful bacteria are no longer inhibited, so they can reproduce and instigate an infection. In fact, if it was not for the disease-causing yeast, harmful bacteria would have little chance of surviving within the bladder. In some people, the disease-causing yeast can invade into the bladder wall, encouraging inflammation and sites of reinfection. In addition, a persistent infection with disease-causing yeast can inflame the urethra and bladder wall, promoting the retention of urine and increasing the likelihood of reinfection. It can also impair the immune system (chapter 14), hindering the body's ability to combat UTIs.

How can disease-causing yeast access the bladder and urinary tract? After initially infecting the urethra, their growth can spread upward into a woman's bladder and progress further. Alternatively, since disease-causing yeast can colonize the tissues and blood of *systemic* candidiasis sufferers, they can enter the vasculature of the kidney, take up residence, and colonize the urinary tract downward, toward the bladder and urethra. Either way, the result is the same. Does this mean every woman with repeated UTIs is a candidiasis sufferer? Most likely, yes. Moreover, this problem is not exclusive to adults; children and infants can also develop UTIs that are precipitated by disease-causing yeast.

In addition to the infection, there is another side to UTIs. This brings us to a question: When is a UTI *not* a UTI? The answer: When it is an allergy. The perpetual symptoms that relate to UTIs can readily reflect the presence of allergies. Normally, the interior of the bladder is supposed to be sterile. Like any other body surface, the colonization of disease-causing yeast (and harmful molds) can instigate inflammation and allergic reactions within the tissues and linings of the bladder and urethra. So, even after the infection is gone, many UTI sufferers still have symptoms until their allergies to disease-causing yeast and harmful mold are appropriately addressed. Some cases are exceptionally complicated, and many layers must be peeled away to achieve success (appendix).

Recurring or chronic UTIs are not normal. Undeniably, candidiasis is the underlying cause of repeated UTIs, with its *infectious* and *allergic* consequences. Yes, harmful bacteria contribute their ill effects, but their mischief is greatly amplified when these troublemakers act together. To achieve long-term wellness, the harmful bacteria and disease-causing yeast must both be treated and eliminated. Therefore, an understanding of this *candidiasis–urinary tract infection connection* will now make it possible to treat most women who suffer with repeated UTIs, freeing them of this annoying problem forever.

INTERSTITIAL CYSTITIS

According to the Mayo Clinic, *interstitial cystitis* (IC) is a chronic condition causing bladder pressure and pain, and sometimes pelvic pain, ranging from mild discomfort to severely debilitating. Since many cases are not diagnosed, the actual number of people who suffer with it worldwide varies from 4 to 12 million. Research indicates that it occurs in about 2 percent of women. Its exact cause is unknown, but many factors are thought to contribute. As an example, a defect within the bladder wall surface may create a "leak" that allows toxic substances within the urine to irritate the wall. Supported by the information in the previous sections, this implicates candidiasis.

Surveys among IC sufferers reveal that their symptoms are more than just pain. For example, one survey showed that they have numerous symptoms, including waking at night two or more times to urinate (85%), urinary urgency (84%), urinary frequency of 15 to 50 times in 24 hours (80%), bladder, urethra, or vagina pain (78%), pain relieved by urinating (57%), painful intercourse (57%), difficulty emptying the bladder (51%), and difficulty initiating urination (47%). In short, IC involves urinary urgency, frequency, and pain that ranges from mild burning or discomfort to excruciating, which can be felt within the bladder, lower abdomen, perineum, pelvis, lower back, and thighs. It often occurs when the bladder is full and is relieved with urination. Menstruation and intercourse appear to aggravate these symptoms, suggesting an endocrine connection.

In the past, IC was not well known and thought to rarely occur, so it is really a recent diagnosis. Despite this, *ulcers* on the floor of the urinary bladder were observed and described by a French physician in 1836. Guy Hunner, a Baltimore gynecologist, reported ulcerative lesions on the urinary bladder wall in 1914, which were later named "Hunner's ulcer." Over the years, these *ulcerative lesions* have become known as IC.

Since the bladder wall inflammation is *not* associated with a bacterial infection, IC is not a common form of cystitis. In fact, this is readily supported because antibiotic therapy routinely *fails* to eliminate the symptoms of IC.

Again, according to mainstream medicine, the cause of IC remains unknown. Although an autoimmune process is suspected, sufferers do not improve with anti-inflammatory or immune-suppressing drugs. Since one-third to one-half of sufferers have *mast cells* (chapter 4) within their bladder wall, it indicates the presence of an allergic process. Mainstream medicine cannot explain what causes this reaction. Lacking further information or insight, IC remains a mystery among mainstream physicians.

Yet, more compelling evidence does exist when you know what to look for. Surveys show that IC sufferers commonly manifest irritable bowel syndrome, spastic colon, abdominal cramping, rheumatoid arthritis, fibromyalgia, asthma, hay fever, and food allergies. All these medical maladies are *strongly associated* with candidiasis (chapters 4, 6, and 9), so IC sufferers appear to be candidiasis sufferers. Is this possible? Yes, because candidiasis is an *infection* with *allergic* consequences. Moreover, chronic UTIs and IC are closely related; their major characteristic symptoms include pain with urination, frequent urination (frequency), and a sudden urge to empty the bladder (urgency). Since there is a *candidiasis–urinary tract infection connection*, this supports the existence of a *candidiasis–interstitial cystitis connection*. The difference is UTIs do not cause ulcerative lesions within the bladder wall, while IC does.

How does candidiasis lead to IC? Like the sufferers of chronic UTIs, the urinary tracts of IC sufferers are also colonized with disease-causing yeast. In IC sufferers, rather than just colonizing the bladder wall surface, the disease-causing yeast invade into, and even through, the bladder mucosa. Like leaky gut syndrome within the gut (chapters 3 and 4), the insults and injury to the bladder wall can progress to *ulcerative IC*, which has been visualized as a fibrous, contracted bladder with a pale surface and ulcers. Since the bladder is supplied with nerves, stretching a bladder with this condition is likely to stimulate the nerves, producing pain, whereas emptying it relieves the pain. Moreover, the presence of allergy-inducing infectious invaders within the bladder wall (mucosa) is likely to cause inflammation and allergic reactions, explaining the presence of mast cells. Since allergies do not arise in every IC sufferer, some sufferers are more susceptible than others. Simply put, IC is a persistent infection with disease-causing yeast within the urinary tract and bladder, involving their invasion into the bladder wall, with or without an allergic response.

There is more evidence to support an association between candidiasis and IC:

- Antibiotics are usually given to most IC sufferers as the first line of therapy. If there is no bacterial infection, why are antibiotics even used? Studies suggest that this approach may additionally damage the bladder wall, but no reasons are given. Antibiotics are a risk factor for the further colonization of disease-causing yeast within the body.
- IC sufferers are suspected of having a history of chronic childhood UTIs, with a parallel history of receiving antibiotics, providing more opportunities to promote the colonization of disease-causing yeast. This implies that chronic UTIs lead to IC. Candidiasis can cause both problems, so it must precede both as well.
- Since disease-causing yeast can colonize and invade into the bladder wall, causing *infectious* and *allergic* consequences, the inflammation that arises can easily represent the body's attempt to confine and combat the disease-causing yeast. Unfortunately, this may cause the generation of self-reactive cells or autoantibodies that mistakenly assault the bladder wall and tissues, promoting injury and damage. The presence of a *candidiasis–autoimmune disease connection* (chapter 14) is consistent with this and readily explains what occurs in some women.
- Toxic substances within the urine can irritate and/or harm the bladder lining. When an external collection bag is surgically implanted to divert urine from the bladder, the inflammation often abates. This sounds like the vulvodynia patients with elevated levels of *oxalate* within their urine, encouraging epithelial reactions that promote inflammation and pain. There is no reason why this metabolic abnormality cannot occur in IC sufferers as well. Alternatively, there may be another reason: the disease-causing yeast may produce substances that are irritating to or cause an inflammatory allergic reaction within the urethra, instigating symptoms.

- Reports from independent physicians confirm that long-term treatment with systemic antifungal medication (Diflucan) aided their IC patients in reducing their symptoms. When IC is treated, eliminating the disease-causing yeast is likely to heal the bladder wall, but it may not stop the IC sufferers' allergies and their symptoms. So, it is important that IC sufferers have their allergies addressed as well, especially their allergies to disease-causing yeast and harmful molds. Therefore, the dual nature of candidiasis, its infectious and allergic contributions, makes a comprehensive approach essential.

When IC is treated, eliminating the disease-causing yeast is likely to heal the bladder wall, but it may not stop the IC sufferers' allergies and their symptoms. So, it is important that IC sufferers have their allergies addressed as well, especially their allergies to disease-causing yeast and harmful molds. Therefore, the dual nature of candidiasis, its infectious and allergic contributions, makes a comprehensive approach essential.

REMOVING THE "DIFFICULTY" OF BEING A WOMAN

It should not be more difficult to be a woman than a man. Yet, this is not a reality because women seem to suffer with a variety of genitourinary problems, including vaginitis, dysmenorrhea, vulvodynia, endometriosis, infertility, PMS, chronic or recurring urinary tract infections, and interstitial cystitis. Many women accept these medical maladies are the "curse of being a woman." Since these problems are not prevalent among healthy women, it implies that something must be amiss within the bodies of the women suffering with them.

An abundance of evidence supports an association between candidiasis and these medical maladies. The direct and indirect infectious and/or allergic contributions of disease-causing yeast can cause a variety of genital and urinary problems. Typically, this is exacerbated by candidiasis-related endocrine (hormone) disturbances, metabolic (chemical) disruptions, and mineral deficiencies (especially magnesium). Depending on the abnormalities involved, candidiasis of the genital tract instigates or promotes vaginal yeast infections, difficult and painful menstruation, discomfort or pain in the vulvar region, the presence of anomalous uterine tissue in areas where it should not be, an inability to become pregnant, and a variety of premenstrual symptoms. Candidiasis within the urinary tract can cause chronic or recurring UTIs, which may progress to IC. With respect to the *candidiasis-genitourinary connection*, women appear to be at a great disadvantage.

If you are a woman who suffers with any of these problems, you can improve your health. The first step is to realize that your problems exist for a reason. Instead of only treating your symptoms, you must accept that *candidiasis* is your real problem. In other words, your genital and urinary symptoms are manifestations of a bigger problem.

Once your candidiasis is correctly diagnosed, it can be treated. Since most of these medical maladies, if not all, involve the colonization of disease-causing yeast within the genital tract and urinary tract, administering a systemic antifungal medication is essential, and the only way to thoroughly eliminate the infection. In addition, the presence of other infectious invaders must be addressed as well, especially harmful parasites, bacteria, and molds. Most of these infectious invaders reside within the gut and can spread from the anus to infect the genitals and urinary tract. So, the gut must be attended to as well. Most of these medical maladies also involve allergies, especially to disease-causing yeast and harmful molds. In many cases, there may be sensitivities and hypersensitivities to a variety of pollens, dust, foods, and chemicals; these must be properly evaluated and treated accordingly. As a result, desensitization (allergy) injections are typically administered to make the immune system less reactive to these allergy-inducing offenders; if allergies are ignored, the symptoms may never be eliminated.

After your candidiasis is treated, the disturbances it caused, both hormonal and chemical, will often correct themselves. In the meantime, because of the malabsorption that commonly accompanies candidiasis, supplementation with numerous nutrients is recommended. Depending on your symptoms, this is where a candidiasis-minded physician can be especially helpful.

So, these medical maladies can be eliminated, but because of the strong participation of allergies, it may take time to become symptom-free. Fortunately, when your candidiasis is properly diagnosed and treated, the difficulty associated with being biologically female is likely to be removed forever.

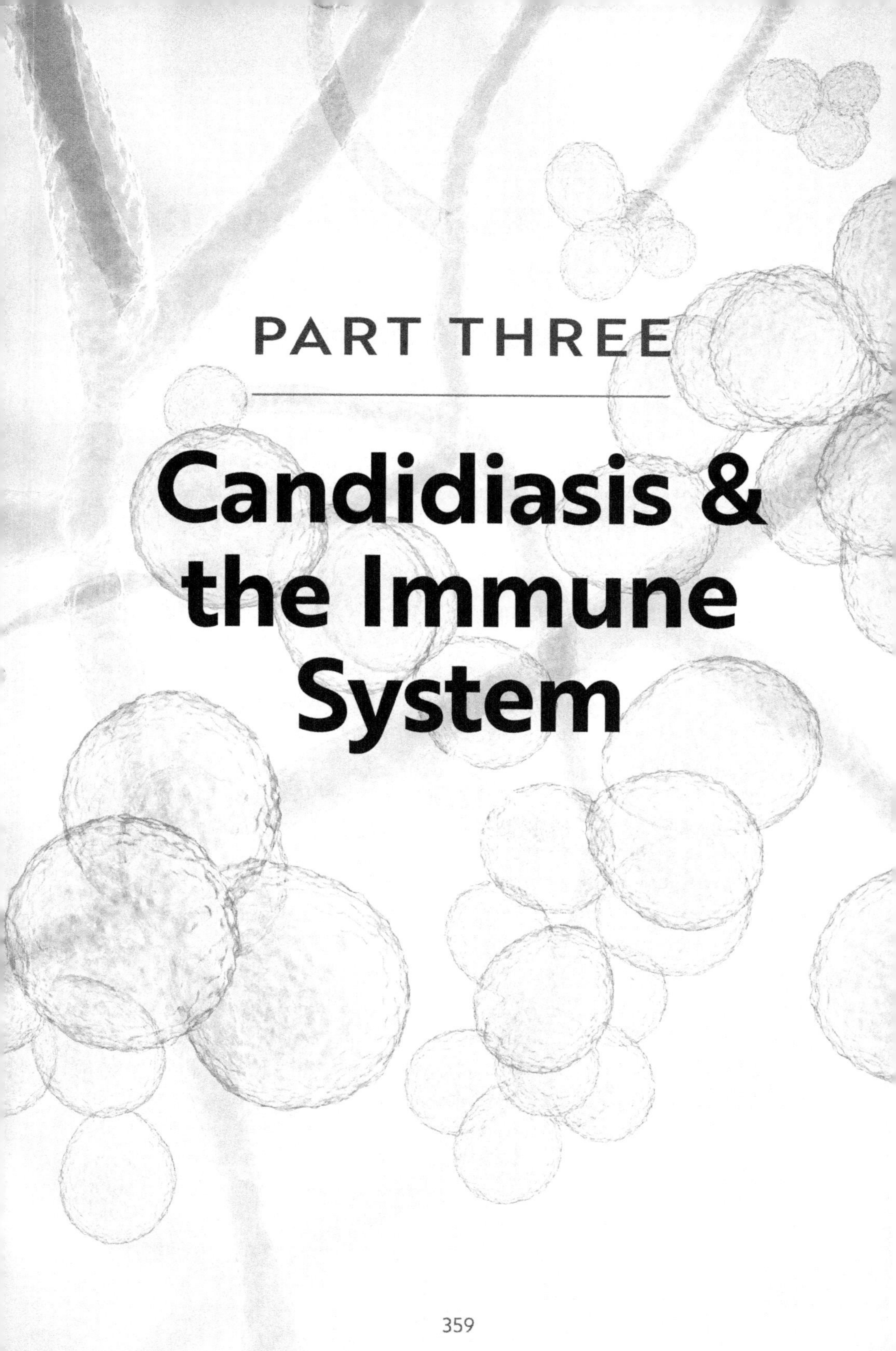

PART THREE

Candidiasis & the Immune System

CHAPTER 14

Immunity, Impaired Immunity & Autoimmunity

Every time you have a "cold" or "the flu," your *immune system* is summoned into action. It functions as your body's "police force," helping you defend against these infections. Unlike real police officers, your immune system is never "off duty." Regardless of whether you touch, inhale, or swallow something harmful, your immune system constantly protects you, keeping you safe.

When your immune system is *competent*, properly performing its duties, you remain healthy. If you are exposed to an infectious invader, like a virus, you might get sick, but your illness is likely to be mild and readily resolved. In contrast, when your immune system is *compromised, deficient*, or *impaired* (slow in responding or performs its duties poorly), you are at risk for developing many undesirable consequences. If your immunity is mildly impaired, you may have prolonged or frequent colds. If it becomes more compromised, significant problems can arise—for example, cancer, chronic viral illnesses, and autoimmune diseases (not to mention allergies). So, your immune system also protects you against disease (as well as tissue damage).

The immune system is so complex that only the basics can be discussed in this chapter. At the simplest level, it has two types of immunity: *Cell-mediated* (cellular) *immunity* involves the *direct* and *indirect activities of certain cells* that regulate the entire immune system, usually without the assistance of antibodies—typically, T lymphocytes, natural killer cells, and mononuclear macrophages. *Humoral* (antibody) *immunity* includes antibodies produced by other cells (B lymphocytes). *Antibodies* are specific types of proteins (glycoproteins) that neutralize or destroy infectious invaders or harmful substances (antigens) in various ways, usually by stimulating other immune-related processes.

Although humoral immunity is typically associated with allergies (chapter 16), it also helps defend the body from infectious invaders and disease. Therefore, both types of immunity overlap, and to regulate the immune system's interactions, immune cells communicate with numerous cellular chemical messengers called *cytokines*; more specifically, *lymphokines* are produced by lymphocytes, and *monokines* are made by monocytes. Basically, the immune system is comprised of cells, antibodies, and the chemical messengers that enable these cells to communicate, regulate, and integrate their activities. However, the immune system is even more complex, involving other participants and contributors as well.

The immune system does not function alone. In conjunction with the nervous system (chapter 10) and endocrine (hormone) system (chapter 11), all three form the *neuroendocrine-immune connection*. This alliance assists the body in maintaining a state of optimal balance, called *homeostasis*. When all three systems are functioning properly and in concert, you are likely to be well, and, if adverse circumstances arise, they are often resolved quickly and efficiently. Yet, disturbances can *directly* impair any or all these systems. Since all three constantly interact, disturbing one system is almost certain to *indirectly* influence the others. If the body can compensate, homeostasis will be reestablished. Unfortunately, some adverse circumstances place great stress on the body, causing disturbances that cannot be readily corrected. Regardless of whether it is appreciated, in many people, candidiasis is such a disturbance.

By definition, candidiasis involves the colonization of disease-causing yeast within the gastrointestinal tract (and other tissues). As a result, an infection with disease-causing yeast can promote a spectrum of symptoms and illness. Even though harmful parasites, bacteria, molds, and viruses are frequent infectious allies, the persistent presence of disease-causing yeast can induce a variety of *infectious* and *allergic* consequences that can adversely affect the *neuroendocrine-immune connection*. As a result, chronic candidiasis often promotes *impaired immunity* and *metabolic disturbances*. Even though many candidiasis-minded physicians appreciate this, its origin has been poorly understood.

In Unraveling Candidiasis, The Perplexing Puzzle of Medical Maladies—Appendix B contains three (of my) articles published in 1996–1997, explaining how chronic candidiasis can cause *metabolic immunosuppression*. It includes blood sugar disturbances (*glucose intolerance*, chapter 11), the increased or prolonged release of insulin (*hyperinsulinism*, chapter 11), elevated amounts of cholesterol and triglycerides within the blood (*hyperlipidemia*, chapter 7), and impaired or defective immunity (immunodeficiencies).

So, candidiasis can precipitate or promote serious immune system disturbances that may have dire, and sometimes deadly, consequences. Is this an exaggeration? No, because candidiasis-related disruptions involving cell-mediated immunity can permit the development of cancerous growths and chronic viral illnesses. In fact, the medical literature recognizes that many of the medical maladies that involve impaired immunity are closely associated with candidiasis. Lacking an appreciation for candidiasis, mainstream physicians assume that disease-causing yeast are simply secondary opportunists; they appear after someone develops impaired immunity. In contrast, candidiasis-minded physicians know that most people with impaired immunity had a history of candidiasis-related signs and symptoms long before their immunity became deficient. In other words, *most people with impaired immunity are really candidiasis sufferers.*

Equally disturbing, candidiasis can instigate abnormal cell-mediated and humoral immunity, promoting autoimmune diseases. The precise process behind autoimmunity remains unresolved, and, although much is known, mainstream medicine claims that this manifestation of abnormal immunity has nothing to do with candidiasis. On the contrary, abundant evidence supports that chronic candidiasis-related mischief participates in this immune system malady.

Therefore, *candidiasis commonly precedes and instigates most immunodeficiencies*. Is this possible? Yes, and it is supported by observation, therapeutic successes, the theory of *metabolic immunosuppression*, and research.

Deficient immunity always has a cause. Although there are exceptions, the presence of an infection with disease-causing yeast is effective at impairing immunity, with or without the assistance of other infectious invaders. In fact, when people with impaired immunity are treated with an anti-candidiasis approach, dramatic improvements often follow. In the bigger picture, an effort to prevent candidiasis or eliminate it before it can impair immunity should significantly reduce the number of people who develop these medical maladies.

METABOLIC IMMUNOSUPPRESSION

Candidiasis sufferers frequently experience metabolic (chemical) disturbances and impaired immunity. The abnormalities that arise range from subtle to overtly obvious. Yet, proving this association has been difficult because the specific research has not been performed. This does not mean the information to connect candidiasis with metabolic disturbances and impaired immunity does not exist. In fact, on a case-by-case basis, it does; after all, when enough candidiasis sufferers are evaluated, this connection is readily evident. Even though the research has been lacking, *metabolic immunosuppression* explains why and how this develops.

Candidiasis sufferers often develop several seemingly unrelated metabolic disturbances, including abnormal blood sugar regulation (*glucose intolerance*), the increased or prolonged release of insulin (*hyperinsulinemia*), and elevated amounts of blood cholesterol and/or triglycerides (*hyperlipidemia*, including *hypercholesterolemia* and/or *hypertriglyceridemia*). Unfortunately, this combination of disturbances can promote cardiovascular illness (chapter 7). Even worse, they can precipitate or cause impaired immunity, leading to immunocompromising medical maladies like cancer, chronic viral illnesses, and autoimmune diseases. At first glance, these abnormalities appear separate. Since their connection to candidiasis is not appreciated, mainstream physicians treat them as independent problems. Yet, every illness must have a cause. Evidence demonstrates that chronic candidiasis can induce these undesirable disturbances, with or without the assistance of other infectious invaders. How was this connection made and why do candidiasis sufferers develop these problems?

At the November 1990 meeting of the American College for Advancement in Medicine (ACAM), Vladimir M. Dilman, M.D., a Russian professor and Chief of the Laboratory of Endocrinology at Petrov Research Institute of Oncology, Leningrad, described his "Four Models of Medicine." Part of his presentation was *metabolic immunodepression*, a phenomenon he claims to have discovered in 1972. Because he was an academic physician with a background in geriatrics, he appreciated that deficiencies in cell-mediated (cellular) immunity were common among the elderly. Since their absolute number of cells was not usually decreased, their impaired immunity must relate to abnormal cell functioning and/or the hormones and metabolic substances that influenced and regulated them. In short, normal numbers of cells are present, but they function abnormally or communicate improperly, leading to impaired immunity.

According to Dr. Dilman, *metabolic immunodepression* involves decreased cell-mediated immunity that *follows* disturbances in *carbohydrate* and *lipid* metabolism. These metabolic disturbances include *glucose intolerance* (reactive hypoglycemia), *postprandial hyperinsulinemia* (elevated insulin levels after eating), *hypertriglyceridemia* (increased free fatty acids and triglycerides within the blood) and/or *hypercholesterolemia* (elevated LDL cholesterol levels within the blood as well as within the plasma membranes of certain immune cells: T lymphocytes and monocytes). He claimed that these metabolic disturbances impaired the production of subsequent generations of cells—baby lymphocytes (*decreased lymphocyte blastogenesis*). Simply put, abnormalities with sugar and fat metabolism were thought to precede and promote impaired immunity. How did he develop his theory? His research demonstrated that improving one metabolic parameter, namely normalizing insulin levels, strengthened immunity and even reversed deficient immunity. This was the first indication there was a connection between metabolic disturbances and impaired immunity.

How does deficient immunity arise? Since most T lymphocytes (T cells) have a finite life span, constant cell proliferation must occur to replace expiring cells. If this does not happen, the number of cells will decrease. Obviously, immunity can only function optimally when ample amounts of new recruits are produced and available. Yet, even when the number of cells is decreased, immunity can be competent when the cells function normally. So, unless there is a severe shortage, the cells can perform their duties. In contrast, if the cells function inadequately, immunity will be impaired. Instead of a shortage of cells, this is what Dr. Dilman found. What caused the decreased cellular functioning? He thought that excess *cholesterol* was responsible.

Cholesterol is a vital component of all cell membranes, including immune cells. If excess cholesterol is within the blood, it can be incorporated into the cell membrane of T cells. As cholesterol accumulates, the cell membrane becomes more viscous, impairing the cell's ability to move substances into and out of it. In turn, these cells are unable to produce and release adequate quantities of cytokines, especially *interleukin-1* (IL-1), a cellular chemical messenger that is a vital T-cell activator. An IL-1 deficiency hinders lymphocyte blastogenesis, impeding the birth of "baby" lymphocytes. Simply put, he thought that excess cholesterol within the cell membranes of T lymphocytes impairs their functioning and reproduction.

Inspired by Dr. Dilman, at the November 1992 ACAM meeting, Pavel Yutsis, M.D., from Brooklyn, New York, presented his findings. He performed a retrospective analysis of 100 patients (seen between 1991 and 1992) who suffered with candidiasis, chronic fatigue syndrome, and multiple allergies. He noted that 86 percent had two to three aspects of metabolic immunodepression.

Yet, neither Dr. Yutsis nor Dr. Dilman understood how or why this occurred. Since the puzzle pieces appeared unrelated and difficult to connect, this complex and confusing encryption was indecipherable. Having experience in immune system research, I looked deeper.

First, a more appropriate name is *metabolic immunosuppression*, which denotes an immune system that is suppressed (inferior functioning) rather than depressed (fewer immune cells). A *suppressed* system can have *normal* numbers of cells but *functions inferiorly*. In contrast, a *depressed* system has *fewer* cells but behaves *normally* or *abnormally*. So, there are four basic states of immunity:

- **Normal immunity:** normal numbers of cells that function optimally.
- **Suppressed immunity:** normal numbers of cells that function inferiorly.
- **Depressed immunity:** fewer cells that function effectively.
- **Suppressed-depressed immunity:** fewer, inferior functioning cells.

An infinite number of variations can occur. For example, the entire immune system can be adversely affected or just one specific population of immune cells.

Dr. Dilman's theory was simplistic and based on a 25-year-old understanding of immunology. Rather than deficient immunity simply resulting from excess cholesterol, why did these people have elevated cholesterol in the first place? The existence of a *candidiasis-hypercholesterolemia connection* (chapter 7) revealed that the presence of an infection with disease-causing yeast was likely to be the real underlying cause of elevated amounts of cholesterol within their blood. Therefore, the cause of impaired immunity was really candidiasis, although harmful parasites, bacteria, molds, and/or viruses could certainly exacerbate the situation.

There is support for a *candidiasis-immunodeficiency connection*. As an example, Carol Jessop, M.D., treated 1,100 patients with chronic fatigue syndrome (reported in the *American Medical News*, May 26, 1989). Eighty percent had a history of receiving repeated antibiotic therapy for various infections. Since antibiotics are a strong risk factor for promoting candidiasis (chapter 2), it was not surprising that most of the patients had symptoms consistent with candidiasis, including hives, irritable bowel syndrome, vascular-like headaches, PMS, vaginal yeast infections, and tinea (fungal skin infections). When the patients were treated with a systemic antifungal agent (ketoconazole, 200 mg/day) and a sugar-free diet, 84 percent responded favorably. This demonstrated that candidiasis caused illness in at least 84 percent of them.

What does this have to do with metabolic immunosuppression? At their initial presentation, 90 percent had hypercholesterolemia. Since most of the patients were in their mid-thirties, this revealed that metabolic immunosuppression is *not* strictly age-related, which Dr. Dilman professed. In addition, if hypercholesterolemia precedes deficient immunity, as he claimed, it should occur in every patient without exception. In other words, although 90 percent is not far from 100 percent, a one-to-one relationship *must* exist if he is correct. Since all the patients had deficient immunity, but only 90 percent had hypercholesterolemia, excess cholesterol cannot solely cause impaired immunity.

Since an antifungal medication benefited a significant number of patients with impaired immunity, Dr. Jessop's evidence supports candidiasis as the underlying cause of deficient immunity, as opposed to accompanying age-related changes. If a persistent infection with disease-causing yeast is responsible, metabolic disturbances and impaired immunity should also occur in children with candidiasis. After all, children are not immune to disease-causing yeast (chapter 12). In fact, Dr. Yutsis (at ACAM, November 1992) found that 75 percent of children with candidiasis had metabolic disturbances—primarily, glucose intolerance and hyperinsulinism. (In general, children are more resilient than adults and do not manifest as many disturbances.) So, when candidiasis is present, metabolic disturbances and deficient immunity can occur at any age.

Candidiasis participates in causing metabolic disturbances and deficient immunity, but which came first: Did Dr. Jessop's patients have metabolic weaknesses that predisposed them to developing candidiasis *or* did candidiasis develop and produce their metabolic disturbances? Both are possible. The combination of a fragile constitution and an infection with disease-causing yeast can promote the undesirable consequences of candidiasis. Conversely, chronic candidiasis makes the body more susceptible and sensitive to adverse circumstances. Roughly 80 percent of Dr. Jessop's patients had been exposed to repeated antibiotics as well as the other risk factors for developing candidiasis, including birth control pills, corticosteroids, multiple pregnancies, and poor diets. Any of these can promote the colonization of disease-causing yeast as well as many other risk factors (chapter 2). In the bigger picture, whether they knew it or not, all of Dr. Jessop's patients had probably been exposed to one or more risk factors for developing candidiasis. This strongly supports that candidiasis was present first.

However, do not ignore the 10 percent of patients who did not have hypercholesterolemia. What were their cholesterol levels before they developed candidiasis? Was their cholesterol level elevated compared to a state of optimal health but not deemed significant because it was within the range of normal? If this is true, you would *mistakenly* believe that metabolic disturbances precede candidiasis. Yet, even if this is true, the amount of cholesterol within their blood would not be significant enough to fulfill Dr. Dilman's theorized sequence of events. If the only starting condition was hypercholesterolemia, it takes much greater amounts of cholesterol (than measured) to impair immunity.

Is there evidence to support the direct undesirable contributions of disease-causing yeast in this process? It is not a coincidence that glucose tolerance is adversely affected within candidiasis sufferers (chapter 11) because disease-causing yeast preferentially use sugar as their major energy source. For many reasons, these infectious invaders interact and interfere with glucose metabolism, altering the body's ability to process carbohydrates. Research supports the contributions of disease-causing yeast in this process; specifically, *Candida albicans* has been found to have *glucagon receptors* on its cell membrane surface and can produce *insulin-like substances.* This implies that an infection with disease-causing yeast can disturb blood sugar regulation in numerous ways:

- Their production of insulin-like substances can exacerbate a lowered blood sugar concentration, promoting hypoglycemia and glucose intolerance.
- Since glucagon is the body's primary blood sugar–raising hormone, their glucagon receptors may effectively bind any glucagon that is available, making it difficult to raise a lowered blood sugar concentration.
- This subsequently instigates the release of the secondary blood sugar–raising hormones, notably epinephrine and cortisol, promoting their undesirable effects.
- Any disease-causing yeast within the tissues or blood can feed off glucose within these areas, further decreasing a lowered blood sugar concentration.

For these reasons and more (chapter 11), there is a *candidiasis–glucose intolerance connection* and a *candidiasis-hyperinsulinism connection*. Since there is also a *candidiasis-hypercholesterolemia connection* (chapter 7), all the available evidence points to a *candidiasis-immunodeficiency connection*.

How and the reasons why this exists is the story that must be told. Although some candidiasis-minded physicians knew an infection with disease-causing yeast was responsible for the metabolic disturbances and deficient immunity that arises in most people, none of them could explain the process. In fact, the explanation seemed nearly impossible to ascertain because of the great variability that exists among candidiasis sufferers. So, instead of investigating the patients, the available research and science pertaining to candidiasis needed to be addressed. Fortunately, a great deal of scientific information exists to explain the immune system effects of disease-causing yeast within the body. However, with respect to a relationship between candidiasis, metabolic disturbances, and deficient immunity, no one had thought to look at the facts and connect the dots.

In my first article, I described how the liver participates in causing the metabolic disturbances and deficient immunity that arises within candidiasis sufferers. It is common knowledge that the liver is an organ primarily involved with metabolism; it is responsible for most cholesterol production, stores excess sugar in the form of glycogen, and manufactures glucose when needed (when fasting, it helps maintain an appropriate blood sugar concentration). However, *the liver is also a member of the immune system*. During an infection or inflammation, the liver shifts to its *acute phase response*, aka the *acute phase reaction*; it decreases its synthesis of *albumin* (an important carrier protein), while increasing its production and release of *acute phase proteins*. These substances are involved in a nonspecific host defense; they enhance the ability of certain immune cells to ingest (engulf) and destroy foreign material as well as activate complement (using the *complement system*, 18 proteins that assist in fighting infections).

The acute phase response is a normal, beneficial response to combat illness. Although it is meant to be a short-term boost to immunity, chronic candidiasis establishes a continuous acute phase response. The *infectious*, *allergic* consequences and *inflammation* that accompany the persistent presence of disease-causing yeast promote a prolonged acute phase response. Since the liver decreases its metabolic activities to assist the immune system, long-term infections must disturb metabolism; excesses of acute phase proteins instigate and promote glucose intolerance, hyperinsulinism, and hyperlipidemia (hypertriglyceridemia and/or hypercholesterolemia), which can then lead to suppressed immunity, depressed immunity, and suppressed-depressed immunity.

It is important to summarize the theory of *metabolic immunosuppression*. Regardless of whether someone has normal or abnormal glucose tolerance, insulin levels, and cholesterol levels, the presence of an *infection* with disease-causing yeast (candidiasis) either causes these disturbances or exacerbates them. The direct and indirect presence of candidiasis can cause inflammatory reactions, including the excessive generation of *oxygen-based free radicals* (chapter 7). Eventually, this injures and damages the membranes of numerous immune cells, especially T cells. Sensing the body is under infectious and inflammatory assault, other immune cells (monocytes and macrophages) are activated, stimulating the liver's acute phase response. Yet, since candidiasis is rarely eliminated, this promotes the prolonged release of acute phase proteins. By themselves, they are not necessarily bad. Rather, it is the perpetual production of certain cellular chemical messengers (cytokines) that adversely affects the body's metabolism and immune system.

The presence of an *infection* with disease-causing yeast triggers the production of certain *cellular chemical messengers* (cytokines) that are supposed to stimulate the liver's acute phase response. These cytokines also cause the liver to increase its production and release of cholesterol (hypercholesterolemia). The specifics reveal that this can promote increases in ("bad") LDL cholesterol and decreases in ("good") HDL cholesterol as well as increase triglycerides within the blood (hypertriglyceridemia). Even though this is undesirable, it has a purpose. The extra cholesterol is used to repair the membranes of injured cells or to give birth to replacements. Yet, when the acute phase response is prolonged, excess cholesterol may be incorporated within the cell membranes of healthy T cells, impairing their functioning (*suppressed immunity*).

In some people, a decrease in certain cytokines or an increase in others can inhibit the proliferation of T cells, leading to fewer cells (*depressed immunity*). Also, during a prolonged infection, circumstances can cause specific T cells (memory T cells and suppressor T cells) to directly inhibit the proliferation of new cells. While this is occurring, the production and release of numerous cytokines further worsens metabolism, instigating or promoting *glucose intolerance* and *hyperinsulinism*, which also adversely affects immunity. In addition, skin (epithelial) cells and gastrointestinal (endothelial) cells can bind specific proteins. If they bind with disease-causing yeast, they may become sensitive and even hypersensitive to it, inducing *allergies*. This is undesirable because the presence of allergies can cause a shift in cell populations that further impairs cell-mediated immunity. Although complicated, taken together, all of this explains much of the *infectious* and *allergic* complications of candidiasis.

Is there research to support a *candidiasis-immunodeficiency connection*? Chronic mucocutaneous candidiasis (CMCC) sufferers (chapter 8) have altered levels of cytokines, triggering a cellular profile that encourages impaired immunity and a persistent infection. Abundant research with other CMCC sufferers uncovered similar results. What about people with a less severe form of candidiasis? One study included 22 patients with chronic candidiasis of the skin/mucosa and 14 patients with *Candida* vulvovaginitis, discovering their proliferation of lymphocytes was weakened or inhibited. In other words, they manifested decreased lymphocyte blastogenesis.

What about the direct effects of disease-causing yeast? The presence of candidiasis-related antigens, toxins, metabolites, wastes, and byproducts adversely alters the body's metabolism. As a result, these harmful substances can impair the functioning of one or more organs. Since the liver is responsible for clearing these harmful substances, decreases in its metabolic functioning must exacerbate metabolic disturbances, further impairing immunity. (The same can be said for the kidneys.)

In fact, several yeast-produced substances are directly harmful to the immune system. For example, *Candida albicans* and other fungi produce *gliotoxin*, a substance that has been found to suppress immunity. Numerous researchers have discovered that gliotoxin can kill immune cells, including thymocytes, splenocytes, and mesenteric lymph node cells, and can selectively deplete the bone marrow of mature lymphocytes. Even at concentrations well below toxic levels, gliotoxin can induce changes in the functioning and metabolism of macrophages, cells that are essential to defend the body against candidiasis. Moreover, gliotoxin diminishes the ability of neutrophils to respond to inflammation as well as ingest particles. Clearly, gliotoxin can impair immunity in numerous ways.

How significant is this effect? Animals that were infected with non-gliotoxin producing fungi survived significantly longer than those infected with a gliotoxin producer. Gliotoxin also impairs the liver's metabolism by inactivating *alcohol dehydrogenase*, the enzyme responsible for degrading alcohol. Obviously, any ethanol that is consumed will not be eliminated as quickly, causing its undesirable effects to escalate, including its ability to impair immunity. To add insult, disease-causing yeast also manufacture ethanol (alcohol), which can easily be absorbed; in the presence of gliotoxin, the amounts of ethanol can become significant and undesirable. Another harmful substance is *acetaldehyde,* and its adverse effects escalate as its concentration increases (chapter 10).

Specifics aside, abundant evidence reveals that chronic candidiasis can impair immunity and promote metabolic disturbances. Metabolic immunosuppression explains why candidiasis sufferers often manifest metabolic disturbances and deficient immunity. Admittedly, since it is just a theory, it will probably need to be adjusted and fine-tuned as the specifics become known. For example, certain combinations of harmful parasites, bacteria, molds, and/or viruses are likely to be worse than others. In practical terms, metabolic immunosuppression is a state of impaired immunity that places a candidiasis sufferer at risk for developing cancer, chronic viral illnesses, and autoimmune diseases.

CANDIDIASIS-CANCER CONNECTION

Of all the illnesses we can develop, the most frightening is probably cancer. After all, cancer sufferers typically experience constantly worsening debilitation that often culminates in a slow and painful death. The origin of cancer is poorly understood, causing most cancer victims to ask, "Why me?" In addition, the course of cancer is unpredictable, eliciting fear, anxiety, anger, and frustration among its victims and family. Although there have been advances, mainstream medical therapy does not improve or cure everyone. Many cancer victims feel helpless and hopeless. Statistics aside, more people are diagnosed with cancer each day. Although its numbers are increasing, it is far from a new illness. The ancient Egyptians documented cancer about 5,000 years ago, and evidence supports its presence long before that.

Cancer is the general term for a diversity of diseases that involve any type of malignant (or benign) neoplasm. A *neoplasm* is an uncontrollable growth of cells that began within normal tissues. The diagnosis of cancer requires the presence of *abnormal cellular features* and *growth patterns*. Most often, the cells appear variably unnatural, depending on the tumor's mass and rate of growth. In general, *benign* tumors usually appear almost normal, are localized, slower-growing, and less lethal. In contrast, *malignant* tumors range from mildly irregular to rapidly deadly, develop their own blood supply, spread more easily, and encourage growth within distant areas (metastasis). Even though some types are more prevalent than others, cancer may originate within virtually any cell of the body. Cancer harms the body, and even kills, by its localized spread or distant metastasis.

Chemical and physical risk factors are known or implicated to participate in a multitude of malignancies. Examples include exposures to tobacco, alcohol, sun and radiation, occupational and environmental hazards, certain medications, infectious agents, genetics, diet, and more. All of these are known to *transform* healthy cells into their abnormal counterparts. Yet, if these factors were solely responsible, virtually everyone who was exposed to them would develop cancer, but this is not what happens. Even more confusing, numerous cancers are *idiopathic*—that is, *no cause is known*. Some researchers claim there is involvement by cancer-causing viruses and/or genetic material (proto-oncogenes). In contrast, there appears to be a genetic predisposition to develop and manifest certain cancers. Breast tumors are more prevalent among family members with breast cancer. Since women in the same family do not always develop it, the contributions of genetics must be limited or influenced by something else.

It is generally accepted that *host susceptibility* determines whether cancer develops. So, the strength of someone's *immunity* determines whether a cancerous growth blossoms or dies. Why is this important? Many researchers believe that everyone generates cancerous cells all the time. When a person's immunity is competent, these cancerous cells are recognized as *"nonself"* and quickly destroyed. Although there are exceptions, cancer progresses within people who have impaired immunity. As a result, virtually every cancer sufferer has some magnitude of impaired immunity; generally, the severity and type of impairment determine the rate of growth and spread of their cancer.

Although anticancer therapies have improved and death rates have decreased, many sufferers die from their medical malady. Mainstream researchers are always searching for better ways to kill or eliminate cancer. Yes, there has been progress, but it has been slow.

With all the research that is done, why is mainstream medical anticancer therapy less than spectacular? Simply put, treatment is aimed at eradicating the "bad" cells. This is not the best approach because it injures and kills healthy cells during the process, further impairing immunity. Frequently, the adverse effects of chemotherapy, radiation therapy, or some other anticancer therapies are more harmful to the body than the cancer itself. What about surgery? If a cancer is confined, surgery may successfully remove it. Yet, there is often a high frequency of reoccurrence afterward. Yes, many cancerous conditions do benefit from debulking in which one or more growths are removed, decreasing the body's burden of malignant cells. It is not without risk because, during surgery, cancerous cells can pass into the blood, seeding other areas and promoting metastasis. This is not surprising because a cancer sufferer's impaired immunity is rarely addressed. Since deficient immunity permits the generation of subsequent abnormal growths, it implies that deficient immunity precedes and permits the development of cancer.

Therefore, mainstream medicine appears caught in a contradiction. Most mainstream physicians think cancer arises as an entity in and of itself, but they will admit they often do not know why. They also believe the cancer itself is not responsible for the impaired immunity that exists within cancer sufferers. If cancer arises as an entity in and of itself and if it is not responsible for impaired immunity, what is? Indeed, something must promote the deficient immunity that is present within cancer sufferers. Moreover, if deficient immunity precedes and permits cancer to develop, cancer is really a *symptom* of deficient immunity. In other words, instead of cancer being an illness in and of itself, it develops because of deficient immunity. Something must be responsible for the deficient immunity that instigates or promotes cancer.

Metabolic immunosuppression explains how candidiasis can impair immunity. Even though candidiasis causes deficient immunity, can it promote cancer? Is it a coincidence that the chemical and physical risk factors associated with cancer are also candidiasis risk factors (chapter 2)? Mainstream physicians do recognize that many cancer sufferers eventually develop candidiasis. However, they believe the disease-causing yeast are only opportunistic infectious invaders; they appear after the cancer develops, taking advantage of the cancer sufferer's impaired immunity. Is this accurate? Not according to candidiasis-minded physicians; when they take a thorough medical history, it quickly becomes clear that candidiasis existed long before someone's cancer was evident. So, there are excellent reasons to suspect that, in most people with deficient immunity, candidiasis came first. This contradicts mainstream medical thinking.

How does candidiasis cause cancer? Research reveals that candidiasis may play a role in transforming normal cells into abnormal cells. Gliotoxin can produce damaging free radicals within the cells it enters and is able to injure cellular DNA. Since genetic changes within a cell can cause normal cells to transform into abnormal cells, gliotoxin may precipitate cancer. For cancer to bloom, there must be deficient immunity. A persistent infection with disease-causing yeast, with or without other infectious invaders, impairs cell-mediated immunity. As a result, the immune system is unable to appropriately recognize and/or destroy any cancerous cells that arise, allowing malignant cells to grow and proliferate. The type of cancer is basically a reflection of someone's genetic tendencies and environmental exposures, although other risk factors can contribute like diet, alcohol consumption, and so on. This perspective might seem simplistic, but it explains the observations and successes of knowledgeable candidiasis-minded physicians.

Several abstracts and studies support this thinking. *Many antifungal medications have antitumor and anticancer activities*. For example, tamoxifen is useful in treating breast cancer. Research indicates that this drug "protects membranes and lipoprotein particles against oxidative damage." Surprisingly, most mainstream physicians are unaware that it is also an *antifungal* agent, with *antiviral* abilities; it kills disease-causing yeast and suppresses viruses. In addition, other antifungal medications have shown promise in treating breast cancer sufferers. This implies that many anticancer drugs are effective because they *indirectly* assault disease-causing yeast.

If deficient immunity arises first and disease-causing yeast are opportunistic infectious invaders, treating candidiasis should have little or no effect on the health of cancer sufferers. Yet, many cancer patients demonstrate remarkable improvements when their candidiasis is appropriately addressed. The simplest evidence comes from patients who manifest *pre-malignant/precancerous* (dysplastic) changes. Although the changes are considered precancerous, the cells do not become malignant if the stimulus for their transformation is removed. Remarkably, a large percentage of patients with precancerous changes have had their cells return to normal after their candidiasis was treated. If candidiasis encourages impaired immunity and anti-candidiasis therapy transforms precancerous cells back into normal cells (or prevents them from replicating), this provides strong evidence for candidiasis promoting cancer.

Can it be this simple? Yes, because it is no different from the other candidiasis-related maladies. Can you accept that allergies are caused by disease-causing yeast (chapter 16) but not cancer? Although dissimilar manifestations, both are immune system illnesses. Do not be fooled. They have much in common. Can you accept that candidiasis may initiate or promote cancer of the colon? After all, disease-causing yeast live, grow, and reproduce within the gut. Add in a pinch of harmful parasites, bacteria, molds, and/or viruses and this is a wonderful recipe for metabolic disturbances and impaired immunity, the perfect seeds for illness.

By the way, this thinking does not negate the use of mainstream medical therapy. Realistically, both approaches may be required for optimal improvement. Some mainstream medical treatment is beneficial, and when used appropriately, it can be a terrific accomplice. In fact, anticancer therapy becomes the most valuable when the immune system is improved or optimized prior to and during its use.

Unfortunately, scant research has been performed to completely explore this association. Although treating candidiasis may not cure every cancer victim, at least it should strengthen their immunity, preventing the generation of additional cancerous cells. In the bigger picture, eliminating candidiasis should correct the immune impairments that precipitate cancer, which is likely to greatly decrease its prevalence. Unfortunately, many cancer sufferers are unlikely to significantly improve until the *candidiasis-cancer connection* is taken seriously.

CHRONIC VIRAL ILLNESSES

If you ever had mononucleosis, you have been intimately acquainted with a well-known viral illness. Most upper respiratory infections (common colds) involve viruses. Many gastrointestinal illnesses are instigated by viruses. Generally, these are usually acute illnesses that occur suddenly, are combated by the immune system, brought under control, and then resolve. Although most of the population does not develop persistent viral illnesses, some people do. Why can most people effectively eradicate or control these viruses, while other people continuously suffer? In other words, what causes someone to have a chronic viral illness? Before this can be answered, there are some points to understand.

Viruses do not only infect us. They can infect plants, animals, and even bacteria. What are viruses? They are the smallest and simplest of microorganisms. Basically, these infectious invaders are tiny particles that only contain specialized genetic material. Depending on their programming, they attach to and enter host cells (a specific cell or many). This is followed by replication and the release of its progeny. Under various conditions, viruses can exist in a dormant or latent state (sleeping); many viruses are not eliminated but are simply brought under control and maintained under close surveillance by the immune system, like a jailed prisoner.

Several viruses are exclusive to human beings. When exposure occurs early in life, their infections are usually mild and rarely fatal. In contrast, most viruses are not specific to man, and an infection with them is often dangerous and occasionally deadly—for example, COVID-19. Of course, the severity of a viral infection reflects the behavior of the specific virus(es) and the magnitude of their accompanying disturbances as well as the person's current state of health.

If conditions are favorable for its transfer, someone can easily become infected with a virus. This might involve contact with one or more bodily secretions. A mother may pass a virus to her fetus or newborn child. After entering the body and depending on its characteristics, a virus may promote a localized infection or spread systemically. Viruses can journey to other organs by the lymphatic system, blood, or along nerve pathways. Within the blood, viruses can mobilize freely, travel with specific cellular elements, or ride within immune cells (especially macrophages and lymphocytes). The ability of a virus to selectively recognize its target and initiate an infection is determined by certain cell surface *receptors*; a virus can assault and impair a specific cell when there is a compatibility between them.

Many viruses are associated with chronic viral illnesses. The most common include:

- *Herpes simplex virus type 1* and *herpes simplex virus type 2* (HSV-1, HSV-2) are widely prevalent and directly transmitted. Mucous membranes are their common site of attack, and self-inoculation can occur. Their illnesses range from insignificant infections and "fever blisters" to fatal encephalitis. Twenty to 40 percent of their victims experience oral infections, and up to 60 percent manifest genital lesions.
- *Human herpesvirus 6* (HHV-6) is related to the other herpesviruses and is thought to be involved in chronic fatigue syndrome.
- *Cytomegalovirus* (CMV) is usually contracted early in life, with transmission by interpersonal contact or in bodily fluids. Its mischief varies from subtle infections to systemic disease and death.
- *Epstein-Barr virus (EBV)* resides within a large percentage of the population. It typically produces "infectious mononucleosis." It is frequently transmitted by bodily fluids and infection usually occurs early in life. People with viral antibodies are permanent carriers and occasionally excrete the virus. Reactivation is possible, leading to a condition called *Chronic active Epstein-Barr virus* (CAEBV).
- *Varicella-zoster virus* (VZV) is a member of the herpesviruses. It is spread by airborne droplets or interpersonal contact. Varicella (chickenpox) is a childhood illness. Herpes zoster (shingles) often follows the reactivation of the dormant virus, but it can also be an acute disease.
- *Hepatitis A, B, C,* and *delta* are respected for their involvement with liver disease. Each has its own disparate features, but the ability to defend against them, as well as their duration of mischief, is largely determined by the body's immunity.

The persistent presence of viruses within the blood reflects numerous factors; often, it is a contest between the ability of the virus to replicate itself and the host's capacity to remove or inactivate them. This is influenced by immunity, genetics, metabolism, nutrition, and age. Generally, larger viruses are cleared more effectively. Of all the risk factors, impaired immunity predisposes someone to the reactivation of dormant viruses and compromises their ability to combat a primary viral infection. In short, the ability of any virus to initiate illness or infection relates to the body's immunity as well as prior exposure. Normally, within the body, viruses are prohibited from spreading by inhibiting their replication within cells or their passage from cell to cell. Since antibodies are not routinely employed to eliminate an initial infection (except for the enteroviruses), the task falls on cell-mediated immunity, which is essential to combat active viral infections. As a result, *defective cell-mediated immunity encourages recurring or chronic viral infections.*

People with chronic viral illnesses usually have deficient immunity. Most mainstream physicians believe the viral infection impairs immunity, prolonging its presence. This is not surprising because the persistent presence of certain viruses can directly and/or indirectly disturb the immune system. However, most people do not suffer with chronic viral illnesses, which means their immunity is competent enough to control these viruses. We can now return to the question: Why can most people effectively eradicate or control these viruses, while other people continuously suffer?

Sufferers of chronic viral illnesses are either unable to bring an acute viral infection under control or their immune system has allowed a virus to reactivate. If deficient cell-mediated immunity is a risk factor for developing a chronic viral illness, then sufferers must have impaired immunity prior to developing their chronic infection. Therefore, chronic viral illnesses are really a *symptom* of deficient immunity. So, what causes the impaired immunity that predisposes certain people to chronic viral illness?

Impaired immunity indicates that something abnormal is occurring within the body. Once again, metabolic immunosuppression reveals how candidiasis can promote deficient immunity. It can impair immunity, but does it encourage chronic viral illnesses? Like cancer, mainstream physicians appreciate that chronic viral illness sufferers can develop and suffer with candidiasis, but they believe the disease-causing yeast are only opportunistic infectious invaders, taking advantage of the impaired immunity. In contrast, candidiasis-minded physicians know that the candidiasis was present before the chronic viral illness. Their successes indicate that eradicating candidiasis corrects the patients impaired immunity, enabling them to effectively combat their viruses, returning them to dormancy. In short, *most people who suffer with chronic viral illnesses are candidiasis sufferers.* Typically, the candidiasis preceded their chronic viral illness, predisposing them to the reactivation of their dormant viruses.

How does candidiasis encourage chronic viral illnesses? In my second article, I explained how the prolonged presence of disease-causing yeast, with or without other infectious invaders, impairs cell-mediated immunity. Since cell-mediated immunity is essential to combat initial viral insults, it explains why some people have a difficult time recovering from viral infections. Even worse, impaired immunity impedes the immune system from suppressing dormant viruses within the body, which allows them to reactivate and cause chronic viral illnesses. The type of illness depends on the virus(es) present. Once again, this might seem simplistic, but it explains the observations and successes of knowledgeable candidiasis-minded physicians.

Most people do not develop chronic viral illnesses because they have a healthy immune system. In contrast, some people suffer with chronic viral illnesses, and deficient immunity is what prevents them from recovering. Most mainstream physicians believe that deficient immunity results from the viral infection itself. Candidiasis-minded physicians are quick to disagree. They know that candidiasis preceded and predisposed their patients to develop chronic viral illnesses; an infection with disease-causing yeast impairs immunity, encouraging the reactivation of dormant viruses or an inability to recover from an initial infection. The presence of a *candidiasis–chronic viral illness connection* means that people with this problem will now have a way to address it. The good news is that these viruses are usually brought under control and returned to dormancy once a person's candidiasis is treated. (Hint: Long COVID-19 sufferers are likely to be candidiasis sufferers.)

AIDS: A CHRONIC VIRAL ILLNESS

AIDS is defined as an immune system illness that arises from an infection with *human immunodeficiency virus* (HIV). It has been transmitted by sexual contact, sharing contaminated needles, blood (and blood product) transfusions, and from infected mothers to their offspring. The initial, acute infection is usually followed by a lengthy period of apparent dormancy; the virus is thought to proliferate during this time, slowly destroying the immune system. Gradually, suppressed immunity ensues, encouraging opportunistic infections and the development of malignancies (these are the cause of most AIDS victims' debility and death).

A significant percentage of people infected with HIV harbor the virus in its dormant state. Some people succumb, while other people maintain their immunity. So, what shifts the balance toward viral replication and infection? Typically, disease-causing yeast appear to be the causative culprit, with or without the assistance of other infectious invaders. Many of the adverse immune system alterations that arise with an HIV infection are identical to the immune impairment that accompanies severe chronic candidiasis (in people not infected with HIV). Obviously, the presence of HIV only makes immunity more fragile.

Most AIDS patients constantly wrestle with candidiasis. So, if someone with HIV (or another chronic virus) is kept free of disease-causing yeast (and other infectious invaders), they rarely progress from viral dormancy. If their infection is active and their candidiasis is treated, their increased immunity should place their virus into a dormant state. Therefore, if someone has HIV and is treated for candidiasis, they should not develop AIDS. Unfortunately, the virus is unlikely to be eliminated (although anything is possible). Realistically, if a healthy immune system is maintained, the virus should remain in a dormant state. It makes no difference if the virus is in perpetual dormancy or completely eradicated; either way, someone will not die from its presence. Sure, it is preferable to eliminate the virus, but until this can be done safely, lifelong dormancy is the next best thing. That is what some currently available drugs do and, if medicine finds a cure, it would be of great benefit. Until then, anything that poisons the immune system in the hopes of destroying the virus is to be approached with caution. Instead, the goal of HIV-positive people or those with AIDS is to regain and maintain optimal immunity.

Many mainstream physicians know that their patients with AIDS and pre-AIDS often develop candidiasis. Yet, they consider the disease-causing yeast to be secondary trespassers. Even though many of their patients have received antifungal therapy, few demonstrate substantial improvements. Does this mean that treating candidiasis is not the answer? Not necessarily. Most of their patients do not make dietary changes, which are an important part of anti-candidiasis therapy. Over time, disease-causing yeast can also become resistant to antifungal medication. In addition, the less prominent disease-causing yeast are not susceptible to a pharmaceutical agent—for example, *Saccharomyces cerevisiae* and *Rhodotorula*-species organisms. Harmful parasites, bacteria, and molds are commonly overlooked, unless there are overt gut problems, for example, unrelenting diarrhea. Even then, mainstream medicine's methods for identifying these infectious invaders are mediocre (chapter 17), so they are missed. When candidiasis is recognized as a significant contributor, it is often late in the course of the infection.

In contrast, candidiasis-minded physicians are aware of the role candidiasis plays within these people. In my second article, I described how candidiasis can promote AIDS in someone infected with HIV. After HIV enters their body, the virus instigates an infection, which is followed by the immune system's response to HIV. If someone's immunity is competent, the virus is placed into dormancy. Unfortunately, if this person has or develops candidiasis, it can impair immunity, leading to deficient cell-mediated immunity. At a certain point, immunity becomes so deficient that it cannot suppress the dormant virus, allowing it to replicate. As the virus increases its presence, immunity is further weakened, leading to fewer immune cells. This allows opportunistic infections to arise, which is when AIDS is diagnosed. Over time, this only worsens, leading to death unless it is comprehensively treated.

Candidiasis is not the cause of AIDS, but it is certainly a powerful contributing factor. Therefore, candidiasis should not be taken lightly in anyone infected with HIV. At the least, an anti-candidiasis approach will not harm someone with HIV. More likely, it will ensure viral dormancy for years to come. Indeed, even someone with advanced illness can be helped, but it is vital that they pay close attention to all the recommendations in this book and seek help from a knowledgeable candidiasis-minded physician.

AUTOIMMUNE DISEASES

The human body is an incredible, living machine, but it is far from perfect. The immune system occasionally develops a strange glitch in its programming. Some people develop immune disturbances that involve assaults against their body's own cells, tissues, and/or organs. In many cases, this is totally out of control, which can lead to significant bodily damage and disturbances. This is known as *autoimmune disease*. Alarmingly, more people develop this malady every day.

Classically, autoimmune disease arises when the immune system produces *antibodies* targeted to attack one or more of the body's own cells, tissues, and/or organs. Depending on the type of antibody, these may have a diverse effect or be directed specifically. Mainstream medicine believes this happens when the immune system cannot properly distinguish "self" from "nonself." It mistakenly perceives certain "self" elements as being abnormal (or foreign) and manufactures antibodies against them. Some researchers think this is genetically determined; others say it is completely under environmental control, while many are completely unaware of any cause.

If an *autoantibody* is identified, it is easy to diagnose an autoimmune disorder. Yet, autoimmunity does not always require self-reactive antibodies. Instead, *misdirected cell-mediated immunity* can also instigate autoimmune disease. These conditions are more difficult to classify. They are likely to be labeled as *idiopathic* or unknown because, without evidence of autoantibodies, the involved mechanisms are remotely obvious at best.

In general, whenever self-reactive cells or autoantibodies are produced, this usually results in a disturbance or damage. There are a great variety of autoimmune manifestations, with processes ranging from rather innocent to severe impairment. Specifics aside, each illness deals with some form of undesirable self-directed immune assault, with its magnitude and severity reflecting a variety of circumstances. To add confusion, many autoimmune sufferers commonly exhibit flare-ups interspersed with periods of remission. Therefore, the course and progression of each person's illness is rarely consistent.

Autoimmunity is usually directed toward one or more "target" cells, tissues, and/or organs, but its effects may be widespread. Although there are exceptions, the potential exists for *autoantibodies* to be manufactured against almost any cell, tissue, and/or organ within the body; many autoantibodies exist and have been identified. Similarly, *misdirected cell-mediated immunity* can be undesirably aimed at the body's own cells, tissues, and/or organs.

It is not pertinent to list all the known or suspected autoimmune illnesses. Even though each has its own undesirable characteristics, all have related processes. The variations simply reflect a person's genetics and exposures. In general, there is a great diversity of autoantibodies and misdirected cell-mediated autoimmunity. Either may cause autoimmune disease by itself, but most sufferers probably experience both simultaneously: misdirected cell-mediated assaults *and* autoantibodies that are targeted to attack "self" elements (because both immune processes are closely interconnected).

What causes autoimmune disease? Although there are theories, most mainstream physicians will admit they are unsure. Yet, since every illness must have a cause, something must be responsible for autoimmune disease. What instigates this self-directed destruction? In some cases, it reflects exposure to a virus, drug, or toxic chemical/metal. Undeniably, anything that impairs immunity can instigate autoimmune disease. Because most autoimmune diseases do not require autoantibodies and their origins remain unknown, it is extremely likely misdirected cell-mediated immunity is responsible.

Again, metabolic immunosuppression is involved. In my third article, I explained how chronic candidiasis, with or without other infectious invaders, can instigate or promote autoimmune disease. On the surface, autoimmunity and chronic candidiasis have much in common. Autoimmunity can involve autoantibodies and/or misdirected cell-mediated immunity. Candidiasis is an *infection* with *allergic* consequences that can impair cell-mediated immunity and promote allergic reactions that generate antibodies. When a candidiasis sufferer has deficient immunity, they may be unable to appropriately discriminate "self" elements from "nonself." In turn, this can permit and promote misdirected cell-mediated autoimmunity. What about the autoantibodies? Since the body's cells, tissues, and organs share some similar (antigenic) components with disease-causing yeast, especially *Candida albicans*, autoantibodies may arise as a confused (allergic) attempt to eliminate the disease-causing yeast. In other words, instead of the antibodies assaulting the disease-causing yeast, they mistakenly attack "self" elements.

The specifics make this clear. As candidiasis impairs immunity, the amount and variety of beneficial immune cells (T cells) can decrease. At some point, the normal cells can no longer compete with and/or suppress the abnormal cells, allowing the abnormal cells to increase in number. If these cells are programmed to assault "self" elements, this creates a population of self-reactive T cells that promote misdirected cell-mediated autoimmunity. In addition, the immune system can become sensitive to the presence (antigens) of disease-causing yeast. Unfortunately, with impaired immunity, this may encourage the production of autoantibodies. Although the general process is the same, the type of autoimmune disease that arises depends on someone's genetics, environmental exposures, diet, and so on.

Research supports an anti-candidiasis approach. As an example, various studies were performed using a natural antifungal antibiotic called *rapamycin* and some of its newer analogs. These medications have antifungal activity; they kill disease-causing yeast and other fungi. Researchers discovered that these drugs have marked anti-inflammatory effects and hinder harmful immune system activities; notably, they impede autoimmune diseases. Since antifungal medications can improve autoimmunity, this supports a *candidiasis–autoimmune disease connection*. Most likely, the benefits of these drugs occur by reversing the immune impairments that accompany candidiasis. In short, eliminating candidiasis corrects the misdirected cell-mediated immunity. It may also decrease the generation of autoantibodies because the stimulus for their production will be eliminated when the disease-causing yeast are gone. More compelling, some studies note improvements in other prominent candidiasis-related illnesses using these medications, including psoriasis, dermatitis, eczema, seborrhea, reversible obstructive airway disease (asthma), food allergies, and inflammatory bowel disease. One researcher described their antitumor (anticancer) effectiveness. Another study demonstrated that rapamycin inhibits cardiovascular disease (arterial thickening). This supports a cause-and-effect association between candidiasis and illness, especially in conditions that involve impaired immunity.

Regardless of the exact science, great improvements often occur after an autoimmune disease sufferer eliminates their candidiasis. Some mainstream medical skeptics will claim any benefits that arise reflect the waxing-waning nature of autoimmunity. In contrast, once someone eradicates their candidiasis and improves, relapses are uncommon. With this understanding, many candidiasis-minded physicians have helped their patients with autoimmune disease using an anti-candidiasis approach. Yet, once autoimmune disease is present, it is often difficult to stop, which means there is no guarantee of a cure. Many sufferers may demonstrate only moderate improvements. Regardless, eliminating candidiasis is the best way to treat anyone with misdirected immunity. Keep in mind, other infectious invaders regularly contribute to and exacerbate autoimmunity and must be addressed as well, including harmful parasites, bacteria, molds, and viruses. So, the *candidiasis–autoimmune disease connection* has been brought into the light and should no longer be ignored.

IMPROVING YOUR IMMUNITY

The immune system is an incredibly complex network of cells, tissues, and organs. Its goal is to keep the body free from disease. It has an ability to recognize "self" from "nonself." Usually, "self" elements are tolerated, while "foreigners" are eliminated. To accomplish this, the immune system has two prominent interrelated sides: *cell-mediated immunity* and *antibodies*. Cell-mediated activities do not need antibodies, but antibody reactions require cellular assistance. In addition, the *complement system* also participates. These three overlapping pieces determine the body's ability to effectively combat an infection.

During a chronic or recurring infection, the liver decreases its metabolic (chemical) duties to assist the immune system. Using its *acute phase response*, it increases its production and release of numerous *acute phase proteins* involved in a nonspecific host defense; these proteins help the immune system destroy a variety of infectious invaders as well as promote healing during inflammation. Although this is meant to be a short-term boost to immunity, chronic candidiasis promotes a prolonged acute phase response. This disturbs the body's metabolic functioning and instigates or promotes disturbances, including *glucose intolerance, hyperinsulinism*, and *hyperlipidemia* (hypercholesterolemia and/or hypertriglyceridemia). This can adversely affect blood sugar regulation (chapter 11) and encourage cardiovascular illness (chapter 7). Even worse, a persistent acute phase response can lead to deficient immunity, which may involve inferior functioning immune cells (suppressed immunity), fewer immune cells (depressed immunity), or both. This condition, *metabolic immunosuppression*, is common among candidiasis sufferers. Yet, every candidiasis suffer does not develop all these disturbances. Every sufferer is a unique individual, having their own inherent strengths and weaknesses. So, the manifestations of metabolic immunosuppression range from subtle to overtly obvious. Furthermore, the immune system interacts with the nervous and endocrine systems, so there will be numerous other related disturbances (chapters 10 and 11).

Deficient immunity is not to be taken casually because it can allow abnormal cells to arise and proliferate, leading to cancer. It can also permit the reactivation of dormant viruses, causing chronic viral infections. Moreover, impaired immunity can encourage misdirected cell-mediated immunity and/or the generation of autoantibodies, instigating autoimmune diseases. Instead of being illnesses with mysterious or unknown origins, chronic candidiasis is often revealed as their true underlying cause. It is important to appreciate that, although they can impair immunity by themselves, disease-causing yeast are frequently assisted by other infectious invaders, including harmful parasites, bacteria, molds, and viruses.

Mainstream physicians believe that disease-causing yeast are opportunistic infectious invaders that replicate and colonize the human body because of impaired immunity. In contrast, candidiasis-minded physicians are aware that an infection with disease-causing yeast usually *precedes* a person's cancer, chronic viral illness, and autoimmune disease. In other words, candidiasis can instigate and promote the impaired immunity that predisposes a person to these medical maladies. Admittedly, it is not responsible for every case of deficient immunity, but it is probably responsible for most. Since eliminating candidiasis often promotes incredible improvements in immunity, it would seem to be the best way to correct the immune system disturbances that participate in these medical maladies. In many cases, this can induce remission and even a cure. Even if treating candidiasis does not produce a miraculous recovery, it can still be of great benefit.

The best defense is a good offense. In a nutshell, this describes the benefit of eliminating your candidiasis as soon as it is identified. This is your best chance to have a healthy immune system. People with healthy immune systems have fewer colds, and when they do develop an illness, they do not feel as bad and seem to recover rapidly. Even more important, a healthy immune system prevents the impaired immunity that predisposes you to cancer, chronic viral illnesses, and autoimmune diseases. To sum this up: "Treat someone for a cold, and they'll be better for a day, but strengthen a person's immune system, and they'll stay well for a lifetime!"

CHAPTER 15

Chronic Fatigue

Most people know how they feel after work; it involves a tiredness that reflects their efforts and stress during the day. It is normal to be tired after work. A tough week of meetings, traveling, and socializing can make the weekend a welcome respite. Following a night of sleep or a quiet weekend, most people feel moderately to fully rested. In contrast, imagine an exhaustion so profound that it siphons off most or all your strength. A depletion of energy so severe that resting in bed becomes your major occupation. Does this seem exaggerated? For many people, it is a reality. Yes, there is a difference between tiredness and fatigue. Tiredness is part of living and exerting yourself. Tiredness resolves with rest. Fatigue barely improves with rest and tends to worsen over time. Although tiredness involves a lack of energy, you know fatigue is present when your energy cannot be regained. Tiredness is normal. Fatigue is not.

One of the most frequent complaints and concerns among patients worldwide is fatigue. It has no preference with respect to race, creed, color, nationality, religion, economic status, or any other parameter. Yes, certain groups demonstrate a greater prevalence of fatigue, notably women, but virtually everyone is at risk.

Fatigue is extreme tiredness from mental or physical exertion, or illness. People with chronic fatigue often cannot participate in their usual daily activities, while some sufferers are bedridden for most of the day with debilitating exhaustion. Fatigue has a highly variable, *subjective* component. What adversely affects one person may slightly inconvenience another. Physically fit people might consider their fatigue insignificant compared to others. Regardless, once fatigue is accepted as legitimate, its actual magnitude is irrelevant.

For a long time, mainstream medicine did not take persistent fatigue seriously. Chronic fatigue was described in a paper published in 1869 and was noted to be a major feature among outbreaks of illness in Los Angeles in 1934, at London's Royal Free Hospital in 1955, and in the United Kingdom in 1956. Even though fatigue is a common complaint voiced by patients, mainstream medicine continued to ignore it. Finally, because of an infectious mononucleosis-like illness in the Lake Tahoe area of California-Nevada in 1987 that involved severe fatigue, the Centers for Disease Control and Prevention was forced to define chronic fatigue syndrome (CFS) in 1988.

Also called myalgic encephalomyelitis (ME), CFS is considered a long-term illness that affects many bodily systems. Its symptoms include a six-month or longer history of fatigue of new onset that causes a significantly lowered ability to participate in normal activities. In addition, it involves a worsening of symptoms after physical or mental activity that would not have caused a problem previously. CFS is not just a "you feel tired" illness because there are other signs and symptoms that vary from one sufferer to another. It is important to know that CFS is a diagnosis of exclusion; someone can only be diagnosed with CFS when their fatigue is not the result of any other chronic clinical disorder. According to a 2015 report by the National Academy of Medicine, CFS affects as many as 2.5 million Americans and 17 to 24 million people worldwide.

With respect to naming a condition that involves persistent fatigue, mainstream medicine has gone through many iterations. Names aside, one thing is clear, CFS is a condition involving *fatigue* as its prominent and prime manifestation. It's not just ordinary tiredness but a debilitating, nagging, and miserable exhaustion that lasts at least six months.

Other symptoms and signs of CFS include (in decreasing frequency) low-grade fever; muscle aches (myalgias); joint pains/stiffness; sleep disorders; mental fatigue, poor concentration, and/or decreased memory (cognitive impairment); depression/anxiety; inability to tolerate extremes of heat, light, or noise; ocular symptoms; irritability/panic disorders; headaches; mouth ulcers and sore throat (pharyngitis); muscle weakness; post-exertion malaise; worsened PMS; anorexia and/or nausea; cough; swelling of the hands or feet; painful lymph nodes; drenching night sweats; sensitivities to foods, drugs, alcohol, and chemicals; and balance problems. This variability is a large reason why CFS is confusing and poorly understood.

Mainstream medicine has looked for a cause and, for all the research that has been done, it has no definitive answers. Numerous viruses have been identified within CFS sufferers (also *Mycoplasma genus* and *Mycoplasma fermentans*), but they do *not* appear to cause this condition. Yet, giving CFS a definition has prevented mainstream medicine from appreciating its true cause. If mainstream physicians realized all the symptoms associated with CFS are readily associated with candidiasis, the real perpetrator of this malady would be evident. Chronic candidiasis sufferers often experience persistent or recurring fatigue as a debilitating symptom. So, most CFS sufferers are really candidiasis sufferers. Candidiasis-minded physicians know that more than 80 percent of CFS sufferers are found to be candidiasis sufferers, and this is a lowball estimate. Yes, disease-causing yeast are not the only culprits because they are frequently assisted by harmful parasites, bacteria, molds, and/or viruses.

How is candidiasis responsible for chronic fatigue? Their prolonged presence creates a long-term *infection* with *allergic* consequences that causes inflammation and stresses the body, promoting exhaustion. Moreover, numerous cofactors and other infectious invaders contribute their ill effects, which has caused candidiasis to be consistently overlooked.

How are disease-causing yeast involved? Do not ask mainstream physicians. After all, they accept CFS as being an independent and serious disorder. For many years, they thought CFS was a psychological manifestation of stress and/or other emotional problems. Eventually, its various associations with impaired immunity were appreciated and studied, which has given CFS some credibility. Abnormalities involving both *cell-mediated immunity* and *humoral immunity* (antibodies) are common among CFS sufferers. Chronic candidiasis can instigate and promote similar immune system disturbances (chapter 14). In addition, it can disturb the nervous system (chapter 10) and endocrine (hormone) system (chapter 11), which are usually adversely affected in CFS sufferers. So, it should be clear that chronic candidiasis and CFS share many similarities, and not just the word "chronic."

CFS is no longer a mysterious condition. Disease-causing yeast are the prime culprits with respect to causing it. The following evidence will make the *candidiasis–chronic fatigue syndrome connection* more understandable and should provide hope for CFS sufferers.

VIRUSES OR DISEASE-CAUSING YEAST?

To determine the prevalence, characteristics, and outcome of CFS patients in primary care, researchers have found that 20 to 25 percent of their CFS patients complained of fatigue as a major problem. However, this is basically the only thing researchers and physicians readily understand and agree about CFS. Even so, it has not stopped researchers from searching for a cause.

With respect to the cause of CFS, mainstream medicine has focused on a wide array of culprits as well as a variety of metabolic (chemical) and environmental contributors. Yet, the exact origin of CFS currently remains unknown. Since it typically arises after a flu-like illness, this implies that CFS has an infectious origin, especially involving viruses. As a result, numerous researchers have been busy looking for the "virus" that causes CFS.

Because resources are limited and research is time consuming, different investigators concentrate on one virus or another. For all the effort, studies have not definitively proven that a virus causes CFS. So, rather than focusing on a specific virus, it is important to consider how viruses are thought to contribute to CFS. Some researchers believe viral illness leads to impaired immunity. Research reveals that CFS patients have abnormal cell populations; increased numbers of *cytotoxic T* cells (to combat intracellular infectious invaders) and decreased amounts of *suppressor T* cells (that terminate the attack when it is over). These researchers think an infection with one or more viruses promotes deficient immunity; combating a prolonged viral infection causes persistently hyperactive immune functioning, leading to the excessive production of cellular chemical mediators (cytokines) thought to induce CFS symptoms.

Numerous researchers agree with this thinking. They found that CFS sufferers demonstrate impaired immunity and hypothesize that an improperly functioning immune system cannot combat an offending virus and it also permits the reactivation of dormant viruses. So, deficient immunity is thought to precede the persistent viral infection(s) that participates in CFS. In short, a chronic viral infection is the effect of abnormal immunity, not its cause. Regardless of the viruses involved in CFS sufferers, it seems the impaired immunity must come first.

If viruses do not cause the impaired immunity, what does? Research reveals that *Candida albicans* depresses T cell and natural killer (NK) cell function. Similar immune abnormalities occur in CFS sufferers. The functioning of cytotoxic T cells, T-helper cells and NK cells is important in preventing reactivation of viral infections. So, if reactivated or persistent viral infections contribute to CFS symptoms, chronic candidiasis can participate in causing CFS.

An infection with disease-causing yeast can severely compromise immunity, impairing the body's ability to defend against an acute viral illness and permit the reactivation of dormant viruses (chapter 14). Although there are exceptions, a persistent infection with disease-causing yeast can cause *suppressed immunity* (inferior functioning cells), *depressed immunity* (fewer cells), or both *suppressed-depressed immunity* (fewer, inferior functioning cells). Regardless of the magnitude, *disturbed cell-mediated immunity encourages a persistent viral infection*, whether it reflects an infection with a recently acquired virus or the reactivation of a dormant virus. Yes, this can include the proliferation and mischief of one or more of the fatigue-associated viruses. Even though this is summarized in a single paragraph, the evidence indicates that viruses are not the cause of chronic fatigue. Rather, viruses are opportunists that instigate trouble *after* candidiasis impairs immunity. Once again, most of the population harbors one or more viruses in a dormant state, but only a small percentage of people develop CFS.

Candidiasis can promote suppressed, depressed, or suppressed-depressed immunity. Many sufferers often experience fatigue and other CFS symptoms without the participation of viruses. Although viruses can contribute their ill effects, disease-causing yeast are the primary infectious invaders that cause CFS. This means a chronic viral illness, whether a new infection or a reactivated dormant virus, occurs because of the impaired immunity promoted by chronic candidiasis. There are exceptions, but candidiasis must precede a chronic viral infection(s). Yes, the specific behavior of a virus may contribute to the variability of symptoms among CFS sufferers, and the more infectious invaders present, the greater the disturbances and variability that will arise. To prove this point, candidiasis-minded physicians know that most fatigue-causing viruses (as well as harmful parasites, bacteria, and molds) can be effectively combated and controlled by a CFS sufferer's immune system after their disease-causing yeast are eliminated.

How does candidiasis cause CFS? In short, suppressed immunity, with or without depressed immunity, can decrease the number of good immune cells, called T lymphocytes (notably, helper T cells). In turn, this can induce a decrease in natural killer cells and cytotoxic T cells as well as an increase or decrease in suppressor T cells. Under these conditions, initial viral insults are not effectively controlled, and dormant viruses will be able to reactivate. This can cause a chronic viral illness, contributing to fatigue. Some researchers believe that the cellular chemical mediators (cytokines) produced when the immune system is hyperactive are responsible for a CFS sufferer's symptoms. Although these cytokines enable the immune cells to communicate and may be responsible for CFS symptoms, they are far from the only cause. Indeed, most symptoms related to CFS mirror the symptoms associated with the infectious and allergic consequences of candidiasis. So, rather than reflecting an excess of cytokines, the symptoms of CFS result from candidiasis, with or without other infectious invaders. Moreover, research reveals that an infection with disease-causing yeast can easily alter the production and presence of cytokines, explaining the disturbances that occur within CFS sufferers (chapter 14).

The symptoms of CFS may appear at any time, depending on the severity and duration of someone's candidiasis as well as on the presence of other infectious invaders. Therefore, with respect to CFS, the disease-causing yeast are the primary troublemakers. So, how are disease-causing yeast able to promote fatigue? There are numerous possibilities.

HORMONE DISTURBANCES & MENTAL MANIFESTATIONS

Research reveals that CFS sufferers have disturbed immunity. Yet, the immune system does not function alone. Together with the nervous (chapter 10) and endocrine systems (chapter 11), all three form the *neuroendocrine-immune connection*. This helps explain why CFS sufferers routinely have endocrine (hormone) and neurological (mental) disturbances. Candidiasis sufferers also regularly manifest the same disturbances.

Many CFS symptoms accompany hormone disturbances, especially problems with the *adrenal glands*. CFS patients are often found to have low levels of *cortisol*—typically, a 30 to 40 percent decrease in production (hypocortisolism). Cortisol is a glucocorticoid manufactured by the adrenal gland *cortex* (chapter 11). The *glucocorticoids* help the body cope with stress and regulate the metabolism of fats, carbohydrates, and proteins as well as sodium and potassium. Cortisol has immune-suppressing and anti-inflammatory activities. When it is present in sufficient amounts, it assists in calming a hyperactive or aggressive immune system, especially in someone with a fatigue-inducing infection. Normally, as its amount decreases, the anterior pituitary releases *adrenocorticotropic hormone* (ACTH), stimulating the adrenal cortex to produce and release more cortisol (and other glucocorticoids). Unfortunately, decreased amounts of cortisol (and other glucocorticoids) promotes inflammation, abnormal metabolism, and impaired immunity. Because of its actions, a cortisol deficiency also frequently causes fatigue.

Investigators at the National Institute of Mental Health determined that most CFS patients have abnormally low levels of cortisol (glucocorticoids) and ACTH. Many studies have measured lowered evening levels of glucocorticoids and a decreased 24-hour excretion of cortisol within their urine as well as an increased sensitivity to administered (exogenous) ACTH. So, in addition to having difficulty manufacturing and releasing cortisol, their anterior pituitary gland appears unresponsive to their lowered levels or is suppressed. In short, these findings represent *adrenal cortex exhaustion* (hypoadrenocorticism). Although mainstream medicine is unsure why this happens, candidiasis sufferers regularly develop suppression, and even exhaustion, of their adrenal cortex without glandular destruction—*hypoadrenalism* (or hypoadrenocorticism). There is a *CFS–adrenal cortex exhaustion connection* and a *candidiasis-hypoadrenocorticism connection*, so a *candidiasis-hypoadrenocorticism-CFS connection* is supported. Furthermore, ACTH is manufactured by the anterior pituitary, and an abnormal metabolism can hinder its production, which can occur in candidiasis sufferers. Therefore, candidiasis can impair production of the adrenal cortex hormones as well as ACTH.

The disease-causing yeast may *directly* be responsible for this disturbance. Research reveals that *Candida albicans* has a *corticosteroid-binding protein* with a high affinity for binding with human *corticosterone* (chapter 11). This implies that disease-causing yeast, especially *Candida albicans*, can interact with and disturb the production of cortisol and other related steroid hormones within candidiasis sufferers. Other research found that disease-causing yeast can produce *steroid-like substances*. This may explain why candidiasis can cause hypoadrenocorticism and an insufficiency of ACTH. In a sufferer, disease-causing yeast may bind cortisol and other steroid hormones, reducing their amounts and efficacy. In addition, since disease-causing yeast can produce steroid-like substances, the anterior pituitary may be fooled; it does not receive a signal that more cortisol is needed. If the steroid-like substances are not active within humans, which is likely, it can cause a deficiency of adrenal cortical hormones and a decrease of ACTH.

Moreover, the adrenal gland *medulla* may contribute to fatigue. Its two hormones (*epinephrine* and *norepinephrine*) participate in blood sugar regulation as well as in the well-known fight-or-flight response that occurs when we feel threatened, excited, apprehensive, scared, and so on. They also stimulate metabolism, increase blood pressure, and depress the appetite. If candidiasis disturbs the functioning of the medulla (chapter 11), the production of its hormones can decrease. In combination with other disturbances, this can encourage a lowered blood sugar concentration, leading to an inappropriate supply of energy for the body's cells and tissues, especially the brain. A lack of available glucose can contribute to fatigue and promote mental manifestations (chapter 10). Since these symptoms are common among candidiasis sufferers and CFS sufferers, this further connects them.

Other glands also contribute. There is a *hypothyroidism-CFS connection*. Decreased functioning of the *thyroid gland* can cause *hypothyroidism*, underactivity or decreased functioning of the gland and its hormones. Since thyroid hormone is vital for the body's optimal metabolism (chemical activities), hypothyroidism will promote deficient metabolism. Typically, someone with hypothyroidism is easily tired and frequently feels cold, especially in their hands and feet. Hypothyroidism also impairs immunity and induces various other problems. Fortunately, this is usually discovered by routine thyroid hormone laboratory testing. Why do CFS sufferers have thyroid gland problems? Most CFS sufferers are candidiasis sufferers who have an undeniable *candidiasis-hypothyroidism connection* (chapter 11). So, candidiasis can contribute to fatigue by adversely affecting the thyroid gland. More often, it disrupts the metabolism without obvious thyroid gland disturbances. This condition, called *hypometabolism*, arises when there is an insufficient conversion of thyroid hormone from its less active to more active form (chapter 11). Since the more active form is essential for optimal metabolism, its deficiency can promote fatigue.

Another likely participant are the parathyroid glands. Although they are less commonly involved with CFS, candidiasis can adversely alter the functioning of the pituitary gland and/or sex glands. Therefore, other hormone disturbances (chapter 11) can readily instigate or promote fatigue.

Since the *neuroendocrine-immune connection* is comprised of three parts, the nervous system readily contributes to CFS. A large percentage of sufferers develop symptoms related to abnormal nervous system functioning, including mental fatigue, poor concentration, loss of memory, depression, anxiety, irritability, panic disorders, headaches, and sleep disorders. Research indicates that CFS sufferers may have *defective monoamine metabolism*. In short, CFS sufferers have abnormal chemical functioning within their brain and nervous system. Although mainstream medicine is unsure why this occurs, many of the CFS mental manifestations are common among candidiasis sufferers. There is a *candidiasis–psychological connection* (chapter 10), and the presence of an *infection* with disease-causing yeast can adversely affect the neurotransmitters within the brains of candidiasis sufferers. In addition, candidiasis has *allergic* consequences, and the presence of numerous harmful candidiasis-related substances can undesirably influence the brain's functioning, both directly and indirectly. This promotes the mental manifestations associated with candidiasis and contributes to fatigue.

So, the fatigue that arises can be instigated and promoted by the immune, endocrine, and nervous systems. Rather than being separate, the *neuroendocrine-immune connection* is an interconnected entity. Each system interacts with and depends on the others, and disturbances involving one are readily reflected within the others. In the bigger picture, this explains the variety of symptoms among CFS sufferers. Every sufferer is a unique individual with their own bodily strengths and weaknesses. So, in addition to the infectious invaders, their symptoms reflect the ability of their *neuroendocrine-immune connection* to withstand insults and injuries. For example, one CFS sufferer may have a susceptible endocrine system, causing hormone disturbances to be more prevalent, whereas another may have more notable nervous system problems, while a third CFS sufferer may have significantly impaired immunity.

CFS sufferers and candidiasis sufferers have much in common. Candidiasis sufferers often experience fatigue as well as the other disturbances common among CFS sufferers. These findings strengthen the case for a *candidiasis-CFS connection.*

SUPPORTING THE CANDIDIASIS-CFS CONNECTION

Although mainstream medicine acknowledges that candidiasis can contribute to CFS, they do not believe it is the major cause. Instead of embracing the *candidiasis-CFS connection*, researchers search for the ever smaller, "missing pieces" of the CFS puzzle. Yet, most of the pieces they find are associated with candidiasis in one way or another, whether or not they know it.

For example, under the premise that fatigue results from an inability to produce enough cellular energy, researchers have examined the human cell's intracellular organelles called *mitochondria*. They are specialized parts that function like little power stations, generating most of the cell's energy. The *number* of mitochondria a cell contains is usually in proportion to its *aerobic capacity*; the greater the cell's workload, the more mitochondria it often has.

Acylcarnitine is a substance within the mitochondria that assists in its generation of energy. Research shows that the *amount* of acylcarnitine correlates with a cell's ability to *generate energy*. Researchers found CFS patients have a deficiency of serum acylcarnitine. Moreover, their concentration of serum acylcarnitine tends to increase to normal as they recover from their fatigue. Therefore, the fatigue that arises in CFS appears to reflect a *mitochondrial disturbance*. Since CFS is associated with a *decrease* of acylcarnitine within the mitochondria, it implies that CFS sufferers cannot generate enough cellular energy. More specifically, this decreases the body's ability to generate energy (aerobically) using oxygen, so a shift toward *anaerobic* metabolism must occur (generating energy without oxygen). Energetically, anaerobic metabolism is wasteful and frequently unable to meet the body's needs. Even worse, it often leads to the production of toxic substances that effectively poison the body's cellular processes—notably, lactic acid. Since mitochondrial functioning is a chemical process that is adversely altered, CFS appears to be a metabolic (chemical) disorder.

Yet, the presence of a mitochondrial disturbance does not explain why it occurs in the first place. To put things in perspective, consider Reye's syndrome, which follows a viral infection that insults the liver, impairing its functioning and promoting fatty infiltration. During the process, the liver's mitochondria become disturbed, impeding their production of energy. Japanese researchers have shown that CFS and Reye's syndrome have many similarities. As a result, the mitochondrial disturbance that occurs in CFS is thought to follow a viral insult. However, this is a bold conclusion because both medical maladies have significant differences. Reye's syndrome commonly occurs within children and is much more fatal, whereas CFS most often manifests within adults and is rarely lethal. If they survive, Reye's syndrome sufferers frequently have a good prognosis for a quick and complete recovery. In contrast, CFS requires a minimum of at least six months of unrelenting fatigue before it is officially diagnosed. Why are these differences important? If the mitochondrial disturbance in CFS *only* reflected a viral insult, then all CFS sufferers would have viral infections, but this is not the case. In addition, if a virus was solely responsible for CFS, most sufferers should be able to mount an effective immune response and recover from the infection (chapter 14), but this does not happen. More revealing, the mitochondrial disturbance that occurs with Reye's syndrome is more pronounced than in CFS. Since Reye's syndrome sufferers can recover from a significant viral insult, while CFS sufferers are unable to recover from a milder offender, it implies that something is compromising the immunity of CFS sufferers, preventing them from effectively combating their viral insult.

Candidiasis is an *infection* with disease-causing yeast that can suppress (and depress) the immune system (chapter 14). As a result, its sufferers frequently have deficient immunity, which encourages frequent or continuous viral infections. It is also a metabolic disorder because a multitude and variety of chemical disturbances regularly occur among its sufferers. Disease-causing yeast can produce numerous harmful substances that must be detoxified and/or cleared from the body by the liver (and kidneys).

Increased amounts of these harmful substances can injure and damage the liver's functioning, leading to mitochondrial disturbances. For example, *gliotoxin* is a harmful substance produced by disease-causing yeast and other fungi. Abundant research reveals that gliotoxin can impair immunity (chapter 14) and adversely affect the liver's functioning (chapters 10 and 14). Research reveals low concentrations of gliotoxin stimulate the release of calcium ions from mitochondria. Why is this significant? In short, calcium plays an indirect role in the generation of mitochondrial energy. So, a loss of calcium disturbs mitochondrial functioning, impairing its ability to generate energy. Therefore, a mitochondrial disturbance is readily consistent with the mischief of candidiasis.

Instead of mitochondria, some researchers focus on other aspects of metabolism, including *glucose intolerance* and *abnormal lipid metabolism*. Are these conditions specific to CFS? No, candidiasis is at work. Candidiasis sufferers frequently develop *metabolic immunosuppression*, a condition that involves *glucose intolerance*, *hyperinsulinism*, *hyperlipidemia*, and/or *impaired immunity* (chapter 14). How does this arise? A long-term infection with disease-causing yeast can stimulate the liver's *acute phase response*; to combat a persistent infection or inflammation, the liver decreases its metabolic activities to assist the immune system. As a result, the liver's metabolic duties are compromised, especially its ability to detoxify harmful substances. In turn, this encourages more generalized metabolic disturbances, which can easily include fatigue. Moreover, a continuous acute phase response also promotes glucose intolerance, the excess release or prolonged presence of insulin, abnormal lipid metabolism, and impaired immunity. So, rather than being isolated findings, these disturbances are secondary to candidiasis, adding further support for the *candidiasis-CFS connection*.

Candidiasis and CFS share many similarities. Candidiasis sufferers and CFS sufferers both have an impaired lymphocyte responsiveness to *mitogens* (substances that induce or stimulate cell division), indicating that their immune disturbances are related. Both have been found to have altered amounts of intracellular chemical messengers (interleukins and interferons), which strongly suggests the presence of infectious and/or viral immune system challenges. In CFS, hyperactivity of a specific enzyme depletes the body of available energy, but this also occurs within candidiasis sufferers with fatigue. Therefore, both illnesses share many common characteristics.

Fortunately, there is more compelling evidence to support a *candidiasis-CFS connection*. At the First International Conference on Chronic Fatigue Syndrome in San Francisco, California, on April 15, 1989, Carol Jessop, M.D., of El Territo, California, presented an analysis of 1,100 patients, including subjects with multiple complaints, especially fatigue, who were treated for more than nine years. About 80 percent of the patients had a history of receiving repeated courses of antibiotics for acne, urinary tract infections, bronchitis, and upper respiratory infections. Most of them experienced sugar and alcohol cravings. Impressively, following 3 to 12 months of treatment with ketoconazole (Nizoral, 200 mg/day, a systemic antifungal medication) as well as a yeast-free/sugar-free diet, 84 percent of the subjects noted significant improvement; most of their symptoms were eliminated, especially their fatigue. As a result, Dr. Jessop concluded that an infection with *Candida albicans* must have predominantly contributed to their symptoms and proposed that CFS reflected the colonization of disease-causing yeast within the gastrointestinal tract, with the subsequent release of a systemic toxin. Dr. Jessop's work strongly supports the *candidiasis-CFS connection*.

Since many studies have demonstrated that ketoconazole increases the immune system in various ways, some researchers believe Dr. Jessop's patients improved from the medication itself. Yet, this does not apply to real life. It does not explain what caused Dr. Jessop's patients to develop CFS in the first place or how boosting immunity corrected their ill health. With all the available evidence revealing candidiasis as the true cause of CFS, with or without the assistance of other infectious invaders, the benefits of ketoconazole really occur indirectly. In other words, instead of the immune improvements being a direct effect of the medication, eliminating the disease-causing yeast corrects the impaired immunity and fatigue. The majority of Dr. Jessop's patients had one or more risk factors for developing candidiasis (chapter 2), implying that candidiasis preceded their CFS. Since their improvements followed the use of a medication that kills disease-causing yeast, their recovery was almost certainly due to eliminating their candidiasis. Moreover, numerous studies demonstrate how improvements within the gut, notably the correction of leaky gut, caused a remission in CFS sufferers. Since *gastrointestinal candidiasis* is the primary instigator of leaky gut syndrome (chapter 4), the disease-causing yeast are the primary problem, not the immune system.

If you understand the *candidiasis-CFS connection*, you know more than most mainstream medicine CFS experts. Unfortunately, mainstream physicians continue to search for increasingly smaller pieces of the CFS puzzle, while completely missing the big picture. Sad to say, their anti-candidiasis bias prevents most CFS sufferers from being appropriately treated and wastes a lot of time and money on obscure and misdirected research.

LYME DISEASE & FATIGUE

What about Lyme disease being the cause of CFS? After all, *Lyme disease* has been linked to CFS for decades. Research has found a relationship between the infectious invader that causes Lyme disease and CFS because some sufferers have positive anti-*Borrelia burgdorferi* antibodies. Is *Borrelia burgdorferi* responsible for CFS? It is unlikely because the fatigue that accompanies Lyme disease is rarely caused by this infectious invader. Instead, the development of CFS is frequently a result of treatment. In a September 1994 article, *"Disarming Lyme Disease,"* in *Scientific American*, Professors of Medicine Fred S. Kantor and Paul B. Beeson at Yale University stated, "Antibiotics are usually curative. A vaccine is in clinical trials. Next on the research agenda: how to help people suffering from chronic symptoms." If antibiotics are usually curative, then Lyme disease is, at best, infrequently responsible for CFS. So, is the fatigue that does arise in chronic cases of Lyme disease because of the illness itself, or is something else going on?

Lyme disease is a complex, immune-mediated, multisystem disorder. Transmission of the infectious invader, the spirochete *Borrelia burgdorferi*, usually involves a tick bite. Soon after, the victim may develop the hallmark manifestation, an expanding "bull's-eye" skin lesion or rash; as it expands outward, it clears in the center. The first set of symptoms (initial infection) may disappear. If no treatment is rendered, it may be weeks to months until a sufferer manifests neurologic, cardiac, and/or joint abnormalities. Arthritis and musculoskeletal problems are the most common disturbances. Typically, these begin as vague, migrating pains within the tendons, muscles, and joints. The temporomandibular joint (opens the mouth/jaw) is often involved. Roughly 50 percent experience arthritis with swelling and discomfort, especially within the knees. In about 10 percent of the victims that are *not* treated, this can become a chronic illness.

Lyme disease sufferers may manifest a diversity of nervous system symptoms. Bell's palsy (facial nerve paralysis) can arise, with one or both sides of the face being paralyzed for several weeks. Inflammation of the brain's protective membrane can produce meningitis, notable for its ability to cause neck stiffness, a sensitivity to light, headaches, and vomiting. This can progress to the brain (encephalitis), instigating memory loss, sleepiness, irritability, and moodiness. Radiating nerve pain may occur within areas affected with impaired nerve sensitivities. There can be numbness and tingling within the extremities. Moreover, Lyme disease may disturb heart functioning, and irregular cardiac rhythms (arrhythmias) are common. Usually, the ability of the heart muscle to conduct an appropriate stimulatory signal is disrupted, leading to heart rhythm disturbances (atrioventricular blocks).

Although a vaccine may prevent Lyme disease, *antibiotics* are the only effective arsenal against active Lyme disease, especially in its acute stage. Because it takes time to eradicate this infectious invader, these pharmaceutical agents are regularly prescribed for lengthy periods. Yet, the evidence is lacking to support a longer course of antibiotics for Lyme disease sufferers who are more severely affected.

Fatigue may arise during Lyme disease, but it is not a typical symptom until a sufferer is treated with a prolonged course of antibiotics. Does the fatigue result from persistent Lyme disease or is something else occurring? Once again, since antibiotics frequently destroy the infectious invaders, their use is usually curative. If the infectious invader is resistant to the antibiotic used, a sufferer's symptoms will persist, and most physicians will prescribe a different antibiotic. The fatigue that occurs usually arises slowly over time—typically, in proportion to the amount of antibiotics used and tends to be more noticeable as a sufferer's symptoms decrease. Why? In addition to killing harmful bacteria, antibiotics kill beneficial bacteria. As a result, the prolonged use of antibiotics strongly promotes the colonization of disease-causing yeast, leading to candidiasis (chapters 2, 3, and 4). Rather than the fatigue arising because of a persistent infection with *Borrelia burgdorferi*, Lyme disease sufferers who develop CFS should be considered candidiasis sufferers until proven otherwise.

Although there are exceptions, Lyme disease is *not* the cause of CFS. Yes, CFS can arise during Lyme disease, especially during treatment. However, antibiotics typically eliminate the infectious invader and are curative. Since the fatigue persists, it cannot result from the persistent presence of *Borrelia burgdorferi* and must occur for another reason. In most Lyme disease sufferers who develop CFS, the long-term use of antibiotics promotes candidiasis, leading to CFS. In fact, this is a great example of "cause and effect"—that is, how candidiasis precedes and promotes CFS—and highlights the risk of taking an abundance of antibiotics.

GETTING ENERGIZED

Do you have low energy? Do you frequently feel tired? Do you have trouble making it through the day without resting or taking a nap? Yes, everyone gets tired at one time or another. Fortunately, a little relaxation and rest replenishes most people's energy.

In stark contrast, if you have been diagnosed with CFS, your fatigue must have been present for at least six months. CFS sufferers do not feel energized, even after sleeping for hours and hours. Many sufferers spend exceptional amounts of time in bed. Some sufferers are likely to require lengthy and frequent periods of rest just to survive, as minor exertions can sap their strength and deplete their remaining energy. Depending on someone's responsibilities and social support, CFS can range from disturbing to debilitating to devastating.

Why does CFS occur? Although mainstream researchers believe that many viruses participate and are responsible for the deficient immunity and fatigue that arises, they are not any closer to preventing or treating CFS.

What are your options? There is only one. All the evidence supports a *candidiasis-CFS connection*. Rather than being a mysterious illness, candidiasis-minded physicians know that CFS is a *symptom* strongly associated with chronic candidiasis. Since CFS sufferers and candidiasis sufferers often have identical disturbances, CFS is a manifestation of candidiasis that involves severe fatigue. In short, most CFS sufferers are really candidiasis sufferers, although there are exceptions. To make matters worse, disease-causing yeast may be assisted by other infectious invaders, including harmful parasites, bacteria, molds, and/or viruses. Obviously, the more infectious invaders present, the greater the toll it takes on someone's body.

How does candidiasis cause CFS? There is no one specific way. Yet, candidiasis and CFS are *primarily* metabolic (chemical) and immune system disorders. The presence of an *infection* with disease-causing yeast can suppress, and even depress, the immune system, allowing persistent viral infections to continuously harm the body (chapter 14). Disease-causing yeast produce harmful substances that are injurious or poisonous to the body, especially the liver. In turn, this compromises the liver's ability to detoxify harmful substances and provide sufficient energy. Impaired liver metabolism can promote abnormal glucose tolerance (glucose intolerance), hyperinsulinism, and hyperlipidemia (chapter 14). Moreover, altered liver functioning will indirectly affect other metabolic processes and pathways. Any or all of this can impair or injure the functioning of the mitochondria within the cells of the body, especially the liver. Since these intracellular organelles are the cell's *power stations*, a mitochondrial disturbance decreases the body's ability to generate enough energy, which additionally disturbs numerous other metabolic processes.

Candidiasis can cause other problems that contribute to fatigue. It can instigate and promote a variety of sensitivities and hypersensitivities, leading to inflammation and allergies (chapter 16). Its *infectious* and *allergic* consequences can induce an abundance of *inflammation*, localized and systemic. The colonization of disease-causing yeast can establish conditions that encourage malabsorption and nutritional deficiencies (chapter 4), making it difficult to function and generate sufficient cellular energy. Their presence increases the generation of harmful oxygen-based free radical reactions with their accompanying cellular insults and injuries (chapter 7). Immune impairments may precipitate autoimmune activities (chapter 14) that cause cellular or glandular stimulation, inhibition, or destruction, promoting substantial disturbances. Candidiasis can directly or indirectly cause dysfunction, suppression, or exhaustion of the pituitary gland, thyroid gland, parathyroid glands, adrenal glands, and/or sex glands; any of these can contribute to fatigue (chapter 11). Candidiasis can promote neurological disturbances (chapter 10); these frequently involve neurotransmitter abnormalities that directly disturb the brain's functioning and indirectly disturb the rest of the body. In short, candidiasis can disturb the *neuroendocrine-immune connection* in a variety of ways, with CFS being the undesirable and unpleasant consequence.

It is no coincidence that most CFS sufferers also have numerous symptoms that are typical of candidiasis. Most CFS sufferers have some magnitude of impaired gastrointestinal permeability, implying the presence of leaky gut syndrome (chapters 3 and 4). Since it is a consistent manifestation of candidiasis, a CFS sufferer is almost certain to be a candidiasis sufferer. Yet, candidiasis is not always obvious, especially if you do not know what you are looking for. Although you must have a high index of suspicion, there are numerous tests that can confirm your suspicions.

With all the available evidence strongly supporting a *candidiasis-CFS connection*, it is unfortunate that most physicians do not consider candidiasis or ignore it completely. An anti-candidiasis bias dooms CFS to remain a mysterious medical malady and forces many CFS sufferers to continue to be prisoners of their own beds. Fortunately, there are candidiasis-minded physicians who think otherwise and consistently help CFS sufferers get well. So, if you are a CFS sufferer, or just feel tired, appropriately addressing your candidiasis will give you the greatest chance of getting energized.

CHAPTER 16

Allergies

You may have been an allergic child with frequent ear infections and food intolerances. As a teenager, you might have woken up one morning with watery eyes and a scratchy throat. Your exercise-induced asthma may have developed after you had a chest cold. Your allergy to cats may have only been recently noticeable. Allergies can develop at any time. They can range from insignificant to debilitating. Even though a few lucky people seem to outgrow their allergies, most people's allergies only worsen over time.

What about allergy symptoms? You may suffer with the classical symptoms of sneezing, a runny nose, watery eyes, and a scratchy throat. Or you might have postnasal drip, coughing, and congested ears. Typically, these symptoms are easy to diagnose as allergy related. In contrast, a great number of allergic manifestations are not so obvious. Most people, and many physicians, are unaware that there is a large diversity of allergic manifestations that can adversely affect virtually every part of your body. Allergies can instigate or promote a variety of gastrointestinal symptoms. Acne, hives (urticaria), and other skin disturbances are often allergy related. Allergies can instigate or promote many mental manifestations, including concentration difficulties, memory problems, moodiness, depression, anxiety, and more. They can contribute to chronic fatigue. Joint pain is frequently the result of allergies. Even palpitations may be allergy related. On and on it goes. Allergies are not just a black-or-white issue because there is an incredible amount of variability. Although seasonal allergies are common, other allergic manifestations are equally prevalent and frequently less than obvious.

More than 50 million Americans suffer with allergies of one type or another, but these statistics only include people who have been diagnosed with commonly accepted allergies. Since 32 million Americans have food allergies, and pollen allergies are the most prominent, it means most allergy sufferers have multiple allergies. The amount of allergy sufferers worldwide is many times this amount and only increasing. Some allergies are so common that a physician is not required to diagnose their presence. In contrast, many allergies are atypical or uncommon, and numerous illnesses involve their undesirable contributions and effects. Allergies range from subtle to obvious, insignificant to incapacitating. Why is there such diversity? Everyone is different and, although there are often similarities, no two allergy sufferers can experience the same exact allergy symptoms and disturbances.

Simply put, an *allergy* arises when someone becomes sensitive or *hypersensitive* to the presence of substances that are normally harmless. This occurs for our protection, but it can cause problems because they can induce allergic responses with undesirable consequences.

Why and how do allergies arise? When you are exposed to something new, your immune system has two choices: respond or do not respond. If Shakespeare's Hamlet was an allergist, he would have said, "To react or not to react, that is the question." To accomplish this, your immune system must first decide whether a foreign substance is harmful to your body or if it can be ignored. In addition, to prevent your immune system from perpetually reacting to the same substances, it must have a capacity to remember (memory) how to distinguish between new and previous exposures. These are not conscious decisions because your immune system functions using cells and chemical messengers. When it is optimally functioning, your immunity effectively assists in your survival and ensures your well-being.

In general, your immune system (chapter 14) involves a defense network of cells that cooperate to protect your body from inopportune substances, like harmful bacteria and the byproducts of cancerous cells. Yet, your immune system does not function alone. Together with your nervous (chapter 10) and endocrine (hormone) systems (chapter 11), all three form your *neuroendocrine-immune connection*. So, your immune system can be influenced by your brain and nervous system as well as by the amounts and activities of your hormones. Typically, positive emotions strengthen immunity, while negative emotions impair it. Similarly, a healthy endocrine system supports immunity, while hormone disturbances compromise it. A healthy body functions in a state of harmony (homeostasis); all three systems balance each other and compensate for each other's weaknesses. In contrast, an unhealthy body must have disturbances that are likely to involve all three systems. Therefore, mental-emotional problems and endocrine disturbances can precede and contribute to the development of allergies.

How reactive is your immunity? If you are to remain healthy, your immune system must function between two extremes. If a substance is harmful and your immune system does not react, damage or destruction of your cells, tissues, and organs is likely to follow. Conversely, if a substance is relatively insignificant and your immune system overreacts, sensitivities and hypersensitivities (allergies) can arise. So, either extreme of immunity (underactivity or overactivity) can be harmful. To avoid the adverse consequences that accompany these extremes, a healthy immune system must operate between them. Fortunately, a healthy immune system is effective, and mistakes are uncommon.

How does your immune system know when to react or not? To avoid confusion and inappropriate assaults, your immune system can determine the difference between *"self"* and *"nonself."* When all is well, it recognizes your cells, tissues, and organs and does not react against them, while exposures to foreign material are considered harmful. Yet, the immune system can sometimes make a mistake. For example, autoimmune diseases can occur when someone's immune system mistakes their own cells, tissues, and/or organs as being foreign and assaults them (chapter 14). So, the immune system's ability to appropriately distinguish "self" from "nonself" is essential for your well-being.

If a healthy immune system promotes wellness, chronic or recurring illness must reflect unhealthy immunity. Why? Since immunity is defined as "the body's overall capacity for preserving health," any state of ill health must represent abnormal immunity. For example, deficient immunity can promote cancer, chronic viral illnesses, and autoimmune diseases (chapter 14). What about allergies? When your immune system responds appropriately to substances you are exposed to, you will not develop allergies. This means allergy sufferers are unhealthy, and their allergies reflect the presence of *abnormal immunity*. In other words, allergies occur when your immune system responds inappropriately, becoming hypersensitive to certain substances. Thereafter, exposure to these substances triggers an *allergic reaction*, involving chemical and cellular responses. This can promote a variety of unpleasant symptoms, either immediately or later. So, rather than being an independent illness, allergies are a *symptom* of abnormal immunity. Moreover, the state of "allergy" can be expanded to include a larger and diverse group of symptoms and illness, including alcoholism, acne, bed-wetting, depression, chronic fatigue, muscle pain, anxiety, abdominal pain, chest pain, irregular heart rhythm, ear infections, hyperactivity, autism, learning disabilities, arthritis, and many others.

What causes immunity to become abnormal? An *infection* with disease-causing yeast can promote *suppressed immunity* (inferior functioning cells), with or without *depressed immunity* (fewer cells). This sets the stage for allergies. Disease-causing yeast, especially *Candida albicans,* are among the most allergy-inducing (antigenic) microorganisms that exist. Their presence within the body frequently stimulates allergy-related immune system reactions that arise to help eliminate them. Unfortunately, most candidiasis sufferers cannot eliminate their disease-causing yeast using only their immune system (at best, their condition is stabilized), which permits perpetual allergy-related reactions. Initially, the persistent presence of candidiasis can trigger sensitivities and hypersensitivities to the disease-causing yeast themselves. Over time, a sufferer's allergies can become more generalized, leading to a diversity of sensitivities and hypersensitivities to foods, pollens, dust, chemicals, harmful molds, and more. What does all this mean? In short, most allergy sufferers are likely to be candidiasis sufferers.

Is candidiasis responsible for most people's allergies? Not according to mainstream medical allergists. They think allergies are triggered by environmental stimuli. If this was true, then most of us (if not all) should be burdened with allergies. Since everyone is exposed to pollen, grass, dust, and millions of other potential allergy-inducing substances virtually every moment of every day, and only a percentage of the population develops allergies, candidiasis-minded physicians know the environment, by itself, cannot be blamed. Mainstream medicine also believes that allergy sufferers must be susceptible to developing allergies; they must have a genetic weakness. Candidiasis-minded physicians agree that genetics contributes, but everyone with this tendency should develop allergies if genetics were solely responsible.

To prove their point, candidiasis-minded physicians recognize not everyone with a genetic susceptibility develops allergies, and many allergy sufferers have no family history of allergies. By itself, genetics cannot explain why allergies arise. In contrast to mainstream medicine, candidiasis-minded physicians appreciate that something is responsible for allergies. Something is occurring within an allergy sufferer's body that makes them more susceptible to external environmental stimuli. This is how candidiasis participates. Yet, with respect to illness, disease-causing yeast have been controversial contributors and their allergy-inducing abilities are no exception. Since seemingly obvious relationships continue to be hotly debated, like leaky gut syndrome (chapter 4), it is understandable that the association between candidiasis and allergies is an area of great confusion and misunderstanding among mainstream physicians.

The *candidiasis-allergy connection* is real. It is so notable and prevalent, the association was incorporated into another name for candidiasis, *candidiasis hypersensitivity syndrome*. Indeed, candidiasis-minded physicians know that candidiasis sufferers consistently manifest a variety of typical and atypical allergies. In return, the existence of these allergies helps explain most of the symptoms and illnesses that occur among candidiasis sufferers.

BASICS OF ALLERGIES

Allergic disease has plagued human beings since the dawn of humanity. Yet, a scientific understanding of allergic phenomena only surfaced during the nineteenth century, and it was not until the early twentieth century that the first descriptions of "harmful elements" were mentioned, referring to the foreign particles (antigens or allergens) that initiate the allergic process.

An *antigen* is anything that can stimulate the immune system to produce antibodies. It may be something harmful like a virus, bacteria, fungus, parasite, or tumor cell (it can be the entire infectious invader or only a specific part). To protect you from infectious invaders and tumor cells, you want your immune system to identify these antigens as foreign, so this is a good thing. In contrast, you do not want your immune system to recognize and react to harmless or insignificant substances all around us, like food particles, dust, pollen, and more. If your immune system becomes sensitive or hypersensitive to these commonly encountered substances, it may manufacture antibodies against them, triggering allergic reactions. In short, this is how allergies arise. Confusingly, what induces an allergic response in one allergy sufferer may not bother another. Indeed, someone's reactivity to all the substances they encounter is likely to be as unique as they are.

Basically, *antibodies* are molecules (glycoproteins) made by certain immune cells (*B lymphocytes*) in response to an antigen's presence. Each is targeted to recognize only the antigen it was designed for, giving it incredible specificity. In fact, the human immune system has the potential to produce a specific antibody to almost anything it encounters. Using *immunoglobulins* (Ig) as building blocks, five basic antibodies (IgA, IgD, IgE, IgG, IgM) can create a seemingly infinite number of antibodies in response to a corresponding number of antigens. They exist for our protection—to neutralize or destroy antigens. This can occur in many ways. Depending on their need, antibodies exist and travel within the blood, can enter damaged tissues, or are secreted and located on the body's mucosal surfaces.

How do antibodies protect us? If an antigen contacts and adheres to its corresponding antibody, it forms an *antigen-antibody complex*. This triggers a series of events that destroys and eliminates the complexed components, clearing them from the body. Alternatively, certain cells have receptors on their surface that can recognize and bind antigens. If this occurs, it stimulates the direct destruction of an antigen and/or the release of substances that signal other immune cells to join the fight. This is called *cell-mediated immunity*. Although it is essential for our health, it does not usually participate in allergic reactions.

Furthermore, the *complement system* contributes to immunity. It consists of more than 25 proteins that are inactive within the blood. As a rule, each protein serves a different purpose and is activated in sequence, producing a cascade reaction that leads to its intended effect. The complement system participates in the destruction of different infectious invaders but has its limitations, as some bacteria are resistant to it. Complement also contributes to autoimmune activities and their accompanying adverse effect. What does this have to do with allergies? Complement can play a role in *allergies*. Although it can stimulate B lymphocytes to produce antibodies, it is more notable for its ability to cause the release of reactive substances (*chemotaxins* and *anaphylatoxins*), promoting inflammation. For example, the complement system stimulates certain allergy-related immune cells (*mast cells*) to release *histamine*, a substance that precipitates the inflammation that contributes to several types of allergies. In addition, mast cells release other substances (*leukotrienes*, *platelet-activating factor*, and *prostaglandins*) that may also participate in allergies. So, the complement system has its good points and its bad.

Clemens von Pirquet, an Austrian pediatrician, described allergy as "the altered reactivity of the host after exposure to a foreign substance (allergen)." This involves *antigen-antibody complexing* and the *complement cascade*. Since more than one response can occur at the same time, attempts have been made to understand their differences. Only one classification has received true recognition and wide acceptance. In 1963, P.G.H. Gell and R.R.A. Coombs described four types of *hypersensitivity*, based on the speed of the reaction and the mechanisms involved. Subsequently, a fifth member was added.

- *Type 1* (*immediate*) reactions include allergic asthma, hay fever, and eczema. The reaction involves mast cells and usually occurs within seconds to minutes after exposure to an antigen. Symptoms can recur one to four hours later and last for several days.

- *Type 2* (*cytotoxic*) reactions arise when antibodies interact with certain cell surface antigens (antibody-mediated); these cells are stimulated to directly assault an antigen.
- *Type 3* (*immune complex–mediated*) reactions occur with persistent infections, exposure to inhaled antigens, and most autoimmune diseases. Excesses of antigens promote the formation of antigen-antibody complexes, which are "deposited" within the tissues and blood vessels, activating the complement cascade, and causing inflammation. When severe, this can cause "serum sickness," a reaction involving the accumulation of immune complexes within the joints and skin, leading to irritation and swelling, especially of the face and neck, accompanied by malaise and other symptoms like fever, as well as an enlarged spleen and lymph nodes.
- *Type 4* (*delayed*) reactions comprise skin contact reactions and a response to some chronic infectious invaders. It usually arises at least 24 hours after exposure to an antigen and involves antigen-reactive cells. Antigens can trigger certain immune cells (*T lymphocytes*) to release chemicals (*lymphokines*) that signal other immune cells (*macrophages*) to their location. Once present, macrophages are activated, which enhances their antimicrobial or antitumor activity. Unfortunately, this may cause localized inflammation and tissue damage. When severe, it can cause chronic granulomas, nodules of dead cells, and scarred tissue. Many substances promote this, including harmful fungi and various foods.
- In contrast, *type 5* (*stimulatory*) reactions occur when autoantibodies stimulate a specific tissue. For example, they can bind to the thyroid gland, mimicking thyroid-stimulating hormone, promoting excesses of thyroid hormone to be produced and released, which can lead to hyperthyroidism.

So, there are five different types of allergic responses. This variety explains why some allergy sufferers respond immediately after being exposed to an antigen, while the responses of others are delayed, as well as why some sufferers' allergic reactions resolve quickly, and others react for days, taking as long as two weeks to dissipate. Clearly, allergies are not a black-or-white ("you have them, or you do not") illness.

In addition, the variety of antibodies contributes to the variability of allergies:

- IgA is the principal antibody in secretions, so it protects mucosal surfaces. As examples, it is present in saliva, tears, and intestinal and respiratory mucus.
- IgD is found on the surface of B lymphocytes and acts as an antigen receptor and may play a role in immune cell activity, but its function has not been fully established.
- IgE is produced by the cells lining the gastrointestinal and respiratory tracts. Most IgE is bound to the surface of allergy-related immune cells—mast cells and basophils. IgE-mediated allergy occurs when these cells interact with antigen and release inflammatory substances; compared to other antibodies, IgE is usually present in minimal amounts within the blood and exists for a short time (two to three days), so this interaction amplifies IgE's influence.
- IgG is the major antibody within the blood and intestinal fluids. It adheres to and stimulates certain immune cells (macrophages and neutrophils) to attack, engulf, and digest particles identified as foreign. An elevated IgG level implies a chronic exposure or infection.
- IgM is a five-unit grouping (pentamer) of the basic four chains of immunoglobulins. It is the first antibody produced during the primary response to any antigen, so it helps confer early protection from an infection.

Of all the antibodies, IgE is the most associated with allergies. In 1966, research proved that the allergic skin reactivity in ragweed sufferers was due to IgE. Later, it became clear type 1 (immediate) reactions are mainly IgE-antibody interactions. How does IgE participate? First, someone must become hypersensitive to an antigen. This involves the generation of mast cells with IgE antibodies attached to their surface. When an antigen binds to two IgE molecules, it triggers a series of reactions, culminating in the release of the cell's chemical-containing granules. Histamine directly promotes inflammation and indirectly generates other chemicals involved in type 1 (immediate) reactions.

Most mainstream physicians, including allergists, believe that IgE-mediated reactions are solely responsible for allergies. Yet, the situation is not this simple. Allergies involve four, and maybe five, types of allergic reactions, five types of antibodies, and the participation of the complement system. This is enough to explain a great amount of the variability and symptoms that occur among allergy sufferers. Since antigen-antibody reactions and the complement system are only involved in about 50 percent of allergic reactions, what is responsible for the rest?

There are other mechanisms that can cause allergic reactions; some are known, while others are waiting to be uncovered. In fact, certain chemicals, foods, and drugs can directly trigger allergic reactions. When someone is hypersensitive, the presence of these substances can encourage the release of specific cellular chemicals that directly instigate or promote allergic reactions, especially *lymphokines* and *prostaglandins*. As a result, some foods and chemicals are directly poisonous to immune cells and platelets. This phenomenon is called a *cytotoxic reaction*, which can be confirmed by a cytotoxic blood test (chapter 17). Allergic reactions are more complicated than most mainstream physicians appreciate because they can be antibody-mediated, complement-mediated, or involve the undesirable actions of cellular chemicals.

Does candidiasis directly or indirectly cause allergies? The human body readily interacts with disease-causing yeast as well as with their metabolites, toxins, and waste products. This involves immune and/or non-immune mechanisms. An abundance of research and clinical experience repeatedly demonstrates that the presence of disease-causing yeast within the human body can instigate and promote a variety of sensitivities and hypersensitivities in candidiasis sufferers.

CONFUSION SURROUNDING THE CANDIDIASIS-ALLERGY CONNECTION

With the amount of allergy sufferers in the world, there is big money to be made from selling allergy medication, especially the expensive prescription drugs, with their fancy "designer" names. At best, allergy medications *impede* the allergic response. They do not eliminate the allergy because they do not address what is precipitating or causing it. So, the question should really be: Why did someone develop allergies in the first place and what caused them? In the bigger picture, why are increasing numbers of people suffering with allergies?

Candidiasis-minded physicians appreciate that most allergy sufferers are candidiasis sufferers. With more people developing candidiasis every day, it is no surprise that the number of allergy sufferers is increasing. Candidiasis is an *infection* with *allergic* consequences. Disease-causing yeast, especially *Candida albicans*, have numerous cell surface molecules that are strongly antigenic (allergy-inducing). Their persistent presence within the body can cause numerous immune system reactions that directly promote allergies. In addition, disease-causing yeast within the gastrointestinal tract can invade into and through the gut wall, causing leaky gut syndrome (chapters 3 and 4). As the gut wall weakens, undigested food particles and other substances can enter the tissues and blood, promoting inflammation and allergic reactions.

A multitude of research has revealed that *Candida albicans* can stimulate the formation of antibodies, increase the numbers of certain immune cells (lymphocytes and macrophages), and increase the activity of others (natural killer cells). *Candida albicans* can induce type 1 (immediate) and type 4 (delayed) hypersensitivity reactions. So, it can strongly stimulate the immune system, affecting both cell-mediated and antibody-mediated (humoral) immunity. Moreover, cells of disease-causing yeast and extracts containing some of their cell surface components can stimulate the attraction of certain immune cells to specific locations by activating the complement cascade. It seems clear that *Candida albicans* and other disease-causing yeast are involved in allergic reactions.

Yet, the effects of candidiasis on the immune system and the responses that arise is an area of great confusion, even among candidiasis-minded physicians. Most of them know their patients demonstrate a spectrum of immune system responses, ranging from insignificant to debilitating. They are aware that the *infectious* and *allergic* tendencies of candidiasis can cause manifestations that vary from one extreme to the other—from being an infectious condition to an allergic condition, although most sufferers fall somewhere in between. Even the most knowledgeable candidiasis-minded physicians have been fooled and misled by this variability, and mainstream physicians claim this lack of consistency argues against candidiasis being a legitimate condition. So, this variability is probably the biggest reason why candidiasis has yet to be fully appreciated. Why does this confusion exist?

Research demonstrates that cell surface components from disease-causing *Candida*-species organisms, especially *mannoproteins*, can produce either *stimulatory* or *inhibitory* effects on the immune system, depending on their concentration. In short, the presence of disease-causing yeast can activate or impair immunity during different stages of illness. This explains why some sufferers can mount an immune response against their disease-causing yeast, while other sufferers cannot defend themselves. This adds support for the variability that presents.

Other evidence indicates that the results relate to the dose and viability of *Candida albicans* administered. A high dose of living *Candida albicans* impairs antibody production and cell-mediated immunity, while lower levels only hinder the production of antibodies. In contrast, a high dose of dead *Candida albicans* promotes antibody production and impairs cell-mediated immunity, while a lower dose stimulates cell-mediated immunity and antibody production. These observations mirror reality. Similar variations occur among candidiasis sufferers. There is no one rule. Although it can be confusing, it should not dismiss the reality of candidiasis.

With respect to anti-*Candida* antibodies, the variety of responses has only added to the confusion. Although most candidiasis-minded physicians are aware that all sufferers do not have significant amounts of anti-*Candida* antibodies, few of them know why. This variability exists for several reasons and can be explained (chapter 17). In short, anti-*Candida* antibodies should not be solely relied on to make the diagnosis of candidiasis. When the anti-*Candida* antibodies are positive, the diagnosis is obvious. In contrast, when the anti-*Candida* antibodies are negative, candidiasis may still be present, but *Candida albicans* is not likely to be the primary, prevalent disease-causing yeast.

Moreover, all the antigenic (allergy-inducing) components of *Candida albicans* are not on the cell surface. *Enolase* is an internal enzyme used to generate energy. It has been measured in the blood of patients with candidemia; *Candida albicans* resides within their blood. This enzyme is highly antigenic and human anti-enolase antibodies have been discovered. It has also been found to stimulate cellular immunity. This is one example of disease-causing yeast substances or components that can induce an immune response. The presence of anti-enolase antibodies implies that the immune system is trying to clear enolase from the blood. As a result, the formation of antigen-antibody complexes is certain to contribute to or cause allergic reactions and inflammation. Another possibility is that enolase may stimulate the complement cascade, encouraging additional allergic reactions.

To add confusion, there may be another reason why sufferers have a variety of immune responses. *Candida albicans* is known to induce type 1 (immediate) and type 4 (delayed) reactions. This alone can explain the allergic reactions that occur within most sufferers. Yet, a persistent infection with disease-causing yeast can also cause type 3 (immune complex–mediated) reactions. After all, anti-*Candida* antibodies do not arise for no reason. In fact, these antibodies are present to combat the infection. If the antigens of disease-causing yeast enter the blood and IgG antibodies are present, these can form immune complexes that can be deposited within the tissues and blood vessels, activating the complement cascade, causing inflammation. When severe, this can lead to a candidiasis-related version of "serum sickness," involving the deposition of antigen-antibody immune complexes within a sufferer's joints and skin, which promotes skin irritation and swelling as well as more general problems like malaise, fever, and an enlarged spleen and lymph nodes. In fact, the amount of *Candida albicans* antigen and immune complexes within a sufferer's blood can be measured (chapter 17). The presence of increased amounts indicates some magnitude of type 3 (immune complex-mediated) reactions are occurring. Again, if *Candida albicans* is not the primary disease-causing yeast, this test may not be helpful, but the process may still be happening, nonetheless.

Type 1 (immediate) and type 4 (delayed) reactions explain why many sufferers feel better when they ingest a yeast-free diet. Eliminating disease-causing yeast decreases their antigen exposure and associated allergic reactions. In short, the fewer antigens consumed, the less allergic responses that occur. Moreover, type 3 (immune complex-mediated) reactions may be equally important. As the antigen load decreases, the amounts absorbed into the blood lessens, allowing any existing antibodies to readily eliminate their presence. This is likely to make a sufferer feel better, but it is often a temporary solution. Over time, as the demand for anti-*Candida* antibodies decreases, so will their amount. If the amount drops significantly and a sufferer starts to consume foods containing their problematic antigens, their symptoms will quickly return. This explains why some sufferers feel better on an anti-candidiasis diet at first, and then later feel sick again, unless they are comprehensively treated.

Type 1, type 4, and type 3 reactions can all participate in promoting allergic reactions in candidiasis sufferers. What about type 2 and type 5 reactions? Type 2 (cytotoxic) reactions involve the direct interaction of antibodies with specific cell surface antigens. Disease-causing yeast have numerous cell surface molecules that are strongly antigenic, so type 2 reactions can contribute as well. Although type 5 (stimulatory) reactions are likely to occur much less frequently, some sufferers have autoimmune disease (chapter 14), mediated by autoantibodies, so type 5 reactions may play a role in their symptoms and illness.

Although the *candidiasis-allergy connection* can be confusing, it does *not* negate the existence of candidiasis. It supports and explains the vast diversity of symptoms and illness among sufferers. The confusion can be exacerbated by the presence of other infectious invaders, which can promote or inhibit immunity. In return, this can increase or decrease a sufferer's allergic reactions. On a practical level, what does all this mean? Since every person is a unique individual, no two sufferers can ever have the exact same symptoms and illness. Allergies are no exception. With the seemingly infinite number of antigens within our internal and external environment, no two sufferers can ever have the exact same (antigen-for-antigen) sensitivities and hypersensitivities. Does this mean candidiasis sufferers cannot be treated for their allergies? No, it only means an individualized approach is essential.

THE VARIETY & VARIABILITY OF ALLERGIES

Our internal metabolic (chemical) functioning, external environment, personality, and so on combine to make each of us a unique individual. Allergies are no exception. Genetics do play a role in the allergic process; your tendency to react or not react to one substance or another is likely to depend on your inherited strengths, weaknesses, and susceptibilities. However, even the most resilient person can become allergic to a variety of things they did not react to previously, once the straw breaks the camel's back.

This explains why allergies, without treatment, only tend to worsen over time. Similarly, if candidiasis remains untreated, it will also worsen over time. Since most allergy sufferers are candidiasis sufferers, as someone's candidiasis worsens so will their allergies. If you are a candidiasis sufferer and the amount of your disease-causing yeast increases and/or if you become more sensitive to their presence, you are likely to develop chemical sensitivities and hypersensitivities. This also works in reverse because developing allergies can make you more sensitive to disease-causing yeast. Simply put, as your allergies worsen, so will your candidiasis. The *candidiasis-allergy connection* is more than just a chance association. It works both ways, with each side readily exacerbating the other.

By definition, candidiasis is an *infection* with disease-causing yeast. Moreover, disease-causing yeast are highly antigenic (allergy-inducing) infectious invaders. As a result, candidiasis frequently promotes *allergic* consequences. Research reveals candidiasis does not even have to invade into the tissues and blood to promote allergy-related illnesses.

Most mainstream allergists would agree that fungal organisms can instigate allergies because molds are known to contribute to asthma and allergic rhinitis worldwide. What about disease-causing yeast? Although they are much less appreciated, some mainstream physicians have investigated skin moniliasis (thrush) resistant to antifungal therapy and have discovered its relationship to the presence of *Candida albicans* antigens. Their results indicate the use of desensitization (allergy) injections, containing *Candida albicans* antigen, are a valuable weapon against this cutaneous, medication-resistant manifestation of candidiasis. Mainstream physicians have admitted that immunotherapy is beneficial in "nail involvement with deep-seated lesions out of the reach of topical agents." In addition, an increasing number of reports demonstrate that the antigens of *Candida albicans* and their allergic consequences are strong instigators of irritable bowel syndrome (chapter 4). British researchers found that similar disturbances can be promoted by *Saccharomyces cerevisiae* (baker's and brewer's yeast) in Crohn's disease, an inflammatory bowel disease (chapter 4). Therefore, it seems that some mainstream physicians do respect the allergic consequences of candidiasis. In fact, an incredible number of reports describe an association between *Candida albicans* and allergies. In the bigger picture, the list of chronic, and sometimes acute, illnesses related to the presence of disease-causing yeast and their induced allergies appears almost endless.

The *candidiasis-allergy connection* is not a revolutionary insight. After all, disease-causing yeast are strongly antigenic (allergy-inducing) infectious invaders. In turn, candidiasis can involve sensitivities and hypersensitivities to foods, pollens, dust, and chemicals. Even more common, it instigates and promotes sensitivities and hypersensitivities to the disease-causing yeast themselves as well as to many harmful molds. Although there are similarities, every sufferer is unique and will have different symptoms and illness. This is especially true with respect to the way each candidiasis sufferer manifests their allergies. So, with respect to candidiasis sufferers, especially those with allergies, allergy testing and immunotherapy are beneficial and often essential (chapters 17 and 18).

HARMFUL MOLDS

Experience reveals that candidiasis sufferers can have allergies to fungal organisms other than *Candida albicans*. They often have allergies to baker's and brewer's yeast (*Saccharomyces cerevisiae*), *Rhodotorula*-species organisms, the antigenically similar molds *Trichophyton, Oidiomycetes, and Epidermophyton*, and a variety of harmful molds; the most prominent are *Aspergillus, Alternaria*, *Cephalosporium*, *Hormodendrum*, and *Penicillium* (chapter 17).

Why do these sufferers have mold allergies? It may simply reflect the antigenic (allergy-inducing) similarity between disease-causing yeast and certain harmful molds—their tendency to induce similar allergies. More often, it is because one or many molds are also present within their body.

There is a difference between molds and *harmful molds*. Although both can trigger allergic reactions, harmful molds can cause disease. Yet, with respect to their ability to instigate illness, most harmful molds are ignored or overlooked. Some of them are notably detrimental and even deadly within the human body, but they are only a relatively small percentage of the entire mold population (experts claim there are more than 10,000 molds).

Disease-causing yeast and harmful molds have much in common. Both are defined as parasitic organisms (fungi) that can grow on dead and/or decaying matter. Yet, molds can produce airborne *spores* that frequently induce allergic reactions within many human beings. Even though some species are prevalent during specific times of the year and are indigenous to certain geographical locations, molds are continuously present within our environment and found virtually everywhere (because of their ability to easily travel within the air). Molds prefer moist and warm conditions, which is why the worst time of the year for a mold-sensitive person is the summer (hot and humid) and the winter (windows are closed, the indoor humidity increases). Unfortunately, it is difficult to eliminate molds entirely; they are durable, and their spores can frequently resist freezing, extreme heat, and even drying.

Although it is still considered controversial, numerous physicians profess that some harmful molds grow on and within the human body. There is a big difference between disease-causing yeast and harmful molds within the human body. Disease-causing yeast have proteinases and other enzymes that can digest bodily proteins, enabling them to invade deeper into adjacent tissue. In contrast, harmful molds mostly reside on surfaces, growing upward and outward. Yet, there are similarities because both are *antigenic* infectious invaders; they can directly or indirectly induce allergies. This is likely to first involve the disease-causing yeast and harmful molds themselves, before progressing to more generalized allergies. Like disease-causing yeast, harmful molds can enter the body when someone inhales them or eats contaminated foods. For example, *Aspergillus* is a common mold that can be consumed and then live within the gut. *Aspergillus* has been found to produce *oxalic acid* and *calcium oxalate*. Since some types of kidney stones are comprised of these substances and they have also been discovered within the urine of women with vulvar pain/burning, the mischief of *Aspergillus* has been implicated in these medical maladies. Here is another example: some harmful molds can manufacture *uric acid crystals* that are thought to instigate or promote gout.

Coccidioides immitis and *Histoplasmosis* are harmful molds that live within the soil. Inhaling their airborne spores brings them into someone's lungs, where they can cause an infection. The resulting illness is usually confined to the respiratory tract. Since molds acquired by inhalation are not typically invasive, the immune system often keeps the infection confined. In return, after recovering from what seemed like bronchitis or a "chest cold," many people unknowingly harbor these trespassers forever. Unless the illness progresses systemically (with increased symptoms) or there is a high index of suspicion, a chronic, low-grade infection ensues that typically precipitates a multitude of allergic and inflammatory consequences.

Alternaria is one of most common species of molds. It can cause hay fever symptoms (allergic rhinitis). In addition, it happily inhabits house dust, so it can trigger allergic reactions all year long in numerous geographical environments. Two other prevalent mold species, *Hormodendrum* and *Cladosporium*, are typical residents within the soil that have been associated with exacerbations of asthma and allergic rhinitis. Therefore, molds must be considered as participants in the symptoms and illness of any candidiasis or allergy sufferer. After all, the most frequent and common mold-related symptoms include headaches, sinus problems, skin conditions, urinary tract infections, and much more.

Like disease-causing yeast, molds are known to produce one or more toxins, called *mycotoxins*. These substances are strongly associated with illness and disease. For example, *Candida albicans* and other fungi (molds) produce *gliotoxin*, a substance that impairs (suppresses) immunity, inhibits alcohol dehydrogenase (the liver enzyme that degrades alcohol), and can injure brain cells and alter the brain's chemistry (chapter 10). Some mold toxins can promote severe mental disturbances (psychoses); for example, the *trichothecene mycotoxins* produced by the mold *Stachybotrys chartarum (atra)*. A multitude of mycotoxins are strong promoters of cancer because they are carcinogenic; notably, *aflatoxin* is a respected liver carcinogen that grows on peanuts as well as on other foods. As more supporting evidence surfaces to link mold toxins with illness, the connection between molds and disease becomes difficult to ignore.

Harmful molds are synergistic with disease-causing yeast, parasites, and bacteria. Each helps the other to its advantage, with their combined effects being worse than the effect of either infectious invader alone. It does not matter which arrives first; all these infectious invaders cooperate in causing disturbances and illness as well as promoting an environment (microbiome) that is mutually advantageous for their continued survival and mischief.

A significant percentage of candidiasis sufferers are frequently found to be infected with one or more harmful molds. They contribute their ill effects with their infectious tendencies, and many of them can trigger allergic reactions. Some harmful molds are antigenically like disease-causing yeast, and these cross-reactive molds can induce virtually identical allergies. Since the symptoms of many sufferers are related to mold allergies, it is negligent to ignore these harmful molds. So, if a physician administers allergy shots for disease-causing yeast and not harmful molds, their patients will perpetually manifest mold-related allergy symptoms.

This explains why candidiasis-minded physicians who administer allergy injections containing a combination of disease-causing yeast and harmful molds have a 150 to 200 percent greater success rate compared to physicians who only use *Candida albicans*. Since candidiasis sufferers regularly test positive for allergies to a multitude of common, harmful, and cross-reactive molds, it is essential to test their reaction to *Trichophyton, Oidiomycetes, Epidermophyton, Alternaria, Aspergillus, Cladosporium, Cephalosporium, Hormodendrum,* and *Penicillium*. In addition, an assortment of other molds readily contributes their mischief and should be similarly addressed (chapter 18).

Although harmful molds are frequently ignored, they should be accepted and recognized as a great health hazard. More to the point, their universal presence makes the contributions of harmful molds a consideration in virtually every candidiasis sufferer.

ELIMINATING YOUR ALLERGIES

To cut to the chase, the good news is that your allergies can be eliminated. Before this can occur, you must first understand why your allergies exist.

To protect you from disease, your immune system must be able to distinguish "self" from "nonself." This enables it to defend your body against foreign invaders. Allergies arise when it reacts or overreacts to substances that are harmless or frequently encountered. Since the human body has the potential to respond to virtually anything that is "nonself," the potential exists to develop allergies to all sorts of things.

A *classical* allergy reaction involves an antigen and antibody. An *antigen* is any substance that can stimulate the formation of antibodies. When your immune system is healthy, it can discriminate "self" from "nonself," responding only against foreign substances. An *antibody* is a protein produced by certain immune cells targeted to bind with a specific antigen. Antibodies are highly specified. Using only five basic antibodies, an almost unlimited number of antibodies can be produced in response to a corresponding number of antigens. Like little tags, antibodies bind with antigens, forming *antibody-antigen immune complexes* that can be recognized by immune cells. Once this occurs, attempts are made to clear them from the body.

Since IgE is the antibody most associated with allergies, excesses indicate a *classical* allergy response. Other antibodies can also promote antigen-antibody complexes and participate in the classical allergy response. In addition, the *complement system* can contribute. Yet, only about half of all allergic reactions involve these "classical" responses. What about the other half? These "nonclassical" reactions do not involve antibodies or the complement system. Instead, they involve other mechanisms. For example, some immune cells directly interact with chemicals, foods, or drugs, which triggers the release of cellular chemicals, causing inflammation. Under certain conditions, foods and chemicals may be directly injurious (cytotoxic) to immune cells and platelets. Furthermore, there are five *types* of allergic reactions. All of this contributes to the variety and variability of symptoms and illness that occurs among allergy sufferers.

Since healthy people do not develop allergies, sufferers must be unhealthy. In other words, allergies have a cause. Most candidiasis-minded physicians are aware that most allergy sufferers are candidiasis sufferers. The presence of disease-causing yeast frequently causes immune system responses in candidiasis sufferers, with both *infectious* and *allergic* consequences. Disease-causing yeast are among the most antigenic (allergy-inducing) infectious invaders known, and their persistent presence induces a diversity of allergic problems. A great deal of research supports the participation of *Candida albicans* in a variety of allergic reactions within human beings. The list of symptoms is extensive; examples include alcoholism, acne, depression, irritable bowel syndrome, fatigue and malaise, bed-wetting, postnasal drip, bronchial asthma, vulvovaginitis, prostatitis, PMS, and many others. Although most candidiasis-related allergic reactions are type 1 (immediate) or type 4 (delayed), the variety of symptoms and illness implies the other three allergic reactions also contribute.

Disease-causing yeast have two sides to their mischief. If their infectious personality is dominant within a sufferer, antifungal therapy and an anti-candidiasis diet should produce substantial improvements. In contrast, when they are causing allergic reactions, as they often do, immunotherapy is warranted, including desensitization (allergy) injections or drops containing the appropriate antigens (chapter 18). Although this involves allergies to foods, pollens, dust, and chemicals, it also includes hypersensitivities to the disease-causing yeast themselves as well as to many harmful molds. Since most sufferers have both infectious and allergic consequences, immunotherapy is typically required and of great benefit.

If you are an allergy suffer, you can take one or more medications to eliminate your symptoms. This may make you feel more comfortable, but it will *not* cure your allergies because their effect is aimed at inhibiting the allergic response, not treating its cause. What about allergy shots or drops? They may make you less reactive or completely desensitize you against your allergy-inducing substances, but they will not prevent you from developing additional allergies. This occurs because allergy shots or drops work by blocking the allergic reaction to a specific antigen, rather than treating its true cause.

Eliminating your candidiasis is the best way to address the cause of your allergies. Although antifungal medication can eradicate your disease-causing yeast and improve your symptoms, it is unlikely to eliminate your sensitivities and hypersensitivities. In fact, even after their infection is gone, most sufferers have residual sensitivities and hypersensitivities. Therefore, a program of desensitization (allergy) immunotherapy using injections or drops will most likely be required to gain substantial improvement in your overall health, especially if you have numerous candidiasis-related symptoms and significant allergies. Since other infectious invaders, including harmful parasites, bacteria, molds, and viruses may also contribute their ill effects, exacerbating your allergies, they must be revealed and appropriately addressed as well.

Compared to the other manifestations of candidiasis, allergies and allergic manifestations often require more time to resolve and eliminate. Rather than being a result of the disease-causing yeast, this has more to do with the nature of allergies and allergic reactions. Fortunately, your investment is almost certain to be worth your time and effort. After all, this is the only way to cure your allergies and ensure that you do not develop others. So, if you are an allergy sufferer and want to eliminate your allergies for good, you would be wise to seriously consider the *candidiasis-allergy connection* and seek a candidiasis-minded physician for treatment.

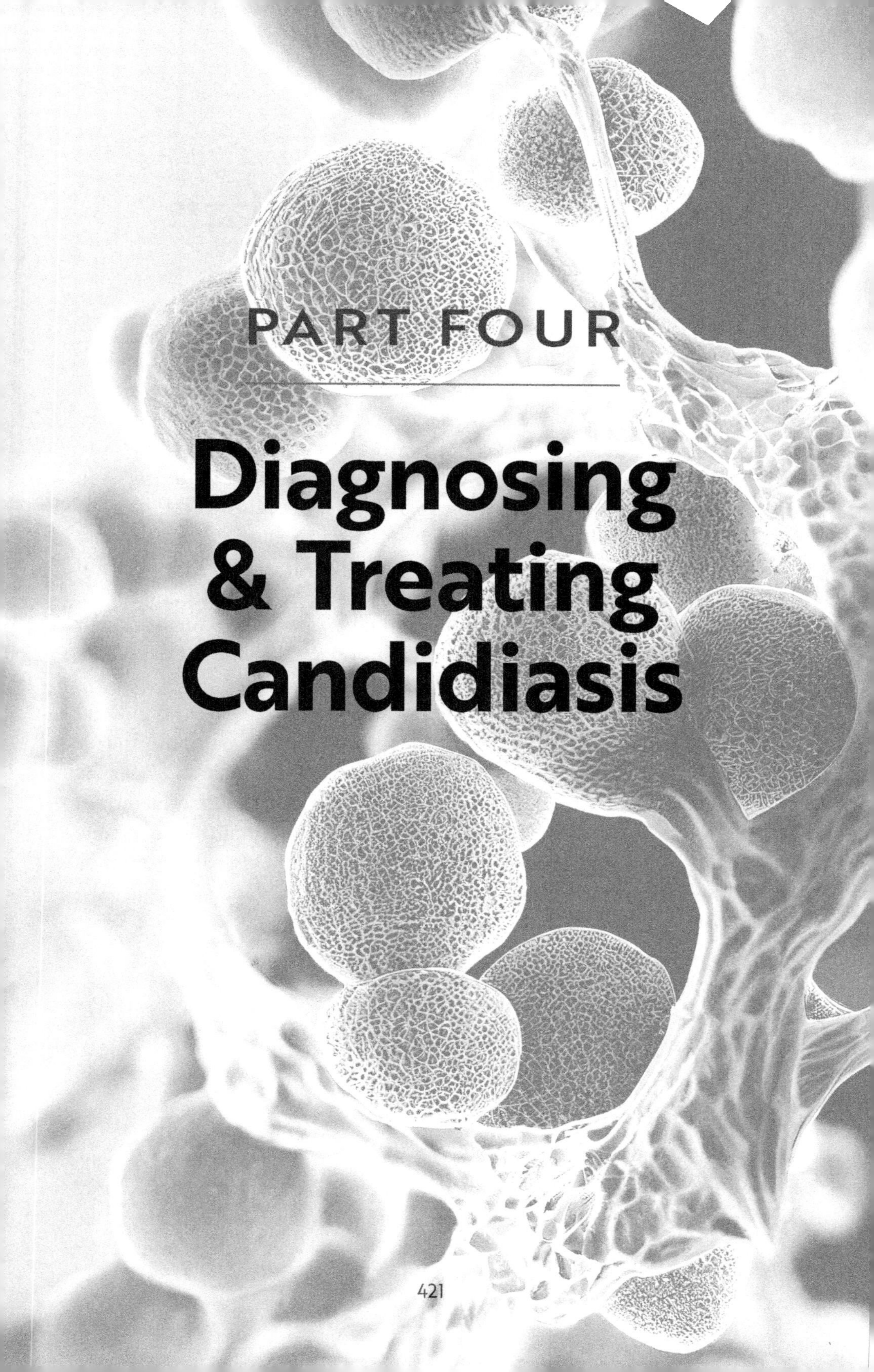

PART FOUR

Diagnosing & Treating Candidiasis

CHAPTER 17

Diagnosing Candidiasis

The proponents and opponents of candidiasis criticize the absence of an "ultimate laboratory test" that conclusively provides a diagnosis. Yet, once you understand the complexity of candidiasis, its variability and diversity, the existence of any one definitive test is impractical, if not impossible. Most of the confusion exists because candidiasis is an *infection* with *allergic* consequences. To add insult, a sufferer may be adversely affected by other infectious invaders, including harmful parasites, bacteria, molds, and/or viruses. Along with stress and the environment, genetics plays a prominent part. Since the diagnosis is not simply a black-or-white issue, suspicion and vigilance are part of the decision-making process.

Fortunately, candidiasis is not doomed to remain a mysterious medical mystery because numerous laboratory tests can readily support and/or confirm the diagnosis. So, it is essential to know when to employ each as well as how to interpret their results. Since it is impractical and inefficient to administer all these tests to any sufferer, it is important to appreciate that some tests are better than others, with each having its usefulness and drawbacks. In most cases, a sufferer's symptoms and illness are the deciding factor.

Note: *The following discussions and interpretations of abnormal laboratory values are not meant to replace physician judgment. Rather, it is for educational purposes. There are always exceptions and professional guidance is essential.*

HISTORY & PHYSICAL EXAM

Currently, with science progressing rapidly, most mainstream physicians spend less time focusing on a patient's past medical history and often only examine a patient with respect to their medical complaint. As an example, if a patient complains of an ear infection, the physician will examine their ears and throat. Yet, the history and physical exam are more important than most physicians realize. Since the risk factors for developing candidiasis and its onset of symptoms involves a cause-and-effect illness, the patient's history alone can often support the presence of candidiasis. Moreover, if you understand that candidiasis can adversely affect the entire body with its *infectious* and *allergic* consequences, evidence of its mischief can be found in one or more areas, increasing the likelihood of illness with disease-causing yeast.

Past Medical History

Past medical history is the single-most essential tool for diagnosing candidiasis (and probably will always be). It should be performed by a qualified health practitioner, preferably a candidiasis-minded physician, inquiring about the history and course of a person's illness and their symptoms. This includes the chief complaint(s) and history of present illness, followed by a review of bodily systems, past medical and surgical history, family history, a list of medications, drug allergies, drug or alcohol abuse, tobacco use, sleep, diet, and exercise. To help obtain a thorough patient history that is candidiasis-oriented, the *candidiasis questionnaire* (chapter 1) can be consulted. Furthermore, an awareness of the *candidiasis risk factors* can aid in making a diagnosis (chapter 2). For example, since antibiotics are one of the greatest risk factors, if someone has taken numerous courses, candidiasis is highly likely.

Nothing is more valuable for uncovering a "candidiasis connection" than determining someone's history of illness and their associated risk factors for developing candidiasis. This helps create a candidiasis sufferer's problem list of their diagnoses and symptoms. It also has a greater purpose because it can serve as a reference point to assess a sufferer's recovery. Later, after treatment, their problem list can be consulted. This is usually when significant beneficial changes are readily evident.

Physical Examination

Physical examination reveals the bodily manifestations of candidiasis. Since every person is a unique individual, their exam is likely to reflect this diversity, but there are some common candidiasis-related findings, including (from head to toe, not by prevalence) seborrhea, psoriasis, eczema, conjunctivitis (inflammation of the eyes), congested nasal passages and ears, oral thrush (white patches in the mouth or on the tongue), swollen and/or tender cervical lymph nodes (in the neck), wheezing in the lungs, irregular heart rhythms, hyperactive (or hypoactive) bowel sounds, abdominal tenderness, abdominal bloating, swollen and inflamed rectal tissues, a groin rash or jock itch, muscle and/or joint tenderness, athlete's foot, and fungal toenails and/or fingernails. Because of mineral deficiencies and malabsorption, decreased tendon reflexes can occur. Moreover, the presence of aberrant growths (benign or malignant) supports the presence impaired immunity and/or endocrine (hormone) disturbances. A lowered body temperature, loss of hair (especially in women), dry or brittle nails or skin, and many other findings are indications of malabsorption and/or hormonal problems.

(Clinical hint: A universally overlooked location is the iris, the colored tissue at the front of the eye. The area around the pupil can often reveal the presence of yeast and mold within the body. White deposits suggest *Candida albicans*, yellow pertains to other disease-causing yeast, and brown correlates with mold. In people with brown eyes, a light held sideway can make this easier to see. When the iris deposits are correlated with the results produced by intradermal testing for yeasts and molds, observing the iris adds diagnostic evidence.)

Some sufferers have normal physical exams, which does not help make the diagnosis. In contrast, other sufferers have obvious signs and symptoms of candidiasis. There is a great diversity of manifestations, even among sufferers with the same complaints. In general, the longer someone has candidiasis, the greater the toll it takes on their body. Typically, the physical exam confirms what was revealed in the history.

ROUTINE TESTS

If a physician knows how to interpret the results, many standard blood tests can be valuable with respect to supporting a diagnosis of candidiasis. They should always look for *metabolic immunosuppression* (chapter 14): glucose intolerance, hyperinsulinism, hyperlipidemia (hypercholesterolemia and/or hypertriglyceridemia), and impaired immunity.

- **Complete blood count (CBC) with differential** analyzes the amounts, proportions, shapes, and sizes of a person's immune (white blood) cells and red blood cells. A low red blood cell count, hemoglobin, and/or hematocrit indicates anemia; although there are different types, malabsorption and nutritional deficiencies are often the cause, so this may reflect leaky gut syndrome. An elevated number of *eosinophils* suggests allergies and/or an infection with parasites. Increased numbers of *basophils* typically accompany allergies and allergic inflammation. A decrease in the total number of *lymphocytes* signifies *depressed immunity* (fewer immune cells). Yet, if someone has frequent infections, even with a normal number of lymphocytes, they have *suppressed immunity* (inferior functioning cells). Even worse, fewer lymphocytes and frequent infections represents *suppressed-depressed immunity* (fewer, inferior functioning cells). To determine this, the total white blood cell count is multiplied by the percentage of lymphocytes, giving the *absolute lymphocyte count*.

- **Erythrocyte sedimentation rate (ESR) or sedimentation rate** is a non-specific test; it cannot pinpoint the cause of a problem. An elevated ESR indicates inflammation. If the ESR is used to assess someone's progress, it typically improves more slowly than their symptoms because inflammation often takes a long time to resolve.
- **Blood chemistry tests (various)** include a variety of tests that quantify various substances within someone's serum. It reflects what is within their body and is an assessment of their metabolism. The fasting *glucose* concentration establishes someone's fasting blood sugar; a decreased value implies hypoglycemia, while an elevated amount suggests diabetes (chapter 11). Kidney functioning can be ascertained by *creatinine* and *blood urea nitrogen* (BUN) levels. Liver activity or impairment is assessed by measuring *bilirubin* (total and direct), *SGOT*, *SGPT*, and *LDH* (liver enzymes). *Calcium* and *magnesium* levels can help determine if there is functional hypoparathyroidism, but their values are far from reliable to make the determination (chapter 11). In addition, elevated *cholesterol* and/or *triglyceride* levels indicate metabolic disturbances, and strongly suggest there is some overt or hidden cardiovascular compromise (chapters 7 and 14). An elevated *uric acid* may accompany or be an omen of impending gout (chapter 9). In the big picture, the presence of numerous disturbances, especially mineral deficiencies, may reflect malabsorption.
- **Five-hour glucose tolerance test, with insulin levels** can determine someone's glucose tolerance. Since most sufferers have some magnitude of *glucose intolerance* (chapter 11), this test is often informative rather than diagnostic. After blood is drawn to determine the fasting blood glucose concentration, the patient receives a drink containing a measured amount of glucose, in proportion to their body weight. Blood

glucose concentration samples are obtained at 30 minutes, hour 1, hour 2, hour 3, hour 4, and hour 5. In addition, fasting and hour-two insulin levels should be measured. A properly performed test will reveal and/or confirm the presence of glucose intolerance—notably, reactive hypoglycemia, prediabetes, and mild diabetes. Moreover, elevated insulin levels indicate *hyperinsulinism*. In contrast, normal insulin levels with a prolonged decrease in the blood sugar concentration may suggest *functional hyperinsulinism*—the prolonged release of mildly elevated amounts of insulin or an inability to inactivate it may cause the same problems as short-term excesses. Alternatively, it may indicate there is a disturbance with the blood sugar–raising hormones. During the test, candidiasis sufferers often experience one or more adverse symptoms, providing further evidence of their condition and the relationship between their blood glucose concentration and symptoms.

- **Thyroid gland testing** can help assess if there is increased or decreased thyroid functioning by measuring the major thyroid hormones, *triiodothyronine* (T3) and *thyroxine* (T4), and *thyroid-stimulating hormone* (TSH). Yet, even with normal results, someone can still have a thyroid hormone disturbance, which can be determined by measuring their *basal body temperature* four days in a row; their temperature is taken upon awakening, before getting out of bed, and then three more times later in the day. A low basal body temperature indicates Wilson's thyroid syndrome, a thyroid hormone abnormality that causes *hypometabolism* (chapter 11). Since it often involves excesses of *reverse triiodothyronine* (RT3), testing for its level can make this disturbance more evident. Moreover, *thyroid autoantibodies* will confirm autoimmune disease of the thyroid (especially, *antithyroid microsomal antibodies*). A qualified physician should determine if there is a thyroid dysfunction and what should be done about it.

- **Other endocrine (hormone) tests** can uncover numerous hormone dysfunctions. A variety of hormones can be measured, *steroids* and *polypeptides*. Depending on the abnormalities that appear, endocrine disturbances can be revealed. For example, adrenal hormone disturbances indicate impaired adrenal gland functioning. Like thyroid gland functioning, a qualified physician should make these determinations.

- **Immunologic tests** can expose a variety of problems. When joint pain is a symptom (chapter 9), autoimmune disease is a consideration. The presence of one or more autoantibodies supports this diagnosis—notably, *antinuclear antibodies* (ANA) and *rheumatoid factor* (RF). Although *C-reactive protein* (CRP) was only found in the active phase of certain acute illnesses, it is being expressed more frequently. CRP, an acute phase reactant, is a general marker for systemic inflammation, but increases in its level are being associated with cardiovascular illness. Since autoimmune disease is not confined to the joints, autoantibodies can be measured for virtually every cell and tissue within the body—for example, gastric parietal cells, smooth muscle cells, mitochondria, interstitial cells of the testes, ovarian cells, skeletal muscle cells, and cells of the adrenal gland (and more). After candidiasis sufferers with autoimmune disease are treated, their symptoms often improve, while their titers of autoantibodies can remain unchanged. What if a sufferer has symptoms, but their autoantibody titers are normal; does this rule out autoimmune disease? No, because most autoimmune disturbances involve *cell-mediated* destruction that does not require autoantibodies (chapter 14).

- **Lyme titers** should be done if there is a suspicion or risk of Lyme disease.
- **HIV serology** will reveal if someone has been infected *with HIV*.
- **Venereal Disease Research Laboratory test (VDRL)** can help uncover these infectious invaders. Since *syphilis* commonly varies in its mischief (it can masquerade as numerous illnesses), it is often valuable to check for the presence of *Treponema pallidum*. A positive VDRL supports a history of infection with syphilis and should be treated. Because VDRL is usually a screening tool, other tests are typically employed to confirm the diagnosis of syphilis.
- **Purified protein derivative testing (PPD)** is a clinical test that is practical when weight loss and/or fever are part of the history because it assesses an infection with *tuberculosis* organisms. The prevalence of tuberculosis has increased, so candidiasis sufferers can benefit from this test. If the test is positive, appropriate therapy should be instituted by a health practitioner who knows how to manage this organism, especially because of the increased incidence of antibiotic-resistant organisms. In addition, when positive, family members and close contacts must also be tested and treated, and even if their results are negative, family members are often treated.
- **Immunological profile** measures specific subpopulations of immune cells (white blood cells). Typically, it is an expensive test used to evaluate

people with impaired immunity (chapter 14) as well as follow their progress. A decrease in specific immune cell subpopulations can identify the type and extent of someone's immune deficiency.

- **Cancer markers** have their usefulness. Several laboratory tests can measure tumor activity in cancer sufferers (chapter 14). *Carcinoembryonic antigen* (CEA) is a general marker for tumor growth. *Lipid associated sialic acid* (LASA) is also a general marker, although it is used less frequently. *Alpha-fetoprotein* (AFP) is not commonly measured; it can be useful to assess liver cancer, although elevated levels are associated with gastric and testicular cancers. *Prostate-specific antigen* is routinely used to detect prostate cancer. Although many tests measure cancer-associated antigens, they are helpful in uncovering cancers before they are clinically evident and following the progress of patients with cancer.
- **Virus titers** can assess the presence and contributions of one or more viruses, especially in patients with impaired immunity (chapter 14) and/or chronic fatigue (chapter 15). The prominent viruses to consider are *Epstein-Barr virus* (EBV), *cytomegalovirus* (CMV), *human herpesvirus 6* (HHV-6), *human herpesvirus 1* (HHV-1), *human herpesvirus 2* (HHV-2), and the *hepatitis viruses* (A, B, C, and delta). Depending on circumstances and a patient's risk factors, other viruses may be worth considering.
- **Cardiovascular blood tests** can reveal if disease-causing yeast are participating in metabolic disturbances that adversely affect the cardiovascular system. Research has associated some laboratory abnormalities with cardiovascular disease, especially levels of *homocysteine, red blood cell magnesium*, and *lipoprotein(a)*.
- **Urine testing** is often not that helpful. Of course, the exception occurs when an abundance of disease-causing yeast is found within a "clean catch" urine sample.

ADVANCED TESTS

These tests are usually not considered by mainstream physicians. In contrast, candidiasis-minded physicians are aware of their importance in supporting a diagnosis of candidiasis.

- **Dark-field microscopy** can determine the presence and aggressiveness of disease-causing yeast within the blood. In a significant percentage of candidiasis sufferers, especially those with impaired immunity, disease-causing yeast assault and invade into their gut wall, enter their tissues, and gain access to their blood. So, *gastrointestinal* candidiasis progresses to *invasive* candidiasis, AND then to *systemic* candidiasis.

The test involves taking a sample (one drop) of blood, placing it on a microscope slide, and adding a special stain (mycostain) that reacts with disease-causing yeast to make it fluoresce. A protective cover slip is placed on top, and the specimen is examined under the dark field of a microscope, using yellow and blue filters; the light shines from the sides, producing a "dark" field. Any disease-causing yeast floating within the specimen are illuminated against a dark background (like a plane in the sky, reflecting sunlight at sunset). Positive fluorescence indicates that there are disease-causing yeast within the blood (systemic candidiasis). In addition, numerous forms of disease-causing yeast can be visualized, including the invasive form (mycelia), the ovoid form, and the immature form (syncitia).

The severity of a sufferer's candidiasis and accompanying gut disturbance is consistently reflected by their dark-field test. Greater than 20 disease-causing yeast indicates severe colonization. In addition, the form plays a role; an abundance of the invasive form implies a more advanced case. This test can also be used to follow a sufferer's progress. For example, if their initial results predominantly demonstrated the invasive form, but after a month on an anti-candidiasis program they only have the ovoid form, some improvement has occurred. Obviously, the preferred finding is an *absence of disease-causing yeast.* Even when this occurs, it reveals limited information about the localized colonization of disease-causing yeast within the gut and/or colonization within other areas, like the lungs and sinuses. It provides no insight about the presence of harmful parasites, bacteria, and molds. By the way, this test primarily addresses the *infection* and has nothing to do with the *allergic* consequences of candidiasis.

- **Cultures** can be obtained from the skin, throat, vagina, urine, stool, and so on. To be useful, these must be acquired using *sterile* technique. This can establish the presence of disease-causing *Candida*-species organisms. Unfortunately, they are rather slow to grow in culture, so it may take two weeks to a month to demonstrate a positive reading, especially if there is light colonization. The downside is, rather than respected as legitimate infectious invaders, many mainstream physicians contend that the presence of yeast within a culture is evidence of a contaminated specimen (except in the most severe cases). On the upside, the advantage of a culture is that the disease-causing yeast can be grown in the laboratory and tested for their sensitivity to various antifungal agents, especially since disease-causing yeast are becoming increasingly resistant to some of these substances. Research indicates the *buffy coat*, a layer of immune (white blood) cells and platelets separated by centrifugation, can be cultured and is highly sensitive for detecting an infection with disease-causing yeast within the blood. Cultures can also be used to assess the presence of harmful bacteria and molds, while they are almost useless for detecting parasites.

- ***Anti-Candida antibodies, Candida-antigen, and Candida immune complexes*** can be assessed. (If you are a resident of New York State, New Jersey, or Rhode Island, these tests are unavailable.)

  When the immune system is healthy and functioning normally, disease-causing yeast are usually recognized as *foreign*. This occurs because disease-causing yeast are strongly antigenic, especially *Candida albicans*, and they can stimulate antibody responses. This is often related to the presence of specific cell surface components called *mannan polysaccharides*. One of the ways the immune system combats the presence of disease-causing yeast is by producing *anti-mannan antibodies*. Since small amounts of disease-causing yeast are present in everyone, anti-mannan antibodies to *Candida albicans* appear in all normal people, although usually in minimal amounts. In contrast, candidiasis sufferers, both adults and children, often have increased titers of these antibodies.

  Depending on where the disease-causing yeast reside and the length of a sufferer's infection, one or more anti-mannan antibodies can be produced. Typically, *IgA anti-Candida antibodies* are created during an active infection involving the mucous membranes, including the gastrointestinal tract, lungs, mouth, sinuses, and vagina. *IgM anti-Candida antibodies* arise early in the infection and are confined to the blood, assaulting disease-causing yeast within the circulation; their presence reveals recent activity, and supports a diagnosis of invasive and/or systemic candidiasis. *IgG anti-Candida antibodies* target infectious invaders within the tissues and blood; elevated amounts can appear with invasive and/or systemic candidiasis. Since IgG anti-*Candida* antibodies take longer to appear, they indicate a prolonged infection. These anti-*Candida* antibodies can be measured, and their levels often correlate with the severity of someone's candidiasis. For example, if all three antibodies are elevated, it means a patient's candidiasis has been present for a long time (IgG), is still active (IgM), and their disease-causing yeast are assaulting their mucous membranes (IgA).

Confusingly, some sufferers demonstrate minimal or nonexistent amounts of anti-mannan antibodies. Why does this occur? First and foremost, anti-*Candida* antibodies only measure antibodies against the mannan of *Candida albicans* as well as any disease-causing yeast that has similar mannoproteins. So, if *Candida albicans*, or an antigenically similar relative, is not a sufferer's prominent infectious invader, they may not have elevated titers. Second, if a sufferer has impaired immunity, their immune system may be unable to respond to the presence of *Candida albicans*, and antibodies may not be produced. This can potentially be a problem because, as their immunity improves, anti-*Candida* antibodies may begin to arise, exacerbating their symptoms and/or instigating new manifestations, especially *allergic* consequences. Third, a sufferer's immune system may not recognize their disease-causing yeast as foreign. There is antigenic similarity between various disease-causing *Candida*-species organisms, other molds, some enteric bacteria, and human blood group H antigen. Most notably, human *blood group H antigen* is the primary antigen expressed by people with type O blood. So, the immune systems of sufferers with type O blood may mistake their disease-causing yeast as "self," rather than "nonself," and not produce antibodies. In contrast, if their immune system produces antibodies targeted against the antigen on disease-causing yeast that corresponds to their blood group H antigen, the antibodies that arise may mistakenly assault their own cells, tissues, and/or organs, promoting autoimmune disease.

Less likely, but possible, if a sufferer is colonized with some harmless (enteric) bacteria within their gut that is antigenically like their disease-causing yeast, their immune system may be so used to its presence that their disease-causing yeast may not be noticed as foreign. Even with significant colonization within the gut and mucous membranes, IgA antibody titers can be low or insignificant, reflecting the ability of disease-causing yeast to bind with and/or destroy this antibody as fast as it is produced. Research reveals that *Candida albicans* has secretory *proteinases* (enzymes) that can degrade IgA, enabling it to neutralize this antibody. Fortunately, the body can compensate by creating antibodies aimed to attack these enzymes; for example, patients with severe candidiasis have been found to have high titers of *Candida albicans anti-proteinase antibodies*. When this occurs, it creates a constant struggle with both sides being injured. Alternatively, low IgA levels may simply reflect a deficiency of this antibody, which may involve a nutritional shortage of its precursors. So, anti-*Candida* antibodies are helpful but tend to be misleading when low. (Anti-mannan IgE anti-*Candida* antibodies can also be measured, but they are often of little help in making a diagnosis because they correlate with a sufferer's allergies rather than their infection.)

In addition, *Candida* mannan antigen can be measured; the major allergy-inducing part of *Candida albicans*. Elevated amounts reveal pieces of *Candida albicans* (or the entire organism) are within the blood. This occurs because excessive amounts can be absorbed from the gut and/or there is a significant infection within the tissues and/or blood. Since free *Candida* mannan antigen is harmful, the immune system tries to eliminate it by forming *Candida IgG immune complexes*, which consist of *Candida*-specific IgG, *Candida* mannan antigen, and fragments of complement proteins bound together; this enables the antigen to be removed by the spleen. The presence of elevated *Candida* immune complexes indicates active illness. Increased amounts of *Candida* mannan antigen reveal that the immune system is unable to effectively combat the infection. Either presentation reveals candidiasis is present. Yet, if *Candida albicans* is not the prominent disease-causing yeast, these values may be normal.

If the anti-*Candida* antibody levels are not notable or the sufferer is not responding well to anti-candidiasis treatment, other antibodies can be checked. Some laboratories offer anti-*Candida* antibodies targeted against various disease-causing yeast. Examples include *C. krusei*, *C. tropica*lis, *Saccharomyces cerevisiae*, and other available tests.

In some sufferers, anti-*Saccharomyces* antibodies may be worth measuring. Researchers have associated high titers of these antibodies with Crohn's disease, a form of inflammatory bowel disease (chapter 4). Since elevated titers signal an *infection* with *Saccharomyces cerevisiae*, a less prominent species of disease-causing yeast, it reveals that this organism is causing or exacerbating illness. Some sufferers can have elevated anti-*Saccharomyces* antibodies without elevated anti-*Candida* antibodies, implying that their illness is related to the presence of *Saccharomyces cerevisiae* and not *Candida albicans* (although the previously mentioned reasons may be responsible for a lack of anti-*Candida* antibodies). *Rhodotorula*-species organisms, another less prominent disease-causing yeast, can also often be present. Yes, it is candidiasis, but instead of being caused by the major species of disease-causing yeast, the less prominent species are the mischief makers. I use the term *atypical candidiasis* to describe these patients.

- **Other antibody tests** can provide additional support. Although *glucan polymers* within the cell wall of *Candida albicans* are more abundant than the mannoproteins, they are weakly antigenic or even non-antigenic. Nevertheless, since antibodies to *beta-glucan* have been measured within the blood of patients with *Candida albicans* infections, *anti-beta-glucan antibodies* can be used to confirm a diagnosis of systemic candidiasis.

  All the antigenic (allergy-inducing) parts of *Candida albicans* are not on its cell surface. *Enolase* is an internal (cytoplasmic) enzyme that helps it generate energy. It has been measured within the blood of patients with candidemia (a blood infection with *Candida albicans*), so it is an indicator of invasive candidiasis. Since this enzyme is strongly antigenic, human *Candida anti-enolase antibodies* have been discovered. However, the presence of anti-enolase antibodies is more nonspecific than anti-mannan antibodies because it can be present during infections with numerous disease-causing yeasts.

  Other research reveals that immune complexes are produced when human beings are exposed to *Candida albicans*. Called *heat-labile antigen* or *CANDTEC antigen*, these molecules are 3,000–4,000 kilodaltons in size, with a unique 200 kilodalton component. Heat-labile antigen is measured by the Cand-Tec assay, and elevated amounts suggest invasive candidiasis.

  When disease-causing yeast, especially *Candida albicans*, invade into and through the gut wall, they usually transform from their less-aggressive ovoid form into their invasive form, called a *mycelium*. Typically, a mycelium has root-like projections, *germ tubes*, that enable the disease-causing yeast to invade deeper into the tissues. *Anti-germ tube antibodies* have been detected and indicate invasive candidiasis.

- **Candi-sphere enzyme immuno-assay (CEIA)** can measure antigenic proteins that exist within some disease-causing yeast. Normally, these proteins are kept hidden from the immune system, and antibodies targeted at these antigens are not manufactured. However, during candidiasis, disease-causing yeast cells are constantly dying, liberating their cellular contents within the body, especially into the surrounding tissues and blood. These antigenic proteins can instigate the production of specific antibodies. The CEIA can reveal the amount.

- **Monoclonal antibody detection** involves specific antibodies of high purity. They have been produced against cell wall extracts of *Candida albicans*, and more. For example, a monoclonal antibody was created to recognize mannoproteins of high molecular mass in the cell wall of *Candida albicans*. Research showed that the antibody specifically detects *Candida albicans* within the tissues, especially the invasive (mycelial) form, but is less likely to reveal the noninvasive (ovoid) form. Clinically, it can be used to diagnose invasive candidiasis.

- **Immunofluorescent assay (IFA)** using *buffy coat* smears can identify the presence of disease-causing *Candida*-species organisms within the blood (candidemia). This test is less sensitive than buffy coat cultures, but much more sensitive than blood cultures. Since disease-causing yeast within the buffy coat is evidence of an infection within the blood, IFA detects invasive and systemic candidiasis.

- **Polymerase chain reaction (PCR)** is a process that allows unlimited copies of genes to be made in a laboratory. Beginning with a single molecule of genetic material (DNA), billions of copies can be made within hours. As a result, PCR has been used to detect *Candida albicans* within specimens of blood, cerebrospinal fluid, sputum, and urine with great sensitivity. Therefore, it is useful for diagnosing invasive or systemic candidiasis, including urinary tract infections with *Candida albicans*. It has been used to identify many other disease-causing yeast and harmful molds.

- **Other tests to identify the species-strain of disease-causing yeast** exist or are in development but are beyond the scope of this discussion.

- **Chitin assay** assesses a unique substance. *Chitin* is a structural polysaccharide found within fungi. Its presence reveals a fungal infection, but it is a nonspecific test.

- **Plasma (1→3)-beta-D-glucan levels** measure the amount of a common cell wall component present in virtually all fungi. Research demonstrates that its presence within the blood can be markedly elevated in systemic candidiasis and less so in invasive aspergillosis (an infection with the harmful mold *Aspergillus*).

- **Blood alcohol levels** can provide indirect evidence of the colonization of disease-causing yeast within the body because they produce ethanol (chapter 10). First, a sample of a patient's fasting blood is taken to measure their glucose and alcohol concentrations. Then, the patient swallows a gelatin capsule containing one gram of glucose, followed by four grams of glucose dissolved in water. A blood sample is drawn at hour 1 to measure their glucose and alcohol concentrations. A significant increase indicates that their gut microorganisms have been fermenting glucose into alcohol. Furthermore, *Candida albicans* and other fungi produce gliotoxin, which is known to inhibit *alcohol dehydrogenase*, the liver enzyme that degrades alcohol. So, repeating this test an hour or more later provides evidence of how effectively someone's alcohol dehydrogenase is functioning; if their blood alcohol levels are not lower, there is a problem with the enzyme. Although the results often correlate with the severity of someone's candidiasis, this test has limited usefulness. Its greatest value seems to involve people with psychological manifestations of candidiasis (chapter 10).

- **D-arabinitol/L-arabinitol ratio** helps reveal systemic candidiasis. *D-arabinitol* is a unique metabolite of disease-causing *Candida*-species organisms that can be detected within the urine and serum. In contrast, human beings make *L-arabinitol*. As a result, an increased ratio of D-arabinitol to L-arabinitol provides evidence of systemic candidiasis. More specifically, some investigators found that an increased ratio within the urine correlates with *Candida* pyelonephritis, an infection or inflammation of the kidneys and renal pelvis with disease-causing yeast (chapter 13).

- **Organic acid test (urine)** assesses a urine sample for numerous metabolites. Specifics aside, many *yeast/fungal* metabolites and *bacterial* metabolites are measured, including their amounts, revealing what infectious invaders are present (chapter 12).

- **Intestinal permeability and leukocyte adherence** can provide evidence of leaky gut syndrome. Antibodies against gliadin and casein are used to measure intestinal permeability (chapters 3 and 4). *Gliadin* is a protein found within the alcohol soluble fraction of wheat flour. *Casein* (found in milk, cheese, beans, and nuts) is a mixture of phosphoproteins that are closely related. Normally, these large molecules cannot pass through the gut wall. Increased intestinal permeability can allow these proteins to pass through the gut wall and initiate an antibody response; usually, in proportion to their allergy-inducing ability (antigenicity) and dietary presence. An increase in IgA antibodies titers to gliadin and/or casein reveals increased intestinal permeability. In contrast, an elevation in IgG antibodies suggests long-term or prior intestinal permeability. Research reveals that candidiasis sufferers often have a high incidence of both IgA and IgG antibodies against both gliadin and casein, evidencing leaky gut syndrome. (This is not the only test to assess intestinal permeability; others are just as useful.) Moreover, the ability of *leukocytes* (immune cells) to adhere to latex beads decreases in people with increased intestinal permeability, providing evidence of impaired immunity.

UNCOVERING OTHER INFECTIOUS INVADERS

Numerous tests reveal other infectious invaders, including harmful parasites, bacteria, molds, and/or viruses. Certain bacteria and molds can be found by using the (urine) organic acid test (chapter 12). Viral titers are mentioned in the routine blood section. Nevertheless, some tests are specific for harmful parasites and bacteria.

- **Urine indican test (Obermeyer test)** can assess the presence of harmful bacteria within the gut. Virtually every candidiasis sufferer has harmful bacteria within their gut. This creates a *dysbiosis* that can progress to *dysbacteriosis* (chapter 4). The urine indican test can estimate the magnitude of colonization. Harmful bacteria are often able to convert *tryptophan* (essential amino acid) into *indole,* which is further metabolized to *indican.* If it is present within the gut, it can be absorbed and enter the blood, where it remains until it is filtered out by the kidneys and excreted within the urine. The more harmful bacteria within the gut, the greater the amount of indican created and available for absorption. This test involves mixing a sample of a patient's urine with a specific reagent. After 10 minutes, it is observed and graded from 0 (no reaction) to 4 (severe). The result reflects the severity of a patient's dysbiosis as well as dysbacteriosis. This test may also be used periodically to follow a patient's progress.

- **Stool samples** are typically acquired to check for parasites and harmful bacteria. They are best at identifying harmful bacteria and testing their sensitivity to antibiotics and other substances. Stool samples often reveal the presence and colonization of disease-causing yeast and harmful molds, which can be tested for their sensitivity to antifungal agents. Yet, contrary to their intended purpose, stool samples are a poor diagnostic tool for revealing parasites. Unless someone is suffering with a significant infection, most protozoa parasites (chapter 5) are *not* detected by routine stool samples; usually, the parasites die and break apart within the stool and/or they are not present in significant amounts. From clinical experience, stool samples reveal parasites in fewer than 5 percent of patients. Moreover, they are inconvenient to obtain; three samples are collected over three days and should be refrigerated until processed. However, there is another important reason to obtain stool samples: to determine and assess someone's population of beneficial bacteria. During/after therapy, testing can reveal the status of a sufferer's beneficial bacteria. Some healthcare practitioners advise their patients to repeat their stool cultures a minimum of every six to eight weeks until at least two consecutive stool samples demonstrate that they have reestablished normal (healthy) amounts of beneficial bacteria.

- **Anoscopy** is the best method for identifying parasites. If disease-causing yeast or significant amounts of harmful bacteria are growing within the rectum, they will be noted as well. It is a painless procedure, taking one to two minutes. After an anoscope (a small funnel) is inserted into a patient's rectum, a technician *vigorously* rubs three sterile cotton-tipped swabs (or a cytology brush) against the mucosa all around and from top to bottom, making sure to collect a specimen from the *deep* rectal mucosa. The swabs (or brush) are removed and each one is separately placed in a test tube (containing a 10 percent formalin solution). The swab tips (or brush bristles) are squeezed against the inside and bottom of each tube, ensuring that most of the rectal material remains within the tube and is prepared for the test. After discarding the swabs (or brush), each test tube receives a different stain, including *trichrome new formulation* (for parasites), *immunofluorescence* (for *Giardia duodenalis* and *Cryptosporidium*), and *crystal violet* (for disease-causing yeast). The samples are centrifuged, placed on slides, and examined under a high-quality microscope (in addition, an instantaneous wet prep can be done). When performed correctly, the anoscopy is exceptionally accurate for identifying parasites and for revealing the presence of disease-causing yeast. Yet, if disease-causing yeast are not seen, it does not rule out candidiasis. It only indicates that disease-causing yeast are *not* colonizing the rectal tissues and can be growing elsewhere.

- **Other tests to support the presence of parasites** are available. Although elevated *IgE antibody titers* can accompany allergies, they may also represent an antigen-antibody immune response aimed against one or more parasites. The presence of *eosinophilia*, an elevated number of eosinophils (immune cells) within the blood, is consistent with an excess of antibodies to parasites (and/or allergies). *Leukopenia*, fewer lymphocytes (immune cells) within the blood, can arise if parasites are impairing immunity, especially when they cause depressed immunity (fewer cells). In contrast, *leukocytosis*, an increased number of lymphocytes within the blood, can occur when there is significant inflammation or a parasitic infection that stimulates immunity. Positive *anti-amoeba antibodies* or *anti-Giardia antibodies* suggest an ongoing, or prior, infection with the parasite corresponding to the positive antibody. A *positive reaction* to *amoeba* by the *cytotoxic test* can denote present or previous exposure. *Positive skin reactions* to specific *parasite antigen testing* can provide evidence of present or prior exposure.

TESTS TO DETERMINE CANDIDIASIS-RELATED ALLERGIES

Disease-causing yeast are highly *antigenic*; they have a strong ability to induce *allergies*. So, candidiasis is an infection with a diversity of allergic consequences (chapter 16). Typically, this includes sensitivities and hypersensitivities to the disease-causing yeast themselves, antigenically similar molds, and many harmful molds. In addition, sufferers can become sensitive or hypersensitive to various other substances, including foods, chemicals, pollen, dust, or anything else within their internal and external environments. So, with respect to treating candidiasis, it is vital to appreciate both of its sides, *infectious* and *allergic*. Most sufferers manifest their infection and numerous allergies at the same time; they rarely have one or the other. Treating their infection and ignoring their allergies is likely to produce mediocre improvements and, in some cases, none. Therefore, it is important to test most (if not all) sufferers for allergies to *Candida albicans*, other disease-causing yeast, and the antigenically cross-reactive molds *Trichophyton, Oidiomycetes, Epidermophyton* (TOE) as well as other harmful molds (chapter 16). A significant percentage of sufferers also benefit from accurately identifying their allergies to foods, environmental substances, and chemicals.

- **Intradermal skin testing** has been used to determine allergies for over 100 years. In 1915, Robert Cooke injected the epidermis or topmost layers of skin. In 1930, a French otolaryngologist (ear, nose, and throat), named Hansel, tried skin testing with various dilutions of antigens, obtaining more information than a single test, by finding that the size of the skin reaction correlated with the dose of antigen administered. In 1937, a general allergist named Herbert Rinkel refined this further, introducing the concept of skin endpoint titration.

- **Serial dilution endpoint titration (SDET)** is related to traditional skin testing, except that the antigens (extracts) are serially diluted by one-fifth (instead of one-tenth). For example, the initial extract is diluted five times (one part extract to four parts diluent) to make dilution number one. Then, dilution one is similarly diluted to yield number two (now, one part in 25), and so on as needed. The physician decides what dilution to start with, and it is injected intradermally. The tests are read at 10 and 15 minutes. Depending on the size of the initial response (wheal), weaker or stronger dilutions are subsequently given until the endpoint is reached. The *endpoint* is defined as the weakest dilution to initiate a *progressive positive wheal;* the first dilution to cause a wheal to form that is at least two millimeters larger than the previous unreactive wheal, but before the next stronger dilution produces a two millimeter or larger wheal. The endpoint correlates with a person's hypersensitivity and becomes their starting dose for immunotherapy, desensitization (allergy) injections. The advantage of this test is that it can measure allergies quantitatively and qualitatively, it is highly reproducible, extremely sensitive, and safe. On the downside, it is time-consuming, and its results can be questionable when someone's allergies are extremely mild. This way of allergy testing is especially good for assessing allergies to disease-causing yeast, harmful molds, and environmental inhalants, including dust and pollen. It can also detect food allergies, but some physicians contend it should not be used because it involves a high rate of false positives; a patient is not allergic, but tests positive anyway. Although this method is best for determining *type 1* (*immediate*) reactions (chapter 16), it is important to reassess patients two to three days later because it can reveal *type 4* (*delayed*) reactions. Since type 4 reactions are not initially noticeable, a patient's allergies can be overlooked if they are not rechecked. Type 4 reactions are also treated with immunotherapy.

- **Provocative neutralization testing (PNT)** is more accurate for revealing allergies to foods and chemicals. After a patient's baseline symptoms are known, a dose of antigen is injected intradermally. During the test, in addition to measuring the magnitude of their resulting skin reaction (wheal), their symptoms are also noted. Following this, weaker dilution's (at a one-to-five ratio) are administered every 10 minutes until their allergy symptoms appear. The injections are continued, using greater dilutions, until their symptoms abate. This provides the starting point for immunotherapy. Patients can also be tested by placing antigen under their tongue (sublingually). Once again, this tests type 1 (immediate) reactions, so patients should be assessed two to three days later to check for any type 4 (delayed) reactions.

- **Food allergy testing** helps determine if foods are contributing to a sufferer's symptoms. The concept of food allergy has been known for over 70 years, if not longer. In 1950, Dr. Theron Randolph (a clinical ecologist) began "challenge testing" to determine a patient's food allergies. His patients were only allowed to drink filtered or spring water until they were symptom-free (usually, this took five to seven days). After the fasting phase, they would eat three meals a day for 25 days. Their symptoms would return when an offending (allergic) food was introduced into their diet. Although crude, if it is carefully and systematically done, accurate results are possible. Moreover, the results are directly related to the actual person, representing both their *IgE-mediated* and *non-IgE mediated* reactions (chapter 16). Challenge testing is often a frustrating, difficult, and laborious process. Alternatively, it can be performed by placing various foods in opaque capsules. A patient swallows a capsule and waits. If there is no response, another capsule is swallowed. This continues until all the capsules are ingested. Once again, this is time-consuming and expensive.

- **Cytotoxic test/ALCAT:** Arthur Black, M.D., was searching for a better, simpler, and less expensive way to recognize reactions to foods. He established the *cytotoxic test* (*cyto* = cell, *toxic* = poison). Immune cells (white blood cells) protect the body from foods and other substances that inappropriately gain access to areas where they should not. Immune cells that are sensitive or hypersensitive to certain allergy-inducing foods can be damaged or destroyed by *non-IgE medicated* reactions (chapter 16). So, it seems logical to observe the interaction between immune cells and specific food antigens to determine someone's food allergies. The test can assess this interaction; a patient's white blood cells and specific food antigens are mixed, incubated for four hours, and then observed under a microscope. Research was published in 1956, so it has been used for a long time. Despite its reasoning and scientific support, this test continues to be ignored by the most mainstream physicians, even though studies of other immune cell interactions (for example, lymphocyte blastogenesis, antibody-dependent cellular-mediated cytotoxicity, natural killer cell activities, and others) are similarly performed and trusted.

William Bryan, M.D. and his wife made various improvements in the cytotoxic test and introduced it to Europe, Australia, and the United States. Mark Lovendale modified the test, creating the *prime test* or *leukocyte antigen sensitivity test* (LAST).

After assessing hundreds (if not thousands) of cytotoxic tests, they have proven to be a valuable tool. The findings are usually graded from 0 (none) to 4 (severe). The results tend to be reproducible and fairly accurate, but there are some caveats. Since the maximum strength of the reactions can vary from patient to patient, the test should only be considered on an individual basis and in relation to someone's symptoms. For example, if person A's strongest response to a specific food is 4 (severe), it is obvious they have a food allergy. However, if person B's maximum response is 2, they appear only half as allergic as person A. Yet, this may be misleading; since candidiasis can cause impaired immunity, person B may be just as allergic as person A and have a weaker reaction. Indeed, a response of 1 is significant in person B (a 50 percent reaction), but it is unimportant in person A (25 percent their maximum response). What about person C? They may have a 0 reaction to everything. Does this mean they have no food allergies? Yes, unless their candidiasis is severe, and their immune system is so impaired it is unable to react. So, even though they may have many allergies, there is no measurable response; in technical terms, this produces a *false negative*. This explains why cytotoxic test results must be considered in the context of a person's symptoms and illness. For these reasons, although great in theory, the cytotoxic test is not totally infallible in practice.

The *antigen leukocyte cellular antibody test* (ALCAT) is a variation of the cytotoxic test that uses electronic hematological instrumentation. Computers analyze cell counts to determine the effects of food extracts on cellular elements, white blood cells, platelets, etc. Basically, it is a computerized version of the cytotoxic test that eliminates technician bias.

The cytotoxic test and ALCAT can also assess sensitivities and hypersensitivities to molds (and yeast). Greater than 10,000 species of molds are known (chapter 16). The most common readily antigenically cross-react with disease-causing yeast or are problematic by themselves; so, it is worthwhile to evaluate some of them. During the ALCAT, various molds are incubated with a sample of a patient's blood. Any change that occurs to the white blood cells is considered a positive reaction. The ALCAT electronically detects and measures the amount.

- **ELISA:** Russell M. Jaffe, M.D., developed the ELISA (*enzyme-linked immunosorbent assay*). It is a laboratory tool that determines if excessive or chronic exposures to reactive foods and chemicals are compromising someone's immunity. It also indicates if this is contributing to their symptoms. The test can investigate delayed reactions to more than 200 substances. After receiving the results, the patient is told to completely avoid strongly reactive foods for six months, and intermediate-reactive foods for three months. More specifically, this test can evaluate a delayed reaction to *Candida albicans*. Alternatively, RAST (*radioallergosorbent test*) is a test that can be used to assesses specific IgE-mediated reactions to foods.

These tests should be considered and employed when food allergies and/or intolerance is suspected. Although some are better than others, no test can provide all the answers. The choice resides with the healthcare practitioner who orders and evaluates them.

MAKING THE DIAGNOSIS

It is one thing to be a candidiasis sufferer. It is another for a physician to make a formal diagnosis. Since a single, infallible test does not exist to make the diagnosis, candidiasis is often overlooked, ignored, or confused. This makes therapy difficult and sometimes impossible.

The good news is that most sufferers can be easily diagnosed. Initially, they should receive a thorough medical history and complete physical exam by a candidiasis-minded healthcare provider. In fact, the history and physical exam are often more revealing than the most sophisticated test.

Numerous tests can assist in identifying the presence of disease-causing yeast and reveal the extent of the infection. In addition, a variety of disturbances tend to accompany candidiasis and should be considered as well: malabsorption and metabolic abnormalities are common, as well as disturbances involving the nervous, endocrine (hormone), and immune systems. Since candidiasis has two sides, *infectious* and *allergic*, addressing a sufferer's allergies is essential. The infectious and allergic consequences of disease-causing yeast would seem to be bad enough, but the situation is often worse. Most sufferers frequently have one or more other infectious invaders present, including harmful parasites, bacteria, molds, and/or viruses. Because of their ability to exacerbate illness and directly cause harm, a search for these troublemakers must be undertaken and appropriately addressed.

So, if you are a candidiasis sufferer, you need to appreciate both its *infectious* and *allergic* consequences. A complete workup will reveal all your infectious invaders and any accompanying disturbances. If you do not want to throw your money away on unnecessary tests, consult with a knowledgeable and experienced candidiasis-minded physician because they are likely to know which tests will be most appropriate; it usually depends on your specific symptoms and illness. This is not just an academic exercise because your results will enable your healthcare practitioner to design and administer the most effective therapeutic program to improve your health and well-being.

CHAPTER 18

Treating Candidiasis

Warning: *During anti-candidiasis therapy, many candidiasis sufferers get worse before they improve. This is a normal consequence of eradicating disease-causing yeast as well as other infectious invaders. This effect, called a die-off reaction, most often lasts for hours to days, rarely up to a week or longer. Therefore, you should not be scared or panic if your symptoms and illness intensify. There are rare exceptions, but this is a good sign and a strong indicator of the beneficial changes that are certain to follow.*

Disclaimer: *Although self-diagnosis and treatment are possible, supervision or management by a knowledgeable candidiasis-minded physician is recommended and, in some cases, essential. Without experienced guidance, your results are likely to be less than optimal, and you might make mistakes that slow or impede your return to wellness.*

Note: *If you are a candidiasis sufferer, you should read the introduction and first three chapters; they contain the general information you need to know. You might also consult the chapter(s) that pertain to your symptoms and illnesses.*

Candidiasis is an *infection* with disease-causing yeast and its *allergic* consequences. The colonization of disease-causing yeast within the gastrointestinal tract, as well as their invasion into and through the gut wall, commonly causes malabsorption and nutritional deficiencies. To add insult, they can advance to infect the tissues and blood as well as virtually every tissue and organ within the body. Metabolic disarray, as well as disturbances involving the nervous, endocrine (hormone), and immune systems, is common. In addition, the presence of one or more other infectious invaders (harmful parasites, bacteria, molds, and/or viruses) is certain to exacerbate a sufferer's health further.

Until now, treating and managing candidiasis rarely reflected science. Due to a lack of available information and an absence of well-constructed and properly conducted research, candidiasis has been treated in a variety of ways. For every person who has been helped, this "trial and error" approach has produced as many or more failures. Because of this lack of success, mainstream medicine contends that candidiasis is a fictitious illness. Yet, there are some candidiasis-minded physicians who know what they are doing and are successfully treating their patients.

In contrast, some healthcare practitioners claim to understand candidiasis but lack the information and experience to do so. At best, instead of eliminating their patient's candidiasis, it is only controlled. It might make them feel better, but it also dooms them to perpetual treatment, or they are likely to relapse. Even worse, many sufferers do not get better using inappropriate or scientifically unsound therapies, causing them to doubt whether they had candidiasis in the first place. Beware of any healthcare practitioner who does not understand the science of candidiasis. They will be easily recognizable when they say, "Let's try this and see how you feel." Rather than using science to their advantage, they are treating by trial and error. This may have been okay 20 or even 10 years ago, when candidiasis was much less understood. Since the information now exists to provide a scientific and logical way of treating sufferers, a rational and scientific approach should standardize the way it is treated and even cured.

Most military strategists know that the best way to win a war is to study the enemy, discover their weaknesses, and then use this information against them. Disease-causing yeast are the enemies of our good health. Like any living organism, they have their strengths and weaknesses. The secret to designing appropriate anti-candidiasis therapy is to use their weaknesses against them. The enemy has been thoroughly studied. Science and research involving disease-causing yeast along with clinical experience have enabled the creation of a comprehensive anti-candidiasis program. This chapter describes the most appropriate and effective ways to combat candidiasis. It is not meant to be the ultimate authority or last word about treatment. As time passes, new medications and herbal preparations are certain to appear. Additional information and insights will come to light. More *candidiasis connections* will be revealed. Yet, enough is known to help most sufferers, and cures are possible.

Since every person is a unique individual, what works for one person may not work for someone else. Yes, there will be differences. For example, some sufferers are allergic to certain foods and must eliminate them from their diet. Other sufferers may be taking one or more medications that need to be adjusted. For these and other reasons, you would be wise to seek professional guidance. This will help you avoid making mistakes and enable you to have the speediest recovery. However, there are no guarantees. If you do not uncover and treat all your infectious invaders, address your allergies, correct your nutritional deficiencies, or ignore many other recommendations, do not expect success.

Anti-candidiasis therapy is meant to be comprehensive, addressing your infectious invaders, allergies, nutritional deficiencies, and so on. You cannot do it 50 or 70 percent and expect a full recovery. It is essential to be 100-percent compliant because digressions only ensure failure. An anti-candidiasis treatment program is difficult for many people. Just staying on a strict anti-candidiasis diet seems to be challenging. Yet, therapy does not have to be torturous, difficult, or even unpleasant. All it takes is the right attitude. In fact, a good attitude is essential. Typically, the sufferers with the best attitudes are the most ill; they usually feel so bad, they are willing to do anything to feel better. Unfortunately, when these sufferer's do begin to feel better, they tend to become more liberal, straying from their program and sabotaging their recovery. Whether you are severely ill or just suffer with a few problems, please make the effort to avoid having this type of attitude. Once you start anti-candidiasis therapy, you should see it to its rightful conclusion.

Yes, candidiasis is a legitimate condition. It can be treated and even be cured. In some cases, this might even save your life.

PROGRAM BASICS

Every candidiasis sufferer needs to know what they are treating and why; otherwise, they may have little incentive to be compliant. The following information outlines the basics of a comprehensive anti-candidiasis program, including the elements to be considered and addressed.

Diagnosing Your Candidiasis

The initial step is to properly *diagnose* your condition (chapter 17). The questionnaire in chapter 1 can reveal your likelihood of having candidiasis, but it is only a tool and there will always be exceptions; for example, some people may have low scores, but be sufferers, nonetheless. Regardless of your score, if you suffer with any of the symptoms or illnesses discussed in this book, you would be wise to consult with a knowledgeable, candidiasis-minded physician.

What can you expect? You should first have a thorough medical history and physical exam. Then, depending on your symptoms and illness, you would receive one or more laboratory tests to verify whether you have an *infection* with disease-causing yeast (and other infectious invaders). Because candidiasis is also an allergy-inducing condition, most sufferers should be evaluated for sensitivities and hypersensitivities to disease-causing yeast and harmful molds. Again, depending on your symptoms, you might also be tested for allergies to foods, pollen, dust, chemicals, and more. A couple of weeks later, when all your results are in, you will know what you have and what you are up against.

Starting an Anti-Candidiasis Program

Your results reveal that you have an infection with disease-causing yeast (and maybe one or more other infectious invaders). What next? Initially, you begin with an anti-candidiasis diet (chapter 20) as well as eliminate your allergy-producing foods. This is critical because it decreases the inflammation within your gut. Normally, your gut produces some mucus, forming a protective layer. As the inflammation within your gut increases, so does your amount of mucus. This can act as a barrier, preventing antifungal therapy from killing your disease-causing yeast, encouraging a relapse. Similarly, an increased amount of mucus inhibits antiparasitic medications from killing parasites and antibiotics from killing harmful bacteria. It will also prevent you from reestablishing a population of beneficial bacteria. Inflammation hinders the absorption of essential nutrients, encouraging malabsorption and nutritional deficiencies. It also stresses the immune system, which can cause numerous, unpleasant secondary consequences and impede your recovery.

Why is the diet so vital for a therapeutic success? Sugars and simple carbohydrates feed your disease-causing yeast, so they must not be consumed. Foods and beverages that contain living disease-causing yeast and/or harmful molds can colonize your gut with more infectious invaders. Even the spores of dead organisms can germinate within your gut and cause problems. Regardless of whether they are alive or dead, ingesting disease-causing yeast and harmful molds can precipitate allergic reactions in sensitive and hypersensitive people. Similarly, allergy-inducing foods can promote adverse immune system reactions and inflammation. To add insult, foods and beverages containing disease-causing yeast and/or harmful molds can be contaminated with their harmful toxins and metabolites.

At the same time, you want to start *detoxification* to help decrease and eliminate as many harmful toxins as possible from your body. Although the diet helps, the liver and kidneys must be specifically addressed.

The liver is an essential organ with dual functions. Its metabolism and detoxifying abilities are well known. Yet, during any chronic infection, the liver produces numerous substances that assist the immune system in combating infectious invaders. Sometimes the liver's participation is successful. More frequently, a chronic infection becomes a continuous, long-standing battle, with both opponents sustaining casualties and damage, but neither side wins. Liver disturbances are common among candidiasis sufferers; their liver functioning is often impaired, which can progress to injury and eventually damage. Since the liver detoxifies harmful substances and eliminates waste from your body, it needs to be strengthened. Therefore, an herbal program that regenerates liver tissue is recommended (chapter 19).

The kidneys are also vital for eliminating wastes and should be strengthened; at least one herb consistently appears to benefit kidney functioning (chapter 19). While the liver can be regenerated rather quickly, the kidneys are slower to improve.

Chronic candidiasis takes its toll on these organs, so detoxification is critical. You must strengthen your metabolism and organs so your body can adapt to the burden of eliminating your disease-causing yeast. Usually, detoxification lasts from one to two weeks, but some sufferers benefit from a longer cleanse.

A good therapy program should initially address and correct a sufferer's malabsorption and nutritional deficiencies. The diet helps improve absorption, but it will not correct long-standing nutritional deficiencies. A nutritional program that contains a variety of supplements is recommended. A knowledgeable candidiasis-minded physician with experience in nutrition would decide which supplements you should take and how much you need. Depending on their medical maladies, some sufferers benefit from receiving additional supplements. As an example, people with cardiovascular disease have special requirements. Like any other tissue within the human body, the cells that comprise the arteries and veins need specific nutrients to optimally function. When these substances are lacking, cardiovascular fragility, injury, and damage are likely (especially occurring secondary to oxygen-based free radical activities). The micronutrients within these herbs and supplements strengthen arteries-veins and are also potent antioxidants. Anyone with cardiovascular illness should consider using them regularly (chapter 19). Yet, their greatest benefit is likely to occur in the long run by preventing illness in the first place.

Some sufferers cannot tolerate the herbs used to detoxify their liver and kidneys. Other sufferers cannot tolerate vitamins, minerals, or any supplements. Clinical experience reveals they have many infectious invaders inflaming their gut, making them unable to tolerate supplements. These sufferers, as well as anyone with notable malabsorption, will benefit from an intravenous nutrition program; vitamins, minerals, and amino acids are administered into a peripheral vein and enter their circulation, where they can get to their cells and tissues unimpeded. Depending on the extent of someone's ill health, this can be done one to three times a week. As they improve, the frequency is decreased and then discontinued when they can tolerate oral supplementation.

Next Step: Anti-Candidiasis Therapy

You are on the anti-candidiasis diet. You are strengthening your liver and kidneys. You are correcting your nutritional deficiencies. One to two weeks have passed, or more. What happens next?

The first goal is to *kill* your disease-causing yeast. Because of their infectious and allergic tendencies, they should be eliminated first. Of all the infectious invaders that assault your gut, although they may not be the nastiest, disease-causing yeast are certainly the most invasive. Some of them can invade into and through your gut wall, causing an increase in intestinal permeability—leaky gut syndrome (chapters 3 and 4). Their direct allergy-inducing tendencies can cause profound inflammation that will not decrease until your disease-causing yeast are eliminated.

What if you have parasites or harmful bacteria, should these infectious invaders be killed first? Unless you have a *severe* infection with one or more of them, you would be wise to wait. Disease-causing yeast can form colonies, as well as biofilms, that can protect these infectious invaders; any of them residing underneath or within these colonies will be shielded from the agents used to kill them. Yes, antiparasitic or antibacterial agents may decrease your number of parasites or harmful bacteria, but you are unlikely to eliminate their presence. After you complete therapy, a relapse is likely. Even worse, there is a good chance the infectious invaders that escaped death may have become resistant to the agents used.

So, if parasites or harmful bacteria are present, it is wise to wait until your disease-causing yeast are eliminated before treating them. What about harmful molds? In general, harmful molds are *not* invasive. Instead of invading into and through the gut wall, they tend to grow on or off its surface. Yet, there is a big exception. Leaky gut syndrome can allow harmful molds to enter the tissues as well as blood. Since disease-causing yeast are responsible for leaky gut syndrome, the first goal is to heal the gut wall. Again, the way to do this is to kill the disease-causing yeast.

Nonabsorbable antifungal agents, whether medications or herbs, are curative when disease-causing yeast are solely confined within the gastrointestinal tract. However, this rarely occurs. Most sufferers have some amount of disease-causing yeast invading into and through their gut wall. So, why do many sufferers feel better after using a nonabsorbable agent? Because they killed a significant amount of disease-causing yeast. Yet, these antifungal agents do not eradicate their infection completely because the disease-causing yeast have not been eliminated from their tissues and blood. Sufferers who use nonabsorbable antifungal agents usually must periodically or continuously take some form of antifungal agent forever to avoid relapse. Many herbs are not well absorbed or potent enough to kill disease-causing yeast within the blood and tissues, so they are no more effective than nonabsorbable antifungal agents.

Research and clinical experience support the use of *systemic* antifungal agents. Most sufferers have disease-causing yeast within their gut wall, which is *invasive* candidiasis. In addition, a significant percentage have disease-causing yeast within their blood and other tissues, creating *systemic* candidiasis. Systemic antifungal medications are absorbed, enter the tissues and blood, and kill disease-causing yeast within these and other locations (for example, the lungs and sinuses). In most sufferers, this is the only way to eliminate the disease-causing yeast from these areas. Using a systemic agent also eradicates disease-causing yeast within the gut tissues, which enables the gut wall to heal from its exterior to its interior. The cells of the gut wall grow from the outer (tissue) side inward toward the lumen (center). When the disease-causing yeast are killed, the gut wall can heal. This decreases inflammation, eradicates leaky gut syndrome, eliminates malabsorption, and restores the gut barrier.

From clinical experience, not using a systemic antifungal medication is the most frequently made clinical mistake. Usually, this happens because a physician does not appreciate the extent of their patient's infection or there is a fear (by them or the patient) to use a systemic antifungal medication (chapter 19). Why? Like any pharmaceutical agent, drugs have unwanted effects and side effects. If a sufferer is on one or more medications, physicians must know whether there are interactions to be concerned about or contraindications to their use. This is the first concern, but adjustments can be made in most cases, and these medications can be successfully employed. Yet, research with these medications has revealed that there is a tiny chance of inducing liver disturbances. It has been thought that these medications, since they must be cleared by the liver, are directly injurious to the cells of the liver. On the contrary, experience reveals that these medications are safe and reliable, especially if your liver has been strengthened prior to their use.

The problem tends to occur in patients with severe candidiasis and impaired liver functioning. Why? These medications kill disease-causing yeast, and, as they die, they liberate their cellular contents. Regardless of whether they are within the gut and absorbed or are colonizing the tissues and blood, their contents are highly toxic and allergy-inducing. These substances need to be cleared from the body by the liver and kidneys. When someone has severe candidiasis and impaired liver functioning, the death of their disease-causing yeast can overwhelm their liver, injuring its cells and tissues. In most cases, this appears to be reversible after the systemic antifungal medication is stopped. Again, this almost never happens when the body is detoxified and the liver is strengthened prior to using these medications.

Research reveals that systemic antifungal agents are safe when used properly. In 1997, K. H. Duswald et al. found that Diflucan (fluconazole) can be used in dosages much greater than recommended. After reviewing roughly 900 cases with dosages greater than 800 mg and up to 2,000 mg used on the first day of treatment, they commented, "These study results indicate that higher daily doses of fluconazole than are currently approved for these indications are well tolerated and tend to provide better clinical efficacy in selected patient populations." Most candidiasis-minded physicians normally give 400–600 mg of Diflucan a day, with some patients needing more. If dosages 4 to 10 times the normal amount (200 mg) are considered safe, then the drug itself is not likely to be the culprit. Once again, the blame is likely to rest with impaired liver functioning, which is why it is essential to detoxify and strengthen the liver.

Another mistake is to use a systemic antifungal medication but only for a short period. It takes about five days for the gut wall to replace its cells and heal, and longer when there is severe inflammation. It can take up to two weeks to eliminate disease-causing yeast from the upper and lower respiratory tract, and longer if there is severe inflammation. If disease-causing yeast are infecting a sufferer's toenails, it can take four to six months to fully eradicate them. Therefore, systemic antifungal agents should be used for a minimum of two weeks, with three to four weeks being the average length of time. If a sufferer needs to remain on medication for a prolonged period, they should adhere to the diet and continue to strengthen their liver throughout. In addition, they should have their liver functions checked (by laboratory testing) about every four weeks.

A big mistake is to use small doses of a systemic antifungal medication. In 1997, P. G. Flanagan et al. demonstrated that inadequate doses of Diflucan (fluconazole) in patients with systemic candidiasis did not eliminate their infection. In 2022, Meng-Si Ye et al. reported that *Cancidas* (caspofungin) at subinhibitory concentrations promotes the formation of *Candida albicans* persister cells. Short course therapy or low dosing are to be avoided because they do not eliminate the infection completely. Even worse, any disease-causing yeast that remain can become resistant to the systemic antifungal medication that was used. In fact, a growing body of research reveals that numerous disease-causing yeasts are resistant to one or more systemic antifungal agents.

For these reasons (and more), systemic antifungal agents are vital to completely eradicate candidiasis. Typically, a candidiasis-minded physician will decide which medication you need and for how long. This is not a simple decision because disease-causing *Candida*-species organisms other than *Candida albicans* commonly contribute to causing infections within human beings. There are 8 major disease-causing *Candida*-species organisms and 17 less prominent disease-causing *Candida*-species organisms. Although their harm varies, all are associated with illness. So the medication you use will depend on which disease-causing yeast you have, their location within your body, and their susceptibility to a drug. Equally concerning, new species and strains of disease-causing yeast may be a problem. Research by numerous investigators revealed that *Candida dubliniensis* is associated with mucosal candidiasis in HIV-infected people. *Candida auris* has caused outbreaks in healthcare settings, is often multidrug resistant, and is difficult to identify with standard laboratory methods. Therefore, with respect to treating your candidiasis, you are strongly recommended to seek professional guidance.

Suppose you start a systemic antifungal agent. What happens next? You will probably experience the die-off of some disease-causing yeast on the first day. Usually, this involves the medication killing disease-causing yeast within your gastrointestinal tract. It also includes the disease-causing yeast killed within your blood after the medication is adsorbed. Over the next couple of days, you might feel better, the same, or worse. Then, about day four or five, you may have a flare-up as the medication is eradicating disease-causing yeast within your gut wall and tissues. After that, you are likely to feel better until about the eighth to tenth day, when disease-causing yeast within your sinuses and lungs begin to die. It takes a good two weeks to kill most of the disease-causing yeast that are susceptible to the antifungal agent being used.

Yet, systemic antifungal medications do have a downside. For numerous reasons, they may not completely kill all the disease-causing yeast within your gut. So, it is wise to add a nonabsorbable antifungal agent about 10 days after starting a systemic antifungal medication. At this point, your gut wall should be healed, and your inflammation should have decreased. As an example, Fungizone oral suspension (chapter 19) is an effective nonabsorbable antifungal medication that kills disease-causing yeast as well as some harmful molds. It has proven to be a great weapon in the fight against candidiasis. It is usually taken four times a day for 8 to 10 days (two to three bottles). After a few days, there should be few major disease-causing yeasts residing within your gut. This is a good time to eradicate parasites and kill harmful bacteria.

It is important to note that some sufferers will not have a significant infection with *Candida albicans* or another major disease-causing yeast. Instead, they tend to be colonized with one or more of the less prominent disease-causing yeast, especially *Rhodotorula*-species organisms and/or *Saccharomyces cerevisiae* (baker's and/or brewer's yeast). These sufferers tend to not be as ill. I refer to them as having *atypical candidiasis*. They are revealed with allergy testing. If a sufferer appears sensitive or hypersensitive to the antigen of *Rhodotorula* and/or *Saccharomyces cerevisiae* (as well as to other harmful molds), but not *Candida albicans*, there is an excellent chance they have atypical candidiasis. Since these organisms are rarely susceptible to pharmaceutical agents, these sufferers tend to experience little to no die-off symptoms from a systemic antifungal medication or even a nonabsorbable medication. Yet, this does not mean these medications should not be used. On the contrary, these patients do appear to have some amount of major disease-causing yeast within them, although present in small numbers. If they are not eliminated and the opportunity arises, they will become more aggressive and invade into the gut wall and tissues, causing leaky gut syndrome. So, regardless of whether candidiasis or atypical candidiasis is noted, anti-candidiasis therapy should be the same up to this point.

What should sufferers with atypical candidiasis do? All candidiasis sufferers probably have some amount of the less prominent disease-causing yeast within their gut. Once their gut wall is healed and the major disease-causing yeast are eliminated, it is time to eliminate their less prominent disease-causing yeast. One or more herbs have proven to be effective at doing this. In fact, these herbs have the added advantage of killing a variety of disease-causing yeast and harmful molds, including disease-causing yeast resistant to medication, so they really clean out the gut. This is when sufferers with atypical candidiasis are likely to have a significant die-off reaction. Herbal therapy may require two or more weeks. Once again, a candidiasis-minded physician is the best person to know which herbs you need, how much, and for how long.

GENERAL CONSIDERATIONS

The preceding discussion is the most common course of anti-candidiasis therapy. Since every person is a unique individual, every sufferer will be given a different program, even if the differences are slight. There are numerous considerations to be considered when planning or undertaking anti-candidiasis therapy.

Infection versus Allergies

Candidiasis has two prominent sides, infectious and allergic. Even though one may be more prominent, most sufferers often manifest both. This usually reflects the length of time they have suffered with candidiasis and the organisms present.

The *infectious* side involves the colonization of disease-causing yeast, including their ability to initiate and promote a variety of harmful disturbances within the body. In turn, a diversity of symptoms and illness may arise, which tends to vary from one sufferer to another. The infection exists when the disease-causing yeast have assumed prominence within the gut, causing *gastrointestinal candidiasis*. Thereafter, their invasion into the gut wall and tissues creates *invasive candidiasis*. When the disease-causing yeast enter the blood and take up residence within areas away from the gut, *systemic candidiasis* is present.

Fortunately, numerous substances can kill disease-causing yeast, including natural preparations and pharmaceutical drugs. Systemic antifungal medication is initially preferable because it consistently kills disease-causing yeast within the tissues and blood. Yet, the infection can be treated with one or more other anti-candidiasis agents. Soon after an appropriate therapy is instituted, the infection will begin to resolve. The speed the infection abates depends on the species of disease-causing yeast present, their location within the body, and the agents used (as well as the sensitivity of the disease-causing yeast to the agent).

The *allergic* side involves the allergy-inducing tendencies of disease-causing yeast (chapter 16). In contrast to their infectious nature, their allergic effects tend to arise slowly. They are also likely to persist if left untreated. At first, sufferers often develop sensitivities and hypersensitivities to the disease-causing yeast themselves, some molds that are antigenically similar, and one or more harmful molds. Over time, as leaky gut syndrome develops, increased intestinal permeability can allow undigested food particles and other substances to enter the tissues as well as blood, triggering allergic reactions to these foods and substances. In addition, sufferers tend to become sensitive or hypersensitive to environmental substances, like pollen and dust, and a variety of chemicals. Almost any substance a sufferer is exposed to can induce allergic reactions.

Compared to the treated infection, allergies are usually long-term symptoms. The infection can be eliminated in a relatively short period, whereas allergic reactions will continue to occur every time a sufferer is exposed to some offending substance, even long after their infection is gone. Therefore, allergy testing with the antigens of disease-causing yeast and harmful molds is essential. Depending on a sufferer's reactions, they would receive immunotherapy, desensitization (allergy) injections or drops, containing appropriate amounts of their allergy-inducing antigen(s). Immunotherapy is used to make a sensitive or hypersensitive immune system less reactive when it is exposed to one or more offending substances. In addition to decreasing someone's symptoms, it removes stress from their immune system, allowing it to function more normally. This indirectly benefits their endocrine (hormone) and nervous systems. Since a multitude of symptoms are related to allergies, whether appreciated or not, most sufferers benefit from immunotherapy. For other sufferers it is essential, and they will have little to no improvement without it. There are exceptions, but most sufferer's allergy-related symptoms will perpetually persist if left untreated.

Gastrointestinal versus Invasive versus Systemic

The primary location for the colonization and mischief of disease-causing yeast is within the gut and the mucous membranes. When they have colonized your gut, you have *gastrointestinal candidiasis*. Yet, in most sufferers, the disease-causing yeast are more problematic. For numerous reasons, they will invade into and through the gut wall, and enter the tissues, promoting *invasive candidiasis*. To add insult, they can enter the blood, creating *systemic candidiasis*. Within the blood, they can create cardiovascular harm (chapter 7). Their presence within the circulatory system also provides them with access to other areas of the body, which they can colonize when the conditions permit. Alternatively, since they can be within the air we breathe, disease-causing yeast can be inhaled and colonize your lungs and sinuses. They can also migrate, especially *Candida albicans*; this ability, called *thigmotropic behavior*, enables them to move toward something that touches them. As a result, they can travel up the common bile duct to colonize and infect the liver, gallbladder, and/or pancreas. They can spread from the mouth and nasal passages into to the sinuses or downward into the lungs. They can advance from the anal area to the vagina or move up a woman's urethra to colonize her bladder and urinary tract; on the other hand, disease-causing yeast can travel within the blood, enter the kidneys, and similarly end up within the urinary tract. Generally, the more widespread their infection, the more severely ill the sufferer. There are exceptions because the disease-causing ability of the specific infectious invader(s) contributes to the magnitude of problems that arise.

If you only have gastrointestinal candidiasis, nonabsorbable antifungal agents should be able to eliminate your disease-causing yeast. It is essential to swish and swallow whatever agent you are using to make sure you kill the disease-causing yeast within your mouth and esophagus, or a relapse is certain. Yet, if you *only* have gastrointestinal candidiasis, consider yourself lucky. Most sufferers are less fortunate because they have some magnitude of invasive candidiasis, with a significant percentage having systemic candidiasis. Therefore, a systemic antifungal medication should be used. This is the only proven way to eliminate disease-causing yeast within the tissues and blood. Some antifungal herbs may kill disease-causing yeast, but they are not 100-percent effective, and their systemic effects are inconsistent. Unless there are strong contraindications, invasive and systemic candidiasis mandate the use of a systemic antifungal agent that effectively kills disease-causing yeast within the tissues and blood.

Some physicians take a different approach and treat candidiasis sufferers according to their symptoms. For example, significant symptoms and illness necessitate a systemic antifungal medication, whereas those with minor symptoms or complaints may be given a nonabsorbable antifungal agent. Cautious physicians might provide a nonabsorbable antifungal agent first and then, if needed, progress to a systemic antifungal medication. A sufferer's symptoms alone should never dictate the type of antifungal agent used. Sufferers with invasive and systemic candidiasis with minimal or few symptoms can easily fool physicians into thinking a systemic antifungal medication is not needed. Since most candidiasis sufferers appear to benefit from at least one course of a systemic antifungal medication, healthcare practitioners and patients should be more open-minded about using them.

Nature versus Nurture

Different people can suffer with similar symptoms and illness. Close relatives may develop completely disparate medical maladies. Your genetics and environment participate in promoting illness. Your *genetics* are your inherited strengths and weakness. Your genetic material contains the tiny blueprints that determine how your body grows, develops, and matures. Your *environment* has two components, internal and external. It encompasses what is within your body as well as what is around you. So, your environment includes the contents of your body, especially your gut microbiome, and everything you are exposed to. Your genetics and environment can affect each other. As a result, your genetics influence what is within your body and how you react to what is in your external environment. In return, your environment, internally and externally, can alter your inherited strengths and weaknesses.

This is a prime reason why candidiasis is so variable. It is an infection within your internal environment that adversely affects your body as well as your ability to fight the disease-causing yeast. The symptoms and illness that arises often depend on your genetic weaknesses; you are likely to manifest the medical maladies you are the most susceptible to develop. With respect to all sufferers, rather than causing one symptom or problem, candidiasis promotes a diversity of symptoms and illnesses. This point continues to confuse mainstream physicians. Why is it important? Candidiasis can manifest in a variety of different ways. Basing someone's diagnosis solely on one test or another will miss or overlook candidiasis in a large percentage of sufferers. Similarly, treating candidiasis without taking this information into consideration will not be in each sufferer's best interest.

GOALS OF THERAPY

Like any battle, fighting the enemy is much more successful when you have a strategy. The following information incorporates research and clinical experience to explain how to increase the effectiveness of your anti-candidiasis therapy. It also explains the reasons why the battle against disease-causing yeast and other infectious invaders is fought in a particular way.

Kill Your Disease-causing Yeast

Everyone has a small amount of disease-causing yeast within their gastrointestinal tract. If you have enough beneficial bacteria, they are kept from causing harm. For many reasons, the beneficial bacteria can be injured or killed, allowing the disease-causing yeast to reproduce and colonize their surroundings. Since this creates an *infection*, it must be treated, and eradicating the disease-causing yeast is the primary goal.

If you are a candidiasis sufferer, you must kill your disease-causing yeast, and you are likely to have to do it more than once. This is the only way to ensure your infection is gone. The most thorough approach involves using systemic antifungal medication in every sufferer. This is the only way to eradicate disease-causing yeast residing within the gut wall and tissues, blood, and other areas of the body. Admittedly, a systemic anti-candidiasis assault is not completely risk-free. As mentioned, many physicians and sufferers have been cautious (and even scared) to administer and use a systemic antifungal medication because they have been considered potentially harmful and occasionally dangerous—most notably, rare liver disturbances. Fortunately, the rationale behind this discretion is not justified, and this almost never occurs with proper precautions, especially when the liver is strengthened before instituting therapy. Yes, it is prudent to recommend their cautious application and close monitoring in sufferers with liver disease.

Normally, the liver is an organ primarily concerned with metabolism; it processes carbohydrates, proteins, and fats. It also detoxifies many chemicals and drugs by neutralizing their harmful effects. Many drugs inauspiciously affect the liver, usually in direct proportion to their concentration or amount. Drugs are responsible for most liver damage; for example, consider the inflamed and/or scarred livers of alcoholics and drug abusers. Fortunately, systemic antifungal medications do not act the same way.

The research and data of systemic antifungal agents is a product of mainstream medical studies that treated patients with severe candidiasis; typically, these people were chosen because they were resistant to other medications available at the time. Since mainstream physicians do not recognize candidiasis until it is advanced, the patients studied were certain to have fragile, and even impaired, liver functioning. So, when a patient took the investigated medication and exhibited a liver disturbance, it was assumed to result from the drug. Since the researchers did not understand the full nature of candidiasis, they had the wrong conclusion. It is important to appreciate that disease-causing yeast produce harmful substances that can impair, and even injure, the liver's functioning (notably, ethanol, acetaldehyde, and gliotoxin).

Rather than a direct effect of the drug, the liver disturbance that arises from the use of a systemic antifungal medication is the undesirable result of having severe candidiasis. When disease-causing yeast are killed, their cellular contents are liberated into their surroundings. If this happens in large amounts, like a flood, an impaired liver can be overwhelmed and functionally suffer. Moreover, certain metabolites of disease-causing yeast are directly toxic to the liver's cells and enzymes. In short, in sufferers with impaired liver functioning, the die-off of disease-causing yeast is to blame, not the medication itself. The good news is that liver disturbances are rare among sufferers who receive systemic antifungal medication, especially if their liver has been strengthened prior to its use. If a liver disturbance does arise, it usually resolves after the drug is discontinued. With few exceptions, *the benefits of using a systemic antifungal medication greatly outweighs its risks.*

The liver is also an essential immune system participant that produces many substances that assist in combating chronic or extended infections, including long-term candidiasis. Yet, this shift toward immunity impedes the liver's metabolism and detoxifying abilities. Given enough time, chronic candidiasis severely stresses the liver and eventually damages it as well. In return, the more severe or prolonged someone's candidiasis, the more likely they will have fragile or decreased liver functioning. In addition, chronic infections with harmful parasites, bacteria, and/or molds can similarly stress the liver. Any alliance between them multiplies their individual effects. Candidiasis is more stressful to the liver than the use of systemic antifungal medications. Again, the benefit of systemic antifungal medication greatly surpasses its risk.

With the appropriate insight and precautions, systemic antifungal medications are safe and effective. Even when there is impaired liver functioning, experience reveals that systemic antifungal agents may still be used safely, although vigilance is required. After all, research shows that the liver can rejuvenate and restore itself even after as much as 90 percent of it has been damaged. Some specific herbs strongly induce liver regeneration by accelerating the repair and reproduction of liver cells. Whether or not there is a notable liver problem, these herbs should be used to strengthen the liver before and during antifungal medication, unless someone is intolerant. Since the liver's activities are essential to good health, most sufferers will benefit from strengthening their liver regardless of the severity of their candidiasis.

An important point: It is worse to undertreat than to overtreat. For example, disease-causing yeast within the gut that mildly invade into the gut wall may become more aggressive and invade further if a sufferer is only treated with an anti-candidiasis diet and nonabsorbable antifungal agents. Drugs like nystatin frequently do not work or promote greater illness in the long run, which additionally argues for the use of systemic antifungal medications. Actually, an optimal anti-candidiasis program will employ both systemic and nonabsorbable agents to their greatest advantage (chapter 19).

Starve Your Disease-causing Yeast

Another essential aspect is to deprive your disease-causing yeast of any source of energy. Starving them effectively decreases their functioning, metabolic activities, and rate of reproduction. Since they readily feed on simple carbohydrates (sugars), any foods that contain them must be eliminated from your diet. In addition, many complex carbohydrates are broken down to simple carbohydrates and have the same effect. These high "glycemic index" complex carbohydrates must also be avoided (chapter 20).

The anti-candidiasis diet by itself will not eliminate your disease-causing yeast; it will not eradicate your infection. Yes, you may feel better after starting the diet, sometimes significantly. This occurs because you are starving your disease-causing yeast, decreasing their metabolic activities. You will also feel better after eliminating foods and beverages that contain yeast and molds, decreasing your allergy-induced inflammation. Yet, if an antifungal agent is not used, you will eventually feel worse. Why?

When disease-causing yeast experience prolonged starvation, they can become more aggressive and invade deeper into the tissues and blood to obtain nutrition and survive. So, without antifungal therapy, your candidiasis is likely to worsen if it is treated by diet alone. For example, research reveals that *Candida albicans* can alter its metabolism to use protein as an energy source when carbohydrates are scarce, so a low-carbohydrate diet alone will not kill it. These conditions also encourage *Candida albicans* to increase its production of *proteinases*, digestive enzymes that degrade tissue protein, which enables it to invade deeper into the tissues. Using diet alone, a sufferer who previously felt better is destined to feel worse sooner or later; in fact, they can become more ill than they were before they started the diet, making anti-candidiasis therapy more difficult. Yes, diet is an integral aspect, but it is foolish to use it as your only weapon.

Moreover, diet cannot address the presence of harmful parasites, bacteria, molds, and/or viruses. All these infectious invaders must be properly identified and appropriately eliminated. Therefore, it is wishful thinking to believe a dietary approach by itself is a magical cure.

Identify and Eradicate Your Harmful Parasites

Unless someone has severe diarrhea or some overtly obvious symptom, parasites (chapter 5) are likely to be overlooked or unsuspected. In most people, their immune system controls the initial infection, the parasite is not eliminated, and they become chronic carriers of one or more parasites. If the gut's immunity is competent, these infectious invaders are suppressed and few to no problems occur. Someone can exist like this for years, until their immunity faulters or another infectious invader arrives. In addition to their inherent harm, parasites adversely alter the gastrointestinal microbiome, upsetting the beneficial bacteria. As a result, parasites are strong risk factors for the development of candidiasis.

Parasites can instigate their own symptoms and illness. In some cases, parasitic illness can be life-threatening and must be treated immediately. More often, people with parasites do not know they even have them. Typically, the presence of one or more parasites will exacerbate your candidiasis. The presence of disease-causing yeast and parasites, a mixed infection, amplifies their infectious effects. In other cases, the presence of disease-causing yeast helps to keep the parasites confined because there is a limited amount of space to inhabit within the gut. Identifying and eradicating parasites is of utmost importance. Until proven otherwise, you should always suspect you have a parasite, especially if your symptoms are significant. Ignoring parasites will guarantee that your anti-candidiasis therapy will not be successful or ensure a relapse. Treating your disease-causing yeast, while ignoring your parasites, can give your parasites the freedom to reproduce and you may become worse than before you started your program.

Mainstream medicine antiparasitic medication can be used. Flagyl (metronidazole) is commonly used to treat amoebiasis and giardiasis, but it can treat some other parasites as well. Unfortunately, it is rather toxic in the amounts that must be used, and many parasites are proving to be resistant to it. Fortunately, an alternative is Fasigyn (tinidazole), which is a much less toxic derivative of Flagyl. Other antiparasitic medications are also available. The advantage of an absorbed drug is that it can kill any parasites that reside beyond the gut; for example, amoebas can migrate up the common bile duct and infect the liver, gallbladder, and pancreas. A medication that is not absorbed will not kill parasites within these and other locations.

To avoid the potential for drug allergies, toxicity, and resistance to medication, various herbs with potent antiparasitic properties can be employed. These often require a longer course (and are typically more expensive), but they are often less toxic.

Parasites are a strong risk factor for promoting candidiasis. If left untreated, they are also responsible for impeding a sufferer's recovery. If you have any chronic or recurring medical malady, the chance of being infected with a parasite is high. Depending on the patient population, anoscopies performed on candidiasis sufferers reveal that 50 to 90 percent harbor one or more parasites. Confusingly, their presence is often not associated with significant gut symptoms, so they are frequently missed or overlooked. So, regardless of opinions to the contrary, it is always wise to assume you have a parasite until proven otherwise.

Eliminate Harmful Bacteria (and Potentially Harmful Bacteria)

Research demonstrates that disease-causing yeast, especially *Candida albicans*, can successfully coexist with one or more harmful bacteria within the body. Even worse, this relationship is often *synergistic*; the mischief of both infectious invaders escalates their harm beyond their individual effects combined. Although the gut is the most prominent location for this conspiracy, other areas similarly affected include the sinuses, lungs, bladder, and vagina. Therefore, some sufferers can develop a bacterial infection soon after beginning antifungal therapy; as the disease-causing yeast are killed, harmful bacteria that coexist within these locations are no longer competitively inhibited, which allows them to reproduce and instigate illness. Many harmful bacteria are known or suspected of being synergistic with disease-causing yeast, including *Staphylococcus aureus*, *Streptococcus* species, *E. coli*, *Proteus*, and *Pseudomonas* species.

Some harmful bacteria are blatantly troublesome and must be eliminated immediately. Yet, there are many more bacteria that are potentially harmful. Under normal circumstances, like disease-causing yeast, these potentially harmful bacteria cause few problems when they are present in small numbers. However, if the beneficial bacteria are injured or killed, they can readily reproduce and promote illness.

Since a mixed infection with disease-causing yeast and harmful bacteria is much worse than either alone, wellness cannot occur until both infectious invaders are gone. So, it is vital to identify and eliminate any harmful bacteria present. Because harmful bacteria are a strong risk factor for promoting candidiasis, a relapse is virtually guaranteed if these infectious invaders are not appropriately eliminated.

Antibacterial agents are typically used to kill harmful bacteria; antibiotics are primarily employed, although some herbs may do the job. Since antibiotics are probably the strongest risk factor for promoting candidiasis, there appears to be a paradox; they kill the harmful bacteria, but they also kill the beneficial bacteria, encouraging candidiasis. Does this mean that antibiotics should not be used by candidiasis sufferers?

On the contrary, antibiotics can be safely employed when a systemic antifungal medication is simultaneously being taken, if there is not an allergy to a prescribed antibiotic(s). You cannot promote the colonization of disease-causing yeast when they are dead. Clinical experience with sufferers demonstrates that antibiotics are more effective after their disease-causing yeast have been killed. Disease-causing yeast can grow in colonies that physically protect (biofilms and inflammation) any harmful bacteria living within or underneath them from an administered antibiotic. Once the disease-causing yeast are eliminated, these harmful bacteria will be exposed, making the antibiotic more efficacious. In any case, if you do take antibiotics, you would be wise to increase your intake of probiotics to replenish your population of beneficial bacteria.

Harmful bacteria are exceedingly prevalent among sufferers, regardless of whether it is obvious or not. In fact, when tested, most sufferers are found to have one or more harmful bacteria present within their stool samples. So, you would be wise to assume you have one or more harmful bacteria until proven otherwise.

Eliminate Harmful Molds

Molds encompass a diverse category of fungal organisms (chapter 16). A large percentage are not harmful. Yet, because of their allergy-inducing abilities (*antigenic potential*) even the most seemingly innocent molds can trigger allergic reactions within sensitive or hypersensitive people. So, molds are problematic for their ability to instigate and/or promote allergic reactions within susceptible people. In fact, many molds are readily associated with allergies, harmful and innocent.

Many *harmful* molds can cause overt illness within human beings. Because of their association with disease, some examples include *Aspergillus* species, *Cryptococcus neoformans, Histoplasma capsulatum, Coccidiomyces immitis*, and *Sporothrix schenckii*. Many more harmful molds are less aggressive, but equally troublesome in the long run; although the disturbances they cause are subtle, their adverse effects are cumulative. Many harmful molds (aggressive and less aggressive) are problematic because they produce injurious toxins, *mycotoxins*, known or suspected of contributing to chronic illness. Unfortunately, many of these infectious invaders are not taken seriously by mainstream medicine.

How do harmful molds get into your body? Since they are virtually everywhere, they can infect the foods and beverages you ingest (as well as be within the air you breathe). Like disease-causing yeast, harmful molds prefer warm and moist environments, so these infectious invaders can colonize and infect the human body. The gut is a wonderful microbiome for harmful molds, although the mucous membranes, respiratory tract, and skin can also be colonized. When there is a healthy population of beneficial bacteria, these infectious invaders are inhibited and/or suppressed, causing few to no problems. If the beneficial bacteria are injured or killed, harmful molds can reproduce and instigate illness. Candidiasis encourages conditions that permit the colonization of one or more harmful molds. Disease-causing yeast and harmful molds can happily coexist, creating a microbiome that encourages their combined presence. In some sufferers, the harm of both infectious invaders is worse than their individual activities combined. In other sufferers, the disease-causing yeast compete with the harmful molds, keeping them from reproducing in large numbers.

Unlike disease-causing yeast, harmful molds tend to grow on surfaces and do not invade the tissues. Unless the gut wall is weakened, they are usually unable to enter the tissues and blood. If they do gain access, it is common to find them infecting the skin and nails. In this case, systemic antifungal medications with activity against both disease-causing yeast and harmful molds is needed (for example, Sporanox); otherwise, a relapse is likely.

Fortunately, most sufferers with harmful molds have them confined within their gut. So, the same nonabsorbable antifungal therapy used to eliminate their disease-causing yeast can combat their harmful molds (for example, Fungizone oral suspension and Miconazole). In contrast, several harmful molds do not respond to medication, requiring the use of antifungal herbal preparations instead.

Like disease-causing yeast, harmful molds are infectious invaders that have allergy-inducing abilities. Some molds are indirectly troublesome because they cross-react with disease-causing yeast, instigating allergic illness within susceptible people. Either way, to reduce your mold-related inflammation and its associated symptoms, you must eliminate mold from your diet and your external environment when possible. If a mold-free diet is not followed, the accompanying inflammation may make it difficult, if not impossible, to eliminate your disease-causing yeast. Also, avoiding moldy foods eliminates the chance of being reinfected with their spores and/or contaminated with their injurious toxins.

Harmful molds must be eliminated without hesitation. When the disease-causing yeast are killed, any harmful molds that remain can reproduce and directly instigate illness, unless they are similarly eliminated. Since they are usually slow growing, illness associated with their presence often arises over weeks to months or longer. Equally problematic, they can be responsible for relapses among sufferers. Since there is only so much space available, the continuous presence of harmful molds within the gut makes it difficult, if not impossible, to reestablish a healthy population of beneficial bacteria. Since a healthy population of beneficial bacteria prevents the colonization of disease-causing yeast, the presence of harmful molds is a risk factor for relapses of candidiasis. Harmful molds must be addressed and eradicated.

Eliminate Cell Wall–Deficient Forms: The Stealth Pathogens

Certain undesirable conditions can cause infectious invaders to transform from one form into another. To survive, some harmful bacteria, disease-causing yeast (including *Candida albicans*), and other fungal organisms can change from their regular (parent) form to a *cell wall–deficient* form (and then back again when conditions improve). Like the transformation of Dr. Jekyll into Mr. Hyde, compared to their wall-bearing counterparts, these cell wall–deficient forms are often troublesome. When this occurs, these wall-less delinquents tend to be present in much greater amounts than their parent forms; in fact, there can be as many as 2 to 10 times the number of cell wall–deficient forms. Unlike their parent forms, cell wall–deficient bacteria have been found to evade the immune system by hiding and surviving within fungal organisms (and possibly some immune cells).

Mycoplasmas are perpetual cell wall–deficient organisms that do not have wall-bearing parents. They are thought to participate in numerous chronic illnesses and are often overlooked. These infectious invaders tend to be slower growing, which means they must be cultured longer and treated with antibiotics for an extended period. The presence of mycoplasmas warrants a great deal of suspicion. When found, they should be identified and eliminated.

With respect to treatment, cell wall–deficient organisms and their parent organisms are often resistant to different medications. As a result, a combination of antibiotics is essential to totally eradicate both forms.

Since clinical labs do not test for these stealth pathogens and few universities research them, these infectious invaders consistently remain undetected. As a result, cell wall–deficient organisms should be *suspected* when there is an infection or significant symptoms and the laboratory culture fails to identify the presence of any infectious invader (negative culture). Nevertheless, evidence indicates that cell wall–deficient organisms are likely to contribute to numerous chronic illnesses, which implies that greater efforts must be made to reveal them. (Clinical hint: a *cold agglutinin titer* test might reveal their presence in some sufferers.)

Subdue and Control Associated Viral Illnesses

Some viruses are blatantly harmful and can cause illness of one type or another. Some examples include upper respiratory infections, mononucleosis, gastroenteritis, hepatitis, chicken pox, and meningitis. In most cases, a healthy immune system can transcend the initial infection and the virus is eradicated or it enters a dormant state.

As a result, many of us perpetually harbor one or more dormant viruses. For example, Epstein-Barr virus, responsible for mononucleosis, is present in over 95 percent of adults. Under normal circumstances, these viruses are suppressed; they are kept dormant and unable to cause problems. In contrast, viral gastroenteritis will upset the gastrointestinal microbiome and its population of beneficial bacteria, so it is a risk factor for developing candidiasis.

Candidiasis sufferers often develop impaired immunity (chapter 14), allowing dormant viruses to awaken, replicate, and cause mischief. Depending on the viruses present, a variety of disturbances can arise. The combined presence of disease-causing yeast and a virus may be worse than the troublemakers' contributions simply combined. Typically, their associated mischief creates conditions that encourage their continued presence. In most cases, the presence of an active, replicating virus further impairs immunity. If this occurs, disease-causing yeast may be able to invade deeper into the tissues and blood as well as colonize other areas. So, a chronic viral infection encourages candidiasis to worsen, impairing immunity even more.

If you have a chronic viral infection, what should you do? You can take supplements or receive intravenous support to enhance your immunity (as well as some medications). However, since an infection with disease-causing yeast (and other infectious invaders) was probably responsible for your impaired immunity in the first place, eliminating your candidiasis is essential to restore the health of your immune system. In most sufferers, once this occurs, their immune system can bring their active viruses under control, returning them to a dormant state.

Reestablish a Healthy Population of Beneficial Bacteria

During therapy, it is essential to reestablish a healthy population of beneficial bacteria within the gut. These microorganisms are exceedingly important (chapter 4) because many of them produce substances that are vital to our health. With respect to candidiasis, the beneficial bacteria compete with, suppress, and inhibit the colonization and mischief of disease-causing yeast (and other infectious invaders). Therefore, without the presence of a healthy population of beneficial bacteria, candidiasis sufferers will relapse.

There may be 400 or more different strains of bacteria within the gut. Ideally, they all happily coexist, and interact to ensure our continued good health. Since the beneficial bacteria can be perturbed, injured, and killed for numerous reasons (chapter 2), they must be replenished. If long-term wellness is your goal, ingest one or more beneficial bacteria on a regular basis.

Eliminate Toxic Heavy Metals

Many heavy metals, including aluminum, arsenic, beryllium, cadmium, lead, and mercury, are blatantly toxic to the human body, especially the immune system. In addition, gold, silver, nickel, and copper can harm susceptible people. Since they can be present within food and water, anyone can be contaminated with these toxic metals.

If heavy metals are suspected, a hair analysis can be performed to measure their presence, although some practitioners claim that this test is far from accurate. A better way to determine if you are contaminated with heavy metals is to receive a *diagnostic chelation*—a slow intravenous infusion of a chelating agent that grabs on to (chelates) heavy metals within your blood. After the infusion, the chelating agent is cleared by your kidneys and eliminated from your body within your urine. Your urine is collected for the next 24 hours and then sent to the laboratory. If heavy metals are present, they will be measured within your urine. Since the body bioaccumulates heavy metals within its cells and tissues, rather than remaining within the blood, the best way to assess your toxic heavy metal burden is a *provoked chelation*. From clinical experience, a patient takes a 1,000 mg D-penicillamine loading dose an hour or more before breakfast and then 500 mg every six hours (empty stomach), until 4,000 mg have been consumed. Urine is collected same as above, starting the morning of day two.

Many sufferers have not significantly improved until their mercury-dental fillings were removed. If you suspect heavy metals or have mercury-containing silver dental amalgams, you would be wise to consult with a healthcare practitioner experienced in this area.

ALLERGIES AND IMMUNOTHERAPY

Since candidiasis is a two-sided condition, an *infection* with *allergic* consequences, most sufferers have allergic reactions to one or more substances when tested. Since their sensitivities and hypersensitivities can instigate and/or promote a variety of symptoms and illness, clinical evidence and research demonstrates that immunotherapy is of great benefit.

This involves administering natural and synthetic substances to stimulate or suppress the immune response and inflammation. Although many substances have proven to be of benefit in modulating the cell-mediated immune response in people with fungal infections, they are not routinely employed to treat candidiasis sufferers. In contrast, stimulating the production of *antibodies* that protect against disease-causing yeast is a type of allergy immunotherapy called *desensitization*.

Typically, a patient receives regular injections containing a dilute solution of one or more allergy-inducing substances (antigens). Instead of promoting symptoms, exposure to small amounts of the antigen enables their immune system to become tolerant to its presence. The antigen stimulates the generation of blocking (IgG) antibodies that prevent IgE (the major allergy-related antibody) from attaching to mast cells, triggering an allergic response. Simply put, allergy immunotherapy suppresses a sufferer's allergic reactions. Research reveals allergy immunotherapy also works by altering the balance of *T lymphocytes* (immune cells); antigen stimulation shifts the power away from allergy-inducing T cells (TH2) toward cell-mediated T cells (TH1). This illustrates that allergy immunotherapy works in many ways and there is more to be learned. In short, allergy immunotherapy benefits immunity through both antibody-mediated and cell-mediated activities. Many studies demonstrate the benefits of generating protective antibodies against *Candida albicans*.

Candidiasis-minded physicians test sufferers for sensitivities and hypersensitivities to disease-causing yeast and harmful molds. In return, each patient receives desensitization (allergy) injections containing their appropriate reactive antigens. Depending on a sufferer's symptoms, they will also be tested for other allergies, including pollens, dust, foods, and/or chemicals. If a sufferer reacts to an antigen, it is included in their desensitization program. Clinical experience demonstrates that sufferers benefit by 30 to 90 percent from immunotherapy, typically lasting from four months to two years. Keep in mind, sufferers who are not compliant or inconsistent with their immunotherapy usually have limited success or none.

Desensitizing sufferers against their allergy-inducing substances blocks their allergic reactions to a variety of substances and protects them against the infectious invaders that induced these reactions in the first place. Initially, candidiasis tends to precipitate allergies to the disease-causing yeast themselves. Because of their allergy-inducing (antigenic) similarity, cross-reactive molds can trigger identical reactions. Numerous harmful molds can also be problematic. As candidiasis progresses, the disease-causing yeast can invade into the gut wall, creating leaky gut syndrome. So, food allergies are common among sufferers. Disease-causing yeast can colonize and infect the upper and lower respiratory tract, promoting allergic reactions within these areas. In turn, allergies to environmental substances are common among sufferers, including sensitivities and hypersensitivities to pollens, dust, and chemicals.

Before allergy immunotherapy can be started, sufferers must be appropriately evaluated for their sensitivities and hypersensitivities. During testing, almost all sufferers demonstrate sensitivities or hypersensitivities to one or more antigens, especially to disease-causing yeast and harmful molds. There are exceptions; some sufferers appear to be allergy-free even with significant symptoms. This is possible but highly improbable. Most likely, these sufferers have severely impaired immunity, making them unresponsive to testing. How can this be ascertained? Although their routine laboratory blood tests may reveal suppressed and/or depressed immunity, it may reveal nothing; typically, more sophisticated immune testing is required. Yet, anti-candidiasis therapy may make this obvious clinically; eliminating their infectious invaders will improve their immunity, unsuppressing their allergic reactions. At this point, it is not uncommon to have a flare-up of allergy-related symptoms and illness. If this occurs, allergy testing is appropriate and highly beneficial.

Many symptoms improve with antifungal therapy by eliminating the infection. Since allergic reactions contribute or are responsible for many sufferers' symptoms, without appropriate desensitization, they will not improve or may only partially improve. Even if a sufferer's allergic reactions do not cause significant symptoms, allergy immunotherapy can still benefit their immunity; it has both antibody-mediated and cell-mediated benefits. Therefore, in most sufferers, if a complete recovery is desired, it is important to address both their infection and allergies.

Identify Allergies to Disease-causing Yeast & Harmful Molds and Eliminate Their Antigens

Because of their strong *allergy-inducing abilities* (antigenic potential), disease-causing yeast can instigate and/or promote allergies to themselves, cross-reactive (antigenically similar) molds, and many harmful molds. So, sufferers should be tested for sensitivities and hypersensitivities to a variety of disease-causing yeast and harmful molds (chapter 17). When tested, virtually every sufferer will be sensitive or hypersensitive to at least one disease-causing yeast or harmful mold.

Sensitivities and hypersensitivities to disease-causing yeast and harmful molds can cause significant localized and systemic allergic reactions within sufferers. Treating these allergies alone can bring great relief. In addition to allergy immunotherapy, eliminating these offenders from your external environment is important. Although it may be impossible to totally eradicate their presence, you can certainly reduce your exposure. You need to clean up areas that are prone to grow disease-causing yeast and harmful molds. For example, under the refrigerator, the air ducts, the laundry hamper, and other warm and moist locations.

Fermented foods have disease-causing yeast within them. Foods and beverages that contain *dead* yeast (for example, bread) can trigger allergic reactions within sufferers who are sensitive or hypersensitive to them. Foods with *living* disease-causing yeast on or within them can repopulate a sufferer's gut with these infectious invaders. Foods and beverages that contain harmful molds, whether alive or dead, can precipitate similar consequences. To add insult, many foods and beverages can be contaminated with the toxins and metabolites of disease-causing yeast and harmful molds. Foods containing disease-causing yeast and harmful molds are a large reservoir for undesirable allergic reactions among sufferers, and many symptoms directly or indirectly result from these reactions. Therefore, sufferers must avoid foods and beverages that contain disease-causing yeast and harmful molds.

Identify and Eliminate Environmental Antigens (Biological and Chemical)

The world is full of substances that may instigate unfavorable allergic reactions. These range from botanical byproducts to synthetic chemicals. Almost anything in our external environment can instigate and/or promote undesirable allergic reactions within susceptible people and their accompanying symptoms. These antigenic participants should be identified and, if possible, eliminated. Depending on your symptoms, you can be tested for environmental antigens, including pollens, dust, and chemicals. Allergy immunotherapy may then be administered. You cannot eliminate all the offending antigens from your environment, but you can reduce your exposure to certain chemicals, clean dust with a special vacuum cleaner, and use air filters in your home.

Identify and Eliminate Allergic Foods

During candidiasis, especially when there is leaky gut syndrome, it is common to develop food allergies. When disease-causing yeast invade into the gut wall, increased intestinal permeability allows undigested food particles to enter the tissues and blood. As a result, a sufferer can become sensitive or hypersensitive to the presence of these undigested food particles. Thereafter, every time an allergy-inducing food is consumed, it will instigate or promote symptoms and stress the immune system. In addition to the immediate reactions they produce, allergic foods can cause delayed reactions, lasting for days to weeks. Since some foods are more antigenic than others, they have a greater potential to cause allergic reactions and symptoms. Some foods are commonly associated with allergies, including corn, eggs, fish, cow's milk, peanuts, shellfish, soy, and wheat.

Every person will have different sensitivities and hypersensitivities. The amount of an allergic food that produces and/or sustains an allergic reaction varies from one sufferer to another (even within the same person from week to week, day to day, and hour to hour). Foods that are highly allergic require tiny exposures to generate significant symptoms, whereas mildly allergic foods can trigger substantial symptoms if they are consumed in large quantities.

Allergic food reactions can cause two major adverse consequences. Their *localized* effect involves their presence within the gut, including the inflammation and allergic reactions that arise. Their *systemic* effects include the indirect reactions they cause elsewhere within the body; examples include nasal congestion, wheezing, lethargy, depression, and many other symptoms. In all cases, allergic reactions to foods can be stressful for the immune system.

Within the gut, allergic food reactions can induce significant inflammation and, with its accompanying mucus, can further compromise the gastrointestinal microbiome, worsening candidiasis. These circumstances can make it more difficult to eliminate disease-causing yeast; antifungal agents may not be able to effectively enter areas that are highly inflamed or have excess mucus/biofilms. Significant inflammation and mucus also prevents the reestablishment of a healthy population of beneficial bacteria. So, food allergies are a risk factor for developing and promoting candidiasis as well as any future relapses.

Confusingly, sufferers frequently crave their most allergic foods, creating a vicious cycle. Terminating this pattern is vital for recovery, so the inciting foods must be identified and eliminated from the diet. Fortunately, after the gut wall is healed and time has passed, many allergic foods often become less inciting. In most cases, after sufferers are desensitized to their problematic foods, many of these foods can be consumed with little to no ill effect.

Several tests can identify if you are allergic to one or more foods (chapter 17). The best involves mixing your immune cells (white blood cells) with suspected or common antigenic foods. A positive response indicates an allergy. Critics contest, "What occurs in a test tube does not accurately apply to the human body." Until better methods arise, this is the most precise way of rapidly determining a sufferer's food allergies. Alternatively, sufferers can be tested for sensitivities or hypersensitivities to food antigens by intradermal skin testing or placing drops under their tongue. Using their own immune system as the testing grounds, food allergies can be revealed. Some critics argue against this form of testing, claiming that it tends to be overly sensitive; someone tests positive but is not allergic to the food tested (false positive). Regardless, food allergies can be detected by one or more tests. Once identified, these foods should be eliminated from the diet. Given enough time, a sufferer's allergies can abate and, eventually, these foods can be reintroduced—generally, one at a time and no sooner than every four days. In addition, allergy immunotherapy can also be administered and is highly recommended.

Allergy (Desensitization) Immunotherapy

If you are like most people, you probably hate getting shots. Even an injection on rare occasion is likely to be unpleasant. So, how will you feel when you are told you must receive an allergy shot one or more times a week? For most sufferers, this is a reality whether they like it or not. If allergy immunotherapy is omitted, desensitization cannot occur, and you will continue to have allergic reactions whenever you are exposed to an allergy-inducing substance. Yet, allergy immunotherapy does not have to be taken forever when it is done correctly.

The goal of desensitization is to produce lifelong immunity to specific allergy-inducing substances (antigens). Once it is achieved, anytime someone is exposed to that specific antigen, they will not inappropriately react. The average length of therapy varies and depends on a sufferer's initial sensitivities and hypersensitivities. Although some sufferers will tell horror stories of having to take allergy shots for incredible lengths of time, allergy immunotherapy can often be accomplished in 6 to 18 months.

There are two preferable methods of allergy testing. Serial endpoint dilution titration (SEDT) and provocative-neutralization testing (PNT) and each has its usefulness (chapter 17). These methods are the quickest way to determine the most effective starting dose of an antigen. Depending on someone's sensitivities and hypersensitivities, the corresponding antigen is administered one or two times a week.

Initially, allergy immunotherapy may instigate and/or exacerbate symptoms. When a specific dose no longer produces a reaction, the amount of antigen is increased—usually by about 2.5 to 5 percent. Retesting occurs when the dose is equivalent to the next higher (more concentrated) dilution. Eventually, a one-to-one dilution of antigen will be tolerated. If someone is then retested and does not respond, they are immune and can discontinue desensitization therapy. Research reveals that once this occurs, it benefits the immune system for many years.

COMPONENTS OF THERAPY

The therapeutic approach to anti-candidiasis treatment varies widely. Until antifungal medications were available, the only choices for therapy were natural preparations in one or more forms. With scientific advances and a greater understanding of candidiasis, including the *infectious* and *allergic* contributions of disease-causing yeast, it seems the best approach is a holistic-integrative one, as described in this chapter. Since every candidiasis sufferer is a unique individual, in addition to the general components of therapy, specific components should be appropriately used. Moreover, many cases are complex, and, like peeling an onion, there are many layers to be revealed and addressed.

Antifungal Agents—Medications versus Herbs

Because candidiasis is an *infection* with disease-causing yeast, one or more antifungal agents should be used. If this is not done, your disease-causing yeast will not be eliminated. The two categories are medications and herbs (chapter 19). Both have their advantages and disadvantages. No one antifungal agent is perfect.

Since most sufferers appear to have some magnitude of *invasive* candidiasis, a systemic antifungal medication should initially be used to eradicate disease-causing yeast within their tissues and blood, which allows their gut wall to heal. This should be followed by a nonabsorbable antifungal agent to eliminate the disease-causing yeast that remain within their gut. Thereafter, harmful parasites, bacteria, and molds can be treated.

Numerous disease-causing yeast and harmful molds are becoming resistant to antifungal medications and combinations of certain medications can have positive or negative effects. Therefore, a knowledgeable candidiasis-minded physician should preferably decide what you are going to use, the dosage, and for how long.

Probiotics: The Good Bacteria

In short, *probiotics* are supplements that contain beneficial bacteria, substances that encourage their growth, or other substances that inhibit the growth of harmful bacteria. What makes the beneficial bacteria helpful? They protect our gastrointestinal tract and mucous membranes from the colonization of infectious invaders. They also directly support our digestion and absorption, and indirectly benefit our immunity. Some of them produce vitamins, short-chain fatty acids, and proteins that are absorbed by us. Short-chain fatty acids (such as *acetic, propionic, butyric, lactic,* and *formic* acids) are particularly important because they increase blood flow within the colon, simulate the secretion of pancreatic enzymes, encourage the absorption of sodium and water, and promote the growth of the gut wall (mucosa). Certain strains of beneficial bacteria assimilate cholesterol, reducing its absorption. They also help reduce the activity of bacterial enzymes (for example, *beta-glucuronidase, nitroreductase,* and *azoreductase*) that convert precancerous substances (procarcinogens) into cancerous substances (carcinogens), so they may protect us against colon cancer and maybe other cancers. They may prevent the small bowel from being colonized with harmful bacteria, decreasing the generation of toxins and cancerous substances within this area.

With respect to candidiasis, their presence is vital to prevent the colonization of infectious invaders. How is this done? Certain probiotic microorganisms produce organic acids that lower the pH within the gut, making it more acidic. This simple act limits the growth of any acid-sensitive, harmful bacteria. For example, *lactic, propionic,* and *acetic* acid are injurious to harmful bacteria, but their effect depends on the acidity of the environment. Equally important, *lactobacilli* have been found to produce certain metabolites (*endotoxins*) that can kill harmful bacteria, disease-causing yeast, and harmful molds, including *lactocidin, lactobicillin, lactobreven,* and *acidolin.* The beneficial bacteria also actively compete for space, preventing infectious invaders from taking up residence.

Which beneficial bacteria should you take? Several factors will decide how effectively a probiotic microorganism can colonize your gut. It must first be able to adhere to your gut wall, or it will be eliminated within your stool. If it is unable to reproduce rapidly, it will be diluted out before it can establish a sufficient population. The microorganism must be able to withstand the extremes within your gut, including exposure to your gastric juice and bile. It should be able to suppress and/or inhibit harmful bacteria, or it will be unable to assume prominence. If it cannot meet these criteria, it may not survive or do you any good. All of this assumes you have a probiotic microorganism that is viable in the first place. If you take a supplement that contains dormant microorganisms, it is likely to be ineffective. A product containing dead microorganisms will do you no good at all.

Many people have heard of "acidophilus," formally called *Lactobacillus acidophilus*, a widely used probiotic microorganism that is rather inexpensive. Yet, it is far from the best microorganism. Clinical experience shows that a significant percentage of candidiasis sufferers do not appear to benefit from supplementation with *Lactobacillus acidophilus* alone because it cannot colonize their gut. This may be due to the strain used. Since some strains are better than others, choosing a different supplement may make a substantial difference. In addition, the gut disturbances and inflammation that accompany candidiasis may injure the gut wall, including the cell surface receptors that bind to *Lactobacillus acidophilus*. Alternatively, some sufferers may develop sensitivities or hypersensitivities to *Lactobacillus acidophilus*. The presence of increased intestinal permeability, leaky gut syndrome, may allow antibodies to be produced against it, preventing it from colonizing their gut. Regardless, supplementation with acidophilus alone often promotes failure, or incomplete success, in many sufferers.

Since different beneficial bacteria manufacture specific substances, the presence of many probiotic microorganisms is often better than one alone. Each has its own characteristics, so the more species and strains present the better. This diversity enables the probiotic microorganisms to function more efficiently, and the metabolic deficiencies of one microorganism are negligible if another can produce substances that compensate. In return, this establishes a gastrointestinal microbiome more resistant to assault by infectious invaders.

Clinical experience demonstrates that the best probiotic supplements contain a variety of living microorganisms. Some products have as many as nine or more different beneficial bacteria. Some examples include *Bifidobacterium longum, Bifidobacterium breve, Streptococcus thermophilus, Lactobacillus acidophilus, Lactobacillus rhamnosus A, Lactobacillus rhamnosus B (bifidus), Lactobacillus bulgaricus, Lactobacillus casei*, and *Lactobacillus sporogenes*. This ensures that at least one member will survive and colonize the gut. Moreover, in these supplements, all the beneficial bacteria do not perform the same function; some physically colonize the gut and are classified as "residents," whereas others are considered "transients," because they assist the residents to move in.

In addition to supplements, yogurt is typically used as a source of beneficial bacteria. Depending on the brand and its pasteurization, if it is heated to kill harmful bacteria, it may contain no living organisms or only minimal amounts. Like probiotic supplements, the best yogurts have many different living organisms. Since most yogurt is made from cow's milk, people who are lactose-intolerant are frequently unable to consume it, even though its lactose is often altered to a more digestible form during manufacturing. In addition, yogurt frequently contains significant amounts of simple sugars that may nourish disease-causing yeast. In the early stages of anti-candidiasis therapy, when diet is most critical, yogurt should be avoided (unless your doctor allows it). If you can tolerate it, in the long run, yogurt is recommended. The same can be said for kefir (fermented milk). Clearly, people with allergies to cow's milk should avoid these. Although other foods can contain probiotics, they are less effective at reestablishing the gastrointestinal microbiome and are not recommended as a therapeutic modality.

What about "soil-based organisms"? Clinical experience indicates that they help some patients with significant digestive problems. *Soil-based organisms* do not colonize the gut and cannot become residents. Instead, they remain temporarily and are considered *transients*. Like an army unit that enters an area to secure it, soil-based organisms alter the gastrointestinal microbiome, assisting the colonization of its residents. Some examples include *Bacillus laterosporus, Bacillus subtilis, Lactobacillus sporogenes* (*Bacillus coagulans*), and bacteria that are found in yogurt (*Lactobacillus bulgaricus* and *Streptococcus thermophilus*).

If *Saccharomyces boulardii* is a species of yeast, why do some candidiasis-minded experts recommend its use as a probiotic supplement? Since you are not supposed to ingest any disease-causing yeast, is this a contradiction? Not necessarily. *Saccharomyces boulardii* is an acid-tolerant (and even acid-loving) species of yeast that does not cause disease. On the contrary, its metabolic activities assist in lowering the acidity within the gut, making it hospitable for the colonization of the beneficial (acid-loving) bacteria. It is also thought that the presence of this good yeast is likely to compete with and hinder the colonization of disease-causing yeast. These reasons seem logical, but they do not take the big picture into account.

Although it may have its benefits, a great deal of caution is warranted when using *Saccharomyces boulardii*. Because it is a yeast, it may cause allergic reactions, inflammation, and symptoms in susceptible candidiasis sufferers. Sufferers with sensitivities or hypersensitivities to baker's or brewer's yeast, *Saccharomyces cerevisiae*, are most likely to be affected. Less troublesome, but annoying nonetheless, as the acidity within the gut decreases, there is a temporary period during which intestinal gas is markedly produced, causing unpleasant symptoms. This cannot be rushed by increasing the amount of this supplement or intestinal *obstruction* might follow. With so many other choices available, *Saccharomyces boulardii* should not be widely recommended or casually taken.

Old-fashioned, naturally leavened sourdough bread contains a different strain of *Saccharomyces cerevisiae* present in small amounts (about 1 percent). Microscopically, this "wild" strain of yeast appears to have a different shape than its commercially employed cousin. It is acid-tolerant (adapted to an acid environment) and happily coexists with the beneficial lactic acid–producing bacteria and acetic acid–producing bacteria that comprise 99 percent of the organisms within sourdough bread. Although this strain of *Saccharomyces cerevisiae* may not be disease-causing, anyone with allergies to disease-causing yeast is wise to avoid it, especially sufferers with allergies to baker's yeast. In fact, sooner or later, despite your best efforts, some disease-causing yeast is going to recolonize your gut. Since the beneficial species of yeast compete with disease-causing yeast, once your allergies have been treated, you might want to eat some yeast-free, naturally fermented sourdough bread.

Should probiotic supplements containing human strains or nonhuman strains be used? Some supplements contain nonhuman strains of microorganisms. Many physicians suspect that these nonhuman microorganisms do not readily colonize or survive well within our gut. So, to avoid confusion and ensure the best therapeutic results, products containing human strains should be used. Moreover, sufferers with lactose intolerance may discover they are allergic to cow's milk–based probiotic supplements; these should be avoided, and nondairy products should be used instead. Products that require refrigeration usually have more viable bacteria.

Probiotics supplements often include substances that support the growth of beneficial bacteria. Numerous complex carbohydrates, called *oligosaccharides*, cannot be absorbed, including *raffinose*, *stachyose*, *isomalto-oligosaccharides*, *galacto-oligosaccharides*, and *fructooligosaccharides*. Since our digestive enzymes have little or no effect on them, they functionally behave like fiber. *Fructooligosaccharides* are short-chain polymers of simple carbohydrates (fructose and sucrose) that are present in asparagus, bananas, beer, Chinese chive, honey, Jerusalem artichoke, maple sugar, oats, onion, and rye. Research reveals that ingesting them can increase your population of *bifidobacteria* tenfold. Yes, they are sugars and taste sweet, but they are not absorbed. As a result, they feed the beneficial bacteria, especially the *bifidobacteria*, but they cannot be absorbed to nourish disease-causing yeast within your tissues and blood. Lactulose is another sugar that appears to have a similar function. Some sufferers may not tolerate oligosaccharides, and they should be excluded until their gut has started to heal and can tolerate their presence.

Other physicians insist that dietary *fiber* is essential because it improves the balance of power within the gut in favor of the beneficial bacteria. Fiber also helps to maintain the integrity of the gut wall, preventing disease-causing yeast and harmful bacteria from invading the tissues.

Probiotics should also include substances that inhibit the growth of harmful bacteria. *Lactoferrin* is a bioactive protein like secretory IgA, the antibody found within external secretions. Lactoferrin can bind iron, depriving infectious invaders of this essential nutrient. *Lactoperoxidase* in an enzyme present within various secretions that encourages hydrogen peroxide to oxidize *thiocyanate* into *hypothiocyanite*, a substance with potent antibacterial activity. These are two brief examples of a growing area of research.

Okay, you have chosen your probiotic supplement. When is the best time to take it? Probably, just at the start of a meal. If antibiotics or antiparasitic medication are being used, it should be taken at least an hour after they are consumed. How much do you take and for how long? Of course, this will vary from one sufferer to another. There is no concrete rule. In general, early in therapy, probiotics are taken two to three times a day. It is best used at breakfast if you take it once a day, breakfast and dinner when used twice, and add it at lunch if used three times. After a healthy population of beneficial bacteria is established, your amount can be decreased to once a day (sometimes, even every second or third day). If tolerated, yogurt/kefir can be consumed. You always want to maintain a population of beneficial bacteria, especially if you are taking antibiotics or antiparasitic medication. This is the best way to prevent the colonization of disease-causing yeast, avoiding relapses.

Nutritional Supplements

Numerous vitamins, minerals, and oils are essential for your health and well-being. Do you need *minimal*, *optimal*, or *super* nutrition? Since deficiencies of one or more nutrients will instigate and/or promote illness, the proper performance of the human body is dependent on the dietary presence of specific substances. Although insufficient amounts are guaranteed to be detrimental, excesses may be better, neutral, or worse, and this depends on the actual role of a specific nutrient. Regardless of opinions, optimal nutrition is crucial, and super nutrition is often preferable, especially for active or stressed people.

Nutritional supplements are an important part of the program. Because most sufferers have some amount of malabsorption, one or more nutritional deficiencies are common. Supplements help correct these deficiencies. Yet, some sufferers have difficulty tolerating supplements. If this occurs, they should start with small amounts and increase their intake as tolerated. As their candidiasis improves, their intolerance frequently resolves, and optimal doses can be consumed.

Since some supplements can interfere with anti-candidiasis therapy, a candidiasis-minded physician should decide what you need, how much you take, and how often.

Intravenous Nutritional Supplementation

Regardless of the preachings of alternative medicine practitioners, a large percentage of sufferers do not require intravenous nutritional therapy. Yet, the greater the gut disturbance and malabsorption present, the more a sufferer needs this type of therapy. Intravenous nutritional supplementation's biggest advantage is the nutrients bypass the gut, placing vitamins and minerals directly into the blood. As a result, insufficient consumption and malabsorption are no longer a problem.

During the earliest stages of anti-candidiasis therapy, many sufferers would probably benefit from intravenous supplementation, although it is not recommended for everyone. Sufferers with difficulty tolerating oral supplements, impaired immunity, and moderate to severe bowel problems are likely to benefit the most.

Intravenous nutritional supplementation should only be done under medical supervision. A candidiasis-minded physician decides what you need and their amounts as well as how often intravenous therapy is to be administered.

IMPORTANT CONSIDERATIONS

Classically, candidiasis has been treated with a spectrum of approaches. This has reflected the lack of understanding involving the science of disease-causing yeast and the diversity of infectious invaders that can participate in this medical malady. Although there have been successful treatments of candidiasis sufferers, it is important to understand what to expect to avoid sabotaging your recovery or quit for the wrong reasons.

You Will Probably Feel Worse at First

During anti-candidiasis therapy, it is exceedingly common to feel *worse* before feeling better. Sometimes, this effect can be severe. This deterioration is a *die-off* reaction, called the *Herxheimer reaction* (a term that was originally used to describe the rapid death of organisms, with the release of their antigens, in syphilis patients). A more accurate term for candidiasis sufferers is "fungal neutralization," which is shortened to *fungalization*, describing the accelerated destruction (neutralization) of fungal organisms with the release of their cellular metabolites, toxins, and antigens.

So, why do you feel worse? When disease-causing yeast die, their cells break apart, liberating their cellular contents. Within the gut, these harmful substances can be absorbed and enter your blood. Normally, this is occurring all the time in sufferers but not in overwhelming amounts. Yet, when an antifungal agent is used, significant amounts of disease-causing yeast are killed in a short period. In turn, you will absorb increased amounts of their harmful substances. The more disease-causing yeast present, the more harmful substances you will absorb. Sufferers with the most disease-causing yeast often have a severe die-off. Before these harmful substances are cleared from your body (by your liver and kidneys), their increased presence can make you feel much worse. If you do not feel worse, you should be suspicious about whether you are killing any disease-causing yeast at all; they may be resistant or insensitive to what you are using.

How long will your die-off last? It depends on the severity of your candidiasis and where the disease-causing yeast are within your body. The more disease-causing yeast to kill, the longer it will take. In addition, the more inflammation and mucus you have, the longer it takes to kill all your disease-causing yeast. Similarly, the more infectious invaders present, the more difficult it will be to eradicate your disease-causing yeast.

If everything was perfect, the disease-causing yeast within your gut can be killed in a few days. Using a systemic antifungal medication, disease-causing yeast within your blood may be eradicated in one to two days. Disease-causing yeast within your gut wall and tissues can be cleared out in about five days, or a little longer. In contrast, disease-causing yeast within your upper and lower respiratory tract may not be eliminated for up to two weeks. Usually, you can notice a die-off each time the disease-causing yeast are killed within these areas. If you have disease-causing yeast infecting one or more toenails, it can take three to four months or longer to eradicate them. Does this mean you have to use a systemic antifungal agent for this long? No, because pulse dosing at intervals can be equally effective and less toxic to the body.

The magnitude of your die-off reaction will also reflect the specific disease-causing yeast infecting you. For example, the major disease-causing yeast, being more harmful, tend to produce a more notable die-off reaction compared to the less prominent ones. Therefore, the worst cases of candidiasis are likely to experience the most significant die-off reactions. With this understanding, the worse you feel, the better you are likely to feel in the future.

What die-off symptoms can you expect? It is difficult to say because they can vary greatly from one sufferer to another as well as in their magnitude. Fatigue and lethargy, as well as headaches and an upset gut, are common for a few days. Some sufferers may develop a "common" cold. Typically, most sufferers experience an exacerbation of their usual symptoms and illness. For example, a sufferer with arthritis is likely to have worse joint pain, and a sinusitis suffer may develop a sinus infection, requiring decongestants and antibiotics. Even so, there is no way to know for certain what symptoms will arise. Most die-off symptoms are annoying but rarely incapacitating. In general, try to start treatment when you have nothing essential to do for the following few days and you can remain at or close to home to avoid unnecessary complications.

The symptoms of die-off can arise slowly or rapidly. They can last from hours to days but rarely more than a week or two. Unfortunately, this is a necessary evil. You cannot avoid a die-off reaction if you want to eliminate your disease-causing yeast. Regardless of how bad you feel, your die-off reaction should be a sign of hope because, when this adjustment period is over, you should begin to feel better. Moreover, this is only the beginning and consistent improvement is likely to follow as your anti-candidiasis therapy continues.

It Takes Time to Heal Leaky Gut Syndrome

Since every sufferer is different, this will vary. Leaky gut syndrome and its accompanying increase in intestinal permeability arises when disease-causing yeast invade into and through the gut wall. The time it takes to heal will mirror the extent of your gastrointestinal damage and inflammation as well as how deeply the disease-causing yeast have invaded within your tissues. It also depends on the amount and type of other infectious invaders present, including harmful parasites, bacteria, molds, and viruses.

Most sufferers notice substantial improvements after a few days of systemic antifungal medication. Bloating, gas, diarrhea, and/or constipation are usually the first symptoms to resolve and disappear. More complicated manifestations, like inflammatory bowel disease or ulcers, require more time for reparations; usually, other medications or herbs are needed to address the presence of other infectious invaders.

Although the gut wall can be reestablished as a barrier in a relatively short time, its functioning may require a prolonged period to improve. The gut enzymes do not return to normal until the mucosal cells of the gut wall are healed. For example, lactose intolerance that arises because of candidiasis may takes weeks to months to resolve (chapter 4).

An essential part of healing your gut wall is to adhere to the anti-candidiasis diet, which will decrease your inflammation. You must also replenish your beneficial bacteria. The better your compliance, the more complete your recovery will be. The presence of persistent symptoms, even after all your infectious invaders are eliminated, usually indicates an ongoing allergic reaction. This typically includes sensitivities and hypersensitivities to disease-causing yeast, harmful molds, and/or allergy-inducing food.

If You Have Cancer or Autoimmune Disease

These medical maladies usually, but not always, arise secondary to impaired immunity. A persistent infection with disease-causing yeast, with or without other infectious invaders, can cause a variety of metabolic disturbances, leading to impaired immunity (chapter 14). Admittedly, candidiasis may not be the sole cause of these illnesses, but it is a strong contributor or promoter at the least. So, if disease-causing yeast and any other infectious invaders are responsible for your impaired immunity, eliminating their presence will correct this effect.

Treating Your Symptoms

If there are no contraindications to their use, symptom-relieving medications can be used to alleviate discomfort—for example, an antihistamine or decongestant to relieve nasal allergies. These should be appropriately used, with the least amount possible, and it is wise to eliminate their use as soon as possible. Medications that suppress your immune system should be taken sparingly. You should always consult your doctor before you take or change medication while you are on an anti-candidiasis program. Even over-the-counter medications can be a problem in some people.

If You Are Taking Other Medications

WARNING: *You should never adjust your medications without the supervision of a physician. If you are receiving prescription drugs and being treated for candidiasis, you must be regularly monitored by a health professional.*

People with chronic or recurring medical maladies who take medication on a regular basis may discover that their drug requirements change during and after anti-candidiasis therapy. In many cases, the dosage previously prescribed becomes too strong and must be adjusted by a physician. Sufferers who have experienced irreversible damage (for example, cardiovascular disease) will benefit from anti-candidiasis therapy, but their improvement may not be as significant, so their drug requirements may not change all that much. In any case, you must be monitored.

During treatment, your medication requirements can change or vary significantly. If you take prescription drugs, or even some herbal and homeopathic remedies, you must be regularly evaluated. You and your doctor should know the interactions of antifungal agents (medications and herbs) with your prescribed drugs. Under these circumstances, it is critical to maintain a close working relationship with your physician.

Typically, the sufferers who must be closely supervised have cardiovascular illness. Diabetics are also at high risk because the diet eliminates sugar and other simple carbohydrates; this frequently improves their ability to maintain their blood sugar concentration, decreasing their need for insulin and other medications. This can be dangerous in unsupervised sufferers.

For many reasons, a sufferer's metabolism and functioning of their *neuroendocrine-immune connection* will often improve with therapy. This is certain to decrease their required dose of one or more medications. This must be evaluated by a physician on a case-by-case basis. Dosages should be reduced whenever possible. In many sufferers, improvements are so drastic that the use of medication is no longer necessary.

Colonics: Pros and Cons

Many sufferers inquire about the value of *colonics*, the irrigation of the colon, with or without antifungal remedies. When performed properly (a high colonic with a good flow rate), the rapid removal of harmful infectious invaders along with their metabolites, toxins, and antigens often precipitates an immediate improvement in someone's symptoms.

Yet, the risks of colonics frequently outweigh the benefits. During a colonic, lots of fluid can be absorbed and, in those with high blood pressure, it may cause a cardiovascular disaster (for example, a stroke or heart failure). In the process of cleansing the colon, an abundance of harmful metabolites, toxins, and antigens can be absorbed, which may exacerbate someone's symptoms. Due to the volume and pressure of fluid used, any gut abnormalities or inflammation that exists, common among sufferers, increases the likelihood of perforating the colon. A colonic is an aggressive treatment that may spread infectious invaders to the small intestine, blood, other organs, or even to other people. The result of a colonic is often temporary, as all the infectious invaders are not completely removed, and illness is destined to return.

In short, colonics are a temporary solution. They may decrease the amount of the infection within your colon, but they cannot eliminate it completely. Moreover, they cannot eradicate the disease-causing yeast from within your gut wall, tissues, blood, and other areas of your body. Considering the success of the other recommendations in this chapter, colonics are unnecessary. After all, a thorough anti-candidiasis program eliminates your infectious invaders from your colon and everywhere else.

To Use or Not Use Vinegar

German anti-*Candida* experts believe a more acidic environment within the gut hinders the ability of disease-causing yeast to change from their less-aggressive (ovoid) form into their more-invasive (mycelial) form. In addition, vinegar is believed to impede the adhesion enzymes of disease-causing yeast, the glue-like chemicals that allow them to adhere to the gut wall. These same experts recommend that their patients consume vinegar (apple cider or wine, but *not* distilled). Although their reasoning is correct, caution is required. Regardless of whether apples or grapes are initially used, the resulting product can be contaminated with disease-causing yeast (as well as harmful molds). Since most sufferers have sensitivities or hypersensitivities to one or more disease-causing yeast, vinegar may trigger allergic reactions and symptoms. So, the use of vinegar should be avoided, at least until their allergies are eliminated. Besides, there are better therapeutic alternatives than vinegar.

Rather than used for treatment, the German approach is beneficial for *diagnostic* purposes. If a sufferer consumes one tablespoon of vinegar a day at bedtime for three days prior to their stool test, in combination with a high-fiber diet, the number of disease-causing yeasts within their stool sample becomes more significant and will be easier to identify.

Photoluminescence/Photo-Oxidation

This is a controversial form of therapy. A medical professional removes approximately 100 milliliters of a patient's blood using a sterile syringe. Next, the blood is put in a tube and is passed through a special machine that irradiates it with ultraviolet light (UV-C). Finally, the sterile blood is reinfused back into its original donor.

Many harmful microorganisms are sensitive to UV light, including disease-causing yeast. There is a rational to this treatment. It is thought that killing them halts their infectious behavior; however, since their allergy-inducing ability is conserved, it is hoped this will permit the development of immunity against the culprit. So, the dead cells act like allergy-inducing substances (antigens) that, hopefully, stimulate the production of corresponding protective antibodies as well as cell-mediated immunity aimed to assault these infectious invaders.

If this therapy works at all, it is usually a slow process as well as expensive. More notably, disease-causing yeast often invade into areas that are difficult for antibodies to reach or locations where cell-mediated immunity may be weak or ineffective. More concerning, several conflicting conditions make this type of therapy high risk. Because there are better methods and ways of treating your illness, this type of intervention is not recommended.

To Treat or Not Treat Your Intimate Contacts

Like a game of tennis, where the ball bounces back and forth between opponents, infectious invaders can be passed between sexual partners as well as from one family member to another. In 1998, W. Mendling et al. investigated

22 women with recurrent vulvovaginal candidiasis. Disease-causing yeast were found within the vaginas and guts of these women, and their male partners often had the same strains inhabiting their guts. More startling, identical strains of disease-causing yeast were grown from the sperm of four men. To prevent relapses, it makes sense to treat both partners.

Harmful parasites, bacteria, molds, and/or viruses can also be passed from one person to another. In addition to sex, they are frequently passed by unwashed hands, directly and indirectly. Therefore, many family members often harbor identical infectious invaders.

So, if you are a sufferer and do not want to be reinfected, you should ask your sexual partner and intimate contacts to be evaluated for candidiasis, including the presence of other infectious invaders. Often, it is safe to assume that whatever you have, they have. Although your sexual partner or family members are not likely to be happy about being treated, it will save *you* years of needless suffering. Besides, once they appreciate the health benefits of anti-candidiasis therapy, they are unlikely to stay angry at you for long.

Talking to Others about Candidiasis

If you are a sufferer, you will discover that there is a diversity of opinions about candidiasis. Some people are enthusiastic. Other people are simply compassionate. Many people are skeptical, and a small percentage will think you are crazy.

Since candidiasis is not well accepted, many sufferers find it difficult to discuss it openly. Attacking your infectious invaders is one thing. It is another to wage an intellectual and psychological battle with friends, neighbors, doctors, and anyone else who wants to prove you wrong. As a result, many sufferers discover that it is easier to keep their condition a secret.

Yet, times are changing. More people are embracing non-mainstream medicine. So, it is getting easier to talk openly about candidiasis with others. Since most people are unaware of it, spreading the word alleviates ignorance and provides assurance that this epidemic really exists. In return, an open forum means more candidiasis sufferers will be able to benefit.

You should not be shy. Candidiasis is supported by an abundance of science and information. If you are armed with the appropriate knowledge, you should never be uncomfortable discussing candidiasis openly. Yes, there is much more to be learned, but there is no longer a reason to doubt the existence of candidiasis.

Exercise

Exercise should be a part of any wellness program. Although it has numerous health benefits, candidiasis sufferers should be cautious. Just because you started an anti-candidiasis program and are restoring your health does *not* mean that you should go out and train for a marathon. Therapy is time to heal. You are healing your gut, correcting your nutritional deficiencies, eliminating your infections and allergies, strengthening your metabolism, immunity, and so on. It is not a time to push yourself to exhaustion.

So, if you are a sufferer, how much exercise should you do? The answer is do what you can tolerate. For sufferers with severe fatigue, this may involve getting out of bed and walking around the house. If your candidiasis is mild, you may not be tired at all. Yet, you should avoid extreme exhaustion. Sometimes, less is more. A one-mile run might be sufficient. If you feel like you can do more, do not be afraid to push a little. However, you do not want to become worse or get injured. You need to find a compromise—that is, an amount of exercise that brings benefits and does not impede your recovery.

Preventing Relapses

Amazingly, many sufferers sabotage their own recovery. Dietary noncompliance, forgetting to take antifungal agents or supplements, ignoring their allergies, and many other oversights all decrease or destroy the effectiveness of therapy. If the program is not followed completely, optimal results cannot be expected. There may be setbacks, like parasitic infections and allergy symptoms, but these complications can be resolved. Your candidiasis did not arise overnight and will not disappear in a day. You must accept that there is a mandatory period when sacrifices must be made; this is essential for your recovery. Sadly, many sufferers liberalize their programs too early, especially their diets. Although you may look and feel better, this does not mean you should quickly resume your previous ways because they are what got you into trouble in the first place. So, if you return to the behaviors and risk factors that instigated your candidiasis, you will have an extremely high chance of a relapse.

Compliance aside, the primary cause of relapse is reinfection or an untreated infectious invader. Harmful parasites, bacteria, molds, and viruses can easily be acquired from food and water or passed back and forth between loved ones. The same can be said for disease-causing yeast. On the other hand, eliminating one infectious invader can encourage others to assume prominence; for example, killing off disease-causing yeast may no longer competitively inhibit or suppress the other remaining infectious invaders. This usually occurs because one or more infectious invaders are overlooked or ignored. Moreover, sometimes a relapse can involve allergic reactions, especially when certain allergic foods are reintroduced.

Like most sufferers, you want your therapy to produce lifelong benefits. Yet, you do not live in a sterile bubble. The world is full of infectious invaders, allergy-inducing substances, toxic materials, and other harmful things. Accidents happen and so do mistakes. Therefore, sooner or later, you may manifest symptoms again. They are not likely to be as severe, but they will be noticeable regardless. What should you do? Treat them, and the sooner the better. When attended to promptly, a subsequent anti-candidiasis program can be easier and shorter in length. If your allergies have been treated, your diet does not have to be as strict. What is the best treatment of all? Prevention. Your candidiasis is not forever, but your vigilance should be.

BEATING YOUR CANDIDIASIS

There is no longer a doubt. Your laboratory tests are in. Your diagnosis has been made. You have candidiasis, an infection with disease-causing yeast. If you want to beat these infectious invaders, what needs to be done?

The first step is to prepare your body to eliminate your infectious invaders. Since your liver and kidneys are vital for removing toxins and wastes from your body, these organs need to be strengthened (there are other reasons). Since candidiasis often promotes malabsorption, nutritional deficiencies are common and must be corrected. Most sufferers can tolerate oral nutritional supplements. Sufferers who cannot tolerate oral supplements, those with severe malabsorption or impaired immunity, will benefit from intravenous supplementation instead.

Most often, the next step is to eradicate your disease-causing yeast, your *infection*. Typically, this involves killing disease-causing yeast within your tissues and blood with systemic antifungal medication, while nonabsorbable medication can help eliminate the disease-causing yeast residing within your gut. In addition, if you have any other infectious invaders, they must be addressed, including harmful parasites, bacteria, and molds; in some cases, cell wall–deficient organisms must be considered. Fortunately, some anti-candidiasis medications also have some anti-mold activity as well, making it easier to simultaneously eliminate disease-causing yeast and harmful molds (there are exceptions).

Since candidiasis involves *allergic* consequences, sufferers often have a variety of sensitivities and hypersensitivities. It is essential to be tested for allergies to disease-causing yeast and harmful molds. Depending on your symptoms, you may also be tested for reactions to foods, pollen, dust, chemicals, and more. Since your allergic reactions are likely to be lifelong, an allergy immunotherapy program is the only way to desensitize you against your allergy-inducing instigators. In fact, many sufferers demonstrate minimal improvement in their symptoms, and sometimes none, until their allergies are addressed. If possible, you should also eliminate as many of your allergy-inducing culprits from your diet and surroundings.

Speaking of diet, in addition to killing your disease-causing yeast, you must starve them. Eliminating sugars from your diet and decreasing your intake of complex carbohydrates will help slow their metabolism and reproduction, impeding the generation of additional disease-causing yeast. Your diet must also be yeast-free and mold-free. This prevents allergic reactions and reinfections with these troublemakers and eliminates their harmful toxins and metabolites from your food supply. Of course, you must also eliminate your allergy-inducing foods.

To prevent a relapse, you must replenish your population of beneficial bacteria. Initially, this should be done at least twice a day with a probiotic supplement containing multiple microorganisms. If tolerated, yogurt/kefir can be used for the same purpose, in moderation.

If you have symptoms or illness that require the use of one or more medications, you *must be medically supervised*. In fact, all sufferers are cautioned against undertaking anti-candidiasis therapy without appropriate medical supervision. Guidance by a knowledgeable and experienced candidiasis-minded physician can prevent you from making mistakes, avoid undesirable consequences, and save you from wasting time and money. Appropriate medical care is not just recommended, it is often essential.

Yes, you can beat your candidiasis. After all, disease-causing yeast and other infectious invaders are not invulnerable. Understanding their weaknesses will ensure your success. You need to know what you are doing and why. Your infectious invaders, allergies, nutritional deficiencies, metabolic disturbances, impaired immunity, and so on can all be corrected once you are armed with the appropriate knowledge. Thereafter, all you need is desire, determination, perseverance, and patience. Many sufferers have beaten their candidiasis. If you follow these recommendations, you are certain to be one of them.

CHAPTER 19

The Anti-Candidiasis Arsenal

Candidiasis is an *infection* with *allergic* consequences. It involves the colonization of disease-causing yeast within the gastrointestinal tract. They can also invade into and through the gut wall, colonizing and infecting the tissues and blood. In addition, they can directly and indirectly gain access to and infect the upper and lower respiratory tract, urinary tract, and other tissues. Eliminating the infection necessitates killing the disease-causing yeast. It is essential to kill virtually all the disease-causing yeast—otherwise, a relapse is destined.

Since the major disease-causing yeast are most associated with illness, these infectious invaders must initially be addressed and eliminated, including *Candida albicans, Candida glabrata, Candida guilliermondii, Candida kefyr, Candida krusei, Candida parapsilosis, Candida tropicalis*, and *Candida viswanathii.*

Furthermore, clinical experience with sufferers reveals the less prominent disease-causing yeast must also be eliminated when present, including *Candida catenulata, Candida ciferii, Candida famata, Candida inconspicua, Candida intermedia, Candida haemulonii, Candida lipolytica, Candida lusitanae, Candida norvegenesis, Candida pulcherrima, Candida rugosa, Candida zeylanoides, Cryptococcus albidus, Cryptococcus laurentii, Rhodotorula glutinis, Rhodotorula rubra*, and *Saccharomyces cerevisiae* (baker's and brewer's yeast). Yes, they may be less troublesome, but they still have the potential to cause illness when present in large numbers. In some sufferers, the less prominent disease-causing yeast do promote blatant illness. In other sufferers, they may exist in small amounts but gain the freedom to reproduce and cause problems when other infectious invaders are killed.

Unfortunately, no one antifungal agent is perfect; not one kills every species of disease-causing yeast. Yet, when chosen wisely and used properly, great success can be achieved with certain combinations. Obviously, the antifungal agents used during therapy should depend on a sufferer's infectious invaders and targeted against them.

Disclaimer: This chapter describes the antifungal agents that can be used to kill disease-causing yeast, including their strengths and weaknesses. The information is for reference. It is *not* meant to replace a physician's guidance. In fact, if these weapons are used inappropriately or indiscriminately, they have the potential to make you worse, not better. Therefore, it is strongly recommended that a candidiasis-minded physician be the one who chooses and prescribes your antifungal agents. Prior to their use, you should improve your capacity to tolerate the die-off of your disease-causing yeast by strengthening your liver and kidneys. In addition, sufferers with cardiovascular disease can also benefit by strengthening their arteries and veins.

(With new antifungal agents being researched and discovered, both medicines and herbs, the information within this chapter includes what was available by early 2023.)

"GET OUT & STAY OUT" APPROACH

If you are a candidiasis sufferer, disease-causing yeast are infecting your gastrointestinal tract. If this is the only place they reside, treatment would be relatively simple; you could use a nonabsorbable antifungal agent to eliminate their presence. However, in most sufferers, disease-causing yeast have invaded into their gut wall, causing some magnitude of leaky gut syndrome with its increased intestinal permeability and malabsorption. Even worse, a large percentage of sufferers have disease-causing yeast within their tissues, organs, and blood. Disease-causing yeast anywhere other than within the gut will require the use of a *systemic* antifungal agent—that is, an agent that is absorbed, killing disease-causing yeast within the tissues and blood.

Clinical experience with sufferers reveals that using nonabsorbable antifungal agents alone (for example, nystatin) has limited benefits and rarely cures their candidiasis. They do not effectively assault disease-causing yeast within their gut wall, tissues, and blood. Many sufferers do feel better after using nystatin because they have reduced the amount of disease-causing yeast within their body, decreasing the burden of their infection. Yes, this may be all some sufferers need. More often, sufferers treated with only nonabsorbable antifungal agents will feel worse, sooner or later, when the disease-causing yeast within their tissues and blood become more aggressive. This explains why many sufferers are forced to take nystatin or other nonabsorbable antifungal agents forever, whether constantly or periodically.

In addition, clinical experience with sufferers reveals that most systemic antifungal agents (for example, Diflucan) cannot eliminate all the disease-causing yeast that reside within the gut. Typically, most of the systemic antifungal agent is absorbed, leaving little to combat the disease-causing yeast within the interior (lumen) of the gut, especially the lower portions. Yes, they do kill disease-causing yeast within the tissues and blood, but they are not as effective against the same infectious invaders residing within the lumen of the gut. So, when the systemic antifungal agent is finished, the disease-causing yeast that remain can become more aggressive and colonize their surroundings, promoting a relapse.

Also, the less prominent disease-causing yeast require a different arsenal. Most nonabsorbable and systemic antifungal agents do not have activity against most of the less prominent disease-causing yeast. After the major disease-causing yeast have been eliminated, the less prominent disease-causing yeast can gain the freedom to reproduce and colonize their surroundings—that is, if they were not causing problems initially. This encourages a relapse (*atypical candidiasis*) involving the mischief of the less prominent disease-causing yeast, notably *Saccharomyces*-species and *Rhodotorula*-species organisms.

Antifungal agents have their advantages and disadvantages. Each is only as good as its spectrum of activity and is only useful for the infectious invaders it can kill. As a result, both systemic and nonabsorbable antifungal agents can be used in combination to compensate for each other's deficiencies.

This brings us to the "get out and stay out" approach. It involves using both a systemic and a nonabsorbable antifungal agent, like a one-two punch. You begin initially with a systemic antifungal agent to completely saturate your tissues and blood, killing the disease-causing yeast within these areas, especially *Candida albicans*. As your gut wall regenerates, replacing its cells, the disease-causing yeast within your gut wall will be killed and pushed into the interior (lumen) of your gastrointestinal tract. After roughly five days (four to six), your gut wall and tissues will be saturated with the systemic antifungal agent. If the medication did its job, there should be no disease-causing yeast remaining within your gut wall, allowing it to heal. Any disease-causing yeast that are still present within your gastrointestinal tract will be unable to invade your gut wall, confining them within your gut interior (lumen), unless they are resistant to the systemic antifungal agent. Since most of the systemic antifungal agent is absorbed, these medications do not eliminate all the disease-causing yeast within your gut (especially the less prominent disease-causing yeast). If systemic antifungal agents are not used initially to heal your gut wall, substantial amounts of inflammation and mucus can form a barrier that protects your disease-causing yeast from any nonabsorbable antifungal agents used. Therefore, it is best to initially employ a systemic antifungal agent and then subsequently add a nonabsorbable antifungal agent to eliminate the remaining disease-causing yeast. So, with the systemic antifungal agent you pronounce, "Get out," and with the nonabsorbable antifungal agent you add, "and stay out." Then, a couple of weeks later, you can use broad-spectrum antifungal herbs to eliminate your less prominent disease-causing yeast, saying, "And don't come back."

Since it takes roughly five days to saturate the gut wall with a systemic antifungal agent, nonabsorbable antifungal agents should preferably be added about 7 to 10 days after beginning therapy. Besides, there is another advantage to waiting. If a systemic antifungal agent and nonabsorbable agent are started at the same time, a sufferer's die-off reaction can be severe. Waiting to add other antifungal agents reduces this unpleasant complication.

Clinical experience with sufferers reveals that, although some can get by without a systemic antifungal agent, most of them benefit substantially from its use. Undeniably, sufferers who have disease-causing yeast within their tissues or blood should receive a systemic antifungal agent. The length of time it is used will vary, but three to four weeks is about average. However, if disease-causing yeast are infecting the toenails or skin, a systemic antifungal agent should be used longer, and probably switched to one that also kills harmful molds. In contrast, sufferers who have disease-causing yeast mostly confined within their gut can benefit from a two-week course of a systemic antifungal agent to ensure that the disease-causing yeast within their gut wall are eliminated. Using this approach, a nonabsorbable antifungal agent tends to be most effective during its first week and can be discontinued by two weeks.

So, there is no longer a reason to take nystatin or another nonabsorbable antifungal agent forever. If you eliminate the disease-causing yeast within your tissues and blood, and then eradicate the ones within your gut, why should you have to take any antifungal agent? Indeed, if you do not feel better after doing this, there are a few possibilities. You are harboring disease-causing yeast resistant to the antifungal agent used. The dose was ineffective. Or disease-causing yeast are not your only problem, and other infectious invaders may be responsible for your ill health, including harmful parasites, bacteria, molds, and/or viruses. If they were not initially considered, these must be identified and treated.

Most medications and supplements (in a tablet or pill form) are more effective or absorbed better when they are bitten or broken before swallowing. Many sufferers have an absence or insufficiency of their gut acid and enzymes. Since the outer coatings of some medications and supplements may not be fully digested, poor absorption can occur. As a result, mechanically breaking medications and supplements indirectly aids their efficacy. In addition, whether you like their taste or not, most antifungal agents should be kept within your mouth for a short period before swallowing, particularly the nonabsorbable agents. Although some have a nasty taste, this ensures the disease-causing yeast that reside on the surface of your mouth and esophagus are also killed. Moreover, taking antifungal agents when your stomach is empty will prevent them from being diluted with food—usually, about an hour before or at least three hours after a meal. Typically, an empty stomach increases their bioavailability and effectiveness, as more is absorbed. (Although Sporanox is supposed to be absorbed better when administered with food, clinical experience demonstrates sufferers should take it when their stomach is empty.)

German anti-candidiasis experts agree with the simultaneous use of both systemic and nonabsorbable combination therapies. Yet, they have a difference of opinion about what medications should be given. There are two general types of anti-candidiasis medication that are commonly used in clinical practice. The *polyenes* are nonabsorbable antifungal agents that adversely affect sterols within the cell membranes of disease-causing yeast, whereas the *azoles* are systemic medications that inhibit sterol synthesis within the cell's interior (cytoplasm). Some German experts claim the two different classes should never be given together because their combined effects hinder each other, while the opposing side says it is vital to use a systemic and nonabsorbable agent even if they are from different drug classes.

Since every sufferer is different, there is no one right way. Yet, one combination seems to make everyone happy: using a systemic antifungal medication (an azole) with miconazole (even though it is also an azole, it is poorly absorbed and essentially acts like a nonabsorbable antifungal agent). This combination appears to have helped some particularly resistant cases of candidiasis, probably because of its broad spectrum of activity against molds. Alternatively, combining a systemic antifungal agent with Fungizone oral suspension (amphotericin B) appears to be easier and more effective. Research demonstrates fluconazole (Diflucan) and amphotericin B can be used additively. In contrast, itraconazole (Sporanox) and amphotericin B appear to be antagonistic, so they should not be taken together. (The *echinocandins* are a third class of drugs that are used less frequently in outpatient clinical practice.)

Therefore, it is important to use both systemic antifungal agents and nonabsorbable antifungal agents. The combinations chosen and the length of time used will depend on your species (and strain) of disease-causing yeast as well as where they are within your body. To prevent mistakes and mishaps, it is vital to be supervised by a candidiasis-minded physician. With the right guidance, it is only a matter of time before you tell your disease-causing yeast to "Get out, stay out, and don't come back."

PHARMACEUTICAL AGENTS

Pharmaceutical anti-candidiasis agents are synthetic substances. Since disease-causing yeast are classified as *fungi*, these substances are technically termed *antifungal agents*. Many of them are refinements of what occurs in nature. In fact, most medications are derived from natural substances and then purified to achieve a consistent potency.

There are two general categories of antifungal medication: systemic and nonabsorbable. *Systemic* antifungal medications can be absorbed by the gastrointestinal tract, saturate the tissues and blood, and destroy disease-causing yeast residing within those locations—if the infectious invader is not resistant to the medication. *Nonabsorbable* antifungal agents are not absorbed, or poorly absorbed, and only kill disease-causing yeast on the mucous membranes and within the interior (lumen) of the gut. Each type has its usefulness.

It is important to consider if someone has or will develop an allergy to a medication(s). In some cases, a sufferer's allergies are minimal, and the drug can be continued. Sometimes an offending medication needs to be discontinued, and the sufferer should be switched to another drug. A physician should always question for drug allergies before instituting treatment, and you should always reveal your allergies to medication. Moreover, it is your responsibility to inform your physician about adverse reactions to any medications they prescribed.

Disease-causing yeast have the potential to become, or can be, resistant to one or more systemic antifungal medications. If the infectious invaders you are trying to kill are resistant to a medication, your recovery will be delayed or even sabotaged. Yet, there is a more troublesome consequence of antifungal resistance. A lack of improvement may make you think you have been improperly diagnosed and abandon anti-candidiasis therapy. So, you must be closely monitored by a candidiasis-minded physician. If you do not experience a die-off reaction or do not feel better after taking an antifungal agent, a different medication should be used. In rare cases, sufferers do not respond to a second drug, and a third must be given. A knowledgeable candidiasis-minded physician should make this decision. In addition, the presence of other infectious invaders may be responsible for your lack of improvement and must also be addressed accordingly.

SYSTEMIC ANTIFUNGAL MEDICATIONS

Although these drugs are the most frequently prescribed and employed, the following information is intended as a quick reference. The unpleasant effects that accompany the die-off reaction are common (chapter 18) but adverse side effects are rare. Since their benefits greatly outweigh their risks, you should *not* be afraid to use these systemic antifungal agents.

Warning: Any physician or healthcare provider who prescribes these medications should be familiar with their precautions, contraindications, and so on. They can be found in the *Physician's Desk Reference* (PDR) or a similar medical source.

Diflucan (Fluconazole)

Diflucan (fluconazole) is a synthetic triazole. It is "a highly selective inhibitor of fungal cytochrome P-450 sterol C-14 alpha-demethylation." It interferes with fungal metabolism, killing disease-causing yeast and other harmful fungi.

It is primarily active against *Candida*-species organisms and *Cryptococcus neoformans*. Activity has also been noted against *Aspergillus flavus, Aspergillus fumigatus, Blastomyces dermatitidis, Coccidioides immitis,* and *Histoplasma capsulatum*.

Unfortunately, disease-causing *Candida*-species organisms can become resistant to Diflucan. Usually, resistance is associated with its prior or continuous use. Giving it with amphotericin B appears to enhance its effectiveness.

Adult doses typically range from 50–400 mg daily. Yet, from clinical experience, most sufferers benefit from 400–600 mg daily, with a *double* (loading) dose on day one. Children receive an amount in proportion to their body weight. (In 1999, R. Schawarze et al. determined that it appears to be well tolerated and efficacious in children below one year of age, including neonates and low-birthweight infants.) Diflucan seems to be the best systemic antifungal agent to initially use during anti-candidiasis therapy.

Nizoral (Ketoconazole)

Nizoral (ketoconazole) is a synthetic, broad-spectrum azole. In vitro studies suggest that it impairs the synthesis of *ergosterol*, a component of fungal cell membranes. In short, it weakens the cell membranes of disease-causing yeast and other harmful fungi.

It is primarily active against *Blastomyces dermatitidis*, *Candida*-species organisms, *Coccidioides immitis*, *Histoplasma capsulatum*, *Paracoccidioides brasiliensis*, and *Philophora*-species organisms. It also has activity against *Trichophyton* species, *Epidermophyton* species, and *Microsporum* species. Other research demonstrates activity against *Malassezia furfur*.

The recommended starting dose is 200 mg. However, 400–600 mg have been used for serious infections or when no response occurs within a reasonable time. In general, 400 mg a day is effective for most sufferers. The dose for children is adjusted for their body weight. This medication has been around longer and is less expensive than Diflucan. Unfortunately, many sufferers have disease-causing yeast and harmful fungi that are resistant to Nizoral.

Sporanox, Onmel, and Tolsura (Itraconazole)

Sporanox (itraconazole), as well as brands Onmel and Tolsura, is a synthetic triazole that inhibits the cytochrome P-450-dependent synthesis of *ergosterol*, a vital component of fungal cell membranes. Basically, it impairs the cell membranes of disease-causing yeast and harmful fungi. Classically, its broad-spectrum activity makes it useful for fungal infections, especially involving the lungs. Its value in treating candidiasis is obvious and has been increasing.

It is primarily active against *Blastomyces dermatitidis*, *Histoplasma capsulatum*, *Histoplasma duboisii*, *Aspergillus flavus*, *Aspergillus fumigatus*, *Candida albicans*, and *Cryptococcus neoformans*. It has varying activity against *Sporothrix schenckii*, *Trichophyton*-species organisms, *Candida krusei*, and other *Candida*-species organisms. It has also been noted to be active against *Coccidioides immitis* and *Paracoccidioides brasiliensis*.

Itraconazole is supposed to be taken *with* food to ensure its maximal absorption and blood plasma levels, which is an exception to other medications. Yet, experience with sufferers reveals that it may be better to take it on an empty stomach. The typical adult dose is 200 mg once a day. If there is no improvement or evidence of progressive disease, the dose can be increased in 100-mg increments to 200 mg twice a day, equaling a total dose of 400 mg a day. Children receive an amount in proportion to their body weight. Because it is effective at killing both *Candida albicans* and *Aspergillus*-species organisms, its ability to kill infectious invaders within the lungs may be highly valuable for sufferers with asthma and other respiratory illnesses.

Lamisil (Terbinafine Hydrochloride)

Lamisil (terbinafine hydrochloride) is a synthetic allylamine derivative. It inhibits *squalene epoxidase,* a key enzyme in sterol biosynthesis within fungi, causing a deficiency of *ergosterol,* leading to excesses of sterol within the cell. So, a buildup of metabolites poisons the cell, resulting in death.

Since it has broad-spectrum activity against fungi, it is commonly used to treat fungal nail infections. Because many sufferers have mixed infections, it can be useful. It is primarily active against *Trichophyton rubrum* and *Trichophyton mentagrophytes.* It also has activity against *Epidermophyton floccosum, Microsporum gypseum, Microsporum nanum, Trichophyton verrucosum, Candida albicans,* and *Scopulariopsis brevicaulis.*

The typical adult dose is 250 mg per day, although some take 500 mg a day. Its broad-spectrum activity makes it a good choice when mold infections are also present. Clinical experience has shown that sufferers with allergies to *Trichophyton* and/or *Epidermophyton* often benefit from its use.

Ancobon (Flucytosine)

Ancobon (flucytosine) is a fluorinated pyrimidine, an analogue of cytosine. It is thought to disturb fungal metabolism by competitively inhibiting the uptake of purine and pyrimidine as well as by being metabolized within the cell to 5-fluorouracil, which is incorporated into fungal RNA, inhibiting the synthesis of both RNA and DNA. Simply put, it causes unbalanced cellular growth, leading to cell death.

It has a narrow spectrum of activity, primarily against *Candida*-species organisms and *Cryptococcus neoformans.* Some other fungi are frequently susceptible, including *Fonsecaea pedrosoi, Fonsecaea compacta,* and *Cladosporium carrionii*. Varying susceptibility occurs with *Aspergillus*-species organisms. Resistance to it can readily arise.

It is rapidly and almost completely absorbed when given orally. The usual daily dose is approximately 100 (50–150) mg/kg of body weight a day, divided into four equal doses, given at six-hour intervals. Although it can precipitate some undesirable disturbances, it should present little problem for sufferers without major compromise. It has few adverse drug interactions and appears to increase the efficacy of other systemic antifungal agents. Sufferers who have disease-causing yeast with low susceptibilities or are resistant to other systemic antifungal agents could benefit from using it.

Amphotericin B

Amphotericin B (intravenous) is a polyene, antibiotic obtained from a strain of *Streptomyces nodosus*. It binds to the cell membrane, which alters its permeability, leading to cell death. It can also bind to cholesterol within mammalian cells, so it is potentially toxic to these cells. When used as a systemic antifungal agent, it must be given intravenously (IV). American physicians consider this drug highly toxic and only administer it in the worst cases, especially when there is a progressive and potentially life-threatening fungal infection.

It has broad-spectrum activity against many fungi, including *Aspergillus* species, *Candida* species, *Cryptococcus neoformans*, and *Blastomyces dermatitidis*. It also has activity against *Coccidioides immitis, Histoplasma capsulatum, Paracoccidioides brasiliensis, Leishmania donovani*, and *Leishmania infatum*. Resistance can occur from its use.

It only administered intravenously under *medical supervision*. A total daily dose of 1.5 mg/kg should not be exceeded for any reason. Although it sounds dangerous, European doctors prescribe the oral form for sufferers with remarkable success. From clinical experience, numerous patients have received one or more systemic antifungal agents, but only substantially improve after taking the oral form of amphotericin B (Fungizone oral suspension); since it is not absorbed or poorly absorbed, it has proven to be safe and effective.

Grifulvin V/Gris-PEG (Griseofulvin)

Grifulvin V/Gris-PEG (griseofulvin) is a broad-spectrum antibiotic derived from a species of *Penicillium*. It is fungistatic; it inhibits the growth of fungi.

Since it is deposited within the skin and nails, it is used to treat fungal infections in these locations.

It is fungistatic against species of *Microsporum*, *Epidermophyton*, and *Trichophyton*. It is primarily employed to treat ringworm infections of the skin, hair, and nails.

Unfortunately, it has no effect on other fungi, so it is useless against disease-causing yeast. Why is it being mentioned? Some sufferers have noticed substantial benefits when taking this drug for their fungal nail infections, implying that harmful molds have been contributing to their ill health.

Less Commonly Used Systemic Antifungal Agents

From clinical experience, candidiasis-minded physicians use the following agents infrequently, so they will only be mentioned briefly. Interested practitioners should do their own research.

- **Brexafemme (ibrexafungerp):** a triterpenoid that inhibits *glucan synthetase*, which is involved in the formation of *1,3-beta-D-glucan*, an essential fungal cell wall component, so it prevents the formation of the fungal cell wall. It is primarily used for vulvovaginal candidiasis. It is active against a wide range of *Aspergillus*-species and *Candida*-species isolates, including those resistant to azoles and echinocandins.
- **Cancidas (caspofungin):** a lipopeptide in the class echinocandins. It inhibits the enzyme *1,3-beta-D-glucan synthase*, which disturbs the fungal cell wall integrity. It is effective against *Aspergillus* species and has broad-spectrum activity against all *Candida* species.
- **Cresemba/Isavuconazole (isavuconazonium sulfate):** an extended spectrum triazole with activity against yeasts, molds, and dimorphic fungi. It inhibits the enzyme *lanosterol 14 alpha-demethylase*, depleting *ergosterol* and accumulating *lanosterol*, compromising the fungal cell wall structure. It is used to treat invasive *Aspergillus* and *mucormycosis* (a rare, serious infection with a group of molds called mucormycetes).
- **Eraxis (anidulafungin):** an echinocandin, which inhibits the synthesis of beta-glucan within the cell wall by noncompetitive inhibition of the enzyme *1,3-beta-D-glucan synthase*. It has activity against some yeast—most *Candida* species, but not *Cryptococcus*, *Trichosporon*, and *Rhodotorula*. It has activity against *Candida* biofilms, synergistically with amphotericin

B, and additively with Diflucan. It is fungistatic against some molds and somewhat active against dimorphic fungi.

- **Mycamine (micafungin):** an echinocandin, which inhibits the enzyme *1,3-beta-D-glucan synthase*, disturbing the fungal cell wall integrity. It has been found to have activity against hundreds of clinical isolates of fluconazole-resistant *Candida*-species organisms. It is administered intravenously for the treatment of candidemia, acute disseminated candidiasis, *Candida* peritonitis, abscesses, and esophageal candidiasis.
- **Noxafil (posaconazole):** a triazole that inhibits the enzyme *lanosterol 14a-demethylase*, depleting *ergosterol* and accumulating *lanosterol*, compromising the fungal cell wall structure. It has broad-spectrum activity against most *Candida* species, *Cryptococcus neoformans*, *Aspergillus* species, *Fusarium* species, *zygomycetes*, and endemic fungi.
- **Vfend (voriconazole):** a triazole with broad-spectrum activity that inhibits the enzyme *lanosterol 14a-demethylase*, depleting *ergosterol* and accumulating *lanosterol*, compromising the fungal cell wall structure. It is active against *Candida albicans*, especially fluconazole-resistant isolates and other *Candida*-species organisms. It is also active against *Cryptococcus neoformans*, *Aspergillus*-species organisms, and many other molds.

ORAL NONABSORBABLE ANTIFUNGAL MEDICATIONS

Nonabsorbable antifungal agents are efficacious for noninvasive gut infections with disease-causing yeast (and harmful molds). Clinical experience reveals that most sufferers have some magnitude of invasive candidiasis, so they will benefit from using a systemic antifungal agent, at least initially. After the disease-causing yeast within their gut wall and tissues has been addressed, oral nonabsorbable antifungal agents can be added to remove the disease-causing yeast (and harmful molds) that remain within their gastrointestinal tract. Although there are a limited number of these agents, their use benefits candidiasis sufferers.

Nystatin

Nystatin (various brands) is a polyene ionophore obtained from a mold, *Streptomyces noursei*. It is a mixture of substances. Nystatin A1 is closely related to amphotericin B. It is not absorbed and relatively nontoxic. It binds to sterols within the fungal cell membrane and alters their permeability, causing leakage of the cell's internal contents. It is used for oral cavity and gut infections caused by *Candida albicans*.

It is fungistatic and fungicidal against a variety of *Candida* species, *Cryptococcus neoformans, Histoplasma capsulatum, Coccidioides immitis, Blastomyces dermatitidis*, and the dermatophytes *Epidermophyton, Trichophyton*, and *Microsporum*. Resistance can occur.

From clinical experience, nystatin is taken four times a day with these amounts: Adults use 1 million units, children receive between 400,000–600,000 units, and infants get 200,000 units. It appears to be more effective when it is retained in the mouth before swallowing.

Fungizone Oral Suspension (Amphotericin B)

Fungizone oral suspension (amphotericin B) is a polyene antibiotic antifungal agent obtained from a strain of *Streptomyces nodosus*. It binds to sterols within the cell membranes of susceptible fungi, altering their permeability, leading to leakage of their cells' contents. It is poorly absorbed orally, making it safe and efficacious. It was available by prescription, but now is primarily obtained from a compounding pharmacy.

It has broad-spectrum activity against numerous fungi, including *Aspergillus* species, *Candida*species, *Cryptococcus neoformans*, and *Blastomyces dermatitidis*. It is also active against *Coccidioides immitis, Histoplasma capsulatum, Paracoccidioides brasiliensis, Leishmania donovani*, and *Leishmania infantum*. Resistance can occur.

Adults and children can take 100 mg (1 ml) four times a day. Preferably, it is taken an hour before or three hours after meals to permit prolonged contact with the mucous membranes. Typically, treatment lasts two weeks. Clinical experience proves its use consistently helps candidiasis sufferers.

Miconazole

Miconazole (various brands) is a synthetic imidazole mononitrate agent. It inhibits the enzyme *Sterol 14a-demethylase*, reducing *ergosterol* production, which impairs the fungal cell wall structure. It is commonly used topically, but it has been used orally and benefitted candidiasis sufferers. Although there is some absorption, it only occurs in tiny amounts, paralleling the presence of leaky gut syndrome. For all purposes, it acts as an oral antifungal agent. It is effective and inexpensive but must be obtained from a compounding pharmacy.

Miconazole inhibits the growth of *Candida albicans*, *Trichophyton rubrum*, *Trichophyton mentagrophytes*, *Epidermophyton floccosum*, and *Malassezia furfur*. It also has antibacterial properties, notably anti-*staphylococcal* activity.

The dosage is 1,000 mg a day, divided into two to four doses. To prevent severe die-off symptoms, start with a 125 mg capsule and build up. Capsules are usually emptied in the mouth and then swished and swallowed.

(**Note:** There are many topical antifungal medications. Since they are not used to treat the infectious aspect of candidiasis, they will not be discussed in this chapter.)

NATURAL PREPARATIONS

***Warning*:** Herbs can be of great benefit, but they should be used appropriately. You would be wise to consult with your doctor before ingesting any herbs, especially if you are taking medication for a chronic or recurring medical problem. More specifically, if you are using herbs to treat candidiasis, you should consult with a candidiasis-minded physician. Any physician or healthcare provider who prescribes these herbs should be familiar with their precautions, contraindications, warnings, and so on.

***Notable warning*:** Pregnant women and nursing mothers should not take the herbs listed in this section without their doctor's permission and supervision.

Herbs are nature's drugs. They can be used in their fresh or dried state. Commercial products that contain one or more herbs are processed in a way that is supposed to yield more consistent and stable concentrations or amounts, such as essential oils, tinctures, and more. They do not require a prescription because they are considered a food or dietary supplement.

In their whole state, most herbs are rarely toxic. Yet, do *not* think that herbs are harmless. When used indiscriminately or inappropriately, problems can and will develop. Moreover, some herbs are dangerous, while others have proven to be deadly. Although most harmful herbs are not available or have been taken off the market, do not assume that just because something is available or widely known, it is right for you. In fact, specific herbs are useful for certain problems, meaning various herbs are better for some people. Unfortunately, some herbs are contaminated with or contain molds (harmful and innocent), so people with mold sensitivities or hypersensitivities can be adversely affected. In addition, various herbs have been found to contain toxic heavy metals, so you must be vigilant about where your herbs originated, how they were processed, and which ones to avoid.

With respect to candidiasis, some sufferers and candidiasis-minded physicians prefer herbs, believing they are safer and more "natural" than drugs. Yet, when used appropriately, medications are safe and usually much more effective at consistently killing disease-causing yeast, especially the major disease-causing yeast. In contrast, many anti-candidiasis herbs are weak or ineffective in their systemic effectiveness; although they may destroy disease-causing yeast on the mucous membranes and within the gut, they cannot harm disease-causing yeast within the tissues and blood. In some cases, this worsens candidiasis; as the disease-causing yeast within the tissues are starved, they become more aggressive, advancing their infection.

Many sufferers benefit from natural anti-candidiasis agents. However, if the disease-causing yeast within their gut wall, tissues, and blood is not eliminated, they must constantly be vigilant. These agents are not recommended for initial treatment unless a sufferer's candidiasis is strictly limited to the interior (lumen) of their gut. Since the goal is to eliminate all the disease-causing yeast, natural agents are more effectively employed after the disease-causing yeast within your tissues and blood are killed, and your gut wall is healed.

Candidiasis-minded physicians commonly prescribe antifungal medications initially to heal the gut wall and eradicate disease-causing yeast from the tissues and blood. Thereafter, clinical experience demonstrates that one or more herbs can be effectively used, and although they do have some systemic effects, their benefits involve eliminating the less prominent disease-causing yeast, including *Saccharomyces*-species and *Rhodotorula*-species organisms as well as many harmful molds. This is not a universal effect, and some sufferers respond better than others.

Herbs are usually taken two to three times a day. Liquid preparations (essential oils and tinctures) should be swished in the mouth before swallowing, followed by a few sips of water. Other herbs are more effective when made into a tea. In most cases, herbs should be taken when your stomach is empty, at least 30 minutes before or three hours after a meal. Unless a physician advises otherwise, you should only take the amounts recommended on their labels.

The following list includes the most employed natural preparations. (They are listed alphabetically, not by potency or effectiveness.) Many other herbs exist and are used in various types of medicine throughout the world but are beyond the scope of this chapter.

- ***Artemisia annua*** is primarily used to treat parasite infestations, especially amoebiasis and giardiasis. However, its broad-spectrum activity makes it useful for most other parasites as well. In addition, it has antifungal activity. It generally works by its peroxide activity, so antioxidants should not be taken simultaneously. It is frequently mixed with other herbs to produce different antiparasitic formulas. The only undesirable effect is some tiredness during or after vigorous aerobic exercise.
- **Bitter herbs** (alkaloid-containing herbs) are natural antifungal agents. They have been used for centuries as food preservatives. Unless you are allergic or they are contaminated with mold, they can be used for their anti-candidiasis activity.
- **Black walnut** *(Juglans nigra)* has antifungal, antiseptic, and antiparasitic properties.
- **Boric acid** was tested as a vaginal douche against *Candida glabrata* vaginitis in a group of women who failed azole antifungal therapy. The dosage was 600 mg a day for two weeks, which improved or cured roughly 80 percent of the women treated. It may be useful against other disease-causing yeast. It should *not* be ingested.
- **Caprylic acid** is a food-related, short-chain fatty acid with strong anti-*Candida* properties. It is sold in different forms, with coconut being its preferred source. It can be irritating to the stomach (gastric) lining, so you should take it under the guidance of a physician.
- **Cat's claw** *(Uncaria tomentosa)* is the Peruvian herb called "una de gato." It has immune-enhancing, antimicrobial, antioxidant, antiviral, anti-inflammatory, and antitumor activities. Because of its diverse effectiveness, especially with a variety of gut disorders, it is believed to have antiparasitic, anti-*Candida*, and antibacterial properties.
- **Cinnamon oil, Ceylon cinnamon** *(Cinnamomum zeylanicum)* has antifungal activity against *Candida albicans.*
- **Coconut butter,** a tropical fat, is a source of caprylic acid and lauric acid. Caprylic acid has anti-*Candida* activity, while lauric acid has antiviral activity. Rather than an anti-candidiasis agent, sufferers use it to supplement their diet, especially in their cooking.

- **Cumin oil** *(Cuminum nigrum)* is a potent antifungal agent with activity against harmful parasites and bacteria. Cumin oil is rich in *cuminaldehyde,* a powerful antioxidant that benefits the functioning of the liver and pancreas.

- **Echinacea** *(Echinacea angustifolia)* boosts immunity. It has antibacterial, antiviral, anti-*Candida*, and some anticancer activity. It is used cyclically; take it for three weeks, stop for two, and so on. Regular use can decrease fertility in men. Some people are allergic.

- **Essiac** *(burdock root, sheep sorrel, turkey rhubarb, slippery elm bark)* is a blend of four herbs that are brewed as a tea. Since it has been used to successfully treat cancer, it is believed to have antitumor properties. Because there is a *candidiasis-cancer connection* (chapter 14), part of its effectiveness may be due to antifungal activity.

- **Garlic** *(Allium sativum)* has a variety of beneficial effects, including antibacterial, antiviral, antihelminthic, antifungal, anti-*Candida*, anti-inflammatory, anticoagulant, and some anticancer properties. Its active ingredient is *allicin*, a sulfur-containing compound. It also contains the antioxidant minerals *selenium* and *germanium*. Beneficial effects of its regular use include decreased blood pressure and lowered cholesterol (decreased LDL, increased HDL). **Warning:** more than 10 raw cloves a day can cause toxicity. In addition, breastfeeding women should limit their use because large amounts may instigate colic in their breastfed infant. Like all foods, sufferers can develop an allergy to garlic; bloating, gas, and other gut upsets occur no matter how little or much garlic is used.

- **Goldenseal** *(Hydrastis canadensius)* is not primarily used to treat candidiasis but has beneficial properties. Its active ingredient is *berberine*, a substance that has anti-inflammatory, antiparasitic, and some antifungal actions. It is also good for "colds" and the "flu," so it must have antibacterial and antiviral properties as well. It can be used as a douche for vaginal yeast infections. It should *not* be used for more than two weeks at a time. **Warnings:** People with hypertension should be cautious because it can increase blood pressure. It not recommended for pregnant women or nursing mothers. It may interfere with the metabolism of B vitamins.

- **Grapefruit seed extract** contains strong antifungal substances. It is active against many infectious invaders, notably *Candida*-species organisms, *Geotrichum*-species organisms, and hemolytic *E. coli*. It can be used orally in capsule form or liquid. The liquid is highly effective but tastes nasty; it frequently contains glycerin, which should be avoided by sufferers who are allergic. As a liquid, it is used to de-mold produce (chapter 20).

- **Horseradish** *(Armoracia lapathifolia)* has antifungal activity. It is a good expectorant and beneficial for digestion. Large amounts can cause diarrhea and excessive perspiration.
- **Kombucha** is an ancient, fungus-like, living organism that is usually made into a tea. It is thought to improve immunity. Being a fungus that is cross-reactive with disease-causing yeast and harmful molds, sufferers should be cautious to avoid triggering allergic reactions and inflammation. Homemade kombucha can be contaminated with mold. Commercially produced kombucha does contain some probiotics, but with so many better probiotic alternatives, there is no reason to consume it as its risks outweigh its benefits.
- **Licorice** *(Glycyrrhiza glabra)*, as an herb, has numerous beneficial effects, including anti-*Candida*, antibacterial, antiviral, anti-inflammatory, and anti-allergic activities. Its major ingredient is *glycyrrhizin*, which can increase cortisol and aldosterone levels. **Warning:** In large amounts, it can increase sodium retention and decrease potassium levels. It should not be used if you have hypertension, renal failure, or take heart medications. Women who suffer with notable PMS symptoms can experience increased water retention and bloating. Pregnant women and nursing mothers should not use it. Consequently, its risks frequently outweigh its benefits.
- **Lemon grass oil** *(Cymbopogon citratus)* has antifungal activity, notably against *Candida albicans*, *Candida tropicalis*, and *Aspergillus niger*. It has potent anti-inflammatory effects.
- **Myrtle oil** *(Myrtus communis)* is a potent, broad-spectrum antifungal agent with activity against a variety of fungi. It benefits pancreatic functioning and has antidiabetic actions.
- **Olive leaf** *(Olea europaea)* uses the leaf of an olive tree to make an extract. It decreases intestinal inflammation. It has antioxidant, anti-inflammatory, and anti-fibrotic properties.
- **Onion** *(Allium cepa)* is related to garlic; it has antifungal, antimicrobial, some antiviral, and some antitumor activities. It also beneficially affects

blood pressure and cholesterol levels. **Warning:** Nursing mothers should avoid this herb to prevent colic in their infants.

- **Oregano oil** *(Origanum vulgare)* greatly benefits most sufferers. Its major constituent is *carvacrol,* which kills numerous infectious invaders. It has strong antifungal activity, including killing *Candida* species, *Geotrichum* species, *Rhodotorula rubra, Saccharomyces cerevisiae, Aspergillus parasiticus,* and other harmful molds. It is also active against a diversity of parasites and harmful bacteria. In addition, it has antiviral, analgesic, and antispasmodic activity. Research reveals that it inhibits *Candida*-species biofilms.

- **Pau d'arco** *(Tabebuia impetiginosa, Tabebuia avellanedae, Tabebuia ipe)* is a South American herb with many names, including "Taheebo," "Lapacho," and "Ipe Roxo." Its active ingredient is *lapachol,* a substance with antifungal, anti-*Candida,* antiviral, antibacterial, antiparasitic, and some antitumor activities. It also has a blood sugar–lowering effect.

- **Pycnogenol** is extracted from pine bark. Although it is primarily known for its anti-inflammatory and antioxidant activity, it inhibits *cyclooxygenase,* a vital enzyme in fungi. As a result, it has antifungal activity. Unfortunately, large amounts are needed for it to be clinically effective, and its high cost makes this prohibitive.

- **Sage oil** *(Salvia officinalis)* improves intestinal inflammation and diarrhea, implying that it has antifungal activity, even though it is frequently used for parasites. It supports the adrenal glands, which are often impaired in sufferers, as well as their sex glands. Since it boosts mood and stimulates the mind, it has been used to treat depression and apathy. **Warning:** Since sage oil affects hormone activity, pregnant women and nursing mothers should not use it. Commercial or aromatherapy sage oil may contain increased amounts of *thujone,* a potentially toxic substance, and should *not* be used.

- **Tea tree oil** *(Melaleuca alternifolia)* has antifungal activity against *Candida* species. It is used *topically* for superficial *Candida* infections, including fluconazole-resistant organisms. It is given as an oral solution, to swish and expel, for infections of the mouth, and is used as a vaginal douche for infections. Some alternative physicians prescribe diluted tea tree oil for internal use. Research reveals that tea tree oil can cause allergic reactions in susceptible sufferers, especially in women who use it vaginally.

Until more research is done, use tea tree oil only for its recommended purposes. In other words, it should *not* be ingested.

- **Thyme oil** *(Thymus vulgaris)* has anti-inflammatory, antiviral, and antibacterial activity. Research reveals its anti-biofilm, anti-leishmanial, antiviral, and anticancer properties.
- **Undecylenic acid** is a medium-chain fatty acid obtained from castor oil with antifungal activity. It is similar to caprylic acid but is much more potent. It is often found as an ingredient in many anti-candidiasis products.
- **Wormwood** *(Artemisia absinthium)* has antioxidant, antiparasitic, antibacterial, antifungal, antiviral, and antitumor properties. Long-term use can have neurotoxic effects. **Warning:** It should not be used by pregnant women and nursing mothers or by people with hyperacidity and peptic ulcers.

Suggested Combinations

From clinical experience with candidiasis sufferers, if needed, these are recommended to be used after medication. They are usually taken as tinctures or essential oils two to three times a day. Their specific warnings are listed in their previous descriptions.

- **Broad-spectrum cleanse, especially against medication-resistant parasites:** *Artemisia annua,* black walnut *(Juglans nigra),* cat's claw *(Uncaria tomentosa),* olive leaf *(Olea europaea),* pau d'arco *(Tabebuia impetiginosa, Tabebuia avellanedae, Tabebuia ipe),* and *wormwood (Artemisia absinthium).*
- **Broad-spectrum cleanse, especially against the less prominent disease-causing yeast and many harmful molds:** cumin oil *(Cuminum nigrum),* myrtle oil *(Myrtus communis),* oregano oil *(Origanum vulgare),* and sage oil *(Salvia officinalis).*

HERBS TO SUPPORT YOUR LIVER AND KIDNEYS

Various herbs are valuable for candidiasis sufferers. Because of their synergistic activity, many herbs are more efficacious when combined. Although these are commonly used, others are available that are equally beneficial. For further information, contact an herbal-minded physician or other healthcare practitioner.

Liver Detoxification and Regeneration

Almost all sufferers have some magnitude of liver congestion and impairment. The liver is primarily an organ of metabolism, so compromised functioning causes metabolic disturbances. Since it is also responsible for detoxifying and eliminating harmful (toxic) substances, disturbed functioning allows toxins to accumulate within the body, with their adverse effects. Moreover, during an infection and/or the presence of inflammation, the liver can assist the immune system, but if it is prolonged, chronic candidiasis promotes impaired immunity (chapter 14). Therefore, before and during anti-candidiasis therapy, all sufferers should strengthen their liver. This can be accomplished with the use of one or more herbs.

The easiest choice is to take the four herbs listed below. Although some physicians only embrace milk thistle, studies show that it is more effective when administered with dandelion root and turmeric. Capsules are preferred, taken three times a day on an empty stomach. Generally, a course is one month followed by one to two weeks off, which prevents the liver from becoming dependent on the presence of these herbs. Liver detoxification can be repeated as often as, and as long as, necessary. In fact, patients with chronic hepatitis frequently use these herbs for life.

Your liver enzymes can be measured to assess the effectiveness of your herbal therapy. Commonly, markedly elevated levels will dramatically improve, even returning to normal, reflecting improved liver functioning. Occasionally, a sufferer's enzyme levels increase, and they eventually decrease; this seems to represent substantial tissue regeneration and cellular activity until the liver becomes normal. There are no adverse effects worthy of caution.

- **Beet root** *(Beta vulgaris)* protects the liver and effectively prevents fat from being deposited within it. By activating the liver enzymes and increasing bile, it increases the liver's detoxification abilities.

- **Dandelion** *(Taraxacum officinale)* protects the liver and gallbladder with its choleretic and cholagogue activities; it stimulates the flow of bile. It also has diuretic actions, making it good for hypertension, aids digestion, may protect against iron-deficiency anemia, and is used for urinary tract infections.

- **Milk thistle** *(Silybum marianum, Carduus marianus)* is a powerful liver rejuvenator; it primarily benefits hepatocellular reproduction and activity as well as increases the production of bile. It is also helpful for psoriasis. Its active ingredient is *silymarin*, containing *silybin*, *silydianin*, and *silychristin*, which have antioxidant activity, inhibit the formation of leukotrienes, and stimulates protein synthesis.

- **Turmeric** *(Curcuma longa)* is good for liver function or disease. It prevents gallbladder disease by its choleretic actions; it stimulates bile. It decreases blood cell aggregation as well as improves arthritis symptoms by the potent anti-inflammatory actions of *curcumin*. It has a synergistic effect when used with milk thistle.

Kidney Strengthening

Your kidneys are notable for their ability to excrete waste from your body. Blood passes through your kidneys where many harmful substances are filtered out and then eliminated within your urine. They have many other functions as well; for example, they regulate your electrolyte balance, maintain your acid-base balance (pH), regulate your blood pressure, produce certain hormones, convert inactive vitamin D to its active form, and maintain your body's water balance.

Years of improper eating, heavy drinking, exposure to harmful substances, recurring or chronic infections, stress, and so on take a toll on your kidney functioning. As an organ, they have a lot of resilience, so impairment may not even manifest until a significant amount is damaged. Given their vast importance, especially involving the elimination of wastes and toxins, your kidneys should be strengthened prior to and during therapy. However, compared to the liver, the kidneys take an incredible amount of time to improve, so extended therapy is frequently needed.

Many herbs benefit kidney functioning, either directly or indirectly, but they are not commonly used in Westernized holistic/integrative medicine and are beyond the discussion in this book. There is one herb, however, that is highly recommended:

- **Parsley** *(Petroselinum crispum)*—curly leaf, not Italian, or flat leaf—is a diuretic and highly regarded for its ability to stimulate the kidneys. It may assist in restoring kidney functioning, improving its metabolic activities. It is thought to clear the kidney's filtering apparatus and even dissolve kidney stones. Moreover, parsley settles the stomach, decreases congestion, cleanses the blood, and enhances immunity. It works best when prepared properly and consumed as a tea.

To prepare: Bring one quart of water to a boil. Turn off heat and add one quarter cup of fresh organic parsley (washed, demolded, and chopped). Cover and steep exactly eight minutes and then strain out the parsley. (Dried parsley tea bags can be used, but fresh is better.) Try to drink at least six to eight cups a day (48–64 ounces) during therapy.

Cardiovascular Strengthening

Many supplements and herbs can strengthen your cardiovascular system. If you suffer with cardiovascular disease of any type, you would be wise to take the supplements listed below prior to and during anti-candidiasis therapy. Since it is primarily a gut condition, malabsorption and nutritional deficiencies are exceedingly common among candidiasis sufferers. In turn, you are likely to be deficient in nutrients needed for the strength of your arteries and veins. In addition, given all the evidence (chapter 7), candidiasis sufferers with cardiovascular disease are exceedingly likely to have disease-causing yeast living within their blood, so taking these herbs helps alleviate inflammation within their circulatory systems.

At the minimum, try to take at least 1,000 mg of vitamin C and 1,000 mg of citrus bioflavonoids, three times a day. The following herbs are recommended and can be used continuously. In fact, when started early in life, their greatest benefit may be in preventing cardiovascular disease.

- **Bilberry** *(Vaccinium myrtillus)* helps preserve eyesight and prevent eye damage. It is useful for eyestrain, myopia, and poor night vision. It is used to treat retinopathy, macular degeneration, cataracts, glaucoma, and varicose veins as well as arthritis and gout. It contains *anthocyanosides*, which have many activities, including antiplatelet aggregation, smooth muscle relaxation, promotion of collagen synthesis and strengthening, and antioxidant and anti-inflammatory actions. In essence, it strengthens arteries and veins, especially the small blood vessels of the microvascular circulation.

- **Butcher's broom** *(Ruscus aculeatus)* strengthens arteries and veins. Its benefits include improving circulation within the hands and feet, decreasing edema within the legs and feet by constricting veins, anti-inflammatory activity (alleviates swelling of arthritis), improving the pain of hemorrhoids, and decreasing constipation.

- **Ginkgo** *(Ginkgo biloba)* assists the circulation, increases mental functioning and concentration, decreases the symptoms of tinnitus and vertigo, is an antioxidant that may slow aging and prevent cancer, relieves hemorrhoids, and may improve vascular forms of impotence. It is also used to treat asthma, respiratory disease, urticaria (hives), migraines-headaches, and depression. It should *not* be used by people who have a bleeding disorder or pregnant women.
- **Gotu kola** *(Centella asiatica)* increases circulation by strengthening the capillaries and veins. It assists wound healing, varicose veins, and scleroderma as well as recovery after childbirth. It decreases the pain and swelling of phlebitis as well as leg cramps, swelling, and tingling. It may increase memory and mental functioning and has a calming effect. It is a good expectorant, in addition to decreasing congestion from colds. It is a mild diuretic. It has a synergistic effect when taken with ginkgo. It should *not* be used by pregnant women or people with hyperthyroidism.

CHOOSING YOUR ARSENAL

Yes, you have candidiasis and want to treat it. What weapons do you choose? Ultimately, the choice depends on your infectious invaders you have. After the appropriate workup and thorough laboratory testing, your infectious invaders should be revealed. Although disease-causing yeast are your primary opponents, you may also have to combat harmful parasites, bacteria, molds, and/or viruses.

Unfortunately, many sufferers try to treat themselves. They often do not know the full extent of their infectious invaders or how to eradicate them completely. If you want to eliminate your infectious invaders and get well, you are cautioned to avoid self-treatment because it frequently leads to relapses that become more difficult to treat. Yet, this problem need not exist. Armed with the proper information, a candidiasis-minded physician will be able to choose your best arsenal of weapons.

Typically, the disease-causing yeast within your gut wall, tissues, and blood are initially addressed with a systemic antifungal medication. Days later, you would add a nonabsorbable antifungal agent to eliminate the disease-causing yeast that remain within the interior (lumen) of your gut. You might also need a second course with a different medication to move forward.

Once the bulk of your disease-causing yeast are eliminated, your other infectious invaders can be combated more easily. Antiparasitic agents, antibiotics, and antifungal herbs are more effective when they are sequentially employed, leaving little time for any infectious invader to reproduce and rise to prominence. Moreover, your less prominent disease-causing yeast should also be targeted with one or more antifungal herbs.

The good news is that, in most cases, your infectious invaders can be eliminated in less than two months. And even if it takes longer, the guidelines within this book will make it easier to avoid the detours that may arise as you travel along the Candidiasis Highway from illness to a town called "Wellness."

CHAPTER 20

The Anti-Candidiasis Diet

Warning: Diet is essential, but it is ***not*** an effective way to combat candidiasis by itself.

Diet is one of the biggest risk factors for candidiasis. Ingesting living disease–causing yeast or their spores directly adds them to your gastrointestinal tract and mucous membranes. Sugar and other carbohydrates you ingest feed them, keeping them well nourished. A lack of beneficial bacteria, whether absent from your diet or various substances killed them, allows disease-causing yeast to reproduce and colonize their surroundings.

Therefore, the anti-candidiasis diet must be an essential part of your therapy. Yes, soon after starting the diet most sufferers feel better—sometimes remarkably. This usually occurs because a deficiency of sugar slows the metabolism and mischief of their disease-causing yeast. The diet also eliminates a significant amount of disease-causing yeast and harmful mold *antigens*—allergy-inducing substances that promote inflammation and allergic reactions. In addition, the diet helps stabilize a sufferer's blood sugar concentration, preventing their sugar "highs" and "lows," which frequently calms their mood, increases their concentration, and so on.

Regardless of how good you initially feel, without appropriate antifungal therapy, your disease-causing yeast will eventually become more aggressive, invading deeper into your tissues and blood to survive and obtain nutrition; in fact, *Candida albicans* can alter its metabolism to use protein as an energy source when carbohydrates are scarce as well as increase its production of digestive enzymes that consume tissue protein (proteinases). So, if you do not receive antifungal therapy, you will eventually feel worse, and possibly even worse than you did before starting the diet. Yes, the diet is an integral part of anti-candidiasis therapy, but it is foolish to believe a dietary approach alone is the magical cure. Furthermore, the diet cannot address the presence of harmful parasites, bacteria, and molds. All these infectious invaders must be appropriately identified and eliminated.

On the other hand, you can learn everything there is to know about candidiasis and visit many candidiasis-minded physicians. You can receive the best antifungal medications, herbs, and other therapies. Yet, if you do not follow the diet, you are doomed to failure. By ingesting disease-causing yeast, knowingly or unknowingly, your diet helped you develop candidiasis in the first place. By consuming sugar and other carbohydrates, your diet encouraged the colonization of your disease-causing yeast, promoting your candidiasis. By eating the same way for years, you maintained and even advanced your candidiasis. Like it or not, the diet is an essential part of your anti-candidiasis therapy.

Okay, you are willing to follow the diet. How long must you adhere to it? Candidiasis is a complex and intricate illness. Since it usually develops over months to years, it is wishful thinking to hope it will disappear in a day or two. Depending on your symptoms and illness, therapeutic and dietary intervention can last from weeks to well over a year. Strict dietary adherence is mandatory, or you are likely to sabotage your own recovery.

The good news is that most sufferers usually follow the diet for two to six months. The length of time reflects the severity of your candidiasis—your infection, other infectious invaders, metabolic disarray, *neuroendocrine-immune connection* disturbances, and allergies. Obviously, if your immunity is impaired, you will benefit from a longer period of strict adherence and vigilance.

For the sufferers who eat anything and everything they desire, the diet can be a shock. It is not the easiest diet, but it is not the most difficult. It is all a matter of perspective and attitude. If you accept and believe the diet is beneficial, you will be less likely to deviate from it. In fact, some people enjoy the diet because they feel better when they adhere to it.

Yet, talk is cheap and saying something is easier than doing it. Many sufferers will be tempted to cheat. For example, what happens when you are at a dinner party? You are likely to think "I'll just have a taste," which escalates to "I'll just have a little bit," to "I'll just have a small serving," and onward to "If I only eat this today and go back on the diet tomorrow, I should be okay."

That might work for a common diet, unless you have food allergies and allergies to disease-causing yeast and molds within the foods you consume. Yes, you might get away with a digression or two if they are few and far between. However, you are only hurting yourself. At best, you are impeding your own progress. At worst, you are assuring your own failure. Regardless of the length of time on the diet, it is only a small amount of time in your entire life.

WHAT TO ABSOLUTELY AVOID!

Many candidiasis sufferers have difficulty understanding and adhering to an anti-candidiasis diet, especially when the recommendations are constantly changing or contradictory. The confusion exists because of misinformation and a lack of understanding. This has led to more than one version of the diet. To set the record straight, these are the things to avoid:

- **Living yeast, mold, or fungi!** These provide a source for their continuous colonization and overgrowth, promoting their infectious and allergic consequences.
- **Ingesting dead organisms!** In most cases, cooked or processed yeast-containing foods must not be eaten. These have antigens that promote allergies in sensitive sufferers, overt and subtle. In addition, some organisms can survive preparation in a desiccated or dormant state, so after ingestion, they can germinate, reproduce, and promote colonization.
- **Foods fermented with yeast!** These may contain living and/or dead organisms as well as yeast-produced toxins, metabolites (chemicals), antigens, and more.
- **Mold-containing foods!** Many molds have antigens that cross-react with yeast, promoting inflammation and allergies. Many sufferers have sensitivities to molds. Equally notable, these foods often contain harmful mold toxins that have adverse effects. Molds prefer to live in warm and moist environments, so when consumed, they can germinate, reproduce, and take up residence within your gut when one or more infectious invaders are killed. Some foods are notably moldy; do not assume that if it cannot be seen, it is not there.
- **Sugar!** This includes all forms of sugar as well as most complex carbohydrates that are degraded into sugar. It is also preferable to reduce your intake of dietary carbohydrates. Emphasis is shifted more toward proteins, vegetables, whole grains, and the "good" fats. Athletes and other active sufferers need more complex carbohydrates, whereas weight loss requires less. In fact, the diet is a highly effective weight-loss diet when carbohydrates are reduced or eliminated. In contrast, to maintain or gain weight, food containing "good" fats can be appropriately increased, especially avocados and the permitted nuts, as well as some whole grains. Vegetarians often have difficulty with this part of the diet because they emphasize carbohydrates, especially fruit; regardless, if they hope

to improve and regain their wellness, they must adjust their attitude and thinking to follow these guidelines.

- **Allergy-causing foods!** This decreases inflammation within the gut as well as throughout the entire body, aiding the healing process.
- **Vegetables, legumes, and whole grains that can be contaminated!** If it cannot be peeled or scrubbed, it must be soaked within grapefruit seed extract (or Clorox) and thoroughly rinsed. Vegetable washes are also recommended to decrease pesticide and chemical content. (De-molding is explained at the end of this chapter.) **Note:** Since they are often stored for long periods in less-than-perfect conditions, many grains tend to become moldy or yeasty, requiring de-molding. Depending on the conditions, especially the humidity, after grains are ground to flour, their mold count can increase remarkably.

EATING FOR WELLNESS

Some people approach a yeast-free diet as an all-or-nothing endeavor. Even though many separate the diet into several components, three phases are enough to achieve results.

The diet begins by eliminating. All foods containing yeast, dead or alive, are removed. In addition, anything with sugar and simple carbohydrates is forbidden. If a sufferer knows (or suspects) their allergic foods, they must be avoided. Even though most sufferers are initially frustrated, there is plenty to eat, but they must be willing to open their mind and taste buds.

Laziness or ambivalence should not get in the way; the diet does not have to be bland and boring. Numerous herbs and spices can readily be incorporated into the menu unless there are questionable ingredients. Preferably, these flavorings should be fresh; otherwise, there is a risk of mold contamination. Some dried spices can be used if they have not been stored for too long (although this is debatable).

The diet has an ample to abundant amount of protein. This includes virtually any animal or vegetable protein, depending on other added ingredients and a sufferer's allergies. Dietary protein is *essential* for the construction of bodily proteins and other vital substances. In addition, protein does not disturb the body's blood sugar concentration. The only exception involves kidney disease, where it may be necessary to avoid too much protein (obviously, this is determined by a physician who carefully assesses the risks versus benefits).

Unless weight loss is the goal, the body needs some dietary carbohydrates. Moderation is the key. Complex carbohydrates with a low-glycemic index are preferred, as they are more slowly absorbed, with less of an effect on glucose intolerance. Brown rice is the favorite; yes, it eventually breaks down into sugar, but it is not metabolized as rapidly as white rice or potatoes. Inflammatory bowel sufferers need less fiber and can try basmati rice. Yet, German candidiasis authorities disagree; they found that *Candida albicans* cultured on rice agar (a laboratory culture medium) forms *chlamydospores,* its dormant, cyst-like version. Even though the whole grain is different from its agar derivative, they eliminate rice from their anti-candidiasis diet to avoid the potential of ingesting these yeast "seeds," and their caution might seem warranted. In other words, the rice fed the yeast, but so do other carbohydrates. A good compromise is to extensively soak and de-mold the rice, and then rinse it thoroughly before cooking.

Most grains are okay, unless a sufferer is allergic; testing can verify this. Adverse grain reactions are not just due to an allergy or intolerance to the grain itself; yeast and molds, as well as their toxins, can grow on the grain and be the real cause of symptoms. De-molding grains can help reveal whether the problem is because of the grain or the yeast/mold growing on it.

Moreover, a serving should be proportional to a sufferer's body weight and activity. This is especially important for children. For example, one cup of brown rice for a child weighing 50 pounds is equivalent to three cups for a 150-pound adult.

Bread is another story. It is made with a commercial yeast called *Saccharomyces cerevisiae* (baker's and brewer's yeast), which was previously thought to be unable to cause disease. On the contrary, evidence indicates that this yeast can invade into tissue, so consuming brewer's yeast supplements must be avoided. Regardless of whether it is alive or dead, *Saccharomyces cerevisiae* antigenically cross-reacts with some *Candida*-species organisms. This means that exposure to this yeast is highly likely to induce allergies and inflammation, even if it has been killed by baking (or fermenting). So, bread is initially forbidden.

Note: A different strain of *Saccharomyces cerevisiae* is within old-fashioned, naturally leavened sourdough bread in small amounts (about 1 percent). Under a microscope, this "wild" strain of yeast has a different shape than its commercially used cousin. More important, this strain is acid-tolerant (adapted to an acid environment) and happily coexists with the beneficial lactic acid–producing bacteria and acetic acid–producing bacteria that comprise the 99 percent of the organisms within this type of bread. Even though this strain may not be disease-causing, anyone with allergies to yeast is wise to avoid it. However, some sufferers may be allowed to have yeast-free, naturally fermented sourdough bread, especially after the first phase of the diet is complete. In fact, sooner or later, despite the best efforts, some yeast is going to recolonize a sufferer's gut. The key is to favor the presence of the helpful species and strains of yeast, not their disease-causing relatives. Because they compete with the disease-causing yeast for space, once a sufferer's allergies have been treated, it would be wise to regularly eat some yeast-free, naturally fermented sourdough bread.

Limiting complex carbohydrates is vital. Although yeast prefer simple carbs (like sugar), they will use complex carbs when deprived, as many are degraded into simple carbs. Decreasing the "enemy's" supply of carbs limits their productivity and inhibits their proliferation. In addition, this minimizes any symptoms that are related to glucose intolerance. Blood sugar disturbances are associated with a diversity of symptoms and illness, primarily and secondarily. These decrease and/or disappear when a sufferer's diet shifts from carbs toward proteins and vegetables. In addition, fats must not be avoided, especially the "good" or "healthy" ones. Sufferers unable to tolerate complex carbs may need some honey to prevent weight loss.

You must eliminate alcohol-containing beverages. These and many drugs are detoxified by the liver. Chronic candidiasis is highly stressful to the liver. Consuming alcohol with compromised liver functioning is far from wise and occasionally hazardous. Eliminating alcohol is vital while taking a systemic antifungal medication because the die-off of yeast stresses the body. Since many alcohol-containing beverages contain sugar, yeast, and mold, they feed yeast and induce allergic inflammation. *Candida albicans* and other fungi make *gliotoxin*, a substance that inhibits *alcohol dehydrogenase*, the liver enzyme that degrades alcohol, so ingesting even small amounts of alcohol can impair liver functioning and lead to trouble.

Finally, the diet appears to allow moderate amounts of fats. Even though current thinking claims a low-fat diet is healthy, everyone needs *essential* fatty acids. In fact, research reveals a diet high in "good" fats is beneficial. The monounsaturated fats are emphasized. Some examples are olive oil, avocado, almonds, and flax seed oil. Studies indicate that these good fats lower cholesterol levels. Moreover, they are required to produce hormones and other vital bodily substances. Lecithin (a combination of phospholipids) is a component of every cell membrane within the body and should be consumed daily (it is in several foods, but supplements are easier).

Warning: Since some vegetables tend to be highly moldy and must be avoided, oils made from them are just as likely to contain molds and their toxins and should similarly be eliminated—examples include corn oil and peanut oil, but other oils may be contaminated.

DIETARY CONSIDERATIONS

Your dietary choices contribute to your nutritional well-being. If your diet lacks one or more essential nutrients, it will cause deficiencies and metabolic disarray. Sparse or excessive consumption favors nutritional derangements. Even a "perfect" diet does not guarantee optimal nutrition because gut disturbances can promote inadequate digestion, insufficient absorption, and/or poor utilization. Therefore, nutritional deficiencies must be corrected, and the addition of supplements is considered highly valuable. A candidiasis-minded physician will usually provide a list of recommended supplements.

Basically, the diet is high in protein, low in carbohydrates, and moderate in fats. Although this approach starves the disease-causing yeast, it is integral to managing glucose intolerance, metabolic disturbances, and allergies. For many sufferers, this means consuming three well-balanced meals daily. In addition, certain vegetables and high-protein snacks may be eaten between meals and after dinner. Severely hypoglycemic patients may benefit from as many as six smaller "feedings" a day. The time interval between meals and snacks provides a relatively constant source of proteins, fats, and some carbohydrates. You should eat enough to avoid hunger. Breakfast is important, so it should not be skipped. Thoroughly chewing food and eating slowly assists digestion. Pancreatic enzyme supplements are often helpful.

Vegetarians often feel cursed by the diet because they usually consume an abundance of carbohydrates, especially fruit, and a paucity of protein. This explains why many vegetarians develop candidiasis in the first place. They must learn to shift their diet toward proteins. In addition, vegetarian diets are consistently high in *phytases*, found in soy and soy products, that inhibit the absorption of essential minerals, promoting deficiencies that exacerbate ill health.

Since sugar, processed starches, and most complex carbohydrates are initially forbidden, all food labels must be read with caution. Many foods contain some form of sweetener. It is easy to be fooled or misled. Ignorance is not an excuse. You must be responsible for your health and know the nutritional content of the foods you consume. Please read labels to obtain the information, but realize that mistakes are often made or something is purposely omitted. Be suspicious: if it tastes sweet, it probably contains sweetener. When in doubt, leave it out!

Although a small percentage of people are legitimately "salt sensitive," salt intake should be decreased, especially for sufferers with fluid retention, high blood pressure, and/or heart problems. Despite this recommendation, sufferers with low blood pressure may consume too little salt and might benefit from more. (When in doubt, ask your physician.)

GUIDELINES DURING ALL PHASES

Do not panic! There is plenty to eat, especially if you are willing to adapt your taste buds to new flavors and textures. Many candidiasis cookbooks are available, and their recipes will provide ample variety to your meals. Yet, keep in mind, not all the books are in alignment with the information within this book, so please adjust the ingredients accordingly.

Note: Follow these guidelines unless you are allergic to something specific!

Proteins

This includes free-range meat and poultry, deep sea fish from far offshore, and certain farm-raised fish. Organic is preferred. Meat, fish, shellfish, fowl, and eggs are excellent sources of protein. Since body fat is where animals tend to accumulate and store consumed chemicals, hormones, and toxins, lean cuts of meat are recommended. Note: Just because a particular protein is listed, it does not mean that it must be eaten. Rather, these are just choices.

Fish: Fresh water and saltwater varieties. Canned is *not* recommended, but if consumed, it should be drained and rinsed thoroughly. Eating too much seafood may provide toxic heavy metals and numerous chemical-plastic toxins. Any harmful substance dumped into water finds its way into seafood. So, eat in moderation (a couple of times per week).

Shellfish: Abalone, clams, crab, lobster, mussels, oysters, scallops, and shrimp.

Fowl: Chicken, Cornish game hen, duck, goose, pheasant, squab, and turkey. The skin is almost all fat and not recommended. Also, the dark meat has a higher amount of fat.

Organ meats: Brains, gonads, heart, liver, lung, pancreas, and sweetbreads. Our society has an overt aversion to these proteins. Yet, they are relatively inexpensive and may be better nutritional sources than muscle meats. They are often used in soups and stews as well as mixed with chopped meat and cooked.

Meats: Muscle cuts like chopped meats, chops, roasts, steaks, etc.

Eggs: A complete protein. If you are concerned about fat, yolks may be removed, but this decreases the bioavailability of protein and the egg's total nutritional benefits.

Avoid: Processed, pickled, and smoked fish and meats. Examples include bologna, corned beef, hot dogs, lunch meats, pastrami, salami, sausages, and similarly prepared foods.

Nuts and Seeds

Nuts and seeds are good sources of protein and are usually high in monounsaturated fats. Limit to 2 tablespoons or less per day, unless allowed more. It is easy to overindulge, so be conscious of consumption. Since preshelled or processed nuts often have mold or yeast on them, it is better to eat fresh nuts from the shell. Their nutritional value (in order): pignolias (pine nuts), Brazil nuts (butternuts), pumpkin or squash seeds, sesame seeds, almonds, walnuts, pecans, toasted soybeans, sunflower seeds, and hazel nuts (filberts). Others nuts and seeds are not permitted! (For example, cashews, peanuts, and pistachios are often high in mold and their toxins.) If no sweetener is added, nut butters of the permitted nuts are allowed in limited quantities.

Dairy Products

All cow's milk and milk products, especially cheese, cottage cheese, kefir, sour cream, and yogurt are *forbidden* in the initial phase (except clarified butter). If tolerated, they may be added back to the diet (except cheese). The best products are unprocessed. When allowed, goat milk is okay. Some sufferers may be allowed to have heavy cream, while others can eat some yogurt or kefir.

Vegetables

Several vegetables are great sources of protein. They are separated by their carbohydrate content: 3 percent, 6 percent, and 10 percent. Sufferers may consume unlimited amounts of the 3 percent and 6 percent vegetables. The 10 percent group must be limited to one cup per day. In addition, the starchy vegetables are mostly carbohydrate and should be avoided; if it is not listed, it is not allowed. Note: If you have mold allergies, avoid vegetables that cannot be peeled or scrubbed, unless they are de-molded before consumption. (De-molding is explained at the end of this chapter.)

3 percent: Bean sprouts, beet greens, celery, chicory, Chinese cabbage, chives, cucumbers, endive, escarole, fennel, gherkins, lettuce, parsley, radishes, rhubarb (raw), and watercress.

6 percent: Asparagus, bamboo shoots, broccoli, cabbage (raw), cauliflower, chard, collard greens (raw), dandelion greens, eggplant, green onions, kale, leeks, lettuce, mustard greens, okra, peppers, rhubarb (cooked), spinach, summer squash, tomato (a fruit), turnip greens, turnips, water chestnuts, and zucchini.

10 percent: Artichoke, beans (green/string or wax), Brussels sprouts, cabbage (cooked), carrots (raw), chervil, collard greens (cooked), garden cress, kohlrabi, onion (raw), and rutabaga.

Higher carbohydrate: Beans or legumes; black beans, black-eyed peas, chickpeas (garbanzo beans), fava beans, Great Northern beans, kidney beans, lentils, lima beans, navy beans, peas, pinto beans, soybeans, and white beans. These should be avoided until the later stages and must be de-molded before consumption.

Avoid: Beets, corn, mushrooms, pickles, potatoes, relishes, sweet potatoes, winter squash, and yams. These are high in carbohydrates and/or fermented. Carrots, onions, and tomatoes should be consumed sparingly.

Cereal Grains

Grains are often referred to as cereals, which are the seeds of grasses, such as wheat, rye, oats, rice, and barley. Although they are an important source of nutrition and fiber, they are initially excluded because of their carbohydrate content and potential for allergies. Sooner or later, whole grains are gradually introduced. These include barley, buckwheat (kasha), chia seeds, flaxseed, millet, oats, quinoa, rice, rye, sesame, and wheat. Unfortunately, grains are a prominent source of food allergies for many sufferers.

If a sufferer is allergic, a specific grain and its products must be avoided. Rotation of grains may be necessary to decrease or eradicate symptoms. Labels must be read to ensure there are no restricted ingredients. More important, the portions of these foods must be limited to avoid excess carbohydrate consumption.

Whole grains: Amaranth, barley, basmati rice, brown rice (short-, medium-, and long-grain), buckwheat groats (kasha), bulgur wheat, couscous, cracked wheat, millet, oats, quick-cooking rice, quinoa, soft wheat, spring wheat, and wild rice. These should be rinsed thoroughly with water before cooking, and de-molding is recommended.

Breads: These must be yeast-free and include chapati, flour tortillas, matzah, soda, and sourdough. They must also be sweetener-free. Note: Some sourdough breads contain yeast. Corn tortillas are not permitted.

Cereals, unsweetened: (cold) corn, millet, puffed wheat, rice, shredded wheat, (hot) bear mush, brown rice cream, cracked wheat, creamy rice, oat bran, oatmeal, and seven grain hot cereal. Note: Most commercial products contain yeast and sweeteners and must be avoided. They may also be contaminated with mold.

Whole grain pasta: Artichoke, buckwheat (soba), rice (wheat-free), and whole wheat. Note: Most pasta is yeast-free but made from refined flour, so allergies must be considered. Corn pasta is not allowed.

Crackers: If they are yeast-free, these can be consumed in moderation. Yeast-free versions include rice cakes, rye, wheat, and various other whole grains. Once again: consider allergies.

Fats and Oils

Fats and oils are permitted in reasonable amounts. If a sufferer has an elevated blood cholesterol level, some caution is warranted. Yet, the human body requires a certain amount of essential fatty acids. Flax seed oil (liquid or capsules) is a relatively inexpensive choice. Others include almond, macadamia, olive, safflower, sesame, sunflower, and walnut.

Several vegetables tend to be highly moldy and must be avoided, so oils made from them are just as likely to contain mold and mold toxins and should similarly be eliminated (obvious examples are corn oil and peanut oil, but other oils may be similarly contaminated).

Beverages

Although most foods contain water, everyone needs fluids for adequate hydration. Increased amounts of fluids must be ingested in hotter or drier climates. Generally, a sufferer is well hydrated when their urine is almost clear. Conversely, if it is noticeably yellow, they are not consuming enough fluids (unless they take lots of B vitamins). Caffeinated drinks and alcohol act as diuretics, causing a loss of water and eventually dehydration.

Water: This is nature's best fluid. Unfortunately, tap water is often a disaster, and most water filters are virtually worthless. The best filters may have a pore size of 5.5 microns and remove 99.99 percent of almost everything. Since microplastics have been found within water bottled in plastic, it should be avoided. In contrast, spring water or imported water is okay when it is stored within glass. Anything else is a compromise.

Clear broth: Choose only organic broth for use in preparing sauces or soup.

Herbal teas: Teas without caffeine (as opposed to decaffeinated) are okay but may be contaminated with molds and fungi. Teas made from bark and twigs are best for avoiding mold.

Coffee: Coffee (including decaffeinated) is made from beans. It may be contaminated with mold and should be avoided. People who insist on having coffee should de-mold their beans, dry them in an oven, grind, and then brew.

Carbonated soft drinks: These typically have an abundance of sugar and other ingredients that may promote problems in candidiasis sufferers. Moreover, since artificial sweeteners are not recommended, diet drinks should also be avoided. Naturally flavored carbonated beverages without sweeteners can be consumed in moderation.

Avoid: Alcohol-containing drinks, caffeine-containing beverages, cider, cocoa, fruit juices and drinks, rice milk, soy milk, and other similar products. (Caffeine stimulates the release of adrenal hormones, which elevates blood sugar levels and nourishes any yeast within the tissues and blood.)

Note: Although prepared vegetable juices are not allowed, home juicing is okay, depending on the ingredients used.

Condiments

Salad dressing should be homemade from fresh herbs or spices, mono- or polyunsaturated oils, and lemon juice. Vinegar and vinegar-containing condiments are *forbidden* because they contain yeast. A large percentage of sauces and condiments are made with some form of sweetener and should not be consumed.

Avoid: Catsup/ketchup, mustard, Worcestershire sauce, Accent spice brand or any spice that contains MSG, soy sauces, pickles and pickled vegetables, relishes, sauerkraut, horseradish, mincemeat, and tamari. Most commercial mayonnaise is made with vinegar and some sugar and should therefore be avoided.

Fruits

Although a source of nutrition, fruits are abundant in sugar. They are not permitted until the disease-causing yeast are eliminated. Fresh raw fruits are better than cooked or processed because their nutrients are more vitalized, as they have not been pasteurized nor do they contain preservatives. The permitted fruits are listed by carbohydrate content below. All servings are one small piece or a half cup. Even when they are feeling well again, at most, sufferers should have two to three servings a day from the 7 percent or 10 percent groups or one serving from the 15 percent group. Any fruit that is not peeled must be washed thoroughly, and de-molded if needed.

7 percent: Avocado and rhubarb.

10 percent: Cantaloupe, casaba melon, coconut (fresh), cranberry (raw), fruit salad (no grapes), gooseberry, honeydew melon, lemon (juice of two fresh), muskmelon, and strawberry.

15 percent: Apple, apricot, blackberry, cherry, dewberry, elderberry, grapefruit (one half), loganberry, orange, peach, plum, raspberry, pineapple (two slices), tangerine, and youngberry.

Note: Banana contains 23 percent carbohydrates and is not permitted. Fruits that are frozen, dried, or packed in syrup are forbidden.

Sweeteners

Are artificial sweeteners really "a government plot to control our lives" as one patient succinctly put it? Well, maybe not, but there is substantial evidence that artificial and/or refined sweeteners are not harmless. If you do consume them, use only small amounts.

Avoid: Dextrin, dextrose, maltodextrin, malt, barley malt, fructose, glucose, galactose, lactose, maltose, brown sugar, invert sugar, confectioners' sugar, raw sugar, turbinado sugar, white sugar, hexitol, mannitol, sorbitol, sucrose corn syrup, corn syrup solids, corn sweeteners, corn starch, beet sugar, date sugar, molasses, sucanat, honey, maple syrup, rice syrup, and other syrups. All of these are sugar in one form or another. Any prepared food has the potential to contain sugar. If it is not listed here, do not assume it is allowed. Once again, when in doubt, leave it out!

FOODS TO AVOID

The following foods contain yeast and/or molds and should not be consumed:

Anything fermented: Vinegar (all types) and vinegar-containing condiments (examples: catsup/ketchup, mayonnaise, olives, pickles, sauerkraut, horseradish, commercial salad dressings, coleslaw, potato salad, and more), wine, beer, and anything made with these foods. Also, soy sauce, tamari, and miso. Sour cream and other sour milk products are not permitted.

Yeast breads, pastries, and raised baked goods: Breads, crackers (and crumbs), croutons, stuffing, pizza crust, rolls, buns, biscuits, pretzels, doughnuts, cakes (and mixes), pies, cookies, and pastries. Although "salt-raising" breads do not contain yeast, they are raised by bacteria and should be avoided. In phase two, whole grain "soda" breads are acceptable, but only if they are made without sugar (most are made with it).

Malt products: All malted milk drinks, cereals, candies. (Malt is a common food ingredient.)

Nondairy substitutes: May contain a form of sugar or other undesirable ingredients.

Mushrooms: These are fungi that produce toxins and create allergic reactions in sensitive people. This also includes truffles.

Sprouts: The sprouting process encourages the growth of molds.

Dried, smoked, fermented, or cured foods: All contain or have been exposed to bacteria, yeast, or molds.

Processed foods: Especially canned soups and frozen foods containing citric acid and/or MSG (byproducts of fermentation).

Hydrolyzed vegetable protein: It is produced by fermentation.

Nuts, seeds, and beans: Be wary; these are often warehoused and exposed to molds.

Leftovers: Cool extra food as quickly as possible. Refrigerate temporarily and then freeze. This retards the growth of undesirable organisms. Frequent refrigerator cleaning is prudent.

Dried herbs and spices: These are often infested with mold. Fresh is greatly preferred.

Anything labeled "enriched": These usually contain B-complex vitamins originally manufactured by yeast.

Supplements not "yeast-free": Most are, but unless it says so, do not assume it is.

Over-the-counter medications: Many of these preparations contain sugar in one form or another.

PHASING IN

Phase one may seem extreme, but when it is combined with antifungal therapy, the disease-causing yeast (as well as molds) are more easily killed when the appropriate medication is used. In return, this gives the gut time to heal, which is especially important in sufferers with bowel problems. In addition, eradicating the yeast-related infection alleviates stress on the body's nervous, endocrine (hormones), and immune systems. Typically, this permits the resolution of a variety of metabolic (chemical) disturbances over time. Eliminating the infection places a sufferer in the strongest position for recovery. So, phase one is the most extreme level of the diet, and it is usually a waste of time to start anywhere else.

Phase two, the challenge phase, tests a sufferer's progress. Allergic foods are reintroduced on a rotation basis to determine tolerance—usually, no sooner than every fourth day. In fact, allergic foods often become less allergic over time. After the gut wall becomes healthy, problematic foods cannot leak through it and will be appropriately digested and absorbed; they are reduced to particles small enough to be tolerated and will not induce allergies.

Phase One

The initial phase (one) of treatment allows these foods (The FAVER Diet):

Fish: All types of fin fish. Be cautious about eating swordfish and other fish that have notable levels of toxic heavy metals, especially mercury. Shellfish are permitted if someone is not allergic.

All meats: Almost any fresh meat, including chicken, beef, pork, turkey, duck, goat, venison, rabbit, frog legs, pheasant, quail, lamb, and veal. The meat must not be dried, smoked, pickled, or cured in any way. Any form of processing is certain to add sugar.

Vegetables: Most fresh and frozen vegetables are okay unless a sufferer is allergic. Starchy vegetables (like potatoes, rice, and beans) must be limited. Sugary vegetables (like beets, carrots, corn, and peas) are eliminated. Vegetable soups are okay, if prepared at home. Yeast and sugar are sometimes used in the recipes of commercially produced soups and vegetables. Any vegetable that cannot be peeled or scrubbed should be de-molded.

Eggs: Unless allergies are a problem, most people can eat as many as they want, but moderation is wise. These can be prepared almost any way, but adding cheese is forbidden.

Rice and rice cakes: These are a substitute for bread. Limit to two or three rice cakes each meal or one-half cup of cooked brown rice. Whole grain rice is soaked and de-molded, and then rinsed before cooking. According to German candidiasis-minded physicians, rice and rice cakes should be eliminated, which may be a smart choice for some sufferers.

Beverages: Any mineral or spring water is good. Because of their contamination with mold, coffee (including decaffeinated) and many soft drinks (especially colas) must be avoided. Teas and herbal teas are problematic because they are often contaminated as well.

Cow's Milk and milk products: Dairy should be excluded because of its carbohydrates, yeast and mold, and antigens. During this stage, the only dairy product allowed is clarified butter, which is almost pure oil (unlikely to trigger an allergic reaction).

Phase Two

Foods are added back one at a time to identify food allergies. Grains may be included, choosing from oatmeal, oat bran, millet, rye, and buckwheat. The original form is preferred (not as a bread or other product); this is the only way to isolate a grain to determine if it causes an allergic reaction, as opposed to some other problematic ingredients. A small portion should be eaten by itself early in the day, and then wait to see if you have symptoms. If none arise, a similar portion is consumed at lunch, and so on. If nothing unusual develops within 48 to 72 hours, the food is not likely to be an allergic culprit.

Low-gluten grains should be added back first: millet, buckwheat, quinoa, amaranth, oat bran, and rice bran. If these are tolerated, the gluten grains (wheat, rye, and oats) can be tried. Once a grain is shown to be innocent of causing allergies, some of its yeast-free products can be tried.

Depending on a sufferer's allergies, permitted cereals may be eaten at breakfast, but protein and/or fat should be added to slow its absorption and any adverse blood sugar effects. (If allowed, some sufferers consume small amounts of organic, plain, sugar-free yogurt or kefir.)

Remember, portion control is crucial. Never exceed more than one cup of grain or its equivalent at any meal. If symptoms are experienced, the amounts must be decreased. If problems are still evident, a return to phase one for two to four weeks is usually needed before a sufferer should attempt phase two again.

Phase Three

Most sufferers rush to this stage too quickly, so it is usually the area of major difficulty. A sufferer must be stable and feeling well before attempting this stage. This is where, depending on preferences, fruits and sugary vegetables are consumed in moderation. In addition, previously allergic foods are rotated in on a trial basis.

FOR VEGETARIANS

A vegetarian approach to a yeast-free diet takes longer to achieve results and is more tedious. Moreover, evidence indicates that people with blood type O and those of Mediterranean heritage benefit from some fish or poultry in their diets. Unless this conflicts with religious or other deep-seated beliefs, these should be consumed during phase one. Otherwise, the only difference in the vegetarian diet is the choice of proteins. These include eggs, tofu, lentils, soaked and sprouted beans (three times per week), and nuts and seeds (or unsweetened nut butters). Sufferers may also purchase an unsweetened (or artificially sweetened) protein powder that can be made into a drink. Note: Beans, seeds, and nuts must be de-molded before ingestion. Also note: Any soy product is a strong source of allergies, in addition to containing an abundance of *phytases*, which inhibit the absorption of many essential nutrients.

IS IT POSSIBLE TO EAT OUT?

Of course! Just order carefully. Skip the alcoholic beverages. Ask for oil and lemon juice on the salad or, better yet, skip the salad and ask for cucumber slices or another peeled vegetable. Order entrées prepared without marinades, sauces, gravies, sugars, mushrooms, wheat as a thickener, or other detrimental ingredients. The safest choice is always broiled or plain items. Depending on the choice, steamed vegetables are fine. Ignore the bread, crackers, and dessert. It might be helpful to repeat this phrase, "I'm eating to get well."

Always be vigilant. If a restaurant appears unclean, it probably is! In certain situations, the odds of obtaining a parasite or harmful bacteria are rather high. Unfortunately, improper handling of food leads to a high transmission rate of these disease-causing invaders. Certain foods are more likely to transmit disease than others. Foods that are improperly handled or washed, like salads, are more suspect than their cooked counterparts. Does it mean someone never eats these foods in a restaurant again? Yes, if wellness is the goal, because reinfection is one of the greatest causes of relapse.

IF YOUR CHILD IS BEING TREATED

Children can just as easily follow the diet. Unless they are old enough, they cannot do it on their own or lack the self-control to follow the diet.

Watching their friends eat anything they want does not help. Advertising that pushes junk food and drinks makes matters worse. So, children usually consume foods loaded with sugar, disease-causing yeast, harmful molds, chemicals, and more. These can negate the benefits and effectiveness of the diet. Clearly, when other children are eating anything and everything, a child needs to understand why a special diet must be followed, especially when they are suffering with candidiasis.

Suppose you have a picky eater? Rather than feeling guilty or sorry and giving into your child's demands, be firm and insist that your child eats for wellness. Your child may temporarily become angry and obstinate, but they are unlikely to harbor long-lasting hate. A good parent is loving, caring, and sets firm boundaries.

You must avoid rewarding good behavior with sweets, especially early on. Later, if sweets are allowed, the portion must be adjusted to your child's size. For example, a small child eating one apple is equivalent to an adult eating three. Parents wonder why their children are overweight; in fact, there are more overweight children in the United States than ever. For the most part, fat is *not* the major cause of obesity. The current trend toward an abundance of carbohydrates, especially sugary foods, is making children fat, as excess dietary sugar and carbohydrates turn into body fat. Moreover, excess sugar promotes blood sugar disturbances, leading to problems like attention deficit disorder, with or without hyperactivity (chapter 12).

The ingestion of sugar has become an epidemic. It is worse for children because sugar seems to be in almost everything they eat. Not all the blame rests with parents, as this problem involves a great deal of peer pressure and brainwashing by advertisers. Therefore, it is essential for adults to educate children about diet. Children must understand that their diet contributed to their ill health and it will again if they eat indiscriminately.

STAYING ON THE DIET

You have candidiasis. You want to eliminate it, so you start an anti-candidiasis program. Like it or not, you are forced to be on the anti-candidiasis diet. Unfortunately, this is how many sufferers approach the diet. They consider it to be a chore or a curse. Keep in mind, you do not have to do the diet. You do not have to get well. You can stay sick. No one is forcing you. Getting well is a choice. Starting anti-candidiasis therapy is a choice. Staying on an anti-candidiasis diet is a choice. You might think, "I have no choice." Yet, you do have a choice. You can choose to stay sick. In contrast, if you choose to get well, you must take responsibility for your health, including your diet. If you choose to get well, following the diet is a commitment you must make. You should come to peace with your choice. It will make your time on the diet all that much easier.

The diet is a vital component of an entire anti-candidiasis program. If you want to regain your wellness, a yeast-free, mold-free, sugar-free diet is essential. You must avoid ingesting foods and beverages that contain disease-causing yeast and harmful molds, whether they are alive or dead. Eliminating sugar and decreasing your intake of complex carbohydrates will slow the mischief and metabolism of your infectious invaders as well as help stabilize your blood glucose concentration. This, alone, is likely to make you feel better, especially if you have severe allergies to disease-causing yeast and harmful molds. More specifically, an anti-candidiasis diet will decrease inflammation and allergic reactions within your gut wall and tissues, which will enable your gastrointestinal tract to heal. Not only will this improve your digestion and absorption of nutrients, but it will also make it easier to eliminate your infectious invaders. Taste buds aside, there are many benefits to the diet.

Although you may find the recommendations unpalatable, they are still important to follow. Since your diet helped to get you sick in the first place, you must eat carefully to regain your health. This is critical to a therapeutic success. Initially, this means absolute adherence. Yet, in time and with improvement, your diet can be liberalized. Foods can be reintroduced slowly, one at a time. Eventually, after your infectious invaders and allergies are gone, you can return to a "normal" diet. When you are done and look back, the amount of time you spent on the diet was not that long.

If you are a candidiasis sufferer and do not follow the diet, do not expect success. You may even be wasting your time as well as making it more difficult to eradicate your candidiasis in the future. Fortunately, most sufferers have incredible improvements and attain substantial benefits when they follow the diet. Although it may require some patience and an adjustment in attitude, following the diet is certain to be well worth your time and effort.

De-Molding Vegetables, Beans, Fruits, and Nuts

1. Add 20 to 30 drops of grapefruit seed extract (or 1 capful of Clorox) to each 1 gallon of (preferably filtered) water.
2. Soak items for 20 to 30 minutes.
3. Rinse thoroughly, preferably in filtered water.

De-Molding Grains

1. Soak the grain in filtered or (glass) bottled water until it hydrates (absorbs water).
2. Add 20 to 30 drops of grapefruit seed extract, similar to above. Do not use Clorox because it can be absorbed by the grains!
3. Soak for 20 to 30 minutes.
4. Rinse well, preferably in filtered water.
5. Cook in filtered or (glass) bottled water.

Vegetable Preparation for Those with Gut Symptoms

This type of preparation, which is especially good for IBS and IBD suffers, will make digestion easier and allow more nutrients to be absorbed by the body:

1. Peel, scrub, or de-mold vegetable.
2. Steam until soft.
3. Purée in food processor or with hand processor; add oil or clarified butter as tolerated.
4. Put servings into parchment paper, insert into freezer bags, seal, flatten, and freeze.
5. Remove, thaw, and serve as desired. Freezing and thawing break the cells, increasing digestibility and nutritional content.

CONCLUSION

A Word to Physicians, the Medically Wise & the Curious

Dear fellow physicians, healthcare practitioners, and anyone interested:

Do you have patients with chronic or recurring medical maladies? Obviously, or the incidence of illness would be decreasing, not increasing. Have you had great success in treating them? It is doubtful because the number of prescriptions written each year continues to escalate. If patients were truly getting better, the use of medication would be decreasing, not increasing.

Although many patients do benefit from using one or more medications, there is a big difference between alleviating symptoms and curing illness. Medications have their intended purpose, but their persistent use means that the cause of an illness is not being corrected. As a result, most people who suffer with chronic and recurring medical maladies experience only mediocre improvements with a drug-oriented approach. Their symptoms tend to wax and wane. They get worse and then better. On and on it goes. More disturbing, patients who have little to no improvement are often prescribed additional medication. They continue to remain sick, developing one problem after another, like a car stuck spinning its wheels in the mud.

This is not about the medical care someone receives after being injured in a car accident. For the most part, acute injuries and illnesses are well managed by mainstream medicine. The medical profession deserves high praise because, in many cases, the outcome of their efforts seems almost miraculous.

In contrast, people who suffer with chronic and recurring medical maladies are not as fortunate because the incidence of these illnesses is greater than ever and rapidly increasing. Some physicians claim this is the result of modern living, including stress, drugs, rock-and-roll, and so on. Other physicians say it is a byproduct of more people living on this planet as well as our increased life span. Some health professionals add, as our ability to identify and diagnose illness has become more precise and refined, mainstream medicine understands more problems and their subtleties. Regardless, an intricate dissection misses the point. Even with the increase in medical sophistication, more people are joining the ranks of the chronically ill.

Disturbingly, many patients go to their physicians and leave, feeling like they were improperly treated. Often, they are told, "You should learn how to live with your condition." Yes, human beings are known for their great ability to adapt. Yes, this ability has elevated us from cave dwellers to skyscraper inhabitants. Yes, people can learn to live with their condition, but why should they have to? With all the advances in medicine, more cures should exist.

Most physicians truly believe they are doing all they can for their patients. They hope that someday every problem will be better understood, and a medication or vaccine will exist to cure it. This thinking has evolved from a cause-and-effect approach to a disease-and-illness approach. If a cause exists, someone will search until a cure is found. The goal is the "magic bullet," a cure aimed at a specific problem. This philosophy is mostly the result of medical specialization, and it has led to the use of symptom-specific pharmaceutical agents.

In fact, true wellness should not require the use of *any* medication. In contrast to mainstream medical thinking, treating candidiasis regularly corrects a variety of medical maladies, frequently decreasing a patient's need for medication or eliminating it entirely.

IDIOPATHIC ILLNESSES

Even though modern medicine has achieved incredible sophistication in its scientific thought and methods, there are a multitude of diseases, disorders, illnesses, conditions, and syndromes that have elusive, unidentifiable, or mysterious origins. By present-day scientific standards, this seems negligent. After all, researchers can split genetic material into its smallest parts. So, it is difficult to believe that a multitude of medical maladies lack causation or evade detection.

Idiopathic is the term assigned to virtually all the medical maladies with an unknown cause or obscure origin. For example, *idiopathic edema* is fluid retention or swelling that occurs without a clear cause.

Can a medical malady arise for no reason? No, something does not and cannot come from nothing. Abnormalities cannot and do not arise from nothing or nowhere, or magically "pop" into existence for no reason. With respect to the human body, the law of "cause and effect" applies, and every effect must have a cause. So, a cause must exist for anything that disturbs the human body, regardless of how subtle it is.

When mainstream physicians and researchers cannot uncover the reasons for something being wrong, they assume there is no explanation, and the medical malady is termed *idiopathic*. Some physicians joke that the word means some "idiot" was not able to determine the "pathology." This is the outcome of mainstream medicine's efforts to pinpoint every symptom or illness and the result of specialization looking at ever smaller pieces and parts.

Many mainstream medical researchers are searching for the elusive "holy grails"—the specialized genetic material and/or hidden infectious invaders responsible for idiopathic illnesses. Some researchers are looking at chromosome defects, others are investigating "stealth" organisms, like *mycoplasmas* and *spirochetes*, while others focus on specific viruses. Unfortunately, mysterious genetic material and elusive infectious invaders are not likely to be the sole instigators of idiopathic illnesses. Yes, one or more of them may contribute to a few or many illnesses, but they are not likely to be the real cause.

If specialized genetic material was responsible for idiopathic illnesses, then everyone with the same genetic material would develop the same malady. If certain "stealth organisms" were responsible for idiopathic illnesses, every person who harbored them should also succumb the same malady. Not everyone with the same genetic material develops the same illness. Similarly, many people are unknowingly infected with "stealth organisms," but only a percentage of them develop idiopathic illnesses. Therefore, most idiopathic illnesses must arise from something more definable.

Ignorance plays a large part in the health of the average person. The same predilection contributes substantial bias with respect to defining illnesses that appear to have no causation. If the reason is commonly accepted or easily overlooked, it will not be related to the big picture. This approach is more than an oversight. It is negligent. Regardless of personal preferences, health professionals have a responsibility to do the best they can for their patients. This becomes a conflict of interest when they are told to think one way, positively reinforced if they do and ridiculed or scorned when they do not. For them, it is almost impossible to see the big picture and small details at the same time. This is how medical specialization has arisen. As the treatment and management protocols have become increasingly specific, thinking has shifted away from generalization and an approach that considers the whole body, embracing specific organs and systems instead. This further promotes a microscopic view.

It is easy to understand how candidiasis can be readily overlooked. Mainstream physicians state, "Doesn't everyone have yeast?" The answer is, "Yes, but it's kept in low amounts until there are enough organisms to upset the body's internal balance." Even though the presence of some yeast within the body is normal, an infection with disease-causing yeast is *not*. The doubters quickly add, "It's too obvious; it can't be that simple." Undeniably, there are other factors to consider, including the participation of harmful parasites, bacteria, molds, and/or viruses. In addition, there are other contributors, including genetic, environmental, and psychological components. Candidiasis is not a simple black-or-white issue because the interplay of all these contributors determines a sufferer's specific symptoms and illness. This is how one candidiasis sufferer develops endocrine (hormone) disturbances, another has autoimmune disease, and a third is burdened with psychological manifestations. Since the number of sufferers is approaching epidemic proportions, it has become more important than ever to recognize, diagnose, and properly address candidiasis.

Idiopathic illnesses are a prominent example of how candidiasis remains present without detection. Some mainstream physicians are beginning to appreciate the results of treating candidiasis-related maladies like asthma, allergies, and bowel problems. Imagine what happens when this is widened to a larger arena, including the other *candidiasis connections*? Chronic and recurring medical maladies will be much less prevalent. We will all feel better and get sick less often. Everyone should look forward to that day.

WHICH TYPE OF MEDICINE IS BETTER?

Candidiasis is an *infection* with disease-causing *Candida*-species organisms with *allergic* consequences. Experience with its sufferers demonstrates that treating their candidiasis produces the greatest benefits to their health. In fact, many mainstream medical treatments for chronic and recurring medical maladies are successful because they unknowingly eradicate disease-causing yeast and one or more other infectious invaders, including harmful parasites, bacteria, and/or molds.

Yet, mainstream physicians continue to ignore candidiasis. *Mainstream* means a strong and powerful trend and course. Mainstream medicine is also called conventional or orthodox medicine. *Conventional* means formed by agreement, arising out of custom or usage, and depending on or conforming to accepted models or traditions rather than nature; that is, it is not natural, original, or spontaneous. *Orthodox* means conforming to the usual beliefs or established doctrines. Basically, a conventional, orthodox, or mainstream physician practices according to well-accepted guidelines. At one time their decisions were based on what worked, but science is the present-day focus. By its definition, it ignores or dismisses original, nonconforming, or unproven treatments and management.

In contrast, *alternative* means providing or necessitating a choice between two things. Unconventional, unorthodox, or alternative physicians approach care from the point of nonaccepted practices. Science may or may not be behind their methods. Sometimes, common sense is their guide. At other times, there appears to be no logic at all. Even without proof, if something is efficacious, an alternative physician is likely to embrace it. Since they are not deterred by an absence of scientific information, these practitioners are not the most respected. Charlatans aside, the biggest problem with alternative physicians is that there is little consensus among them. Their practices and views vary greatly.

Complementary means helping to fill out or mutually making up what is lacking. Similarly, *integrative* means to make whole or complete by adding or bringing together parts. In principle, physicians who practice complementary and integrative medicine are trained in mainstream medical science and its methods. They are not afraid to use alternative means when mainstream methods fail or are ineffective. They embrace what benefits their patients the most. Although they desire to understand the science and are not put off by its absence, they bridge the gap between mainstream and alternative medicine. (To be complete, *holistic* medicine believes the parts are interconnected and can be explained only by reference to the whole. However, as a term, its use is decreasing and being replaced by *integrative* and/or *functional* medicine.)

Many physicians and healthcare professionals have tried to understand candidiasis. Their discoveries have been limited and not well explained or combined into a comprehensive whole. Like a Rubik's Cube, all the sides must be aligned to see the bigger picture. Therefore, this book had to include the scientific support to explain candidiasis, integrate its parts, present clinical examples, and recommend a way to standardize an approach to its therapy and management. If you scan the references, you will see there is an incredible amount of information supporting the topics in this book. Yet, this approach to health can only move forward when other members of the medical community advance these topics further.

Increasing numbers of people are turning to alternative, complementary, and integrative physicians and its healthcare practitioners for answers or, at least, hope. Most people do not enjoy being ill and have lost faith in mainstream medicine because of its lack of cures and/or poor understanding about chronic and recurring medical maladies. So, there really is no choice. If someone wants to get better, they have been forced to look elsewhere. Yet, non-mainstream medicine has its problems. Physicians practicing alternative, complementary, or integrative medicine often lack standardization and consistency. Typically, the science behind their methods is missing or poorly understood. Moreover, there is a great difference between their various schools of thought, especially with respect to treating candidiasis.

Although many patients do improve with non-mainstream medicine, better is not to be equated with optimal health, or even a cure. Almost any reasonable intervention is likely to have some positive effects, even though most are short lived. Unfortunately, many people continue like this for years at a time, achieving benefits but never becoming truly well.

The bottom line is that good care is good medicine, regardless of its origin. Yes, medicine should have science behind it. However, do not lose sight of the fact that, since every person is a unique individual, there must also be an art to medicine.

MEDICAL SCIENCE VERSUS THE ART OF MEDICINE

An incredibly famous quote is, "I think, therefore, I am." The medical version for doctors translates; "I think, therefore, I practice." This emphasizes their confidence in their mental abilities and knowledge. Turning it around, the quote further transforms into "I practice, therefore, I think." Now, you would believe that every medical decision involves some mental effort. If this were the case, why do most patients receive treatment like they are traveling along an assembly line? Studies reveal that the average office visit only lasts about six minutes, or shorter. If a patient's illness has been seen before, most doctors know exactly what to do for it—no arguments, questions, discussions, ifs, ands, or buts. Undeniably, this often precludes freethought from entering the management process.

Science is a state, fact, or knowing. It is knowledge, as opposed to intuition and belief. Systematized knowledge is derived from observation, study, and experimentation to determine the nature or principles of what is studied. Mainstream medicine has become increasingly science-oriented, and rightly so. The core of their thinking embraces the human body as a machine capable of (eventually) being fully disassembled and understood; the more the parts are dissected and examined, the greater their knowledge. It is a logical viewpoint that is not always useful in practice. It creates a narrow-minded approach because each part is assumed to perform in a certain way, but its conclusions are based on what is measurable. Subtle or undeniable occurrences are often dismissed as unproven. Knowing the pieces is helpful, but this may be of little value when they are applied to the big picture. For example, studying a brick will not explain the operation of a building. It is more worthwhile to obtain a broader understanding to appreciate how all the combined parts contribute to the finished product. Therefore, a microscopic view is frequently misleading and occasionally dangerous.

More problematic, scientific thinking is becoming increasingly complex. Technical reports on the news further brainwashes many people toward a scientific approach to medicine. New discoveries seem exciting and intricate, but the reporters and investigators often overstate their value. The wellness of a patient should be the goal. Unfortunately, many physicians and researchers try to turn medicine into an exact science. Modern physicians want to qualify and quantify every scientific fact, so no guesswork remains. Sadly, this eliminates the "art of medicine." If only it were this simple.

Art is the disposition or modification of things by human skill, to answer the purpose intended. In this sense, art stands opposed to nature. Art is also skill, dexterity, or the power of performing certain actions that are acquired by experience, study, or observation. You would think art is the opposite of science. Yet, from its definition, art complements scientific thinking; you make certain conclusions or discoveries based on your previous experiences, observations, and studies. Therefore, mainstream medical science should embrace art as a component. Yes, the "art of medicine" should have a scientific basis. Art and science do not have to be mutually exclusive. Each can happily coexist to the benefit of the other. Both should go hand in hand. In fact, the most significant breakthroughs have often occurred by artistic-intuitive investigators, especially the ones with open minds.

With respect to describing chronic and recurring medical maladies, the appropriate quote should really be, "There are none so blind as those who will not see." Something cannot and does not spontaneously arise or magically appear. There must always be an origin for every medical malady. If it cannot be seen, it does not imply there is no cause. You cannot see oxygen, but it exists within the atmosphere. You cannot see gravity, but it keeps you from flying off the Earth's surface into outer space. You cannot see the electricity that heats a light bulb filament, causing it to glow. Although it may not be obvious, something must be responsible for instigating and promoting illness. In most chronic or recurring medical maladies, especially those with an obscure origin, candidiasis is often the culprit, with or without the help of other infectious invaders, including harmful parasites, bacteria, molds, and/or viruses. Candidiasis is sitting right under the noses of most mainstream physicians, but they cannot see it. Other mainstream physicians choose to ignore it. In many cases, it is even totally maligned. Yet, all that is required is an open mind.

Many years ago, human beings realized that air and water were essential ingredients for life. Most accepted this and did not know why. It was not until the scientific revolution that an understanding started to surface. Similarly, a minority accept candidiasis as being a real medical malady, but do not know why. More information appears every day to lend further support for it. With every sufferer treated, a little more is learned. Since it is in its relative infancy, numerous pieces of the candidiasis puzzle are still missing. This lack of knowledge fuels the fire for the proponents of "The Candidiasis Inquisition." Currently, a lack of acceptance pervades the mainstream medical community. Yet, many physicians know these infectious invaders exist and reside within and on the body of human beings (and animals). With an abundance of case reports staring them in the face, mainstream physicians will still not accept candidiasis as being more than a fashionable or trendy illness. This is not surprising. At one time, even the most educated people believed the world was flat, while others knew it could not be. History has proven time and time again that human beings can be greatly misinformed until the true answer is uncovered, studied, accepted, and explained to the public. History has also shown that open-minded thinkers are quicker to realize and appreciate the truth.

The intent of this discussion is motivated by the concern and well-being of everyone who needlessly suffers with chronic and recurring medical maladies. Yes, treating symptoms can improve a patient's comfort, but the overall approach should be aimed at eliminating the infectious invaders and allergies that cause their ill health. Hopefully, the realizations and insights in this book will encourage others to further align and assemble the pieces of the candidiasis puzzle so that medicine can evolve in a new direction.

LESSONS FROM MICROBIOLOGY

In the 1860s, Louis Pasteur, one of the pioneers of biological science, developed the "germ theory of disease." Basically, he believed illness is solely caused by one or more "germs" within the body. His thinking was a cause-and-effect, black-or-white approach. If someone harbored an infectious invader, illness followed. Otherwise, they should remain healthy.

In the early twentieth century, German microbiologist Günther Enderlein observed *Candida albicans* organisms within samples of human blood. He subsequently noted that it was present in every human being he tested. Obviously, if everyone harbors *Candida albicans*, but only some people succumb to its mischief, there had to be more going on than Pasteur's germ theory of disease. The overwhelming presence of disease-causing yeast within the sick motivated him to find a way to treat it. Since homeopathic remedies were commonly used in Germany, he created homeopathic solutions containing cell wall fragments of *Candida albicans*. Without a full understanding of the intricacies of candidiasis, he employed injections and oral drops of these solutions. Even though he did not understand the reasons why, his homeopathic solutions helped a great number of his chronically ill patients.

These scientists, as well as others, realized that infectious invaders readily instigate illness within the human body. It was not until Dr. C. Orian Truss, a clinically oriented physician, that the connection between the microbiology of disease-causing yeast and chronic illness was made in 1961. Although an understanding of science is important, an appreciation of the bigger picture had more profound consequences, and this could have only occurred with an open mind.

LESSONS FROM GENETICS

Gerald Fink was a geneticist at the Whitehead Institute for Biomedical Research at MIT in Cambridge, Massachusetts. He began studying yeast in 1962 because "the yeast's cells and genes are astonishing like ours but much easier to study." For example, baker's yeast has about 6,000 genes, and most are thought to correspond with genes within human beings.

Even though he knew just about everything there is to know about this class of fungi, a laboratory finding surprised him. In the spring of 1991, he noted a strain of *Saccharomyces cerevisiae* (baker's or brewer's yeast), an innocent laboratory organism, when placed under stressful conditions "reverted to the long-lost behavior of its wild ancestors."

What made this discovery startling was that *Saccharomyces cerevisiae* was thought to be a stable organism, only existing in one shape, *ovoid* without the ability to form filaments (*mycelium*). Under laboratory conditions, this is what is universally seen. Moreover, when placed within an environment containing a low concentration of nitrogen, an essential nutrient, the organism was expected to starve and stop growing. In contrast, a batch of these cells behaved abnormally by forming filaments "that snaked over the plate like unruly lines of conga dancers," and invading into the surface of the culture medium. To rule out contamination, the experiment was performed repeatedly with the same results.

These cells behaved like *wild* disease-causing yeast searching for its food. To assist their mobilization, disease-causing yeast form filaments that branch outward to adjacent areas, like tree roots. This is thought to be the way most disease-causing yeast invade into and through the gut wall, creating leaky gut syndrome. *Saccharomyces cerevisiae* was not known to have this capability, which is why geneticists used this organism; that is, it was stable. Here was evidence that this yeast could transform itself into mycelia, its invasive form. Was this a new mutation? No, Gerald Fink realized *Saccharomyces cerevisiae's* ability to form filaments had been eliminated a long time ago by previous scientists. Since strains lacking that ability were used in the laboratory, it was universally assumed that it was a noninvasive, innocent yeast. It was luck to find a strain that acted like its wild ancestors, proving that *Saccharomyces cerevisiae* can be invasive and readily contribute to candidiasis.

This is not new information; it was just overlooked. In general, disease-causing yeast are not well understood because they are not cooperative laboratory organisms; they readily switch from their ovoid shape to their filamentous form. Confusingly, both forms have been demonstrated to participate in human disease, and many factors contribute to their associated disturbances. Alan Ezekowitz, M.D., a Harvard immunologist, insists that it is likely both forms can cause disease, "although with different degrees of severity." He states, "Fungi cling to cells. They are more difficult to eradicate than bacteria." Candidiasis is not as simple or as easy to define as some might like. There are also two possible additional variants: *Candida albicans* also forms a *cell wall–deficient form* and a *chlamydospore* (cyst-like), and both may elicit illness, confusing the issue further.

The symptoms and illness of candidiasis vary among its sufferers, and there is a lot left to be learned. According to Gerald Fink, "There's an embarrassing paucity of information about what makes *Candida* pathogenic." Until this is clarified, for the sake of those with chronic and recurring medical maladies, do not totally disregard the existence of candidiasis. Once again, you should open your mind to the possibilities.

LESSONS FROM PATHOLOGY

At a meeting in Mallorca, Spain, in June 1996, A. V. Constantini, M.D., presented his work, based on research in peer-reviewed literature. His interest involves *mycotoxins*, an area of pathology. He claimed, "Mycotoxins in human health is a new field in medicine. It brings to the scientific community, particularly the medical community, a new etiologic concept which implicates the toxigenic fungi and their specific toxins (mycotoxins) as the cause of the major non-communicable diseases. Mycotoxins is the generic term to describe a fungal-produced toxic metabolite which can cause disease leading to death."

Dr. Constantini founded the Center for Mycotoxins in Food in Freiburg, Germany. He analyzed many medical conditions and their possible relationship to mycotoxins. For example, mainstream medicine thinks that gout is related to abnormal *purine* metabolism. He believes differently, stating it is "an infectious, granulomatous disorder based on abnormality of mycotoxicity due to exposure to fungus." When animals were given mycotoxin, they developed gout. Rather than uric acid tophi within their joints, the findings are consistent with massive granuloma and the presence of *ochratoxin*. In addition, an analysis of the anti-gout medication "colchicine" lends further support for his thinking; it is well established that colchicine has *no* specific activity against uric acid. According to his literature review, colchicine has antifungal activity. Griseofulvin is another antifungal drug that "has a remarkable effect against gout." Dr. Constantini suspects that fungi may play an important role in causing some forms of cancer, cardiovascular disease, alcoholism, psoriasis, irritable bowel syndrome, and so on.

Despite the complexity of his work, molds live on surfaces and rarely take up residence within the body when there are enough beneficial bacteria; typically, molds need something to anchor on, unless they are virulent. Since disease-causing yeast can exist within and infect the human body, causing the same illnesses he claims are created by mold toxins, his work is included to show that there are different ways to look at chronic and recurring medical maladies. Since his work is based on mycotoxins, it does not lend support for all the allergy-related illnesses. Yes, harmful molds contribute to the disease process, but disease-causing yeast seem to be the most likely cause of chronic and recurring medical maladies, with harmful molds being infectious allies in most cases.

Disease-causing yeast can *invade* into the tissues and blood. In contrast, harmful molds tend to grow on tissue surfaces, unless there is a portal for their entry into the tissues and blood. Although there are exceptions, illness from harmful molds and their mycotoxins should be primarily confined to the gastrointestinal tract and mucous membranes as well as respiratory tract. Candidiasis is an *invasive* infection with *allergic* consequences. In fact, Dr. Constantini's work may have been successful because, at the same time they eradicated harmful molds, they were killing disease-causing yeast. In addition, destroying harmful mold eliminates any synergism between it and disease-causing yeast. Regardless of whether the causative culprits are disease-causing yeast or harmful molds, both are related, act together to instigate illness, have similar nutritional requirements, and can be destroyed by antifungal medication and an anti-candidiasis approach. An open mind does not always mean someone is looking in the right place or reaches the most accurate conclusions.

In fact, *Candida albicans* was found to produce its own toxin, called *canditoxin*. The research performed on canditoxin was Japanese, being published by two investigators: K. Iwata and K. Uchida. Their first paper on canditoxin was released in June 1967. Twenty more papers were released over the following years, until April 1978. These researchers were open-minded enough to discover and investigate canditoxin. After 21 articles, their research stopped.

Since 1993, numerous papers have been published on *gliotoxin*, a mycotoxin. Are gliotoxin and canditoxin one and the same? This is not clear without further research. More to the point, the research on gliotoxin proves that it has numerous harmful effects. It has been associated with *aspergillosis*, a mold-related illness, even though many fungi manufacture it, especially *Candida albicans*. If you enter "gliotoxin" in a PubMed search, there are almost 800 references. Yet, if you enter "gliotoxin and candida" only 13 articles appear. It seems the research is funding investigations into the role of gliotoxin in aspergillosis and other molds, *not* disease-causing yeast. Clearly, an open mind is important, but it will do you little good if no one else is willing to back you up.

An abundance of research proves that disease-causing yeast and harmful molds do produce harmful toxins. These can adversely affect the human body and our health, but there is more to be learned. However, must we wait before we treat people who harbor these infectious invaders? Although

awareness of the public. Although he was iculed, criticized, and insulted, some people and physicians listened.

Since then, scientific research and ckal experience have provided more insight into the participation of case-causing yeast instigating illness within human beings. The mainstm medical community would be wise to open their minds to the existerand prevalence of candidiasis. Even if they resist, mainstream physiciawill have to eventually accept candidiasis or risk losing increasing nbers of their patients. Some physicians will think they are exemptr example, ophthalmologists believe cataract surgery will always be nled. Yet, if the public embraces candidiasis, people will seek treatment, gvell, and cataracts will develop less frequently. This is because candidis relates to wellness, which is something most doctors overlook or ignc So, if wellness is to prevail, we must all work together for the benefit of patients. Self-serving interests must be put aside.

On the surface, candidiasis appear be a simple topic. When this book was initially conceived in 1994, I l not appreciate the scope and complexity of this medical malady. I h no idea disease-causing yeast could cause so many problems and disbances within the human body. Although other physicians claimed to h great success in treating candidiasis sufferers, I was not about to treat th without studying the research. More knowledge led to more questionsnich led to answers and further questions. With clinical experience, maquestions have been concretely answered. Some questions have generattheories, hypotheses, or speculation that is based on the available informn. Yet, even though many holes in the Swiss cheese have been filled, tanswers to many questions are elusive or mysterious. And speaking ab an elusive problem like chronic fatigue syndrome, I believe most long VID sufferers will be revealed to be candidiasis sufferers.

This book was written to educate ers, not create controversy. Even though candidiasis may not be apprecia for years, substantial effort went into creating this book to provide as m information and clarity as possible. Hopefully, there are some open-ided physicians who are willing to help unravel and align "The Perplg Puzzle of Medical Maladies" to usher in a new direction for medic and create greater wellness for everyone.

A Complex Caseminating Recurrent Urinary Tractections—Forever

by MBielski, M.D.

This contributed article by Dr. Marc Bielski, practices medicine in New York City, illust the importance of *aggressive* therapy using antifungals and antibacterial antibiotics. It s as a provocative challenge to our general " antibiotic" mentality. -- Editor

Eliminating Recurrent Urin Tract Infections -- Forever !

by
Marc J. Bielski, MD

Why am I writing this article? I am r urologist, nor have I ever had a urinary infection myself. Moreover, urinary infections are, in fact, rather rare am men. Admittedly, I do not consider my to be an expert. To the contrary, I am r of a generalist, looking at the human bod an entire organism. With this in min became a *clinical ecologist* -- that i search for the underlying causes of illn including what is in your internal external environments. Undeniably, illi does not arise from nowhere or magic "pop" into existence by witchcraft sorcery. Therefore, I attempt to underst the underlying "hidden" pathology and turn, use an appropriate therapeutic appro that is aimed at correcting it. The bott line is that, in an effort to get people we am trying to beat Nature at its own gai The opponents that I am constantly battl are pathogenic (disease-causing) yea molds, parasites, bacteria, and viruses -- other words, any organism that can inva and infect the human body, causing illne regardless of whether its adverse effects obvious or subtle.

Urinary tract infections are primarily health issue among women. Some wom seem to develop one infection after anoth as soon as one infection is finished bei treated, the next one starts. Other wom seem to get a urinary tract infection eve time they have sexual intercourse, which c psychologically and/or physically ruin, or even destroy, their love-life. The more fortunate women develop urinary tract infections only once or twice a year, which is something they are able to tolerate and, consequently, learn to live with.

What is a urinary tract infection (UTI)? By definition, a UTI occurs when the urinary tract -- usually, the bladder and urethra -- becomes infected with microorganisms. UTIs are not dangerous -- that is, unless the infection progresses up the ureters, infecting one or both kidneys, which can instigate severe illness that may even become life-threatening. Although a UTI may be asymptomatic, especially during pregnancy, its most common symptoms are:

1. *dysuria* (pain with urination)
2. urinary *frequency*
3. sudden *urgency* to empty the bladder.

UTIs can occur for a variety of reasons. A one-time infection is usually not of great concern; frequently, it is treated and subsequently forgotten. On the other hand, chronic, recurrent, or frequent UTIs are *not* normal. Indeed, something must be going on in the urinary tracts of women who suffer with repeated UTIs. What could this be?

The most well-known answer is anatomical -- that is, women have a shorter urethra than men do, making it easier for bacteria to spread from the opening of the female urethra, upwards into the bladder. Furthermore, since the most prevalent infecting microorganisms are notable inhabitants of the gastrointestinal tract (for example, *E. coli*, *Staphylococcus*, *Klebsiella*, *Proteus*, and others), the close proximity of a woman's anus to her urethra permits these microorganisms to readily spread from her anus to the opening of her urethra. Understandably, women who have anatomical disturbances are at a much greater risk for UTIs. Typically, their bladders do not empty completely, or else

S.L. had some typical yea psychological symptoms, moodiness, mood swings, mental difficulty concentrating, anxie depression. Her history also inclu year history of birth control although these had been discontinu earlier. Like most young ca sufferers, her physical examinat unremarkable.

In my opinion, candidiasis wa behind her problems. Rather than word for it, we proved it. Lil candidiasis sufferers, the routine blo were also unremarkable; her chemi CBC were within normal limits. If stopped here, as most mainstream practitioners do, one would conclu nothing was wrong, dooming S.L. t with UTIs forever. Fortunately for S searched further. Her anti-*Candid* bodies were elevated: IgG = 6800 (range: 800-3200); IgM = 4100 (norn 4000); IgA = 3000 (norm: 800- *Candida* antigen = 80 (norm: 0-50 *Candida* immune complex = 120 (no 50). The results are interpreted as a *Candida albicans* infection of her membranes that had spread to involv tissues and bloodstream.

Stool testing revealed few yeasts a ova/parasites. Yeast culture of the showed 1+ *Candida*-species orga (normal range: 0 to +4). Bacterial culture demonstrated: 4+ *Ga streptococcus*; 1+ *Citrob ammalonaticus*; 2+ *Mucoid E. coli*; *Bacillus cereus*; and 3+ *Pseudomo* species organisms. The last two organ were sensitive to Cipro (ciprofloxaci newer fluoroquinolone, which n antibiotic-sensitive patients generally ten tolerate relatively well). These find verified mild candidiasis, as well as presence of pathogenic bacteria in her tract, a condition called *dysbacteriosis*. Anoscopy (rectal swabbing for parasites) identified *ameobiasis (Entamoeba coli* cysts), in addition to 1+ true hyphae of *Candida albicans*. It is important to note that the stool sample lab test had been negative for parasites -- that is, the amoebic cysts had *not* showed up in the stool specimen.

Yeast and mold antigen skin testing, using the serial dilution endpoint titration technique was significant for moderate allergies to *Candida albicans*, baker's yeast, brewer's yeast, T.O.E. (the antigenically cross-reactive molds *Tricophyton*, *Oidiniomycetes*, and *Epidermophyton*) and to another mold, *Alternaria*. Her environmental allergies included moderate reactions to English plantain, Chenopodium, and ragweed, and a severe reaction to grass smut mix (which is really just another form of mold allergy).

Undeniably, S.L. had candidiasis, dysbacteriosis, and ameobiasis. Accordingly, S.L. was started on a yeast-free/sugar-free/mold-free diet with nutritional and probiotic supplements, including some herbs to detoxify her liver and kidneys. She was also given systemic anti-fungal medication (Diflucan 200 mg. once a day). I almost always administer a systemic antifungal *first*, in an effort to saturate the tissues and bloodstream, because killing the pathogenic yeasts in these locations is the best way to heal the patient completely, as well as to prevent rapid relapses. S.L. was also started on an allergy desensitization program (allergy shots), using the appropriate antigens.

During the first week, S.L. experienced a Herxheimer "die-off" reaction -- that is, an increase in symptoms, including weakness, achy muscles and tiredness. These started on the first day and worsened by day two. S.L. was urinating every hour during the day

some people try to hide the truth, it still exists. Eventually, the truth will surface. An open mind will allow this to happen more quickly.

LESSONS FROM DENTISTRY

Jerry Pollock, Ph.D., of the Department of Oral Biology & Pathology at SUNY, Stony Brook, New York, and his colleagues investigated antifungal activity within the saliva of AIDS patients. He concluded, "Defective salivary antifungal activity may contribute to oral candidiasis." Research revealed the existence of "yeast cell conversion to pseudo-mycelial forms of *Candida albicans* with invasion of the oral mucosa and the development of candidiasis." So, in the case of the *candidiasis-AIDS connection*, which was first, the chicken or the egg? According to Dr. Pollock, "It is tempting to hypothesize oral candidiasis or high oral yeast cell load contributes to the progression of AIDS."

Although HIV-positive patients have diminished antifungal activity, oral thrush does not develop in every HIV-positive person. When it occurs, it represents a grave prognostic sign. Every mainstream physician would agree. Since HIV-positive people have decreased antifungal activity, every one of them should develop thrush, but this is not what happens. Something else must be occurring, or this must be the wrong way of looking at the problem. This is cause-and-effect thinking. Conversely, consider metabolic immunosuppression (chapter 14). Many viruses are infectious invaders that are controlled when a person's immune system is healthy. In the presence of chronic candidiasis, the immune system can become suppressed and even depressed. This inauspicious pathologic process is what allows these opportunistic pathogens to evade the body's normal defense mechanisms and cause havoc. The continuous presence of an infection with disease-causing yeast impairs a candidiasis sufferer's immunity. Once again, it took an open mind and a different way of looking at the problem to appreciate that candidiasis precedes the impaired immunity, as opposed to following it.

UNRAVELING & REALIGNING THE CANDIDIASIS PUZZLE

Candidiasis has a long history. Oral thrush has been known for thousands of years, but it was not until C. Orian Truss, M.D., that an association between disease-causing yeast and illness within human beings was discovered. In the late 1970s and early 1980s, Dr. Truss brought this medical blight to the awareness of the public. Although he was ridiculed, criticized, and insulted, some people and physicians listened.

Since then, scientific research and clinical experience have provided more insight into the participation of disease-causing yeast instigating illness within human beings. The mainstream medical community would be wise to open their minds to the existence and prevalence of candidiasis. Even if they resist, mainstream physicians will have to eventually accept candidiasis or risk losing increasing numbers of their patients. Some physicians will think they are exempt; for example, ophthalmologists believe cataract surgery will always be needed. Yet, if the public embraces candidiasis, people will seek treatment, get well, and cataracts will develop less frequently. This is because candidiasis relates to wellness, which is something most doctors overlook or ignore. So, if wellness is to prevail, we must all work together for the benefit of all patients. Self-serving interests must be put aside.

On the surface, candidiasis appears to be a simple topic. When this book was initially conceived in 1994, I did not appreciate the scope and complexity of this medical malady. I had no idea disease-causing yeast could cause so many problems and disturbances within the human body. Although other physicians claimed to have great success in treating candidiasis sufferers, I was not about to treat them without studying the research. More knowledge led to more questions, which led to answers and further questions. With clinical experience, many questions have been concretely answered. Some questions have generated theories, hypotheses, or speculation that is based on the available information. Yet, even though many holes in the Swiss cheese have been filled, the answers to many questions are elusive or mysterious. And speaking about an elusive problem like chronic fatigue syndrome, I believe most long COVID sufferers will be revealed to be candidiasis sufferers.

This book was written to educate others, not create controversy. Even though candidiasis may not be appreciated for years, substantial effort went into creating this book to provide as much information and clarity as possible. Hopefully, there are some open-minded physicians who are willing to help unravel and align "The Perplexing Puzzle of Medical Maladies" to usher in a new direction for medicine and create greater wellness for everyone.

APPENDIX

A Complex Case: Eliminating Recurrent Urinary Tract Infections—Forever

by Marc J. Bielski, M.D.

This contributed article by Dr. Marc Bielski, who practices medicine in New York City, illustrates the importance of *aggressive* therapy using both antifungals and antibacterial antibiotics. It serves as a provocative challenge to our general "anti-antibiotic" mentality. -- Editor

Eliminating Recurrent Urinary Tract Infections -- Forever !

by
Marc J. Bielski, MD

Why am I writing this article? I am not a urologist, nor have I ever had a urinary tract infection myself. Moreover, urinary tract infections are, in fact, rather rare among men. Admittedly, I do not consider myself to be an expert. To the contrary, I am more of a generalist, looking at the human body as an entire organism. With this in mind, I became a *clinical ecologist* -- that is, I search for the underlying causes of illness, including what is in your internal and external environments. Undeniably, illness does not arise from nowhere or magically "pop" into existence by witchcraft or sorcery. Therefore, I attempt to understand the underlying "hidden" pathology and, in turn, use an appropriate therapeutic approach that is aimed at correcting it. The bottom line is that, in an effort to get people well, I am trying to beat Nature at its own game. The opponents that I am constantly battling are pathogenic (disease-causing) yeasts, molds, parasites, bacteria, and viruses -- in other words, any organism that can invade and infect the human body, causing illness, regardless of whether its adverse effects are obvious or subtle.

Urinary tract infections are primarily a health issue among women. Some women seem to develop one infection after another; as soon as one infection is finished being treated, the next one starts. Other women seem to get a urinary tract infection every time they have sexual intercourse, which can psychologically and/or physically ruin, or even destroy, their love-life. The more fortunate women develop urinary tract infections only once or twice a year, which is something they are able to tolerate and, consequently, learn to live with.

What is a urinary tract infection (UTI)? By definition, a UTI occurs when the urinary tract -- usually, the bladder and urethra -- becomes infected with microorganisms. UTIs are not dangerous -- that is, unless the infection progresses up the ureters, infecting one or both kidneys, which can instigate severe illness that may even become life-threatening. Although a UTI may be asymptomatic, especially during pregnancy, its most common symptoms are:

1. *dysuria* (pain with urination)
2. urinary *frequency*
3. sudden *urgency* to empty the bladder.

UTIs can occur for a variety of reasons. A one-time infection is usually not of great concern; frequently, it is treated and subsequently forgotten. On the other hand, chronic, recurrent, or frequent UTIs are *not* normal. Indeed, something must be going on in the urinary tracts of women who suffer with repeated UTIs. What could this be?

The most well-known answer is anatomical -- that is, women have a shorter urethra than men do, making it easier for bacteria to spread from the opening of the female urethra, upwards into the bladder. Furthermore, since the most prevalent infecting microorganisms are notable inhabitants of the gastrointestinal tract (for example, *E. coli, Staphylococcus, Klebsiella, Proteus,* and others), the close proximity of a woman's anus to her urethra permits these microorganisms to readily spread from her anus to the opening of her urethra. Understandably, women who have anatomical disturbances are at a much greater risk for UTIs. Typically, their bladders do not empty completely, or else they may have defects that promote re-infection, like a *cystocele*. Although I am not a big proponent of invasive modalities, an anatomical disturbance is likely to warrant surgical correction and must not be quickly dismissed or casually overlooked.

If women with anatomical defects are at greater risk for urinary tract infections, do the majority of women with chronic, recurrent, or frequent UTIs have an underlying anatomical problem that predisposes them to developing repeated UTIs? The answer depends on how you look at it. Speaking purely anatomically, there is usually not much happening in the urinary tracts of the vast majority of women. In other words, everything is where it should be, with no anatomical abnormalities. Functionally, however, something must be amiss -- that is, something is occurring inside the bladders of susceptible women that causes them to develop repeated urinary tract infections. What could be going on in the bladders of these women?

Before this question is answered, I have a more pressing question: Is it a coincidence that the majority of UTI sufferers also have some type of gastrointestinal (GI) disturbance? No, because the micro-organisms that infect their urinary tracts have to come from somewhere, and the GI tract is a colossal breeding ground for these infectious invaders, readily spreading them from the anus to the urinary tract. Nevertheless, once antibiotics are taken for an infection, it should be gone for good. Yet, this is not what happens in these women, implying that there is still an underlying problem that is not being addressed. What is being missed? Similar to the GI tract, the urinary tract can become colonized with pathogenic yeasts as well as harmful molds, creating an environment that is predisposed to developing repeated bacterial infections. Gastrointestinal candidiasis and "leaky gut syndrome" are well-known terms among the readers of this newsletter and do not need to be explained. Even so, what you might not know is that certain pathogenic yeasts are capable of colonizing the urinary tract and appear to be responsible for most repeated urinary tract infections.

Classically, bacteria are accepted as the sole cause of UTIs, while pathogenic yeasts and harmful molds are consistently overlooked or ignored. Regardless of this bias, similar to the GI tract, pathogenic yeasts can infect the bladder and urinary tract; for example, *Candida albicans* and *Candida glabrata* are the number one and number two most common fungi that are involved with UTIs. However, when these organisms are noted in a urine culture, they are quickly dismissed as being "contaminants" -- even when the woman who collected the sample swears that she carefully followed directions required for a proper sample collection.

In fact, research shows that *C. albicans* and *C. glabrata* are co-conspirators, being synergistic in their behavior; that is, *C. albicans* releases enzymes that aid the adherence of *C. glabrata* to the surface of the bladder wall. After colonizing the urinary tract, pathogenic yeasts are able to enter into a synergistic relationship with a variety of harmful bacteria, each benefiting from the other's presence, as well as keeping the other from taking over completely. When antibiotics are administered, they might kill the bacteria, but they do not kill the pathogenic yeasts, which can form colonies that can grow in layers or sheets. The presence of the yeast may protect some bacteria from the ill effects of the antibiotics, explaining why a UTI can reappear as soon as the antibiotics are discontinued. Although the active infection is reduced by the antibiotics, some bacteria survive to re-infect the urinary tract, possibly becoming resistant to the antibiotic in the process. I suspect that pathogenic yeasts are also able to invade into the wall of the urinary bladder, encouraging inflammation and sites for re-infection. In addition, a persistent infection with pathogenic yeast can inflame the urethra and bladder wall, promoting the retention of urine, a condition that increases the likelihood of re-infection. In the bigger picture, a chronic infection with pathogenic yeasts can weaken the body's immunity, hindering its ability to combat UTIs.

How do the pathogenic yeasts get into the bladder and urinary tract? After initially infecting the urethra, their growth can spread upwards into the bladder, and even further. Alternatively, since pathogenic yeasts are routinely noted to colonize the tissues and blood of candidiasis sufferers, it is not that difficult for them to enter the vasculature of the kidney, take up residence, and colonize the urinary tract downwards, towards the bladder and urethra. Either way, the result is the same. Am I saying that every woman with repeated urinary tract infections is a candidiasis sufferer? Most likely, yes. When a candidiasis-minded physician or other health caregiver approaches UTIs from this point of view, UTIs can be eliminated forever.

Case Report:

As an example, consider S.L., a 28 year old technical recruiter. S.L. came to me on February 2, 1998 complaining of a two-year history of frequent UTIs that had been treated with numerous courses of antibiotics. Past history revealed that S.L. underwent bilateral ureteral re-implantation at age three. Except for rare infections, S.L. did well until about 1994, when she started having frequent urinary tract infections after sexual activity. At the time, her only solution was to take a sulfa pill after sex, which appeared to work well -- that is, until her infections became resistant to their use. During 1995, S.L. had no infections, but she was not sexually active either. The happy news is that she met her fiance in January, 1996. Unfortunately, she developed urinary tract infections every two months thereafter, which warranted appropriate treatment. After an infection with *Staphylococcus haemolyticus* at the end of November, 1997, S.L. visited a urologist in early December. Her workup included an IVP (intravenous pyelograph with contrast -- an x-ray study of the kidneys, renal pelvis, ureters, and bladder) that revealed a depressed bladder base that was consistent with a cystocele, but none was found by sonogram. Due to her history and findings, S.L. was told that she had "honeymoon cystitis" -- a diagnosis of exclusion that does not explain what is really going on. Other history that is worth noting is the repair of an umbilical hernia at age 24. In 1996, she was diagnosed with *Trichomonas vaginalis* (a vaginal infection with a parasite) and was treated with Flagyl (metronidazole).

Being candidiasis-minded, I was able to elicit information that helped support a candidiasis-connection to her recurrent UTIs. I discovered that S.L. also developed the symptoms of a vaginal yeast infection with each urinary tract infection. However, this had been missed because there was no discharge, just pain. These episodes were self-treated with over-the-counter medications. Further questioning revealed that S.L. experienced mild nasal congestion with excessive mucus that was consistent with her history of environmental allergies to grass and trees. S.L. also had constipation with infrequent diarrhea, evidencing irritable bowel syndrome (IBS). Since I am well aware of the candidiasis connection to IBS, I was not surprised when S.L. told me that her symptoms decreased on a yeast-free diet.

S.L. had some typical yeast-releated psychological symptoms, including moodiness, mood swings, mental fogginess, difficulty concentrating, anxiety, and depression. Her history also included a five year history of birth control pill use, although these had been discontinued a year earlier. Like most young candidiasis sufferers, her physical examination was unremarkable.

In my opinion, candidiasis was clearly behind her problems. Rather than take my word for it, we proved it. Like most candidiasis sufferers, the routine blood tests were also unremarkable; her chemistry and CBC were within normal limits. If we had stopped here, as most mainstream medical practitioners do, one would conclude that nothing was wrong, dooming S.L. to suffer with UTIs forever. Fortunately for S.L., we searched further. Her anti-*Candida* antibodies were elevated: IgG = 6800 (normal range: 800-3200); IgM = 4100 (norm: 800-4000); IgA = 3000 (norm: 800-2000); *Candida* antigen = 80 (norm: 0-50); and *Candida* immune complex = 120 (norm: 0-50). The results are interpreted as a mild *Candida albicans* infection of her mucus membranes that had spread to involve her tissues and bloodstream.

Stool testing revealed few yeasts and no ova/parasites. Yeast culture of the stool showed 1+ *Candida*-species organisms (normal range: 0 to +4). Bacterial stool culture demonstrated: 4+ *Gamma streptococcus*; 1+ *Citrobacter ammalonaticus*; 2+ *Mucoid E. coli*; 3+ *Bacillus cereus*; and 3+ *Pseudomonas*-species organisms. The last two organisms were sensitive to Cipro (ciprofloxacin, a newer fluoroquinolone, which many antibiotic-sensitive patients generally tend to tolerate relatively well). These findings verified mild candidiasis, as well as the presence of pathogenic bacteria in her GI tract, a condition called *dysbacteriosis*. Anoscopy (rectal swabbing for parasites) identified *ameobiasis (Entamoeba coli* cysts), in addition to 1+ true hyphae of *Candida albicans*. It is important to note that the stool sample lab test had been negative for parasites -- that is, the amoebic cysts had *not* showed up in the stool specimen.

Yeast and mold antigen skin testing, using the serial dilution endpoint titration technique was significant for moderate allergies to *Candida albicans*, baker's yeast, brewer's yeast, T.O.E. (the antigenically cross-reactive molds *Tricophyton, Oidiniomycetes*, and *Epidermophyton*) and to another mold, *Alternaria*. Her environmental allergies included moderate reactions to English plantain, Chenopodium, and ragweed, and a severe reaction to grass smut mix (which is really just another form of mold allergy).

Undeniably, S.L. had candidiasis, dysbacteriosis, and ameobiasis. Accordingly, S.L. was started on a yeast-free/sugar-free/mold-free diet with nutritional and probiotic supplements, including some herbs to detoxify her liver and kidneys. She was also given systemic anti-fungal medication (Diflucan 200 mg. once a day). I almost always administer a systemic antifungal *first*, in an effort to saturate the tissues and bloodstream, because killing the pathogenic yeasts in these locations is the best way to heal the patient completely, as well as to prevent rapid relapses. S.L. was also started on an allergy desensitization program (allergy shots), using the appropriate antigens.

During the first week, S.L. experienced a Herxheimer "die-off" reaction -- that is, an increase in symptoms, including weakness, achy muscles and tiredness. These started on the first day and worsened by day two. S.L. was urinating every hour during the day and twice at night. She also complained of yeast infection symptoms that were "not bad,...just twinges." On the bright side, although S.L. still had some post-nasal drip, her nasal passages were less congested. Undoubtedly, we were on the right path. During this second visit, I prescribed Fungizone Oral Suspension (1 ml. orally, swish and swallow -- four times a day for two bottles) to start on day ten while still continuing, Diflucan -- in order to eliminate yeast and mold *within* the fecal stream of the gastrointestinal lumen, thereby making it easier to eradicate the parasites and pathogenic bacteria later on. On day fourteen, Fasigyn (tinidazole, a less-toxic, newer relative of Flagyl that is produced by Pfizer, but not available in the US) was to be added to destroy the amoebas (1000 mg., twice a day, for four days). By the way, in addition to killing amoebas and *Giardia lamblia* (a common parasite), Fasigyn is also cidal (deadly) to *Clostridia*-species organisms (an anaerobic bacteria that is known to cause pseudomembraneous colitis and other difficult problems and which can impede a patient's progress if it is not treated) as well as to other pathogenic bacteria. Since Fasigyn is usually taken for a brief period and only kills the *trophozoite* (the active form of the parasite), its use should be followed by another anti-parasitic drug tailored to destroy any remaining parasite *cysts* (the inactive stage) so that they cannot repopulate the GI tract again later. Therefore, Humatin was started on day eighteen (500 mg., three times a day, for seven days). (Since a number of parasites now seem to be resistant to Flagyl, you would be well advised to try to obtain Fasigyn, if you can. It is legal to import non-FDA approved drugs for personal use with a prescription.) Alternatively, numerous anti-parasite herbal preparations can be used, but I have not found them to be as consistently reliable. Therefore, I personally prefer prescription medications as the most effective approach to eliminate the infection and I reserve herbal therapy for use later, to complete the program.

S.L. was seen two weeks later (Diflucan day nineteen, Humatin day three). She complained of being tired a lot, but she had not developed a urinary tract infection. Her constipation had improved, but was not gone. To treat her dysbacteriosis (altered gut bacterial flora), Cipro was prescribed (500 mg., twice a day, for five days).

Unfortunately, when treating candidiasis, there are often bumps and potholes in the road. Three days later, S.L. called from San Francisco (she was there on business), complaining of urinary tract symptoms. Since it was a weekend, another physician was on call and switched her antibiotic to Macrobid (100 mg., twice a day, for seven days). S.L. called me a few days later to say that she was doing better. I recommended that she add the herb cranberry, in capsule form, as prevention against further infections (two capsules, three times a day). I said to see how it goes and to return in a few weeks. I also told her that I was not at all surprised that she had developed another UTI, because after the yeasts are eliminated from the urinary tract, the pathogenic bacteria are no longer competitively inhibited, enabling them to reproduce freely and readily to instigate another infection. Although I had administered Cipro for her GI dysbacteriosis, I had hoped it would also eliminate the pathogenic bacteria that were colonizing her urinary tract. Unfortunately, in this case, however, the microorganisms that infected her urinary tract were resistant to Cipro, which permitted her infection to develop. Urine culture results revealed a mixed infection -- 10,000-50,000 colony forming units (CFU) per mililiter (ml) of *E. coli* that was sensitive to most drugs except tetracycline, as well as 10,000 - 50,000 CFU/ml of *Enterococcus*-species organisms that were sensitive to ampicillin, penicillin, and nitrofurantoin, but resistant to Cipro.)

Three weeks later, S.L. returned, having finished all the medications. She said that she was feeling "great, for the most part." Her energy was "so much better." On the downside, S.L. still complained of minor "bladder problems" that had improved with the use of cranberry capsules. She had also experienced some gastrointestinal bloating in the last few days and constipation that began the prior week. We went over the results of her recent urinary tract infection, and I prescribed Ampicillin (500 mg., four times a day, for five days) to make sure that all the pathogenic bacteria were gone from her bladder. Because of her ongoing bladder symptoms, I suspected that her infection was not completely gone, since the *Enterococcus*- species organisms had not yet been appropriately treated. In fact, gram positive cocci, a group to which the *Enterococcus* species belong (together with *Streptococcus* and *Staphylococcus* strains) are known to be frequent co-colonizers together with *C. albicans*, and they are also becoming notorious for their resistance to many antibiotics.

S.L. returned in a month. Having been on the program for two months, she said that she felt "good." Her energy was "good, except when I am hungry." Since she had no more complaints, I told her to continue on, but to return again in four to six weeks. She was to repeat her routine blood tests and undergo a follow-up anoscopy exam (rectal swabbing procedure) prior to her next consultation with me.

Once again, there were bumps and potholes in the road. S.L. returned a month later, complaining that her bloating was "worse than ever." She experienced constipation alternating with loose bowel movements. Her routine blood tests revealed a cholesterol level of 119 (somewhat low, but in the normal range), with an HDL (high density lipoprotein, the good form of cholesterol) of 63. Her CBC (complete blood count) showed a total white blood cell count of 3.8 with an absolute lymphocyte count of 1254, as well as evidence of anemia. At this point, it was obvious that S.L. suffered with immuno-depression. Microscopic urinalysis revealed moderate bacteria, but nothing grew when the sample was cultured. Anoscopy showed no ova/parasites, although there were a few mycelia of yeast, as well as a few true hyphae of *Candida albicans.*

Because of her reaction to Diflucan, I was certain that we had treated the pathogenic yeast in her tissues and bloodstream. In my opinion, the yeast was not completely eliminated from her GI tract because there was something else that required treatment. What was being missed? Obviously, there was still some dysbacteriosis, but this was not the ultimate problem. I looked back at S.L.'s history and the picture suddenly became clear. In February, 1997, after getting drunk with martinis, S.L. experienced the symptoms of a urinary tract infection, but the culture was negative. Although wine and beer are known to be produced by brewer's yeast, distilled alcohol is notorious for its contamination with mold. Were harmful molds contributing their ill effects? S.L. did not have onychomycosis (toenail fungus). On the other hand, she was allergic to some common molds. In addition to the martini episode, S.L. had also had a more recent flare-up of urinary tract infection symptoms a couple of days after ingesting vodka at an art exhibition, also with negative cultures. Therefore, this provided evidence that mold-related *allergies* were a contributing factor in her problems. With this in mind, I prescribed

Sporanox (200 mg. every morning, for thirty days).

One week later, S.L returned (Sporanox day eight). She felt "better...really good," and her energy was similarly "good." However, she still complained of some mild urinary tract symptoms. I explained that these were probably related to the Herxheimer "die-off" reaction to the molds, not only within her GI tract, but also in her tissues and urinary tract. I considered the probability that some *Enterococcus*-species organisms remained in her urinary tract. Accordingly, I again placed her on Fungizone Oral Suspension (same dose, amount as before) to kill any remaining mold or yeast within her GI tract. After three days, she was to take Ampicillin (500 mg., four times a day, for three days), then to skip a day and then to take Cipro (500 mg., twice a day, for three days). This was to eliminate the dysbacteriosis in her urinary tract and then her GI tract. She was told to schedule a follow-up visit in about a month, if needed.

One month later, S.L. proclaimed that she felt "so good." Her energy was "really good" also. She had not been tired since somewhere between the second to third week of Sporanox. No vaginal yeast infection symptoms either. No symptoms of allergic rhinitis or post nasal drip. Her anxiety, depression, and other cerebral symptoms were gone. All in all, S.L. was greatly improved. I then placed her on an herbal maintenance regimen (including oil of oregano, cat's claw, black walnut, and grapefruit seed extract) that was aimed at eliminating any remaining pathogenic yeasts or harmful molds.

S.L. returned two months later, saying that she felt "great." Her energy was also "great." She was still on the diet, and even though she might cheat a little now and then, she did not experience any unpleasant symptoms. She was told to continue with her allergy shots until completed. It was also a good idea to continue with the oil of oregano for a few more weeks, and to use the cranberry capsules until she felt that she no longer needed them.

It is now almost two months since her last visit. S.L. wrote me a thank you card, stating that "I feel better than I can ever remember." This is a happy ending to a you'll-have-to-learn-to-live-with-it kind of problem that had previously been considered "incurable."

S.L. is not alone. I have numerous other patients who have taken similar twists and turns during their courses of treatment. The key to their recovery involves understanding their underlying pathology and its assortment of possible illness-instigating contributors. Among these, candidiasis is probably the most significant (and the most frequently ignored) underlying problem. After all, pathogenic yeast are capable of invading into the gastrointestinal wall, colonizing the tissues and entering the bloodstream. Therefore, the pathogenic yeast needs to be dealt with *first*. This is the quickest way to heal the gastrointestinal wall, eliminate "leaky gut" problems, and decrease malabsorption. In my experience, the use of a *systemic (absorbable)* antifungal medication is the best way to eliminate pathogenic yeast from all of these areas. After the tissues are saturated with an absorbable, systemic antifungal medication, Fungizone (a polyene that is much better than Nystatin) or another *non-absorbable* antifungal medication should be added to eradicate any gastrointestinal candidiasis that remains. Herbs can be added as well. Moreover, do no overlook the adverse contributions of harmful molds, because molds *do* cause illness and they must be addressed accordingly. Sporanox (itraconazole) is an azole relative of

Diflucan (fluconazole) which is much better for use against *molds* because it is lypophilic (fat-soluble). Diflucan is hydrophilic (water-soluble) and it is better to use to treat pathogenic yeasts, such as *Candida* species.

Parasites and pathogenic bacteria must also be identified and appropriately eradicated.

Candidiasis and complex mixed fungal-bacterial co-infections do not have to be treated as mystery illnesses any longer. Cultures and other laboratory test methods are highly recommended to verify your suspicions, as well as to aid you in prescribing therapy. Sometimes, however, the causative culprits are not easily identified or do not readily reveal themselves. Consequently, your therapy may have to be based on intuition and experience, especially when laboratory methods are inadequate to define the problem completely. As an example, routine stool specimens are consistently poor when it comes to revealing parasites. That is why the rectal swab method (anoscopy) is a much better diagnostic tool. In my practice, roughly 90% of the patients are shown to have parasites by anoscopy, compared to fewer than 10% by stool specimens. In contrast, stool specimens are infinitely superior at identifying pathogenic bacteria. So there is often a need for *both* diagnostic tests. In any case, frequent, recurrent, or chronic urinary tract infections should *never* be thought of as normal. There are often numerous infectious organisms contributing their mischief, all of which need to be identified and eliminated.

In addition to the infection, there is another side to UTIs. This brings us to a question: When is a urinary tract infection not a urinary tract infection? The answer: When it is an *allergy*. Is this possible? Yes, the perpetual symptoms that relate to UTIs can readily reflect the presence of allergies. Normally, the inside of the bladder is supposed to be sterile. Like any other body surface, the overgrowth of disease-causing yeasts, harmful molds, and pathogenic bacteria can instigate inflammation and allergic reactions -- sensitivities and hypersensitivities -- in the tissues and linings of the bladder and urethra. This is why, even though the actual *infection* is eliminated, many sufferers of repeated UTIs are unable to eliminate their symptoms completely -- that is, at least not until their yeast and mold *allergies* are appropriately addressed as well.

Either way, whether by infection and/or by an allergic process, yeast-related illness appears to be a prominent instigator of repeated UTIs. Obviously, harmful bacteria contribute their ill effects as well, but their mischief is greatly amplified whenever both bacterial and fungal pathogens are co-conspirators Therefore, to achieve long-term wellness, the pathogenic yeast *and* the pathogenic bacteria must *both* be dealt with and eliminated. Hopefully, an understanding of this complex *candidiasis-urinary tract infection connection* will now make it possible to treat the majority of women who suffer from repeated UTIs, freeing them of this annoying problem forever.

Contributed to the Candida & Dysbiosis Information Foundation Newsletter. P.O. Box Drawer JF, College Station, TX 77841; Vol. 4, No. 1 (March 2000)

(For help in obtaining non-FDA approved prescription drugs, contact the Persons with AIDS (PWA) Health Group in New York City at 212-255-0520. The internet is another source for locating international pharmacies to import medications from outside the US. Two books titled *How to Buy Almost Any Drug without a Prescription* and *Mexican Pharmacies* are available from LMB Enterprises, P.O. Box 5342, Sarasota, Fl 34277. -- Editor)

About the Author

Marc J. Bielski, M.D., is a holistic-integrative physician, licensed in New York State. He graduated from the Bronx High School of Science in 1976, receiving the Excellence in Microbiology award. He then attended the University of Rochester, earning a BA in Biology with honors (1980), including minors in chemistry, physics, and philosophy.

From 1980 to 1982, Dr. Bielski worked at the MD Anderson Cancer (Hospital and Tumor) Center in Houston, Texas, in their Department of Immunology & Immunotherapy. After his successful research with stem cells, he joined the cell-mediated immunity division, focusing on antibody-dependent cellular (ADCC) and natural killer (NK) immunity. He contributed to and authored numerous published articles involving cellular immunity and participated in early investigations involving the immune dysfunctions in people with AIDS.

From 1982 to 1986, he attended the University of Texas Health Science Center (Joe R. & Teresa Lozano Long) School of Medicine at San Antonio, graduating with a Doctor of Medicine degree. His fourth-year electives included emergency medicine in San Antonio, Pediatric Infectious Disease at the New York University School of Medicine, and an extended elective in Pediatric Cardiology at the Mount Sinai School of Medicine in New York City.

After a year of postgraduate training in the Department of Pediatrics at New York University, in 1987, he shifted his focus to adult general internal medicine, gaining experience at multiple medical centers and private offices, including an apprenticeship in the office of a cardiologist, where he learned about the diagnosis and treatments of acute and chronic cardiovascular problems.

Being an athlete since childhood along with his interest in sports medicine, from 1986 to 1994, he was a senior medical staff member of the New York City Road Runners Club. He attended races and assisted in the care of injured runners, as well as performed triage at the finish line of the New York City Marathon. From 1990 to 1991, he participated in an orthopedic practice, performing intake histories and physicals, and served as a part-time attending physician for the New York City Emergency Medical Services (EMS), performing histories and physicals on their new EMS applicants.

Since orthodox-traditional medicine could not explain why increasing numbers of people were developing frequent, recurrent, and chronic medical problems, Dr. Bielski became interested in alternative-complementary medicine and attended numerous conferences from 1988 to 1994. Initially, as his holistic-integrative interests increased, he realized that a technical approach to wellness included a diversity of contributors to illness, including diet, nutrition, and more.

From 1991 to 1995, Dr. Bielski worked at the Atkins Group for Complementary Medicine in New York City. His interests led him to study nutritional and herbal medicine, homeopathy, acupuncture, and other alternative-complementary modalities. In early 1993, he received an article on yeast-related illness, and, after reading it, he was inspired to learn more. Since this was before the internet was established, he searched through the medical libraries in New York City, finding compelling evidence for candidiasis. He also began to establish a basis for understanding the science and approach to treatment. Initially, he treated patients only with non-pharmaceutical methods, with good-to-acceptable results. Since Dr. Atkin's focus was on blood sugar disturbances and Dr. Bielski believed they were the result of a cause rather than an isolated problem, Dr. Bielski left the Atkins Group to devote his studies to candidiasis.

From 1995 to 1997, as he was researching and writing about candidiasis, he was a part-time consultant for a complementary medicine center in Brooklyn, New York, providing outpatient follow-up care. With the help of a medical contributor, he created a manuscript on candidiasis to be published by Avery Publishing, but the rights were returned to him when the publisher was acquired by another house. Also, during this time, three of his articles (chapters) about candidiasis and immuno-compromise were published in *EXPLORE! For the Professional* (see appendix B of *Unraveling Candidiasis: The Perplexing Puzzle of Medical Maladies*).

Dr. Bielski's articles attracted the attention of Maggie Burston, the founder and director of the Burston Clinic for Complementary Medicine in Toronto, Canada. In 1997, he was invited to provide a two-day workshop about candidiasis for numerous local and international medical caregivers, as well as Elizabeth Naugle—the creator/editor of the *Candida & Dysbiosis*

Information Foundation Newsletter, based in College Station, Texas. From 1997 to 2001, in addition to being a consultant for the Burston Clinic, he gave numerous lectures at the University of Toronto on yeast/mold-related health issues for medical professionals and the public.

From 1998 to 2011, Dr. Bielski practiced holistic-integrative medicine in New York City. During this time, he was recommending that people with frequent, recurrent, and chronic medical maladies receive a comprehensive evaluation and diagnostic approach to assess subclinical infections, allergies, and so on, as well as created a standard of care for treatment. In 2001, he relocated his private practice to the Olive Leaf Wholeness Center to combine holistic-integrative medicine into a multi-practitioner setting. In 2004, he realized his consulting skills were needed elsewhere and left to pursue that path until 2011 when he moved to Arizona.

Other activities included: In 2000, Dr. Bielski became a Diplomate of the American Board of Integrative Holistic Medicine. Also, in 2000, he began incorporating manual therapy into his practice, including osteopathic-chiropractic adjustments and bioenergetic craniosacral therapy. In 2001, he received his Certificate of Chelation Therapy from the American College for Advancement in Medicine, involving advanced knowledge about the treatment of intravascular and extravascular toxic heavy metals for numerous medical problems, especially EDTA for cardiovascular compromise. From 2002 to 2004, he was an associate professor, providing preceptorships for student nurse practitioners attending the New York University School of Holistic Nursing.

In 2009, Dr. Bielski cofounded MyoCardioCare, Inc. (www.myocardiocare.com) with Frank Terrizzi to develop and commercialize cardiac assist devices for cardiac arrest and support, and he is on the board of directors. From 2011 to the present, Dr. Bielski continues to be a private consultant and has several other books in development.

ALSO BY DR. MARC J. BIELSKI

UNRAVELING CANDIDIASIS

The Most Comprehensive Discussion of the Variety of Expressions and Manifestations of Candidiasis with a Holistic-Integrative Medical Approach to Diagnosis & Treatment

What is mainstream medicine missing? Why is the incidence and prevalence of frequent, recurrent, and chronic medical illnesses increasing?

People are suffering with medical maladies such as allergies, asthma, cardiovascular disease, depression, diabetes, gastrointestinal disorders, and headaches more than ever before. What's the missing piece of the health puzzle?

Rather than being an obvious infection, candidiasis is often a subclinical problem that is readily overlooked. Candidiasis is an infection involving one or more species of disease-causing yeast. Their physical presence within the body creates disturbances, directly and indirectly. In addition to their metabolites and toxins, they are also strong allergy-inducing microorganisms. Their adverse effects produce numerous medical maladies with or without the assistance of harmful parasites, bacteria, molds, and/or viruses. Other factors, like toxins, also contribute to the disarray.

Unraveling Candidiasis: The Perplexing Puzzle of Medical Maladies has four parts. Part 1 contains general information for practitioners and patients. Part 2 discusses the various candidiasis connections within the body. Part 3 explains how candidiasis impairs the immune system, creating immunocompromise, chronic fatigue, and allergies. Part 4 includes information related to the diagnosis and treatment of candidiasis. Three appendices provide supplemental information, and an extensive list of supporting references concludes the book.

ISBN: 979-8-9888309-0-0 • 8.5" x 11" • 566 pages • Available on Amazon.com

Printed in Great Britain
by Amazon

32350914R00314